The
Oxford Dictionary
of
NEW WORDS

Edited by Elizabeth Knowles

with Julia Elliott

Oxford   New York
OXFORD UNIVERSITY PRESS
1997

Oxford University Press, Great Clarendon Street, Oxford OX2 6DP

Oxford New York
Athens Auckland Bangkok Bogota Bombay
Buenos Aires Calcutta Cape Town Dar es Salaam
Delhi Florence Hong Kong Istanbul Karachi
Kuala Lumpur Madras Madrid Melbourne
Mexico City Nairobi Paris Singapore
Taipei Tokyo Toronto Warsaw
and associated companies in
Berlin Ibadan

Oxford is a trade mark of Oxford University Press

Published in the United States by
Oxford University Press Inc., New York

© Oxford University Press 1997
First edition 1991
This new edition 1997

British Library Cataloguing in Publication Data
Data available

Library of Congress Cataloging in Publication Data
Data available
ISBN 0–19–863152–9

10 9 8 7 6 5 4 3 2 1

Typeset by Selwood Systems, Midsomer Norton

Printed in Great Britain by Biddles Ltd.,
Guildford & King's Lynn

Preface

The *Oxford Dictionary of New Words* covers new words which have been 'in the news' in the decade and a half between the beginning of the eighties and the mid-nineties. The book follows the pattern set by the ground-breaking first edition, published in 1991, in aiming to provide an informative and readable guide to about two thousand high-profile words and phrases which have come to public attention in the past fifteen or sixteen years. The purpose is to tell the story of each item treated, by explaining the events that brought it to prominence. Each story is illustrated by examples of actual use in journalism (including electronic publications and online postings) and fiction. The vocabulary covered provides an overview of the given period, by high-lighting historical, cultural, and social concerns and by reflecting the effects of technological development and scientific discovery.

For the purposes of this dictionary, a 'new word' is any word, phrase, or sense that came into popular use or enjoyed a vogue in the given period. Vocabulary thus covers completely new coinages such as *Aga saga* and *pharm*, and new uses of existing terms, such as *dragon* and *rage*. A minority of items covered in the first edition claim a place here because their stories have continued to develop (*BSE* is an example of this).

Politics is always fertile ground, and our period has added a number of phrases to the general stock. *Clear blue water*, *green shoots*, and the *vision thing* have become clichés of modern political life. More seriously and sadly, the break-up of the former Yugoslavia has given us the unwelcome concept of *ethnic cleansing*, as well as famil-iarizing us with such compounds as *Bosnian Serb* and *Bosnian Muslim*. An earlier conflict, the Gulf War of 1991, is still with us in the term *Gulf War syndrome*. The reunification of Germany in 1990 made 'East German' and 'West German' historical terms, but added *Ossi* and *Wessi* to our vocabulary.

The concept of *political correctness* has gained a high profile during our period, to the point at which *PC*, for *politically correct*, may be used pejoratively as well as approvingly: in social terms, for example, the concept of the *New Man* is now questioned (and often juxtaposed with the very un-*PC New Lad*). Usages such as *African-American*, *First Nations*, and *Native Canadian* represent more serious instances of attempts to coin terms which are free from traditional stereotypes.

The business world is well represented here, with terms such as *downshifter* and *presenteeism* suggesting current pressures and anxieties; the concept of *dress-down Friday*, intended to reduce stress, is not likely to address underlying concerns about the *glass ceiling* or the *marzipan layer*.

The world of computing and communications has a constantly developing vocabu-lary; we are now used to seeing *e-mail* addresses, and for many people the *Internet* is already a major resource: whether or not we believe in some of the more extravagant claims made, we are likely to be familiar with the concept of the *information super-highway*. But the words we use also reflect an anxiety about the social impact of the electronic revolution: *mouse potato* and *otaku* are two terms which suggest the downside of over-reliance on modern technology.

For some people, *surfing the Net* may be a preferred form of activity; others may limit themselves to *fantasy football* and the *rotisserie league*. But the eighties and nineties have also seen the development of *extreme sports* such as *canyoning* and *jet-skiing*, as well as the spread of the more traditional *dragon-boat racing*.

Environmental concerns continue to contribute to our vocabulary, many of them associated with travel and transport. *Speed bumps* and *speed cameras* are only two of the *traffic calming* measures proposed in recent years. The use of *RME* (*rape methyl ester*) to replace fossil fuels has also been proposed. Some campaigners, on the other hand, direct their efforts towards a reduction in road-building programmes; reports of such protests have referred to the *twigloos* and *benders* in which protesters live.

In one sense the fact that we are dealing with 'new words' places no chronological limit on the range of entries. *Boxgrove man* and *Iceman* reach back into prehistory, while the vocabulary associated with the *dinomania* of *Jurassic Park* goes back further still: *raptor* (for *velociraptor*) properly claims its place in this book. Anxieties about the *millennium bug*, on the other hand, look to the future.

Much of the pleasure and interest in compiling a book of this kind derives from the opportunity to watch the ebb and flow of language, and to enjoy the endless inventiveness with which vocabulary adapts to changing situations. We hope that the results allow us to share some of this pleasure with our readers.

Acknowledgements

Our first and greatest debt must be to Joanna (Sara) Tulloch, whose original conception this book was, and who edited the first edition in 1991. She compiled the first headword list on which this text is based before moving to her current position as Consultant Editor to the *Oxford English Dictionary*, and subsequently read and commented on early drafts. Our second major acknowledgement is to Michael Proffitt and his *OED* New Words editors, Matthew Fletcher, Neil Fulton, Emma Lenz, Jennie Miell, Danuta Padley, Eleanor Rands, and Judy Selfe. Much of what is written here is based on their draft entries for the *OED*, and we were constantly sustained by their generous and willing cooperation. Michael Quinion was a valued assistant editor. We are also grateful to Yvonne Warburton for providing access to the quotation and library research carried out by Melinda Babcock, Nancy Balz, David Banks, Jane Brownlow, George Chowdharay-Best, Julia Esplen, Sally Hinkle, Gigi Horsfield, Rita Keckeissen, Catherine Malone, and Jon Ross Simon. Patrick Hanks, Judy Pearsall, John Simpson, Bill Trumble, and Angus Stevenson provided valuable constructive comments on early drafts of the text. We were fortunate that Trish Stableford was once again able to take on the proof-reading.

The subject icons were designed by Information Design Unit.

Elizabeth Knowles
Julia Elliott

January 1997

How to Use this Dictionary

The entries in this dictionary are of two types: **full entries** and **cross-reference entries**.

Full entries

Full entries contain up to five sections:

1 Headword section

The first paragraph of the entry, or *headword* section, gives

- the main headword in **large bold type**

  Where there are two different headwords which are spelt in the same way, or two distinct new meanings of the same word, these are distinguished by superior numbers after the headword.

- the pronunciation in the International Phonetic Alphabet and enclosed in oblique strokes /prəˌnʌnsɪˈeɪʃ(ə)n/ (see the key to the symbols which follows)

- the part of speech, or grammatical category, of the word in *italic type*

  All the names of the parts of speech are written out in full, as *adjective*, *adverb*, *noun*, *pronoun*, and *verb*. There are also entries for word-forming elements (*combining form*, *prefix*, and *suffix*) and for *abbreviations* and *acronyms*.

  When a new word or sense is used in more than one part of speech, the parts of speech are listed in the headword section of the entry, and a separate definition section (see below) is given for each part of speech.

- other spellings of the headword (if any) follow the part of speech in **bold type**

- the subject area or areas to which the word particularly relates are shown at the end of the headword section in the form of one or more graphic icons, for example

  Ⓧ ✷ (see the key to the icons which follows).

  The subject icons are only intended to give a general guide to the field of use of a particular word or sense. In addition to the icon, the defining section of the entry often begins with further explanation of the headword's application.

2 Definition section

The *definition* section explains the meaning of the word and when appropriate includes information about the level or type of language in which it is used ('in US slang', for example) or its more specific application in a particular field; it may also include phrases and derived forms of the headword (in **bold type**) or references to other entries (in SMALL CAPITALS). References to specific phrases at other headwords are given in *italic* and SMALL CAPITALS. Thus a reference to EXTREME *sports* indicates that this compound is dealt with under the headword EXTREME.

3 Etymology

The *etymology* section, starting a new paragraph and set in smaller type, explains the origin and formation of the headword where this is not transparent. In cases where an explicit statement would involve repetition, there is no separate etymology section, and the information appears in the history and usage section (see below). Words and phrases in this section may be in *italic type*, showing that they are the forms under discussion. Cross-references to other headwords are printed in SMALL CAPITALS.

4 History and Usage

This section, also in small type and starting a new paragraph, gives an account of the *history and usage* of the word or phrase. The circumstances in which the headword entered the language and came into popular use are described, and compound and derived forms of the headword (together with some other related terms) are considered. These are given in **bold type**, and are accompanied by their own definitions and histories. As elsewhere in the entry, words printed in SMALL CAPITALS constitute cross-references to other headwords.

5 Illustrative quotations

The final section of the entry, in condensed type, contains the *illustrative quotations*. These are arranged in a single chronological sequence, even when they contain examples of a number of different forms. Their primary purpose is to illustrate usage rather than to provide date evidence, and therefore the earliest example is not necessarily given. The sources quoted represent English as a world language, and the book includes well over 2,000 quotations from the UK, the US, Australia, Canada, and other English-speaking countries. They are taken for the most part from newspapers, popular magazines, and works of fiction, with emphasis on accessibility; some electronic publications and online postings are also cited.

Cross-reference entries

In order to make best use of this dictionary's ability to give an expansive account of the recent history of words and phrases treated, there is some grouping together of related pieces of information in a single article. To ensure that the required information can be found, cross-reference entries have been inserted in the alphabetic sequence of headwords, leading the reader to the article under which the particular word or phrase is discussed. Cross-reference entries are single-line entries containing the headword (with a superior number if identical to some other headword), a subject icon or icons to give some topical orientation, the word 'see', and the headword (in SMALL CAPITALS) under which the information can be found. For example:

Tiger² 🏛 see TAMIL TIGER

A cross-reference is given when there is a significant distance between the alphabetical places of the cross-referenced headword and the full entry in which it is mentioned. Thus the compounds and derived forms of a full headword are not given their own cross-reference entries because these would immediately follow the full entry; the same is true of the words which start with one of the common initial elements (such as *Euro-* or *hyper-*) which have their own full entries listing many different formations. On the other hand, forms grouped together by their final element (for example, words ending in *-size* or *-ware*) appear as cross-reference entries in the main alphabetical sequence.

Alphabetical sequence

The full and cross-reference entries in this book are arranged in a single alphabetical sequence in *letter-by-letter* alphabetical order (that is, ignoring spaces, hyphens, and other internal punctuation). The following headwords, taken from the letter B, illustrate the point:

babe
baby buster
back to basics
badger-watch
bad hair day
baggy
bail bandit
batch file
BBS
beardism
beast
been there, done that
beetle bank
be good news
Beltway Bandit
benchmark

• •

Note on Proprietary Status

This dictionary includes some words which are, or are asserted to be, proprietary names or trade marks. Their inclusion does not imply that they have acquired for legal purposes a non-proprietary or general significance, nor is any other judgement implied concerning their legal status. In cases where the Dictionary Department has evidence that a word is used as a proprietary name or trade mark this is indicated in the text of the entry, but no judgement concerning the legal status of such words is implied thereby.

Pronunciation Symbols

In the International Phonetic Alphabet, the characters b, d, f, h, k, l, m, n, p, r, s, t, v, w, and z have their normal English sound values.

The other consonant sounds are represented by

g	as in go	ŋ	as in sing	ʃ	as in she	x	as in Scottish loch
tʃ	as in chip	θ	as in thin	ʒ	as in decision		
dʒ	as in jar	ð	as in this	j	as in yes		

The vowel sounds in English are represented as follows:

a	as in fat	ʌ	as in dug	aʊə	as in sour
ɑː	as in cart	ʊ	as in put	eɪ	as in fate
ɛ	as in met	uː	as in boot	ɛː	as fair
ɪ	as in bit	əː	as in fur	ɪə	as in pier
i	as in cosy	ə	as in ago	ɔɪ	as in boil
iː	as in meet	ʌɪ	as in bite	ʊə	as in tour
ɒ	as in got	aʊ	as in brow	əʊ	as goat
ɔː	as in port	ʌɪə	as in fire		

Additional symbols, not representing actual sounds, are:

ˈ   the stress mark, which appears before the syllable carrying the main emphasis

ˌ   the secondary stress mark, which appears before the syllable carrying the next degree of emphasis (when, in words with several syllables, this might be in doubt)

:   the length mark, indicating that the preceding vowel is long (shown above in the explanation of the long vowels)

( )   parentheses, used round any sound that is optional

Icons

The graphic icons at the end of the headword section of each entry indicate the broad subject field to which the headword relates. The icons used are

Art and Music: words to do with the arts

Computing: words to do with computing and associated technology

Environment: words to do with conservation and the environment

Business World: words to do with work, commerce, finance, and marketing

Health & Fitness: words to do with conventional and complementary medicine, personal fitness, exercise, and diet

Lifestyle & Leisure: words to do with homes and interiors, fashion, the media, entertainment, food and drink, and leisure activities in general

Politics: words to do with political events and issues at home and abroad

Popular Culture: words which have entered the general vocabulary through their use in popular culture

People & Society: words to do with social groupings and words for people with particular characteristics; social issues, education, and welfare

Sports: words to do with sports of all kinds

Science & Technology: words to do with any branch of science (other than computing) in the public eye; technical jargon that has entered the popular vocabulary

• •

A

abled /'eɪb(ə)ld/ *adjective* 【

Able-bodied, not disabled. Also (especially with a preceding adverb): having a particular range of physical abilities.

Formed by removing the prefix *dis-* from *disabled.*

The word *abled* was first used in print in the US in the early eighties; the usage had spread to the UK by the end of the eighties, but was only really in use among disabled people until well into the nineties. It is sometimes qualified by a word indicating the particular type of ability in question, as in **hearing-abled**. The euphemistic **differently abled** and **otherly abled** were coined in the US in the mid eighties as part of the general trend towards POLITICAL CORRECTNESS. They were specifically intended as more positive official terms than *handicapped* (then the official term in the US) or *disabled* (the preferred term in the UK during the eighties). *Differently abled* was the more successful, although it was criticized for ungrammatical formation, for example in the *Los Angeles Times* soon after its official coinage:

> In a valiant effort to find a kinder term than handicapped, the Democratic National Committee has coined differently abled. The committee itself shows signs of being differently abled in the use of English.

Other similarly euphemistic coinages intended to serve the same purpose were later formed on CHALLENGED and (to a lesser extent) *inconvenienced.*

> Predominantly middle-aged, fully abled, self-consciously heterosexual married membership.
> —Virginia Mollenkott *Godding* (1987), p. 39

> I was aware of how truly frustrating it must be to be disabled, having to deal not only with your disability, but with abled people's utter disregard for your needs.
> —*San Francisco Chronicle* 4 July 1990, Briefing section, p. 7

> All the young members of this group suffer from cerebral palsy but insisted 'We are not disabled, we are differently abled.'
> —*Amateur Stage* Sept. 1990, p. 5

> The politically correct send their children to schools like Smith College, where they can learn about *ableism* ('oppression of the differently abled by the temporarily abled').
> —*Boston* June 1991, p. 82

> Deaf dogs should have the same right to compete against their hearing-abled peers.
> —*Dog World* June 1993, p. 46

ableism /'eɪb(ə)lɪz(ə)m/ *noun* Also written **able-ism** 【

Discrimination in favour of the able-bodied or against the disabled; the attitude or assumption that it is only necessary to cater for able-bodied people.

Ableism was a term first used in print by feminists in the US in 1981; it is one of a long line of serious and not-so-serious formations in -ISM that are associated with POLITICAL CORRECTNESS. While the proliferation of terms of this kind may have resulted in the trivialization of issues such as *ableism*, widespread discussion also took place (in the UK, especially in connection with the failure of a private member's bill designed to combat *ableism* in 1994). The two adjectives corresponding to this noun are **ableist** and *disablist.*

> The cover design appears to be rather male-dominated, white, ableist.
> —*Rouge* Winter 1990, p. 27

A panelist named Angela took the mike to tell about 'ouch experiences'. An 'ouch' is when you experience racism, sexism, classism, homophobia, ableism, ageism, or lookism.

—*New Republic* 5 Oct. 1992, p. 30

abortion pill /əˈbɔːʃ(ə)n pɪl/ *noun* Ⓧ ▣

A progesterone-blocking drug that is used to induce an early abortion by preventing implantation of the embryo in the womb; specifically, the drug RU–486.

The search for a contraceptive pill that could be taken after intercourse has been going on for several decades: a *morning-after pill*, as it was then known, was being developed in the second half of the sixties. The term *abortion pill* only arose in the mid eighties, however, with the development of the substance RU–486 (see MIFEPRISTONE) by French pharmacologists; the substance itself was first described in 1982, but it did not acquire the name *abortion pill* until the mid eighties. This drug is designed for use in the early stages of pregnancy and causes the womb lining to be shed, as in normal menstruation; according to its advocates it is as safe and effective as a surgical abortion. It has nevertheless caused considerable controversy both in the US and in the UK.

Why no explicit reference to the increasing ethical dilemmas raised by modern science, from animal rights to the abortion pill RU486? —*New Scientist* 20 July 1991, p. 13

Some brand it the 'death pill'. Others declare it the 'moral property of women'. But after years of controversy, an abortion pill that is almost totally effective is finally coming to America.

—*US News & World Report* 22 Mar. 1993, p. 32

abortuary /əˈbɔːtjʊəri/ *noun* Ⓧ

In the language of anti-abortionists: a clinic at which abortions are carried out.

A blend of *abort* and *mortuary*, designed to emphasize the death of the foetus.

A US coinage dating from the early to mid eighties, *abortuary* is a deliberately emotive word used almost exclusively by the pro-life movement. It is well established in Canadian as well as US usage, but is only rarely found in British sources.

After all she's going to get the truth, which she doesn't get at the abortuary.

—*New York Times* 16 July 1986, section B, p. 2

The book opens with Grant fleeing from the pistol-wielding guard of a Planned Parenthood abortuary—a fully formed, aborted, dead infant in the author's arms.

—*Christianity Today* 19 Mar. 1989, p. 58

As a result of the decision we're left where 100 children a month will be killed at the abortuary.

—*Vancouver Sun* 27 Oct. 1990, section A, p. 8

He kills 10 to 20 babies a week in his 'abortuary' and then puts them in his incinerator and burns them. —*Time* 9 Sept. 1991, p. 19

abuse /əˈbjuːs/ *noun* ▐▌

As the second element of a compound:

(when the first element is the name of a potentially harmful substance or activity) a fashionable synonym for 'addiction';

(in the context of human relationships, when the first element may either be a noun designating a person, or an adjective) physical—especially sexual—maltreatment of another person;

(in a wide variety of other contexts) wrongful use of, or harm caused to, whatever is named in the first element.

These are not so much new meanings of the word as new constructions in which it is used; *abuse* has meant 'wrong or improper use, misapplication, perversion' since the sixteenth century, but not until the late twentieth century was it used in apposition to another noun.

2

Abuse began to be used as the second element in compounds in 1969; during the seventies this was largely limited to official reports on such subjects as **alcohol abuse**, **drug abuse**, **narcotics abuse**, **solvent abuse**, **substance abuse** (covering all types of harmful substances), and **child abuse**. During the eighties the usage was taken up by the media generally and there followed a fashion for compounds of this type.

New compounds of the eighties and nineties included **cocaine abuse**, **crack abuse**, **laxative abuse** (in connection with the EATING DISORDERS anorexia nervosa and bulimia nervosa), and **hormone** or **steroid abuse** (usually in sport). More colloquially, there was recognition of **snack abuse** as a contributory factor in obesity.

With reference to physical maltreatment of another person, there were a number of formations with an adjective as the first element, pinpointing the particular type of abuse being discussed (**physical, sexual, emotional, psychological, ritual**, and **satanic abuse**) or the relationship involved (**incestuous abuse, spousal abuse**, and even **cohabitational abuse**, of a live-in lover). Following on from *child abuse*, there was **sibling abuse** and **wife abuse**; from **elder abuse** there developed the ambiguous term **old age abuse**, which illustrates the syntactic confusions that began to arise (it does not mean 'abuse of old age', but has been used to mean both 'maltreatment of the old' and 'abuse of a carer by an elderly person').

Soon the first element began to name animals or things to which harm was done (**horse abuse, racket abuse** in tennis, **river abuse** by the environmentally irresponsible, even **car** and **vehicle abuse**) or the means of causing the harm (e.g. **aerosol, chemical**, and **mercury abuse** to the environment). Occasionally there were elliptical formations such as **safety abuse**, where it is not the safety that is being abused, but those safeguards put in place to ensure it. In science, the word is becoming a fashionable term for 'distortion': examples include **chart abuse**, in which graphs are distorted to give a 'better' result; **computer abuse**, in which computing facilities are misused in order to 'massage' data; and **math(s) abuse**, in which the rules of number are ignored.

During the same period, the adjective **abusive** also developed its meaning in keeping with the new uses of the noun. Whereas in the past a person who was described as *abusive* was using language (*verbal abuse*) to vent feelings, the implication now became that of being given to physical or sexual abuse; the adjective also came to qualify new nouns in the sense 'involving abuse', for example in the term **abusive relationship**.

> But the needle never flickered past the red zone on the McEnroe dial; and not once did the umpire, Richard Kaufman, intone that glorious phrase 'racket abuse'. —*Guardian* 6 July 1989, p. 16

> As the workforce grows, so does the difficulty and expense of monitoring, training, and protecting it and the likelihood that safety abuses will occur.
> —Catherine Caufield *Multiple Exposures* (1989), p. 211

> People should be made aware of both actual and potential old age abuse, its causes and ways of preventing it. —Alison Froggatt *Family Work with Elderly People* (1990), p . 51

> People for whom cold, cruel homelessness was preferable to their colder and crueler domesticities: their abusive husbands, molesting parents, fleabag orphanages, hellish reformatories.
> —J. Morrow *Only Begotten Daughter* (1990), p. 243

> Binges are accompanied by feelings of loss of control, self-induced vomiting, laxative abuse, vigorous exercise, or strict dieting to prevent weight gain. —*Nursing Times* 11 Nov. 1992, p. 30

> Casual use of snacks or the use of unhealthy snacks can lead to 'snack abuse', resulting in obesity and other health problems.
> —*Food & Living* (supplement to *Albuquerque Journal-Tribune*) 10 Jan. 1993, p. 9

abzyme /ˈabzʌɪm/ *noun* Ⓧ ▣

An antibody that has been altered to give it some of the properties of an enzyme.

Formed by combining the *a* and *b* of *antibody* with the last syllable of *enzyme*.

Abzymes are products of BIOTECH. The research that made it possible to create artificial antibodies sharing the catalytic properties of enzymes was first reported in the middle of the eighties, and it was the research scientists themselves who nicknamed the result an *abzyme*, and then suggested the name as a serious term in the scientific literature.

These catalytic antibodies—or 'abzymes'—look promising to doctors for such tasks as gobbling up blood clots or scar tissue, and to industry for producing certain sorts of bulk chemicals.

—*Economist* 18 Nov. 1989, p. 109

The new 'artificial enzymes'—catalytic antibodies which some researchers nicknamed abzymes. —*New Scientist* 24 Mar. 1990, p. 38

acceptable /ək'septəb(ə)l/ *adjective* {{

In the phrase **the acceptable face of —**: the more acceptable parts or aspects of something that might otherwise be considered unpopular or unpalatable.

The phrase *the acceptable face of —* entered the language in the early eighties, initially used with an implicit and ironical nod towards the words *the unacceptable face of capitalism* made famous by the former British Prime Minister Edward Heath. Speaking in the House of Commons in May 1973, of the large pay-offs made by the international mining and trading company Lonrho and the exploitation by the beneficiaries of tax loopholes, he said:

It is the unpleasant and unacceptable face of capitalism, but one should not suggest that the whole of British industry consists of practices of this kind.

The acceptable face of — is now established as a catchphrase, used, often ironically, to emphasize a positive quality discernible within a negative or disagreeable context. As it becomes more familiar the phrase **acceptable face** may also be found outside this construction.

After years of trans-manche misery, Sealink's superferry turned out to be the acceptable face of Channel crossings, even in November, giving my daughter her first untroubled passage in 12 years. —*The Times* 19 Oct. 1991, Saturday Review, p. 38

The Big Issue seems a very Nineties way of making begging a little more respectable; with its entrepreneurial benevolence, its 'feel-goodishness', it can at times look like the acceptable face of destitution. —*Independent on Sunday* 5 Dec. 1993, Review section, p. 18

If there is an acceptable face to G-funk—the West Coast rap sound whose slick, oleaginous melodies are the diametric opposite of its bawdy, sometimes startlingly brutal lyrics—it belongs to Warren G. —*The Face* Jan. 1995, p. 92

access¹ /'aksɛs/ *noun* {{

In educational jargon in the UK: the principle of making education available to those who might normally be excluded from it. Widely used in compounds, especially **access course**, a course designed to provide a student who does not hold the normally required entrance qualifications with essential background information and skills.

Access in this sense is recorded from the beginning of the eighties; it became a key word in educational philosophy in the UK in connection with concern about the opportunities being offered to ethnic-minority students, women, and the disabled, who for one reason or another might not have been able to benefit fully from the school system. For this reason the courses are sometimes referred to as *second chance* courses. *Access* is used mainly with reference to higher education. Apart from *access course*, formations include **access scheme**, **access studies**, and **access student** (a student who is either studying on an *access course* or gained admission to a degree course in this way).

Some critics point out that calculations for jumble sale accounts, DIY wallpapering and placing bets are among the skills required for access schemes. Supporters of access point out that such calculations require sophisticated maths. Next week a conference at North London...will bring the leading supporters and critics face to face. —*Independent* 12 Feb. 1987, p. 11

On any one day they might start someone off on the first step to basic literacy and numeracy or introduce another to an access course leading eventually to a degree.

—*Times Educational Supplement* 8 Mar. 1991, p. 26

access² /'aksɛs/ *transitive verb* ⓧ

To get in touch with (one's deepest inner feelings or subconscious desires); to experience at a deep level.

In the sense defined here, *access* is a vogue term in popular psychology, used particularly since the late eighties and originating in American English. The word was first used as a transitive verb (abbreviating the phrase *gain access to*) by computer scientists in 1962; by the late seventies this specific use (in which the object of the verb was the computer system or data held in it) had spread into more general contexts in the sense 'gain access to, reach, make contact with', and this usage gradually became less concrete, as the following examples from 1990 show:

> Signed interpretation…is often the only way of accessing television for pre-lingual deaf people, whose only language it is.

> It's not acceptable to me that there are frail aged across the border who can't access our services.

The usage in psychology may have begun with a specific use of the computing metaphor: from the late eighties there are examples referring to the process of *accessing* a word or other specific piece of information in the memory bank, as though the human brain were being regarded as a large computer in which many individual pieces of information are stored. The usage defined above principally refers to the process of gaining access to what was once locked up in the subconscious, but here too the contexts became more general, so that ultimately *access* meant no more than 'get in touch with, feel, express'.

> Certain self-help experts and New Age gurus…seem to have a taste for computer language. They are likely to tell us that we need to 'access' our inner children or 'interface' differently with our families and co-workers. —*New York Times Book Review* 17 May 1992, p. 44

> You know the scene: racing around the heath in the middle of the night, shouting at the skies and beating his chest and hanging out with some Fool who probably did a Shamanism seminar at Esalen once. Deciding all of a sudden that he's got to do some grieving, learn to access his rage. —*New Republic* 1 June 1992, p. 12

acid jazz /asɪd 'dʒaz/ *noun* Also written **acid-jazz** 🎵 ᴾᴼᴾ

A style of popular music in which elements of jazz, blues, and soul are fused with a steady, rhythmical, funky beat.

Acid jazz, a musical style which became popular in the late eighties and early nineties, has only its name in common with *acid* HOUSE. It eschews the electronic drum machine in favour of the live drummer. It is characterized by a steady, funky beat and a laid-back style.

> Two years ago, at the height of the acid jazz phenomena, the ICA hosted an anarchic evening of jazz meets beats. —*Straight No Chaser* Winter 1991, p. 15

> In the fickle world of Toronto clubdom, acid jazz music is now the 'vibe' of choice…a combination of '70s funk and velvety jazz retooled and remixed with R&B and hip hop. —*Toronto Life* June 1994, p. 11

> The jazz of 9 Lazy 9 lounges across the cusp separating the brash fusions and musical dexterity of Acid Jazz from the altered states weirdness and streetwise cool of the Mo Wax label. —*The Wire* Jan. 1995, p. 12

acquaintance rape /əkweɪnt(ə)ns 'reɪp/ *noun* ⓵

The rape of a woman by someone who is known to her.

The term *acquaintance rape* has been recorded since the early eighties. It is used synonymously with the term *date rape*, which was first recorded in the mid seventies, although the latter is narrower in its application. *Date rape*, the rape of a woman by a man she is dating or with whom she is on a date, became a matter of concern particularly within university campuses in the US during the eighties. Both *date rape* and *acquaintance rape* are now broadly acknowledged, and have been given emphasis by a number of high-profile trials in the US in recent years. Both forms of rape are associated with the difficulty experienced by women in reporting the crime and the complexities involved in proving that rape has taken place.

> Incidents of sexual abuse and 'acquaintance rape' continued to blight the female undergraduate's college experience at Rutgers...in the 1980s.
> —Michael Moffat *Coming of Age in New Jersey: College and American Culture* (1989), p. 48

> The term date rape is itself a relatively new entry into the compendium of sexual crimes. 'There was a time not so long ago when a fair number of people thought you couldn't rape somebody you knew,' says Mary P. Koss, a professor of psychiatry and psychology at the University of Arizona and the author of a national survey on acquaintance rape.
> —*Newsweek* (Canadian edition) 16 Dec. 1991, p. 22

> 'Acquaintance Rape: Is Dating Dangerous?' is a pamphlet commonly found at counseling centers. The cover title rises from the shards of a shattered photograph of a boy and girl dancing. Inside, the pamphlet offers a sample date-rape scenario.
> —*New York Times Magazine* 13 June 1993, p. 28

acquired immune deficiency syndrome see AIDS

actioner /ˈakʃ(ə)nə/ *noun* 🦆 POP

An action film; a thriller.

Actioner is recorded from the first half of the eighties as a designation for a film characterized by a sustained degree of (often violent) physical action. The term is sometimes used dismissively, the implication being that, however well-made or exciting the *actioner*, it is by nature no more than a vehicle for the depiction of sequences of violent action.

> In the typical actioner, the victims are undifferentiated cannon fodder: terrorists, one dimensional bad guys. —*etc Montréal* 15 Feb. 1994, p. 40

> Carefully-made actioner with lots of well-timed shocks. —*Guardian* 22 Dec. 1995, p. 20

> It's *The Sweeney* which lives on in this smash-bang-wallop actioner...about the work of the Met's Armed Robbery Squad—the Flying Squad to you and me.
> —*Independent* 25 Jan. 1996, supplement, p.36

ADD ⊗ ⚔ see ATTENTION DEFICIT DISORDER

add-in /ˈadɪn/ *noun* and *adjective* 🖥

noun: Something which is added to a computer or other system to improve its capabilities or performance.

adjective: Concerning or describing something which is so added.

In the early eighties personal computer systems were developed whose capabilities could be extended by plugging additional electronic circuit cards into EXPANSION SLOTS; an example was the IBM PC. This ability gave rise to *add-in* as an adjective to describe such cards, which for example can improve the resolution of the display, control external devices, provide network connections, or produce audio output. The word was also used from the early eighties for software which extends the functions of computer systems, particularly small programs which added extra features to other applications software (such as a spelling checker added to a text editor). By the late eighties a noun had developed; this referred to the circuit card or computer software itself. The word has on occasion been applied to areas outside computing, but this is comparatively rare.

> There are less costly ways to provide revitalising water therapy, from simple bathtub air-mat add-ins to double-sized, air-jetted baths. —*Choice* Mar. 1991, p. 75

> This Visual Basic add-in can double the productivity of almost any VB programmer...with features that make designing, coding, and managing projects amazingly easy.
> —*Compute* Sept. 1993, p. 4

This isn't the first or only computer with a TV inside. For years, add-in cards containing a TV tuner have been available. —*Wall Street Journal* 4 Nov. 1993, section B, p. 1

adhocracy /adˈhɒkrəsi/ *noun* ⚡

A flexible organizational system designed to be responsive to the needs of the moment.

From the phrase *ad hoc* 'formed or arranged for a particular purpose; happening as necessary and not planned in advance', ultimately from Latin meaning 'to this'.

The term *adhocracy* was first popularized in *The Future Shock* (1970) by the American writer Alvin Toffler. Since the early nineties the word has gained fresh currency, in discussions of managerial systems based particularly on Japanese models such as KAIZEN. In an *adhocracy*, small teams of managers and workers are typically brought together for a limited period to resolve a defined problem; once the problem has been dealt with, the task force can be dissolved, and the effort of the individual members redirected. The term is now spreading from business vocabulary into more general discussions of organizational systems, and there is some evidence of pejorative usage: the *ad hoc* nature of the system has been seen as indicating disorganization rather than a praiseworthy flexibility.

As information technology reduces communication costs, the nonhierarchical structures (such as markets and adhocracies) may help overcome the limitations of hierarchies. —*Scientific American* Sept. 1991, p. 97

Adhocracy. The Clinton administration's way of working: based on a kitchen cabinet that is loosely organised around an influential inner circle...It's now increasingly seen by critics as the cause of the president's naïve decision-making. —*Guardian* 18 June 1994, Weekend section, p. 68

administrator /ədˈmɪnɪstreɪtə/ *noun* ⚡

An agent appointed by the courts to administer the affairs of an insolvent company.

A specialized use of the noun *administrator*. Since the mid nineteenth century the terms *administration* and *administration order* have been used to denote the control and direction of the property of an insolvent company or individual, and the court order requiring it.

It was not until the early eighties that the term *administrator* in this specific sense was applied to the agent appointed to administer the affairs of an insolvent company under the terms of an administration order. The *administrator* appointed in such circumstances combines the roles of receiver and manager, having the power to carry on the business of the company and to borrow for that purpose. This new role has been given a public profile in recent years in major collapses such as that of the Maxwell business empire.

Administrators are 'an entirely new concept within the framework of the insolvency legislation in Great Britain,' say PW. —*Financial Times* 19 May 1987, p. 9

The Commons Social Security Committee is to call administrators of the Maxwell companies to give evidence. —*Independent* 9 July 1992, p. 7

advance directive ⟨⟨ see LIVING WILL

adventure /ədˈvɛntʃə/ *noun* ▣

A type of computer game in which the player plays a role in a story involving simulated danger; an instance of playing this kind of game.

The original adventure game, called *Adventure*, written in the late sixties, and transferred to one of the first microcomputers in 1976, was essentially a puzzle-based game. The player had to explore an imaginary landscape (called Colossal Cave) in search of treasures, all the time being presented with situations that had to be solved by logic or guesswork. Many such text-based **adventure games** were written as personal computers became more common, this general term for them appearing in the early eighties; an important influence was the series of paper- or board-based role-playing games generically known as *Dungeons and Dragons*. As computers have become more powerful, the games have become more complex, introducing graphics and sound and permitting a much greater degree of interaction with computer-generated characters and, more recently, with other players linked through networks. A player of these games is sometimes called an **adventurer** and the playing of them **adventuring** or **adventure gaming**. This type of game is distinct from the action (or *shoot-em-up*) game in which agility in destruction of the opposition is the key to success, and the simulation game (also known as the *god game*), in which the player manipulates the environment within which computerized agents 'live'.

> If you are GM'ing a horror campaign, encourage players to set objectives and make sure they stick to them throughout the adventure. —*GM* Nov. 1989, p. 20

> We've broken down the Gamesworld into easy-to-define categories. Now you can tell at a glance which is the best shoot-em-up, the best fighting game, the best adventure and so on.
> —*ACE* Feb. 1991, p. 4

> The Eye of Traldar was designed to help entry-level gamers get started with the basics of advent-uring in the D&D game. —*Dragon Magazine* Feb. 1992, p. 48

> A MOO operates much like text-based adventure games such as Infocom's Zork.
> —*Internet World* July 1994, p. 18

aero /ˈɛːrəʊ/ *adjective* ▨ ⊛

In colloquial use: aerodynamic in design or appearance, streamlined.

An abbreviation of the adjective *aerodynamic* 'of or having a shape which reduces the drag of air moving past'.

Use of the abbreviation *aero* has been recorded since the late eighties. It is used particularly of elements combining fashion and function, such as the sleek new lines of contemporary car designs. It is also used of car or cycle parts, and of cycling appurtenances such as helmets. The adjective is commonly used in the compound noun **aero bar**, denoting an attachment to or replacement for the handlebars of a racing cycle, allowing the cyclist to adopt a more aerodynamic, forward-sitting posture.

> Users of aero bars wanting to try the forward-sitting position favored by triathletes can do so without buying a new steep-seat-tube frame. —advertisement in *Bicycling* Feb. 1991, p. 12

> New 8 speed cassette freehubs had their proving ground in the Tour de France this year, as did a very promising looking aero wheel. —*Bicycle* Feb. 1992, p. 15

> In the last 18 months we've made changes that our customers want and need. We lowered the front end for more visibility, and softened the lines for a more aero look.
> —advertisement in *New Republic* 18 May 1992, p. 12

Aerobie /ɛːˈrəʊbi/ *noun* ▨ ⊛

The proprietary name for a toy for catching, consisting of a thin plastic ring which is cast horizontally through the air in a spinning motion.

The *aerobie* was invented in the US in the early eighties and patented in 1985. It travels through the air faster than its predecessor the *frisbee*, which was invented in the fifties, being lighter and having a flatter shape and a thin rim.

> World Frisbee champion eight of the last nine years, Zimmerman also holds the record for an Aerobie throw of 377 metres.
> —*Kitchener-Waterloo Recorder* (Ontario) 8 June 1988, section E, p. 6

> Throwing discs long distances means doing without a thick rim, which generates drag. In the late 1970s, Alan Alder…began to investigate the possibilities. Nearly a decade later, he had abandoned the disc for a ring, which he calls the Aerobie ring. —*New Scientist* 28 July 1990, p. 40

aerosol abuse ⦚ see ABUSE

affinity card ∿ see LOYALTY CARD

African-American /ˌafrɪk(ə)nəˈmɛrɪk(ə)n/ *noun* and *adjective* Also written African American 🏠 ⟨⟩

noun: An American citizen of African descent; a black American.

adjective: Of or relating to African-Americans.

African-American was adopted as the preferred term for US blacks in the second half of the eighties. Hitherto *black* had been the favoured term, although both *Afro-American* and *African-American* had been in formal use since the mid nineteenth century. The use of the abbreviation in the former term was felt by some to be derogatory, whereas *African-American* was considered to give proper recognition to the African heritage. Adoption of the term was given significant impact by the plea for its use made by the politician Jesse Jackson, in a speech made during ceremonies held in honour of Martin Luther King. He said:

> Just as we were called colored, but were not that, and then Negro, but were not that, to be called Black is just as baseless. Every ethnic group in this country has reference to some cultural base. African Americans have hit that level of maturity.

The term is now established and in widespread use. In Canada *African-Canadian* has been recorded since the early nineties.

> They must also deal with at least three of five major ethnic groups—African Americans, American Indians, Asian Americans, Chicano/Latinos, and European Americans.
> —*Change* Mar. 1991, p. 21

> 'Justice Marshall has long avoided using the term *black*, preferring *Negro* or, more recently, *Afro-American*'. Jesse Jackson has been pressing the appellation *African-American*.
> —*New York Times Magazine* 28 July 1991, p. 10

> Then again, gangsta-jungle may fare better with the US hip hop audience if it sheds altogether any taint of rave, which most African-American youth regard as a strictly Caucasian affair.
> —*Muzik* July 1995, p. 41

Aga saga /ˈɑːgə sɑːgə/ *noun* Also written Aga-saga POP

A form of popular novel typically set in a semi-rural location and concerning the domestic and emotional lives of middle-class characters.

A *saga* of family life set against a comfortable background typified by possession of a kitchen with an *Aga* stove, notionally an emblem of middle-class life, and representing a sustained cosiness.

In genres of popular fiction, the consumer boom of the eighties was marked by the development of SEX AND SHOPPING. As the recession grew, the fictional appeal of the glitzy, high-fashion world lessened, to be replaced by more domestic interests.

The novels of Joanna Trollope and others depict articulate middle-class characters who, while often maintaining successful careers, are firmly centred on the home. *Aga sagas* do in fact deal with many of the painful problems of modern life (and are likely to give a realistic treatment to depictions of redundancy, illness, and old age), but their essential appeal probably lies not so much in the stories of individual characters as in the creation of their own secure microcosm. In some contexts, *Aga saga* is now synonymous with a sanitized and prettified picture of rural life.

> The success of Joanna Trollope's rural novels led to a whole wave of Aga Sagas from publishers hoping to cash in but today's best-selling formulaic products are legal thrillers, featuring powerful lawyers struggling against adversity and conspiracy.
> —*Independent on Sunday* 11 Dec. 1994, review section, p. 37

> There's a copious literature outlining the drawbacks of rural life, a sort of ongoing anti-Aga-saga which city-dwellers ignore at their peril; the cannier ones give it a fair trial, a weekend say, and flee back to the city, screaming.
> —*Guardian* 25 Mar. 1995, p. 7

When contemporary women writers publish novels about other women of a certain class the critics call them 'Aga Sagas' and throw them on the fire.　*—Daily Telegraph* 6 Oct. 1995, p. 29

See also BONKBUSTER

ageful /'eɪdʒfʊl/ *adjective*

Advanced in years, old.

Formed by analogy with *youthful* and perhaps also *ageless*.

The word *ageful* was coined in the US in about 1990 as a deliberate attempt to make a positive characteristic of age (so as to combat *ageism*); however, it has a euphemistic quality that places it in a long line of alternatives for 'old'. It does not so far appear to have become established in the language.

'Old? Deaf?' snapped the voice. 'Ageful, we prefer. I'm ageful myself and this is a hearing-assisted telephone so if you'd speak slowly and loudly...'　*—Guardian* 4 June 1990, p. 18

Agenda 21 /ə,dʒɛndə twɛntɪ'wʌn/ *noun*

A schedule drafted at the EARTH SUMMIT in Rio in 1992, for implementing action agreed on at this conference.

Agenda 21 represents a prioritized agenda for implementing action to safeguard and improve the world environment for the twenty-first century. In 1996, it is still not clear to what extent the aspirations expressed by *Agenda 21* will have been put into effect in the time envisaged.

And that's before they go on to discuss what has been dubbed 'Agenda 21', a comprehensive greenprint for transforming the world economy.　*—BBC Wildlife* Jan. 1992, p. 51

The June 1994 deadline for drawing up the desertification treaty and action plan called for in Agenda 21 was not met, but the convention was agreed and signed in October.

—Britannica Book of Year (1994), p. 185

agent /'eɪdʒ(ə)nt/ *noun*

A semi-independent computer program which can carry out specified tasks, give assistance or advice, or seek desired information without continual reference to the user.

A figurative use of the word in the sense 'a person who acts for another'; non-human *agents* previously existed only in the sense 'a thing which brings about an effect or exerts power' (as, for example, in the chemical *Agent Orange* in the former case or a grammatical agent in the latter).

In the eighties the concept of the **autonomous agent** grew out of artificial intelligence work dating back to the sixties, and by the mid nineties it had become a key area of research in computing. Its proponents claim the approach may soon radically alter the way in which we interact with computers. Currently, **intelligent agents** have been created that actively and independently monitor communications networks such as the INTERNET to discover useful information; others provide a responsive link between a computer system and its user (these are usually called **interface agents**); yet others undertake specific sub-tasks within a computer system (such as obtaining information from databases), making independent decisions and if necessary consulting other *agents*. Such computer programs are commonly referred to in general as **software agents**; the word *agent* is also used attributively, as shown in the examples below.

The project used sophisticated 'agent' programs to search thousands of sources and select likely stories to include in new editions published hourly at the convention, editions that could include material customized to each reader's interest.　*—CompuServe Magazine* Sept. 1994, p. 25

Programmers are trying to design better and better software agents that can seek and sift, filter and find, and save us from the awful feeling one gets when it turns out that the specific knowledge one needs is buried in fifteen thousand pages of related information.

—Howard Rheingold *The Virtual Community* (1994), p. 57

Managers with e-mail addresses on their business cards have given up waiting for 'intelligent agents' to filter through the resulting flood of messages. They are crawling back to their neglected secretaries instead. They may not be the future, but they work.   —*Economist* 1 Apr. 1995, p. 85

Interface agents are semi-intelligent systems which assist users with daily computer-based tasks...Such agents learn by 'watching over the shoulder' of the user and detecting patterns and regularities in the user's behavior.   —21 Apr. 1995 online posting

Aids /eɪdz/ *acronym* Also written **AIDS** Ⓧ

Short for **acquired immune deficiency syndrome**, a complex condition caused by HIV, which destroys a person's immune system—their body's ability to fight infections.

An acronym, formed on the initial letters of *Acquired Immune Deficiency Syndrome*.

The condition was first noticed by doctors at the end of the seventies and was described under the name *acquired immune deficiency state* in 1980. Later research has shown that the illness, if not the name, was far from new: a person had died from *Aids* as long ago as 1959, and the virus which causes *Aids* may have existed for a hundred years or more in Africa. The US Center for Disease Control first used the name *acquired immune deficiency syndrome* and the acronym *Aids* in September 1982.

At first *Aids* was identified as principally affecting two groups: drug users who shared needles, and male homosexuals. Once the virus which causes the immune breakdown that can lead to *Aids* was identified and it became clear that this was transmitted in body fluids, sexual promiscuity in general was blamed for its rapid spread.

The acronym soon came to be used attributively, especially in **Aids virus** (a colloquial name for HIV) and **Aids-related**. By 1984 doctors had established that infection with HIV could precede the onset of any symptoms by months or years. The Center for Disease Control created a carefully-organized vocabulary for the spectrum of stages: absence of infection was named *HIV antibody seronegativity* (i.e. the absence of antibodies against HIV in the blood), initial infection was *HIV antibody seropositivity* (the presence of antibodies), followed by *HIV asymptomaticity* (initial infection but no symptoms) and *lymphadenopathy syndrome* (the first appearance of symptoms in the lymph nodes), then by **Aids-related complex** (ARC), a phase in which preliminary symptoms of fever, weight loss, and malaise become apparent. The final phase, always ultimately fatal, in which the body's natural defences against infection are broken down and tumours may develop, came to be known as **full-blown Aids**.

While researchers continue to search for an **Aids vaccine**, no cure has yet been found. Public awareness of the impact of the illness remains high, with the terms **pre-Aids** and **post-Aids** indicating the watershed social effect of the disease. Much effort has also been put into **Aids awareness**, and a small loop of **red ribbon** may be worn as an indication of sympathy and support for sufferers.

The staggering economic toll of caring for AIDS victims...has prompted the health care industry...to seek more cost-effective and humane ways of providing care for the critically ill.

—*Omni* Dec. 1989, p. 58

Nearly 40 countries now demand certificates from certain categories of visitor showing a negative result of a recent blood test for HIV antibodies. The World Health Organisation is strongly opposed to 'AIDS-free' certificates being used as a condition of entry and is campaigning against such policies.   —*Traveller* Spring 1991, p. 11

It seems more than passing strange that...even the tiny Caribbean island of Dominica...has seen fit to post large billboards counselling both safe sex and compassion for people with AIDS.

—*New Yorker* 16 Sept. 1991, p. 23

He claims reporters have been manipulated by the combined efforts of AIDS activists (who want to keep AIDS from being ghettoized as a gay disease) and medical researchers (who know the media frenzy makes it easier for them to get funds).   —*Playboy* Sept. 1992, section A, p. 31

When the [T cell] count dips below 200, one of three drugs can prevent *Pneumocystis carinii* pneumonia, a defining condition of full-blown AIDS.

—*US News & World Report* 10 May 1993, p. 86

In 1988 his first novel, The Swimming Pool Library, provoked admiring—if stunned—reviews with its enthusiastic account of homosexual pre-Aids orgying. —*Guardian* 6 Sept. 1994, p. 20

Air Miles /'ɛː maɪlz/ *plural noun* Also written **air miles, air-miles** ⟨⁓⟩

A proprietary name for a consumer incentive scheme under which credits redeemable for free air travel are issued to frequent flyers, or to people taking part in designated transactions; such credits may also be given as a bonus by some employers.

A specialized usage of the established compound *air mile* 'a nautical mile used as a measure of distance flown by aircraft'. In this usage the free *air* travel is measured in *miles* corresponding to air miles.

Air Miles was launched in the early eighties and quickly proved popular.

Air Miles will be awarded for every eligible journey participants make on British Airways scheduled services, so the more flights that a passenger makes, the more Air Miles are accumulated—building up for a leisure trip or even a complete holiday.

—*Highlife* (British Airways) May 1991, p. 7

The air-miles plan is fantastic—one point for every dollar you spend. The fee is $120 per year, but for frequent flyers looking to upgrade from a basic VISA to one with an air-miles option, Royal Trust is a good place to start looking. —*Onset* Oct. 1994, p. 19

Estate agents are offering free air miles to homeowners in an attempt to get more houses on the market. —*Daily Telegraph* 16 Jan. 1995, p. 6

A property developer has picked up more than 2.4 million air miles with his American Express card—enough to circumnavigate the globe 99 times. —*Daily Telegraph* 20 Jan. 1995, p. 3

The accumulation of air miles has become one of the ruling obsessions of modern American life. —*Guardian* 29 Nov. 1995, section 2, p. 5

airport fiction /'ɛːpɔːt fɪkʃ(ə)n/ *noun* ▓

The form of popular fiction typically sold at airports for in-flight reading.

From the late seventies, *airport fiction* has been somewhat disparagingly referred to in discussions of popular writing. The typical **airport book** (such as a CELEBRITY NOVEL) is a best-selling novel of reasonably substantial length, characterized by an exciting plot and narrative flow rather than by subtle analysis of situation or character. **Airport novels** are seen as essentially disposable: suitable for whiling away time on a long flight, but likely to be discarded when the journey is over. It is however recognized that in the field of popular fiction the most successful **airport novelists**, while not trying to produce lasting literature, display considerable skill in satisfying their readers' needs.

Reading for distraction—which is what makes the airport book so popular.

—Neil Postman *Conscientious Objections* (1988), p. 54

In publishing they call them airport novels—those silly, trashy books that will amuse you just until your plane lands. —*People* 25 Nov. 1991, p. 13

The reigning king of airport novelists, specializing in a kind of suspense fiction meant to be read by tired businessmen taking the red-eye. —*Chicago Tribune* 5 June 1992

air quotes /'ɛː kwəʊts/ *plural noun* ⟨POP⟩

Quotation marks represented by the movement of a speaker's fingers in the air, indicating that what is being said is ironic, should not be taken seriously, or is not a word or phrase he or she would usually employ.

The use of the gesture referred to as *air quotes* is a device which creates a distance between words and the ideas or things that they symbolize; use of the word NOT is another. The term *air quotes* has been recorded in print since the late eighties, but the gesture itself, used as an accompaniment to speech, is likely to be much older. The gesture is formed by holding the fingers up in the air, notionally around the word or phrase being simultaneously expressed. The fingers are curled in the shape of quotation marks: use of the middle finger with the forefinger perhaps represents double quotation marks, while use of the forefinger alone may represent single quotation marks. The phrase *quote unquote* has a similar function, appended to or preceding a statement, word, or phrase to indicate that the opinion expressed or the choice of words are not of the speaker's making.

> Betty tells friends she's 'ultra-Type A' and, with air quotes, 'a yuppie madwoman', so they won't imagine she actually enjoys her 12-hour days at the firm. —*Spy* Mar. 1989, p. 98

> This hugely successful new publication mixes beer, birds and bad language into a nauseatingly laddish concoction which Young insists is just for laughs. 'It's like the Sun with air quotes around it.'…The legend on the masthead gestures towards the ironic escape route: 'For men who should know better.' —*Guardian* 10 Oct. 1994, section 2, p. 11

alcohol abuse ▐▌ see ABUSE

alcoholic /alkə'hɒlɪk/ *adjective* ▨

Designating a traditionally soft drink, such as lemonade, which has an alcoholic content.

Alcoholic soft drinks were first developed in the late seventies, but it is in the nineties that increased promotion has made such drinks as **alcoholic lemonade**, under a variety of brand names, fashionable among the young. The successful marketing of these **alcopops** has raised public concern in the area of health and safety, with considerable debate focusing on the propriety of making alcohol more accessible to young people, while by the use of such terms as **alcoholic soft drink** effectively reducing awareness of the *alcoholic* content of the chosen beverage.

> The product…has since spawned some 23 other brands of alcoholic 'soft' drinks from manufacturers anxious to emulate the brewer's success. —*Independent* 3 Jan. 1996, p. 13

> There are circles among the twenty-somethings in which alcoholic lemonade is all the rage. —*Daily Telegraph* 27 Mar. 1996, p. 18

alderperson ▐▌ see PERSON

aliasing ▣ see ANTIALIASING

a-life ▣ see ARTIFICIAL LIFE

allophone /'aləfəʊn/ *noun* ▣ ▐▌

A person living in French Canada who speaks a language (and is of ethnic descent) other than French or English.

A transferred use of the English and French noun *allophone*, used in linguistics to mean 'any of the variant sounds forming a single unit of sound in a specified language'.

The word *allophone* has been recorded in its new sense in both Canadian French and in English since the late seventies. However the usage first developed in the language of the French Canadians and it may be seen as a significant feature of the resurgence of French separatism centred in Quebec. Initially referring both to immigrant and indigenous peoples, it now largely denotes those people who have emigrated to Canada from European countries such as Germany, Poland, and Ukraine, also known as *non-native Canadians*. The constituent groups within Canada may now somewhat neatly be listed as *francophone, anglophone, allophone*, and the *First Nations* or NATIVE peoples.

> Gunn also criticized a proposal before the Montreal Catholic School Commission to ban 'allophone'

students – those whose mother tongue is neither English nor French – from speaking languages other than French on school property.   —*Maclean's Magazine* 11 June 1990, p. 36

French-Canadian nationalists contended that British-Canadian leaders were deliberately trying to swamp Canada with a policy of massive immigration of anglophones and allophones.
  —M. D. Behiels *Quebec & Question Immigration: From Ethnocentrism to Ethnic Pluralism,*
                  1900–1985 (1991), p. 6

The integrity of an independent Quebec cannot be challenged by the claims to 'self-determination' by allophones or natives as they do not constitute distinct 'nations' or 'peoples'.
            —*Canadian Geographic* May 1993, p. 94

all-singing, all-dancing /ɔːlˌsɪŋɪŋ ɔːlˈdɑːnsɪŋ/ *adjectival phrase* Also written all singing, all dancing; all singing and dancing 🔊

Having many attributes or features. Also used ironically with the suggestion that these attributes or features are gimmicky or otherwise dubiously desirable.

The source of the term may be a series of posters produced in 1929 to promote the new sound cinema such as that advertising the Hollywood musical *Broadway Melody*, which proclaimed the words *All talking All singing All dancing*.

The phrase became prominent in the very late seventies, when it was used particularly to describe new designs and technical gadgetry. It quickly became a popular catchphrase, and its use rapidly extended to embrace abstract ideas and attributes as well as physical features. There is nearly always an implied scepticism in its use, the suggestion being that the many features and additions may be merely showy rather than really useful or effective.

As a welcome antidote to the all-singing, all-dancing sales effort, the stockbroker James Capel's oil team has produced a timely and sober BP/Shell comparison.
          —*The Times* 28 Sept. 1987, p. 26

Most, if not all, of the various manufacturers of backline equipment are currently offering a fairly bewildering range of all singing, all dancing models with umpteen switchable channels, reverbs, loops, hoops and a teasmade for the interval.   —*Guitarist* Sept. 1994, p. 190

Trifle is not a dish that pulls on looks. Michael Smith offers an all-singing, all-dancing 18th-century version in *Fine English Cookery*, where decoration takes the form of a mandala of glacé cherries, toasted almonds, Carlsbad plums, crystallised pears and chestnuts, and ratafia biscuits.
          —*Independent* 27 May 1995, p. 32

all-terrain bike 🔊 see ATB

alphabetism 🔊 see -ISM

alternative fuel /ɔːlˈtɜːnətɪv ˌfjuːəl/ *noun* 🔊 🔊

A fuel other than petrol for powering motor vehicles.

The term *alternative fuel* has recently gained a high profile as a result of the environmental concerns of the eighties and nineties. The quest for a satisfactory *alternative fuel* has taken place in a context of increasing anxiety about air quality. Unleaded and SUPERUNLEADED petrols, by reducing harmful levels of lead particles in the air, have brought some improvements, but concerns remain about emissions even from vehicles using these petrols. Many of the products of conventional fuel combustion, such as benzene and carbon monoxide, are known to be hazardous to health. It is hoped that *alternative fuels* such as BIO-DIESEL, ethanol, and methanol will pave the way towards a healthier environment, and research into the manufacture and use of such fuels, and modifications to the design of cars to be run on them, known as **alternative fuel vehicles** or *AFVs*, continue as the nineties advance. It remains to be seen whether a satisfactory fuel will be found, or whether a more radical solution may be offered by the ZERO-EMISSION VEHICLE.

Alternative fuels such as ethanol and methanol have gained ground in California as part of a strategy

to achieve air quality standards, but serious issues relevant to the conversion of agricultural output from 'food for people' to 'food for cars' remain unaddressed.
—*Impact of Science on Society: Science, technology and transport (UNESCO)* 1991 Vol. 41, No. 2, p. 98

Even though today's gas engines burn cleaner and more efficiently than ever, we're looking at alternative fuels like methanol-gasoline mixtures, natural gas, and electricity to power our vehicles in the future. —*Earth* Oct. 1995, p. 3

ambient[1] /'ambɪənt/ *adjective* and *noun* 🎵 POP

adjective: Of a style of largely instrumental music characterized by predominantly electronic textures and the absence of a persistent beat, and designed to create or enhance a particular atmosphere or mood.

noun: Ambient music.

A specialization of sense of the adjective *ambient* 'surrounding', used in terms such as *ambient sound* and *ambient noise*. These terms denote the acoustic quality of a particular environment as reproduced in a recording, and also an enhancement of sound produced intentionally in the recording process.

Ambient music has developed as a musical genre since the late seventies. Its emergence is associated particularly with the popular musician Brian Eno, who said in a record sleeve note in 1978:

> Over the past three years I have become interested in music as ambience…To create a distinction between my own experiments in this area and the products of various purveyors of canned music, I have begun using the term Ambient Music.

Eno confirmed the distinction between his *ambient music* and canned music or muzak by pointing out that canned music is intended to regularize an environment by blanketing its acoustic and atmospheric idiosyncrasies, whereas *ambient music* is intended to create or enhance such idiosyncrasies. It is associated predominantly with the creation of a mood of relaxation or contemplation.

In the nineties *ambient music* has combined with a number of existing musical styles, forming hybrid styles such as **ambient house**, **ambient rap**, and **ambient techno**. The noun **ambience** has also developed as an alternative term for *ambient music*.

> This is ambient music that dissolves regional idioms in a suspension of a 'virtual reality' production; a kind of 'new age' world music. —*Folk Roots* Sept. 1992, p. 54

> Initially popular as music for ravers coming down after a night's mayhem, ambient has become a booming album-based genre. —*New York Times* 13 Mar. 1994, section 2, p. 32

> Ambience doesn't have its immediate roots in the chill-out rooms of danceterias: its connection to the original vision of Cage and Eno is far more explicit. —*The Face* Jan. 1995, p. 47

> Ambient music looks to have a future in this country as the official artform of the cyberpunks, who are very much on the ascendant right now. —*The Face* Jan. 1995, p. 47

ambient[2] /'ambɪənt/ *adjective* ▨

Of or related to goods that can be stored at room temperature; especially designating food stored without refrigeration.

Goods were described as being stored at *ambient* or surrounding temperature; then *ambient* was applied to the form of storage, and then to the goods themselves.

The phrase **ambient warehousing**, denoting warehousing maintained at ambient temperatures, was recorded in the early eighties. From this there soon developed the phrase **ambient food**, food which may be stored within such warehousing. This compound noun provides an equivalent term, economically expressed, to *chilled food* and *frozen food*. Use of the term is still restricted to retailing jargon; it appears not to have moved into popular use.

> John Harding…decided with John Capito there was a market for gourmet ambient meals in this

country.   *—Retail & Distribution Management* 27 July 1985, p. 22

A series of 'composite' warehouses, he added, will come on stream…supplying frozen, chilled and ambient goods.   *—The Times* 14 Apr. 1988

amnio /ˈamnɪəʊ/ *noun*

Short for **amniocentesis**, a test that may be carried out in pregnancy to determine the condition of the foetus and that involves drawing off a sample of the amniotic fluid through a hollow needle.

The term *amniocentesis* is recorded in medical literature from the fifties although it did not enter the general language until the procedure became more widely known, in the late seventies and eighties. From the eighties in the UK the test was made routinely available to women over the age of 35 as a means of detecting abnormalities, especially Down's syndrome, associated particularly with babies born to older women. Factors associated with the test were an increased risk of miscarriage, and the ability to discover the sex of the unborn baby. These factors, along with the widespread availability, and take-up, of the test made the term *amniocentesis* a familiar one in the late eighties and nineties. The development of the shortened form *amnio* was a natural consequence of this familiarity.

> We can now reassure an older woman that if the amnio is OK, she should feel just as optimistic about the outcome of her pregnancy as a younger woman.
>   *—Chicago Tribune* 3 Mar. 1991, section 1, p. 5

> I agonised for days about whether to have an 'amnio'.   *—Independent* 11 Feb. 1992, p. 13

> Ultra-sound prenatal diagnosis is now used in more than eighty-five per cent of Canadian pregnancies. One former cabinet minister told me that she was treated 'like a social traitor' by a specialist when she refused to have an amnio for her 'high-risk' pregnancy at the age of thirty-eight.   *—Saturday Night* June 1993, p. 66

anchor 🖳 see HTML

Anglo-Irish agreement 🗒 see DOWNING STREET DECLARATION

animal companion /ˌanɪm(ə)l kəmˈpanjən/ *noun* 🐾

An animal kept as a pet.

The notion of a dog, cat, or other animal providing companionship is of course traditional, but in recent years concern about the role of animals in human society has caused some people to reject the use of the word 'pet' as reflecting an inherently exploitative view. *Animal companion* is recorded from 1980 as a usage intended to avoid derogatory implications that the animal so designated is seen merely as a possession, or as a member of an inferior species.

> There's now even a Pet Lovers' Helpline one can call for information about the health and behavioural problems of one's animal companions (the term now used by those who regard the word 'pet' as patronizing).   *—Globe & Mail* (Toronto) 26 Nov. 1991, section D, p. 1

> Cardinal Newman, who had the intriguing idea that those humans who live more or less virtuously endow their animal companions with personhood and an accompanying share in immortality.
>   *—Guardian Weekly* 10 Oct. 1993, p. 30

anime 🐾 see JAPANIMATION

annus horribilis /ˌanəs hɒˈriːbɪlɪs/ *noun* 🗯

A dreadful year.

A modern Latin phrase, modelled on the established *annus mirabilis* 'a remarkable or auspicious year'.

The term *annus horribilis* has been recorded since the mid eighties. Its early use tended to be in conscious juxtaposition with *annus mirabilis*, but as it became more established it began to stand alone. The term was given a high profile when Queen Elizabeth II used it to describe the year 1992, in the wake of the fire in Windsor Castle and the breakdown of the marriages of Prince Charles and Prince Andrew. She said:

> 1992 is not a year I shall look back on with undiluted pleasure. In the words of one of my more sympathetic correspondents, it has turned out to be an 'annus horribilis'.

This use by the Queen established the term *annus horribilis* within the popular language, and since 1992 it has been used freely in a broad range of contexts.

> If last year was the *annus mirabilis* of the oil sector of the unlisted securities market, this year is looking more like the *annus horribilis*. —*Financial Times* 23 June 1990, section 2, p. 2

> Much attention has been focused on the Queen's account of her *'Annus Horribilis'* and her plea for understanding and compassion. —*Independent* 25 Nov. 1992, p. 24

> My league has suffered an *annus horribilis*—being rocked by drugs, bribes and non-attendance. —*Maxim* July 1995, p. 115

anorak /'anərak/ *noun* POP

A derogatory or jocular term for a person who pursues an interest with obsessive dedication.

Such a person is popularly caricatured as wearing an *anorak* (a garment traditionally considered to be unfashionable and boring), especially while waiting in the open to see a celebrity or get an autograph. In the mid nineties the *anorak* was adopted by some young people as a fashion item, probably with conscious irony, though possibly as an extension of the *mod* fashions of this time, characterized by features traditionally associated with sportswear.

The term *anorak* is recorded in this sense from the early eighties. Initially it denoted a physically unprepossessing, introverted individual engaged, like the TRAINSPOTTER, in the obsessive pursuit of a special interest, especially a solitary and unfashionable one. In the early nineties the range of the term's reference broadened to include the computer buff and INTERNET enthusiast, bringing it closer in sense to TECHIE. It is still used to denote an obsessive enthusiast, and the appellation remains largely derogatory. However, the term's contextual use has broadened and the *anoraks* of the mid nineties have become less isolated in pursuit of their interests and less socially inept, including now amongst their obsessions approved if not positively 'cool' areas of interest, notably film and popular music. People may now jocularly describe themselves as *anoraks*.

Usage appears to be restricted to the UK, where it continues to gain rapidly in currency. Attributive uses such as **anorak book** and **anorak pop** are found, and a number of derivatives have developed: the adjectives **anoraked**, **anoraky**, and **anorakish**. Creative coinages including **anoraksia** and **anoraknophobia** have also been recorded.

> 'Cyberspace' is no longer the preserve of techno-nerds and anoraks. —*Guardian* 1 Jan. 1994, p. 11

> The Beatles have become almost an obsession. I try to get studio out-takes and rare records, I'm almost anorak level about it—getting really excited if I can hear John Lennon cough. —Jayne Miller *voXpop: The New Generation X Speaks* (1995), p. 170

> Women seem to be less anoraky about their music, whereas men pursue this rather sad interest in the minutiae of music to a much later age and are therefore more likely to consider DJ-ing as a career option. —*Independent on Sunday* 14 May 1995, p. 22

> It is, of course, in the end just a film about film, made by and for the irredeemably anoraked, and its commercial bellyflop at the US box office is as unsurprising as its critical overpraise. —*Interzone* June 1995, p. 38

> Some God-forsaken anorak with a portable satellite dish intercepted one of our calls, recorded it, set up a meet with the reptiles on a clifftop just down the road from Sandringham and tried to flog them a tape for £50,000. —*Independent* 1 Feb. 1996, section 2, p. 7

See also OTAKU

antialiasing /ˌʌntɪˈeɪliː(ə)sɪŋ/ *noun* Also written **anti-aliasing** 🖳

The process of making less noticeable the jagged edges or lines which appear in visual images that have been created by, or displayed on, devices of insufficient resolution.

The *alias* in this case is the false representation of the image.

The term *aliasing* was first used in 1958, applied to the introduction of distortions into speech or music when they are converted from analogue to digital format by a system which does not sample the original sufficiently often (an effect that has sometimes been employed deliberately in pop music). Later, the term was applied to the equivalent problem with visual images: this shows itself as a stepping effect on sloping lines and edges, rather like a staircase; such inaccuracies are often referred to as *jaggies*. The process of minimizing the appearance of these jagged edges by various smoothing techniques was named *antialiasing* in print in 1978. The term became more common through the eighties and nineties because of the rapid expansion of computer graphics techniques and the need to overcome limitations in the technology; *antialiasing* techniques are routinely applied to video pictures, computer-generated art, laser-printed pages, and other images. The term is also applied, but less often, to the correction of digital audio signals.

> The traditional cure for jaggies is antialiasing. Technically, antialiasing is the process of removing spurious signals resulting from undersampling, typically with a low-pass filter, but in the context of graphics, antialiasing has come to mean any process that helps eliminate jaggies.
> —*Dr. Dobb's Journal* May 1991

> Another feature that many users want is the ability to work with composite images. To offer this capability, a program must support at least one alpha channel, an antialiased mask that is included in the rendered image. —*MacWorld* June 1992, p. 180

> Voice I/O applications require a linear voice-band codec that provides a direct interface with a signal processor, a microphone, and an amplified speaker. The codec should offer on-chip anti-aliasing and anti-imaging filters. —*Byte* Nov. 1992, p. 187

antibody-positive /ˌʌntɪbɒdɪˈpɒzɪtɪv/ *adjective* ⊗

Having had a positive result in a blood test for *antibodies* to HIV; at risk of developing AIDS.

The term *antibody-positive* has been in technical use to denote the result of any blood test for antibodies to a virus since 1969. Its specialized sense arose in 1985, when fear of Aids was at its height. Since infection with HIV could precede the onset of any Aids symptoms by many years, health officials emphasized the need to avoid over-reacting to a positive test and tried to prevent discrimination against those who were known to be *antibody-positive*. The adjective **antibody-negative** is less common.

> Without testing facilities at, say, clinics for sexually transmitted diseases, 'high-risk' donors might give blood simply to find out their antibody status (and possibly transmit the virus while being antibody-negative). —*New Statesman* 27 Sept. 1985, p. 14

> This longstanding concentration on the clinical manifestations of AIDS rather than on all stages of HIV infection (i.e., from initial infection to seroconversion, to an antibody-positive asymptomatic stage, to full-blown AIDS) has had the…effect of misleading the public.
> —Susan Sontag *Aids & its Metaphors* (1989), p. 31

antichaos 🧪 see CHAOS

anti-Maastrichtian 〽️ 📇 see MAASTRICHT

anti-viral 🖳 see VIRUS

applet /'aplət/ *noun* 🖳

A small computer program, particularly one executing a single task within a larger suite of applications.

A blend of *application*, in the sense of a computer program, and the diminutive suffix *-let*.

The word *application* became associated with computer software in the mid sixties, when a distinction needed to be made between *systems software*, which controlled the operation of the computer system as a whole, and *applications software*, which was designed to carry out some specific task for a user. By the late eighties, it was common to speak of an *application* in the latter sense. With the growth of complex personal computer applications in the late eighties and nineties, particularly in windowing environments, it became standard practice to provide small programs to execute sub-tasks within the application as a whole; these might include formatting page layout, setting user-defined values, or controlling a printer. These small programs became known as *applets*. The term is also applied to any small application, particularly one which executes a single task.

All in all then, the very epitome of a shareware applet; small, tidy, catering to an untended niche, and—once registered—discreet. —*Personal Computer World* Apr. 1992, p. 282

All the basics are there, including an audio control applet, for altering recording and playback volume. —*Computer Buyer* Feb. 1994, p. 123

applied kinesiology ⊗ see KINESIOLOGY

aquacise /'akwəsʌɪz/ *noun* and *verb* ⊗ ✸

noun: Physical exercise carried out in shallow water.

intransitive verb: To practise aquacise.

Formed by substituting the Latin word *aqua* 'water' for the first two syllables of *exercise*.

The benefits of exercising in water have been recognized for many years and the practice is an established part of physiotherapy, occupational therapies, and, increasingly in the eighties and nineties, of fitness regimes. Following the development in the early eighties of the term *aquarobics*, the noun and verb *aquacise* and a number of related terms including *aquajogging* and *watercise* have developed in the nineties.

Aquacise teachers use routines devised by ex-swimming instructress/synchronised swimmer Jennifer Horrocks; physiotherapists at local hospitals and GPs have also created some routines. —*Essentials* Sept. 1990, p. 158

Aquajogging gets the heart pumping, and it's okay if you look like a geek. —*Minnesota Monthly* Feb. 1994, p. 18

Golf putting green, croquet lawn, badminton and volleyball, daily classes of aerobics and watercise are all available at the Four Seasons on Maui. —*Freedom: Canada's Guide for Disabled* Spring/Summer 1995, p. 58

ARC ⊗ see AIDS

Archie /'ɑːtʃi/ *noun* Also **archie** 🖳

A computerized Internet tool designed to simplify searches of multiple FTP (file transfer protocol) servers.

Named to suggest the word *archive*. Despite the existence of a US comic strip of the same name, apparently its designers did not have this in mind.

There are many thousands of public FTP sites on the INTERNET containing millions of files which can be retrieved by anybody. There are so many sites that it is often impossible to know where a particular item may be found, if it exists at all. *Archie* was designed in early 1991 to be an archive of FTP sites. At off-peak times, an *Archie* server's software polls sites that offer files; it gathers all the file details into a central database. That database is then indexed, and can be searched by an *Archie* client.

Using the Gopher protocol, WinGopher supports Archie, Veronica, and WAIS searching.
—advertisement in *Internet World* July 1994, p. 5

My next attempt was to use archie to see if there were any ftp sites that might have information on video stores. —*Internet World* July 1994, p. 76

See also FTP, VERONICA

Arpanet 🖳 see NET

artificial life /ˌɑːtɪfɪʃ(ə)l ˈlʌɪf/ *noun* 🖳

A field of research which seeks to understand how lifelike processes such as replication and independent behaviour can be embodied in computer systems and to create artificial organisms with lifelike properties.

The phrase *artificial life* has certainly been used before in other contexts; however, its specific application to the new field in computing is recorded from 1987. The phrase is frequently abbreviated to **a-life** or **alife**, while a practitioner may be known as an **a-lifer**. Rather than attempt to construct complex, human-level thinking systems from scratch, *artificial-life* researchers aim to simulate simple natural behaviours—such as movement and the sensing of surroundings—with the expectation that more complex 'intelligent' abilities will emerge, in the same way that the flocking of birds and the collective abilities of bees and ants emerge from the simple behaviour of individuals. Some *a-life* research involves simulations in computers of lifelike systems; some aims to develop autonomous robots and industrial control systems. Another goal is to illuminate Earth's biology by providing alternative models for evolution. The research has close links with several other fields: cellular automata, genetic algorithms, NEURAL networks, nanotechnology (see NANO-), VIRTUAL *reality* and intelligent AGENTS.

Many a-lifers think that their field will fare better than that of 'classical AI' (whose results are acknowledged to be disappointing). —*Whole Earth Review* Summer 1991, p. 124

Artificial Life, or A-Life as it calls itself, arrives as the newest wave of computer-driven science. A-life's objects are virtual creatures: patterns of activity that occur inside a computer, represented for us by bug-like, bird-like, plant-like assemblages of pixels which undergo electronic versions of growth, procreation, death, birth and evolution. But real robots that mimic living creatures are not excluded. —*Times Literary Supplement* 15 Apr. 1994, p. 30

A typical gathering of a-life researchers includes biochemists, computer wizards, game designers, animators, physicists, math nerds, and robot hobbyists. The hidden agenda is to hack the definition of life. —Kevin Kelly *Out of Control: The New Biology of Machines* (1994), p. 349

assisted suicide ⊗ 🍴 see DOCTOR-ASSISTED SUICIDE

ATB /eɪtiːˈbiː/ *abbreviation* 🎽 ✠

Short for **all-terrain bike**, a sturdy bicycle designed to be ridden in off-road locations.

The initial letters of *All-Terrain Bike*.

The terms *ATB* and *all-terrain bike* were first used in the early eighties to denote a type of lightweight but rugged bicycle with a broad, deeply-treaded tyre and a sophisticated gear system. Such a bicycle was originally, two or three years earlier, called a *mountain bike*, a term which continues to be used synonymously with *ATB* and *all-terrain bike*. The broader terms developed perhaps to express the notion that the bicycles, originally designed for use in mountainous terrain, had come to be ridden in a variety of off-road locations. *All-terrain cycling*, cycling on cross-country trails rather than roads, has remained a popular sport and leisure activity in the nineties. In the early nineties the *cross bike* was introduced; this offers a combination of the rugged toughness associated with the *ATB* and the sleeker styling of the conventional road bike or racer.

The abbreviation *ATB* is used attributively in noun phrases such as **ATB tyre**, **ATB frame**, and **ATB glove**, also called an *all-terrain bike glove*, a padded glove which affords protection against branches and brambles.

> Mountain bikes, also known as all-terrain bikes (ATBs), borrow sophisticated metal alloys, titanium lugs…and other materials from the aero-space industry for lightweight strength.
> —*Time* 19 Aug. 1991, p. 43

> The mountain or all-terrain bike (ATB) is a more rugged, off-road machine…They have a smaller frame, wide knobbly tyres to get a good grip in the mud, good ground-to-pedal clearance and a lot of low gears for negotiating steep hills.　　　　　　　　　　—*Which?* Aug. 1991, p. 440

ATM 〰 ▨ see HOLE-IN-THE-WALL

attention deficit disorder /əˌtɛnʃ(ə)n ˈdɛfɪsɪt dɪsɔːdə/ *noun phrase* ⊗ ⁑

Any of a range of behavioural disorders, occurring especially in children, symptoms of which include poor concentration, hyperactivity, and learning difficulties. Often abbreviated to **ADD**.

References to a *disorder* associated with *attention deficit* have been recorded in the specialist literature of child psychology and in studies of learning difficulties since the late seventies. *Attention deficit disorder* (with the alternative form **attention deficit hyperactivity disorder**, used in North America) and the related term *hyperactivity* (when used specifically of children) are broadly employed as synonyms for the medical term *hyperkinetic syndrome* 'a disorder of children marked by hyperactivity and inability to attend'. Treatment for the condition may involve the administration of drugs such as amphetamines, or therapeutic approaches including behavioural and family therapies.

The term *attention deficit disorder* spread beyond specialist terminology and into general use in North America in the early nineties, *hyperactivity* being more commonly used in the UK. By the mid nineties its use has spread to the UK, where it is frequently accompanied by the expressed or implied suggestion that the term and the condition are American inventions. Such suggestions form part of a debate within the UK centred on the validity of the condition as a genuine psychological disorder, a debate which similarly attended the spread of the term *hyperactivity* in the eighties, despite the medical recognition of *hyperkinetic syndrome*.

> If any of this sounds familiar, then don't panic. Certainly don't relax either, because you might have the latest vogueish condition, Attention Deficit Disorder. ADD, a kind of grown-up version of childhood hyperactivity, is only just being recognised in Britain as a genuine medical syndrome and a potential nightmare of late-twentieth century living.　　　　　—*The Face* Sept. 1994, p. 29

> Stan Mould wondered why he was so disorganised—impulsive, easily distracted, unable to plan ahead. Then he discovered Attention Deficit Disorder, a condition diagnosed in the United States.　　　　　　　　　　　　　　　　—*Guardian* 14 Sept. 1994, section 2, p. 7

> Jerad's teacher…suggested he be tested for attention deficit disorder. Jerad indeed was diagnosed with ADD, and began getting treatment.　　　　　　　—*Pacific Current* Mar. 1995, p. 23

> The symptoms are some of the characteristics of attention deficit disorder—ADD—a condition which is either a fancy, mumbo-jumbo American excuse for parental failure or the real reason so many young people underachieve at school.　　　　　—*Scotland on Sunday* 22 Oct. 1995, p. 6

See also DYSPRAXIA

attitude /ˈatɪtjuːd/ *noun* ▨

A highly independent or individual outlook and approach; assertiveness; style, panache. Especially in the phrase **with attitude**.

A specialized sense of *attitude* which represents an extension of the meaning 'truculence; a lack of cooperation; arrogance'.

The noun *attitude* was first used in this sense in the vocabulary of North American slang, intermittently in the seventies and becoming more frequent in the eighties. By the early nineties it had spread to the UK and gained rapidly in currency. Its particular sense embraces an assertiveness without hostility or arrogance, and a lively individuality. People have *attitude* and increasingly, as the nineties advance, so do things.

> In the early '70s, crepes were the foodstuff that ushered in the eating revolution—the pancake with attitude that took us from meat and potatoes into the modern world of gastrohype.
>
> —*Toronto Star* 30 July 1994, section G, p. 2

> Logic and gravity are of no consequence to the sagging lines, the bordacious cuts, and the grievous colours and patterns; to be worn with bandanas, caps (of various variations), major boots, leather pouches, and plenty, plenty attitude. —*City Life* 24 Aug. 1994, p. 17

> With glittering shards of sampled melodies, backwards delirium and a B-line with attitude, his alchemical mixing skills transfix. —*The Wire* Jan. 1995, p. 64

> We in the Carlton television area are currently being treated to late night 'television with attitude' consisting of programmes like *God's Gift* in which several charm-free yobbos perform various activities to a room full of squealing women in an attempt to discover which one of them is God's gift to women. —*Independent* 13 Jan. 1996, p. 15

See also 'TUDE

Audit Commission /ˈɔːdɪt kəmɪʃ(ə)n/ *noun* 〰️ 📷

In the UK: an independent body which monitors public spending, especially that by local government, on behalf of the government.

Under the Local Government Finance Act of 1982 the *Audit Commission* was established to take responsibility for local authority audits. These audits, prepared either by district auditors or independent approved auditors from private firms of accountants, are open to public inspection. Since its inception the *Audit Commission* has also carried out a number of special investigations, including in 1990 a review of state primary schools and in 1996 a survey of police performance and an evaluation of GP FUNDHOLDERS. This developing role has been assigned to the Commission within a climate in which there is a growing belief in the need for assessment of existing systems and new practices in local government and in education and health.

> They are all full-time classroom assistants at Sir James Smith's School, Cornwall, where we have found the recent Audit Commission suggestion that classroom assistants can improve efficiency in primary schools is no less true in secondary.
>
> —*Times Educational Supplement* 8 Feb. 1991, p. 20

> The question of the role of the member in the modern, enabling, local authority has been put on the agenda by a 1990 report from the Audit Commission. —*Independent* 23 July 1992, p. 22

> In the first objective evaluation of fundholding, a linchpin of the NHS reforms, the Audit Commission says that most fundholders have made few changes and are not giving value for money.
>
> —*The Times* 22 May 1996 (electronic edition)

authoring /ˈɔːθərɪŋ/ *noun* 💻

The process of creating or compiling MULTIMEDIA documents or page layouts for electronic publishing.

When the first practical MULTIMEDIA compilation packages began to appear in the mid eighties, people were faced with finding a simple term to describe the process of creating a document which might contain graphics, sound, animation, and video in addition to text; all of these could be linked together by hypertext links (see HYPER-) to create a non-linear document which the user could browse at will. The terms *programming* and *compiling*, though not entirely inappropriate, were not really the right words (and in any case already had specific meanings in computing), nor was *writing*, because origination of text was only sometimes involved. The new word *authoring*, first seen in 1985, seemed a better fit and is now the standard term; it is also frequently used attributively, as in **authoring system**, **authoring package**, **authoring tools**, and **authoring software**. The term *authoring* is also used for the process of creating complex page layouts for electronic publishing and is applied attributively to the systems involved in this.

> In order to profit from the possibilities of hypertext, teachers have to be provided with powerful authoring environments which allow them to create complex hypertexts while concentrating fully on the contents and didactic aspects.
> —*Literary & Linguistic Computing* Vol. 2, No. 2 1992, p. 125

> The 840AV is well suited for multimedia authoring, and it's the best choice for demanding production applications, such as color prepress and publishing, where more processing horsepower quickly pays for itself. —*MacWorld* Dec. 1993, p. 20

auto bra ⚗ see CAR BRA

automagically /ɔːtə(ʊ)ˈmadʒɪk(ə)li/ *adverb* 🖳

In informal usage, concerning an automatic process, especially in computing, which is sufficiently complex or incomprehensible that it appears to happen by magic.

A blend of *automatically* and *magically*.

This blend seems to have been first used in the US in the late eighties and is still mainly confined to technical computing contexts, frequently on the INTERNET and Usenet (see NET). It is often used by specialists about some process which is too complicated to explain at the moment. It reflects the dictum of Arthur C. Clarke that

> Any sufficiently advanced technology is indistinguishable from magic.

Though initially humorous in intent, it now appears in neutral contexts. The derived adjective and noun **automagic** are also fairly common online.

> Techies (and journalists in their turn) shrug their shoulders and report simply that this behaviour occurs 'automagically' (to use the American term for it).
> —*Personal Computer World* Mar. 1992, p. 383

> I do this editing from within the kludgy bookmark editing window though, actually using it to automagically generate the hotlist for my homepage. —10 Mar. 1995, online posting

> The List Designer, Manager, Browser, and Connect utilities are integrated as extensions, and many of the field classes have some fresh automagic. —9 Mar. 1996, online posting

automated teller machine 〰 ▓ see HOLE-IN-THE-WALL

autonomous agent 🖳 see AGENT

autostereogram /ɔːtə(ʊ)ˈstɛrɪəgram/ *noun* 🖳 ▓

An image, generated by a computer, consisting of a pattern of dots and lines which are perceived as three-dimensional by focusing one's eyes in front of or behind the plane of the image.

Although the word was first used in 1957 (of a photographic image), its current usage in computing dates from the early nineties. The pictures look like random collections of coloured lines and dots, but by deliberately uncrossing the eyes most people can resolve them into a three-dimensional image. The pictures actually consist of a pair of images, one arranged and coloured for the right eye, the other for the left, printed together but slightly offset; the process of calculating the correct separations for the elements of the images is so complex that only a computer can do it. *Autostereograms* became a craze in the early nineties, first in Japan and then in the US and the UK, appearing as glossy images on market stalls, in books and magazines, and latterly in advertisements; many computer programs for generating them also appeared. The technical name has been widely abbreviated to **stereogram**; in popular usage, the images are often known by the trade mark *Magic Eye*.

I am inclined to agree with…the only British company making the posters (properly called autostereograms), that unless there are dramatic improvements in the technology, they are liable to be an 18-month wonder.   *—Independent on Sunday* 23 Jan. 1994, p. 17

Stereogram images, in general, have become a social phenomenon inspiring a number of books (including three New York Times' bestsellers), posters, postcards, and national syndication in the Sunday comics.   *—The HiTek Report* 17 Apr. 1995, online newsletter

awesome /'ɔːs(ə)m, in the US 'ɑːs(ə)m/ *adjective* POP

In North American slang: marvellous, great, stunningly good.

Awesome originally meant 'full of awe', but by the end of the seventeenth century was also used in the sense 'inspiring awe, dreadful'. The apparent reversal of meaning that has now taken place started through a weakening of the word's meaning during the middle decades of the twentieth century to 'staggering, remarkable'; this was then further weakened and turned into an enthusiastic term of approval in the eighties.

Awesome was taken up in the eighties as one of the most fashionable words of general approval among young Americans. The first printed use appears in the *Official Preppy Handbook* (1980). It is particularly associated with *preppies* and the New York smart set, often appearing as part of a fixed phrase, preceded by *totally*. It has remained popular into the nineties, and has spread outside the US to Canada and Australia.

That night I *freebased* a *fractal* of *crack* and *blissed out* on *E*. It was *awesome*. It was *ace*. It was *wicked, bad* and *def*. It was twenty quid. OUCH!   *—Blitz* Dec. 1989, p. 130

Now the rock world is reeling from the most awesome teenage heart-throbs of the lot – the Turtles.   *—Daily Star* 23 Oct. 1990, p. 19

The girl hooked me onto the bungy rope…'You did it, Mom! You bungeed! You were awesome!'   *—Beautiful British Columbia* Fall 1994, p. 4

AZT /eɪzɛd'tiː, in the US eɪziː'tiː/ *abbreviation* ⓧ

Short for **azidothymidine**, a drug used in the treatment of AIDS to stop HIV from replicating itself within the patient's body; now officially known as *Zidovudine*.

Azidothymidine was developed in the US in 1974 as a treatment for retroviruses (viruses replicating by means of RNA). In 1985, soon after HIV was identified as a retrovirus, *azidothymidine* was tested against it; it was found to prevent the virus from copying itself and so helped to prolong the life of infected patients. For a while it was promoted in the press as a 'wonder drug' and even—quite incorrectly—as a cure for Aids. Once the drug was in regular use for treating HIV-positive individuals, from 1986 onwards, the name *azidothymidine* was usually abbreviated to *AZT*. This is still the name by which the drug is known colloquially, despite the fact that its official name was changed to *Zidovudine* in 1987 and it is marketed under the trade mark *Retrovir*. Although other treatments, such as DDI, DDC, and *3TC* (or *Lamivudine*), have since become available, it continues to be used, often in combination with 3TC in particular.

The US National Institutes of Health have apparently spent US$1 billion on HIV treatment research since 1984 and have produced no treatment (AZT, DDI and DDC have all come from the private sector).   *—Outrage* Feb. 1991, p. 22

Patients with HIV have responded well to a combination of therapies…It is thought that a combination including the drug Retrovir (AZT), from Wellcome, and a treatment called Lamivudine (3TC), by Glaxo, is 10 times more effective than any one therapy.   *—Daily Telegraph* 21 Nov. 1994, p. 5

B

babe /beɪb/ *noun*

A slang term for an attractive young woman.

Babe meaning 'a pretty girl' is recorded (especially in US English as a term of address) from 1915, but has been repopularized in the nineties, especially through the 'Wayne's World' sketches and films (see NOT), with an extra emphasis on the element of sexual desirability. (In the film *Barb Wire*, the heroine, played by Pamela Lee Anderson, habitually demands, 'Don't call me babe!') Some uses of *babe* applied to an attractive man are recorded, but in the main a *babe* is assumed to be female, and may be described by the adjective **babelicious**.

He has gray hair, is on the short side and is not what I would refer to as a babe.
—*Sassy* Aug. 1991, p. 110

Wayne and Garth yearn for 'babes—in the land of Babe-a-lonia, where Julia Roberts is babelicious'. 'A babe with major lippage', says Wayne. —*Premiere* Mar. 1992, p. 19

Sean said, 'You look good, Mom. A little modern, but good. David thinks you're a babe'.
—*Harper's Magazine* June 1992, p. 62

Women are classified by male colleagues on the basis of attractiveness, availability, age, clothes and make-up, as 'babes', 'one of the boys', a 'bit of a mum', a 'lesbian', or a 'dragon', and are treated accordingly, regardless of their job status. —*Independent* 21 Dec. 1995, p. 1

baby buster POP see GENERATION X

back to basics /bak tə 'beɪsɪks/ *noun phrase*

As a political catchphrase: embodying a conscious return to what are seen as fundamental principles of self-respect, decency, and honesty.

A particular use of an existing formulation.

The current association of *back to basics* with the British Conservative Party derives from a speech made by John Major to the Party Conference in 1993. The Prime Minister said:

It is time to get back to basics: to self-discipline and respect for the law, to consideration for others, to accepting responsibility for yourself and your family, and not shuffling it off on the state.

The emphasis of the original statement was thus on personal responsibility, but from the beginning *back to basics* has been associated in the public mind with a call to return to the moral values of an earlier period (perhaps comparable with the *Victorian values* of the Thatcher era). It has accordingly been used somewhat mockingly in situations in which Conservatives are deemed to have fallen short of the aspirations embodied by the phrase.

'Back to Basics' has so far involved three resignations, nine girlfriends, one close male friend, two violent deaths and two...'love children'. —*Vanity Fair* Apr. 1994, p. 139

Back to basics, newly billed as the defining slogan of Majorism, begins its political life in contradictory spirit. —*Guardian* 9 Nov. 1994, p. 20

badger-watch POP see -WATCH

bad hair day /bad 'hɛː deɪ/ *noun phrase* POP

A day on which everything seems to go wrong.

Bad hair day, a day on which one's hair is particularly unmanageable, has become a succinct phrase used to describe a day on which nothing seems to be properly in one's control.

Soon you will notice how much less complaining you do, even on bad hair days.
—*Post* (Denver) 8 Feb. 1994, section B, p. 7

On a 'bad hair day' when you just know that you look terrible and you think that everyone else notices it as well. —*Independent* 13 Aug. 1996, section 2, p. 26

baggy /'bagi/ *noun* and *adjective*

noun: A style of British popular music combining the guitar-based melodies of indie pop with dance rhythms. Also the culture associated with this music, characterized by the wearing of baggy clothes.

adjective: Belonging to this music or culture.

The name is taken from the *baggy* clothing worn by followers of the music.

Baggy music and culture marked the closing years of the eighties. Popular particularly in northern Britain, the music was characterized by a loose, funky feel and the use of a live drummer rather than an electronic drum machine. The individualism and exuberance of *baggy* music, the use by its followers of drugs such as ECSTASY, and the code of dress, suggest that the *baggy* culture developed in contradistinction to the spirit of the eighties. Some however suggest it may have sprung from the confidence and optimism of that decade.

I think Baggy was definitely a product of 10 years of Thatcherism, a kind of euphoric finale to Eighties optimism. —*Melody Maker* Dec. 1991, p. 9

He wrote the magnificent 'There She Goes', but that was a hit at the tail end of baggy over four years ago. —*Select* Mar. 1995, p. 8

Back when the Stone Roses' first album appeared, the Madchester scene was at its height. They were the first of the 'baggy' bands, combining rock and dance music into a new, sweaty whole that raved and clubbed and lived on Ecstasy. —*Alternative Press* May 1995, p. 47

bail bandit /'beɪl bandɪt/ *noun*

A person who commits a crime while on bail awaiting trial.

Use of the slightly archaic term *bandit* is no doubt influenced by the attraction of the alliteration (see also BELTWAY BANDIT).

Increasing recognition of a perceived rise in crime committed by those on bail and awaiting trial led to the development of the term *bail bandit* in the early nineties. Measures taken under the terms of the Criminal Justice and Public Order Act of 1994 were intended to reduce the potential for such crime. These included new restrictions on the powers of the courts to grant bail, and new police powers to attach conditions to police bail after a defendant has been charged, to arrest an offender without warrant for breach of police bail, and to detain a person after charge to prevent further offending.

After a police campaign against 'bail bandits'—who commit fresh offences while awaiting trial—ministers are considering forcing a suspect to prove he would not be dangerous if allowed to wait at home instead of in jail. —*Independent on Sunday* 3 Oct. 1993, p. 5

The party supported elements of the 27-point package, such as giving courts new powers to lock up persistent 12 to 14-year-old offenders and to curb 'bail bandits'. —*Guardian* 12 Jan. 1994, section 1, p. 6

New bail powers…would help tackle the 'scandal of so-called bail bandits'. —*Daily Telegraph* 10 Apr. 1995 (electronic edition)

ball-tampering /'bɔ.ltamp(ə)rɪŋ/ *noun*

In cricket: illegal alteration of the surface of a ball to affect its movement in the air when bowled.

The phenomenon of *ball-tampering*, disturbing the surface of the ball especially by fingering, rubbing, or even cutting its seams, was a matter of considerable controversy within cricket circles in the first half of the nineties. It fuelled hostility between some opposing teams, particularly Britain and Pakistan. Some players and commentators perceived a disinclination on the part of umpires to report to the cricketing authorities observed instances of such tampering, although when it was reported and proven it did incur fines. In one instance unauthorized revelations of *ball-tampering* were made to the press; the fine imposed by the Test and County Cricket Board in response to this created a furore. The alternative terms *ball-doctoring* and *ball-gouging* have also been recorded.

> Pakistan are far from damaged by the allegations of ball-tampering. Let him who has never lifted the seam of a cricket ball cast the first stone. —*Daily Mirror* 1992 (BNC)

> There was nothing about ball-tampering in the umpires' report from Ilkeston.
> —*Guardian* 28 May 1994, p. 22

> He added that, if ball-tampering spread, the balance of power in the game would shift decisively against batsmen, reducing scores and shortening matches.
> —*Independent on Sunday* 7 Aug. 1994, p. 1

> It emerged that just last week Khan's defence team had announced it was making fresh allegations—this time of ball-tampering. —*Independent* 16 July 1996, p. 3

balsamic vinegar /bɔːl‚samɪk 'vɪnɪgə/ *noun* 🎲

A dark, sweet Italian vinegar, matured in wooden barrels.

Balsamic here comes from *balsam* in its sense 'an aromatic resinous exudation, obtained from various trees and shrubs and used as a base for certain fragrances and medical preparations'.

Balsamic vinegar was originally, and still is largely, produced in Italy. The resin from the wooden barrels in which it is matured gives it its distinctive dark colour and rich, aromatic, sweetness.

The influence of Italian cooking on the cuisine of the UK and North America has been increasingly apparent in the eighties and nineties. Not only have foods such as CIABATTA and TIRAMISU become widely available, but also ingredients essential for Italian recipes, such as pesto, sun-dried tomatoes, and mascarpone. *Balsamic vinegar* is one of these, widely used in marinades, to flavour sauces, and with oil to form **balsamic vinaigrette**.

> An acquaintance with rocket, pine nuts and balsamic vinegar becomes essential before eating out. —*New Scientist* 15 Oct. 1994, Future supplement, p. 13

> A beautiful iced plate of Connecticut Candy oysters was served with balsamic vinegar and shallots. —*New Jersey Monthly* July 1995, p. 82

bancassurance /'baŋkəʃɔːrəns, baŋkə'ʃɔːrəns/ *noun* Also written bankassurance 〰

The selling of insurance products and services, especially life assurance, by banking institutions.

Of uncertain origin, perhaps a borrowing from French.

It has been established practice for some time for banks and building societies to act as financial advisers to their clients, recommending investment and insurance policies with companies with whom they have links. In the nineties major banking institutions have taken this a step further and have established their own insurance services, in competition with insurance companies, selling life assurance policies directly to their customers. This marks a further blurring of the distinction between banks and building societies, at a time when many services, such as mortgage provision, are now offered by both. *Bancassurance* is a growing trend both in the UK and in the rest of Europe, no doubt reflecting a widespread increase in the market for reliable life assurance.

> The job losses stem largely from the amalgamation of TSB's bank and insurance operations into a unified 'bankassurance' business. —*Guardian* 25 June 1993, section 1, p. 17

> The banking and insurance community is familiar with the company, as the Netherlands' third-

largest bank, a fast-growing organisation that is following the same successful bancassurance route as Lloyds Bank and TSB. —*Independent* 3 Mar. 1995, p. 33

banoffi pie /bənɒfi 'pʌɪ/ *noun* ❌

A dessert having a pastry base and a filling consisting of bananas, toffee (made from condensed milk heated with sugar), and cream.

A blend of *banana* and a phonetic respelling of *toffee*.

References to *banoffi pie* were recorded intermittently in the seventies and eighties, but the dessert did not become generally known until the start of the nineties. In recent years it has become very popular and is now widely available in restaurants, delicatessens, and supermarkets. References to *banoffi cheesecake*, a cheesecake made with bananas and toffee, have also been recorded. Increasing familiarity has led to instances of the noun **banoffi** used alone to denote the pie.

Few can resist sticky, mouth-watering banoffi pie…The secret to the perfect banoffi is to bake the pastry first. —*Daily Express* 6 May 1994, p. 17

Puddings are of the banoffi pie/tarte tatin variety. —*GQ* Jan. 1995, p. 119

barfly jumping /bɑːflʌɪ 'dʒʌmpɪŋ/ *noun* POP

An activity involving jumping at a Velcro-covered wall with the aim of sticking to it, usually practised in bars.

A *barfly* is 'a person who frequents bars'; the idea of a fly landing on the surface of a wall is also present.

An activity, like CANYONING and STAGE DIVING, in which participants hurl themselves bodily forward despite the attendant risks of pain and injury. In this case the aim is to stick, like a fly, to a velcro-covered wall. There is evidence that *barfly jumping* has caught on in various parts of the world, but it has not achieved widespread popularity. It seems unlikely that it will become an established activity.

Life assurance companies may reduce payments to those fatally injured while barfly jumping. —*Daily Telegraph* 4 Sept. 1992, section 2, p. 3

New Zealand's gifts to the world: Katherine Mansfield, Janet Frame, mooning and barfly jumping…Participants wear a Velcro suit, bounce on a trampoline, and compete to see who can stick himself highest to a Velcro-covered wall. —*Guardian* 18 Mar. 1994, section 2, p. 3

basehead /'beɪshɛd/ *noun* Also written **base-head** POP 🍴

In US slang: a person who habitually takes cocaine in the form of freebase or CRACK.

From *base*, the second element of *freebase* 'cocaine that has been purified by heating with ether, and is taken by inhaling the fumes or smoking the residue', and *head* in the sense 'a habitual taker of drugs; a drug addict'.

Use of the noun *basehead* has been recorded since the late eighties (an American rap band called *Basehead* was performing at that time). The term *basehead* denotes users of both freebase and crack; its use tends to be derogatory, with an implication of dependency or addiction.

Dirty, skinny, disordered base-heads yelling at each other and us and people who aren't there. —*P. J. O'Rourke Parliament of Whores* (1991), p. 131

That part of a basehead's time not actually involved in the preparation and ingestion of the drug is spent in the search for and acquisition of more of it. —*New York Review of Books* 16 July 1992 , p. 23

BASE jump /'beɪs dʒʌmp/ *noun* and *verb* Also written **base jump** POP ⚽

noun: A parachute jump from a fixed point, especially a high building or promontory, rather than from an aircraft.

intransitive verb: To make a BASE jump.

The acronym *BASE* is formed from the initial letters of *Building, Antenna-tower, Span, Earth*. The strong formative and semantic influence of the noun *base* in its standard senses is reflected in the increasing occurrence of the acronym in lower case.

The phenomenon of **BASE jumping** is thought to have started in the US in the very late seventies. It developed out of the desire to conduct parachute jumps without a need for aircraft. The locations sought by *base jumpers* include high *buildings*, the *antenna-towers* of radio stations, the *spans* of high bridges, and the cliffs provided by the *earth* itself. As the sport took hold records were set for the lowest possible jump, at one time recorded as 190 feet. By the nineties the activity had spread to the UK. It appears to be shunned by the British Parachute Association.

It might not sound safe, but BASE jumpers—4,000 worldwide—say this is the second safest site, behind El Capitan in California's Yosemite National Park.
—*USA Today* 19 Oct. 1989, section C, p. 10

He had already completed four base jumps before the Hilton leap and was not challenged when he entered the hotel through a back door. —*Independent* 18 June 1992, p. 6

Both could climb the Tower and Base jump from the top, 20,000 feet above sea level, onto the glacier below. —*Radio Times* 26 June 1993, p. 79

Base jumping wears a very different aspect from the public face of daredevilry: the laughing bungee jumper, the boasting sky diver. —*Guardian* 5 Aug. 1994, section 2, p. 5

See also BUNGEE JUMPING

basic pindown ⁅ see PINDOWN

basuco /bəˈzuːkəʊ, bəˈsuːkəʊ/ Also written **basuko, bazuco**, or **bazuko** *noun* POP

A cheap, impure form of cocaine, made by mixing coca paste with a variety of other substances, which is extremely addictive when smoked for its stimulant effects.

A Colombian Spanish word; perhaps connected with Spanish *basura* 'sweepings, waste' (since the drug is made from the waste products of refined cocaine) or with *bazucar* 'to shake violently'. Alternatively the connection could be with *waste, rubbish* generally, just as other drugs have in the past been referred to collectively in slang as *junk*. A quite different derivation comes from the suggestion that there have actually been two stages of borrowing here: first the English weapon-name *bazooka* was borrowed into Spanish, then it was applied figuratively to the drug (with its explosive effect), and finally the word was re-borrowed into English in a slightly altered form.

Basuco is the South American equivalent of CRACK, and has been smoked in Latin American countries for some time. The drug first appeared in the English-speaking world in 1983 and at first was also known as *little devil* or *Suzuki*, but *basuco* now seems to be its established name.

Police and drug enforcement agencies [in Florida] believed basuco had the potential to create a bigger problem than crack…The cost of using basuco was as little as $1 a dose.
—*Courier-Mail* (Brisbane) 15 Dec. 1986, p. 6

While it takes two years of regular cocaine use to become addicted, it takes only a few weeks to become hooked on *bazuko*, a mind-blowing mix of coca base, marijuana and tobacco containing such impurities as petrol, ether and even sawdust. —*The Times* 14 Sept. 1987, p. 10

Fernando…lost his wife and a high-ranking civil service job after starting to smoke basuco.
—*Observer* 22 May 1994, p. 20

batch file /ˈbatʃ faɪl/ *noun* ▣

A computer file in which is stored a list of commands to be carried out in sequence when the name of the batch file is typed at the operating system's command prompt.

The word *batch* has long been a common term in computing for 'a group of items which are to be processed as a single unit'; *file* is used in the standard computing sense of 'a collection of data stored and accessed under one name'.

Various compounds in *batch* have been common in computing for several decades, particularly *batch processing* and, more recently, *batch job*. However, the term *batch file* came into use only in the early eighties as one specific to the MS-DOS operating system (though the concept is much older, and names such as *macro* and *script* have been used in other systems and continue to be so). It is relatively simple using a text editor to create and store a list of commands for the computer to carry out; this makes it easy to repeat such sequences quickly and accurately and to use complicated commands without having to re-type them each time. The usefulness of *batch files* has greatly decreased with the introduction of graphical interfaces, such as Microsoft Windows, in which they are not used.

It includes a superior script language that lets even nonprogrammers write quick-and-dirty batch file utilities. —*PC World* Oct. 1989, p. 236

Programmer Kris Jamsa packs everything you could want to know about DOS batch file programming into this hefty edition. —*Compute* Nov. 1991, p. 128

BBS /biːbiːˈɛs/ *abbreviation* 🖳

Short for **bulletin board system**, a non-profit, computer-based forum which may permit discussion, the exchange of electronic mail, or access to software and other electronically-encoded material by means of telephone lines and modems.

The initial letters of *Bulletin Board System*; in the full phrase, *bulletin board* (the US equivalent of the British *noticeboard*) is used metaphorically to refer to the 'posting' of information in a place to which many people have access.

It was at the end of the seventies that computerized *bulletin boards* began proliferating. Initially, each *BBS* system was separate, but since the mid eighties they have been increasingly connected through non-profit links such as *FidoNet*; many now have access to the INTERNET. A *BBS* is usually small, often run on a single personal computer as a hobby by its operator, or SYSOP; there may be as many as a hundred thousand of them worldwide (*Boardwatch* magazine estimated in 1993 that there were more than sixty thousand in the US alone). Many serve groups with special interests: for example, there are boards for computing enthusiasts, religious organizations, and political activists; others cover health and medical issues, earthquake preparations, gun control and civil liberties, and so on. The concept of *bulletin boards* has given rise to suspicion, as they have become popularly associated with the illegal exchange of computer software and pornography, as well as subversive activity by terrorists and extremists. The term is sometimes employed by companies providing access to information or software updates stored on stand-alone computers, for security reasons kept separate from their main networks. Another name for the concept is **electronic bulletin board**, which first appeared in print in the early eighties; the abbreviation *BBS* is sometimes expanded to **bulletin board service**.

Most people think of BBSs as crude hacker forums where computer nerds trade tips on how to pirate software or break into the Pentagon's computers. —*Computer Buyer's Guide and Handbook* (1990), Vol. 8, p. 34

Founded in 1988 to keep guild members posted on developments in the lingering writers strike, the BBS has since evolved into a kind of electronic agora. Cars are sold, restaurants reviewed, serious political arguments are waged. —*Premiere* Sept. 1991, p. 25

Virtual communities are not utopias…Electronic bulletin board systems can bring people together, but the computer screen can be a way of controlling relationships, keeping people at a distance. —*Newsweek* 6 Sept. 1993, p. 49

beardism 🖰 see -ISM

beast /biːst/ *noun* 🖳 🖰

In UK prison slang: a person convicted of a sexual offence.

A specialization of context of the noun *beast* in its transferred sense 'a brutal person'.

The use of the noun *beast* to denote a sex offender entered the vocabulary of prison slang in the late eighties, joining the earlier *nonce*, which has a similar usage. Those considered by fellow inmates to be *nonces* or *beasts* are held to be at the bottom of an implicit hierarchy of respect. They are regarded as at risk from assaults by other prisoners (and allegedly by officers also), as a consequence of which they tend to be housed separately, often in isolated or even solitary conditions.

> The arrival of a police van at a prison might often be accompanied by comments such as 'a couple of beasts for you', with the result that the prisoners are immediately identified.
> —*Daily Telegraph* 29 Nov. 1989, p. 8

> When I heard what happened I felt a bit rotten…Then I heard he was a beast, and I felt better…It might sound rotten, but I don't feel sorry for him. I would rather have a murderer on the loose than a child molester or a pervert. —*Guardian* 28 Feb. 1995, section 2, p. 2

been there, done that /ˈbiːn ðɛː ˌdʌn ðat/ *interjection* POP

In humorous or ironic use: an assertion that the speaker knows from personal experience everything of interest about a particular place or topic.

A statement that one has *been* to a particular place and *done* everything of interest there.

Been there, done that as a jocular expression of world-weariness in response to suggestions that a particular place or action might be of interest has been current since the late eighties. The extension, **been there, done that, got the T-shirt**, reinforces the notion of the jaded tourist who has relentlessly visited sites of interest and bought souvenirs. Originally used in the context of proposed visits, **been there, done that** as an expression of weary familiarity may now be employed as a way of refusing to participate in any suggested form of activity or entertainment.

> I can assure you and them that I've been there, done that, got the video and the T-shirt.
> —*Big Issue* 22 Nov. 1994, p. 13

> But Mutombo has been there, done that, bought the T-shirt.
> —*Post* (Denver) 23 Apr. 1995, section B, p. 1

> So let those who want to remember, do so. But not me. Not anymore. Been there, done that.
> —*Guardian* 6 May 1995, Outlook section, p. 25

beetle bank /ˈbiːt(ə)l baŋk/ *noun*

A strip of land sown with perennial grasses and other plants to create an environment in which aphid-eating insects can thrive.

Partly with a playful allusion to *bottle bank*.

In the nineties, the development of *beetle banks* represents one of the ways in which farmers are encouraged to manage their land in an environmentally sensitive way. The policy is one which is intended to benefit both farmers and wildlife: the *beetle banks*, while re-establishing a traditional environment, can reduce crop infestation by harbouring aphid-eating insects.

> Further on we come to a new farm track, and Bruce points out the 'beetle bank', lush with grass and nettles, that lies along its edge. —*Scotland's Natural Heritage* June 1994, p. 21

> Extended five metre-wide 'beetle banks', a recent initiative by the Game Conservancy Trust, would also help encourage ground-nesting birds while creating cover for aphid-eating bugs with more pay-off in savings on aphicides. —*Guardian* 12 Oct. 1994, Society section, p. 4

be good news /biː gʊd ˈnjuːz/ *verbal phrase* POP

To be an asset; to be commendable, admirable.

A transferred usage, recorded since the early eighties, in which a person or thing, rather than information or tidings, represents *good news*. This development has followed the comparable *be bad news*, which had become established by the sixties.

He's good news. I get very good vibes from him.

—Erica Jong *Parachutes & Kisses* (1984), p. 209

This man is good news. I haven't read it [*sc.* his book] but I most certainly will.

—*Bookseller* 1 Jan. 1993, p. 32

Beltway Bandit /'bɛltweɪ ˌbandɪt/ *noun* Also written beltway bandit ⚡ 🖭

In US slang: a company or individual, frequently one formerly employed by a US government agency, hired by a corporation to assist in securing government contracts.

The noun *beltway* has been in use in the US since the fifties to denote a ring road, especially that around Washington, DC. In a transferred sense, usually as *Beltway* with an initial capital, it also denotes Washington, DC itself, especially as representing the perceived isolation of the US government and its agencies from the rest of the country. In an early usage of the term at the start of the eighties *Beltway Bandit* denoted simply one of a cluster of firms located along the Washington ring road. Subsequent use reflected the transferred use of *Beltway* to denote the enclosed world of the US government, the notion being that of pirates or *bandits* roaming the highway of government influence, exploiting their links with government agencies by selling their knowledge to those firms keen to secure government contracts.

Morris is not a...'Beltway Bandit' cashing in on a study subsidized by the government, but an objective and courageous free-lance writer. —*Washington Post* 3 July 1988, section 10, p. 4

Rosslyn, Virginia...[is] virtually deserted today: all the beltway bandits, procurement-consortium consultants are drinking Bloodies at brunches.

—Ron Rosenbaum *Travels with Dr. Death* (1990), p. 104

benchmark /'bɛntʃmɑːk/ *verb and noun* 💻

transitive verb: To measure the performance of (a computer system) in certain well-defined situations, such as intensive calculation, sorting, or text formatting, by running a specially-designed computer program or suite of programs.

noun: The result of such a test; a numerical value for the performance of a computer system in relation to others.

A specialized figurative application of the word. Originally a *benchmark* was a horizontal wedge-shaped incision cut by surveyors, for example in a wall, so that an angled bracket could be inserted to form a *bench* or support for the surveying equipment at a reproducible height. By the 1880s it had taken on the figurative sense of 'a point of reference; a criterion, a touchstone' of which the computing sense is a specific usage.

With the rise in number of models of microcomputers from about the end of the seventies onward, manufacturers and computer enthusiasts increasingly found a need for independent measures of the power of competing systems. The obvious solution was to run a computer program on each system which carried out some repetitive task and compare the time each took to complete. This process was termed **benchmarking** in 1976 and the noun and verb first appeared in print in the early eighties. A large number of such *benchmarks* have appeared, but their results are often distrusted because they are necessarily measures taken in artificial situations which may not correspond to real working conditions.

Figure 1 also shows results of the Whetstone test, a floating-point intensive benchmark, for both single- and double-precision arithmetic. —*UNIX Review* Sept. 1991, p. 55

We haven't had a chance to completely benchmark the new low-cost Mac models with the 68LC040 processor against competing 486SX machines, but early testing indicates that these new Macs may actually be faster. —*MacWorld* Dec. 1993, p. 19

bender 🌻 see TWIGLOO

benefit tourism /'bɛnɪfɪt ˌtʊərɪz(ə)m/ *noun*

The practice of travelling to or within Britain in order to claim social security benefits.

Formed from the idea of TOURISM undertaken so that one may qualify for *benefits* such as social security payments.

The term *benefit tourism* derives from a speech made to the British Conservative Party conference in 1993 by Peter Lilley, Secretary of State for Social Security, in which he highlighted what he saw as abuses of the system by would-be beneficiaries, or **benefit tourists**. Both terms have occasioned considerable debate, with some favouring what is seen as the identification of unexceptable exploitation of income support and other benefits, and others centring their concern on increased pressure on those who are seen as some of the most vulnerable members of society.

> Mr Lilley's clampdown on 'benefit tourism' has been attacked by the Government's own social security advisory committee. —*Independent on Sunday* 10 July 1994, p. 1

> The reason for changing the rules was Peter Lilley's desire to win over the Conservative Party conference in 1993, when he promised to stamp out 'benefit tourism', as foreign idlers were supposedly drawn to exploit the British welfare state. —*Independent* 27 Mar. 1995, p. 14

> As for EU citizens using their right of entry to become 'benefit tourists', on March 20th the High Court upheld Britain's right to deny income support to unemployed EU citizens if they were not seeking work. —*Economist* 1 Apr. 1995, p. 29

be there for /biː 'ðɛː fɔː/ *verbal phrase*

Be available to provide support and comfort for (someone), especially in a period of particular difficulty or stress.

The phrase *be there for* has been popular since the late eighties as encapsulating a view of personal support and sympathy readily available from another in time of need.

> I want to be there for her because she'll be there for me when Dean and his replacement and the guy after that are all history. —Jay McInerney *The Story of My Life* (1988), p. 92

> Mr. Bon Jovi's face and smile became tokens of the late 80's easy promises. He…was at his best wringing out anthems like 'I'll Be There for You'. —*New York Times* 15 Nov. 1992, section 2, p. 30

> He knows that Mum and Dad are always going to be there for him. —*Daily Mail* 2 Jan. 1995, p. 37

bhangra /'baŋgrə, 'baːŋgrə/ *noun* and *adjective* Also written **Bhangra**

noun: A style of popular dance music which fuses elements of Punjabi folk music with features of Western rock and disco music.

adjective: Belonging to this style of music or the subculture surrounding it.

A direct borrowing from Punjabi *bhāngrā*, a traditional Punjabi folk dance associated with harvest.

Bhangra music originated in the UK in the late seventies or early eighties, when pop musicians with a Punjabi ethnic background started to experiment with westernized versions of their parents' musical traditions. The term first appeared in English sources in this meaning in the late eighties when the style's popularity with Asian audiences had begun to attract a more general following. By the early nineties it had moved beyond Britain and, in particular, had returned to its north Indian roots. This new form, sometimes labelled **bhangra beat**, spread into the Indian subcontinent during the mid eighties and influenced the traditional styles it was derived from. As with many current forms of popular music, *bhangra* has been combined with other styles to form fusions such as **techno-bhangra**.

> This was not the middle of a feverish Saturday night, but a Wednesday mid-afternoon excursion for devotees of the Bhangra beat, the rhythm of the Punjabi pop…An up and coming group…turned

in a performance which set the seemingly incompatible rhythmic stridency of funk and Bhangra dance to a compulsive harmony.   —*Independent* 30 June 1987, p. 12

The bhangra is a Punjabi dance which has now become standard at all north-Indian weddings and has deteriorated into a hybrid pop form heavily influenced by Western jiving and Indian film choreography.   —Mark Tully *No Full Stops in India* (1992), p. 40

Maybe he'd have been more inspired by the ragga music of Shabba Ranks, or the 'bhangramuffin' of Apache Indian, whose roots lead circuitously back to Jamaica, among other places.
                    —*Guardian* 27 Jan. 1995, Friday supplement, p. 11

bimbo /'bɪmbəʊ/ *noun* ▌▌

In media slang: an attractive but unintelligent young woman.

This was originally a direct borrowing from Italian *bimbo* 'little child, baby'. The word was in use in English in other senses before this one developed (see below); in all of them the original Italian meaning has been lost, but in this case there may be some connection with the use of *baby* for a girlfriend, and possibly some influence from *dumbo* as well.

Bimbo first came into English in the early twenties, when it was used on both sides of the Atlantic (although mainly in the US) as a contemptuous term for a person of either sex; ironically, P. G. Wodehouse wrote in the forties about 'bimbos who went about the place making passes at innocent girls after discarding their wives'. By the end of the twenties it had developed the more specific sense of a stupid or 'loose' woman, especially a prostitute. In the late eighties, *bimbo* started to enjoy a new vogue in the media, this time without the implication of prostitution, but often with the suggestion that the typical *bimbo* was likely to 'kiss and tell' by selling her story to the popular press. In the US *bimbos* cost politicians their careers; Britain also had its own 'battle of the bimbos', when the affairs of certain rich men were exposed and the lifestyle of the *bimbo* was discussed in court. The word started to acquire derivatives: a teenage *bimbo* came to be known as a **bimbette** and a male *bimbo* as a **bimboy** (but see also HIMBO), while having an affair with a *bimbo* was even described as **bimbology** in one paper.

In the nineties the word has undergone a further development: **power bimbos** and **killer bimbos** are seen as women who combine the traditional attractions of a *bimbo* with career success on their own terms.

A gathering of playboys just wasn't a party unless there was at least one…scantily clad bimbette swimming around in a bathtub of shampoo.   —*Arena* Autumn/Winter 1988, p. 157

The Chanel-clad Queen of the Killer Bimbos has got her man by the short and curlies.
                    —*Daily Star* 16 Jan. 1992, p. 9

Stone's outrage at *VF*s topless cover seems bizarre for an ex-*Playboy* cover girl, but it is also symptomatic of the New Power Bimbos's quest for legitimacy.   —*Spy* July 1995, p. 45

bi-media /bʌɪ'miːdɪə/ *adjective* Also written **bimedia** ▓

Involving, or working in, two of the mass communication media (especially radio and television) at one time.

Although the word was first used in the US in the mid eighties, it only became widely known in the UK at the end of the decade. The BBC, led by its Director-General John Birt (see BIRTISM), streamlined its news-gathering and presentation by having staff work in both radio and television, a change that aroused much controversy by going against long-standing tradition. In the UK the term is strongly associated with the BBC, as it is the only organization running both television and radio operations in the UK; it is applied very occasionally to other pairs of media, usually print journalism and broadcasting. The noun for this concept is **bi-medialism** or **bi-mediality**; rarely an adverb **bi-medially** is also seen.

This bi-media approach has seen star correspondents performing on a range of programmes, from the *Nine O'Clock News* to Radio 4 phone-ins.   —*Independent* 8 Jan. 1993, p. 8

But nothing would divert attention from the open BBC wound, and there was a feeling that Birt, despite an impressive speech, hadn't done enough to acknowledge the pain of Producer Choice and 'bimedialism'. —*Guardian* 14 July 1993, section 2, p. 17

bio-diesel /ˈbʌɪə(ʊ)ˌdiːz(ə)l/ *noun* Also written **biodiesel** 🌱 🔋

A fuel made at least in part from organic products and intended as a substitute for diesel fuel.

The concept of a *biofuel*, one derived from organic material rather than mineral oil, dates back to the seventies; in the eighties, various attempts were made to create a fuel oil which could be used in place of diesel fuel or to dilute it. In Europe, the emphasis since about 1990 has been on using a processed rape-oil; this is sometimes called *RME* (an abbreviation of *rape methyl esters*, from the end products of the chemical processing of the oil). In the US, *bio-diesel* is usually a mixture of diesel fuel with processed vegetable oils of various types, such as soya bean and peanut oil.

Proponents of the fuel claim it burns more cleanly and is better for the environment because it is a renewable resource and the fuel itself is biodegradable in the event of a spill; it has been claimed that diverting only 10 percent of America's cropland to the production of *bio-diesel* could provide all the fuel needed for agriculture throughout the country. Others are unconvinced, arguing that the land needed to grow the biofuel crops could be better used and that the fuel is in any case far from pollution-free.

But ironically, the environment pressure group Greenpeace is opposed to research into bio-diesel. Though it believes in principle in bio-fuels, in practice it believes there are better ways to spend Government money. —*Farmers Guardian* 7 Aug. 1992, p. 8

Biodiesel, the alternative fuel derived from rapeseed, has few advantages over conventional diesel fuel, according to a study released…by Germany's Federal Environment Office (UBA).
—*New Scientist* 6 Feb. 1993, p. 19

Not only have their bio-diesel producers secured government support, they are also convincing the public that growing rapeseed for fuel is an environmentally-friendly option.
—*Farmers Weekly* 21 July 1995, p. 5

biodiversity /ˌbʌɪə(ʊ)dʌɪˈvəːsɪti/ *noun* Also written **bio-diversity** 🌱

Diversity of plant and animal life.

In the late eighties and nineties there has developed an increasing awareness both of the richness and variety, the *biodiversity*, of the natural world, and of the growing threat posed to it both in agriculture's intense cultivation of particular species and in the destruction of the world's rainforest. Adoption of the term *biodiversity* in the mid eighties was given impetus by its use at a forum held in Washington, DC in 1986. A broadly-based campaign to protect the earth's *biodiversity* began at around this time, identified particularly with efforts to protect the rainforest. A number of *biodiversity* programmes and conventions were established, and a **National Institute of Biodiversity** was founded in Costa Rica. The issue was given a high profile in the EARTH SUMMIT in Brazil in 1992. This led eventually, after commercial considerations prevented the signature of the US President George Bush, to the signing of the international **Biodiversity Treaty** in 1993, President Clinton signing for the US.

A conflict may be perceived between the desire to protect the planet's *biodiversity* and the need to supply humankind's food, water, and energy requirements. Another enemy of *biodiversity* is the potential manipulation of the environment consequent on the late twentieth-century sciences of biotechnology, or BIOTECH, and GENETIC ENGINEERING.

There is a common tendency to suppose that less-than-lush landscapes are somehow short on biodiversity. Indeed, such 'trash' landscapes may well invite the traditional attitude…that it is an act of virtue to convert them for the benefit and profit of humanity.
—*New Scientist* 2 Mar. 1991, p. 34

Action on biodiversity must shift from the present overemphasis on tropical forests to a more realistic target of protecting, managing and increasing resources of the 'agrobiodiversity' needed for future global food security. —*New Scientist* 18 Jan. 1992, p. 8

The Biodiversity Legal Foundation had petitioned to add the southern Rocky Mountain population of the boreal toad to the endangered species list. —*Post* (Denver) 24 Mar. 1995, section B, p. 6

Corals come in many forms, providing living space for a variety of marine organisms—reef ecosystems have probably the greatest biodiversity on the planet, rivalling that of rainforests.
—*Guardian* 4 May 1995, p. 10

The notion of 'Frankenstein's tomato' was resurrected by Prince Charles on Tuesday night, on the eve of a seminar on Britain's disappearing biodiversity. —*Independent* 14 Dec. 1995, p. 5

bioreactor /ˌbʌɪə(ʊ)riːˈaktə/ *noun*

A vessel in which living organisms are cultured, either to grow useful types of cells or to manufacture a chemical product. Also, in a transferred sense, a TRANSGENIC animal viewed as a producer of pharmaceutical drugs.

In the area of BIOTECH, *bioreactors* are key components. They are used to cultivate plant or animal cells (which may have been genetically modified), to grow tissue that can be used for transplantation or grafts, and as reaction vessels to manufacture chemicals by biological processes such as fermentation, or processes which employ bacteria to treat waste water. Considerable research effort has been put into creating more efficient designs: one announced in June 1992 was a spin-off from NASA research into cultivating cells in microgravity, called the **rotating wall bioreactor**, which can cultivate three-dimensional human tissues—such as liver, bone marrow, and smooth muscle—for transplants. Another more recent development is the **hollow-fibre bioreactor**, which permits larger-scale production using a disposable culture medium.

Using a three-dimensional 'bioreactor' for culturing bone marrow tissue, J. H. David Wu and his colleagues...have shown that they can produce almost all of the stages and subtypes of human blood cells. —*Science News* 3 Apr. 1993, p. 214

Now new technologies, such as the hollow-fibre bioreactor, are allowing these antibodies to be produced efficiently *in vitro* and not in the bellies of beasts. —*Economist* 22 Apr. 1995, p. 116

biospherian /bʌɪəˈsfɪərɪən/ *noun* Also written **biospherean** and frequently capitalized

Any one of eight experimenters who were sealed in an artificial habitat called **Biosphere 2** between September 1991 and September 1993; also, a member of a later similar group.

Formed by adding the adjectival suffix *-ian* to *biosphere* 'the regions of the Earth's surface capable of supporting life'. The noun has been in use since 1899 and is employed in such official terms as the UNESCO designation *biosphere reserve* for an area in which there is significant *biomass*, or volume of living organisms, to be conserved.

The idea behind *Biosphere 2* was to test whether an artificial environment could be created and sustained independently of life on Earth, partly as an ecological experiment and partly to determine whether space habitats or colonies on other worlds were practicable. A three-acre environment, looking like a huge greenhouse, was created in the Arizona desert at a cost of about $100 million, completely isolated except for sunlight and electrical power. It was stocked with a carefully selected assortment of plants, insects, birds, and other living organisms to recreate a series of habitats. Eight volunteers spent two years inside, living off crops they cultivated and maintaining the habitats. The environment was named *Biosphere 2* on the assumption that the Earth was *Biosphere 1*. Although the habitat suffered some setbacks (especially with the carbon dioxide levels inside the dome), much was learned about the ecological principles involved. Nevertheless, the experiment caused some controversy, with some observers describing it as a ridiculously futuristic venture (or even as an expensive publicity stunt or theme park) rather than a piece of serious environmental research.

When the eight space-suited 'Biospherians' finally sealed themselves into the stunning 3-acre glass-and-steel bubble of a replicate Earth known as Biosphere 2—some were calling it the most important scientific experiment since the moon launch.   —*Tucson Weekly* 6–12 Nov. 1991, p. 4

In spite of the mechanical intervention, in the form of a carbon dioxide 'scrubber', installed just days before the dome was sealed behind the Biosphereans, the atmospheric level of the gas is now close to 2000 parts per million (ppm), some eight times that in the air outside.
—*New Scientist* 23 Nov. 1991, p. 14

Within great latitudes, the artificial ecosystem of Bio2 [Biosphere 2] ran its own course, but when it veered toward a runaway state, or stalled, the biospherians nudged it.
—Kevin Kelly *Out of Control* (1994), p. 152

biotech /ˈbʌɪə(ʊ)tɛk/ *noun* 🜂

The use of living organisms in industrial, medical, agricultural, and other processes; a firm working in this field.

Though the term *biotechnology* was coined in 1947, it was only in 1974 that the shortened form *biotech* appeared, at the point at which it was first becoming possible to manipulate the genetic make-up of living things. This made it possible to 'customize' micro-organisms capable of producing useful substances which could not readily be manufactured any other way; **biotech companies** can also create plants and animals with valuable characteristics that did not previously exist, such as resistance to disease, better flavour, or increased productivity (see GENETIC ENGINEERING for more details). The ethical and environmental issues raised by the creation and release of modified life-forms have caused immense controversy in the eighties and nineties. A *biotech company* is occasionally known as a *biotech*; the word is also commonly used attributively. A person working in a *biotech* laboratory is a **biotechnician**; the technical processes involved are sometimes generically named **biotechniques** or described by the adjective **biotechnical**.

Biotech firms are creating…genespliced strains of corn that can resist insect pests, thus cutting down on the need for pesticides.   —*U.S. News & World Report* 11 Jan. 1993, p. 27

There is also a need for a policy of 'prior informed consent' whereby exporters of biotechnical products are required to inform an importing country of any restrictions or bans placed on their products.   —*New Scientist* 25 June 1994, p. 47

biotecture /ˈbʌɪə(ʊ)tɛktʃə/ *noun* 🜔

The use of plants as an integral part of the design of buildings.

The idea of *biotecture*, in which plant-life forms an integral part of the design and structure of a building rather than merely providing ornamentation or background, developed in the eighties. It is not yet clear whether interest in *biotecture* represents an essentially experimental phase, or whether the practice will become an established one.

Perhaps the ultimate is the proposal of German architect Rudolf Doernach that we live in 'biotecture plant houses'—houses not only covered with plants but made in and of them.
—D. Pearson *The Natural House Book* (1989), p. 249

It also has roots in movements such as *Baubiologie* (building biology) and biotecture—clothing buildings in living greenery—that have sprung up in Europe, especially Germany.
—*Independent on Sunday* 7 Nov. 1993, p. 12

birthing pool 🜕 see WATER BIRTH

Birtism /ˈbəːɪtɪz(ə)m/ *noun* 🜔

The principles and practices of John Birt, Deputy Director-General of the BBC 1987–92, and Director-General from 1992.

Formed from the name of John *Birt* (b. 1944) and the suffix *-ism*.

Birtism is recorded from 1988 as a term for the policies introduced into the BBC by John Birt. These are characterized by an emphasis on the explanatory function of broadcasting, particularly in the area of current affairs (as exemplified by proposals for a ROLLING NEWS service), and a market-based approach to the elements of programme-making. **Birtian** or **Birtist** policies remain controversial, and **Birtists**, while associated with the BI-MEDIA revolution, have been criticized for an extreme reliance on management theory and jargon, and for adversely affecting PRODUCER CHOICE.

> For many at the meeting, the idea that the flamboyant, original and free-thinking Janet Street-Porter had notions of journalism not dissimilar to those of the allegedly dull and dreary Birtists came as something of a shock. —*Sunday Times* 27 Mar. 1988

> Now an iron structure has been set in place in news and current affairs to make sure that producers do not have freedom, that they conform to what has become known as Birtism.
> —*Guardian* 14 July 1993, p. 6

> A dangerous device, irony, particularly in the Birtian BBC.
> —*Independent on Sunday* 4 Sept. 1994, p. 24

> BBC1's hybrid schedule, mixing Birtist elements with blatantly populist fare, has maintained its 32 per cent share. —*Guardian* 9 Jan. 1995, section 2, p. 14

See also PRODUCER CHOICE

B-ISDN /ˈbiːʌɪɛsdiːˌɛn/ *abbreviation*

A digital communications system capable of high speeds and which can transmit many kinds of information at once.

An abbreviation of *broadband*, 'relating to or using signals over a broad range of frequencies', and *Integrated Services Digital Network*, the name of an existing digital telecommunications system (usually abbreviated to *ISDN*) which offers a variety of facilities at much lower speeds.

The rapid growth in networked telecommunications in the nineties has fuelled demand for digital services capable of carrying very large amounts of different kinds of data quickly and accurately worldwide. Applications include videoconferencing, electronic mail (see ELECTRONIC), MULTIMEDIA, teleshopping, teleworking or other remote access (see TELE-), file transfers (especially in computer-aided design and manufacturing), access to databases, CLIENT-SERVER links, INTERNET access, and the WORLD WIDE WEB. *B-ISDN* is one set of standards for achieving this, which is beginning to emerge from research laboratories into commercial use; an experimental high-speed link has been established throughout western Europe. Other uses are being suggested for the system even before it has come into service, such as high-definition cable television, video-telephones, and remote education.

The older ISDN technology, which is extensively used in France, Germany, Japan, the US, and elsewhere (but rather less so in Britain) is sometimes called **N-ISDN** (**Narrowband ISDN**) to distinguish it; in Europe it is also called **Euro-ISDN** or **E-ISDN** to indicate it conforms to European standards for the system.

> Live video data and multimedia applications will benefit significantly from the data capacity of B-ISDN lines. —*Byte* July 1992, p. 45

> The main initial application of B-ISDN is LAN interconnection, which will require even greater bandwidth on demand as applications like videoconferencing arrive on PCs.
> —*Computer Bulletin* Sept. 1994, p. 8

bit map see RASTERIZE

BITNET see NET

black information /ˌblak ɪnfəˈmeɪʃ(ə)n/ *noun*

Information held by institutions such as banks and credit agencies about people who are considered to be bad credit risks.

The consumer spending boom of the earlier eighties meant that by the end of the decade many people were financially over-extended, and in some cases unable to cope with the debts that had been incurred. *Black information* was coined in the late eighties, as a term for the information held by banks and other institutions about those regarded as bad credit risks, and likely to be 'blacklisted' as regards future borrowing.

The propriety of such information being passed from one institution to another has always occasioned some debate. More recently this has been intensified by the development of the concept of *white information*: a positive statement of a customer's creditworthiness which may be passed on to a credit reference agency without the customer's being informed.

> They will have a chance to inspect similar 'black' information on customers with bad debt records elsewhere.   —*The Times* 4 June 1988, p. 34

> Banks and building societies have hitherto resisted providing 'white information' to the [credit reference] agencies, restricting themselves to defaults—so-called 'black information'. But some banks have started to pass on 'white information' to their credit card operations.
> —*Guardian* 19 Mar. 1994, p. 26

black metal /blak 'mɛt(ə)l/ *noun*

A type of heavy metal music with lyrics which invoke the Devil and celebrate evil.

The harsh and vigorous music of *heavy metal* was recognized by the late seventies as a distinctive form of rock music. *Black metal* as the name of a variety of this, characterized by lyrics invoking the Devil and celebrating evil, is recorded from the late eighties.

> Different types of ritual were performed, varying from the benign such as listening to 'black metal' music to the more serious ones such as the abuse of mixed drugs and sacrifices of small animals.   —*Canadian Journal of Psychiatry* 1988, Vol. 33, p. 199

> Black metal, a form of hard rock that features explicitly Satanic lyrics, was founded by a band called Venom in the early Eighties.   —*Observer* 3 Oct. 1993, p. 3

black section /blak 'sɛkʃ(ə)n/ *noun*

In the British Labour party, a proposed, officially recognized grouping of non-white members at constituency level, designed to represent the interests of non-whites.

Left-wing members of the Labour Party, especially those from the London constituencies, first proposed the formation of *black sections* in the early eighties. They believed that these might act as pressure-groups on behalf of blacks and Asians and would encourage black and Asian involvement in mainstream political life. The proposals were denounced as a form of reverse apartheid by the trade unions and were eventually rejected by the National Executive Committee and the party conference in 1987; nor have they found a place in the NEW LABOUR of the nineties.

> What the party needs is…a black section within as an internal training-ground and pressure group, like the women's section and the Young Socialists.   —*New Statesman* 13 Aug. 1982, p. 9

> The Conference also overwhelmingly rejected proposals to set up Black sections within the party, a matter which had caused difficulty earlier in the year when in April the National Executive Committee had suspended the parliamentary candidature of one leading advocate of black sections.   —*Parliamentary Affairs* 1988, Vol. 41, p. 319

black smoker see SMOKER

black tar /blak 'tɑ:/ *noun*

In the slang of drug users, an exceptionally pure and potent form of heroin from Mexico. Also known more fully as **black-tar heroin** or abbreviated to **tar**.

This form of heroin is dark (*black*) in colour and has the consistency of *tar*; *tar* had also been a slang word for opium since the thirties.

Black tar first became known under this name to drug enforcement officials in Los Angeles in 1983 (though it may in fact be the same thing as *black stuff*, slang for brown Mexican heroin since the late sixties); its abuse had become a serious and widespread problem in various parts of the US by 1986. It is made and distributed only from opium-poppy crops in

Mexico using a process which makes it at the same time very pure and relatively cheap. *Black tar* has a large number of other slang names, including those listed in the *Economist* quotation given below.

DEA officials blame the low price of 'black tar' for forcing down other heroin prices, causing the nation's first general increase in overall heroin use in more than five years.
—*Capital Spotlight* 17 Apr. 1986, p. 22

Black tar, also known as bugger, candy, dogfood, gumball, Mexican mud, peanut butter and tootsie roll…started in Los Angeles and has since spread to 27 states…What makes black tar heroin unique is that it has a single, foreign source—Mexico—and finds its way into Mexican-American distribution networks, often via illegal immigrants. —*Economist* 7 June 1986, p. 37

blades ⬛ see ROLLERBLADE

Blairism /'blɛːrɪz(ə)m/ *noun* ⬛

The political and economic policies of the British Labour politician Tony Blair (Anthony Charles Lynton Blair, b. 1953 Prime Minister since May 1997). Also, a statement or remark expressing such policies.

Blairism, as incorporating the essentials of NEW LABOUR political principles and practices, is recorded from 1994, the year in which Tony Blair was elected as leader of the Labour Party. More recently, the general characteristic of a willingness to combine a concern for social issues with an acceptance of many aspects of market-based economics has been focused in the aspirations enshrined in the concept of a STAKEHOLDER ECONOMY.

The effect of Tony Blair's views and beliefs within his party has been the subject of considerable media attention, and has given rise to a number of associated terms. There are references to **Blairist** and **Blairite** views, and the results of the implementation of such views by **Blairites** (and occasionally **Blairistas**) have even been described as **Blairification**.

A little more exposure to Blairism and evidence that it is not just a leadership phenomenon but running deep in the veins of the party itself, would make the balance of forces much tighter.
—*Guardian* 21 Sept. 1994, p. 9

It is well worth re-reading that compromise text, for it meets virtually all the arguments for modernisation advanced by the Blairites, yet remains true to the spirit of Clause 4.
—*Guardian* 14 Jan. 1995, Outlook section, p. 22

This may not be quite the sort of blood-and-thunder oratory to which we became accustomed when the pre-Blairite Labour Party fell out with itself.
—*New Statesman & Society* 17 Mar. 1995, p. 12

blot /blɒt/ *noun* and *verb* ⬛

noun: The method by which biological molecules are transferred from a gel medium, under the influence of an electric field, to an immobilizing medium (such as a membrane filter) on which specific target molecules can be identified.

intransitive verb: To transfer such material in this way.

A specialized sense of the word; the molecules from the gel are absorbed on to a filter as though *blotting* a spill of ink.

This method is now a standard one in biochemistry for identifying complex biological substances, particularly those related to DNA and other genetic material. In the first stage, electrophoresis is used to separate molecules by placing a voltage across the gel, which forces molecules to move through it at speeds related to their size. The part of the gel containing the molecules of interest can then be physically *blotted* on to a second medium where specific tests, say for genetic sequences, can be carried out by radioactive or other probes. The first such technique, specifically designed to search for rare DNA fragments, was invented by the British biochemist Edwin Southern in the mid seventies and is known as the **Southern blot** method. Shortly afterwards it was applied to identifying RNA (ribonucleic acid) sequences by reacting them with DNA; by extension of the metaphor the name **Northern blot** was given to this. A further modification to identify peptide sequences and amino acids was similarly called the **Western blot**; this is best known as the method for determining whether someone has HIV. The latter two are often written in lower-case. The verbal noun describing the technique is **blotting**, often as a compound with one of the identifying words.

DNA was extracted from...lymphocytes and after restriction enzyme digestion was analysed on Southern blots probed with labelled restriction fragments.
—*British Medical Journal* 6 May 1989, p. 1215

Proteins were blotted onto a nitrocellulose sheet...in a tank blotting apparatus.
—*Serodiagnosis and Immunotherapy in Infectious Disease* 1989, Vol. 3, No. 5, p. 347

Northern blot analysis showed that three discrete bands corresponding to the cloned cDNA were present in different proportions among the tissues. —*Nature* 24 Jan. 1991, p. 344

Positive tests are confirmed with a blood test called the Western Blot, which is more sensitive than the ELISA. —*World-Herald* (Omaha) 24 Dec. 1994, p. 3

blue box /blu: 'bɒks/ *noun* 🌱

A blue-coloured box used for the collection of recyclable items as part of a municipal recycling scheme.

The first municipal recycling scheme involving the collection of goods from easily identifiable *blue boxes* was launched in Kitchener, in Ontario, in the early eighties. Every household was given a blue plastic box into which the residents were encouraged to place recyclable goods such as tin cans, glass jars, and newspapers, for weekly collection. The scheme, which became known as the **blue box scheme**, proved successful, probably because of the ease and convenience for householders. The idea was adopted widely in Canada, where a conscientious approach to recycling has been referred to as a **blue box approach**. Similar *blue box schemes* have been launched in the US and the UK, but they do not appear, outside Canada, to have developed beyond the experimental stage. Although in the UK their success has been heralded by environmental groups, most local authorities favour the use of area collection points such as bottle banks, and recycling facilities at waste disposal sites.

A pilot Blue Box scheme which covers 3,500 homes in Sheffield — the first recycling city — is proving to be the most successful collection method in the UK.
—*Earth Matters* Summer 1990, p. 4

The project's organisers plan to issue each of Cardiff's 110,000 households with a blue box in which paper, glass bottles, tin cans and textiles can be separated before collection.
—*Daily Telegraph* 6 May 1990, p. 9

Just a reminder that corrugated cardboard (ie boxes) must be put in the large blue bins in the arena parking lot. They will not be accepted in your blue box or normal trash.
—*Walkerton Herald Times* (Ontario) 29 June 1994, section A, p. 18

Brimming blue boxes have been plunked at the end of nearly every drive or front walkway.
—*Queen's Q.* Fall 1994, p. 756

blue Brie ▓ see CAMBOZOLA

blush wine /'blʌʃ wʌɪn/ *noun* ▓

A wine with a slight pink tint (or 'blush'), made in the manner of white wines but from red grape varieties (as distinct from *rosé* wines, coloured by only brief contact with red grape skins).

Blush wines were developed in the late seventies, but became really popular in the mid eighties, when they were seen as offering a pleasant light drink in accordance with current concerns about health and fitness. Their commercial success has rested on their suitability as a 'party' drink, rather than on recognition by serious wine-drinkers.

Blush wine is pale pink and made by using black-skinned grapes as if to make white wine.
—Jancis Robinson *The Oxford Companion to Wine* (1995) p. 119

Speaking of sweet: remember sangria and wine coolers from the '60s and '70s? They were replaced, in large part, by a blush wine called white zinfandel, panned by critics but loved by the soda-pop pinheads. —*Houston Chronicle* 17 Apr. 1996, Food section, p. 2

bodice-ripper /'bɒdɪsrɪpə/ *noun* Also written **bodice ripper**

A sexually explicit romantic novel or film, especially one with a historical setting, with a plot featuring the seduction of the heroine.

A characteristic action in the seduction scene in such a novel is the *ripping* of the *bodice* of the heroine's dress by her lover.

The use of the term *bodice-ripper* is a device whereby a critic can dismiss a novel as offering a merely formulaic plot involving explicit but romanticized scenes of sexual seduction in a historical setting. The formula is generally regarded by publishers as commercially successful, and for this reason perhaps is sometimes adopted in the CELEBRITY NOVEL. In the nineties the term has been extended to novels with a contemporary setting, gay novels, and biographical works which include sexual revelations. In works such as these, while the emphasis on sexual seduction remains, the element of costume drama is lost—the ripping of the bodice has become no more than notional.

In Sweet Liberty Alan Alda sees his history of the American Revolution turned into a bodice ripper. —*Empire: The Monthly Guide to the Movies* Apr. 1992

I quote this not only because Ms. Tharp's autobiography turns out to be a bodice-ripper, filled with famous and not-so-famous husbands and lovers (including Mikhail Baryshnikov and David Byrne) alongside alcoholism, feuds and therapy. —*New York Times Book Review* 13 Dec. 1992, p. 13

The inimitable MP-turned-novelist Ms Currie will discuss her Westminster bodice-ripper, *A Parliamentary Affair.* —*BBC Holidays* Oct. 1994, p. 70

As the title might suggest, *Firecracker* is explosive, a real bodice ripper, but ultimately unsatisfying in its strident will to overpower, with characters who never just talk; they scream.
—*etc Montréal* 15 May 1995, p. 21

See also BONKBUSTER, SEX AND SHOPPING

body double /'bɒdi dʌb(ə)l/ *noun*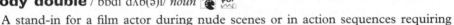

A stand-in for a film actor during nude scenes or in action sequences requiring special skills.

Use of the term was first recorded in film-world jargon at the start of the eighties, though the practice of employing *body doubles* is likely to be older. The term gained in currency after the release in 1984 of a film by Brian de Palma called *Body Double*, a thriller about an out-of-work actor and female striptease artist. *Body doubles* are required when an actor or actress is unwilling to take part in nude scenes and it is work of this sort with which the term is most commonly associated. However *body doubles* are employed in a number of other situations, particularly when specialist skills such as elaborate dancing or playing the piano are required; in such scenes, rather than or as well as the entire body, parts such as hands, wrists, or feet will feature. A *stuntman* or *stuntwoman* is also working as a *body double* but is not normally referred to as such.

Since Brian De Palma's 1984 thriller, 'Body Double', the term has been synonymous with a stand-in during a sex scene. But among casting directors and modeling agents, the job description routinely extends to public exhibition of not-so-private body parts; hips, thighs, abdomen, instep, even wrist. —*New York Times* 19 Jan. 1992, section 2, p. 13

'Usually they'll put out a call for measurements', says Shelley Michelle, who was Julia Roberts's body double in the 1990 film 'Pretty Woman'. 'But a lot of times they're looking for great legs or something like that.' —*New York Times* 19 Jan. 1992, section 2, p. 13

On such large-scale productions body doubles are well paid. But on low-budget British pictures, they are a luxury few directors can afford.   *—Guardian* 19 Jan. 1994, section 2, p. 11

Forget your Best Boys and your Key Grips, the body double is surely *the* most unsung foot-soldier of the entire film industry, *never* getting a credit at the end, and rarely even being acknowledged for the work they do.   *—Empire* May 1995, p. 56

bodyism ⦃ see -ISM

body piercing /ˈbɒdi pɪəsɪŋ/ *noun* Also written **body-piercing** ✗ ᴘᴏᴘ

The piercing of parts of the body other than the ear, in order to insert studs, rings, rods, and other objects usually as a form of adornment and also to enhance sexual pleasure.

Some references to *body piercing* are recorded from the late seventies, when the term was used in an anthropological context with reference particularly to infibulation. The term entered the general language in the eighties and nineties, marking a fashion for a variety of forms of *body piercing* of which the recent roots can be traced back to the punk era of the late seventies. In addition to the established practice of piercing the ears, people began to pierce other parts of their faces, such as nostrils and lips. The practice was then extended to other parts of the body including tongues, navels, and nipples. By the start of the nineties *body piercing* had become widespread, its professional practitioners known as **body piercers**. The range of people who have had their bodies pierced is wide, the piercing of nostrils or navels with small rings or studs being the most commonly chosen form. A more aggressive style of *body piercing* involving the use of heavier and larger metal objects is associated particularly with an alternative nineties punk culture. *Body piercing* has been used as part of their performance by some musicians and performance artists. It is also associated with sado-masochistic sex. In the mid nineties increasing concern has been expressed about possible dangers to health associated with *body piercing* and some discussion about the introduction of legal restrictions on the practice has taken place.

And then at Isaac Mizrahi's show the two came out together, navels bared and beringed between cropped sweaters and ball skirts: body piercing as a supermodel totem.
    —New York Times 21 Nov. 1993, section 9, p. 1

Les Foufounes Electriques…is not the kind of bar where you take your mom for a quiet drink. It's big, loud, and as dark as the psyche of the clientele, which includes a disproportionate number of green-Mohawk-coiffed, body-pierced, leather-clad slam dancers.
    —Globe & Mail 14 June 1994, section A, p. 3

He tells of repeated suicide attempts and of the salvation he found in body piercing.
    —Guardian 6 July 1994, section 2, p. 4

Your dis of body piercing suggests that you've spent too long in Hays, Kansas, yourself and don't know the special bink a pierced tongue adds to oral sex.   *—Spy* Aug. 1994, p. 11

Harmolodic innovator Ornette Coleman raised the stakes for his music as performance art at the San Francisco Jazz Festival in November by presenting a local fakir performing quasi-ritualized body piercing as an entr'acte during his multimedia show *Tone Dialing*.
    —The Face Sept. 1994, p. 81

bog-standard /ˈbɒgstandəd/ *adjective* Also written **bog standard** ᴘᴏᴘ

In slang: basic, standard; unexceptional or uninspired.

The origin of the term is obscure, but it may represent an alteration of *box standard*, an informal term designating a motorcycle or other mechanical device which has no modifications, but which is in the condition in which it came out of the manufacturer's box.

The term *bog-standard* was first recorded in the early eighties. Its use tends to be dismissive—something which is *bog-standard*, as opposed to simply standard, is devoid of any interest.

Like 24 out of 25 people, I carry the intact gene and do not have any of the four mutations. 'Bog standard and boring', was his comment on my genetic fingerprint.

—*Independent* 20 Jan. 1992, p. 14

Heineken now bring over what is in Holland bog-standard bottled lager, re-label it in luxury-suggestive colours and market it as Heineken export.

—*Guardian* 12 June 1993, Weekend section, p. 53

A bog-standard biography with a cheap Psycho sales gimmick, you can't help thinking Perkins deserved better.   —*Empire* May 1995, p. 131

The Coffee shop in the basement is done out in limed oak in arts and crafts style but the rest of the furniture is bog standard café tables and chairs.   —*Time Out* 9 Aug. 1995, p. 39

bonkbuster /ˈbɒŋkbʌstə/ *noun*

In jocular use: a type of popular novel characterized by frequent explicit sexual encounters between the characters.

A blend of *bonk* 'to have sexual intercourse (with)' and *blockbuster* 'something of great power or size, especially an epic film or a best-selling book'.

The term *bonkbuster* entered the lexicon of the fiction critic and the media commentator in the late eighties, where it joined the earlier, and more polite, BODICE-RIPPER. The incorporation in the term of the slang word *bonk* carries with it a suggestion that the descriptions of sexual activity in the novel will be explicit and blatant. The *bonkbuster* is likely to have a contemporary setting, its seduction scenes lacking the romanticism lent by the period setting characteristic of the bodice-ripper. The characters, however, tend to be glamorous and wealthy. Like the bodice-ripper, the *bonkbuster* may be a CELEBRITY NOVEL, written by a well-known person with the aim of making what may be perceived as easy money, the assumption being that the *bonking* will sell the book. The term is still largely restricted to the UK, where familiarity with it has led to the development of the adjectives **bonkbustering** and **bonkbusting**.

As the extra-curricular activities of discomfited Tories continue to entertain the nation, Mrs Currie's 564-page political 'bonkbuster' beds down nicely with the assorted scandals *du jour*.

—*Guardian* 24 Jan. 1994, section 2, p. 10

Trollope whips up a storm of a story. She bridges that important gap between the low-brow bonkbusters and the heavy, unreadable novels which so often win the Booker Prize.

—*Daily Express* 17 Mar. 1995, p. 53

Bookmark (Sat BBC2) visits Rutshire, the Gloucestershire of Jilly Cooper's imagination, as we glimpse Cooper preparing her latest bonkbuster, *Appassionata*.

—*Independent* 16 Mar. 1996, Weekend supplement, p. 32

See also SEX AND SHOPPING

bootable /ˈbuːtəb(ə)l/ *adjective*

Of a computer system: capable of being started up by loading its operating system into its working memory. Of a disk: containing the software necessary to carry out this process.

Formed by adding the adjectival suffix *-able* to *boot*. The latter is an abbreviated form of the verb *bootstrap* 'to initiate a fixed sequence of instructions which itself initiates the loading of further instructions and, ultimately, of the whole system'; this in turn is named after the process of *pulling oneself up by one's bootstraps*, a phrase which is widely supposed to be based on one of the eighteenth-century *Adventures of Baron Munchausen*.

Bootstrap systems have been used in computing since the fifties, but it was not until personal computers (which are started up this way from floppy or hard disks) began to be widely used in the late seventies and eighties that the word was abbreviated to *boot*. *Bootable* itself dates from 1982; when applied to a disk it represents a revival of an old active meaning of the suffix *-able*, since it is not the disk itself that can be booted, but the system that can be booted from the disk.

You can mark one partition as bootable. This means that your machine will boot from the operating system in that partition when you switch on.   *—What Personal Computer* Dec. 1991, p. 117

The installation disk contains the program software and Installer application; the second is a bootable start-up disk.   *—Byte* Oct. 1994, p. 159

Bork /bɔːk/ *transitive verb* 🄰 𝄐

To seek to obstruct the selection or appointment of (a person) by a campaign of systematic public criticism of the person concerned.

The name of Robert *Bork* (b. 1 Mar. 1927), a judge whose nomination to the US Supreme Court in 1987 was rejected following a large amount of unfavourable publicity for his allegedly illiberal and extreme views.

Nominations to the Supreme Court, made by the President, require the 'advice and consent' of the Senate, and over the years there have been a number of challenges to presidential nominees. In 1987, the nomination of Robert Bork by Ronald Reagan resulted in a successful challenge. Bork was widely criticized by his opponents for holding illiberal and extremist views, and there followed a vigorous public campaign against him.

The use of this verb, and of the noun **Borking** for the process involved, is associated primarily with the (ultimately unsuccessful) challenge to the nomination of Judge Clarence Thomas in 1991. No challenge since has generated similar controversy, and it remains to be seen whether the coinage will outlast immediate memories of the hearings involved.

'We're going to Bork him', the National Organization for Women has promised. But if they succeed, liberals may discover that they have Borked themselves.   *—New Republic* 9 Sept. 1991, p. 21

By omitting reference to any of the capital's many conservative interest groups, he gives the humorous impression that defenseless conservative senators have been victimized by this powerful force that coalesced in the fight against Robert Bork, whose nomination to the Supreme Court in 1987 was rejected, and that now goes around 'Borking' politically incorrect nominees.
—New York Times Book Review 23 May 1993, p. 11

Bosnian /'bɒznɪən/ *adjective* 🄰

Of or belonging to Bosnia–Herzegovina, a country in the Balkans, formerly a constituent republic of Yugoslavia. Used especially in:

Bosnian Muslim, a native of Bosnia who is Muslim by religion. Often used attributively.

Bosnian Serb, a native of Bosnia who is of Serbian descent. Often used attributively.

In 1992 Bosnia–Herzegovina followed Slovenia and Croatia in declaring independence. Ethnic conflict amongst Croats, Muslims, and Serbs quickly reduced the republic to a state of civil war, and UN peacekeeping forces were deployed. The terms **Bosnian Muslim** and **Bosnian Serb** have been heard with increasing frequency in reports of the savage conflict that has ensued and the ETHNIC CLEANSING associated with it; *Bosnian* alone is likely to mean someone of Croat origin.

Some Serbs are hinting that they could allow humanitarian corridors, and might even accept Bosnia in the present borders, provided Bosnian Serbs keep the land they have won there.
—Economist 15 Aug. 1992, p. 26

If U.S. aircraft struck siege guns around Sarajevo, he insisted, the Bosnian Serb offensive would collapse.   *—Coloradoan* (Fort Collins) 22 May 1993, section A, p. 16

Serb and Croat nationalists view the Bosnian Muslims as apostates at best, and at worst as a bridgehead of Islamic fundamentalism in Europe.
—New York Review of Books 23 Mar. 1995, p. 57

See also IFOR, UNPROFOR

-bot /bɒt/ *suffix* 🖳

Used to create words relating to automatic systems, self-operating computer processes, and miniaturized semi-independent machines.

From the second element of *robot*, meaning a 'mechanical humanoid', itself derived from the Czech word *robota*, 'forced labour'.

Many transient words have been invented in science fiction works with the second element *-bot*, referring to autonomous or sentient mechanical devices of various kinds. In addition, the word *robot* began to be shortened to *bot*; to start with, an initial apostrophe indicated it was perceived as an abbreviation, but this was quickly dropped.

From the mid eighties onwards, both *-bot* and *bot* began to be used in computing to refer to various types of automatic response programs and intelligent AGENTS, principally associated with networking and the INTERNET. The term **knowbot** (short for *knowledge robot*) appeared in the late eighties to describe an automatic agent which would search electronic networks and return information to the user (with an initial capital it is a US trade mark for a specific search system). With the huge growth of *Usenet* (see NET), problems with irresponsible users flooding newsgroups with unwanted advertising messages (see SPAM) forced a number of people to create **cancelbots**: computer programs that would automatically issue messages cancelling the offending originals (the term was first used in 1994; *cancelbot* is now also used online as a verb).

Mobile devices capable of some measure of independent behaviour are sometimes called **mobots** (*mobile* plus *-bot*). Interest in microminiaturized automatic machines has prompted the creation of the words **microbot** and **nanobot** (see NANO-).

A security mouse scuttled along the floor—nasty-looking little microbot with fretted eyes and a muzzle clotted with dirt. —Bruce Sterling *Islands in the Net* (1989), p. 185

And there would be a bonanza for firms that could design 'knowbots'—software robots—that would search through massive databanks for useful information.
—*Newsweek* 13 Jan. 1992, p. 57

The lawyers who advertised in Usenet newsgroups are getting their comeuppance. A Norwegian hacker has designed a 'Cancelbot' program able to find their adverts and erase them.
—*Guardian* 7 July 1994, OnLine section, p. 6

People will use Usenet for this in some form always—there's very little way of stopping it, short of…cancelbotting all encrypted messages posted to Usenet (not likely).
—10 Apr. 1995, online posting

bounce /baʊns/ *noun* 📪

In US politics: a sudden upward swing in the popularity of a candidate or party.

An early reference to a political *bounce* was made by Jody Powell, press secretary to the former US President Jimmy Carter, who used the phrase 'post-convention bounce' in 1980 in reference to an upsurge in the popularity of the Democratic Party. Since then the term has taken hold in the US, although it does not yet appear to have spread further.

It is rare enough for a candidate not to get a bounce in the polls after winning some major primaries; to lose ground is almost unheard of. —*Time* 20 Apr. 1992, p. 38

Free-trade Republicans were all set to support Clinton on GATT—until it was discovered that the Clinton forces had sneaked in several multi-million dollar subsidies to favored media outlets. The GOP is confident GATT will pass after the election, with no special favors to Katharine Graham—and no election bounce for Clinton. —*American Spectator* Dec. 1994, p. 62

bovine spongiform encephalopathy ⊗ ⁣ see BSE

Boxgrove man /bɒksgrəʊv 'man/ *noun* 🦴

An early human, represented by fragments of a fossilized shinbone and teeth found in a gravel quarry at Boxgrove, a small town in West Sussex, in 1993.

In 1993, two years after the European discovery of the ICEMAN, the fragmentary fossil remains of *Boxgrove man* were unearthed in West Sussex. At the time the assessment was that the fossil remains could be the oldest in Europe by many thousands of years, although two years later much older fossil remains were discovered in a Spanish cave.

Boxgrove man—Europe's oldest human—dined off horsemeat, rhinoceros, giant and red deer, and cave bear. —*Guardian* 10 Sept. 1994, p. 9

To welcome 1996, the Natural History Museum has a new exhibition of an exceedingly old person. It features Boxgrove Man, who lived half a million years ago on the South Downs.
—*Daily Telegraph* 11 Jan. 1996 (electronic edition)

box-shifter ▣ see VAR

boy toy ▯ see TOYBOY

BPR ▣ ⟋ see BUSINESS PROCESS RE-ENGINEERING

break-dancing ▪ POP see HIP-HOP

brewpub /'bru:pʌb/ *noun* Also written **brew pub** ▓

Chiefly in the US: a public house, frequently with a restaurant, selling beer brewed on the premises.

Brewpubs were introduced in North America in the mid eighties, and have become fashionable and popular. *Microbreweries*, established in the same period, had reversed the traditional notion of a brewery as producing beer to be sold over as wide an area of possible through a number of outlets. *Brewpubs* add to the concept of the small, individual brewery the facility of a restaurant which will encourage patrons to eat as well as drink in their favourite resort.

Welcome to the brew pub, one of the hottest concepts in the restaurant industry. A combination of restaurants and microbreweries, brew pubs are capturing the fancy of folks looking to dine out and be diverted. —*Wall Street Journal* 22 Feb. 1990, section B, p. 1

New microbreweries and brewpubs have sprung up. —*Chile Pepper* Feb. 1992, p. 30

It is true that in relation to such other brewing centers as Germany, Britain, and North America, Belgium seems to lag far behind with only five brewpubs. —*Country Living* May 1995, p. 142

The battered red Geo parked out front has a bumper sticker that says it all: 'SAVE THE ALES. Support your local brewpub and microbrewery.' —*Sun* (Baltimore) 8 Aug. 1995, p. 3

bridge /brɪdʒ/ *noun* ▣

An electronic component which connects elements of a digital communications network and supervises the distribution of messages between them.

A device which acts as a *bridge* between parts of a network.

A *bridge* acts as a filter on a local area network or LAN. It looks at each small burst of data (a 'packet'), notes its intended destination, and either accepts it for its local network or forwards it to the next bridge in the system. The effect is to reduce the amount of data each separate local network has to carry, speeding it up.

A bridge was used to divide an overstretched Lan into two separate Lans to bring performance back to acceptable levels. —*Computer Weekly* 9 Dec. 1993, p. 34

Modems are too slow to handle Lan traffic and bridges give no protection against the broadcast storms which can bring down an entire backbone. —*Computer Weekly* 24 Feb. 1994, p. 32

Brit award /'brɪt əwɔ:d/ *noun* Also written **BRIT** ▪ POP

An annual award made in a number of categories for British pop and rock music.

From a blend of the initial letters of *British Record Industry* and the first element of *British*.

The *Brit awards* (occasionally also referred to casually as **the Brits**) have been awarded since the mid eighties to mark British achievements in pop and rock music. In the nineties, the awards have become more high-profile, but within the industry are associated more with mainstream forms than with the radical and unconventional.

> Suede got the covers of *Melody Maker,* the *NME,* and most recently *Q.* Chart success followed…Then came their electric apearance at the otherwise mediocre Brit Awards.
>
> —*Arena* May 1993, p. 26

> An industry gong-fest like…The Brits.　　　　　　　　　　　　　—*Empire* Nov. 1995, p. 147

Britpop /'brɪtpɒp/ *noun* Also written **Brit-pop**, **Brit pop** 🌊 POP

British pop music; specifically, the music of a loose affiliation of independent British groups performing in the mid nineties, showing influences from a variety of British musical traditions.

The term *Britpop* developed in the late eighties as a generic label for British pop. In the mid nineties it came to denote specifically a new wave of music produced in Britain by a number of groups as a self-conscious reaction against the prevalence of American musical styles, showing influences from a variety of specifically British musical traditions such as mod, punk, and NEW ROMANTIC. The success of many of the bands, notably Blur, Elastica, Oasis, Pulp, Radiohead, Suede, and Supergrass, precipitated a resurgence in the popularity of British pop in the mid nineties.

> It's a dead cert that 1995 will be characterised by huge numbers of dodgy combos desperately waving the Brit Pop banner. Also guaranteed…is that 1996 will see the vast majority make their farewell appearances in The Maker's own AWOL column. *Salve et vale,* fame-hungry teenage loudmouths.　　　　　　　　　　　　　　　　　　　—*Melody Maker* 25 Mar. 1995, p. 9

> A call to *Select* magazine's editor suggesting Suede and their peers were all part of a British reaction to the American grunge movement, and Britpop was born.　　—*Arena* Dec. 1995, p. 138

> Britpop…has become the most popular musical form in the country, despite or because of its central tenet: a (very) basic gainsaying of the received wisdom that 'they don't write songs like they used to.'　　　　　　　　　　　　　　　　　　　　　　　—*ikon* Jan. 1996, p. 62

brown dwarf 🜨 see MACHO

browse /braʊz/ *verb* and *noun* 💻

transitive or *intransitive verb*: To read or survey (data files), especially across a computer network; specifically, to do so on the WORLD WIDE WEB.

noun: An instance of this.

A further extension of the figurative use of the verb *browse,* originally meaning 'the action of animals feeding on scanty vegetation' (the implication being they have to search it out), but then extended to the action of looking through (say) a book.

The word has had this sense in the computing context since at least the mid eighties; it is common to find buttons labelled *browse* on visually-oriented computer applications which enable the user to search for relevant files on the local system or across a network. The word took on a new sense and life with the advent of the WORLD WIDE WEB in the early nineties. This interface to the INTERNET requires special computer programs to search out, translate, and display the tagged material in the files being downloaded. These programs were quickly dubbed **browsers** and in computer contexts **browsing** now frequently means using such a program to access the Web. The use of **browsability**, in application to software, has also been recorded.

> The difference between a palette and any other type of window is that the tool for a palette is virtually always the browse tool.　　　　　　　　　　—*HyperLink Magazine* Sept. 1991, p. 50

> The handy viewer lets the user browse the disc reading documents, viewing images, and unzipping program files.　　　　　　　　　　　　　　　　　　　　　　—*CD-ROM World* Apr. 1994, p. 96

When the Netscape browser finds a JPEG file stored in both formats, it first downloads and displays the low-resolution version. —*Data Communications International* Jan. 1995, p. 113

Bruges group /'bruːʒ gruːp/ *noun* 📖

A mainly Conservative British political pressure group set up in 1989 for the purpose of opposing closer ties with Europe.

On 20 September 1988, Margaret Thatcher, then British Prime Minister, made a speech in Bruges in which she said:

We have not succeeded in rolling back the frontiers of the state in Britain, only to see them reimposed at a European level.

This speech, encapsulating a defence of national sovereignty as against what was seen as the growing bureaucracy of Brussels, was widely reported, and warmly received particularly by those opposed to the MAASTRICHT treaty and the creation of a SINGLE CURRENCY. When in the following year a group was formed to argue specifically against British participartion in the creation of a federal European state, the name *Bruges group* was seen as particularly appropriate. The adjective **Brugeist**, designating a politician holding views analogous to those of the *Bruges group*, has also been recorded.

Tomorrow week the Reform Club sees the launch of yet another influential, right-thinking think-tank. It calls itself the Bruges Group after the venue of Mrs T's recent speech at which she put the boot into creeping Euro-federalism. —*The Times* 31 Jan. 1989 (Profile)

Her Bruges speech in the autumn of 1988…which attacked the notion of 'a United States of Europe', aroused much controversy, though the 'Bruges group' of right-wing historians and others declared their support for Mrs Thatcher's stand. —K. O. Morgan *The People's Peace* (1990), p. 498

BSE /biːɛs'iː/ *abbreviation* ⊗ ◖◗

Short for **bovine spongiform encephalopathy**, an incurable brain condition in cattle which causes neurological disorders, and eventually results in death.

The initial letters of *Bovine Spongiform Encephalopathy. Bovine* because it affects cattle; *spongiform* in that it produces a spongy appearance in parts of the brain tissue; *encephalopathy* is a word made up of Greek roots meaning 'disease of the brain'.

Bovine spongiform encephalopathy was first identified in the UK in late 1986. *BSE*—the abbreviation was first used in 1987—quickly became dubbed *mad cow disease* because the symptoms in cattle included staggering and falling down. The infective agent is thought to be a PRION, similar to that causing CREUTZFELDT–JAKOB DISEASE in humans and *scrapie* in sheep, with transmission through animal protein which was fed to cattle in the 1980s. Intense public concern was driven by fear that humans might be infected through eating diseased beef, though such infection has not been proved. Infection has spread to several other countries; the US and several European countries have banned imports of British beef for fear of the disease, and a programme of slaughter of all animals over a specified age has been instituted. The adjectives **BSE-free** and **BSE-infected** are now freqently encountered.

In Britain 'Mad cow' disease may be responsible for a rare brain infection that has affected a 16-year-old girl…The young girl's condition has sparked debates over whether eating beef can cause humans to contract the disease, bovine spongiform encephalopathy.
—*Animals Voice* Ontario, Spring 1994, p. 28

BSE has now leapt the species barrier 15 times since 1986, even infecting the domestic cat—50 have died so far—as well as exotic ruminants such as eland and gemsbok, and even one puma and a cheetah. —*Guardian* 12 May 1994, section 1, p. 22

The genetic differences between humans and cows appears to form such a high 'species barrier' that BSE can not cross it to cause the brain damage typical of BSE and its human equivalent, Creutzfeldt-Jakob Disease. —*Independent* 18 Dec. 1995, p. 3

BTW /ˌbiːtiːˈdʌb(ə)ljuː/ *abbreviation* 🖥

An abbreviated form of the phrase *by the way*.

This is one of a large number of abbreviations used in various online communities, such as bulletin boards (see BBS) and the INTERNET. Originally used to save time when keying, and to reduce the size of messages, they have become (depending on your point of view) either a useful convention, a minor art form, or a contagious nuisance, because some users make a point of creating new ones to entertain, mystify, or annoy. However, only a small group are in regular use. Among these are *FYI* 'for your information' (one of the few that pre-dates the online community, having previously been in office use); *FWIW* 'for what it's worth'; *IIRC* 'if I remember/recall correctly'; *ISTR* 'I seem to remember/recall'; *IMHO* 'in my humble opinion', sometimes written *IMO*, presumably when the writer is not feeling humble; *LOL* 'laughing out loud', an appreciative response to a witticism; a related but stronger term is *ROTFL*, also but less often written *ROFL*, 'rolling on the floor laughing', not usually meant literally; *RTFM* 'read the fucking manual', a dismissive response by an expert to an elementary or stupid question; and *TTFN* 'ta ta for now', a catchphrase in general use since it was popularized by the 1940s BBC radio programme *ITMA*, and adopted for use online.

I think a work should be judged on its own merit. BTW, Kreisler is a favorite of mine!
—*New York Times* 1 Dec. 1992, section C, p. 14

ROTFL! Thanks for today's biggest smile! —12 Apr. 1995, online posting

IMHO the second best electronic newsletter for Information Systems professionals is Ken Laws' The Computists' Communique. —*Infosys* 11 Aug. 1995, online newsletter

I stated I had a problem, and immediately people started calling me clueless and telling me I didn't RTFM when I did very carefully RTFM. —13 July 1996, online posting

See also FAQ and SMILEY

buckminsterfullerene /ˌbʌkmɪnstəˈfʊləriːn/ *noun* 🧪

A stable form of carbon, whose nearly spherical, hollow molecule consists of 60 carbon atoms arranged in a shape with 12 pentagonal faces and 20 hexagonal ones (a truncated regular icosahedron).

Because the shape of the molecule suggests one of the geodesic domes designed by the US architect Richard Buckminster Fuller, its discoverers named it after him (*Buckminster Fuller* plus the suffix *-ene*, a common terminating form for hydrocarbon compounds, strictly here used unsystematically, as *buckminsterfullerene* has no hydrogen in it).

Buckminsterfullerene is a new form of carbon, quite unlike either diamond or graphite. It was discovered by accident in 1985; scientific and public interest in this extraordinary substance grew rapidly in the early nineties after a way was found in 1990 to synthesize it using carbon arcs. It was quickly found that there is a whole class of such hollow spherical molecules, generically called **fullerenes**. They were found to have quite unprecedented properties: in the pure state they are insulators and totally stable; doped with metals, when they are called **fullerides,** they can be semiconductors, conductors, or superconductors; other atoms can be trapped inside them (so they are examples of *molecular cages*); and they can be made magnetic like iron (an unheard of property for a non-metallic material). *Buckminsterfullerene* is usually known under the abbreviated name **buckyball** (coined in 1987), or sometimes *soccerene* or *footballene*, because of the similarity of the molecule's shape to the panels of a soccer ball. In 1991 *Science* magazine named the *buckyball* its choice for 'molecule of the year', calling it 'the discovery most likely to shape the course of scientific research in the years ahead.' It is possible also to create hollow cylinders of carbon atoms, named **buckytubes** in 1991 (they are also sometimes called *nanotubes*, see NANO-). Naturally occurring *buckyballs* have been found as fire products.

Like a newly learned word that seems to jump from every book, molecular cages have become ubiquitous since the existence of buckminsterfullerene's icosahedral carbon cage was confirmed two years ago. First came larger carbon cages, called giant fullerenes; nested cages, known as

Russian dolls; and ultrathin fibers, called buckytubes.   —*Scientific American* Feb. 1993, p. 10

There is a lot of hollow space inside the carbon latticework known as a buckyball—space that can be used to trap an atom or two.   —*Discover* Sept. 1993, p. 32

The fulleride compounds, crystals of carbon-60 molecules doped with alkali atoms such as potassium or rubidium, can become superconducting at temperatures as high as 30K and above, higher than for any other materials except the cuprate superconductors.
                                      —*Physics News Update* 30 Jan. 1995, online newsletter

buddy /ˈbʌdi/ *noun* and *verb* Ⓧ 🍴

noun: Someone who befriends and supports a person with AIDS by volunteering to give companionship, practical help, and moral support during the course of the illness.

intransitive verb: To do this kind of voluntary work. Also as an action noun **buddying**.

A specialized use of the well-known American sense of *buddy*, 'friend'.

For several generations children and adults in the US have been encouraged to follow the **buddy system**—never to go anywhere or take part in any potentially dangerous activity alone, but to take a *buddy* who can bring help if necessary. The scheme to provide *buddies* for people with Aids, started in late 1982 in New York, was an extension of that system, recognizing that these people need friendship that is often denied them once they are diagnosed as having the condition; the word was first used in this sense in print in 1984 and the concept has now spread widely. The American film *Buddies*, released quite early in the Aids era (1985), was surely influential in popularizing this specialized use; it may also be linked to the slang use of *buddy* in the homosexual community for 'lover' and to the term BUDDY MOVIE for a film about same-sex friendships.

I suppose the book wouldn't have been written if I hadn't buddied, because I wouldn't have had a sense of knowing the reality of Aids.   —*The Times* 29 June 1987, p. 16

Colchester Switchboard...Weds. 6–10 pm. Advice, support, information. Aids/HIV counselling and 'buddying' services available.   —advertisement in *Gay Times* Dec. 1990, p. 87

Everyone knows that if you want some work donated to a good cause, you go to someone already busy working hard. These are the people serving on school boards and probation committees...they work on victim support schemes or become Aids buddies.   —*Independent* 10 Feb. 1993, p. 20

bulimic /buˈlɪmɪk/ *noun* Ⓧ 🔀

A person suffering from the EATING DISORDER bulimia nervosa, in which bouts of extreme overeating are followed by self-induced vomiting, purging, and fasting.

Formed by treating the adjective *bulimic* as a noun; the noun *bulimia* from which the adjective derives comes ultimately from Greek *boulimia*, from *bous* ox and *limos* hunger.

Although **bulimia** as a medical condition is recorded from the fourteenth century, *bulimic* as an adjective in this sense only came into use in the late seventies, and the noun dates from 1980. This chronology reflects the growing social awareness of EATING DISORDERS as affecting a wide range of people, and this awareness was heightened when public figures such as Diana, Princess of Wales spoke openly of suffering from *bulimia*.

The risk of suicide among bulimics is high.   —*Woman's Own* 28 Aug. 1982, p. 22

The 46-year-old singer-songwriter said he was a drug addict and alcoholic for 16 years and a bulimic for six.   —*Rolling Stone* 22 Mar. 1990, p. 5

Like bulimics, shopaholics are more likely to 'binge' when under stress or depressed.
                                      —*Guardian* 6 Jan. 1994, section 2, p. 12

bull bar /ˈbʊl bɑː/ *noun* Also written **bull-bar** 🔀

A metal bar or framework fitted to the front of a vehicle, originally to provide protection for the vehicle in the event of a collision with an animal, now frequently as a fashionable accessory.

Formed by compounding: a *bar* fitted as protection against collision with a *bull*, as typifying the animals likely to cause damage to the vehicle. A precedent for the *bull bar* was set in North America in the 19th century, when trains were fitted with an apparatus known as a *cow-catcher*, which removed straying cattle or other obstructions from the rails.

Use of the term *bull bar* was first recorded in the sixties in Australia, where the device, a heavy, horizontal, steel bar, was adopted for use initially on the front of large lorries. In the open spaces of Australia freely roaming animals such as cattle and kangaroos present a regular hazard for motor vehicles and the *bull bar*, also known as a *roo bar*, from the last syllable of *kangaroo*, was devised as a purely functional means of minimizing the nuisance.

In the UK in the late eighties and nineties four-wheel drive motor vehicles, originally designed for off-road use in rough terrain, became popular and fashionable as family cars, frequently being driven in a predominantly urban environment. The *bull bar* was adopted for use on these vehicles, in part because of the protection it affords against damage to the car in minor accidents, and partly, perhaps, because it is felt to enhance the car's rugged appearance. The popularity of *bull bars* quickly spread, and they were fitted to commercial vehicles and even to small domestic cars. However, in the early nineties, very soon after the *bull bar* became fashionable, fears were expressed about the dangers attached to its use in centres of human population. The rigidity and strength of the steel bars result, in the event of even a light collision, in disproportionate injury to pedestrians, and an estimated 70 deaths a year have been attributed to its use. A Private Member's Bill to outlaw *bull bars* was blocked in the spring of 1996, apparently as a consequence of existing European directives which, it was felt, would render it ineffective. As yet the issue remains unresolved.

> Hundreds of ambulances have been fitted with bull bars to protect them in minor accidents even though the bars can easily kill pedestrians. —*Independent on Sunday* 10 July 1994, p. 8

> As well as the physical results of accidents involving bull bars, there is also growing evidence of psychological effect on drivers, turning them into macho maniacs.
> —*Independent on Sunday* 26 Mar. 1995, p. 5

> An increasing number of car manufacturers make the presence of front crumple zones a key part of their safety publicity: the front of modern cars simply folds up in an accident…unless of course a rigid lump of steel called a bull bar prevents that happening.
> —*The Times* 6 Apr. 1996 (electronic edition)

bulletin board ▣ see BBS

bump ♀ see SPEED BUMP

bundle /ˈbʌnd(ə)l/ *verb* and *noun* ∿ ▣

transitive verb: To supply (items of software) with computer equipment at an inclusive price; also, to supply (a selection of software) as a single item, or to include (additional items of equipment) as part of a computer system, similarly at an inclusive price

noun: A package which includes such equipment and software.

Competition among suppliers of personal computers grew dramatically during the late eighties and nineties. As an attempt to distinguish their products from the pack, and to add value, manufacturers and retailers began to include operating systems, applications software, games, and reference CD-ROMs as part of the sales package or **bundle**; they also provided systems enhanced with peripherals such as printers, CD-ROM drives, or modems. The adjective is **bundled**, often in the phrase **bundled software**, and the verbal noun is **bundling**.

> All UNIX reference manuals are included, along with Next documentation and manuals for the bundled software. —*UnixWorld* Sept. 1989, p. 74

These products provide dial-out and dial-in capability through client software bundled with each product. —*Byte* Nov. 1992, p. 269

New, highly-specified multimedia bundles from Compaq and Packard Bell include modems as standard features. —*.net* Dec. 1994, p. 10

bungee jumping /'bʌndʒi dʒʌmpɪŋ/ *noun* Also written **bungee-jumping** POP

The action or practice of jumping from a height while secured by an elasticated rope attached to the ankles or to a harness.

The noun *bungee* (also written *bungie* and *bungy*) has, since the late thirties, denoted an elasticated cord or cable or a spring used in aeronautics and, since the sixties, a fabric-bound rubber strap with a hook on either end, used for securing luggage. Its application to the elasticated rope used in bungee jumping dates from the late seventies when the practice began.

Some have suggested that *bungee jumping* has its roots in Vanuatu in the south-west Pacific, the elasticated cord replacing the liana vines used there. The contemporary sport of *bungee jumping* is believed to have come originally from New Zealand. First references to *bungee jumping* in Europe and North America date from the end of the seventies. By the early eighties it had become a popular and high profile activity, its practitioners purportedly being attracted to it for the adrenalin rush it provides. Occasional tragic accidents, usually resulting from miscalculation of the required length of the rope, have lent the activity a certain notoriety; despite this the sight of an appreciative knot of spectators gathered around a tall crane, from which a tiny figure bounces up and down through the air, has been not uncommon in the late eighties and early nineties. However, the activity, never properly accepted as a serious sport, appears to be declining in popularity as the nineties advance, possibly giving way to newer thrills such as BASE JUMPING and CANYONING.

People who **bungee jump** are **bungee jumpers**, and the elasticated rope is usually called a **bungee cord**, **bungee rope**, or **bungee line**. Frequent figurative use of the term *bungee jumping* has been recorded, expressing the notion sometimes of fickleness, of bouncing back and forth, sometimes of rapid rise to success, but usually of great risk.

A New Zealander bounced back from a headfirst leap from the Eiffel Tower today…He wanted to bring New Zealand's sport of 'bungy jumping' to Paris.
—*Telegraph* (Brisbane) 26 June 1987, p. 11

Bungee jumping and allied activities are not true sports…They require no skill and are devoid of real risk. They are appropriate for beery boys on spring break. —*Utne Reader* July 1992, p. 13

The head of the US delegation at the UN Earth Summit sniped at his White House superiors in a memorandum in which he says leading the delegation was like taking a bungee jump while somebody cut his line. —*Boston Globe,* 1 Aug. 1992, p. 3

Bungee jumping looks and feels a lot more dangerous than it actually is. But don't make a fool of yourself by asking. 'What happens when the cord breaks?' Bungee jumpers delicately refer to this rare occurrence as 'zeroing out'. —*Men's Health* Oct. 1993, p. 70

For people at MTV who have bungee-jumped from intern to P.A. and on to A.P. and producer…the prospect of taking a job at a television network or an advertising agency is not pleasant.
—*New Yorker* 10 Oct. 1994, p. 67

burb /bəːb/ *noun* Also written **'burb** POP

A suburb or suburban area. Usually in the plural as **burbs**.

The abbreviations *burb* and *burbs* were first recorded in US English in the late seventies and had spread to the UK by the late eighties. Their use is somewhat dismissive, suggesting, like *suburban*, an area which is conventional and boring. In the US the word *burb* has started to combine with other nouns to form compounds such as **scrub-burb** and **car-burb**.

Yet, for all our car-burb creations and post-Los Angeles *Angst*, the romance of the city dies hard.
—*New York Times Book Review* 15 Nov. 1992, p. 22

The problem may not be which 'burb to choose, but which to move on from first.
—*Sunday Telegraph* 9 Oct. 1994, section 2, p. 13

The Bradys…live in the same house in a sunny 'burb, sport the same tragic early seventies quiffs, [and] boast wardrobes packed with polyester flares.   —*Maxim* July 1995, p. 129

business process re-engineering /bɪznɪs ˌprəʊsɛs riːɛndʒɪˈnɪərɪŋ/ *noun phrase* 🖳 〰️

The management technique of redesigning the way operations are carried out in a business in the interests of efficiency and reducing costs.

Re-engineering is used in a figurative sense as an elevated alternative to *redesign* or *reorganization*.

The idea of *business process re-engineering* was invented in 1990 by two Americans, James Champy and Michael Hammer, and it was pioneered in practice by a number of US firms. The redesign process seeks to determine how information flows through a business and how it is processed, to search out unnecessary or duplicated operations, and to improve decision-making and the responsiveness and accuracy of the steps involved. This is allied to a number of well-established business ideas: putting customers first; organizing workers into teams, giving them greater individual responsibility, and rewarding performance; and breaking down the traditional barriers between departments. The term is frequently shortened to **business re-engineering** (or just **re-engineering**) or abbreviated to the initials **BPR**. Practitioners of **BPR** are sometimes called **re-engineers**; the technique as a whole is also called **business process redesign**.

Business re-engineering—sometimes called business process redesign (BPR)—looks like being the Next Big Thing. Leading US companies are already using BPR to change the way they work to make their business processes more responsive, more productive, and from 10 to 100 times cheaper.   —*Computer Weekly* 15 July 1993, p. 22

Re-engineering is immensely popular: 69% of the American companies surveyed, and 75% of the Europeans, are already re-engineering, and more than half of the rest are thinking about it.
—*Economist* 2 July 1994

UK corporations are taking advantage of the opportunities presented by business process reengineering, downsizing and re-organisation to rethink their approach to asset management, maintenance and even procurement.   —*Computing* 18 May 1995, p. 6

business tourism 🏙️ 🔲 see TOURISM

• •

C

cable-ready /ˈkeɪb(ə)l ˌrɛdi/ *adjective* 🏙️ 🔳

Designed to be plugged into a cable television network, able to receive cable television.

Cable television (or *cable*) was developed in the US in the sixties and finally adopted in the UK at the beginning of the eighties; the term *cable-ready*, indicating a growing awareness that the ability to access a cable network was likely to be a prerequisite for the user, is recorded from the mid eighties. There is an associated noun, **cable-readiness**.

They live in their parents' cable-ready finished basements and can't get the jobs they want.
—*Playboy* Dec. 1992, p. 6

I became convinced that the TV that angled down from brackets on the wall…*got* cable, wasn't merely cable-ready like mine at home but the real McCoy, that all that was required to activate it was for someone to come in and turn a key. —*Wall Street Journal* 4 Nov. 1993, p. 76

Cadbury Code /ˈkadb(ə)ri kəʊd/ *noun* 〽️

A voluntary code of practice for public companies.

The *Code* of Best Practice was issued by the Committee on Financial Aspects of Corporate Governance, set up under the chairmanship of Sir Adrian *Cadbury* (1929–).

The discovery in 1991 of the misappropriation of the company pension funds of Mirror Group Newspapers generated wide public concern about corporate practice and boardroom power. The **Cadbury Committee** was accordingly set up, with the *Cadbury Code* being published in 1992. Its recommendations paid particular attention to the responsibility of the auditors of a company for testing assumptions and forecasts made in the directors' reports. An adjective **Cadbuarial** has been recorded.

They now have the Cadbury Code to do their thinking for them…The pension funds' association even has a service that marks company accounts for Cadbuarial correctness.
—*Daily Telegraph* 26 Aug. 1994, p. 20

In these slim reports, he looks at compliance with the Cadbury Code and accounting standards, and assesses the overall financial reporting environment. —*Independent* 8 Feb. 1995, p. 27

caffeinated /ˈkafɪneɪtɪd/ *adjective* ⊗ 💢

Containing caffeine, having had caffeine added.

Formed by removing the prefix *de-*, which implies removal or reversal, from *decaffeinated*, to indicate the presence or addition of the alkaloid drug *caffeine*.

Caffeinated is recorded from the early seventies. In the eighties and nineties, while forms of coffee commercially available proliferated (see LATTE), concerns about the effects on health of an excess of the stimulant caffeine increased the popularity of *decaffeinated coffee* (or DECAF), to the extent that a growing need was felt by 'traditional' coffee-drinkers to indicate a preference for the untreated beverage. The heightened awareness of the stimulant properties of caffeine has meant that *caffeinated* has come to mean 'pepped up, with added vigour'.

There is definitely something caffeinated about Nusrat Fateh Ali Kahn. His music acts like a pick-me-up for the soul. —*Interview* Sept. 1991, p. 82

He had spotted *caffeinated coffee*, drunk by those who hate *decaf* but cannot be sure what they will get if they ask only for coffee. —*New York Times* 19 Mar. 1995, p. 23

cambozola /kambəˈzəʊlə/ *noun* Also written **Cambozola** 💢

The trade mark of a type of German blue soft cheese with a Camembert-like rind, produced using Gorgonzola blue mould.

An invented name, formed from the first element of *Camembert* and the final element of *Gorgonzola*.

Since the early eighties, a number of modern cheeses have been developed. *Cambozola*, as the alternative term *blue Brie* indicates, combines a creamy texture with a strong but mellow flavour. First marketed in 1984, it has (unlike the earlier but ultimately unsuccessful LYMESWOLD) proved popular.

Certainly the most successful of the 'modern' Bries has been Cambozola, a German cheese referred to as blue Brie. —R. Moon *Delicatessen* 1989, p. 69

Juicy parmesan-crusted chicken breast is rolled around molten cambozola, over red pepper coulis; heavily buttered couscous seems too much of a good thing. —*Toronto Life* June 1994, p. 81

cancelbot 🖥️ ⚗️ see –BOT

canteen culture /kanti:n 'kʌltʃə/ *noun* 📮 ▮▮

A derogatory term for an established set of attitudes within the police force, characterized by resistance to the introduction of modern managerial standards and practices, and at its most extreme associated with male chauvinist and racist views.

The police *canteen* is the place where those of like mind foregather, giving rise to the characteristic *culture*.

In the late seventies and early eighties, a debate on the role of the police force was fuelled by concerns about public disorder and rising crime rates. In 1981 there were outbreaks of rioting in Brixton, Southall, Liverpool, Manchester, and Bristol; Lord Scarman's statutory report into the Brixton riots subsequently identified the alienation of ethnic communities from the police force as one of the conditions favourable to the outbreak of the riots.

The phrase *canteen culture* has been used since the late eighties to embody what were seen as the two main obstacles to modernization: lack of professional training courses (as opposed to the system of 'learning on the job'), and the apparent perpetuation of racist and sexist attitudes in a culture unlikely to be changed or questioned by recruits absorbed into it.

From the early eighties, effort has been put into both applying modern management techniques to policing, and fostering links between the police and the community, but the *canteen culture* is still seen as hard to eradicate, particularly among the middle ranks of the service, as a number of recent harassment cases have indicated.

Behaviour...had been picked up from police colleagues rather than learned in the training school-...Since 1981, Hendon has tackled this 'canteen culture' directly. Almost half the Met's serving officers have been trained in the new style, known as 'policing skills'.
—G. Northam *Shooting in the Dark* (1988), p. 164

Another officer feels that, however well such courses work, the gulf between the 'equal ops' end of the police and the 'canteen culture' remains wide.
—*Guardian* 28 Sept. 1994, Society section, p. 7

The industrial tribunal...heard disclosures from two witnesses of sexual harassment against male and female officers and a canteen culture where insults and 'mickey taking' are rife.
—*Daily Telegraph* 21 May 1996 (electronic edition)

canyoning /'kanjənɪŋ/ *noun* ▨ ⊙

A mountain sport which involves launching oneself, clad in protective clothing, down a mountain watercourse, through a series of naturally formed gullies, rapids, and falls.

From *canyon*, 'a deep gorge, often with a stream or river'.

In the late seventies and early eighties, leisure activities increasingly included EXTREME *sports*; *canyoning*, which became popular in the early nineties, is one example. In *canyoning*, which bears some resemblance to the more established sport of luge, the participants must rely on their protective clothing and the lubricating force of water to shield them from injury as they are carried downwards at great speed.

In practice, winter canyoning is far more fun than frightening...In the entire 400m pinball ride, you never once touch side or bottom. —*Independent on Sunday* 17 Oct. 1993, Review section, p. 78

Canyoning is another thrilling sport where you are carried along by the power of a waterfall.
—*Daily Mail Holiday Action* Summer 1995, Mountains & Lakes supplement, p. 15

carbohydrate chemistry 🧪 see GLYCOBIOLOGY

carbon tax /'kɑ:b(ə)n taks/ *noun* 🌳 〰

A tax levied on fossil fuels with the aim of discouraging the production of harmful carbon dioxide resulting from their being burnt.

The possibility of a *carbon tax* was first mooted in America in 1986, when anxieties about the *greenhouse effect* and damage to the ozone layer were at their height. However, although anxiety about *global warming* continues, there is as yet no scientific consensus on the likely extent of the increase which is agreed to be occurring. The imposition of a global *carbon tax* would represent one possible remedial measure, but could have a correspondingly adverse economic effect on industry. Although the EARTH SUMMIT of 1992 produced an international commitment to address the general problem, no firm targets for action were set.

Canberra has backed off imposing a 'carbon tax' owing to pressure from industry.
—*Independent* 22 Feb. 1995, p. 14

At Rio, the EU was the world's most forceful advocate of strong targets. Since then sundry proposed EU policies to reduce emissions—a carbon tax, for instance—have been pigeon-holed.
—*Economist* 1 Apr. 1995, p. 67

car bra /'kɑː brɑː/ *noun* ✖

In the US, a protective device to be fitted over the bodywork of the front of a car.

From the notion that such a device fitted over the front end of a *car* resembles a woman's *bra* in form and function.

Car bras (or **auto bras**) were introduced in the US in the second half of the eighties as protection against damage to the paintwork. By the end of the decade the term was being used for a particular form of protective device: a carbon-based cover which fits over the front bumper of a car and absorbs the microwaves used in radar equipment. Use of such **stealth bras** minimizes the risk of detection for a motorist who is speeding.

I keep reading ads for car bras that are supposed to suck up police radar signals and permit one to sail through traps. —*Car & Driver* Sept. 1989, p. 20

Car bra...A close fitting cover to protect the front end of an automobile from insects, flying gravel and from the elements. —*Atlantic* Feb. 1991, p. 112

cardboard city /kɑːdbɔːd 'sɪti/ *noun*

An area of a large town where homeless people congregate at night under makeshift shelters made from discarded cardboard boxes and other packing materials.

First attested in print in the early eighties, *cardboard city* names a phenomenon of the eighties and nineties, and a growing problem in large cities, both in the UK and in the US. It is sometimes written with capital initials, as though it were a place-name in its own right; in the UK this usually refers to the area frequented by the homeless near Waterloo Station in London.

This is not a country where families can live under bridges or in 'cardboard cities' while the rest of us have our turkey dinner. —*Washington Post* 23 Dec. 1982, section A, p. 16

Perhaps, like others, he had dreamed of what London might offer—but the reality of the city was no money, anonymity and a place to doss down in Cardboard City, the black arena by Waterloo Station inhabited by some 200 of London's homeless.
—*Daily Telegraph* 16 Sept. 1989, Magazine section, p. 30

care in the community ⊗ ◖ see COMMUNITY CARE

caring nineties POP see TOUCHY-FEELY

carjacking /'kɑːdʒakɪŋ/ *noun* ◖

The violent abduction or 'hijacking' of a car or its driver. Also, violent theft from a driver in such circumstances.

Carjacking appeared in America in the early nineties, as a form of car crime involving the stealing or commandeering of an occupied car by threatening the driver with violence; the term is also used to cover theft from a driver in such circumstances. In contrast to HOTTING, the levels of violence involved in a *carjacking* or **carjack** have been of considerable concern: the advice has been given that those who find themselves being **carjacked** should not attempt to resist the **carjacker**.

In a week ending Aug. 25, at least 40 people fell prey to carjackers, weapon wielding car thieves.
—*Detroit News* 29 Aug. 1991, section A, p. 1

The victim of the carjack was beaten and stripped of his clothes.
—G. Donaldson *Ville* (1993), p. 44

With new phenomena like carjacking and road rage, there is more to worry about than just the accident factor. —*Independent on Sunday* 6 Aug. 1995, p. 20

cash-back /'kaʃbak/ *noun* ∿

A free facility offered by retailers whereby a customer may withdraw a limited amount of cash when making a credit or debit card purchase, the amount of which is added to the bill. Commonly used attributively in phrases such as **cash-back facility** and **cash-back scheme**.

The *cash-back* facilities and schemes offered by retailers since the late eighties have been made possible by the development of computerized link systems between banks and points of sale, such as SWITCH. *Cash-back* may be used in conjunction with a credit card, but its advent has accompanied the debit card in particular. If a debit card is being used, the amount of cash is simply added to the bill for the goods being purchased and the whole is debited in one transaction from the customer's bank account. The shopper who needs a little extra cash is therefore saved even the small effort of having to make a separate transaction at the HOLE-IN-THE-WALL, which itself offers a convenient method of cash withdrawal. The *cash-back* facility represents one of several ways in which traditional banking facilities are moving beyond the banks themselves.

Nearly one in ten now gets cash elsewhere, often from a supermarket. For example, Sainsbury's has a cash-back scheme, which allows you to add extra to your bill if you pay by debit card.
—*Daily Mail* 10 Mar. 1993, p. 28

cash for questions 🔒 POP see SLEAZE FACTOR

CD /siːˈdiː/ *noun* 💻 🧪

Short for **compact disc**, a disc on which audio or video sequences or other data are recorded digitally and replayed using a laser.

The initial letters of *Compact Disc*.

The standard *CD* is a 12cm diameter aluminium disc, on which data is recorded as a spiral pattern of pits and bumps; to replay it the disc is 'read' by a laser beam inside a **CD player**. Launched in 1982 as a medium for distributing audio recordings, by the end of the eighties the *CD* had almost completely supplanted the older groove-and-stylus LP technology because of the higher quality of its digital reproduction. In 1983, the same technology was used to launch the **CD-ROM** (short for *Compact Disc Read-Only Memory*). This takes advantage of the capacity of a standard *CD* to store large amounts of digital data. Reference works, commercial databases and compilations of computer software soon became available, more recently extended to include **CD-based** games and MULTIMEDIA, though its widespread adoption as a consumer technology had to await the incorporation of **CD-ROM drives** as standard items in personal computers in the mid nineties. Unlike audio *CD players*, many *CD-ROM drives* require the disc to be encased in a **CD caddy** to keep it free from dirt. In the late eighties, the industry created the **CD-R** format (for *CD recordable*), which permits the recording of data on a disc using the WORM principle (see WRITE-ONCE), which can then be read in any *CD-ROM player*; by the mid nineties such recordable *CD-ROM* systems were beginning to be affordable by individual users.

A number of processes have been developed to extend *CD* technology to include pictures as well as sound. **CD-I** (short for *Compact Disc-Interactive*), created in the mid eighties, became widely available in the early nineties. A **CD-I disc** contains digital video, audio, and data; a **CD-I player** is a complete computer system with software that allows the user to control the presentation in an INTERACTIVE way; the format has had considerable impact in training as well as entertainment. **CD video** is a video system in which both sound and picture are recorded on compact disc.

Film and video applications need more space than one *CD* could provide. Two competing proposals were created in the mid nineties for increasing the *CD's* storage capacity, one called **MMCD** (short for *Multi-Media CD*) and another called *SD*; a standards war was avoided by agreement to create a joint format named *Digital Video Disc* (DVD).

> The CDTV system involves a unit the same size as a video recorder which plugs into a standard television set. —*Daily Telegraph* 13 Aug. 1990, p. 4

> Photo-CD allows photographers to shoot their snaps on film and, after the film has been processed, store the images on a 12-centimetre CD for about £10. This disc, which holds about 100 images, will play on either a Photo-CD player, a CD-I player, or future CD-ROM system, which will display images on a TV screen. —*New Scientist* 21 Sept. 1991, p. 36

> A CD-I player is basically a CD player with a micro-computer built in. It can play regular CD's and CD-I's, which carry not only digital audio but also digital video and software used by the player's computer to enable extensive interaction between the user and the disk. —*New York Times* 19 Jan. 1992, section 2, p. 25

> Each of our compact discs has its own Apple CD caddy with the barcode affixed to the outside of the case. —*American Libraries* Mar. 1992, p. 218

> CD-R lets you write data to a specially manufactured writable disc. Any standard CD-ROM drive can read such a disc. —*Byte* Mar. 1993, p. 198

> A year ago, 31 per cent of personal computers sold in Britain had CD drives; now 78 per cent do. There were 375,000 CD-Rom drives in the UK at the start of the year, Mr Tabizel says. Now there are 600,000, and he expects the million mark to be cracked in June. —*Independent on Sunday* 2 Apr. 1995, Business supplement, p. 3

> The new standard is based mainly on the proposed SD format, but uses more robust error correction from the rival MMCD proposal. It will be called the DVD (digital video disc). —*Personal Computer World* Feb. 1996, p. 19

CDM   see COLD DARK MATTER

celebrity novel /sɪˌlɛbrɪti ˈnɒv(ə)l/ *noun*

A novel whose distinguishing feature is its authorship by a 'celebrity', especially one regarded as a non-literary figure.

While the term was first recorded in the late seventies, the *celebrity novel* is a phenomenon of the eighties, when publishing houses would compete to sign up famous names for their publicity value. The work of these **celebrity novelists** was likely to require at least substantial editorial support; in the case of the model Naomi Campbell and the novel *Swan* the book was ghost-written, and it was suggested that the supposed author had not even read it. By the mid-nineties, it had become evident that the appetite for *celebrity novels* had waned, but public interest was revived by the court case in which Random House unsuccessfully attempted to recover from the actress Joan Collins the very substantial advance given for two novels.

> Actress Janet Leigh's first novel…is not a celebrity novel in the sense of the term we have come to understand from the Random House v Joan Collins case. —*The Bookseller* Feb. 1996

See also AGA SAGA, BONKBUSTER, SEX AND SHOPPING

-centric /ˈsɛntrɪk/ *combining form*

As the second element in a hyphenated adjective: centred on the person or thing named in the first word.

A development of the established combining form -*centric*, forming (with other combining forms) adjectives with the sense 'having a (specified) centre', 'having as its centre', such as *Anglocentric*, *anthropocentric*, and *theocentric*.

In the early nineties, -*centric* began to combine freely with a variety of nouns to form hyphenated adjectives such as **customer-centric** and **user-centric** (perhaps on the model of *user-friendly*). The world of computing has been particularly open to such formations, with references to **network-centric** systems and **desktop-centric** and **pen-centric** applications being found in the literature; one text indicates concern that the advice given is **IBM-compatible-centric**.

The use of -*centric* has become increasingly widespread, with forms such as **ghetto-centric**, **liquor-centric**, **male-centric**, and **state-centric** being only some of those recorded.

140 young people turned out. I think that says something about the need for a department that is theatre-centric. —*Times Educational Supplement* 8 Mar. 1991, p. 32

We're very good at it…the best in the industry at user-centric applications or software.
—*MacWorld* June 1992, p. 75

He tried to keep his leisure-centric lifestyle attuned to the passing of the seasons.
—James Finn Garner *Once Upon a More Enlightened Time* 1995, p. 18

It was about time you gave coverage in your clubs section to the opinion that babe-centric flyer art isn't quite the height in (ironic?) erotica. —*i-D* Nov. 1995, p. 5

cerebrally challenged {{ see CHALLENGED

CFC /siːɛfˈsiː/ *abbreviation*

Short for **chlorofluorocarbon**, any of a number of chemical compounds released into the atmosphere through human agency, and known to be harmful to the ozone layer.

The initial letters of the elements which make up the chemical name *chlorofluorocarbon*: compounds of *chlorine*, *fluorine*, and *carbon*.

CFCs have been in use for decades as refrigerants, in aerosols, as dry-cleaning and industrial solvents, and to blow expanded plastics (the term *chlorofluorocarbon* was first noted in 1947, and the abbreviation *CFC* in 1976). After initial environmental research in the seventies, *CFCs* came to wide public notice in the years following the discovery in 1982 of a hole in the ozone layer over Antarctica. Ultraviolet light in the upper atmosphere breaks down the *CFCs* releasing chlorine atoms which react with ozone molecules in the stratosphere. *CFCs* were also found to contribute significantly to the *greenhouse effect*. Concern increased as the ozone hole grew larger each spring, and was later discovered to have a twin over the Arctic. The Montreal Protocol of 1987, reviewed in 1992, aimed to stop the production of several such *ozone depleters* by the year 2000. By 1989, manufacturers had started to produce products labelled **CFC-free**. If not followed by a number or in a combination such as **CFC gases**, the term is nearly always used in the plural, since there is a whole class of compounds of similar structure. The related *HCFCs* (*hydrochlorofluorocarbons*) and *HFCs* (*hydrofluorocarbons*) are currently used as temporary replacements; they affect the ozone layer much less but have an even greater greenhouse effect.

Du Pont has…promised to suspend production of ozone-destroying CFCs by 2000.
—*News-Journal* (Wilmington) 9 July 1990, section D, p. 1

We must hope that equally effective legislation to stop the emission of CFC gases will be pushed through by the Western industrial nations, who do now seem genuinely to have the wind-up about the holes being torn in the Earth's ozone layer.
—*World BBC Magazine of Mankind* Apr. 1992, p. 4

HFCs are produced commercially as a substitute for ozone-depleting CFCs and are also emitted as a by-product of HCFC-22 production (another CFC substitute).
—William J. Clinton and Albert Gore, Jr. *The Climate Change Action Plan* (1993) (electronic edition)

CFTR /siːɛftiˈɑː/ *abbreviation* 🟡

Short for **cystic fibrosis transmembrane regulator**, the gene which causes cystic fibrosis.

The initial letters of *cystic fibrosis transmembrane regulator*.

Cystic fibrosis, a hereditary disease affecting the exocrine glands such as the mucus-secreting and sweat glands, was first recognized in 1938. The disease involves the production of a thick mucus which obstructs the intestinal glands and pancreas, and is particularly associated in young children with respiratory infections and a failure to thrive.

In 1989, researchers identified the faulty gene responsible for the condition. Individuals affected are now known to lack a protein, *cystic fibrosis transmembrane regulator*, that enables the transport of chloride ions across cell membranes. The gene is recessive, so that both parents of a patient can be carriers without being affected by the disease, and genetic counselling is seen as essential, as each subsequent child of carrier parents has a one in four chance of being affected. More revolutionary treatments include heart and lung transplants and attempts to alter the genetic content of faulty cells.

Since last year's discovery of the gene causing cystic fibrosis (CF), researchers have learned that several different mutations in this 'CFTR' gene can cause the inherited respiratory disease.
—*Science News* 20 Oct. 1990, p. 245

challenged /ˈtʃalɪndʒd/ *adjective* 🟡

Especially with a preceding adverb: regarded as lacking a physical or mental attribute, not having a specified skill.

Like ABLED, *challenged* in this sense arose in the US; it has been in use since the mid eighties, and has spread widely to the UK. It was originally intended as another euphemistic coinage, offering a more positive term than *handicapped* or *disadvantaged*, and gave rise to such usages as both the general **physically challenged** and **mentally challenged**, and more specific compounds such as **vertically challenged**.

Despite the originally serious intention, the use of *challenged* with a preceding adverb has increasingly developed a jocular note. Compounds such as **cerebrally challenged** and **culinarily challenged** may still be euphemistic, but the tone associated with them is one of irony, and coinages have become increasingly inventive.

As a pluralistic democracy composed of many minorities, our mission is to attempt to educate *everyone*—the economically disadvantaged, the physically challenged, the learning disabled, the non-English speakers. —D. & T. Seymour *America's Best Classrooms* (1992), p. 22

Sources suggest that there may be well over four million people in Canada considered as challenged due to a wide array of disabilities.
—*Freedom: Canada's Guide for the Disabled* Spring/Summer 1995, p. 34

Though she [the protagonist of the film *Clueless*] may be 'hymenally challenged,' or a virgin, it is only because she is saving herself for the right man. —*Sight & Sound* Oct. 1995, p. 46

Celebrity chefs…take centre stage and teach the culinarily-challenged to cook.
—*Good Food* Easter 1996, p. 101

change management /tʃeɪn(d)ʒ manɪdʒm(ə)nt/ *noun* 🟡 🟡

Controlled identification and implementation of required changes within a system.

The concept of *change management* originated in the world of systems analysis, in discussion of the procedures required for the structured identification and implementation of needed alterations to a computing system. Use of the term then spread through the increasing number of publications on management theory, which from the late seventies reflected a widespread awareness of the need for a more professional and structured approach to management. The term is often used attributively, as in *change management procedures* and *change management objectives*.

> The Endevor change management tools of Legent's Business Software Technology division…include workstation-based products that interact with host-based data center tools.
> —*Software Magazine* Oct. 1990, p. 10

> 'Change management'—the currently fashionable concept that deals loosely with the human side of getting organisations to respond to challenges facing them.
> —*Independent on Sunday* 7 Aug. 1994, p. 11

channel-surf 🔲 POP 〰️ see SURF

chaos /'keɪɒs/ *noun* 🧪

A state of apparent randomness and unpredictability which can be observed in any complex dynamic system that is highly sensitive to small changes in external conditions; the area of mathematics and physics in which this is studied is called **chaos theory**.

A specialized use of the figurative sense of *chaos*, 'utter confusion and disorder' (a sense which itself goes back to the seventeenth century).

The serious study of *chaos* began in the late sixties, but it was only in the seventies that mathematicians started to call this state *chaos* (and to describe the behaviour as **chaotic**) and not until the late eighties that the study of these phenomena came to be called *chaos theory*. It relates to any complex process in which a small change in initial conditions can make a disproportionately large difference to the outcome. An example is a leaf floating down a mountain stream; though at every step its movement is determined by the laws of physics, tiny changes in its starting point can radically alter its exact course because the action of the stream is so complicated. By the beginning of the nineties the study of *chaos* had proved to offer important insights to all areas of science, and more generally to an understanding of social processes. Such **chaotic systems** are said to operate **chaotically**, to show **chaotic behaviour**, or exhibit **chaotic dynamics**. A person who studies *chaos* is a **chaos theorist** (occasionally a **chaologist** or **chaoticist**). Many complex systems seem to exist 'at the edge of chaos'—apparently *chaotic* but showing signs of regular patterns of behaviour; the study of these systems is called *complexity theory*, or sometimes **antichaos**. *Chaos theory* is also called **chaology**, but this word is now more often reserved for the phrase **quantum chaology**, the application of *chaos theory* to events where classical and quantum physics meet; the field of research, and the effect, is also called **quantum chaos**.

> Chaos theorists—the current revolutionaries in science—were all interdisciplinary mavericks, and all met with resistance and hostility. —Philip Slater *Dream Deferred* (1991), p. 78

> The phenomena of quantum chaology lie in the largely unexplored border country between quantum and classical mechanics; they are part of semiclassical mechanics.
> —*The New Scientist Guide to Chaos* (1992), p. 195

> But investigators of chaos theory who turn to patterns called fractals manage to find order in the midst of such unpredictable events. —*Scientific American* Sept. 1992, p. 23

> The Earth-crossing asteroids include rocky and metallic objects derived from main-belt asteroids through collisional fragmentation and chaotic dynamics; others are probably extinct comet nuclei. —*Nature* 6 Jan. 1994, p. 33

charm offensive /tʃɑːm əˈfɛnsɪv/ *noun* 🔲 POP 〰️

A deliberate campaign of using charm in order to achieve a goal, especially a political one.

Charm offensive is recorded from the early nineties, and represents a figurative use of the established military sense of *offensive*: there is an implication that the apparent warmth and friendliness shown are consciously employed as weapons in a campaign to achieve a particular objective, rather than being genuinely felt. The term is primarily associated with politicians attempting to 'win hearts and minds' for support in a particular cause, from Mikhail Gorbachev's attempt to win support for his liberalizing measures, to the PRAWN COCKTAIL OFFENSIVE undertaken by the British Labour Party.

> Instead of taking a hard line, the official expects Hussein to emphasize a new 'reasonableness'...If the 'charm offensive' fails, U.S. officials fear a resumption of military probing and acts of terrorism. —*US News & World Reports* 11 Jan. 1993, p. 18

> Nato's new secretary general...pledged himself yesterday to launch a 'charm offensive' aimed at winning the confidence of Russia. —*Financial Times* 11 Jan. 1996, p. 2

chart abuse ⚗ see ABUSE

Charter /'tʃɑːtə/ *noun* Also written **charter** ⚒ ⫴

The second element, following nouns in the possessive case or used attributively, in names of British government documents concerning the rights of citizens in a specified areas.

A use of the noun *charter*, a written grant of rights, coined in this sense by the British Prime Minister John Major in the House of Commons, when in April 1991 he announced his government's intention to introduce a *Citizen's Charter* which would guarantee that public services met given standards of performance, and would give the public rights of redress when such standards were not upheld.

Further specifications followed: the **Patient's Charter** sets standards for the health service, and the **Parent's Charter** explains the structure and aims of education in schools and the rights of children within that system. A **Charter Mark**, an award granted to institutions for exceptional public service under the terms of the **Citizen's Charter**, has also been established.

The development of such *Charters* may be seen as part of the social climate of the early nineties in which users of public services have increasingly been seen and spoken of as *customers*, whose rights are to be recognized and protected, but it is too early to say whether implementation of the system will be regarded as having made a substantial difference to the perceived standards of performance.

> The Citizen's Charter sets a new Standard for public services. The Charter Mark recognises this Standard. If you think your organisation meets the Standard, why not apply for a Charter Mark?
> —advertisement in *Observer* 2 Feb. 1992, p. 16

> The Post Office Counters Ltd Customer Charter sets several areas for improvement of its service to customers, including the availability of stamp machines. —*Which?* Sept. 1992, p. 480

> Her days in intensive care in an acute ward exemplified what the service did well, but when she moved on to the long, slow process of recovery, then the pointless patient's charter didn't help her, or us, challenge the careless ethic of the asylum. —*Independent* 10 Jan. 1995, p. 15

Chechen /'tʃetʃɛn/ *noun* and *adjective* ⚒

noun: A member of a Muslim Caucasian people inhabiting the Chechen Republic, an autonomous republic in SE Russia. Also, their language.

adjective: Of or belonging to this people or their language.

The obsolete Russian word *chechen* (modern *chechenets*).

Although used in ethnographical works since the beginning of the nineteenth century, *Chechen* became familiar to the general English-speaking world only after the break-up of the former Soviet Union focused attention on unrest in a number of the former Soviet Republics. The *Chechen* Republic, or Chechnya, declared itself independent of Russia in 1991, and Russian troops invaded the republic in 1994. Considerable western media coverage has been devoted to their attempts to crush the resistance with which they were met, and the effect within Russia itself of their failure to achieve a swift and outright victory.

> Costya was surrounded by a dozen Chechens, people from the northern Caucasus.
> —*Independent* 1 Dec. 1992, p. 29

> The best Russia can hope for is to establish enough control over Grozny to impose a puppet administrator, while facing an unwinnable fight against Chechen guerrillas in the hills.
> —*Economist* 7 Jan. 1995, p. 29

See also COMMONWEALTH OF INDEPENDENT STATES

chemical abuse ⟨⟨ see ABUSE

chemoprevention /kiːmə(ʊ)prɪ'vɛnʃ(ə)n, kɛmə(ʊ)-/ *noun* ⊗

The use of medication techniques to prevent the onset of cancer.

Perhaps with allusion to *chemotherapy*.

In the early nineties, medical research into treatments for cancer increasingly highlighted **chemopreventive** agents as appropriate for investigation. *Chemoprevention* was seen as a potentially valuable weapon whereby the onset or development of cancer in its early stages could be substantially inhibited. A process which requires the long-term taking of drugs is inevitably controversial, but it should be noted that *chemopreventive* agents can include natural foods and extracts.

> This is no longer nutritional-food-store stuff…At our hospital, two cancer research sections…have committed themselves to chemopreventive studies. —*Chicago Tribune* 20 Dec. 1992, p. 1

> The tale of tamoxifen has lessons for the new science of chemoprevention—giving people drugs to prevent disease. —*New Scientist* 11 June 1994, p. 44

cherry-pick /'tʃɛri pɪk/ *transitive* or *intransitive verb* ⋀ ⟨⟨

To pick out for oneself (the best and most desirable items); to make such a selection from (a list of possible choices).

Probably a back-formation from *cherry picker*, a hydraulic crane with a platform at the end, for raising and lowering people working at a height, but also with an idea of someone being raised to a position of advantage for picking the best fruit on a tree.

The term is recorded from the early seventies, but seems to have come into widespread general use in the expansionist eighties, particularly as companies diversified. As the term has become more familiar, there has been a further shift in emphasis: a **cherry-picker** may now be a person who selects favourable figures and statistics in order to present biased data.

> We're going to cherry-pick the best of other people's products the first few years until we get into the business. —*Forbes* 12 Nov. 1979, p. 224

> The tobacco industry accuses the EPA of 'manipulating and cherrypicking' data to 'falsely disparage' cigarettes. —*Guardian* 5 July 1993, p. 12

> Odious though it is to cherrypick in such splendid work, a couple deserve special mention.
> —*Q* June 1995, p. 143

child abuse see ABUSE ⟨⟨

Child Support Agency /tʃʌɪld sə'pɔːt ˌeɪdʒ(ə)nsi/ *noun phrase* ⟨⟨

A government agency responsible for the assessment and collection of compulsory child maintenance payments from non-resident parents. Frequently abbreviated to **CSA**.

The term *Child Support Agency* was first recorded in 1990 in reference to a new agency established in Australia as a branch of the Australian tax office.

References were first made to plans for a *Child Support Agency* in the UK in 1990, and these were repeated in the Conservative Party's 1992 election manifesto. The agency was launched in 1993 under the terms of the 1991 Child Support Act. An agency of the Department of Social Security, its role replaced that of the courts in the pursuit of maintenance payments. The agency has wide powers of enforcement; it may, for example, enforce the deduction of payments directly from a person's salary. In practice this has mainly affected absent fathers. No distinction is made between married and unmarried parents, and if necessary the agency may apply to the court for a declaration of parentage (solely for the purpose of maintenance payments). The activities of the *Child Support Agency* have been highly controversial, many people feeling that the level of payments imposed fails to balance the needs of first and second families and to take into account other financial arrangements made at the time of separation. The agency was subjected to a thorough review in 1994, which led to wide reforms of its methods, one of the consequences of which was an acknowledgement of 'clean-break settlements' (those where both partners have agreed to a division of their capital). The agency has, however, continued to attract complaints and criticism. A number of cases of mistaken identity have arisen, leading to the requirement for standardized compensation in such cases. Despite these factors the work of the agency has been broadly welcomed by many as a partial solution to the poverty trap associated with single parenthood.

The CSA will have access to official records for tracing absent parents and collecting and enforcing maintenance payments.   —*Which?* Jan. 1993, p. 25

More than half the maintenance assessments carried out by the Child Support Agency last year were wrong. Auditors found errors were made by staff even when they had sufficient information to calculate the correct amount of maintenance.   —*Daily Telegraph* 19 July 1995, p. 2

Complaints about the Child Support Agency are still 'pouring in' to the ombudsman despite government claims of improvements, MPs were told yesterday.
                                              —*Daily Telegraph* 16 May 1996 (electronic edition)

chipset /'tʃɪpsɛt/ *noun* Also written chip set 💻

A suite of integrated circuits designed to work together to fulfil a particular purpose in a computer system, for example in controlling video displays or communications input and output.

A transparent compound. The term *chip* is used here in its normal sense in the computing industry of 'integrated circuit', so called because all such complex electronic devices are created on the surface of a tiny piece, or *chip*, of silicon.

Although such microelectronic devices have been in use for decades (*chip* itself dates from 1962 and *microchip* from 1975), the compound term *chipset* only appeared in the mid eighties, when the increasing complexity and speed requirements of microcomputers necessitated the creation of suites of microchips which were designed to work as a set. For example, manufacturers commonly produce a set of chips comprising a microprocessor and support circuits which are sufficient to construct a working basic computer.

Intel is pushing vendors to adopt its PCI (Peripheral Component Interconnect) specification and chip set for a mezzanine bus in Pentium systems, and most vendors believe the two will become tightly linked.   —*Byte* July 1993, p. 84

Although it does not offer AVI video capture, the Jazz Multimedia Jakarta board...also uses the Tseng Labs chipset to provide graphics and video playback acceleration as well as MPEG decoding.   —*New Media* Aug. 1994, p. 27

chlorofluorocarbon 🌱 ⚗ see CFC

choker 🌱 see TRAFFIC CALMING

chopsocky /tʃɒpˈsɒki/ *noun* Also written **chopsockey** 🍵 POP

A film or video depicting an excess of bloodshed and mutilation in the context of Oriental martial arts.

Formed as a pun on *chopsuey*, the Chinese-style dish.

Martial arts films featuring elaborately staged fight scenes, such as those starring the American actor and kung fu expert Bruce Lee (1941–73), became popular in the seventies, with the term *chopsocky* being recorded at the end of the decade. By the mid eighties the appetite for cinematic violence had notably increased, as 'slasher' movies and other gory horror films were released for rental through video clubs. By 1994, *chopsockies* combined elements of both genres. The term is also used attributively, as in **chopsocky film**.

> Tarantino adores...all movies. Chop-socky epics from Hong Kong, westerns, the French New Wave, noir thrillers, low-budget exploitation stuff. —*i-D* Oct. 1994, p. 35

church planting /tʃəːtʃ ˈplɑːntɪŋ/ *noun* 🍴

The practice of establishing ('planting') a core of worshippers intended to develop into a congregation.

Since the mid eighties, evangelical Christian congregations have increasingly sought to spread their message by the establishment and fostering of small groups of worshippers intended to form the nucleus of further congregations. Such groups may be seen as offshoots from a parent church where the original congregation has grown too large; more controversially, it has happened that such a **church plant** has been introduced into an existing congregation whose practices are not sympathetic to what is seen as the HAPPY-CLAPPY approach of the parent body.

> The Mission has been actively involved in church planting, and it was a pleasure to worship with one such congregation numbering around 300 of all ages.
> —*Tear Times* (Tear Fund) No. 49 1990, p. 3

ciabatta /tʃəˈbɑːtə/ *noun* 🍽

A kind of moist, open-textured Italian bread made with olive oil. Also, a loaf of this bread.

An Italian dialect word meaning 'a down-at-heel shoe, a slipper', with reference to the characteristic shape of the loaf.

Since the mid eighties, an increasing number of different breads have become commercially available in the UK, not just in specialist bakeries but in general supermarkets. *Ciabatta* has proved particularly popular, and is now often found in savoury varieties, in which herbs, olives, or sun-dried tomatoes have been added to the dough.

> The British high street ciabatta, oozing with oil, soft of crumb and supple of crust, is actually a modern invention. —*Independent on Sunday* 24 Oct. 1993, Review section, p. 65

> The most recent big seller from abroad is ciabatta. —*Today* 27 July 1995, p. 16

CIS 📇 see COMMONWEALTH OF INDEPENDENT STATES

Citizen's Charter 📇 🍴 see CHARTER

CJD ⊗ see CREUTZFELDT–JAKOB DISEASE

clamper /ˈklampə/ *noun* 🍴

A person who clamps a car, or subjects another to the experience of having his or her car clamped.

Formed from the verb *clamp*, to immobilize an illegally parked car by attaching a wheel clamp to it.

From the early eighties, when the term *wheel clamp* began to be widely used for the device designed to be locked to one of the wheels of an illegally parked car, thus immobilizing it until the fine has been paid, it became increasingly common for *wheel* to be dropped, and the simple verb to be employed. Those carrying out the process thus became *clampers*, a term which has come into increasing use in Britain as many local authorities have placed responsibility for such work in the hands of private enterprise.

> Public car parks can seem like a welcome refuge from traffic wardens, double yellow lines, hungry parking meters, and 'clampers' in clogged-up city centres.   —*Which?* June 1990, p. 330

> He was not charged by the police for trying to dump the car clamper and his van in the harbor.
> —*New York Times* 21 Jan. 1992, p. 12

Clause Four /klɔːz ˈfɔː/ *noun* Also written Clause 4 📕

A clause included in the British Labour Party constitution of 1918 (revised in 1929) which contained an affirmation of the party's commitment to the common ownership of industry and services.

In 1995 *Clause Four* was rewritten and the commitment to common ownership finally dropped from the Labour Party's constitution. Originally composed in 1918 by the economist and historian Sidney Webb, the statement appeared thus in the revised constitution of 1929, under the Clause IV heading 'Party Objects':

> To secure for the producers by hand or by brain the full fruits of their industry, and the most equitable distribution thereof that may be possible, upon the basis of the common ownership of the means of production and distribution, and the best obtainable system of popular administration and control of each industry or service.

For several decades, while those on the left of the party have continued to applaud this statement as a socialist ideal, party modernizers have increasingly seen its commitment to nationalization as an albatross around the neck of progress, beginning in 1959 with a demand for its revision by Hugh Gaitskell, the then leader of the Labour Party. It was not until the advent of NEW LABOUR under Tony Blair, with its determined proposals for modernization, that the impetus against the retention of *Clause Four* was sufficiently strong to defeat the considerable number of Labour MPs who continued to defend it. Resolution of the issue was finally achieved by ballot in the autumn of 1995, allowing the party to go on to develop a manifesto free from any doctrinaire obligation to nationalization, and symbolizing the identity and strength of New Labour.

> The more dramatic the battle to defeat the Jurassic Park Socialists who want to retain Clause Four, the more powerful Mr Blair's appeal to the electorate.   —*Daily Mail* 2 Jan. 1995, p. 8

> More than half the Labour Party's 62 Members of the European Parliament subscribed to an advertisement in yesterday's *Guardian* calling for the retention, or at worst emendation, of Clause Four of the party's constitution: the one about common ownership of the means of production, and so on.   —*Daily Telegraph* 11 Jan. 1995, p. 22

> The claim that Mr Blair had changed but Labour had not could no longer be sustained because of the success of the Labour leader's campaign to change Clause Four.
> —*The Times* 2 July 1996 (electronic edition)

cleansing /ˈklɛnzɪŋ/ *verbal noun* 📕

The purging of undesired social or ethnic groups from a geographical area.

A translation of either German *Reinigung* or Serbo-Croat *čišćenje*.

While the forcible displacement of social and ethnic groups from a given area is far from being a new phenomenon, the use of the term *cleansing* is more recent. The process of **social cleansing**, the removal of an identified social group regarded as 'undesirable', was recorded in America in the mid eighties, but in the nineties *cleansing*, and especially ETHNIC CLEANSING, have become familiar terms through reports of the savage conflicts taking place in the former Yugoslavia.

Cleansing activities have to extend first of all to the Bolsheviks and Jews.

—*Independent* 5 May 1991, p. 10

A sentiment has developed among the Lebanese that the communal cleansing was wrong and that the displaced people should return home. —*Economist* 10 Oct. 1992, p. 68

In growing numbers, the unemployed and homeless, thieves, street children, tramps, prostitutes and homosexuals are being murdered by the police and hired death squads. Colombians call it 'social cleansing'...Amnesty puts the numbers killed by social cleansing in the thousands.

—*Independent on Sunday* 30 Jan. 1994, p. 15

The Serbs were keen to ensure the Zepa 'cleansing' operation was less offensive.

—*Today* 27 July 1995, p. 2

clear blue water /klɪə blu: 'wɔ:tə/ *noun phrase* 🔼 POP

The ideological gap between the aims and aspirations of two political parties.

From a blend of *clear water*, the distance between two boats, and *blue water*, the open sea, with a play on *blue* as the traditional colour of the British Conservative party.

The phrase *clear blue water*, used by the British Conservative politician Michael Portillo in a pamphlet outlining the principles and aspirations of the Conservative Right, was given a satirical twist by Geoffrey Howe at the Conservative Party Conference in 1994:

Wrapping ourselves in the Union Jack in the pursuit of a populist chimera would simply be a prelude to a burial at sea—in clear blue water somewhere out in the mid-Atlantic.

The phrase has become a cliché of modern political life, and early in 1996 John Major was confident enough of its familiarity to make allusive use of it in a Commons debate, when speaking of the **clear red water** which he perceived to lie between himself and the Labour leader, Tony Blair.

Fifteen years after the Conservative Party came to power, between us and the party that has sat on the Opposition benches all that time, there stretches still clear blue water.

—*Observer* 8 Nov. 1994

I'm absolutely brassed off with all this talk of green shoots and clear blue water.

—*Independent* 6 May 1995, p. 1

clergyperson {| see PERSON

client-server /klʌɪənt 'sə:və/ *noun* Also written **client/server** 💻

A type of networked computer system which consists of a number of workstations or personal computers (the *clients*) linked to a central computer containing a repository of data (the *server*). Frequently used attributively: being or belonging to this type of system.

The term *client-server* was coined in the mid eighties for a new type of linkage between a central computer system and its peripheral computers. This takes advantage of the processing power of the individual users' 'intelligent' computers, which are able to do much of the calculating, formatting, and display of data; previously this had been the responsibility of the central mainframe computer when terminals had no processing ability of their own. Typically, applications software running on the user's client machine sends a request for data to the central server, which returns it to the user. The technique is increasingly used in business, particularly for database applications, and the move to *client-server* computing away from mainframes is often called *downsizing* (see -SIZE) or *distributed computing*.

This client-server directory application allows Macintosh users to access a central VAX database for company information such as phone number, location, or personnel data.

—*MacWorld* Dec. 1993, p. 44

Every new software product seems to be described as 'client-server', with resulting confusion among IT departments, end-users, consultants and suppliers. The term is now so devalued that anyone attempting to describe any set-up more complicated than linking a single PC to a server now calls the architecture 'true' client-server.   —*Computer Weekly* 24 Mar. 1994, p. 36

The current realization of this model is called 'client/server' because it consists mostly of data models residing on servers and applications (clients) residing on local processors that access the server-based data across a local- or wide-area network.   —*Dr. Dobb's Journal* Oct. 1994, p. 18

Clintonite /ˈklɪnt(ə)nʌɪt/ *noun* and *adjective* 📷

noun: A supporter or adherent of William Jefferson ('Bill') Clinton (b. 1946), American Democratic statesman and President of the United States since 1993, or his policies.

adjective: Of or pertaining to Bill Clinton or Clintonites.

The election of President Clinton in 1993 put an end to the Republican domination of the presidency which had lasted since the election of Ronald Reagan in 1981. Since the beginning of his presidential campaign, perhaps in anticipation of the change, the Clinton name has been notably productive in forming additions to the political vocabulary. The terms *Clintonite* and **Clintonian** carried with them the implications of a new philosophy which would break with the conservatism established in the Reagan years, but attempts to **Clintonize** the prevailing political and economic culture have not been wholly successful. **Clintonization** has been hampered by WHITEWATERGATE and other problems, and **Clintonism** as a philosophy has not achieved the clarity of *Reaganism* for either adherents or opponents. *Clintonite* and other derivatives were widely used in 1996, as the President campaigned successfully for a second term.

It's now clear that the Clintonites were seething while Reaganites presided over eight million new jobs and the eruption of new Edge Cities (new middle-class housing developments, new shopping malls, new school systems, new leagues for kids' soccer, football and basketball) all over America.   —*Wall Street Journal* 19 Feb. 1993, section A, p. 14

Making this emerging Clintonism real has required the building of new, cross-cutting political coalitions by the President, because the old two-party structures forged during the New Deal can no longer answer the challenges of the new world.   —*New York Times* 28 Nov. 1993, p. 1

Clintonite spinmeisters will hail this 'sop to Cerberus' as a summit triumph.
   —*Post* (Denver) 7 May 1995, section E, p. 4

It was a classically Clintonian exercise, so everyone assumed it would end in a classically Clintonian way: with a doughy-thick waffle.   —*Economist* 22 July 1995, p. 47

Almost as remarkable as Mr Dole's emergence as a born-again supply-sider is his own shameless copying of Clintonisms.   —*Economist* 17 Aug. 1996, p. 39

See also CLINTONOMICS

Clintonomics /klɪntəˈnɒmɪks/ *noun* 〜 📷

The economic policies of President Clinton (see CLINTONITE).

Formed on the model of the earlier formations *Nixonomics*, *Reaganomics*, and *Rogernomics* (see -NOMICS).

Clintonomics, centring on the presidential campaign pledge to reduce the large US budget deficit, represent one of the main aspects of CLINTONITE policy. As in other areas, their implementation has been less successful than was originally hoped, and it is not yet clear that the final effect will be marked enough for the term itself to outlast the Clinton presidencies.

Are his positions as a candidate and his overall record accurate guides to what has been called 'Clintonomics'—Clinton's agenda for America's economic future?
   —*Investor's Business Daily* 24 Apr. 1992, p. 1

A favorite of business for tax breaks he backed in the Senate, this consummate insider will try to sell Clintonomics to Congress from his new post at the Treasury.
   —caption in *Newsweek* 25 Jan. 1993, p. 27

The voters cannot be reminded enough that Robb's *aye* gave Clintonomics its one-vote margin.
—*Richmond Times-Dispatch* 5 Oct. 1994, section A, p. 10

Clipper chip /ˈklɪpə tʃɪp/ *noun* Also **clipper chip** 🖳 ⦃⦄

An encryption system for digital telecommunications systems for which there exist special decryption keys that permit law enforcement agencies to intercept such communications.

The term *Clipper* was originally a secret code name in the late eighties within the US National Security Agency, which developed the system; it may have been chosen after the name of the nineteenth-century fast sailing ship. It is combined with *chip* in its normal electronics sense of 'a semiconductor integrated device'.

With the development of highly-secure encryption systems based on PUBLIC KEY ENCRYPTION, and of fast personal computers to run them on, law enforcement agencies fear that criminals may be able to communicate readily without any risk that their messages will be intercepted. The US government attempted to swing the advantage back towards the law enforcers by proposing in April 1993 that all consumer digital telecommunications devices, including telephones, should contain the *Clipper Chip*. This is an encryption device which would be secure for all normal purposes, but which creates messages which could be decrypted and read by agencies which have two special digital keys. To encourage public confidence in the system, it was proposed that the keys should be held securely by third-party government agencies and only made available under certain circumstances (because this process is called *escrow* in law, the system is formally called the *Escrowed Encryption Standard*).

The proposal immediately raised a storm of protest based on civil liberties arguments and fears that a less ethical future administration could use the system to spy on its citizens as a method of social control, raising images of Orwell's *Big Brother* and memories of the McCarthy period. Concern was also expressed because the encryption system was secret, and so its effectiveness could not easily be established. As a result of the controversy the proposals were withdrawn in 1994, but ways of making the scheme acceptable, for example by moving the escrow away from government agencies and using a different encryption system, continued to be sought. The word **Clipper** is also used attributively to refer to the system.

Clipper chip is also a proprietary name in the UK and US for another type of computer chip, and as a result the term is no longer used officially in encryption technology, although it is still common in the media.

The Clinton administration is now peddling its solution. Earlier this year, it began an all-out press to make sure that a new computer encryption device—the Clipper chip—will be buried in all communications equipment, from computers and phones to the PC-TVs we'll use to cruise the info highway. —*Rolling Stone* 19 May 1994, p. 46 (sidebar)

The Clipper chip represents the worst-case scenario for a U.S. intelligence community that has become dependent, as a young child is dependent on breast-feeding, on technical intercepts for its daily bread. The alternatives to Clipper are obvious: Get back in the business of real spying.
—*Rolling Stone* 19 May 1994, p. 46 (sidebar)

Civil rights groups have criticized the Clipper initiative, since the federal government holds a copy of every chip's master key and can use that key to decrypt—or decode—any Clipper-encrypted conversation.
—*Computer News* 17 May 1995, online newsletter

cocaine abuse ⦃⦄ see ABUSE

codec ⚗ see DIGITAL COMPRESSION

codependency /kəʊdɪˈpɛnd(ə)nsi/ *noun* Also written **co-dependency** ⊗ ⦃⦄

In the US: an emotional dependency on supporting or caring for another person or people. Also the state or condition of being dependent in this way.

The term *codependency* and the alternative form **codependence** are recorded in US psychological jargon from the early eighties, and were used initially with particular application to the spouses and relatives of alcoholics. *Codependency* may develop from prolonged exposure to an oppressive routine, frequently accompanied by a lack of compliments and praise, with the result that a person experiences a loss of self-confidence and a reduced sense of individuality. The characteristic essential to *codependency* appears to be the **codependent**'s denial of his or her own individual autonomy. *Codependency*, and the related concept of the *adult child*, have been associated with the *dysfunctional family*. Attempts to address the problems associated with all these have been collectively referred to in the US as the *recovery movement*.

> Out of codependent relationships come dysfunctional families, that is, families where one or both parents are alcoholics, drug addicts...rage-aholics...control-aholics, or caretakers.
> —Erika J. Chopich and Margaret Paul *Healing your Aloneness: Finding Love and Wholeness Through Your Inner Child* (1990), p. 41

> Codependency is one form of the traditional female role in which a woman is encouraged to deny her own identity and live through a man.   —*New York Times Book Review* 18 Mar. 1990, p. 34

> It has to be pretty weird to be a political spouse in the 1990's. It consigns you to a derivative life at the very time that everyone else has concluded that grown-ups are not supposed to be co-dependent.   —*New York Times* 24 Oct. 1993, section 9, p. 9

> As one of the most famous recovering co-dependents in the world, does she think that, freed from personal co-dependent relationships, she is now engaged in 'caretaking' on a much wider scale, through her books?   —*Kindred Spirit* Sept. 1995, p. 36

> Co-dependency support group, 5.30 p.m....The group meets the needs of people in various stages of co-dependency, including but not limited to Adult Children of Alcoholics.
> —*News & Record* (Greensboro, NC) 19 May 1996, p. 4 (Nexis)

cohabitational abuse ⟨⟨ see ABUSE

cold dark matter /kəʊld dɑːk 'matə/ *noun phrase* 🧪

Matter consisting of massive particles with low energy, which is believed by some scientists to exist in the universe but which has not yet been directly observed.

A combination of *matter* with *dark*, in the sense of 'invisible', and *cold* in the physicist's sense of 'lacking in energy', 'slow'.

It has been suggested since the thirties that large amounts of invisible matter must fill the spaces between the stars and galaxies. With the growth in theoretical understanding about the beginning of our universe at the Big Bang two theories have grown up about this **dark matter**. One suggests that the missing mass has not yet been detected because it consists of massive particles that only weakly interact with ordinary matter (see WIMP); because these particles have low energies they have been called generically *cold dark matter* or **CDM** for short. The other theory suggests that the matter was given off at the Big Bang in the form of energetic neutrinos, which have little mass; this matter is called by contrast **hot dark matter** or **HDM**. Recent observations suggest that both types of matter are involved, with the larger part of it *CDM*, a large minority *HDM*, and a small balance ordinary matter; the term **mixed dark matter** has been suggested for this.

> Neither the hot dark matter nor the cold dark matter hypothesis seems to work, at least not in its pure form, but this doesn't necessarily imply that these ideas have to be completely discarded.
> —Richard Morris *The Edges of Science: Crossing the Boundary from Physics to Metaphysics* (1990), p. 108

> If you look at computer simulations of the two scenarios, the cold dark matter universe looks much more like the real thing. Hot dark matter does not make the majestic spiraling galaxies we see. A hot dark matter universe would have incredibly thin walls of galaxies. With cold dark matter so many things match our observations: the size of galaxies, their rotation speeds, the clustering, and the voids.   —*Omni* July 1990, p. 90

One vexing problem is that the observed mass in the universe amounts to only 10 percent of what is needed to form galaxies; the other 90 percent has been considered 'missing matter,' and most recently has been believed to take the form of…cold dark matter.

—S. S. Hall *Mapping the Next Millennium* (1992), p. 363

cold fusion /ˈkəʊld fjuːʒ(ə)n/ *noun*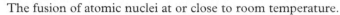

The fusion of atomic nuclei at or close to room temperature.

Nuclear *fusion* which takes place in comparatively *cold* conditions.

Research into controlled nuclear fusion as a possible source of energy has been going on since the fifties, using reaction vessels in which the nuclei of light elements such as helium are brought close together under conditions of high pressure and temperature. Though some fusion has taken place , the energy needed to start the nuclear reaction has so far always been greater than the amount produced. If *cold fusion* existed, taking place at low temperatures and pressures within solid materials, it might provide a cheap and almost limitless source of energy. In 1989, Martin Fleischmann and Stanley Pons from the University of Utah announced *cold fusion* had taken place in the laboratory with simple apparatus. This announcement created enormous interest and controversy, which heightened when other laboratories around the world failed to repeat the result. Most scientists now believe that *cold fusion* of this kind is impossible, though research is continuing in several places. Another type of *cold fusion*, technically known as *muon-catalysed fusion*, is known to exist, but is thought unlikely ever to provide a useful source of energy.

According to this view, the only real question remaining about cold fusion is why two respectable chemists went off the deep end in pursuit of a delusion. —*Reason* Dec. 1991, p. 29

Cold fusion has been dismissed as 'pathological science' by the vast majority of scientists…But the undeniably attractive idea of limitless energy from batterylike cells still has its believers.

—*Scientific American* May 1992, p. 53

Huizenga was co-chairman of the Department of Energy (DOE) panel on cold fusion, assembled to advise the Secretary of Energy on the extraordinary claims of an energy utopia based on experiments using essentially test-tube chemistry. —*Skeptical Inquirer* Summer 1992, p. 348

commonhold /ˈkɒmənhəʊld/ *noun* ✖

In the UK, the freehold tenure of a flat within a multi-occupancy building, but with shared responsibility for common services.

In Britain prior to the late eighties, tenure of property was by *freehold* (in which the property was owned outright), or *leasehold* (in which the property was held by lease, and would at the set time revert to the original owner). Flats were very frequently held by leasehold, often for a substantial number of years; in such a case the owner of the building might set appropriate service and maintenance charges, but would be responsible for the building overall.

Commonhold proposals were brought before the British parliament in 1987. A *commonhold* system makes it possible for the tenants of a building to buy the freehold of their flats; this brings with it a joint responsibility for services and maintenance. Former tenants thus become actual property owners, or **commonholders**, in a change much in tune with the aspirations of Conservative philosophy; it remains to be seen how much difficulty is presented in the long run by the increased financial and management responsibilities entailed.

The Law Commission proposals would enable commonholders collectively to share the benefits and responsibilities of owning the freehold of a block of flats.

—*Independent* 24 Feb. 1990, p. 38

A commonhold association, in which all the flat-owners have a vote, will have certain legal obligations, such as managing a reserve fund for major repairs, and keeping proper accounts.

—*Which?* Oct. 1991, p. 581

The government already has a commonhold bill drawn up (to which a right-to-manage clause could easily be attached). —*Economist* 14 Jan. 1995, p. 26

Commonwealth of Independent States /ˌkɒmənwɛlθ əv

ˌɪndɪˈpɛnd(ə)nt steɪts/ *noun phrase* 📛

A confederation of former constituent republics of the Soviet Union, established in 1991 following the dissolution of the USSR.

A translation of the Russian phrase *Sodruzhestvo Nezavisimykh Gosudarstv.*

The *Commonwealth of Independent States*, or **CIS**, was established in 1991 following a meeting in the Belorussian city of Brest at which the USSR was dissolved. The founding member states were Armenia, Azerbaijan, Belarus, Kazakhstan, Kyrgyzstan, Moldova, Russia, Tajikistan, Turkmenistan, Ukraine, and Uzbekistan.

Dissolution of the apparently monolithic Soviet Union, and the subsequent establishment of the *Commonwealth of Independent States*, seemed to many a harbinger of the NEW WORLD ORDER proclaimed by President Bush. However, as the nineties have progressed, events have not supported the original optimism. Azerbaijan left the **CIS** in 1992, and in 1994 Russia invaded the CHECHEN Republic, where fighting continues. In the mid nineties it is not yet clear how long-lasting the *CIS* will be.

Whether or not the new Commonwealth of Independent States is destined to last...it has already provided a mechanism for the controlled dissolution of the Soviet Union.
—*Economist* 4 Jan. 1992, p. 13

Russia, Ukraine, and Belarus...formed the core of the Commonwealth of Independent States (CIS) that emerged from the ashes of the USSR.   —Martin Ebon *KGB Death & Rebirth* 1994, p. 128

community care /kəˌmjuːnɪti ˈkɛː/ *noun* ☒ 🔩

In the UK: a government programme introduced in 1990 to provide long-term care for the mentally ill, the elderly, and people with disabilities, within the resources offered by the community rather than in hospitals or institutions.

Community care, also frequently referred to as *care in the community*, is not a new idea, and facilities offering such care have existed for many years. However, in 1990 in the UK the government, after a lengthy discussion period, launched a new, far-reaching, national *community care* programme as part of its programme of health service reform. The government's aim was to reduce institutional provision of long-term care and replace it with care schemes offered by the community, including domiciliary and outreach services. The programme was implemented under the terms of the 1990 National Health Service and Community Care Act, which provided for further major reforms including the purchase of care by FUNDHOLDER GPs and the competitive provision of services by HOSPITAL TRUSTS. *Community care*, which has involved extensive reorganization of staffing and resources within the health and social services, has met with considerable criticism on the grounds that, with the closure of many of the old institutions, the overall level of support for people in need of care, especially the mentally ill, has dropped. It is felt that institutional care encompasses both monitoring and treatment, not just restraint, and that *community care* allows for inadequate supervision of the taking of essential medication. Concern has been exacerbated by a number of incidents in which members of the public and care workers have been attacked or killed by people suffering from schizophrenia. Further concerns have been expressed that a greater burden will fall on short-stay hospitals and on non-professional carers, typically the children or spouses of the disabled or elderly. A more positive view expressed is that *community care* offers the long-term patient a better quality of life than that associated with the old institutions.

By uprating the level of community care, more people should be able to stay at home rather than move into residential or nursing homes.   —*Mature Times Monthly* Oct. 1992, p. 1

Hospital trusts are warning that their beds are becoming blocked by patients who cannot be discharged because of the crisis in funding community care for the old and disabled.
—*Guardian* 10 Jan. 1995, section 1, p. 8

The government's failure to make community care work is discrediting a progressive policy. Things are bad enough now, but they will get worse as the asylum closures proceed. More murders will

mean more public outrage, and more pressure to return to the old inhumanity of the loony bins.
—*Economist* 2 Sept. 1995, p. 16

Thus came the first political recognition of one of the main failings afflicting the care in the community programme: the way it fails to cope with schizophrenics and other seriously mentally-ill patients who need long-term, round-the-clock support.   —*Independent* 21 Feb. 1996, p. 17

comper /ˈkɒmpə/ *noun*

A person who regularly enters for competitions in order to win as many prizes as possible; a 'professional' competition entrant.

From *comp* as an abbreviation of *competition*.

The growing number of competitions (especially as promotions for consumer goods) has bred in turn the 'professional' competition entrant: someone who treats entering for competitions in order to win commercially attractive prizes as effectively a full-time occupation. The term *comper*, designating such a person, was coined in the second half of the eighties, and was soon followed by **comping** as a term to describe the activity involved.

Your Health has a quiz with a £100 prize…There are thousands of people who devote their time to such competitions. Known as 'comping', it is a well-established addiction.
—*Sunday Telegraph* 11 June 1989, p. 45

These professional competition entrants—compers—who spend hours hunched over supermarket leaflets, who sweat over nonsensical anagrams and word searches, who dream up witty ways to describe exactly why they enjoy slamming in the lamb.   —*Guardian* 1 Dec. 1993, section 2, p. 8

Entering competitions can be a way of life. David Cohen talks to three die-hard 'compers'.
—heading in *Independent* 1 Jan. 1996, p. 13

complexity theory 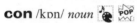 see CHAOS

computer abuse see ABUSE

con /kɒn/ *noun*

A convention or conference, especially one devoted to a particular literary genre.

Formed by shortening *convention*.

The American practice of holding *cons* or **conventions** at which fans (or FEN) of science fiction can meet fellow enthusiasts and discuss their favourite works is now a well-established one. The informal abbreviation is still chiefly used by aficionados, but since the eighties is likely to be recognized by those who do not themselves participate; the custom of holding such gatherings has now spread to other genres.

You here for the con?   —Sharyn McCrumb *Bimbos of the Death Sun* (1988), p. 7

There's plenty of people out there who read sf and fantasy as part of a balanced reading diet and who don't think of themselves as fans, and who'd probably go pale at the thought of spending a weekend at a con.   —*Interzone* Jan. 1994, p. 26

cook-chill /kʊkˈtʃɪl/ *adjective* and *noun*

adjective: Of foods: sold in a pre-cooked and refrigerated form, for consumption after reheating.

noun: The process of pre-cooking and refrigerating foods for reheating later.

The *cook-chill* system had become popular in institutional catering by the early eighties; the phrase itself was first used in written form in 1982. The term became widely known in the UK in the late eighties, when there was an increase in the number of cases of listeriosis, thought to be caused at least in part by failure to store *cook-chill* foods correctly or reheat them thoroughly. Certain groups, especially those ill in hospital, were discovered to be particularly at risk.

The Department of Health has already advised people in at-risk groups not to eat cook-chill foods cold, and—if you buy one to eat hot—to make sure that it's reheated until it's 'piping hot'.
—*Which?* Apr. 1990, p. 206

-core /kɔː/ *combining form*

The second element in compounds for specific forms of popular music.

From the second element of *hardcore*, with allusion to the primary meaning of *core* as the central element of something.

The establishment of HARDCORE in the eighties has led in the nineties to the development of a number of related terms for popular music, including **foxcore**, grunge music performed by female bands, **grindcore**, a type of fast heavy metal music incorporating harsh noise as a musical effect, and QUEERCORE.

Foxcore's been overtaken by the equally absurd 'riot girl' tag.
—*Richmond Times-Dispatch* 15 June 1995, section D, p. 13

A huge mailorder catalog full of great death metal, grindcore, industrial, and alternative.
—advertisement in *Screamer* Nov. 1995, p. 77

Clubbers converge every fortnight on this groovy bar room, listening to lounge-core before midnight and House after.
—*Time Out* 6 Dec. 1995, p. 70

crack /krak/ *noun*

A highly addictive, crystalline form of cocaine made by heating a mixture of it with baking powder and water until it is hard, and breaking it into small pieces which are burnt and smoked for their stimulating effect.

The name arises from the fact that the hard-baked substance has to be *cracked* into small pieces for use, as well as the *cracking* sound the pieces make when smoked.

The substance came to the attention of US drug enforcement agencies in the early eighties, but at that time was generally known on the streets as *rock* or *freebase*. In the mid eighties the name *crack* appeared as slang among drug users, and soon became established as the usual term; since the late eighties, the fuller description **crack cocaine** has tended to replace *crack* alone in official use. Both terms are now in use throughout the English-speaking world. *Crack*'s appearance on the US drug market coincided with a marked rise in violent crime, testifying to its potency and addictiveness, with users prepared to go to almost any lengths to get more. The word *crack* quickly became the basis for compounds, notably **crackhead** (a user of *crack*; see also BASEHEAD), **crack house** (a house where *crack* is prepared or from which it is sold), and **crack pipe** (the home-made device in which *crack* is smoked). The violence associated with the drug was sometimes described in the press as **crack wars**. Addicted women were found to be giving birth, often prematurely, to under-sized children with brain damage and other developmental disorders; these became known as **crack babies**.

In New York and Los Angeles drug dealers have opened up drug galleries, called 'crack houses'.
—*San Francisco Chronicle* 6 Dec. 1985, p. 3

Charlie and two fellow 'crackheads' took me to a vast concrete housing estate in South London where crack is on sale for between £20 and £25 a deal. —*Observer* 24 July 1988, p. 15

The police picked up the body of an unidentified black male in his twenties. He had been shot through the head, apparently another victim of the crack wars.
—R. Stone *Keeping the Future at Bay* in *Best American Essays* (1989), p. 254

In these days of crack babies, Dr. Fleischman says, infants may be born weighing a pound or less, only 20 to 22 weeks gestational age, but having a heartbeat.
—*New York Times Magazine* 5 Aug. 1990, p. 62

Some had started using broken-off car antennas for crack pipes, stuffing the usual bit of Brillo pads into one end to recycle the vapors and provide an extra hit.
—Daniel Coyle *Hardball: Season in the Projects* (1993), p. 134

crack abuse ⟦ see ABUSE

cracker /'krakə/ noun ▣

A person who maliciously or mischievously breaks into a computer system.

From *crack*, in the sense of 'to break open', plus the personalizing suffix *-er*.

The word *cracker* began to be used from the mid eighties onwards because of the shifting sense of the older word HACKER. Some people in computing attempted to restore the older sense by creating the term *cracker* to take over its negative associations, and to make a distinction between (good) hackers and (bad) *crackers*. This has not worked out, and both terms are commonly used in popular sources to refer to persons carrying out such anti-social activities; if there is a difference, it is that hackers explore for the sake of achievement or to demonstrate their skills, whereas the *cracker* is malicious or aiming at personal gain. The verb is **crack**, and the action noun is **cracking**.

> The debate still rages as to what constitutes the difference between hacking and cracking. Some say that cracking represents any and all forms of rule-breaking and illegal activity using a computer. —Rudolf Rucker, R. U. Sirius, & Queen Mu *Mondo 2000* (1993), p. 54

> We work separately and together, and every now and then we do structured cracks for general interest, for example trying to crack British Telecom codes for free transatlantic calls. —*Independent on Sunday* 8 Jan. 1995, p. 23

> CIAC and similar groups fear Satan will make it easy for hackers or systems 'crackers' to use the program to target systems in order to locate weaknesses. —*Computer Weekly* 13 Apr. 1995, p. 4

Creutzfeldt–Jakob disease /krɔɪtsfɛlt'jakɒb dɪˌziːz/ noun phrase ⊗

A fatal degenerative disease, affecting nerve cells in the brian, causing mental, physical, and sensory disturbances such as dementia and seizures. Often abbreviated to **CJD**.

Named after H. G. *Creutzfeldt* (1885–1964) and A. *Jakob* (1882–1927), German neurologists, who first described cases of the disease in 1920–1.

The term *Creutzfeldt–Jakob disease*, recorded since the thirties, has recently received considerable news coverage. In the early nineties it became apparent that growth hormone derived from human sources and administered to children had transmitted the *CJD*. The disease is believed to be caused by PRIONS and to be related to other spongiform encephalopathies; the possibility that there may be a direct link between BSE and new forms of *CJD* is currently a matter of public concern.

> Just a few years ago growth hormone derived from human sources transmitted Creutzfeldt–Jakob's disease. —*Scientific American* Sept. 1992, p. 163

> It is clearly imperative to continue to study closely the epidemiology of CJD, as the long incubation periods in CJD and other prion-protein diseases indicates that it will be many years before a theoretical link between CJD and BSE can be excluded. —*Independent* 17 Nov. 1995, p. 20

> There is the issue of those a-typical, youthful victims of Creutzfeldt–Jacob Disease whose fates so shocked the nation when they were revealed on 20 March, and whose existence provided the first convincing link between mad cow disease and humans. —*Observer* 31 Mar. 1996, p. 16

cross bike ▨ ⊕ see ATB

cruncher /'krʌntʃə/ noun ▣

A computer or computer application which undertakes extensive calculation or processing of data.

A shortened form of the colloquial computing term *number cruncher* 'a machine capable of performing complex operations on large amounts of numerical data'; the full form was first recorded in English in 1966 and relies on the imagery of the computer as 'eating' and 'digesting' large amounts of data and later spewing out the results.

The motivation for a shortened form of the phrase *number cruncher* was perhaps the development of complex computing applications that worked on non-numerical data: for example, literary and linguistic computing contributed the concept of **word-crunching** and the **WordCruncher** (the trade mark of a concordancing package for use on large amounts of free text). The shortened form *cruncher* began to appear in the computing and statistical communities in about the mid eighties, though it has never become particularly common on its own; *number cruncher* is still the most commonly used term, with a few general alternatives such as **data cruncher** and **information cruncher**. There is also a transitive verb to **crunch**.

> Computer aided editing, compiling electronic databases, preparing indices and concordances by crunching words...provide 'tools' for traditional and new methods in textual research.
> —*Literary and Linguistic Computing* Vol. 5, No. 2 1990, p. 172

> This SQL server strips away all the extras and offers the user lean data cruncher.
> —*Publish* Feb. 1991, p. 101

> NAFTA cruncher. According to...Minnesota developer Iconovex, Indexicon, an automatic indexing add-on for WordPerfect for Windows, took just ten minutes running on a 486/66 to automatically generate a back-of-the-book index for the full eleven hundred pages of the NAFTA agreement.
> —*Language Industry Monitor* Sept. 1994, back cover

crusty /'krʌsti/ *noun* Also **crustie** ⚒ POP ⟨⟨

In the UK: a member of a group of young people who have adopted a lifestyle characterized by the wearing of rough, torn clothes, and by matted, often dreadlocked hair; also, occasionally, the subculture belonging to this group.

It is likely that the noun is formed on the adjective in its sense 'hard, crustlike', which has an established transferred use in reference to unwashed skin and clothes.

References to *crusties* first began to appear in the UK in the early nineties. The culture associated with them may be seen to have sprung from the culture of the NEW AGE *travellers*, which developed in the UK in the late eighties. Sometimes the terms *crusty* and *New Age traveller* are used interchangeably, and similarities may be seen between the two groups, particularly in terms of clothing and appearance and in a lifestyle frequently centred around busking or begging in city streets, the participants accompanied by a cluster of dogs kept as pets. New Age travellers are associated with the rejection of conventional and especially materialist values, many choosing to live an itinerant existence on the fringes of society, frequently in old buses converted into makeshift homes. However, although some *crusties* espouse the philosophies associated with the New Age, many are less easily identified with this set of aspirations. *Crusties* are more likely to live in conventional homes and to mix with contemporaries who do not share their culture. Some people have located the deeper roots of the *crusty* culture in the punk movement of the late seventies and early eighties, associating it with punk's apparently more aggressive challenge to conventional society. *Crusties* have also been associated with environmental protest, in particular the campaign against the building of the Newbury bypass in Hampshire in 1995, where the term was applied to many of those living in tree houses and TWIGLOOS.

The noun *crusty* is freely used attributively and there are indications of its development as an adjective in this sense.

> Apart from the dedicated black hip hop fans, the Academy is filling up with white kids too, and they're not all Fila-shod, Raiders-jacketed rap wannabes. There's a decidedly crusty flavour in the audience and all that's missing is a few dogs on string. —*Rage* 24 Oct. 1991, p. 20

> Crusty was born out of punk, nurtured by hippy foster-parents on the free festival scene, and has now come of age. —*Independent* 26 Oct. 1991, magazine, p. 67

> The Levellers got where they are via the ardent support of pop's self-styled underclass—the New

Age travellers, crusties and anarcho-punks who populate the free-festival and squat scenes.
—*Guardian* 31 Aug. 1993, section 2, p. 6

Dreadlocky bloke (15+) needed for a happy girl (15) for gigs, festivals, talking, laughter and pleasure, likes Levellers, NMA, outcast band and crusties.　　—advertisement in *Select* Mar. 1995, p. 99

Amid the 'crusties', white rastas and mud-stained tree huggers, Jeannine, Lady Barber, wife of Sir David, the Baronet of Greasley, cuts a curious figure.　　—*Independent* 19 Jan. 1996, p. 5

CSA ⚄ see CHILD SUPPORT AGENCY

cultbuster /'kʌltbʌstə/ *noun* ⚄

A person who plays a leading part in removing another from the influence of a cult.

The power of a *cult* over a person is reduced or broken by someone acting as a *buster*; there is probably a conscious awareness of the earlier compounds *gangbuster*, *ghostbuster*.

In the late eighties, concerns about the influence on the young and impressionable of religious cults, such as the cult of the Moonies based on Sun Myung Moon's Unification Church, found direct expression in methods by which young people, often those who had been forcibly removed by their parents from what was seen as a dangerous sphere of influence, were subjected to a prolonged process aimed at eradicating implanted beliefs and ideas. This in turn gave rise to misgivings as to whether the methods employed constituted in themselves another form of brainwashing rather than a genuine freeing from an imposed mode of thought. It is likely that a number of incidents in the mid nineties, including the siege and fire at the headquarters of the Branch Davidian cult in Waco, Texas, and the massacre or mass suicide of members of the Order of the Solar Temple in Switzerland and Canada, will be seen by *cultbusters* to provide justification for their actions.

A four-part BBC drama...about a young woman kidnapped by a cultbuster and 'deprogrammed' against her will, raises questions about an individual's right to affiliate to a religion, and the ethics of forcible removal.　　—*Independent on Sunday* 15 Jan. 1995, p. 24

cultural Chernobyl /ˌkʌltʃ(ə)r(ə)l tʃə'nɒbɪl/ *noun phrase* ⚄

A place which in terms of art and culture is regarded as a disaster area.

Something regarded as the *cultural* equivalent of *Chernobyl*, a town near Kiev in Ukraine where, in April 1986, an accident at a nuclear power station resulted in a serious escape of radioactive material and the subsequent contamination of Ukraine, Belarus, and other parts of Europe.

This allusive reference to the mid-eighties disaster dates from 1992, when the French theatre director Ariane Mnouchkine coined *cultural Chernobyl* to express her views of the first European Disneyland, EuroDisney, which had been established just outside Paris. It is not yet clear whether the term will become more generally established.

She referred to Euro Disney as a 'cultural Chernobyl'—a horror of cardboard, plastic, and appalling colors, a construction of solidified chewing gum and idiotic fairy tales lifted straight from comic strips.　　—*Harper's Magazine* July 1992, p. 18

cut and paste /'kʌt (ə)n(d) peɪst/ *verb* and *noun* ⚄

transitive or *intransitive* verb: In computing, to delete (text, data) in a document in a computer application and insert it elsewhere in the same document or into another in the same or a different application.

noun: The action of moving data in this way.

A figurative use of the phrase, derived from the once-common office procedure of creating an edited version of a document by physically *cutting and pasting* sections from a draft, itself based on the action of clipping items such as newspaper cuttings and pasting them into a scrapbook.

The figurative use in computing arose in the early eighties when graphically-based operating systems began to be introduced. A mechanism was provided that enabled users to select material in one document, delete it to a separate area of memory (the *clipboard*) and insert it from there into the new document. A similar function had been available in older word processors, but only readily allowed such moves within one document in one application. The phrase is also applied more loosely to the related action of copying and inserting, which leaves the original material in place. The phrase is frequently used attributively, not unusually in the participial form **cut and pasted**.

> The Edit menu provides you with advanced cut and paste techniques for creating image montages. *—Personal Computer World* Feb. 1991, p. 149

> Styled text cannot be cut and pasted between applications without losing all that neat font and formatting information. *—MacUser* Oct. 1993, p. 165

> Each journalist will have a multimedia PC and will call up the video footage from the server to his or her desktop. The journalist will then cut and paste the footage as one would with a word-processing document. *—Independent* 9 Oct. 1995, section 2, p. 14

cyber- /'sʌɪbə/ *prefix* 🖳

The first element of a wide variety of terms relating to computer-mediated electronic communications, particularly those which came to general prominence in the eighties and nineties, such as ELECTRONIC *mail* and the INTERNET.

Back-formation from *cybernetics* 'the science of communications and automatic control systems in both machines and living things', coined in 1948 and ultimately from the Greek noun *kubernētēs* 'steersman'.

In the following three decades, a few other new terms were based on the same prefix: *cyborg* was invented about 1960 to describe a person whose abilities have been transformed or augmented by mechanical elements built into the body; followers of the BBC television series *Dr Who* will remember the *Cybermen*. However, it remained essentially a niche usage.

The prefix suddenly gained a new vigour following the publication of William Gibson's novel *Neuromancer* in 1984, in which he used **cyberspace**—a word he had actually coined two years previously in a short story in *Omni*—to describe the VIRTUAL *reality* landscape within networked computers that is experienced by humans whose brains are directly connected to it. *Cyberspace* quickly became popular within the science-fiction, computer, and communications communities, and can still refer to virtual reality environments. From about 1990 the word has moved towards mainstream usage, partly because of the rapid expansion of interest in the Internet; its sense has at the same time shifted to refer to the totality of all communications networks without any virtual reality overtones. As Bruce Sterling has put it in his book *The Hacker Crackdown*:

> Cyberspace is the 'place' where a telephone conversation appears to occur...The place *between* the phones.

The adjective formed from *cyberspace* is **cyberspatial**.

The word **cyberpunk** was coined by Bruce Bethke in 1983 and immediately became applied to the subgenre of science fiction of which *Neuromancer* was a canonical example. *Cyberpunk* novels are morally ambiguous, describing marginalized people struggling to survive in bleak urbanized futuristic worlds dominated by global businesses or governments, whose control is enhanced by artificial intelligence; plots often involve electronically-augmented individuals (the 1982 film *Blade Runner* is pure cyberpunk in concept). In the mid eighties, some science-fiction writers and others saw parallels between these future worlds and current society, and began to describe themselves as *cyberpunks*. The related adjective is **cyberpunkish**.

On the model of these two words, a very large number of other compounds beginning in *cyber-* have since been formed, making it the most fecund combining form in the language of the early and mid nineties. Many of the coinages have merely a fleeting existence; some, however, seem to have staying power: a **cybernaut** is a supposed traveller in *cyberspace*—a person who uses computers to communicate; **cyberart** is a body of artistic work created (by a **cyberartist**) using computer-based techniques and, perhaps, transmitted by electronic means; a **cyberbrain** is an artificial intelligence; **cyberculture** is the society of people linked by, and communicating through, electronic means such as Usenet and the Internet; in a **cybercafé** one may take refreshment while accessing the Internet; **cyberdelia** (with its adjective **cyberdelic**) refers to a high-tech, computer-generated form of psychedelia; **cyberfeminism** recognizes the non-discriminatory advantages of cyberspace to women (one holding these views is a **cyberfeminist**); **cyberhippies**, also known as **Cyberians**, are a high-tech development of the 1960s hippy culture, embracing technology rather than shunning it; a **cyberlawyer** is either an expert on the law relating to online communications (**cyberlaw**), or studies the implications of computers and communications for the practice of law; **cyberphobia** is a fear of electronic communications or of its technology (someone who has this is **cyberphobic**); a **cybersurfer** SURFS the Internet in search of interesting things; **cybersex** is either explicit sexual material transmitted by electronic means or, more particularly, simulated sex using virtual reality techniques; a **cybersuit** is a whole-body costume for virtual reality simulations (wired to monitor body movements and feed them back to the computer generating the images); the **cyberworld** is either the whole of *cyberspace*, or that part of it relating to virtual reality environments. **Cyber** appears alone as a noun, adjective and verb, relating generally to computer-mediated communications or virtual sensations; the adjective **cyberish** is sometimes found.

A low-level supervising program woke up a slightly higher-level supervising program deep in the ship's semisomnolent cyberbrain and reported to it that whenever it went *click* all it ever got was a hum. —Douglas Adams *Mostly Harmless* (1992), p. 11

In theory, people will one day be able to fully simulate sex with a computerized being, or with another 'virtual' person over the phone lines...Except for the one-dimensional thrill of Cyborgasm, cybersex does not exist yet. —*Esquire* June 1993, p. 58

Although spatial imagery and a sense of place help convey the experience of dwelling in a virtual community, biological imagery is often more appropriate to describe the way cyberculture changes. —Howard Rheingold *The Virtual Community* (1994), p. 5

But 92 per cent of teen-agers are gadget-friendly, which means that cyberphobics really are making history: Adolescents always have claimed to know more than their parents, but for the first time, they're right. —*CompuServe Magazine* Mar. 1994, p. 18

If anyone could qualify for being a closet cybernaut, Mike Lunch, director of the PC division at Toshiba, has got his diploma. —*Computer Weekly* 28 July 1994, p. 72

From Oct 1 the first photographic gallery of cyberart will be showing at url http://www.pavilion.co.uk/gallery/shot. High culture for the cyber masses.
—*The Face* Oct. 1994, p. 36

Shaw, who waggishly signs himself off in messages to the Net as 'the friendly Internet MP' (as well as, in a touching display of loyalty to his constituency, encouraging France-bound cybersurfers to use the ferry rather than the Chunnel), has been badgering the Government to take an interest in the Info Highway. —*Guardian* 20 Jan. 1995, Friday supplement, p. 17

We are not geeks, we are cyberspace frontiersmen. And when the Net becomes a global community, the frontier will move farther—to some cyberlands yet unknown—or perish if there are no more new lands to explore. —12 Feb. 1995, online posting

One person's 'cyberpunk' is another's everyday obnoxious teenager with some technical skill thrown in, or just someone looking for the latest trend to identify with.
—14 Mar. 1995, online posting

cystic fibrosis transmembrane regulator ⊗ see CFTR

D

DAB ⚗ see DIGITAL AUDIO BROADCASTING

daisy-chaining 🖳 see SCSI

dangerous dog /deɪn(d)ʒ(ə)rəs ˈdɒg/ *noun* 🐾

A dog of a breed notable for its strength and ferocity, legally defined as dangerous to the public in an act passed in May 1991, which set out restrictions as to the import, production, and keeping of a number of named breeds in the UK.

In 1990, public concern about a number of attacks on children by rottweilers and other dogs was exacerbated by reports from the RSPCA that ferocious cross-breeds of fighting-dogs were being bred and used in the UK.

The **Dangerous Dogs Act**, as the bill became known, imposed severe controls on the keeping of certain breeds (such as the pit-bull terrier) and banned others (such as the bandog and the Japanese tosa). Owners of dogs subject to restriction were required to license their animals, and to keep them muzzled in public; unlicensed and unmuzzled dogs were liable to seizure, and could be destroyed. A number of high-profile cases followed, in which dogs identified as pit-bull terriers remained on 'Death Row' for several years, while legal battles took place over whether the classification was in fact correct. To date, with fewer attacks by dogs being reported, the scope and force of the legislation remains controversial, although accounts in 1996 of the breeding and selling of WOLF-DOGS indicated that public anxiety remains alive.

> Charged under the Dangerous Dogs Act for biting a dog warden, Kizzy was likely to be seized by the police to be destroyed. —*Dogs Today* Dec. 1992, p. 6

> The English bull terrier is not one of the breeds singled out for strict curbs by the 1991 Dangerous Dogs Act. —*Daily Telegraph* 24 Dec. 1994, p. 1

> [Bull mastiffs] are not on the dangerous dogs list. —*Daily Telegraph* 20 Mar. 1996, p. 6

dark matter ⚗ see COLD DARK MATTER

DAT ⚗ see DIGITAL COMPACT CASSETTE

data cruncher 🖳 see CRUNCHER

dataglove /ˈdeɪtəglʌv/ *noun* Also written **DataGlove** 🖳

A glove which contains sensors to detect the relative position and movements of the hand and fingers, used to control and manipulate a variety of computer-generated images, especially in VIRTUAL *reality* environments.

The original *dataglove* was developed in the mid eighties. The computer uses the data from the sensors in the glove to insert an image of the user's hand into the scene it is generating and displaying. In combination with other control and feedback systems, such as the EYEPHONE, it permits users to 'handle' objects in the virtual world, and also—by the convention of pointing a finger—to instruct the computer to 'move' through the scene in any direction. The *dataglove* was quickly taken up by research organizations and others because it was a great improvement on previous methods of interacting with computer systems: hand movements are natural, and provide much more detailed information to the computer. It was quickly applied to computer games and is also beginning to have applications in teleoperation (see TELE-) and in other fields.

> Wearing DataGloves and DataSuits, we will 'perform' in our own computer movies, 'choreograph' computer dances, and 'paint' stunning works of computer art. —*Omni* Dec. 1989, p. 148

> The 'dataglove' is VR's equivalent to the PC's mouse, a glove with optical fibres stitched along its fingers so that the position of the hand is turned into a pattern of light.
> —*Economist* 11 Mar. 1995, p. 130

data warehouse /ˈdeɪtə ˌwɛːhaʊs/ *noun* 🖳 ∿

A collection of data which has been brought together from a variety of sources within and outside an organization and processed into a form which gives useful guidance to the organization's decision makers.

A compound of *data*, in a mixture of its general sense of 'known facts used as a basis for inference or reckoning' and its computing sense of 'quantities operated on by a computer', with *warehouse*, 'a store or repository', with the implication of a substantial or complex collection.

The *data warehouse* is a technique which was developed in the US in the early nineties to help organizations spot trends and predict the effect of change on the profitability of the business. It employs fast computers and large amounts of storage; the aim is to copy raw data from various sources, store it, process it, and present it to managers in a form which is easy to assimilate and interrogate. Such systems are regarded as an evolutionary step forward from the *executive information systems* of the eighties and they became something of a fashionable concept in the mid nineties, in part because some early implementers found their systems paid for themselves within months in reduced costs. The technique is called **data warehousing** and a verb **data warehouse** is sometimes seen.

> Data warehousing offers users the possibility of pulling together information held in disparate and potentially incompatible locations throughout an organisation and putting it to good use.
> —*Computing* 8 June 1995, p. 4

> When a data warehouse succeeds, more users than initially planned want to employ data mining to their advantage. Data-warehousing and data-mining applications are usually installed with a specific motive in mind, such as fraud detection or profit generation. —*Byte* Oct. 1995, p. 101

date rape ⁅ see ACQUAINTANCE RAPE

Dayton /ˈdeɪt(ə)n/ *noun* ⁅

An agreement on measures to achieve the ending of hostilities in former Yugoslavia, reached in Dayton, Ohio, in November 1995. Often used attributively, as in **Dayton agreement, Dayton (peace) accord**.

Talks at the Wright-Patterson air base in Dayton, Ohio, between representatives of Bosnia, Croatia, and Serbia, culminated in an agreement on 21 December 1995 which was described by Alija Izetbegović of Bosnia in the following terms:

> And to my people I say, this may not be a just peace, but it is more just than a continuation of war.

The accord was signed on 14 December 1995 in Paris by the Presidents of the three countries; it remains to be seen what long-term success will be achieved.

> However, in line with Pale's attempts to rewrite Dayton, Mr Koljevic said the solution for Sarajevo would be the 'Mostar model' of ethnic cantons—which will not happen.
> —*Independent* 30 Dec. 1995, p. 8

> The incident is a glaring illustration of the failure of Milosevic to honour the pledge he made at the Dayton peace accord to hand over alleged war criminals. —*The European* 30 May 1996, p. 11

See also BOSNIAN

DCC 🔬 see Digital Compact Cassette

ddC /diːdiːˈsiː/ *abbreviation* Also written **DDC** ⊗

A drug used, often in combination with AZT or another drug, as a treatment for the later stages of HIV infection.

The initial letters of *Di-*, *Deoxy-*, and *Cytidine*, which make up the drug's chemical name *dideoxycytidine*.

Dideoxycytidine acts in a similar way to other HIV treatments such as AZT or DDI, by inhibiting the enzyme in the HIV virus which controls the translation of its RNA into the DNA form it needs to replicate inside the infected cell (the general name for such drugs is *nucleoside analogues*). It has been known since the sixties; its inhibitory effects on DNA replication were discovered in the late seventies; clinical trials to see if it could be useful against HIV began in the late eighties. It was provisionally approved by the US Food and Drug Administration in 1992, but only for use in combination with AZT under certain circumstances, because clinical tests showed that *ddC* was less effective alone than AZT but that the two worked well in combination. However, it has been given medical approval for use alone in other countries such as Australia. Like all such drugs, *ddC* has side-effects, in particular causing loss of feeling in fingers and toes.

> So far, the only treatments are nucleoside analogues, drugs like AZT, DDC and DDI.
> —*New York Times* 28 Nov. 1993, p. 58

> I attribute my health, weight and energy to everything from acupuncture to prophylactics, from Chinese herbs and selenium supplements to ddc, septrin and rifobutin.
> —*Guardian* 29 Apr. 1995, Weekend section, p. 5

See also ZALCITABINE

ddI /diːdiːˈʌɪ/ *abbreviation* Also written **DDI** ⊗

A drug which is used in the treatment of AIDS.

The initial letters of *Di-*, *Deoxy-*, and *Inosine*, which make up the drug's chemical name *dideoxyinosine*.

The compound *dideoxyinosine* was first synthesized in 1975 in connection with cancer research. As it is a similar type of compound to AZT (Zidovudine), clinical trials began in the US in 1989 to see whether it could be used as an alternative drug against the Aids virus HIV; trials in the UK followed in 1990. It was quickly shown that, like AZT, *ddI* prevents HIV from replicating itself within the body; the drug was found to be helpful for Aids sufferers who could not tolerate the side-effects of AZT, even though *ddI* can cause liver damage. It is common for patients to be treated alternately with these and other anti-HIV drugs, such as DDC and D4T, to prevent these side-effects becoming too debilitating. In 1990, the alternative full name **didanosine** was adopted.

> A new study suggests that HIV-infected people who have taken zidovudine for at least four months are better off switching to another antiviral agent called didanosine, or DDI.
> —*Science News* 29 Aug. 1992, p. 134

> So far, the only treatments are nucleoside analogues, drugs like AZT, DDC and DDI…which slow the virus by fooling it with a decoy of genetic material it needs to reproduce.
> —*New York Times Magazine* 28 Nov. 1993, p. 58

death futures /dɛθ ˈfjuːtʃəz/ *noun* 〰 📰 ⚔

In US slang: life insurance policies of people who are terminally ill, bought by a third party at less than the mature value as an investment redeemable on the death of the insured person.

These *futures*, stocks sold for future delivery, will be delivered at the time of *death*.

The spread of AIDS has brought with it a heightened awareness of terminal illness in hitherto healthy young people and a recognition of the attendant need for costly long-term nursing care. A person suffering from such illness, especially a young person with no dependants, may choose to sell his or her life insurance in order to benefit from the proceeds while alive. Such an arrangement, known formally as a *viatical settlement* (*viatical* means 'by the roadside'), is of benefit both to the policy-holder, for whom it may provide a vital source of cash, and to the purchaser, or investor, who may pay less than half the mature value of the policy and thus stand to make a substantial return on his or her investment. Such transactions have been reported, predominantly in the US, since the early 1990s. **Death-futures companies** serve this specialized area of the investments market.

> The product has been called 'death futures', or speculating in death—the sooner the policyholder dies, the faster the return. —*Boston Globe* 25 July 1993

> The ideal investment opportunity has finally arrived. Street name: Death futures. Attributes: Uncomplicated, safe, legal and nearly guaranteed to reap you 20 percent annual returns.
> —*Spy* Feb. 1994, p. 14

> In the 'death futures' business, a bad disease becomes a good investment. And a life-insurance policy that normally pays out after death provides cash during life—in exchange for profits for an investor. —*Seattle Times* 25 Nov. 1995, section A, p. 10

decaf /'diːkaf/ *noun* and *adjective* Also written **Decaf, décaf, decaff** ▓

noun: Decaffeinated coffee; a drink of decaffeinated coffee.

adjective: Decaffeinated.

An abbreviation of *decaffeinated*. The name *Decaf* is also a trade mark in the UK.

The term *decaffeinization* was first recorded in the late twenties, and decaffeinated coffee has been available since that time, consumed in the main by people wishing to avoid being kept awake at night by the stimulant effects of caffeine. In the early eighties concerns about caffeine grew as people became aware of further unwelcome effects, including raised levels of stress, an increased heart rate, and palpitations. Decaffeinated coffee became widely available and consumption increased rapidly, although methods by which **decaffeination** is achieved have also given cause for concern.

Familiarity with the product led in the mid eighties to the adoption of the term *decaffeinated* as a noun standing alone, without the need for the word *coffee*. Use of the abbreviation *decaf* naturally followed. It also came to modify names for other forms of coffee, such as cappuccino and LATTE. It is also applied to products other than coffee, from which the caffeine has been removed, such as **decaf Coke**. Meanwhile, the prevalence of *decaf* has led to the need to affirm untreated coffee as CAFFEINATED.

> We care passionately about quality and only used the gentlest method of decaffeination, turning our backs on the more common harsher solvent methods.
> —advertisement in *Health Now* Nov. 1990, p. 1

> She moves to the cash register, orders a decaf cappuccino and picks up one of three free newspapers offered there. —*Pittsburgh* Nov. 1992, p. 61

> Chocolate milk has the same nutrients as plain milk, less sugar than apple juice and an insignificant amount of caffeine—as little as a cup of decaf.
> —advertisement in *Maclean's* 13 June 1994, p. 5

> Decaff doesn't give you a headache. It's the result of the withdrawal symptoms produced by coming off caffeine. —*Independent on Sunday* 3 July 1994, Review supplement, p. 47

> Seated over decaf and lemon meringue pie were…all Surrey parents who were fed up with unionized teachers. —*Pacific Current* Mar. 1995, p. 21

> Noe Valley is a place where a single woman can feel safe going out alone after dark for a decaf latte. —*Mother Jones* June 1995, p. 27

decommunization /diːˌkɒmjʊnaɪˈzeɪʃ(ə)n/ *noun* 🔒

The process of removing the communist basis from a country (especially one in Eastern Europe) or its institutions or economy; loosely, democratization.

The concept has been in use since the beginning of the eighties (the transitive verb form **decommunize** is first recorded in 1980), when the first signs emerged of a willingness in communist countries to allow a small amount of private enterprise in some areas of their economies. Its use became more frequent in the late eighties and into the nineties—first in relation to East Germany, Poland, and Hungary and later to all former Warsaw Pact countries—as the stormy and extended process of converting these countries' economies to varying degrees of democracy and capitalism took place. The noun has become more common in the nineties; an adjective **decommunized** is also found.

'We cannot decommunize a whole society overnight,' says Friedrich Magirius, superintendent of Leipzig's Protestant churches, who notes that East Germany was 'a typical dictatorship'.
—*Time* 9 July 1990, p. 75

Each of these countries is in the midst of a painful economic transition, so politicians are strongly tempted to divert attention from the grim reality to 'de-communization'. If they cannot deliver bread, why not the heads of a few supposedly fat Communists?
—*New York Times Magazine* 31 May 1992, p. 32

decompression 🅰 see DIGITAL COMPRESSION

dehiring 〰 see OUTPLACEMENT

dental dam /ˈdɛnt(ə)l dam/ *noun* ⊗ ▨

A piece of latex held over the mouth as a barrier against infection in oral sex.

A *dam* which shields the *dental* area.

Since the *post*-AIDS early nineties, *dental dams* have frequently been recommended as a sensible protection during oral sex against infection through the medium of bodily fluids.

Dental Dams, various colours and flavours. —*The Pink Paper* 30 Mar. 1991, p. 16

A generation alerted to the dangers of Aids kept itself informed not only about condoms but also about dental dams. —Pauline Adams *Somerville for Women* (1996), p. 361

See also SAFE SEX

dependency culture /dɪˈpɛnd(ə)nsi ˌkʌltʃə/ *noun* 🔒 ◖

A way of life characterized by dependency on state benefits.

The theory of a *dependency culture* was developed by sociologists in the late eighties, and soon became a matter for political debate. While those on the left wing continued to advocate the provision of benefits as an essential of civilized society, right-wing theorists countered with the view that such provision could in fact be damaging to those in receipt of benefits, by conditioning them to such provision, and thus rendering them unlikely or unable to break away from dependence on this form of support.

The term is now an established one, but more recently has broadened to encompass the notion of the situation of any group in a comparable position.

With the present emphasis on avoiding the creation of a 'dependency culture'...the argument is that any receipt of state benefits may lead to an undesirable decline in personal motivation and to increased reliance on state support. —Stephen Smith (ed.) *Economic Policy* (1991), p. 44

During the boom years of the mid-1980s...conservative works chronicling the growth of a black dependency culture in America's ghettos multiplied. —*Economist* 2 May 1992, p. 140

This is what Terry Carlin, northern officer of the Irish Congress of Trade Unions, calls a 'dependency culture' created by the Troubles. —*Independent on Sunday* 11 Dec. 1994, p. 3

derivative /dɪˈrɪvətɪv/ noun 〰

A financial contract whose value derives from and is dependent upon the value of an underlying variable asset, such as a commodity, currency, or security.

As a noun and adjective, *derivative* has long had the meaning '(relating to) something whose origin lies elsewhere; not original'. In the financial sense, the term may in part originate in its mathematical sense of 'a quantity measuring the rate of change of another', such as acceleration being a derivative of velocity (its rate of change).

The concept of *derivatives* has existed for many decades in the currency and commodities markets, but the umbrella term only began to be applied in the mid eighties; before then, each kind of contract was identified separately: *future, option, swap, warrant*. Its introduction reflected the great increase in popularity of such contracts in the world's markets, but it has also contributed to confusion about them, as there are many types of *derivatives*, with new ones frequently being invented for special purposes. The underlying principle in each case is that dealers are not trading in the asset itself—whether this is a currency such as dollars or deutschmarks or a commodity such as grain or copper—but are making a contract based on the future price of the asset. In the simplest case, this could be an option to buy or sell a quantity of a currency at some future date at a given price; such contracts are commonly entered into to reduce, or *hedge*, the risk of unexpected changes in currency rates.

However, by far the greater proportion of such contracts in recent years have been speculative, because the investor can potentially make a large profit for a small outlay (a circumstance known as *gearing* in Britain or *leverage* in the US). Many banks, commodity brokers, companies, and individuals have made and lost extremely large sums on such speculations, an outstanding example being the collapse of the British bank Barings in 1995 and huge losses by a Japanese bank speculating in copper in 1996. Such losses have led to fears that unrestrained trading in *derivatives* might destabilize the world's markets or even lead to their collapse. A particular problem is that newer types of *derivatives* are often extremely difficult to understand, relying on complex statistical techniques that have made mathematics graduates highly employable in such **derivatives markets**.

'Hedge funds'…sprang up in the 1960s as a way for rich investors to pool their money and do all sorts of things that mutual funds, and even registered investment managers, cannot ordinarily do: go long and short, hedge in derivatives markets, borrow lots of money, invest any proportion of their capital in any sort of asset. —*Economist* 5 Oct. 1991, p. 104

Last week, the Bundesbank said unequivocally that derivatives pose a threat to world financial markets. —*Independent on Sunday* 24 Oct. 1993, Business section, p. 3

Put simply, derivatives have flourished because a series of recent developments have transformed them into a cheap and efficient way of moving risk about within the economic system. —*Economist* 10 Feb. 1996, Corporate Risk Management Survey, p. 9

desert fever ⊗ see GULF WAR SYNDROME

Desert Storm syndrome ⊗ see GULF WAR SYNDROME

designer dyke 🄿 ⁊ see LIPSTICK LESBIAN

detectorist /dɪˈtɛkt(ə)rɪst/ noun ※

A person whose hobby is hunting for buried coins and other treasure using a metal detector.

Metal-detecting as a hobby has grown in popularity since the seventies, and in the eighties the terms *detectorist* and **metal detectorist** were coined as designations for enthusiasts of the interest. A number of interesting 'finds' have been made by *detectorists*, but archaeologists among others have expressed concern that in excavating the buried material evidence may be damaged or vital provenance relating to the artefacts lost.

Cut pennies of this reign…had become comparatively common in recent years, as a result of the activities of metal detectorists.   *—Coin News* May 1994, p. 3

About 400,000 finds of historical interest are made each year by detectorists in England, yet of these only a minuscule proportion is reported.   *—Independent on Sunday* 8 Oct. 1995, p. 22

differently abled {{ see ABLED

digital audio broadcasting /ˌdɪdʒɪt(ə)l ɔːdɪəʊ ˈbrɔːdkɑːstɪŋ/ *noun phrase*

A system for transmitting a radio network in high-quality digital stereo, together with associated data, over one or more transmitters operating on a single frequency.

Digital audio broadcasting (**DAB** for short) was developed in the early nineties; the intention was to create a transmission system of high quality that would be easy for listeners to use and would economize on scarce broadcasting frequencies. Various data facilities can be transmitted in association with the broadcasts, particularly MULTIMEDIA (text and graphics linked to the audio). This opens the possibility of a broadcast WORLD WIDE WEB, which some commentators regard as a future component of the information SUPERHIGHWAY. The BBC started its *DAB* service in the London area in September 1995; however, it did not publicize the service, as receivers were not expected to be available until 1998. In Europe, the name is usually applied to the system in which a number of different digital programme channels are broadcast together using MULTIPLEX techniques; in the US it often means a digital radio signal broadcast on the same frequency as an existing AM or FM transmission, or digital radio broadcasts from satellites.

The DAB receiver is based on advanced computer technology that makes it possible to download large quantities of information to program the radio set and the associated equipment, such as the DCC recorder, mini disc or PC.   *—Diffusion EBU* Spring 1993, p. 23

It was timely for the BBC in December to demonstrate the results of its latest experiments in Digital Audio Broadcasting—DAB…One of the benefits of DAB is that only one frequency per radio station is needed to cover the whole country, saving spectrum and making life a lot easier for people with car radios who no longer have to shift frequencies as they travel from one part of the country to another.   *—Television* Dec. 1993, p. 22

Digital Compact Cassette /dɪdʒɪt(ə)l kəmˌpakt kəˈsɛt/ *noun phrase*

A format for tape cassettes, similar to ordinary audio cassettes but with digital rather than analogue recording; a cassette in this format.

A transparent compound: a small, or *compact, cassette* containing recording tape for making recordings in *digital* format (see DIGITAL COMPRESSION).

The audio world has been convinced for nearly a decade, since the launch of CDs, that digital recording techniques produce better quality than analogue ones; users soon wanted to be able to record audio in digital format as well as play pre-recorded material. Though the *Digital Audio Tape* (DAT) system was put on the market in the late eighties, its price and complexity put many users off and the record industry was extremely distrustful of a system which could so easily make perfect copies of its products. The *Digital Compact Cassette*, or **DCC**, was one solution to producing a reasonably-priced digital recorder, first put on the market in 1992. However, a battle for market dominance took place between it and Sony's recordable mini-CD MINIDISC system, launched at about the same time, which has reduced the take-up of both, even though *DCC* machines will also play ordinary compact cassettes.

With Sony's digital audio tapes (DATs) going out like the Strategic Defense Initiative (millions spent, product still remote), and Discmans skipping down the sidewalk to oblivion, DCC is being hyped as an industry saver.   *—Vibe* Fall 1992, p. 34

Updated versions of existing media formats have also fared badly…and Philips' Digital Compact Cassette (DCC) has not had any visible impact on the audio cassette market.
     —Guardian 8 June 1995, OnLine section, p. 9

digital compression /ˌdɪdʒɪt(ə)l kəmˈprɛʃ(ə)n/ *noun* 🅰

A process for reducing the number of pulses needed to transmit a digital image or other data so that the information can be carried on a communications system of lower capacity.

The technique of *digital compression* has become more important in recent years as digitized sound, images, and video have become more common. These media convert into very large amounts of digital data, particularly so for video, making it expensive and difficult to transmit and store them. Techniques have been developed which detect repeated sequences of various kinds, abbreviate them during transmission and reconstitute them at the receiving end. The techniques are used to store and transmit still images, to record audio (for example, on a DIGITAL COMPACT CASSETTE), to record and play television programmes from CD, operate videoconferencing systems, and transmit television signals down telephone lines for on-demand systems (see -ON-DEMAND).

The term *digital compression*, more fully **digital signal compression**, is frequently abbreviated just to **compression**; all three terms can refer either to the complete process of compaction and expansion of signals or, specifically, to the initial compaction stage only; the reverse process at the receiving end is then called **decompression**. The device which actually does the *compression* is a **compressor** and its equivalent for the reverse process a **decompressor**; commonly both functions are combined into a single unit, called a **codec** (an abbreviation formed from the first two letters of *compressor* and the first three of *decompressor*). Digital data in its compacted form is said to be **compressed**; the verbs **compress** and **decompress** are also commonly used.

There are two main types of *digital compression* systems: **lossless compression**, in which the original digital signal is exactly reproduced when expanded again (a necessity for many kinds of computer data), and **lossy compression**, used for audio and video, in which some loss of detail is acceptable. The most common standards for compressing images for video are called **MPEG-1** and **MPEG-2** (from *Motion Picture Experts Group*), generically known as **digital video compression** (**DVC**). The equivalent for still images is called **JPEG** (from *Joint Photographic Experts Group*).

> Lossless-compression algorithms can usually compress digital data up to one-half to one-quarter of its original size. —*Byte* Nov. 1992, p. 162

> One of the technological innovations which prompted the most recent round of CRTC hearings is digital compression, which permits broadcasters to cram several channels into the space currently occupied by one. —*United Church Observer* June 1993, p. 21

> The service, if approved, would let individual customers receive videos by phone in compressed form for viewing later. —*Guardian* 8 Oct. 1993, section 1, p. 16

> The codec is the engine that keeps a desktop videoconferencing application running by compressing and decompressing the heavy streams of video and audio data transmitted over the network. —*Data Communications International* Apr. 1995, p. 67

digital superhighway 🖥 see SUPERHIGHWAY

dino- /ˈdaɪnəʊ/ *combining form* 🅧 🅰

Used as the first element in words relating to dinosaurs.

In the late twentieth century, research on **dinos**, and the suggestion that as active animals they may also have been warm-blooded, has increasingly caught the public attention. Traditional views of known dinosaurs have been reassessed, and new species, such as the MAIASAUR or *good mother lizard*, continue to be identified.

Since the mid eighties, this growing popular interest in serious research has been reflected by the linguistic development of *dino-* as a productive combining form. Numerous books (particularly for children) have been published to answer **dinoquestions**. Museums have put on special exhibitions to explain the latest research, and have even provided **dinostores** in which **dinomaniacs** can purchase associated **dinoproducts**.

Dino- may also be used in more serious scientific terms: **dinoturbation** has been coined for the disturbance of layers of sediment by dinosaur trampling, and the effects of this process on the formation of sedimentary rock.

Dinomania was given a fresh impetus by the publication of Michael Crichton's 1991 **dinothriller**, *Jurassic Park*, based on the premise that modern scientists could use DNA technology to clone dinosaurs; the subsequent film by Steven Spielberg increased **dinofever** through the special effects with which it brought such creatures as Crichton's RAPTORS to the screen.

New fossil evidence suggests that 130 million years ago Earth was ruled not by thundering stegosaurs and tree-munching brontosaurs but by curious dino-midgets, some no bigger than a pigeon. —*Discover* Mar. 1991, p. 2

The enormous success and the hype surrounding…'Jurassic Park' has propelled 'dinomania' to all-time highs. —*Coloradoan* (Fort Collins) 4 July 1993, section C, p. 5

In *Hunting Dinosaurs*, he looks at palaeontology sideways…and positively revels in trivia—historical, scientific and dinomaniac. —*New Scientist* 19 Nov. 1994, p. 48

disablist 〖 see ABLEISM

disco biscuit ᴾᴼᴾ see ECSTASY

diss /dɪs/ *verb* and *noun* Also written **dis** ᴾᴼᴾ

In slang (originally in the US):

transitive or *intransitive verb*: To put (someone) down, usually verbally; to show disrespect for a person by insulting language or dismissive behaviour.

noun: An example of this behaviour; an insult or put-down.

Formed by abbreviating *disrespect* to its first syllable.

Diss originated in US black English in the early eighties and has been popularized through the spread of HIP-HOP. In black culture, insults form an important part of the peer-group behaviour known as *sounding, signifying,* or *playing the dozens,* in which the verbal repartee consists of a rising crescendo of taunts and abuse. The concept of **dissing** moved outside black culture through its use in rap, and is now widely known both in America and in the UK. An adjective **dissed** also exists, often used in the verbal phrase **get dissed**.

As they denounce selected rappers, the [presidential] candidates are learning what rappers have long known: that the right dis is bankable. Dissing is perfect fodder for the age of the sound bite. An insult is short, personal, full of strong emotion and perhaps tied to a celebrity. —*New York Times* 28 June 1992, section 2, p. 20

On TV, one of the Geto Boys justified dissing women because 'in my 'hood, all the women are prostitutes'. —*The Face* Sept. 1993, p. 152

In fact, twentysomethings claim to be the most dissed generation in history. —*Coloradoan* (Fort Collins) 9 Jan. 1994, section E, p. 1

distributed computing 🖳 see CLIENT-SERVER

DNA fingerprinting 〖 🔺 see GENETIC FINGERPRINTING

DNA profiling 〖 🔺 see GENETIC FINGERPRINTING

Doc Martens /dɒk ˈmɑːtɪnz/ *noun* 💢

A type of heavy boot or shoe, usually laced, and with a cushioned sole.

An adaptation, with *Doc* as an informal shortening of *Doctor,* of the proprietary name *Doctor Martens,* ultimately from *Dr K. Maertens,* the name of the German inventor of the sole.

Doctor Martens have been commercially available since the late seventies, but the development of the term *Doc Martens* dates from the eighties, and coincides with their rise as a fashion item for the young, particularly in the area of GRUNGE. In the mid nineties, **Docs** or **DMs** remain popular for their associations of tough and confident IN YOUR FACE informality.

Doc Marten shoes: the status symbol of the young.   —*Homemaker's Magazine* Apr. 1993, p. 22

Madison's own Janeane Garofalo has hit Hollywood with sarcastic lines, Doc Martens and attitude.   —*Madison Eagle* (New Jersey) 21 July 1994, p. 3

Under the patterned skirt, black leather shin-high boots with silver lace-ups. Maybe black flats or big, funky Doc Martens.   —*Wired* Jan. 1995, p. 155

The clunky boots with the heat-sealed rubber soles are known as 'Docs' or 'DMs' to the initiated, and have for decades been standard gear for Britain's skinheads.   —*Forbes* 16 Jan. 1995, p. 42

doctor-assisted suicide /dɒktə əˌsɪstɪd ˈsuːɪsaɪd/ *noun phrase*

The taking of lethal drugs, provided by a doctor for the purpose, by a patient regarded as terminally ill.

In the debate on the legalization of euthanasia, the concept of **assisted suicide** as effected with the assistance of another person has been discussed since the mid-seventies: one expressed view is that the term itself effectively defines euthanasia.

Doctor-assisted suicide identifies more specifically the source of the necessary assistance, and highlights the area of medical ethics where the strongest debate has occurred, the question of whether or not this assistance is in effect a breach of the Hippocratic Oath. Advances in medical science have made it more likely that the question will arise, and a number of high-profile cases in the late eighties and nineties have raised public awareness of the issues involved. (In one case in the United Kingdom, it was regarded as being legally significant that, regardless of the strength of the dose given, the drugs administered could not have had a therapeutic purpose.)

The debate on this specific form of euthanasia continues, but in the meantime several American states have passed laws making *doctor-assisted suicide*, *physician-assisted suicide*, or *medicide* (*medically assisted suicide*) illegal.

A state law that forbids doctor-assisted suicides.   —*Ithaca Journal* 12 Nov. 1993, section A, p. 8

At least three other states…have recently passed laws explicitly banning doctor-assisted suicide; five states have rejected attempts to allow it.   —*Economist* 26 Nov. 1994, p. 66

The proposed law goes further than the practice in Holland, where euthanasia is still technically illegal; and, unlike Oregon's recent doctor-assisted suicide legislation, it would allow people to go to a doctor for a fatal dose and then take it at will.   —*Economist* 18 Feb. 1995, p. 76

double whammy /dʌb(ə)l ˈwami/ *noun*

A twofold blow or setback.

A figurative use of 'two blows resulting in a knockout'; the original (US) sense of *whammy* was 'an evil influence', and in the 1950s was particularly associated with the comic strip Li'l Abner; a *double whammy* in this context was an intense and powerful look which had a stunning effect on its victims.

Double whammy in its current sense entered the language through modern politics. It moved into the general vocabulary in the eighties, and was given a high profile by Conservative campaigning in the British election campaign of 1992. Ian Lang, who as Scottish Secretary would have lost both his seat and his job if he had not been re-elected, told his supporters:

Scotland has rejected separatism. Britain has rejected Socialism. It's a double whammy!

Double whammy subsequently developed a further intensification in the form *triple whammy*.

Like thousands of other women, I cannot identify with a *male* God; and black women of course face the double whammy.   —Virginian Mollenkott *Godding* (1987), p. 58

The Tory Tax Bombshell posters dominated the 1992 campaign and Double Whammy has entered the general vocabulary. —*Guardian* 8 May 1995, section 2, p. 13

Choose orange to feel stimulated, blue to feel relaxed, green to feel healthy—or try all three bath-oil bead colors for a triple whammy! —*Modern Woman* May 1995, p. 10

dove ᴾᴼᴾ see ECSTASY

Downing Street declaration /'daʊnɪŋ striːt dɛklə‚reɪʃ(ə)n/ *noun phrase*

A joint agreement between the British and Irish governments, formulated in 1993, intended as the basis of a peace initiative in Northern Ireland.

A *declaration* issued from 10 *Downing Street*, the official London home of the British Prime Minister.

A forum for greater cooperation between the United Kingdom and the Republic of Ireland on the subject of the future of Northern Ireland was initially established by the *Anglo-Irish agreement* of 1985. The agreement was the subject of some dissension, particularly among Ulster Unionists, who objected to the fact that their political representatives had not been involved in the negotiations. Attempted talks on the future of Ulster in May 1991 sought to involve them in a new agreement.

In the wake of this, the two governments pursued a policy of closer cooperation over Northern Ireland affairs. The *Downing Street declaration* was issued in 1993 by the British Prime Minister John Major and the Irish Taoiseach Albert Reynolds, and was seen as a major contribution to the continuing PEACE PROCESS.

He has, as you know, called for the election of a Free Assembly, the result of which is already foreseeable and the reality of which would be to bring things right back to the situation before the Downing Street Declaration; in short, to internalise the settlement of Ulster and ditch the three-stranded talks. —*Independent* 5 Oct. 1995, Supplement, p. 3

download /daʊn'ləʊd/ *transitive* or *intransitive verb*

To transfer (the contents of an electronic data file) from a larger system to a smaller or peripheral one.

A compound of *down*, in its figurative adverbial sense of 'moving from a superior to an inferior position', and *load*, meaning 'to store data in a computer'.

The term came into use in 1980 to describe the process of obtaining data from a central storage system; the data may be text, graphics, audio, video, or executable software. The source may be one to which the user's computer is connected by means of a local area network (see LAN) or one to which it is linked by telecommunications, such as an ELECTRONIC *bulletin board* or the INTERNET. *Download* is also used for the process of transferring operating data from the user's system to some peripheral equipment: for example, sending fonts to a printer. The action is **downloading** or a **download**; a file is **downloadable** if it is possible to obtain it by *downloading* it; the person who does this is a **downloader**; *downloadable* is sometimes used as a noun, to refer to a file which is available by this means. The opposite is UPLOAD.

They now use a…heart rate monitor that downloads results into a lap-top computer that plots results on a graph. —*Bicycling* Feb. 1991, p. 110

With automated features and other conveniences, and an added bonus that many of these programs are either low-cost or free downloadables, the main problem may simply be choosing one. —*CompuServe Magazine* Aug. 1993, p. 2

The only area where tape would continue to have a future is in archiving, where the low costs of tape as a bulk storage medium would continue to beat disk-based systems, but it is also an area where high speed downloading onto disks for re-use would be required.
—*Television* Feb. 1994, p. 11

Getting bored watching your 14.4 modem limp along the Internet? How about those endless downloads, especially for images and sound clips? Been there, done that.

—advertisement in *Internet World* Feb. 1995, p. 5

downshifter /'daʊnʃɪftə/ *noun* 🔀

A person who makes a change of career or lifestyle to a mode that is less pressured and demanding.

The idea of deliberately **downshifting** one's career, first noted in the mid eighties, has gained ground in the nineties. *Downshifters*, having achieved success, are now questioning the high price paid in relation to personal and family life, and in many cases are choosing to opt for a lifestyle of *voluntary simplicity*, in a trend fostered by the increasing workplace pressures encapsulated by such terms as OUTPLACEMENT and PRESENTEEISM.

In the 1980s there were fast-trackers. In 1991 they will be 'downshifters', who reinvent success by shunning career-track jobs with good promotion prospects for jobs that allow more flexible hours and more time for family and community.   —*US News & World Report* 31 Dec. 1990, p. 84

The newly leisured call themselves downshifters.   —*Guardian* 25 Oct. 1995, p. 4

'Downshifting', i.e. a deliberate decision to reduce or withdraw completely from financially rewarding but stressful work so as to achieve a more meaningful and happy life.

—*Oxford University Gazette* 29 Feb. 1996, p. 814

downsize 🖳 ⤳ see -SIZE

dowse /daʊz/ *intransitive verb* ⊗

To make a diagnosis by dowsing, chiefly with a pendulum attached to a radionic device, over a patient's body. Also as a transitive verb, to diagnose (a patient) by dowsing.

In the field of alternative medicine, diagnosis by *radionics*, the study and interpretation of radiation believed to be emitted from substances, has been practised since the fifties. Since the early eighties, interest in the technique has grown, centring on the use of a pendulum to detect variations in a body's radiation levels as a guide to a person's state of health.

If he [the practitioner] uses a pendulum, for he is literally dowsing for disease, then the pendulum will swing, as a rule, from a simple oscillation to a clockwise movement to give a 'yes'.

— S. Fulder *Handbook of Complementary Medicine* (1989, rev. ed.), p. 265

Once the child has been dowsed, the treatment begins and if necessary specific supplements or remedies are recommended.   —*Here's Health* Dec. 1990, p. 54

dragon /'drag(ə)n/ *noun* ⤳ ⌂

Any of (originally) four Asian countries, South Korea, Taiwan, Singapore, and Hong Kong, which developed booming economies based on high-technology exports.

These countries were named after the *Chinese dragon*, a legendary beast which has for centuries been a symbol of the Orient to Western observers; but as the Western dragon is an aggressive beast, the term also has undertones of assertiveness and competitiveness foreign to its beneficent eastern namesake.

The term entered English in the mid eighties, as a way to describe the heavily industrialized small countries of the western Pacific rim (the **little dragons**). The initial group was later augmented by Indonesia, Malaysia, Thailand, and (more recently still) Vietnam, all of whom have moved rapidly towards industrialization in the late eighties and early nineties. Since the early nineties, the term has largely been replaced by TIGER.

While the dragons were building rapid growth on fast-rising exports, the Latin Americans shielded inefficient local forms behind high trade barriers.   —*Economist* 18 Apr. 1992, p. 12

One of Asia's four rapidly developing 'Little Dragons'—along with South Korea, Taiwan and Hong

Kong—Singapore is the smallest and in some ways most successful.

—Time 18 Jan. 1993, p. 36

dragon boat /'drag(ə)n bəʊt/ *noun* ▓ ✆

A rowing boat of traditional Chinese design, shaped like a large canoe and decorated with a carved dragon's head prow, used in the modern competitive sport of **dragon-boat racing**.

The boats have a distinctive and usually brightly painted carved head of a *dragon*, with horns and open mouth, on the prow of the boat, and a dragon's tail on the stern.

Dragon boats are used in the annual *Dragon Boat Festival*, celebrated in the Far East as a public holiday and said to originate in ancient China. According to legend, the followers of a statesman who had drowned himself as a protest against the corruption of the court took out their boats to search for his body. In order to drive away fishes which might eat the body, they beat drums and hit the water with their paddles.

In the modern sport, crews of twenty-two rowers compete against one another, the time for their paddle-strokes given by a drum beaten by the helmsman sitting on a raised seat in the prow. *Dragon boat racing* is now popular in Western countries with large Chinese communities, and in the eighties was officially established in Canada and the United Kingdom. Those taking part in the sport (also known as **dragon boating**) are **dragon boaters**.

Vancouver has the largest dragon-boat fleet on the continent.
—Beautiful British Columbia Magazine Winter 1990, p. 8

The Chinese Cultural Association in conjunction with Cathay Pacific Airlines posted notice of Canada's first dragon-boat festival…less than a decade later, there are estimated to be more than 8,000 dragon boaters in Canada. *—Equinox* June 1994, p. 31

Throughout China and in Chinese communities worldwide, dragon-boat races are held every May 5 of the lunar calendar. *—Post* (Denver) 15 Jan. 1995, p. 3

The Henley club is one of 70 crews that regularly take part in what is billed as Britain's most colourful water sport—dragon-boat racing.
—Daily Telegraph 6 Jan. 1996, Weekend section, p. 3

dress-down Friday /drɛs daʊn 'frʌɪdeɪ/ *noun* ▓ ᴾᴼᴾ

In the US: a day, usually a Friday, on which it is considered acceptable that office workers dress more casually ('dress down') in the workplace than on other days.

The practice of marking the end of the working week with a relaxation of the dress code is not entirely new, but in recent years in the US it has become much more widespread, recognized as a fashionable new convention and marked by the advent of the term *dress-down Friday* at the start of the nineties. American firms with UK branches have brought the *dress-down Friday* to Britain, where the practice of dressing more informally on a Friday has also been called a *Friday Wear* policy.

TV Guide publisher Mary Benner waltzes into her big corner office wearing bright red Converse high-tops, khaki pants and a cotton oxford. It's a dress-down Friday.
—Inside Media 1 Dec. 1993, p. 40

The problem with dress-down Friday is that it turns offices into minefields of potential disaster. Ask anyone who has ever worked for a company with a Friday Wear policy: the managing director who was mistaken for an intruder and refused entry to the building. *—GQ* Jan. 1995, p. 105

'Dress-down Friday' has become so popular…in the US that it is beginning to spread into the rest of the week. *—The Times* 26 Jan. 1995, p. 2

drive-by /'drʌɪvbʌɪ/ *adjective* and *noun* Also written **driveby**, plural **drive-bys** or **drivebys**

In the US:

adjective: (Of a crime, especially a shooting) carried out from a moving vehicle. Hence figuratively of any activity: carried out in passing or on the run.

noun: A shooting carried out from a moving vehicle. Also known more fully as a **drive-by shooting**.

The full phrase *drive-by shooting* was first noted in print in the early eighties, and by the end of the decade the abbreviated form *drive-by* was frequently seen. It represents a reappearance in American crime of the gang-led murder carried out from a moving car, something more readily associated with the twenties. In its new incarnation, it is linked in particular with rival teenage gangs and with the drug culture. One-off variants of the original phrase, such as **drive-by case**, **drive-by gunfire**, and **drive-by killing**, are common. Indeed, the *drive-by* quickly became such a familiar feature of American urban life that the adjective started to be used figuratively (again mostly in one-off formations), both for other kinds of 'attack' carried out from a vehicle (**drive-by egging**, a **drive-by musical attack** from a car's sound system played at full volume, **drive-by punching** (in fact carried out while passing on foot), etc.) and to imply a hit-and-run approach to a subject, as in **drive-by documentary** and **drive-by journalism**.

> They 'claim their 'hood',—pledge allegiance to their neighborhood gang—and it becomes their whole world, their family...The drive-bys are mostly 'paybacks', revenge killings, sometimes for feuds that started before they were born.　　　　　　　　　　　　　—*Time* 16 Mar. 1992, p. 12

> Broder and...Woodward chide the political press for practicing 'quick, drive-by journalism'.
> 　　　　　　　　　　　　　　　　　　　　　　—*New York Times Book Review* 24 May 1992, p. 5

drop-dead /drɒp'dɛd/ *adverb* POP

In slang use, referring to an attractive person: very, stunningly.

This adverbial use of an existing phrase is recorded from the early nineties, frequently in **drop-dead gorgeous**.

> Priscilla Presley arrives straight from a television interview, looking drop-dead gorgeous.
> 　　　　　　　　　　　　　　　　　　　　　　　　—*Los Angeles* June 1990, p. 136

> She's young, seen as hip, not promiscuous, and drop-dead good-looking.
> 　　　　　　　　　　　　　　　　　　　　　　　　—*Vogue* Dec. 1995, p. 136

> Drop-dead gorgeous Gina G won't be stripping—she wants to work on her new LP despite the mega-offer to reveal all.　　　　　　　　—caption in *Daily Star* 11 Sept. 1996, p. 13

drug abuse see ABUSE

drug mule see MULE

dub poetry see PERFORMANCE POETRY

dude /duːd/ *noun* POP

In slang (originally in the US): a person, a guy, one of the 'gang'. Often used as a form of address: friend, buddy.

Dude is a slang word of unknown origin that was first used in the US in 1883 to mean 'a dandy, a swell' or (as a Western cowboys' word) 'a city-dweller'. By 1967 it had been taken up in US black English to mean 'a man, a cool guy or cat' (and later 'any person'), losing its original negative connotations.

This more general use of *dude* was popularized outside black street slang through the *blaxploitation* films of the late seventies and, more particularly, through the explosion of HIP-

HOP during the eighties. By 1985 it had become an accepted part of surfing vocabulary, and it was through this route and through TV series such as *The Simpsons* that it spread into British English idiom. *Dude* has come to be used as a form of address in just the way that *man* was used in the sixties, but has broken out of its macho ghetto in the female form **dudette**.

> It is the teenage Bart who has caught the public's imagination. With his skateboard and, touchingly, his catapult, he is a match for anyone, not least because of his streetwise vocabulary. 'Yo, dude!' he says; 'Aye caramba!' and—most famously—'Eat my shorts!'
>
> —*Independent* 29 July 1990, p. 17

> The character who beat Agassi was...his former roommate at the Nick Bollettieri Tennis Academy for Baseline Bashers and Awesomely Cool Dudes and Dudettes.
>
> —*Sports Illustrated* 17 June 1991, p. 34

> He pronounced 'dude' like a surfer. Whites had made the word their own. Black guys didn't use 'dude' anymore; they said 'homeboy'.   —Darryl Pinckney *High Cotton* (1992), p. 282

DVD /'diːviːdiː/ *abbreviation* 🖳

A proprietary name for a type of digital recording medium, similar in appearance to a CD but with much increased storage capacity.

According to its manufacturers, the initial letters of *Digital Versatile Disc*. However, the expansion *Digital Video Disc* is commonly encountered, perhaps because a principal reason for developing it was to permit a full-length feature film to be stored on one disc.

The *DVD* standard represents a victory for common sense over commercial rivalry. Two competing but incompatible standards were developed in the early nineties, the SD ('Super Density') system from Time-Warner, Toshiba, and Matsushita and the MMCD ('Multimedia CD') format from Sony and Philips. The two groups compromised on a single standard, thus avoiding a damaging standards battle. The new discs are the same size as CDs but can be double-sided and multi-layered, so permitting them to hold much larger amounts of data. Specifications have been developed for several types of discs for various purposes, including **DVD-Audio**, **DVD-Video**, and **DVD-ROM**, as well as the projected recordable disc types **DVD-R** and **DVD-RAM**. The systems were due to go on sale in late 1996.

> The low expected costs of pre-recorded DVDs, and the fact that they can store five times as much information as current computer CD-ROMs, have led to claims that they will completely restructure both the home entertainment market and information storage systems.
>
> —*Independent on Sunday* 19 Feb. 1995, Review section, p. 15

> The new super-density CD format will be called DVD—for Digital Video Disc—and will hold 133 minutes of MPEG-2 video or 4.7 gigabytes of data...The first DVD players should reach the US market next September, and there is some hope they will reach Europe before Christmas.
>
> —*Guardian* 14 Dec. 1995, OnLine section, p. 8

> The DVD's great weakness is that in its first two incarnations, DVD-Video (which will show films) and DVD-ROM (video games), it cannot record. The disc's supporters reply that, once copyright laws and a few technical problems have been worked out, a recordable version, known as DVD-RAM, will appear in about a year's time.   —*Economist* 1 June 1996, p. 67

dweeb /dwiːb/ *noun* POP

In North American slang: a contemptible or boring person, especially one who is studious, puny, or unfashionable; a 'nerd'.

Of unknown origin; probably an invented word influenced by such existing words as *dwarf*, *weed*, and *creep*.

The term has been in printed use since the early eighties, and may have originated in US prep school slang. The corresponding adjective is **dweeby** or **dweebish**.

Norman, a research dweeb with a rockabilly hairdo.
—*Kitchener-Waterloo Record* (Ontario) 9 Nov. 1989, section C, p. 22

'Wayne's World' is…hosted by two cheery high school headbangers…Wayne…and his borderline dweeby pal Garth. —*Los Angeles Times* 14 Feb. 1992, section B, p. 8

People attired in 3-D glasses still look comically dweebish.
—*Popular Science* June 1993, p. 86

DWEM /dwɛm/ *noun* POP

A derogatory term denoting any of the famous historical personages traditionally forming the accepted canon of European writers, artists, and thinkers.

An acronym for *Dead White European Male*.

In the eighties the traditional teaching of literature, particularly in American colleges, began to be questioned in a central aspect. The overwhelming numerical prevalence, among accepted 'great writers' of the past, of European males, was increasingly criticized as evidence of deliberate neglect of those who could not, through race or gender, belong to this central group.

Coinage of *DWEM* coincided, in many cases, with radical curriculum revision in which concentration on the works of **Dead White European Males** gave place to the study of feminist writers or non-European literatures. The debate continues between those who welcome the widening of the canon, and those who see the process as essentially one of cultural impoverishment which discourages access to great works of art.

Like other terms developed by supporters of POLITICAL CORRECTNESS, *DWEM* is now likely to be used in ironic allusion to, and criticism of, what is seen as a new form of puritanism.

Nothing can be done about the fact that Locke, Montesquieu and other DWEMs (today's academic acronym-as-epithet: dead white European males) were important and African, Latin and Asian philosophers were not, as sources of the American Revolution.
—G. Will *Suddenly* (1990), p. 16

America's largest state spawned some of PC's greatest excesses, from mandatory bilingualism to the labelling of Shakespeare and Milton as DWEMs, Dead White European Males.
—*Guardian* 13 Jan. 1995, p. 25

'This is the call of the Fourth Instinct,' she says thrillingly in nearly every paragraph, neatly stencilling her grab-bag of Greek divinities, folk wisdom and DWEM soundbites with this handy catchphrase. —*Independent on Sunday* 23 Apr. 1995, Review section, p. 38

dyspraxia /dɪsˈpraksɪə/ *noun* ⊗ ⁍

A disorder marked particularly by impairment of the ability to co-ordinate motor movements, and now associated with difficulties in reading and spelling.

From *dys-* 'bad, difficult' and *-praxia* (from Greek *praxis* 'action').

The term *dyspraxia* is recorded in medical literature from the early part of this century, but it is in the nineties that the term has made its way into the mainstream vocabulary. *Dyspraxia* is rapidly becoming as familiar as *dyslexia* in discussions of reading difficulties, although the degree to which its ready use reflects an accurate medical diagnosis is still a matter for debate. Those suffering from *dyspraxia* are described as **dyspraxic**.

The moment my child was diagnosed as slightly dyspraxic and told he could improve with physio-therapy, he threw himself wholeheartedly into the exercises. —*Guardian* 8 Mar. 1995, p. 8

Recently the newer syndrome of dyspraxia has replaced dyslexia in fashionable schools and educational circles as the explanation why little Freddie can't pass into Porridge Court.
—*Daily Telegraph* 16 Nov. 1995, p. 31

E

e- /iː/ *combining form*

From the beginning of the nineties, *e-*, for ELECTRONIC, has been used to form words relating to the publication or exchange of information in an electronic format, such as E-MAIL, *e-text* (see ELECTRONIC), and *e-zine* (an electronically published fanzine), and words relating to electronic financial transactions, such as *e-cash* and *e-money*.

> Please do not hesitate to send any e-texts you might find to the Gutenberg listserver address.
> —*Wired* (Premiere issue) 1993, p. 23

> Given that e-cash will probably depend for its value on convertibility into traditional money, will it not ultimately be the domain of bankers rather than computer scientists?
> —*Economist* 26 Nov. 1994, p. 26

> I click into a stylishly presented and sometimes unwittingly amusing e-zine called @ Fashion.
> —*Time Out* 17 Jan. 1996, p. 173

Earth Summit /əːθ ˈsʌmɪt/ *noun* 🌱

An unofficial name for the United Nations Conference on Environment and Development, held in Rio de Janeiro in Brazil in 1992.

A *summit* conference of nations, held to discuss worldwide matters of environment and development regarded as essential to the future of the *Earth*.

The conference held in Rio was not the first of its kind: a world environment conference had been held in Stockholm in 1972. Twenty years later, however, environmental concerns had gained a much higher public profile, with heads of state attending the *Earth Summit*.
Considerable attention was paid to formal agreements: the *Earth Charter* constituted a statement of intent regarding the rights and obligations associated with responsible management of the Earth's resources, and AGENDA 21 a treaty on more specific points. Negotiations on some agreements continued well after the end of the conference itself: it was not until 1993 that the United States signed the BIODIVERSITY *Treaty*. It remains to be seen whether the high hopes generated will have a real and lasting impact.

> The Earth Summit may present a final opportunity to develop globally coordinated actions to save the rainforest. —*Green Magazine* Apr. 1992, p. 21

> Is anything going to be left of the the high-flown declarations of the Earth Summit two years ago? Although there was never much hope for many of the waffly wish-lists, the two international treaties—the Biodiversity and Climate Change Conventions—should surely have been binding.
> —*Science* 17 Dec. 1994, p. 3

eating disorder /ˈiːtɪŋ dɪsˈɔːdə/ *noun* ⊗ ⚇

Any of a range of psychological disorders characterized by abnormal or disturbed eating habits.

Eating disorders were being discussed in medical literature in the late sixties, but it was not until the late eighties that use of the term became widespread, generally in regard to the problems suffered by anorexics and BULIMICS. The increasing familiarity of the term in lay use may reflect both a growing social awareness of the conditions covered by it, and a wish to be able to refer to them in non-clinical and non-judgemental tones. Sufferers from such conditions may be described in medical terms as *eating disordered*. The alternative term *eating distress* may also now be found.

> She had a severe eating disorder that began shortly after her mother had an affair and her father threatened divorce. —John Bradshaw *Homecoming* (1990), p. 240

> Five years ago, Gondolf went into therapy, hoping to put an end to her chronic binge-and-purge eating disorder. —*Mother Jones* Jan. 1993, p. 26

> A new syndrome—Binge Eating Disorder—in which an individual eats a huge amount without getting rid of it, has been identified in one of the biggest surveys into diet illnesses. —*Daily Telegraph* 26 Apr. 1995, p. 7

EC 🗳 see EUROPEAN UNION

e-cash 🖳 see E-

ecological footprint /iːkəˌlɒdʒɪk(ə)l ˈfʊtprɪnt/ *noun* 🌳

Something which has had a permanent (and damaging) effect on the surrounding environment.

A *footprint* as a permanent mark made on the *ecology*.

A term of the nineties which reflects a growing awareness that any environment is likely to be adversely affected by those living in it.

> This way, they did not overgraze their valley and kept their ecological footprint as small as possible. —James Finn Garner *Politically Correct Bedtime Stories* (1994), p. 17

> Humanity must learn to leave a smaller ecological footprint...or the 21st century will be filled with unpleasant environmental surprises. —*Austin American-Statesman* 25 Apr. 1996, section B, p. 10

economical with the truth /iːkəˌnɒmɪk(ə)l wɪð ðə ˈtruːθ/ *adjectival phrase* 🗳 POP

Only saying as much as is strictly relevant; not telling the whole truth; in wider and jocular use, untruthful.

The notion that a limited truth is to be distinguished from falsehood can be traced back to a similar expression by the eighteenth-century politician Edmund Burke:

> Falsehood and delusion are allowed in no case whatsoever: But, as in the exercise of all the virtues, there is an economy of truth.

In its current form it derives from a statement given in evidence in 1986 by the then British Cabinet Secretary, Sir Robert Armstrong, to the Supreme Court, New South Wales, in the 'Spycatcher' trial (during which the British Government sought to prevent publication of a book by a former MI5 employee. Referring to a letter, Sir Robert said:

> It contains a misleading impression, not a lie. It was being economical with the truth.

The explanation received considerable media attention at the time, and the phrase quickly passed into the language; the MP Alan Clark, under cross-examination at the Old Bailey during the Matrix Churchill trial, made allusive reference to it:

> Our old friend economical...with the actualité.

Economical with the truth has subsequently moved from the world of political cliché to that of more general jocular and derogatory description.

> The world is full of minimisers: civil servants are economical with the truth, engineers want to cut down the weight of aircraft, bees use as little wax as possible. —*New Scientist* 21 May 1994, p. 34

> She now stands accused of being economical with the truth. —*Independent* 16 Oct. 1995, p. 16

Ecstasy /'ɛkstəsi/ *noun* Also written **Ecstacy, ecstacy,** or **ecstasy** 🎵POP

The hallucinogenic drug methylenedioxymethamphetamine or MDMA. Sometimes abbreviated to **E**.

The name refers to the extreme feelings of euphoria and general well-being which the drug induces in its users.

The drug was first synthesized in 1960 and became known as MDMA in 1978; by the mid eighties it had appeared on the streets in the US and was being called *Ecstasy* or *Adam* (from a scrambling of the initials of MDMA; a similar compound became known as *Eve*). It was *Ecstasy* that the media most associated with the introduction of the *acid house* culture to the UK in 1988 (see HOUSE). Energetic dancing in hot and often unventilated club environments, combined with the tendency of *Ecstasy* itself to raise body temperature, led to fatalities from dehydration—causes compounded, it was alleged, by the removal of free drinking facilities by promoters keen to sell packaged drinks. Greater understanding of the problems led to the creation of *chill-out* areas where clubbers could rehydrate, rest, and recover. Impure or deliberately adulterated *Ecstasy* led to further deaths. When it was proved that continual use could do irreversible damage to nerve cells in the brain, it was banned in both the US and the UK. However, it remains one of the most popular illicit drugs of the nineties on the RAVE scene; users are said to **drop an E**. In early 1995, it was reported that an unrelated substance inducing similar effects, called **herbal E**, was being distributed in clubs. Tablets of *Ecstasy* may be referred to variously as *disco biscuits*, *doves*, and *love doves* (see LOVED-UP).

Ecstasy. X. Eve. E. All of a sudden everyone was exciting and beautiful and so much fun to talk to. You never got that bored, tired feeling you usually got at parties after a couple of hours.
—*Details* Dec. 1991, p. 36

When you're doing things like this all the time you've got to be in control of yourself, and the only drug you can do and be in control is coke. You can't really drop an E and do a photo session or something like that. —*i-D* Oct. 1994, p. 26

The drug, herbal E, is being distributed at house parties and raves, and induces a state similar to Ecstasy. It consists of a combination of 10 herbal stimulants which pharmacists say cause dehydration and put strain on the heart and kidneys. —*Independent on Sunday* 26 Mar. 1995, p. 4

edutainment /ɛdjʊˈteɪnm(ə)nt/ *noun* 🔀

Entertainment with an educational aspect; material intended to entertain and to inform.

Formed from the first element of *education* and the final element of *entertainment*, on the model of the earlier *infotainment*.

In the seventies, formations such as *infotainment* (representing a blend of information and entertainment) and *docutainment* (a documentary intended to entertain as well as inform) gave evidence of a conscious desire to inform and educate through the medium of entertainment.

Since the early eighties, *edutainment* has represented a development of this approach, with particular concentration on the interactive capacity of MULTIMEDIA products. For electronic publishing, the **edutainment market** is now seen as being of major importance, although the substantial educational benefits believed to be derived are still a matter of some debate.

'Edutainment'…What that means is a program is as entertaining, enjoyable and motivating as it is an educational learning tool. —*Home* Sept. 1993, p. 71

So much that comes to us out of the culture of computers, especially as the technology moves toward 'edutainment' for the young, grinds away at the already diminished attention span and power of concentration. The essence, after all, of hypertextual surfing is pushing buttons and jumping around. —*Edges* Spring 1994, p. 39

An 'edutainment' centre with motion simulators, interactive games, soft play area, VR games and catering facilities. —*Leisure Management* Apr. 1995, p. 8

elder abuse 🎎 see ABUSE

electronic /ɪlɛkˈtrɒnɪk/ *adjective* 🖳

Relating to activities or processes mediated or enabled through the use of a computer, frequently by means of telecommunications links.

A development of the adjective *electronic* from the original term *electronic data processing*, a synonym for *computing* in the sixties, where *electronic* referred principally to the processing mechanism rather than to the data. It is now applied also to the object of the processing, and in general *electronic* has become a near synonym for *computerized*.

The larger group of new phrases beginning with *electronic* are linked to networking, and in particular to the INTERNET. The first was **electronic mail**, (1977); often abbreviated to E-MAIL. Messages sent by this process may be stored in an **electronic mailbox** (1981), or transmitted through an **electronic bulletin board** (see BBS). *Electronic* SUPERHIGHWAY is one term for a nationwide high-capacity communications network. An application of networking in the US to make politics more accessible and responsive to local opinion—**electronic democracy**—was popularized by Ross Perot during his presidential election campaign in 1992; several experiments in linking members of communities in the US to provide discussion forums on local concerns are in various stages of planning: they are described collectively as the **electronic town hall** or an **electronic town meeting**. The only partly explored potential of the new communications networks is often referred to in the US as the **electronic frontier**, by obvious analogy to the country's physical mid-west frontier of the late nineteenth century.

A variety of terms have been coined for techniques permitting commerce over electronic networks: **electronic banking** (in which an individual maintains a bank account by means of a computer and communications links); **electronic cottage** (a home or personal workplace linked to the outside world by telecommunications; **electronic trading** (buying and selling shares by transactions communicated through computer networks); **electronic transfer** (the direct transfer of money from one bank account to another). In the mid nineties, various schemes have been proposed for carrying money in electronic form in SMART *cards*; this system has been variously named **electronic cash**, **electronic money**, and the **electronic purse**.

Another group of new compounds in *electronic* refer to the production or transmission of computerized documents or similar information. **Electronic publishing** (1977) is the publication of text in machine-readable form rather than on paper (it can also refer to texts published in this way); **electronic text** (often abbreviated to **e-text**), is the machine-readable version of a text, frequently tagged with formatting instructions for display or printing; an **electronic document** is a generic term for any machine-readable text, perhaps an **electronic brochure** or **electronic catalogue**; an **electronic journal** is a scholarly journal published only in electronic form and usually disseminated via the Internet or similar system; an **electronic newspaper** is one produced in machine-readable form and accessible over a computer network, and which may in the future permit readers to receive a personalized selection of news stories. The development of small, lightweight video recording equipment in the mid eighties led to the rise of **electronic newsgathering** (**ENG**), in which news material is recorded in the field directly on to videotape by a small crew; an **electronic newsroom** is one in a radio or television newsroom in which news stories are input, edited and linked to bulletins using computer systems; an **electronic kiosk** is a free-standing display unit, say in a shop or bank, for interactive enquiries and sometimes for placing orders.

An **electronic nose** is a microprocessor-based sensing device designed to identify odours; an **electronic organizer** is a portable computer with software to manage appointments, address book and related information; **electronic tagging** identifies offenders held on remand or on probation in a form of house arrest: a non-removable bracelet or anklet is periodically interrogated by a sensor attached to a telephone and raises the alarm if the person is out of range; **electronic tolling** is a proposed system for charging for road use by detecting the identity of a vehicle at a toll point, with the cost either debited automatically from the driver's bank account or deducted from the balance held on a smart card in the vehicle; **electronic warfare** is the use of electronic surveillance systems and countermeasures as tactical weapons; an **electronic zoo** is an indoor wildlife habitat exhibit using audio, video, and similar techniques to simulate the presence of large animals in a natural environment.

> When bills can be settled by instant electronic transfer and every shop takes plastic, who needs a pocketful of money? —*Highlife* May 1991, p. 26

> First Chicago will also have around-the-clock access to the world's largest financial futures and options markets on the new after-hours electronic trading system.
> —advertisement in *Forbes* 2 Sept. 1991, p. 249

> It's very quiet everyplace these days, what with people locked into their electronic cottages from morning to night, conveniently doing all their banking, shopping, and much of their jobs over the electronic spiderweb that connects all living things on the planet. —*Esquire* Feb. 1994, p. 36

> Ministers have ordered new trials of electronic tagging for offenders to pave the way for the widespread use of curfew orders in Britain for the first time.
> —*Guardian* 6 May 1994, section 1, p. 1

> The electronic frontier needs sheriffs like any other, and the F.B.I. says bills introduced in Congress last week will give it the technological draw on cyberspace bandits.
> —*New York Times* 14 Aug. 1994, section C, p. 2

> If electronic democracy is to succeed, however, in the face of all the obstacles, activists must do more than avoid mistakes. Those who would use computer networks as political tools must go forward and actively apply their theories to more and different kinds of communities.
> —Howard Rheingold *The Virtual Community* (1994), p. 300

> There are two different types of payment. One is the high-volume and low-value, where electronic cash such as Digicash or Mondex will be secure enough. The other is high-value and low-volume, where the credit card route will be appropriate. —*Computing* 16 Mar. 1995, p. 27

> Food, drink and perfume companies are keen to use electronic noses to increase the objectivity and consistency of their quality control. —*Economist* 15 Apr. 1995, p. 110

See also E-

e-mail /'iːmeɪl/ *noun* and *verb* Also written email 🖵

noun: Messages distributed by ELECTRONIC means from a computer user to one or more recipients via a network; a single message of this kind. Also, the system of sending messages in this way.

transitive verb: To send e-mail to (a person); to send (a message) by e-mail.

The term *e-mail* has been in use since the first half of the eighties, and was originally applied to the transfer of messages in this way; as the number of **e-mailers** increased, the term was increasingly applied to the messages themselves.

> He had a long queue of e-mail to read and answer. —*Analog* Feb. 1992, p. 102

> I wrote the user an email saying that I did not approve of the way he had advertised his commercial Web site. —8 May 1995, online posting

> The ex-FBI agent went to the computer on the other side of the room and began E-mailing his sources in Asia and Europe. —Tom Clancy *Op-Center* (1995), p. 93

> What it offers is a little piece of downloadable software that automatically appends a piece of trivia to your e-mail messages. —*Independent* 29 July 1996, section 2, p. 10

See also E-

emergicenter /ɪˈməːdʒɪsɛntə/ *noun* ⊗

A clinic, typically situated in an urban commercial centre, offering immediate or emergency outpatient treatment for minor ailments or injuries. A trade mark in the US.

From a blend of the first elements of *emergency* and *center* (the US spelling for *centre*), on the model of the earlier *surgicenter* 'a surgical unit where minor operations are performed on outpatients'.

Emergicenters were introduced into the US in 1981, with more than two hundred such facilities being established in shopping malls and other commercial centres. Their introduction may be taken to represent a logical extension of the view that healthcare is to be purchased like any other commodity, and that it may effectively be brought to the likely consumer by the establishment of clinics of this kind in busy commercial centres.

A new development...is the rise of the 'emergicenter'...There are more than 250 of these walk-in facilities throughout the U.S., generally located in shopping centers or along highways.
—*U.S. News & World Report* 17 Aug. 1981, p. 52

Hospital emergency room costs for minor injury treatment have skyrocketed in recent years to support the backup facilities needed for major trauma cases, several emergicenter operators said. —*Washington Post* 27 May 1985, Washington Business section, p. 11

Other facilities: Walk-in family care and urgent care at St. Lucie West Emergi-Center and Emergi-Center of Jensen Beach. Out-patient surgery at the Stuart Surgery Center.
—*Palm Beach Post* 22 Oct. 1995

See also URGICENTER

Emily's list /ˌɛmɪlɪz 'lɪst/ *noun* 🗓 POP 🗓

A group whose purpose is to further the political candidature of women.

Acronym for *Early Money Is Like Yeast*; in this context, *yeast* is punningly seen as the agent which makes the dough rise.

Emily's list was launched in America in 1985, in a campaign to develop a political network for Democratic women and fund prospective candidates. The organization swiftly developed a reputation as an effective political action group. In the early nineties it spread to Britain, when *Emily's list (UK)* was founded; it is too early to say whether it will be similarly successful in affecting electoral patterns.

Emily's List spent $3.5 million on candidates and issues and established itself as one of the most effective political action committees in the country. —*The World & I* Mar. 1993, p. 22

That was the moment when Emily's List was born. A campaign to make 50 per cent of MPs women and to do it by raising the money to support them.
—*Times Educational Supplement* 10 Feb. 1995, p. 24

e-money 🖳 see E-

emoticon 🖳 POP see SMILEY

emotional abuse 🗓 see ABUSE

empower /ɪmˈpaʊə, ɛmˈpaʊə/ *transitive verb* 🗓

Give power to, make able to do something.

While *empower* in the sense 'give power to' is recorded from the seventeenth century, it has in recent times developed an extension of meaning. Since the seventies, the questioning (central to the NEW AGE Movement) of the traditional values of Western culture has been accompanied by a growing perception that the acceptance of such values effectively restricts or deprives groups or individuals who do not conform to what is recognized as the dominant tradition.

Empowerment is increasingly seen as a strategy for liberation and restoration, whereby a person may both be freed from the restraints of an imposed tradition, and given back the ability to act independently. In this context, the **empowering** process is seen as one which allows the development of full potential, and in so doing opens up new horizons. A person who is **self-empowered** is thus one whose ability to act independently is not governed by acceptance of an external set of values.

A matching extension of negative terms has also occurred: *disempowerment* is seen as the deliberate removal or restriction of choices and opportunities, reducing the *disempowered* person to a powerless position of deprivation and vulnerability.

I know how gut-wrenching the struggle to find a balance can be. Some of us felt it was our responsibility to assist in empowering those who could not find a clear voice and some of us were disempowered through those attempts. —*Saturday Night* June 1993, p. 9

Self-empowerment comes from awareness and tolerance, spirituality and knowledge of self.
—*Urb* 7 July 1993, p. 12

He called on his managers to adopt a set of 'soft concepts' including such warm, fuzzy notions as having 'the self-confidence to empower others and behave in a boundaryless fashion.'
—*New York Times* 4 Mar. 1995, section D, p. 1

These self-empowered individuals are motivated by teamwork and developing broader skills rather than just achieving conventional status. —*Independent* 12 Oct. 1995, section 2, p. 23

energy audit /'ɛnədʒi ˌɔːdɪt/ *noun* 🌳

A systematic review of the energy needs and efficiency of a building or buildings.

A a result of the increasing costs of energy and the environmental implications of using fossil fuels to provide it, techniques have been developed in the eighties and nineties for assessing the energy efficiency of industrial and domestic buildings and finding ways to improve it. This includes ways to reduce heat losses by insulating walls and roofs, to ensure equipment is working effectively, and to minimize wastage. The concept of the *energy audit* has developed to provide a systematic method of assessing efficiency and make suggestions for reducing waste. A person undertaking such a survey is an **energy auditor**.

She took advantage of a free energy audit and lowered the utility bill by filming windows and getting insulated curtains. —*Richmond Times-Dispatch* 30 July 1995, section G, p. 11

A system of energy audits for all Trust properties has been initiated and staff have been trained to be more energy conscious. —*Independent* 24 Oct. 1996, p. 12

escape key /ɪ'skeɪp kiː/ *noun* 💻

A key on many computer keyboards which causes a special character code to be transmitted which is commonly used to signal that the user wishes to cancel, and thus escape from, the current operation.

The need for a cancel character within computer systems has been recognized at least since the fifties; the term *escape character* for it first appeared in the early sixties, at the time when the standard for the character coding used in most computers today was being established. But a dedicated key on a computer keyboard which produced the escape character was slower in appearing, and *escape key* is not recorded until the early eighties. One reason was that until the appearance of interactive systems based around the windowing concept, there was relatively little need for such a key and a similar function was frequently implemented with other keystrokes. In informal usage and in computer instructions, the term is frequently abbreviated to **escape**, which is also used as a verb with the meaning 'cancel the current operation'.

Pressing the Escape key quits the game and takes you back to the options screen.
—*Amiga Computing* Dec. 1990, p. 100

When I reboot, I get the error message 'Load error—press Escape to retry'.
—*What Personal Computer* Dec. 1991, p. 163

Essex man /'ɛsɪks man/ *noun* 🏚 POP 🍺

A derogatory term for a type of British Conservative voter, in London and the south-east of England (and particularly the county of Essex) in the late eighties.

Formed (perhaps remembering the earlier *Selsdon man*, a name given to a type of Conservative voter of the early seventies) on the model of such anthropological terms as *Peking man* and *Piltdown man*.

Essex man has been noted since the beginning of the nineties as a major factor in Conservative support. *Essex man* is characterized as a brash, amoral, self-made young businessman, of right-wing views and few or no cultural or intellectual interests, who shares some of the characteristics of the earlier *yuppies*, but who concentrates on the acquisition of consumer goods and material wealth rather than on enhanced social status. In the election of 1992, the Conservative victory in the constituency of Basildon, Essex, was seen as early evidence of the importance of **Essexist** support.

Essex man is regarded primarily as the type of a political supporter, but his female equivalent, *Essex girl*, is seen in social terms, being variously characterized as unintelligent, promiscuous, and materialistic, and is the butt of many politically incorrect jokes.

Both terms reflect the financial and political climate of the eighties, and it remains to be seen how durable they will ultimately be.

Too many of her enemies failed to see this. They railed and sneered at the enrichessez-vous spirit of the 1980s, at yuppies and Essex Man, at the greed and self-interest of Thatcherism.
—*Guardian* 22 Oct. 1993, section 2, p. 7

Yet today you hear next to nothing about C2s. Essex man lies unheeded and unloved in the gutter of political history. —*Economist* 8 Apr. 1995, p. 43

An alarming tale of Essex girl jokes and sexual innuendo.
—*Independent on Sunday* 23 Apr. 1995, p. 28

Essex Man represents a new phenomenon in post-war British politics—a potentially violent and very far from respectable, still less guilt-ridden, type of petit bourgeois who bears absolutely no resemblance to the law-abiding middle class which the Attlee Government had to deal with.
—*Sunday Telegraph* 4 Feb. 1996, p. 29

See also NEW LAD

Estuary English / ˌɛstjʊ(ə)ri ˈɪŋglɪʃ/ *noun* 【

A type of English accent identified as spreading outwards from London, mainly into the south-east of England (the area of the Thames Estuary), and containing features of both received pronunciation and such regional accents as Cockney.

The term was coined in 1984 by linguist David Rosewarne, who concluded that the descriptions of English used in applied linguistics did not cover the speech he was hearing every day in London. Popularization of the term in the early nineties was followed by a conscious adoption of *Estuary English* as a feature of a classless society. It may now be regarded as fashionable among certain popular comedians, pop and rock musicians, and presenters of television programmes for the young.

Mr Coggle said yesterday that Estuary English was an 'off-the-shelf' mode of pronunciation from which speakers could pick sounds they thought would move them up or down socially.
—*Guardian* 22 Dec. 1993, p. 18

In England itself, another reversion is under way. The upper-class young already talk 'Estuary English', the faintly Cockneyfied accent of the South-east.
—*Independent on Sunday* 7 Aug. 1994, p. 18

e-text ▣ see E-

ethical investment / ˌɛθɪk(ə)l ɪnˈvɛstmənt/ *noun* 〜

An investment which takes account of the investor's scruples by screening the companies to be invested in for their business morality and social outlook.

The demand for *ethical investment* began in the US in the early eighties, when it became clear that an increasing number of savers wanted to put their money into funds which were managed to invest only in companies whose activities they were happy with. The first *ethical investment* scheme appeared in the UK in 1984 and the concept is now an established part of financial practice worldwide. The person making the investment is an **ethical investor**, the scheme, such as a unit trust, may be called an **ethical fund**, and the practice **ethical investing**. In the US, the concept is also known as a *socially responsible investment*, with similar compounds.

> The US has always been well ahead of the UK in the field of Socially Responsible Investment (SRI. or Ethical Investment as it is known here), with more than 10 per cent of the money passing through Wall Street screened for factors such as involvement in South Africa…nuclear power, the tobacco industry…and gambling. —*BBC Wildlife* July 1990, p. 462

> Ethical investments have become popular with that increasingly large band of savers not prepared to go for a profit at any price. —*Guardian* 4 Mar. 1995, PEPs Report supplement, p. 4

ethnic cleansing /ɛθnɪk ˈklɛnzɪŋ/ *noun* 🖾

The mass expulsion or extermination of people from a minority ethnic or religious group within a certain area.

Ethnic cleansing was reported in 1991, as conflict spread in the former Yugoslavia; more recently, it has been particularly associated with the bitter fighting between BOSNIAN *Serbs* and BOSNIAN *Muslims*, who had apparently lived in amity as neighbours for generations. Despite the hopes raised by the DAYTON *accord* of 1995, it is not yet clear that *ethnic cleansing* in the Balkans can be considered a thing of the past. The full extent of the atrocities committed in the first half of the nineties is not yet known.

> The world still seems helpless to stop ethnic cleansing in Bosnia. —*Imprimis* Sept. 1994, p. 3

> The area has a large number of towns and villages, many emptied of Muslims and Croats in three years of ethnic cleansing. —*The Times* 9 June 1995, p. 11

> The Croatian political and military leadership issued a statement Wednesday declaring that Serbia's 'aim…is obviously the ethnic cleansing of the critical areas that are to be annexed to Serbia'. —*Washington Post* 2 Aug. 1995, section A, p. 22

See also CLEANSING

EU 🖾 see EUROPEAN UNION

Euro /ˈjʊərəʊ/ *noun* Also written **euro** 〰 🖾

The name agreed for the future European currency unit, to replace the ecu after monetary union and establishment of a SINGLE CURRENCY.

Probably an extension of the existing *Euro* 'Eurobond, Eurodollar, or other item traded on the Euromoney markets'; ultimately, formed by shortening *European*.

The designated name (originally proposed in 1971) for the future European currency unit has formed one specific area of controversy in the wider issue of a SINGLE CURRENCY. Before the chosen name was agreed on at a summit conference in Madrid in December 1995, a wide variety of suggestions, including the *euromark* and the *eurofranc*, had been canvassed; the final choice, *Euro*, avoids giving preference to any of the existing national currencies. Designs for the banknotes, showing architectural images of windows, bridges, and gateways, but without individual national symbols, were unveiled at a meeting of finance ministers in Dublin in December 1996.

> The 'Euro'—a currency to replace the franc, the mark, the lire, the peseta, and possibly the pound—was born yesterday. —*Independent* 16 Dec. 1995, p. 1

> The euro is likely to be broken into 100 units, like pence to a pound. The European Commission expects the euro to be known colloquially as the pound in Britain, the mark in Germany and so on. —*Times* 17 Feb. 1996, p. 34

Euroconnector 🖾 see SCART

Euro-ISDN 🔬 see B-ISDN

European Union /jʊərə͵piːən ˈjuːnjən/ noun 🔒

A federation of (originally western) European states, established in 1992, which is co-extensive with the European Community, and whose members send representatives to the European Parliament. Abbreviation **EU**.

The *European Union* was established by the MAASTRICHT treaty of 1992, and came into being with the ratification of the treaty on 1 November 1993. As an organization it comprises the EC together with two intergovernmental 'pillars' for dealing with foreign affairs and with immigration and justice. It is seen by both supporters and critics as an important step on the road to full economic and political integration of the member states, but it is too soon to say to what degree such expectations will be realized.

> Ukraine yesterday became the first republic of the former Soviet Union to sign a partnership and cooperation agreement with the European Union. —*Guardian* 24 Mar. 1994, p. 12

> Finns are expected to say 'yes' to the European Union in a referendum today that would sever Finland's past Soviet ties and strengthen its links with the West.
> —*Boston Globe* 16 Oct. 1994, p. 25

> The UK is the only EU member that still relies on the old-style document licences.
> —*Which?* July 1995, p. 7

> The 15 heads of government of the European Union will formally agree to call the proposed single European currency 'the Euro' when they meet in Madrid tomorrow.
> —*Guardian* 14 Dec. 1995, p. 21

Euro-sceptic / jʊərəʊˈskɛptɪk/ noun and adjective 🔒

noun: A person who is sceptical about the value of closer connection with Europe, particularly in the context of increasing the powers of the European Union.

adjective: Of, pertaining to, or characteristic of Euro-sceptics.

The term *Euro-sceptic* was coined in the mid eighties, and has been freely used as the debate in the UK about the supposed benefits to Britain of increasing cooperation with fellow members of the EUROPEAN UNION has become more intense. Politicians of all parties are now defined in terms of their acceptance or rejection of **Euro-sceptical** views, and **Euro-scepticism** has become particularly fashionable on the right wing of the Conservative Party.

> Reports at the weekend of informal discussions among finance ministers meeting in Luxembourg sounded alarm bells among Labour and Conservative Euro-sceptics.
> —*Guardian* 13 May 1991, p. 1

> Mr Major entrusted much of the sensitive work on his 'hard ecu' alternative to monetary union to the Euro-sceptical Mr Maude. —*Economist* 22 June 1991, p. 34

> It will cheer British Euro-sceptics, who insist the UK could do better as a simple free trade partner of the community. —*Daily Mail* 2 Jan. 1995, p. 5

> Two sentences in Baroness Thatcher's Keith Joseph Memorial lecture reveal the self-delusion at the heart of Euroscepticism. —*Independent* 16 Jan. 1996, p. 14

Eurostar /ˈjʊərəʊstɑː/ noun 🎛

The high speed passenger rail service which links London with various European cities via the Channel Tunnel. Also, a train used on this service. A trade mark in the UK.

Construction of the Channel Tunnel, a railway tunnel under the English Channel, linking the coasts of England and France, was begun in 1987; the tunnel was opened, and *Eurostar* began to operate, in 1994.

Ashford commuters will have to confine themselves to the old Network Southeast trundlers, instead of hopping on the Eurostar trains. *—Independent* 31 Jan. 1995, p. 15

We've hurtled ear-poppingly beneath the sea on Eurostar. *—ikon* Jan. 1996, p. 82

See also LE SHUTTLE

evening primrose oil /ˌiːvnɪŋ ˈprɪmrəʊz ɔɪl/ *noun phrase* ⊗ ▓

An oil for medicinal and cosmetic use extracted from the seeds of the evening primrose, a plant (*Oenothera*) with pale yellow flowers that open in the evening.

The increasing popularity in the early eighties of complementary medicine and its alternative approaches to health was particularly associated with a wish to use natural rather than artificial remedies. *Evening primrose oil*, as containing fatty acids thought able to modify chemicals causing inflammatory skin disease, was of particular interest and soon became the subject of commercial exploitation. Capsules of the oil are sold as dietary supplements, and it is increasingly used as an ingredient of soaps and cosmetics, although its effectiveness as a remedy is still a matter of debate.

Many women today take evening primrose oil to help with the symptoms of PMS or to improve their skin and general well being. *—advertisement in Health Guardian* Nov. 1990, p. 4

The widespread belief that evening primrose oil helps reduce symptoms of eczema and other skin conditions is a myth, according to dermatologists from Leicester Royal Infirmary.

—Guardian 18 June 1993, p. 4

executive information systems ▣ ⋀⋁ see DATA WAREHOUSE

expansion slot /ɪkˈspanʃ(ə)n slɒt, ɛk-/ *noun* ▣

A socket in a piece of computing equipment, especially a personal computer or WORKSTATION, into which an additional electronic circuit board may be plugged to add capabilities to the system.

Soon after the first personal computers became available, it became clear that users often needed additional functions which it would be unnecessary or uneconomic to provide as part of the basic system. So a system of connectors was developed in the late seventies, into which **expansion cards** or **expansion boards** could be plugged (the term *expansion slot* itself dates from 1980). A similar system was later adopted for the IBM PC and other computers. More recently, the term has also been applied to sockets which have connectors rather than slots, but which have a similar purpose. The term is frequently abbreviated to **slot**.

The system also provides two standard 16-bit expansion slots which will accept full-size cards allowing you to add scanners, fax boards…and just about any other peripheral you might want or need. *—Computer Buyer's Guide* 1990, Vol. 8, No. 3, p. 93

What sets the T3300SL apart from the SX machine is the latest industry standard expansion slot, PCMCIA 2.0, which will take credit card-sized cards for add-ons like modems and network adaptors. *—What Personal Computer* Dec. 1991, Issue 29, p. 23

Other vendors combine codec and terminal adapters on a single card, looking to cut down on the number of PC slots they fill up. *—Data Communications International* Jan. 1995, p. 58

export /ɪkˈspɔːt, ɛk-/ *transitive verb* ▣

To transfer (data) out of one computer system into another, or from one application within a computer to another.

A specialist sense of the word *export*, meaning 'to carry something out of one place into another' used as computer jargon.

This jargon sense first appeared in print in the early eighties, but had almost certainly been used in speech for some time before then. Though the data may be **exported** over a LAN or other network, the term, like IMPORT, is more commonly used to refer to the transfer or copying of data from one application to another, especially if some change of format is taking place. For example, a database might be instructed to *export* some records as numbers for manipulation in a spreadsheet, or a user of a word processor might *export* a text file in a different format suitable for another type of word processor.

Most Mac database managers (and spreadsheets) can import and export files with the fields delimited by tabs or commas and the records separated by carriage returns.

—*MacWorld* Dec. 1993, p. 151

These systems generally provide a mechanism to import and export a growing number of de facto standard formats, allowing for limited movement of data between foreign, albeit similar, systems. —*Dr. Dobb's Journal* Dec. 1993, p. 18

extra-virgin /ɛkstrə 'vəːdʒɪn/ *adjective* and *noun* Also written **extra virgin** 🔲

adjective: Denoting a particularly fine ('extra') grade of olive oil.

noun: An olive oil of this grade.

Virgin olive oil is obtained from the first pressing of the olives.

Before the second half of the twentieth century, many households in the UK would have seen olive oil as having primarily a medicinal purpose. This changed in the fifties and sixties with the spread of interest in Mediterranean cookery, and culinary developments in the eighties saw an awakening of interest in the different grades and types. Increasing commercial exploitation of the trend means that recipes are as likely to recommend a specific variety of oil, as delicatessens and supermarkets are to be able to supply it.

Extra virgin is the highest quality, pressed from hand-picked fine olives.

—*Cook's Magazine* Nov. 1981, p. 10

Each has its rightful place in the kitchen, Extra Virgin oil for dressing salads or drizzling on warm, fresh bread, and a more commercial brand for cooking. —*Wine* May 1993, p. 59

The first clue to the quality of the oil you buy is a term you must look for: extra-virgin.

—*Food and Wine* Oct. 1994, p. 67

extreme /ɪk'striːm/ *adjective* 🔲 ⚽

Designating sports performed in a hazardous environment, involving a high physical risk.

Extreme sports, which require a high degree of physical dexterity and nerve, have become increasingly popular as a leisure activity in the early nineties. **Extreme skiers**, like those indulging in HELI-SKIING, pursue their chosen sport on slopes which would be considered too steep for traditional skiing, and BUNGEE-JUMPING, CANYONING, and SNOWBOARDING all provide the desired physical and mental challenge.

The East Coast also offers extreme skiing...In an environment that has recorded the highest wind speed on this planet, devotees pack their backpacks, strap on their skis, and face dangers equal to their Western counterparts. —*Skiing* Mar. 1991, p. 12

Shaun Baker is an extreme kayaker, a masochist who chooses to ride his canoe over waterfalls.

—*Independent on Sunday* 13 Aug. 1992, Real Life section, p. 6

The terrain in the area varies from powder-filled couloirs for the extreme skier, to open meadows suitable for light ski-touring. —*SkiTrax* Dec. 1992, p. 22

The 'extreme sports' of bungee jumping, street luge and mountain biking.

—*Chicago Tribune* 12 May 1996, p. 1

extropy /'ɛkstrəpi/ *noun* Also written **Extropy** ⦗⦘

The concept that life is not limited by entropy, but will continue to expand in an orderly and progressive manner.

The concept of *entropy*, which arose in the nineteenth century as a mathematical quantity in thermodynamics, was later given a physical interpretation as representing the degree of disorder or randomness of the constituents of any physical system. One of the consequences of the Second Law of Thermodynamics is that entropy can only increase, the eventual result being 'heat death', a state in which structure is absent and temperature is uniform. The term *extropy*, coined in 1992, represents a precisely opposite view: **extropians** assert the principle that life, by means of human intelligence and technology, will expand indefinitely and in an orderly, progressive manner throughout the entire universe. There is also an adjective **extropian**, and a noun **extropianism**.

'Extropians', as promoters of extropy call themselves, issued a seven-point lifestyle manifesto based on the vitalism of life's extropy.　　　　　　　　　　　　—K. Kelly *Out of Control* (1994), p. 107

They're devoted to fighting entropy and all that doomy stuff about finite resources and the inevitable heat death of the universe. Instead they're devoted to promoting the forces of Extropy.
　　　　　　　　　　　　　　　　　　　—*Ottawa Citizen* 1 Apr. 1995, section B, p. 4

eyephone /ˈʌɪfəʊn/ *noun* Also written **EyePhone** 🖳

A headset used in VIRTUAL *reality* environments which provides its wearer with stereoscopic visual images and synchronized sound.

Taken literally, the word is meaningless—how can eyes hear? But the name was invented as a pun on *earphone*, because it is an analogous device giving similar private access to information for the eyes instead of the ears.

Early virtual reality systems used a standard computer monitor to display the images generated by the computer, but this could not give the feeling of immersion in the scene required for suspension of disbelief. The *eyephone* was developed in the late eighties to provide a solution; it consists of two small television screens, one for each eye, which are fed slightly different views of the scene so that the wearer perceives a three-dimensional stereoscopic image; standard earphones supply the sound. Wearing the *eyephone* gives the user a sense of being within the computer-generated scene; sensors within it track movements of the wearer's head, so that the scene moves with the wearer; as with a DATAGLOVE, objects can apparently be manipulated within the scene. Such devices are now becoming common in computer games and commercial visualization systems, but in the mid nineties concern began to be expressed about the adverse physiological effects of wearing such devices for extended periods, especially by children. In its capitalized form, the name is a US trade mark.

Using two high-powered computers and software designed to produce three-dimensional images on a screen, a designer can create an environment...on the computer. The user, after putting on...a Dataglove and Eyephone, can then 'walk' through the house, say, and pick things up on the screen and move them around.　　　　　　　　　　　—*Artnews* Apr. 1990, p. 125

The customer can then strap on VPL 'eyephones'—a headset with telescreens providing wraparound stereoscopic views of the kitchen of their dreams and, using the VPL data glove which uses position sensors, the customer can point to objects within the illusory system.
　　　　　　　　　　　　　　　　　　　　　　—*CAD User* Oct. 1995, p. 21

e-zine 🖳 see E-

• •

F

face, in your 🔅 see IN YOUR FACE

fajitas /fəˈhiːtəz/ *plural noun* 🍴

A Mexican-American dish consisting of strips of spicy marinated chicken, meat, or fish, served in a soft flour tortilla, usually with salad and other savoury fillings.

Also, a vegetarian dish consisting of strips of vegetables served in this way.

The singular form **fajita** is a Mexican Spanish word meaning 'little sash or belt' (with reference to the long narrow shape of the pieces of meat or fish).

Fajitas entered the English-speaking world across the Texas-Mexican border, in a style of cooking popularly known as *Tex-Mex* (from *Texan-Mexican*). Based on Mexican concepts and ingredients, this cuisine is adapted to the North American palate by a more moderate use of hot flavourings such as chilli. *Fajitas,* which is quick to prepare and easy to eat, is increasingly familiar in fast-food restaurants in North America and Europe.

The singular form **fajita** is often used in compounds such as **fajita restaurant** and **fajita sauce**.

Tex-Mex evolved from the dishes that crossed into Texas from the Mexican border states and in time developed along the lines of the familiar fajitas, burritos, chili, tacos and nachos.

—*Food & Wine* Aug. 1991, p. 42

Here we'll be serving up an incredible feast of dishes that are all firm favourites in the South West of America. These include tortilla soup, taco salads and sizzling hot chicken fajitas.

—advertisement in *The Times* 12 Sept. 1992, Saturday Review, p. 7

The meat for fajitas is marinated in chilies and cooked over a mesquite fire.

—*Washingtonian* June 1993, p. 71

Two small, overlapping tortillas covered with grilled meat, meant to be sauced…and rolled up fajita-style. —*Washingtonian* June 1993, p. 83

false memory syndrome /fɔːls ˈmɛm(ə)ri ˌsɪndrəʊm/ *noun phrase* Ⓧ 【

The recollection during psychoanalysis of childhood sexual abuse (especially by a relation), which has not in fact taken place.

Realization in the eighties that *child* ABUSE, especially by a relation, is a much more widespread phenomenon than was previously thought, has led increasingly to the development of therapies designed to *recover* memories suppressed by the victim (see RECOVERED MEMORY). More recently, first in the US and then in the UK, concern has developed that persistent questioning might suggest 'memories' of events which did not actually happen. Many parents have claimed their lives have been blighted by false accusations made by their adult children. Recognition of the possibility of **false memory**, and familiarity with the term *false memory syndrome* and its abbreviation **FMS**, were given impetus by the formation in Philadelphia in 1992 of the **False Memory Syndrome Foundation**, which campaigns to support parents who believe they have been wrongly accused. In November 1996, a man in the UK was acquitted of sexually abusing a woman, when the prosecution offered no evidence against him: two psychological assessments concluded that the woman could have been suffering from *false memory syndrome*, and that her 'memories' may have been triggered by storylines in television dramas.

By virtue of his prodding, *both before and after* he devised psychoanalytic theory, to get his patients to 'recall' nonexistent sexual events, Freud is the true historical sponsor of 'false memory syndrome'. —*New York Review of Books* 18 Nov. 1993, p. 66

The accusation that Freud fabricated his evidence is being used to give credibility to what has become known as False Memory Syndrome. This refers to the idea that memories of sexual abuse reported by many people in therapy are not actual memories but rather have been implanted or suggested by the therapist. —*Guardian* 12 Feb. 1994, Weekend section, p. 21

I told Donna that her parents seemed sincerely convinced of their own innocence, which was why they had joined the False Memory Syndrome Foundation in Philadelphia and why they were speaking out about their case. —*Esquire* Mar. 1994, p. 87

If repressed memories pop up years later, brain specialists say, they must be imperfect—and highly vulnerable to outside influence and revision. Elizabeth Loftus, a professor of psychology at the University of Washington, has shown just how easy it is to create a false memory.

—*Time* 17 Apr. 1995, p. 55

It is believed to be the first case in which the defence of false memory syndrome has been used in Britain. —*Guardian* 30 Nov. 1996, p. 1

See also RECOVERED MEMORY

fantasy football /ˈfantəsi ˈfʊtbɔːl/ *noun* 😀 ⚽

A competition in which participants select imaginary teams from among the real players in an actual league and score points according to the actual performance of their players.

Fantasy football started in the US in the eighties in the sport of American football but quickly spread to Britain, where the term applies to soccer. The object of the game is to choose an imaginary team whose members will in real life out-perform those of the other contestants. Scoring is often complex, counting not only goals scored, but other aspects of the **fantasy team**'s performance, such as defensive capability, assists, and bookings. Both in the US and in Britain, *fantasy football* became a craze in the early and mid nineties. The concept has been extended to many other games, including **fantasy cricket** and **fantasy basketball**.

Fantasy football is sweeping the country…In fantasy football, you are the owner, general manager and coach of a team. You decide which players to draft, which players to play and which ones to cut or trade. —*Pro Football Weekly Preview '91* Oct. 1991, p. 37

The cause of these nation-wide palpitations is the impending close of the fantasy football league season, driving the primarily male participants to a frenzy of expectation.
—*Guardian* 6 Apr. 1996, Outlook section, p. 27

See also ROTISSERIE LEAGUE

FAQ /fak, ɛfeɪˈkjuː/ *acronym* 🖥

A document, usually in electronic form online, containing a list of the questions most often asked about a particular subject, usually with answers to them.

Acronym for *frequently asked questions*.

Online discussion groups, particularly Usenet ones, have developed *FAQs* to minimize repetitive discussion about queries which are continually raised, particularly by newcomers; it is a point of Usenet *netiquette* (see NET) to consult the *FAQ* before posting a question. *FAQs* are almost always developed and maintained on a voluntary basis by expert members of a group and often contain considerable amounts of valuable data about the subject. The term shows signs that it may be moving outside the online community. Although it is generally pronounced as an acronym, a significant minority, particularly in Britain, spell it out as an initialism.

Always read the newsgroup FAQ, if there is one, before you start posting.
—*.net* Dec. 1994, p. 51

The 'Great Exploding Whale of Oregon' story has already gained legendary status on the Internet. Regularly queried, it is now enshrined in the 'Frequently Asked Questions' (FAQ) of the *alt.folk-lore.urban* newsgroup—and as several FT readers have asked about it, it is time to record it in these pages. —*Fortean Times* June 1995, p. 17

Please find a solution that I can include in the FAQ and mail it to me.
—21 July 1996, online posting

fattism ⚧ see -ISM

fatwa /ˈfatwɑː, ˈfatwə/ *noun* Also written **Fatwa** or **fatwah** 📿

A legal decision or ruling given by an Islamic religious leader.

A direct borrowing from Arabic; the root in the original language is the same verb *fatā* (to instruct by a legal decision) from which we get the word *Mufti*, a Muslim legal expert or teacher.

Actually an old borrowing from Arabic (in the form *fetfa* or *fetwa* it has been in use in English since the seventeenth century), the *fatwa* acquired a new currency in the English-language media in February 1989, when Iran's Ayatollah Khomeini issued a *fatwa* sentencing the British writer Salman Rushdie to death for publishing *The Satanic Verses* (1988), a book which many Muslims considered blasphemous and highly offensive. *Fatwa* is a generic term for any legal decision made by a Mufti or other Islamic religious authority, but, because of the particular context in which the West became familiar with the word, it is sometimes erroneously thought to mean 'a death sentence'.

> [He]...rejected the findings of a BBC opinion poll which claimed that only 42 per cent of Muslims in Britain supported the fatwah. —*Independent* 16 July 1990, p. 5

> The *fatwa*, or death sentence, imposed on him by Ayatollah Khomeini in retribution for his 'blasphemous' novel *The Satanic Verses*, is still in force.
> —*New York Review of Books* 4 Mar. 1993, p. 34

> Unlike many writers and artists, Chahine hadn't been *fatwa*ed, but he felt threatened nevertheless. —*New Yorker* 30 Jan. 1995, p. 57

fax-on-demand 🖳 🧪 see ON-DEMAND

feeding frenzy /fiːdɪŋ ˈfrɛnzi/ *noun* 🍴

A voracious competition among would-be purchasers or consumers.

Feeding frenzy in its literal sense is recorded from the sixties; in 1962, the journal *Scientific American* noted:

> Frequently three or four sharks will attack the marlin simultaneously. A wild scene sometimes called 'feeding frenzy', now ensues.

By the late seventies the term had taken on a figurative meaning, and was being used to describe episodes of commercial competition in which the rivalries observed reached levels of frenzy.

In this application, the notion of fierce competition between the parties involved was paramount, but as the usage has become established, the idea of live prey being torn apart has also become important: increasingly, *feeding frenzy* is likely to be used to denote furious media attention directed on a hapless victim.

> The agents started calling people up, working up a feeding frenzy by telling everyone that finally there was a new Shane Black script to see. —*New York Magazine* 18 June 1990, p. 43

> Is it a grotesque invasion of privacy, a banal journalistic feeding frenzy, a new benchmark in the tabloidization of American politics? —*Nation* 24 Feb. 1992, p. 220

> There had been a 'feeding frenzy' of speculation and gossip at the House of Commons following news of the MP's death. —*Guardian* 11 Mar. 1994, p. 10

> Next Tuesday is 1 August, the day when the new N-reg plates arrive and the motor trade goes into a feeding frenzy. —*Independent on Sunday* 30 July 1995, Review section, p. 59

feel-bad /ˈfiːlbad/ *adjective* 〰 📑 POP

That induces a feeling of anxiety and depression.

Formed by analogy with FEEL-GOOD.

Feel-bad is recorded from the early nineties, and is used primarily as a conscious modification of FEEL-GOOD, in contexts which specifically contradict the connotations of financial and material well-being; **feel-bad factor** is frequently encountered.

> Another feel-bad week in a feel-bad year: no boomy thing at all.
> —*Independent on Sunday* 18 Dec. 1994, p. 15

> We're all so insecure about our short-term contracts and our feel-bad factors that we're terrified of appearing keen to leave the office. —*Guardian* 28 Jan. 1995, Weekend section, p. 45

> Three years later came *The Birds*...a doom-laden masterpiece sucker-punching movie-goers with that gloriously bleak feel-bad ending. —*ikon* Jan. 1996, p. 47

feel-good /'fiːlgʊd/ *adjective* 〰️ ⌂ ᴘᴏᴘ

That creates a feeling of well-being in people; in financial and material contexts, the opposite of FEEL-BAD.

Dr Feelgood was a name adopted in 1962 by the blues pianist 'Piano Red' (William Perryman), who broadcast and recorded under this sobriquet. Later the name was used (with negative connotations) as a term for a physician who provides short-term palliatives rather than a more effective treatment or cure.

Feel-good in the sense 'creating a feeling of well-being in people' is recorded from the early seventies, but in the nineties it has come increasingly to refer to a sense of financial and material well-being; the presence or absence of a **feel-good factor** is freqently spoken of in discussions of economic recovery as affecting a government's chances of survival. Ostensibly apolitical events such as periods of fine weather and national sporting successes are seen as affecting political fortunes by increasing the *feel-good factor*; the received wisdom is that good results make voters feel good, and that this favours the incumbent party.

> *Frozen Assets*, the first feel-good movie about sperm banks.　　　*—Spy* May 1993, p. 8

> Economic forecasters would look in vain on college campuses for the elusive 'feel-good factor'.
> 　　　*—Guardian* 25 Oct. 1994, Education section, p. 3

> Bad news not only for John Major but for Tony Blair too: the 'feel-good' factor will not return before the end of the century, and may never reappear.　　　*—Independent on Sunday* 14 May 1995, p. 5

feminazi /'fɛmɪnɑːtsi/ *noun* Also written **femi-Nazi** ᴘᴏᴘ ▓

A contemptuous term for a radical feminist.

Formed by combining the first two syllables of *feminist* with the noun *Nazi*, to make a blend.

Use of the word *feminazi*, which has been recorded since the early nineties, is associated particularly with the presenter of popular US radio and television chat shows Rush Limbaugh. The term was used initially particularly within the abortion debate, in which it was applied to those women who support the pro-choice movement. There is some evidence that it has been adopted as a code word by those wishing to deride these women, in an apparent attempt to link them with the militant feminism associated with the seventies. The term is also used to draw a distinction between radical feminism and the perceived POST-FEMINIST ethos of the nineties, with the implication that the latter represents the emergence of common sense and enlightenment, while *feminazis* belong to an outdated and—a notion expressed through use of the element *Nazi*—heinous political tradition.

While some dismay has been expressed about use of the word it has nevertheless begun, in the mid nineties, to spread outside the abortion debate into more general use. Although there has been some dilution of sense, it remains highly derogatory. However, it is sometimes used in self-deprecation by women of themselves, in reference to their continuing espousal of traditional feminist principles. There is little evidence that the word has yet spread outside the US.

> Fortunately, many young women today have little in common with the militants of the 1970s, many of whom are now the embittered feminazis.
> 　　　—Rush H. Limbaugh *The Way Things Ought to Be* (1992), p. 191

> A feminazi is a person who wants rights males don't have, like the legal ability to kill one's own child while it resides in the womb.　　　*—Coloradoan* (Fort Collins) 22 May 1993, section A, p. 14

> Gay women spout the usual 'femi-Nazi' dogma about hard rock being degrading, exploitative and misogynist.　　　*—Spy* Aug. 1993, p. 28

> I may be a left-wing, radical, ACLU card-carrying liberal feminazi who wants to save the whales.
> 　　　*—Post* (Denver), 11 June 1995, section C, p. 8

fen /fɛn/ *plural noun* ▓

A jocular designation for fans (especially of science fiction) considered collectively.

Formed as a supposed plural on the model of *man/men*.

Initially a humorous self-designation among enthusiasts for science fiction (especially those habitually attending CONS), the term became more widely known through accounts of such gatherings written for a wider audience.

All of this had become so familiar to the fen...that it scarcely seemed artificial anymore.
—Sharyn McCrumb *Bimbos of the Death Sun* (1988), p. 165

A public venue was naturally out of the question; and very few fen owned homes large enough to house even a small con.
—Larry Niven, Jerry Pournelle, & Michael Flynn *Fallen Angels* (1991), p. 89

feng shui /ˈfɛŋ ʃuːɪ, ˈfʌŋ ʃuːɪ/ *noun* 🞩

A kind of geomancy, based on Chinese mythology, concerning the choice of sites for houses or graves.

From the Chinese, a compound of *fēng* 'wind' and *shŭ* 'water'.

In Chinese mythology, *feng shui* is the term given to a system of spirit influences, good and evil, which inhabit the natural features of a landscape; in extended usage, it came also to mean the form of divination employed to deal with such spirits when selecting a site for settlement or burial. This form of geomancy is still practised: it is recorded that when the Hong Kong and Shanghai Bank was designed in Hong Kong:

a feng shui master was brought in as part of the design team.

The interest in Eastern religion and philosophy which developed in the seventies and eighties has ensured that the principles and practices of *feng shui* are now a recognized part of NEW AGE culture.

Metz is a practitioner of *feng shui*, the ancient Chinese art of designing homes and workplaces in harmony with the forces of nature. —*New Age* Nov. 1991, p. 50

To San Francisco feng shui guru Steven Post, who has seen interest grow from a 'trickle to a torrent,' the assumption that people are affected by their surroundings is common sense.
—*Newsweek* 23 Dec. 1991, p. 42

Improve your health, relationships and prosperity by clearing stuck energies in the places where you live and work. Karen Kingston blends Feng Shui wisdom with ancient wisdom from Bali and other cultures. —advertisement in *Kindred Spirit Quarterly* Autumn 1994, p. 70

file transfer protocol 🖳 see FTP

film-on-demand 🖳 ⚗ see -ON-DEMAND

First Nations 🏳 ⁅ see NATIVE

flame /fleɪm/ *verb* and *noun* 🖳

transitive verb: In online jargon, to post an electronic message to someone which is destructively critical, abusive, or intended to provoke dissent or controversy.

noun: An example of this.

The impersonal nature of electronic communications can weaken conformity to the social niceties: messages are blunter, abuse or criticism is quicker to appear and more intense in nature, and wild opinions are touted and defended with greater fervour. The first attested uses of *flame* in this sense date from the early eighties. However, the term only began to be known outside the electronic community in the early nineties, as a result of the growth of interest in the INTERNET. A person who *flames* someone is a **flamer,** the collective noun for such messages is **flamage** and the action noun is **flaming**. If argument and abuse become extensive, with many people joining in, a **flame war** is said to develop (also written **flamewar**). A deliberately provocative message, designed to induce someone to retaliate, is

flame bait (or **flamebait**). Necessarily, most *flaming* takes place in public forums (NEWSGROUPS), but sometimes personal electronic mail, or **flame mail**, is sent. A person posting a message may sandwich a section of it between the phrases **flame on** and **flame off** as an indication that it contains material that the reader may regard as controversial or provocative, or perhaps to head off criticism. Inflammatory messages addressed generally are more usually called *trolls*, and those who send them TROLLERS.

It always disappoints me to read some flame from a reader who is mostly demonstrating his lack of tact or inability to express an opinion without insulting anyone.

—*C Users Journal* Jan. 1993, p. 128

The American way of dealing with it is to begin the message with 'Flame on' or 'Flame off'—to show whether it really is an angry message, or whether it's intended as friendly, but could be taken as angry. —*Independent on Sunday* 16 Jan. 1994, p. 22

flatline /ˈflatlʌɪn/ *intransitive verb* Also written **flat-line** Ⓧ ᴾᴼᴾ

To die. Also, by extension, to become unproductive or ineffectual.

With reference to the *flattening*, when a patient dies, of the peaks on the *line* displayed on a heart monitor.

Earliest uses of the verb were recorded in a medical context in the very early eighties. Shortly afterwards, in 1984, it was taken up by the science-fiction writer William Gibson, who used it in his novel *Neuromancer*. However, it was in 1990, with the release of the film *Flatliners*, that the verb and its noun derivative **flatliner** entered the popular language. The film tells the story of a group of medical students who dangerously exploit their ability to control the heart rate by helping each other to *flatline* in order to experience the first few seconds after the moment of death, before being revived (the participants, the *flatliners*, were considerably chastened by the experience). Use in relation to actual death has not become widespread, but the verb in its extended use is growing in currency.

There is some evidence of transitive use of the verb in both senses. There is also evidence of the development of an adjective, especially in the phrase **go flatline**.

He flatlined on his EEG…'Boy, I was *daid.*' —William Gibson *Neuromancer* (1984), p. 50

The yuppies had kneaded [the script] and kneaded it until it became, as Grady Rabinowitz used to say, a piece of shit. It went flatline at Warners.

—Julia Phillips *You'll Never Eat Lunch in this Town Again* (1991), p. 542

The Ronzer had been flatlined for years. Overload on those antique circuits.

—*New Yorker* 9 Mar. 1992, p. 30

To flatline: to show EEG pattern indicating brain death after too long in cyberspace.

—*Independent* 19 May 1992, p. 12

Not that it was a bad magazine, but it was a fiscal flatliner—with one of Brown's early issues …carrying just 14 pages of ads. —*Spy* May 1992, p. 60

flesh-eating disease Ⓧ see NECROTIZING FASCIITIS

FLOPS ▣ see TERAFLOP

Floptical /ˈflɒptɪk(ə)l/ *adjective* Also written **floptical** ▣

The trade mark of a type of floppy disk in which the position of the heads is accurately controlled by a separate optical track, thereby permitting a much higher storage capacity.

A blend of *floppy*, computer jargon for 'a flexible removable magnetic disk for the storage of data' (which continues to be used, though the currently standard 3.5-inch disks are actually rigid) with *optical*, 'constructed to use the principles of optics'.

The *Floptical* disk was developed in the US in the late eighties as one way to increase the storage capacity of floppy disks. It stores its data by a conventional magnetic recording system, but the recording and playback heads are positioned accurately over the tracks by a separate optical sensor which reads a pattern which has been laid down on the disk at the time of manufacture. This permits tracks to be packed much more closely together than in a standard disk, and achieves a storage capacity of about 21 megabytes. The term **Floptical disk** is also used. Occasional use of *Floptical* as a noun is recorded.

> One solution is a marriage of optical and magnetic technologies known as the Floptical disc. It takes only one more manufacturing step to make a Floptical over a standard floppy, which keeps their price-per-megabyte similar.   —*Guardian* 17 June 1993, section 2, p. 17

> Loading these files in from floppy disks can be very time-consuming. Flopticals solved the problem and gave me the added advantage of being smaller and more rugged than other removable storage media.   —*CompuServe Magazine* Aug. 1994, p. 22

> Insite Peripherals made a valiant effort three years ago with its 21MB floptical drive that could read from and write to 1.4MB floppies, and the company pioneered laser-guided track positioning.   —*MacWorld* Oct. 1995, p. 36

fluoxetine ⊗ see PROZAC

flying bishop /flʌɪŋ 'bɪʃəp/ *noun* POP 🎗

An informal term for a bishop in the Anglican Church appointed to minister, within another's diocese, to those who do not accept the ordination of women.

A *bishop* who has an itinerant ministry to those in another bishop's diocese, rather as a *flying picket* would picket premises other than those at which he or she was employed.

The decision in 1993 of the General Synod of the Church of England to authorize the ordination of women did not end controversy over the issue as a whole. Particular concerns were associated with the position of those who were unable to accept the decision of the Synod, or who even regarded it as heretical. *Flying bishops* represent a compromise solution to the problem, whereby priests who feel unable to accept the views of their own bishop on female ordination can be ministered to by one with a more acceptable outlook.

> The compromise reached last week over 'low-flying bishops' gives most of the laity opposed to women priests everything they want.   —*Independent on Sunday* 16 Jan. 1993, p. 6

> Since his appointment as a 'flying bishop' was announced last month, Bishop Gaisford—a fierce opponent of women's ordination—has been deluged with letters.   —*Guardian* 12 Mar. 1994, p. 6

> The Church of England, in appointing 'flying' bishops, is giving its members the chance to deny the priesthood of women.   —*Times* 3 July 1996 (Nexis)

FOB /ɛfəʊˈbiː/ *noun* 📖 POP

A supporter of President William Jefferson ('Bill') Clinton.

An acronym for *Friend of Bill*.

FOB is recorded from 1992, the year in which Bill Clinton was elected President of the US, and implies particularly a personal friend and supporter from his days as Governor of Arkansas.

> Much has been made of the FOBs (Friends of Bill), that large web of contacts Clinton formed as he reached out from Arkansas by way of Georgetown, Oxford, Yale, and the Democratic Leadership Conference.   —*New York Review of Books* 22 Oct. 1992, p. 10

> By all accounts, FOB (Friend of Bill) Strobe Talbot will seize the lead in crafting Clinton's policy.   —*US News and World Report* 8 Feb. 1993, p. 14

> [A] lobbyist and FOB whose Hamptons political salon is in session when Congress isn't.   —*Newsweek* 31 July 1995, p. 42

See also CLINTONITE

foodie /ˈfuːdi/ *noun* ⬚ ▐▐

In colloquial use: a person whose hobby or main interest is food; a gourmet.

Formed by adding the suffix *-ie* (as in *groupie*) to *food*; one of a succession of such formations during the eighties for people who are fans of a particular thing or activity.

Although gourmets have been around for a long time, the term *foodie* is an invention of the early eighties. Its use was encouraged by the food and wine pages of the newspaper supplements and the growth of a magazine industry for which food is a central interest. The *foodie* is interested not just in eating good food, but in preparing it, reading about it, and talking about it as well. The fashion is sometimes referred to disparagingly as **foodie-ism**.

> Foodies are discovering ingredients like red Swiss chard, fresh dates and miniature golden pear-shaped tomatoes. —*Philadelphia Inquirer Magazine* 11 Oct. 1992, p. 38

> It would be very easy for a programme of this sort to lurch from one extreme to another and, as a counterweight to the hamburger culture, lure children into the equally objectionable world of foodie-ism. —*Daily Telegraph* 29 Aug. 1994, p. 15

footballene 🜊 see BUCKMINSTERFULLERENE

for-profit /fɔːˈprɒfɪt/ *adjective* 〰 ▐▐

Intended to make a profit, profit-making.

References to *for-profit* organizations can be traced back to the fifties, but since the beginning of the eighties the term has been increasingly applied in the areas associated with public services, as in **for-profit hospital** and **for-profit school**. In an era of privatization, the identification of an organization providing services as being *for-profit* or NOT-FOR-PROFIT is frequently made.

> The minister made a point of proclaiming her government's support of for-profit child care centres. —*This Magazine* Dec. 1993, p. 16

> The Colorado Springs organization is using a for-profit promoter. —*Fort Collins Triangle Review* (Colorado) 13 Jan. 1994, p. 16

Fourex ⬚ ᴾᴼᴾ see xxxx

Four-x ⬚ ᴾᴼᴾ see xxxx

foxcore 🐾 ᴾᴼᴾ see -CORE

fox-watch ᴾᴼᴾ see -WATCH

freeride /ˈfriːrʌɪd/ *verb and noun* ✪

intransitive verb: To ride on a snowboard designed for all-round use; to practise free snowboarding on and off piste without taking part in races or performing tricks.

noun: A type of snowboard for all-round use on and off piste.

In the nineties, **freeriders** and their chosen pursuit of **freeriding** testify to the growing popularity of SNOWBOARDING as one of the EXTREME *sports* of the decade.

> The board rode well in the soft flats. A great choice for the female free-rider. —*Skiing* Dec. 1990, p. 218

> The slightly longer and stiffer freeride model provides more edgeholding ability for carving turns. —*Playboy* Dec. 1992, p. 172

> You can…freeride those snow-covered hills in street-style oversized clothes that offer the freedom you need and keep you warm too. —*Fresno Bee* 1 Dec. 1994, section E, p. 1

> Freeriding is the heart and soul of snowboarding—and 'free' says it all. —*Arena* Dec. 1995, p. 184

Friday Wear ⚏ see DRESS-DOWN FRIDAY

from hell /frəm 'hɛl/ *adjectival phrase* Also written **from Hell** 🔲 🎸

In jocular use, meaning 'exceptionally unpleasant or bad; doing everything wrong'.

Since the late eighties this term, first used in the US, has spread rapidly to the UK. It is attached freely to a wide range of nouns denoting a particular group or kind of person or thing.

> The Au Pair from Hell...waits to be served dinner with the rest of the family unless asked to help dish up. —*FSAP (Foreign Student & Au Pair Magazine)* Oct. 1992, p. 27

> Nineties SF is eclectic and colourful; it ranges from plots set in the deepest recesses of the mind to futures where no humans exist apart from a group of anoraked and bespectacled science fiction fans from hell. —*GQ* Jan. 1995, p. 37

frozen embryo /'frəʊz(ə)n ˌɛmbrɪəʊ/ *noun* ⊗ ⚗

A fertilized human embryo which has been deep-frozen for storage.

In the eighties, it increasingly became the practice that couples seeking fertility treatment by means of implantation would agree that a number of 'spare' fertilized embryos should be kept for them in a deep-frozen state in case further implantation was required.

It was recognized at an early stage that the eventual fate of these *frozen embryos* might present moral and ethical problems, and this concern was realized when in 1996 it became apparent that a number of clinics which had agreed to hold *frozen embryos* for a stated number of years were no longer in touch with the registered owners or parents. A lively public debate as to the rights of the *frozen embryos* then ensued, with the view being expressed in some quarters that they were effectively **orphan embryos**, and should be made wards of court.

> The Constitution might well prohibit any state decision to discard a frozen embryo rather than to preserve it for future implantation. —L. H. Tribe *Abortion* (1990), p. 124

> A baby who had spent four years and two months as a frozen embryo was born this week in Chester to a surrogate mother. —*Guardian* 29 Mar. 1995, p. 9

FTP /ɛfti:'pi:/ *noun* and *verb* Also written **ftp** 🖥

noun: In computer jargon, a method of transferring files across certain kinds of network (in particular the INTERNET); less commonly, a computer application which supervises the process of obtaining files by this method.

transitive or *intransitive verb*: To transfer (a file) by FTP.

The initial letters of *File Transfer Protocol*, *protocol* being used here in the computing sense of 'a set of rules that govern the exchange of information between computer devices'.

FTP (invented in the early seventies) is one of the most important and oldest techniques of the Internet; the term has become widely known in the nineties as interest in the Internet has increased. It permits an authorized user on one computer system to connect to another, identify files on it, and DOWNLOAD them. The application handling the process takes care of splitting the file into blocks of data (*packets*) for transmission over the network, checking that they have been correctly received and reassembling them in the right order. The source of files accessible in this way is often called an **FTP site** or an **FTP archive**. Users seeking files can often connect to public sites without needing a password, in a process called **anonymous FTP**. The computer programs handling the transfer are frequently referred to as the **FTP server** at the transmitting end and the **FTP client** at the receiving end (see CLIENT-SERVER). A verbal noun **FTPing** and an adjective **FTPable** are occasionally used.

> The FTP daemon responds to a limited set of English-like commands that specify actions such as listing a directory, changing to another directory and receiving or transmitting a file. —advertising insert in *Byte* Nov. 1992

> If you log into a server with anonymous ftp, nobody charges you (by access time, packets down-

loaded, records passed, or some other scheme) for the data that you obtain.
—*Byte* Mar. 1994, p. 70

To get software which will encrypt and decrypt e-mail, ftp to ftp.demon.co.uk and look for the folder marked PGP. —*i-D* Oct. 1994, p. 20

fuck-me /ˈfʌkmiː/ *adjective* 🔀 ᴘᴏᴘ̃

In slang: intended to invite or held as inviting sexual interest; alluring, seductive. Especially in **fuck-me shoes**: sexually exciting or provocative shoes.

Formed by compounding: the verb *fuck* with the pronoun *me*.

First recorded evidence of the adjective dates from the mid eighties. Originally and chiefly used in the phrase *fuck-me shoes*, the adjective is still largely restricted to formulations within the vocabulary of shoes, such as **fuck-me boots** and **fuck-me heels**, often with reference to very high heels.

Evidence of the euphemistic equivalent *do-me* has been recorded in the mid nineties. The notion of *fuck-me shoes* or *do-me shoes* has also been used metaphorically, the shoes representing provocative sexuality.

I come bouncing down the front steps in this strapless number…and a brand new pair of rhinestone fuck-me shoes wobbling under me. —Jane Leavy *Squeeze Play* (1990), p. 228

When her interviewer shows up with a photographer, it's on…with the red fuck-me pumps.
—*Washington CityPaper* 24 Jan. 1992, p. 26

Have you ever looked at old men, the sort of old men who seduce young women? The roguish high-bummed stride, the fuck-me tan, the effulgent cuff-links, the reek of dry-cleaning.
—Julian Barnes *Talking it Over* (1992), p. 43

From what I can gather from reading several decades-worth of eulogising on Blahnik's expert shoemanship, owning a pair of his vertiginous, fuck-me heels is the closest thing to shoe heaven.
—*Guardian* 24 Sept. 1994, Weekend section, p. 45

Desirous of smearing her image as dutiful daughter, she stepped into Drew's do-me shoes with a vengeance. —*Guardian* 13 July 1996, Guide, p. 97

full-blown Aids ⊗ see Aɪᴅs

fullerene 🜹 see ʙᴜᴄᴋᴍɪɴsᴛᴇʀꜰᴜʟʟᴇʀᴇɴᴇ

the full monty ᴘᴏᴘ̃ see ᴍᴏɴᴛʏ

full pindown ⑈ see ᴘɪɴᴅᴏᴡɴ

full-video-on-demand ⛃ 🜹 see –ᴏɴ-ᴅᴇᴍᴀɴᴅ

fully abled ⑈ see ᴀʙʟᴇᴅ

functional food /ˈfʌŋkʃ(ə)n(ə)l fuːd/ *noun* ⊗ 🔀

A foodstuff which contains additives specifically designed to promote health and longevity. Sometimes abbreviated to **FF**.

A translation of Japanese *kinoseishokuhin*.

Functional foods were originally a Japanese idea and by 1990 had an eight per cent share of the Japanese food market. They reverse the negative connotations of food additives by fortifying foods with enzymes to aid digestion, anti-cholesterol agents, added fibre, and similar additions, and by marketing the foods as beneficial to health—much the same idea as the familiar breakfast cereals fortified with vitamins and iron, but taken a stage further. *Functional foods* took some time to be tested on Western markets, but are now receiving considerable attention and being strongly promoted commercially; since the early nineties, *functional foods* have often been referred to as ɴᴜᴛʀᴀᴄᴇᴜᴛɪᴄᴀʟs.

The notion of food as elixir, hand-me-down from antiquity, has reemerged bearing a new set of names; among them are nutraceuticals, designer foods and functional foods.

—*Scientific American* Sept. 1994, p. 86

Functional foods are sometimes wrongly referred to in the media as 'miracle foods', implying they are something of a panacea, negating the need for a healthy diet. —*Grocer* 23 Mar. 1996, p. 45

fundholder /ˈfʌndhəʊldə/ *noun* 〰 ⊗

In the UK: a general practitioner who is provided with and controls his or her own budget.

The health care reforms of the late eighties and early nineties saw the creation of *fundholders* as an integral part of the long-term plan for the health service. **Fundholding** practices, with responsibility for their own budgets, have become purchasers of health care from the newly established HOSPITAL TRUSTS; the perception was that the operation of market forces would be beneficial to both consumer and supplier. The success of the scheme is still a matter of debate; in May 1996, an evaluation by the AUDIT COMMISSION of **fundholding** questioned whether the improvements identified justified the overall administrative costs.

Hertfordshire now has so many fundholding GPs competing and bickering over contracts that cash-strapped hospitals are unable to cope with their excessive demands.

—*Private Eye* 4 June 1993, p. 10

The practice was one of the first 306 fundholders set up in 1991, electing to run a budget to buy non-urgent hospital and community health care for patients in place of the local health authority.

—*Guardian* 7 Apr. 1995, p. 3

In the first objective evaluation of fundholding, a linchpin of the NHS reforms, the Audit Commission says that most fundholders have made few changes. —*The Times* 22 May 1996, p. 11

fundie /ˈfʌndi/ *noun* Also written **fundy** 🌱 ⌂

In colloquial use: a fundamentalist; especially *either* a religious fundamentalist *or* a member of a radical branch of the green movement, a 'deep' green.

Formed by adding the suffix *-ie* to the first four letters of *fundamentalist*.

A nickname which belongs to the political debates of the early eighties, when the Moral Majority and other fundamentalist Christian groups in the US and the Greens in Germany became political forces to be reckoned with. In the green sense, *fundie* has its origins in the arguments from 1985 onwards between the German Greens' *realo* wing, who were prepared to take a normal cooperative approach to parliamentary life, and the more radical fundamentalists, who did not wish to cooperate with other parties and favoured extreme measures to solve environmental problems. With the decline in Green politics in the nineties, the word has lost some of its force in the environmental sense, but continues to be used to refer to religious fundamentalists.

The 'fundies' in the multi-national organisation [Greenpeace] object fiercely to Solo's size and fuel consumption and want a greener, wind-assisted alternative, while the 'realos' say they need something strong and fast enough to compete with naval ships.

—*Guardian* 30 July 1993, section 2, p. 18

I would describe my brothers as apatheists—heck, I'd describe all my family that way. None of them are the firebreathing fundie types. —23 Mar. 1995, online posting

• •

G

gabba /'gabə/ *noun* Also written **Gabba**, **gabber**, **Gabber**

A harsh, aggressive type of HOUSE music with a rapid beat.

A direct borrowing from the Dutch *gabber* 'mate, fellow, lad'.

Gabba is a form of HARDCORE dance music characterized by a particularly rapid beat and an aggressive machismo. Originating in Rotterdam, it crossed the North Sea in the early nineties and has become a part of the British music and club culture; it is especially popular in northern England. The noun is commonly used attributively, especially in the formulations **gabber house** and the one-word form **gabberhouse**.

> So hard it makes Napalm Death sound like the Carpenters, Gabberhouse is the reviled bastard child of the Digital Era...With a devout working-class audience of terrace boys, skinheads and shopgirls based in Rotterdam, Gabber is a Euro-noise phenomenon that remains deeply underground in the UK. —*Guardian* 11 Nov. 1994 Friday Review, p. 19

> In Amsterdam you'll get pretty much what you'd get in a house club in London; in Rotterdam, however, they prefer thrash-metal techno at over 190 beats per minutes (that's, er, like fast). It also has some of the best gabba around (gabba is music over 200 beats per min—that's even faster). —*Smash Hits* 29 Mar. 1995, p. 54

> As happy hardcore scales the charts and jungle gains widespread recognition, the northern rave scene continues to pledge undying allegiance to the impenetrable speedcore of Lowlands gabba. —*i-D* Aug. 1995, p. 85

gagging order /'gagɪŋ ɔːdə/ *noun*

In the UK: an official order forbidding public discussion of a specified subject, in print or by broadcasting.

The implementation of an official ban on public discussion of a given topic is far from new, and the balance between confidentiality in matters of national security and civil liberties has frequently provoked controversy. In the sixties, considerable attention was paid to the circumstances in which it was seen as appropriate that a *D-notice* should be issued; this, more fully a *Defence notice*, was a formal request from the Services, Press and Broadcasting Committee that news editors should observe a ban on the publication of specified subjects felt to have a bearing on national security.

The development of modern communication techniques has made it less easy for outright prohibitions of this kind to be sustained, but in the nineties public attention was once more drawn to the principles involved, and the colloquial term *gagging order* began to appear in the press. This was applied particularly to PUBLIC INTEREST IMMUNITY CERTIFICATES, but has also been used of an order where the principle involved is one of personal privacy rather than national security.

> Kenneth Clarke, then the home secretary, signed a 'public interest immunity certificate' (gagging order) refusing Henderson the necessary documents. —*Private Eye* 27 Jan. 1995, p. 26

gangsta /'gaŋstə/ *noun* and *adjective*

noun: A style of rap music, chiefly from the US West Coast, in which the lyrics are centred on the violence of gang culture; also, a performer of this music.

adjective: Of or belonging to gangsta music.

A development of an earlier sense denoting a member of a black American street gang. The form *gangsta* represents a phonetic respelling of *gangster*, a process, seen also in the development of the term NIGGA, which may be regarded as an affirmation of black culture through use of its dialect.

The term *gangsta* has been recorded in this sense since the late eighties. Frequently used in the phrase **gangsta rap**, the term denotes a tough-talking rap associated with West Coast performers such as Ice-T, Niggaz with Attitude, Ice Cube, Dr Dre (both formerly with Niggaz with Attitude), Tupac Shakur, and Snoop Doggy Dogg. *Gangsta* lyrics appear to celebrate violence, and some *gangsta* performers have become notorious for their possession and use of guns. *Gangsta* is also regarded as misogynous, a tendency revealed in its use of derogatory terms for women such as *bitch* and HO. A derivative noun **gangstaism**, or **gangsta-ism**, has been recorded since the early nineties, suggesting the development of an ethos identified with the musical style.

> After L.A. exploded, though, there was no denying that the brutal rhymes of West Coast gangsta rap weren't just macho posturing; they expressed the hard truths of real life for a segment of society heretofore invisible on the network news. —*Rolling Stone* 10 Dec. 1992, p. 79

> Ms Tucker has launched a campaign to boycott record shops that sell the work of gangsta rap artists whose lyrics glorify violence and denigrate women. —*Guardian* 8 Jan. 1994, p. 10

> Gangsta rap music has been increasingly condemned by politicians and the media conglomerate Time Warner has been accused of failing in its public duty by continuing to market the lyrics of violence and sexual violation. —*Daily Telegraph* 8 June 1995, p. 10

gap year /ˈgap jɪə/ *noun* ⟨⟨

A period of one academic year taken as a break from formal education by a student between leaving school and taking up a place at college or university.

The idea of a year's break (or *year out*) from formal education, which would provide a student with experience of life and interpersonal skills to complement academic achievement, was one which gained ground in the eighties. Organizations were set up to provide applicants with access to appropriate voluntary and charitable work abroad, often in developing countries, and by the early nineties advertisements were appearing for courses which could be taken in the *gap year*: academic studies from a branch of learning other than the student's chosen subject were also seen as valuable in contributing to all-round achievement. It is notable that the popularity of the *gap year* developed against a background of increasing pressure for graduates in the job market: the concept is seen as bringing together the older values of voluntary service with the more modern perception of the importance of demonstrating administrative as well as academic attainments to prospective employers.

> Two-term courses attracted students taking a gap year. —*Independent* 6 Apr. 1995, p. 19

garage /ˈgɑrɑːʒ/ *noun* Also written **Garage** 🐾 POP

A variety of HOUSE music from New York which incorporates elements of soul music, especially in its vocals.

Probably named after the *Paradise Garage*, the former nightclub in New York where this style of music was first played; there may also be some influence from the term *garage band*, which has been applied since the late sixties to groups (originally amateurs who practised in empty garages and other disused buildings) with a loud, energetic, and unpolished sound which is also sometimes known as *garage* or *garage punk*.

New York *garage* developed in the early eighties (principally at the Paradise Garage but later also at other New York clubs), but was not given the name *garage* in print until 1987. The founding influence on the style was the New York group *The Peech Boys*. In its later manifestations *garage* is very closely related to *deep house* (see HOUSE)—indeed some consider *deep house* to be simply the Chicago version of *garage*, incorporating the lyrical and vocal traditions of American soul into the fast, synthesized dance music which is typical of house. The adjective **garagey** is sometimes used to describe the music.

> The void left in trendier clubs following the over-commercialisation and subsequent ridiculing of

'acieed!'…is being filled by 'garage' and 'deep house'.   *—Music Week* 10 Dec. 1988, p. 14

The music is less frenzied than rave music. DJs play a broader range of music, including garage and rare grooves.   *—Independent* 11 April 1992, p. 4

I don't like your normal garagey things at all—they're too slow for me. I like something that's going to make you listen.   *—The Face* January 1995, p. 130

gastric leakage ⊗ ✕ see OLESTRA

gay gene /'geɪ dʒiːn/ *noun* ⊗ ◬

In slang: a sequence or sequences of DNA which, when present in the human X-chromosome, may predispose towards homosexuality.

The question of whether homosexual inclination can be genetically determined is disputed. In 1993, it was rumoured that scientists had found a *gay gene*, and although the announcement itself proved to be premature, the attendant publicity highlighted some of the moral and ethical questions attendant on the research itself, and on any positive outcome of it. In the light of current scientific developments, anxieties were felt and expressed as to the possible role of GENETIC ENGINEERING in relation to any identified *gay gene*. It is apparent that any further results announced by **gay geneticists** will be keenly scrutinized.

Gleeful reactionary bigots, welcoming the discovery of the so-called gay gene, beware.
    —Guardian 7 Aug. 1993, Weekend section, p. 3

Recently, two American psychologists reported evidence for the existence of 'gay genes'.
    —New Scientist Supplement 28 Nov. 1995, p. 6

geek /giːk/ *noun* POP

An unfashionable, boring, or socially inept person.

A particular use of an existing word in the sense 'simpleton' or 'dupe' (in the earlier part of the century a *geek* was an assistant at a sideshow whose purpose was to appear as an object of disgust or derision); *geek* originates as a variant of the English dialect *geck* 'fool', of Germanic origin, and is related to the Dutch words *gek* 'mad, silly', and *gekken* 'to joke'.

Geek, like ANORAK and TRAINSPOTTER, represents a current term of disapprobation for a person regarded as unfashionable, boring, and socially inadequate. A *geek* is also seen as a person likely to have an obsessional interest in a specified hobby: a **movie geek** is absorbed in the minutiae of films, while a **computer geek** shares the TECHIE's interest in and knowledge of modern technology. *Geek* has developed a number of derivatives, with the adjectives **geekish** and **geeky**, the noun **geekiness**, and the adverb **geekishly** all being recorded.

I got a few books that described weird stuff, and I spent the rest of my youth trying to build robots. All my friends thought I was a total geek.   *—Discover* Mar. 1991, p. 47

What I can't stomach, I guess, is the geekiness of so much art-world language which vomits out half-chewed-up bits of theory, blissfully unaware of the context of that theory.
    —Guardian 22 Jan. 1994, p. 27

With his thick specs, shabby Clark's shoes (the laces often undone) and grey suit, he looks a bit of an anorak, a school swot, a computer geek who has somehow strayed into the corridors of power.   *—Independent on Sunday* 27 Nov. 1994, p. 8

I had health benefits and great pay, which went a long way toward making up for the geeky uniform and steel-toed loafers. (There is no such thing as a stylish safety shoe.)
    —Our Times July 1995, p. 43

Generation X /dʒɛnəˌreɪʃ(ə)n ˈɛks/ *noun* POP ◖

A generation of young people perceived to lack a sense of direction in life and to have no part to play in society.

The term may be traced to a novel by Charles Hamblett and Jane Deverson entitled *Generation X*, published in 1964, a science fiction work set in the final decades of the twentieth century.

The term *Generation X* first entered the popular language in the very late eighties and early nineties, in reference to the generation of young adults just coming of age in the closing decade of the millennium, and gained rapidly in currency after the publication in 1991 of Douglas Coupland's *Generation X: tales for an accelerated culture*. **Generation Xers** are sometimes seen as a lost generation, becoming adults at the end of a century that, in the West, has lurched from two world wars into a period of sustained growth and finally into a period of recession. At a time of high unemployment for the young, of accessible entertainment and the readily available escape routes of drugs and alcohol, the *Generation Xers*, like their peers the SLACKERS, are regarded as lacking motivation and shirking responsibility. They have also been called the *baby busters*, in contrast to the *baby boomers*, the group to which their parents are likely to belong, and the *twentysomethings* or the younger *twenty-nothings*. Familiarity with the term *Generation Xer* has led to the use, since the early nineties, of the abbreviation **Xer**. In the mid nineties there have been references to **Generation Y**, the teenagers of the nineties.

Xers like their infotainment. The average Xer logs 23,000 hours in front of the TV before reaching the age of 20. They learned all they need to know about politics from Oliver Stone's *JFK*.
—*Playboy* Dec. 1992, p. 109

Faced with dwindling employment opportunities, the collapse of student aid, a scarcity of affordable housing, the threat of AIDS, draft registration, the omnipresence of media opulence and limited access to mental health care, Generation X has responded by creating an underground slacker culture of pathetic art, rock, comics, fiction, film and fashion that's already begun to affect the mainstream beyond the confines of the music scene.
—*San Francisco Sunday Examiner and Chronicle* 10 Jan. 1993, section D, p. 2

Maybe it's the pandemic shrug of Generation X, the futility felt by the young when analyzed to death by self-styled experts, carpet-bombed by music videos and wired to 157 channels with nothing on. —*Rolling Stone* 19 May 1994, p. 52

A report published today by the independent think tank, Demos, shows that far from being inert slackers, higher-educated Generation X-ers are defining a new work ethic, based on balance and fulfilment, strikingly different from the Protestant work ethic.
—*Guardian* 30 Nov. 1994, section 1, p. 26

genetic engineering /dʒɪˌnɛtɪk ɛndʒɪˈnɪərɪŋ/ *noun* ⊗ 🔬

The deliberate modification of a living thing by changing its genetic structure.

The phrase *genetic engineering* dates from 1969; the process's first products, monoclonal antibodies, were created in 1975. The infant BIOTECH field was given an immense boost in 1980 when the US Supreme Court ruled that engineered living organisms were patentable. By the mid nineties an immense range of products had been developed, from micro-organisms that fabricate human insulin, through flavour-enhanced tomatoes and frost-resistant potatoes, to microbes that eat sewage, and sheep that produce human proteins in their milk. The field has attracted enormous and continuing controversy ever since US scientists proposed a moratorium on genetic research in 1975. Concern focuses both on the ethics of creating new plants and animals (some fashioned to develop diseases for study) and also on the environmental implications of releasing **genetically-engineered** organisms into the wild, where they might mutate or behave differently from the way they do in the laboratory. Even more controversial are proposals to modify human genes to remove susceptibility to certain inherited diseases. A specialist working in the field is a **genetic engineer**.

The decision to grant a patent for the 'Harvard mouse', an animal genetically engineered to develop cancer, was contrary to morality and should be revoked, a coalition of animal welfare groups said Tuesday. —*Chicago Tribune* 4 Jan. 1993, section A, p. 4

Developments in genetic engineering inevitably attract public suspicion and regulation reflects that. —*Guardian* 18 Oct. 1993, section 1, p. 12

If the emerging genetic engineering industry has its way, in the years ahead the world will see massive releases of genetically modified organisms (GMOs) into the environment. These will range from the largest to the smallest organisms: from trees…to viruses that are used among much else as biopesticides. —*New Scientist* 25 June 1994, p. 47

See also PHARM

genetic fingerprinting /dʒɪˌnɛtɪk 'fɪŋɡəprɪntɪŋ/ *noun* ⚗ 🔬

The analysis of genetic information from a blood sample or other small piece of cellular material as an aid to identification.

Genetic fingerprinting as a forensic technique was developed in the UK in 1984; it was discovered that the number and pattern of certain repeated sequences in human DNA appeared to be unique to each individual. It was immediately recognized that the technique (also known as *DNA fingerprinting, DNA profiling,* or *genetic profiling*) provided a powerful new way to identify offenders from samples of blood, semen, skin, or other material that contained body cells and hence DNA. The technique was soon adopted in British courts to secure convictions; the first murder case to be decided on the basis of *genetic fingerprinting* evidence was heard in Bristol in 1987. However, response in the US was more guarded and in some cases courts rejected DNA evidence because of apparent contamination of samples or poor methodology. The assumption that each pattern of repeated sequences (the **genetic fingerprint** or **genetic profile**) was unique turned out not always to be true. *Genetic fingerprinting* can also be used to establish whether two individuals are related; zoos use the technique to confirm that pairs of animals are unrelated in order to maintain genetic diversity in their offspring. The forensic community prefers to use *DNA profiling* and its variants, as being more accurate (the profiles are of DNA sequences, not genes).

> Forensic scientists can also use genetic traits found in blood and other tissues to identify bodies. Sometimes known as genetic fingerprints, these include about 70 inherited enzymes that can be used in a form of extraordinarily detailed blood typing.
> —*New York Times* 8 July 1985, section A, p. 3

> Life and health insurance companies and employers will inevitably demand access to each person's genetic profile, much as they now claim the right to medical records.
> —*Boston Globe* 12 Nov. 1990, p. 34

> Always call the police—and do it within 24 hours. This ensures that samples of the attacker's semen, skin and hair will be found fresh. They can be analysed and the man can be identified by genetic fingerprinting. —*Sun* 16 Sept. 1992, Woman supplement, p. 3

gesture politics /'dʒɛstʃə ˌpɒlɪtɪks/ *noun* 🏛 POP

Political action which concentrates primarily on publicity value and influencing public opinion.

The connotations of *gesture* as implying lack of any real effect are well established, as in this quotation from the early twenties:

> So far as the movement against Prohibition is concerned, the victory of Mr Edwards…is only a gesture.

The era of SOUND-BITES and spin doctors, however, has heightened public suspicions that what seems to be a decisive action may be no more than the appearance of this; the term *gesture politics* has been used from the late eighties to describe the phenomenon.

> There is no room for gesture politics. If we want to open debate about our future and our constitution, that is fine. —*Daily Mail* 2 Jan. 1995, p. 5

> I am not into gesture politics. But I resent the way this is being introduced, with such haste, before the Tory party conference. —*The Times* 25 Sept. 1995, p. 4

get a life /ɡɛt ə 'lʌɪf/ *verbal phrase* POP

In slang (often as imperative): start living a fuller or more interesting existence.

Get a life has been popular since the early nineties as a scornful admonition which at once sums up a view of a person's existence as unacceptably empty or dull, and recommends a change of lifestyle.

> The aristocracy is having to make some hard decisions: whether to pretend that the twentieth century never happened or to jump ship, join the middle class and get a life.
>
> —*Tatler* July 1993, p. 82

> If I'm using e-mail because I can't handle the stress of being in close proximity to other people, then I'm sad and should probably get a life.　　—*Guardian* 24 Nov. 1994, OnLine section, p. 4

> 'Get a life' messages periodically appear—usually in impolite terms—advising *Star Trek* enthusiasts that they could be spending their time better elsewhere.　　—*Internet World* Feb. 1995, p. 80

ghostbuster /ˈgəʊstbʌstə/ *noun* POP

In slang: a person who professes to banish ghosts, poltergeists, and other spirits.

There is probably a conscious echo of the earlier and alliterative *gangbuster*.

The term *ghostbuster* was first recorded in 1920, but the current popularity derives from the 1984 film *Ghostbusters* which presented to the public a group of three specialists combatting a paranormal outbreak which menaced Manhattan; the supernatural element conveyed by the word *ghost* in fact represented not so much the disembodied spirit of a dead person, as in a traditional ghost story, as the kind of destructive supernatural entity represented by a poltergeist. The *ghostbusters* of the story relied on technological devices as well as their own powers to deal with the dangerous forces which manifested as destructive slime.

The film (and its sequel *Ghostbusters II*) proved a great popular success, especially among young people; **ghostbusting** is now an established term for investigation into the paranormal, and **ghostbusting** as an adjective is also recorded.

More recently, the term has developed a transferred use: a *ghostbuster* may be someone such as an Inland Revenue official, investigating people regarded as *ghosts* because they are disembodied in the sense that they do not appear in the Inland Revenue's records.

> Randi is a practising magician, but is probably now better known as a 'ghostbuster', investigating claims of the paranormal.　　—*New Scientist* 13 July 1991, p. 17

> Revenue 'ghostbusters' scour the country seeking 'ghosts' and 'moonlighters'—individuals who have never reported their earnings, or who have second, undeclared, jobs.
>
> —*Guardian* 8 Oct. 1994, p. 35

> There's nothing like a nice crunchy platter of tarantulas after a long day of ghostbusting.
>
> —*Today's Parent* Oct. 1994, p. 96

> What is important about Strange But True is the way that it brings the hoariest ghostbusting tales together with the wilder fringes of the 'alternative health' movement.
>
> —*Guardian* 4 Jan. 1995, section 2, p. 12

GIFT /gɪft/ *acronym* ⊗ 🧪

Short for **gamete intra-fallopian transfer**, a technique for helping infertile couples to conceive, in which eggs and sperm from the couple are inserted into one of the woman's Fallopian tubes ready for fertilization.

The initial letters of *Gamete Intra-Fallopian Transfer*; a *gamete* is a mature cell able to unite with another in reproduction. Like many acronyms of the eighties and nineties, this one seems to be chosen for the significance of the resulting 'word': the technique presents the infertile couple with the much-wanted *gift* of a child.

The technique was developed in the US during the early eighties as a more 'natural' alternative to *in vitro* fertilization. Since, using this technique, it is possible for fertilization to occur within the human body, *GIFT* has proved more acceptable on moral and religious grounds than IVF, the technique which produces 'test-tube babies'.

> Colin Campbell, the chairman of the new Human Fertilisation and Embryology Authority (HFEA), acknowledges that by failing to license GIFT units the authority will be unable to ensure that clinicians transfer no more than three eggs.　　—*New Scientist* 30 Mar. 1991, p. 7

We offer all of the assisted reproductive technologies, including in vitro fertilization, Gamete Intrafallopian Transfer (GIFT), Zygote Intrafallopian Transfer (ZIFT), embryo cryopreservation, sperm banking and egg donation at...Hermann Hospital.   —Mar. 1995, online posting

See also ZIFT

glamour dyke ʀᴏ̃ᴘ ❨❨ see LIPSTICK LESBIAN

glass ceiling /glɑːs 'siːlɪŋ/ noun ⚡ ʀᴏ̃ᴘ ❨❨

An unofficial or unacknowledged barrier to personal advancement, especially in the workplace.

A *ceiling* as something which constitutes a barrier to ascent, but which cannot be seen because it is made of *glass*.

The introduction in the sixties and seventies of equal opportunities legislation and employment practice increasingly made illegal or impracticable institutionalized forms of inequality of opportunity. The perception was that these changes would open the way to advancement for previously disadvantaged groups.

By the early eighties, however, it was clear that there were still barriers to progress, particularly for women or members of ethnic minority groups. The term *glass ceiling* was coined as a name for an invisible but impenetrable barrier, believed to enshrine the traditional prejudices which could not now be openly admitted. It may be noted that as the concept became more familiar, the figurative associations were developed: a *glass ceiling* was taken as something which could be broken.

More recently, there are signs that the usage is being extended. Any person in employment regarded as unlikely to be promoted further may be spoken of as having 'hit the *glass ceiling*', and the term may also be used more generally for a block to a natural upward progression outside the job market.

Sadly, astronomers from all countries report a 'glass ceiling'. The proportion of women is highest for the lower grades.   —*New Scientist* 8 Oct. 1988, p. 62

Once on the corporate ladder, minorities have another challenge—making it to the top or shattering the so-called 'glass ceiling'.   —*Hispanic* Nov. 1991, p. 6

For most top amateurs there is a glass ceiling on the professional circuit, and it does not take them long to hit it.   —*Economist* 7 Jan. 1995, p. 5

After several spirited assaults, the FT-SE's 3200 glass ceiling finally gave way yesterday, allowing the index to close sharply higher after a day of drifting.   —*Daily Telegraph* 25 Aug. 1995, p. 25

glycobiology /ˈglʌɪkə(ʊ)bʌɪˌɒlədʒi/ noun 🧪

The branch of science which studies the role of complex sugars and carbohydrates in living organisms.

A compound of the prefix *glyco-*, meaning 'sugar', with *biology*, 'the study of living organisms'.

Glycobiology is a new and still emerging science whose name was first used only in the late eighties, though the study of sugars and their complex related compounds, the carbohydrates, is as old as organic chemistry; the sugars and starches are among the most important sources of energy for living things. The new interest in these compounds has come about through a growing recognition of the role they play in normal cell functions in the body and also in disease: they are involved in the immune system, the growth of tumours, hormone reactions, and fertilization, among others. Researchers are looking into a wide range of treatments based on this new knowledge, including antibodies for tumour detection, ways to reduce the effect of rheumatoid arthritis, and treatments for HIV. Outside biology, carbohydrate reactions are important in such diverse fields as soft-drink manufacture and papermaking and here the field is known either as **glycoscience** or as **carbohydrate chemistry**. Derivatives formed on *glycobiology*, **glycobiological** and **glycobiologist**, have also been recorded.

Oxford Glycosystems has opened up the potential of glycobiology by developing equipment and techniques for analysing quickly the complex structures of sugars.

—Independent on Sunday 10 July 1994, Business section, p. 4

Although the number of scientists studying glycobiology is still small, interest in carbohydrate analysis is on the rise. *—Genetic Engineering News* 15 Nov. 1995 (electronic edition)

goalposts POP see MOVE THE GOALPOSTS

gobsmacked /'gɒbsmakt/ *adjective* Also written **gob-smacked** ⚏

In British slang: astounded, flabbergasted; speechless or incoherent with amazement; overawed.

From *gob* (slang for the mouth) and *smacked*; the image is that of clapping a hand over the mouth, a stock theatrical gesture of surprise also widely used in cartoon strips.

Although it had been in spoken use for several decades, *gobsmacked* is not recorded in print until the mid eighties. It was then the slang of the football terraces and the yob culture; why it suddenly started to be much more widely used, nobody knows. Surprisingly it was the 'quality' newspapers which took it up—perhaps to show their familiarity with current slang—although it also appeared in the tabloids. It was used particularly memorably in 1991 by Chris Patten, then Chairman of the Conservative Party. Two adjectival synonyms, **gobstruck** and **gobsmacking**, have been formed, as well as an adverb **gobsmackingly**. A verb **gobsmack** was back-formed from the adjective in the late eighties.

The movie—which took a gobsmacking seven years to make…won bundles of Oscars in 1988.

—Fast Forward 15 Nov. 1989, p. 25

The chairman of the Conservative Party admitted on Radio Four's Today programme that he was 'gobsmacked' by Labour's claim that its poll-tax replacement would save the average household £140. *—Independent on Sunday* 19 May 1991, p. 23

The jagged preoccupation with the Trompeta Real and the morbid spotlight on Simeon's gobstruck state might make their point once, but I can't live with them. *—Classic CD* 25 May 1992, p. 66

golden goal /ˈɡəʊld(ə)n ˈɡəʊl/ *noun* ⚽

The first goal scored during extra time, which ends the match and gives victory to the scoring side.

A 'sudden death' system, avoiding the penalty shoot-out, which originated with soccer in the first half of the nineties and has now been extended to hockey.

FIFA have experimented in youth tournaments with sudden-death extra time, where the first team to score within the additional 30 minutes win…The golden goal method has not proved entirely satisfactory, with statistics showing that most games go to the full half-hour goalless, probably because teams are even more frightened than usual about making a decisive error.

—Daily Telegraph 19 July 1994

Ali Raza, Pakistan's full back, made hockey history in the final…when he scored hockey's first golden goal nine minutes into extra time. *—Independent* 19 Aug. 1996

gold standard /ˈɡəʊld standəd/ *noun* ⚏

The example which sets the standard to which other parts of a system must conform.

A figurative use of *gold standard* 'a system by which the value of a currency is defined in terms of gold, for which the currency may be exchanged'.

The use of *gold standard* as a term for something representing an agreed standard of excellence against which other members of a category are measured is recorded from the late eighties. It was initially found particularly in scientific and medical contexts, but is now developing a wider currency; in the nineties, it has frequently been employed in the debate as to whether British public examinations have retained their academic rigour, and whether A-levels can still be held to represent an educational *gold standard*.

Cerebral angiography is the 'gold standard' in the diagnosis of sinus venous thrombosis.
—*Lancet* 13 May 1989, p. 1086

Supporters of the A-level 'gold standard' will find the report reassuring.
—*Times Educational Supplement* 22 Feb. 1991, p. 20

The gold standard for 'online-quality' nonlinear video editing systems is 60-field capture capability.
—*New Media* Aug. 1994, p. 85

gomer /ˈgəʊmə/ *noun* Ⓧ ᴘᴏᴘ

In medical slang: a patient regarded as unlikely through age and ill-health to respond to treatment, who is thus seen as unrewarding of effort.

Formed from the initial letters of the adjuration *get out of my emergency room.*

Gomer is recorded in accounts of US medical slang from the early seventies, and by the nineties had crossed the Atlantic. It remains to be seen whether the term will move from the unofficial jargon of hospital staff into the wider public vocabulary, but it has some relevance to the current debate on the effect of market forces on patient care, as highlighted by the establishment of ʜᴏsᴘɪᴛᴀʟ ᴛʀᴜsᴛs and ꜰᴜɴᴅʜᴏʟᴅɪɴɢ general practitioners.

'Gomer' is shorthand for a patient, typically male, whose senility, chronic illness or lack of compliance promises to make his care troublesome and unrewarding. —*California* Apr. 1990, p. 26

Other perennials in the junior doctor's lexicon, I later discover, are 'turfing'—to transfer responsibility for a patient to another firm, and 'gomer' (get out of my emergency room)—a difficult patient. —*Guardian* 11 June 1990, Weekend section, p. 9

goodfella /ˈgʊdfɛlə/ *noun* ᴘᴏᴘ 🍸

A member of the Mafia, a mobster.

From the title of *Goodfellas* (1990), a film by Martin Scorsese about the world of the American Mafia; a reliable member of the Mafia is seen as a *good fellow* by his companions.

Modern cinema interest in the world of the Mafia may be said to have had its genesis in *The Godfather* (1972) and its two sequels, made by the American film director Francis Ford Coppola; more recently, Martin Scorsese has turned his attention to the same field. His first film on the topic, released in 1990, centred not so much on the fortunes of the rulers of a Mafia 'family' as on the ordinary members or *goodfellas*. The jargon of their violent world has been referred to as **Goodfella-ese**.

Like the goodfellas who become gangsters so they don't have to stand in line to buy bread, Scorsese can get his hands on any film he has a passion for.
—*Village Voice* (New York) 18 Sept. 1990, p. 39

'Collecting juice', in Goodfella-ese, means collecting interest from loan-shark clients.
—*Vanity Fair* Apr. 1993, p. 128

good mother lizard 🦎 see ᴍᴀɪᴀsᴀᴜʀ

gopher /ˈgəʊfə/ *noun* 💻

A system for searching for information on the ɪɴᴛᴇʀɴᴇᴛ.

The name, like so many to do with computing and the Internet, is a pun: the user can tell the system to *go for* the information needed; the *gopher* (the North American hole-digging rodent) was seen as a suitable symbol for a system that 'burrows' through the Internet; and the *gopher* is the mascot of the University of Minnesota, where the system was developed in early 1991.

The Internet contains huge repositories of information, but it is also anarchic and badly organized, so users have the perennial problem of finding what they are looking for. The *gopher* system is one solution. It consists of two parts: a central server which contains indexes to information, and a client application which users run on their own computers (see also ᴄʟɪᴇɴᴛ-sᴇʀᴠᴇʀ). When they connect to the *gopher* server they are presented with a series of

MENUS with categories of information; selecting one leads down through lists of subsidiary options until the information itself is reached or the search fails. There are now thousands of *gopher* servers throughout the world, mostly specializing in some field of knowledge or geographical area; the collective name for all the servers and the information they contain is **gopherspace** (on the model of *cyberspace*: see CYBER-).

> With so many Gopher servers around, many of which are arranged on a voluntary basis, gopherspace is suffering from its success. Navigating gopherspace can be difficult, and the quality of the information retrieved may be dubious. —*Guardian* 30 June 1994, p. 5

> Another resource is Griefnet, a gopher with lists of groups that help one deal with bereavement, suicidal thoughts, serious illness, etc. —*Everybody's Internet Update* 1994, online newsletter

See also VERONICA

goth /gɒθ/ *noun*

A style of rock music characterized by an intense or droning blend of guitar, bass, and drums, often with mystical or apocalyptic lyrics. Also, a performer or follower of this music or the subculture which surrounds it.

A back-formation from the adjective *Gothic*; the style of dress and some elements of the lyrics evoke the style of Gothic fantasy.

Goth grew out of punk in the late seventies, with bands like Siouxsie and the Banshees making the transition; by the mid eighties it had attracted many to its subculture, and by the late eighties it had spread from Britain to continental Europe and the US. As a fashionable genre *goth* had waned by the mid nineties, though interest in it continues; the look has an elaborate and very noticeable dress code, including black leather, crushed velvet, and heavy silver jewellery, combined with white-painted faces and heavy black eyeliner. The genre is also known as **goth rock** or, formerly, **goth punk**, while the cultural milieu is sometimes referred to as **Gothdom**.

> Goth Rock, populated by flaming creatures ashimmer with eye makeup, attitude, and omnisexuality. —*Locus* June 1992, p. 15

> To the new Goths Gothdom is about wearing the blackest black, with a lot of silver jewellery and looking as thin and pale as possible. —30 Aug. 1993, online posting

> 'The idea was to dress in velvet and silk—to be a dark glamorous puss; a Lord of the Night,' says Martin Meister, an Austrian living in London, who has provided the V&A with a goth outfit. —*Independent on Sunday* 21 Aug. 1994, Fashion supplement, p. 32

granny dumping /'grani ˌdʌmpɪŋ/ *noun*

The deliberate abandonment or 'dumping' at an unfamiliar location of an elderly person by those responsible for him or her.

In the early nineties a worrying trend was observed in the US: a number of elderly and confused patients, apparently brought to hospital emergency rooms for immediate treatment, were then abandoned there by those responsible for them. The evidence is still largely anecdotal, and it is too soon to say whether the practice is on the increase, but considerable concern has been expressed in the knowledge that the current social and economic pressures on families and carers can only become more acute as the population ages.

> Hospital staffers call it 'granny dumping': elderly people abandoned in emergency rooms, under the pretext of illness, usually by relatives who are too poor, too tired or too stressed out to continue providing care. —*Newsweek* 23 Dec. 1991, p. 64

> Government policy on community care of the elderly could see the arrival of 'granny dumping', which has occurred in the US, the conference was told. —*Independent* 6 Jan. 1992, p. 7

grant-maintained schools see OPT OUT²

graze /greɪz/ *intransitive verb* ⚒ ◖◗

To flick rapidly between television channels, to zap or *channel-surf* (see SURF).

A figurative use of the verb *graze* 'to feed'.

In the late seventies, *graze* began to be used in the US to refer to the practice of eating lots of snacks throughout the day in preference to full meals at regular times; the word was also applied to eating unpurchased food while shopping (or working) in a supermarket. In the mid eighties the word was applied to browsing or **grazing** among television channels (more fully **channel grazing**). Two factors were particularly significant: the growth of cable television in the US, with the proliferation of channels for **grazers** to graze among, and the popularity of remote control devices (or *zappers*). In the nineties, *graze* has also come to mean browsing information from CD-ROMs (see CD) or the INTERNET (though SURF is the more common term here).

> It's thousands of bits from TV shows within one TV show—a grazer's paradise.
> —*USA Today* 27 Feb. 1989, section D, p. 3

> We used to watch television as a family…When we grazed up and down channels together, we used to stumble over the unexpected. —advertisement in *Toronto Life* June 1994, p. 3

grebo /ˈgriːbəʊ/ *noun* 🎸 ᴘᴏᴘ

A British urban youth cult favouring heavy metal and punk rock music, and long hair. Also, a member of such a cult.

Perhaps formed from a blend of the noun *greaser* in the sense, 'a member of a gang of youths with long hair and riding motorcycles', and *-bo* on the model of *dumbo*.

Grebo is recorded from the late eighties as a term which brings together musical tastes bridging punk or rock, and a social approach combining an apparently aggressive or antisocial manner with long hair and clothes regarded as reminiscent of an earlier 'biker' generation.

> A new cult known as 'grebo'…is a movement of transcending witlessness whose generally youthful protagonists…have appropriated both…punk's anti-social slobbishness and the grimy, anti-chic dress-sense of the hippy biker. —*The Times* 13 Oct. 1987, p. 19

> There can hardly be a town in the country whose civic centrepoint has not, at some time, been graced by a group of spotty grebos admiring each other's chrome and planting the odd flob on the asphalt. —*Guardian* 17 Aug. 1991, p. 22

> 'All That I Ask of Myself…' is a lean, streamlined thrash thing which has more to do with straightedge than it does with grebo. —*Melody Maker* 25 Mar. 1995, p. 34

green shoots /griːn ˈʃuːts/ *noun* 〰 🏠

Signs of growth or renewal, especially of economic recovery.

A figurative use of the established phrase, with the *green shoots* representing new growth on a plant.

This figurative usage is recorded from the mid eighties, but came particularly to public attention in Britain in 1991, when the Chancellor Norman Lamont, speaking at the Conservative Party Conference, said:

> The green shoots of economic spring are appearing once again.

This optimistic view of the coming economic upturn (often misquoted as 'the *green shoots* of recovery') was not universally felt to be supported by events, and *green shoots* has increasingly been used ironically, and is currently (like CLEAR BLUE WATER) regarded as a political cliché.

> Every week in the last four months of 1991 was marked by predictions from one minister or another that the recession was about to end. The 'green shoots' of recovery were now showing.
> —*New Republic* 13 Apr. 1992, p. 19

> Tax increases may be necessary but they carry the risk of jeopardising those fragile green shoots. —*Computer Contractor* 29 Sept. 1993, p. 7

> I'm absolutely brassed off with all this talk of green shoots and clear blue water.
> —*Independent* 6 May 1995, p. 1

grey economy /greɪ ɪ'kɒnəmi/ *noun* Written **gray economy** in the US ⚒

That part of a country's economy relating to commercial activity that is unaccounted for in official statistics.

The term *grey economy* appeared in 1983; the term *grey market*, from which it derives, can be traced back to post-war America, where it described the unscrupulous selling of scarce or rationed goods at inflated prices (a lesser *black market*). As the phrase *grey economy* became established its meaning was extended to cover any unorthodox or unofficial trading which is conducted in the wide grey area between official indicators of economic growth and the black market. In specific applications the term has been used with reference to any unwaged but significant activity (such as housework); to the earnings of those who 'moonlight' by taking a second job, often under an assumed name; and to the practice among small independent retailers in the UK of importing a product direct from its manufacturer or a foreign supplier in order to retail it at a price lower than that of its official distributor.

> They call it the 'grey economy', a halfway house between the dole and the shady world of breadline work…She knows plenty of people in the grey economy who will be unimpressed with the latest scheme. —*Guardian* 14 Oct. 1994, section 1, p. 3

GRID ⊗ see AIDS

gridlock /'grɪdlɒk/ *noun* 🔒 ᴾᴼᴾ

A situation in which no progress can be made, a state of deadlock.

A figurative use of the term in its primary US sense 'a traffic jam affecting a whole network (or *grid*) of streets'.

This figurative use of *gridlock* is recorded from the early eighties, but recently has become increasingly familiar. It has a particular currency in US politics, where it is used to denote a situation in which legislation is making no progress, either because of conflicts within Congress, or because of disagreement between Congress and the Administration. A high-profile use occurred in 1992, when immediately after the election of President Clinton, the Senate Republican leader Robert Dole commented:

> A little gridlock might be good from time to time.

The adjective **gridlocked** has also developed to describe a deadlocked situation.

> A bipartisan coalition in Congress for two to four years could execute real change and cure gridlocked government. —*Wall Street Journal* 4 Nov. 1992, section A, p. 14

> Using these techniques, we can overcome mental gridlock. —*Bottom Line* Aug. 1994, p. 9

> Environmental groups are prepared to work for gridlock if it holds up bills they deem damaging to the environment. —*Star-Ledger* (Newark) 26 Nov. 1994, p. 10

> If Congress reverts to demagoguery and 'sound-bite' politics, the debate could degenerate into gridlock. —*Richmond Times-Dispatch* 23 Aug. 1995, section B, p. 5

grindcore 🎵 ᴾᴼᴾ see -CORE

grunge /grʌn(d)ʒ/ *noun* 🎵 ᴾᴼᴾ

A style of rock music characterized by a raucous guitar sound. Also, a style of dress associated with this music, characterized by layered, often second-hand clothes, and chunky leather boots.

A new development of sense of the noun *grunge*, which appears to have been founded initially on the established sense 'grime, dirt', as evidenced in phrases such as *dirty guitar sound*, used in reference to the music.

Some have traced use of the term *grunge* in relation to informal music back to the late sixties, and recorded evidence of the term dates from the early seventies. However, it was in the early nineties, in relation to the music of popular bands such as Nirvana and Pearl Jam, that the term gained a high profile, often used attributively in formulations such as **grunge rock** and **grunge metal**. Seattle, the home town of both these bands, is frequently regarded as the birthplace of *grunge*.

A transferred use of the noun also developed in the early nineties, applied to the style of dress adopted by the followers of *grunge* music. Features considered to be characteristic of *grunge* included elements traditionally associated with poverty, such as loose-fitting and layered clothing, ripped jeans, shirts with torn-off sleeves, and heavy boots. This code of dress generated a market for second-hand jeans and shirts, and perpetuated the popularity of DOC MARTENS. Though apparently more casual and accidental than STREET STYLE, the look was similarly, though perhaps even more fleetingly, adopted by the fashion industry, and ironical references to **designer grunge** were recorded. The adjective **grungey** developed in reference to both the music and the style of dress, the spelling of the existing adjective *grungy* sometimes also being used. The verb **grunge out** was used of those adopting the look, often called **grunge kids**, **grungers**, or **grungesters**.

Formulations such as **post-grunge** and **after-grunge** in the mid nineties suggested that the culture was in decline, but also attested to its high profile in the first half of the decade.

> She gave lot of interviews and the notoriously fickle British music magazines, who adored her grunge-rock sound and her torn thirties tea dresses, proclaimed her their new genius.
> —*Vanity Fair* Sept. 1991, p. 232

> From subculture to mass culture, the trend time line gets shorter and faster all the time. It was just over a year ago that MTV began barraging its viewers with the sounds of Seattle 'grunge rock', featuring the angst anthems and grinding guitars of bands like Nirvana and Pearl Jam.
> —*New York Times* 15 Nov. 1992, section 9, p. 1

> Still, designer grunge is a concept that doesn't play well in Seattle where the real grunge community wears a 'uniform' of layered, worn clothing.　　—*Chicago Tribune* 4 Jan. 1993, section B, p. 5

> Success seems to rest easily on Tarantino's shoulders. It has not changed his open manner, his naive expectancy, and certainly not altered his dress code. No neo-mogul striving for importance in designer chic, Tarantino still grunges out.　　—*etc Montréal* 15 Feb. 1994, p. 39

> Grunge groups are famous for raucous live performances in small venues, and they launched a revolution in mass street fashion, with a return to rugged, ripped clothing and long hair.
> —*Guardian* 5 Mar. 1994, p. 14

> The group is discussing what it's like to be seen as grunge kids in the reality of post-Nirvana Aberdeen.　　—*Rolling Stone* 2 June 1994, p. 46

> Magnum...are one of those bands who, in the light of post-grunge de-metalisation, have become simply redundant.　　—*Q* June 1995, p. 140

G7 /dʒiː ˈsɛv(ə)n/ *noun* Also written **G-7** 〰 📷

A group of seven leading industrialized nations (Canada, France, Germany, Italy, Japan, UK, US). Often used attributively, as in **G7 countries**.

In 1986, the Finance Ministers of Canada, France, Germany, Italy, Japan, the United Kingdom, and the United States, meeting as a group of seven, issued a joint statement setting out their aspirations to coordination of economic policy in the period ahead. Since then the **G7 nations** have met regularly, and **G7 summits** have attempted with more or less success to deal with the economic problems of a worldwide recession, and to reach economic agreements compatible with individual national interests.

> Unlike the UN, the GATT cannot undermine the values that the G7 champions.
> —*Economist* 22 June 1991, p. 14

> Bentsen flew to Tokyo for talks with fellow G-7 finance and foreign ministers on the Russian aid package.　　—*Washington Post National Weekly* 19 Apr. 1993, p. 5

> Monetary policy around the world is being loosened because of fears that growth in the G7

economies will slow from 3 per cent in 1995 to 2.25 per cent this year and 1.75 per cent next.
—*Sunday Telegraph* 4 Feb. 1996, Business section, p. 4

G-spot /'dʒiːspɒt/ *noun* ⌇POP⌇

A sensitive area capable of overwhelming response to stimulation.

A figurative use of *G-spot* as an informal term for *Gräfenberg spot* 'a sensitive area of the anterior wall of the vagina believed by some to be highly erogenous and capable of ejaculation', named from the German-born American gynaecologist Ernst *Gräfenberg* (1881–1957).

G-spot in its literal sense is recorded from the early eighties, with the figurative sense coming into use in 1988. The term is generally employed with the notion of someone in a public role being able to evoke an uncontrollable response from an audience.

This is what happens when you get carried away in massaging the great American g-spot ('g', in this case, for greed).   —*New Republic* 25 Apr. 1988, p. 42

The sound possesses a fiery physicality and the lyrics an emotional rawness that hits the musical G-spot every time.   —*Q* Jan. 1993, p. 26

Gulf War syndrome /gʌlf 'wɔː sɪndrəʊm/ *noun phrase* Ⓧ

A disorder of the nervous system alleged to have been contracted by soldiers serving in the Gulf War of 1991.

References to *Gulf War syndrome* (also variously referred to as *desert fever*, *Desert Storm syndrome*, and *Persian War syndrome*) are found from 1993, and provide a continuing area of controversy. The main points of debate are twofold: initially, it was questioned whether *Gulf War syndrome* actually existed; once it was generally recognized as an illness, the focus of interest moved on to the cause.

The question is not yet decided, but ex-servicemen have claimed that the illness from which they suffer derives from the anti-nerve-gas medication administered to troops who were to serve in the Gulf, or from exposure to harmful chemicals while on active service. A number of legal actions are impending. In August 1996 the Pentagon notified a number of Gulf War veterans that they might have been exposed to chemical weapons when an Iraqi arms dump was destroyed in March 1991, and in December the US Defense Department said that it would sponsor new private studies of the effects of low-level exposure to chemical nerve agents. In the same month the British Armed Forces Minister told the House of Commons that contrary to previous statements, an official investigation had found that a harmful organophosphate had been used in a toxic delousing powder issued to troops serving in the Gulf War. An official research programme into illnesses suffered by Gulf War veterans was announced.

Persian Gulf War veterans who have experienced any 'Gulf War syndrome' symptoms—including skin rash, headaches, chronic fatigue, stomach problems, breathing difficulties and birth defects in children—should get a checkup as soon as possible.   —*American Health* Sept. 1994, p. 39

The so-called Gulf War syndrome—an unexplained chronic illness which affected some 500 British troops who fought in the Gulf.   —*New Scientist* 7 Jan. 1995, p. 42

One of the many possible causes of desert fever, or Gulf war syndrome…is a combination of vaccinations and anti-nerve gas tablets.   —*Guardian* 19 Jan. 1995, p. 4

[The MP] who has been at the forefront of the campaign to gain recognition of Gulf War Syndrome, first raised the issue of organophosphates in 1994.
—*Daily Telegraph* 16 Dec. 1996 (electronic edition)

• •

H

hacker /'hakə/ *noun*

In colloquial use:

A person who enjoys programming or using computers as an end in itself. Also, a person who uses his or her skill with computers to try to gain unauthorized access to computer files or networks.

Formed on the verb *hack*, in its senses 'to engage in computing as an end in itself' and 'to gain unauthorized access to (a computer system or electronic data)'.

The first recorded uses of the term *hacker* to denote an enthusiastic (if not obsessive) user and programmer of computers appeared in the mid seventies. Since then the word has become the established term for such a person, largely replacing the use of *hack* as a noun (probably because of the strength of the noun *hack* to mean 'a journalist'). By the mid eighties the use of the term *hacker* had begun to reflect the new phenomenon of computer espionage. Increasing numbers of *hackers* were now using their skills in order to circumvent computer security systems, sometimes simply as a display of technical prowess, sometimes with the specific intention of demonstrating lapses in computer security, and sometimes with more serious and damaging intent. This new and rapidly growing threat to the security of military, commercial, and personal data was widely reported in the media during the eighties, and as a consequence it was this sense of the word *hacker* which became popularized, though enthusiasts themselves continued to use the term in its earlier sense (and made an unsuccessful attempt to create a distinction in sense between CRACKER and *hacker*). The world of *hackers*, and their interests and attitudes considered collectively, are referred to as **hackerdom**, a term which embraces both the amateur enthusiast and the highly-skilled professional programmer.

> The main thing you need to know is that you can't skip steps. You don't climb out of the primordial ooze of hackerdom one-day and work on million-line projects the next
> —*Computer Language* Feb. 1991, p. 25

> While hackers have been smeared with broad-brush attacks for illegally entering or destroying computer systems, most are, in fact, careful not to damage information or act illegally. Those who do harm are called 'crackers' by the hackers.
> —Alvin & Heidi Toffler *War and Anti-War: Survival at the dawn of the 21st Century* (1993), p. 150

> The Wall Street Journal reports that hackers used General Electric's Internet connection to penetrate security firewalls at GE facilities in two US cities. —*.net* Feb. 1995, p. 13

hacker-watch POP see -WATCH

hairpin rybozyme ⊗ see RYBOZYME

Hamas /haˈmas/ *noun*

A Palestinian Islamic fundamentalist movement, which calls for the creation of a Palestinian state founded on religious principles, in all of Palestine, and opposes peace with Israel.

Arabic *hamas* 'enthusiasm, zeal'; also interpreted as an acronym for the full name of the movement, *ḥarakat al-Muqawama al-Islamiyya*, 'Islamic Resistance Movement'.

Hamas came to prominence in the Gaza Strip in the late eighties, against a background of populist political activity inspired by the INTIFADA, and the negotiations with Israel being conducted by the Palestine Liberation Organization (PLO). An impetus was given to the movement's campaign in 1988, when the PLO explicitly recognized Israel's right to exist. *Hamas* rejected the idea of a negotiated settlement with Israel, declaring that the surrender of any part of Palestinian soil would be tantamount to giving up an aspect of the Islamic faith. This *rejectionist* view was shared by another fundamentalist group with which *Hamas* was associated, the Palestinian arm of the ISLAMIC JIHAD. *Hamas* has continued to oppose both Israel and the PLO since the Israel–PLO peace accord (signed in Oslo in 1993 and implemented in 1994) which led to partial Palestinian autonomy. The organization boycotted the first Palestinian elections in January 1996.

> The charter of Hamas, the Islamic resistance group in the occupied territories, states that if an enemy is on Muslim land 'there is no higher peak in nationalism or depth in devotion' than the obligation on every 'Muslim and Muslimah' to fight that enemy.
>
> —*Economist* 24 Aug. 1991, p. 47

> Threatened by peace, leaders of the two major Palestinian fundamentalist groups, the Iranian and Saudi-financed Hamas and the Iranian-backed Islamic Jihad, have unsheathed their knives.
>
> —*U.S. News & World Report* 11 Jan. 1993, p. 28

> Many more people in the Autonomy sympathise with Hamas's condemnation of the peace process than the electoral figures would suggest.　　　　　　　—*Independent* 26 Feb. 1996, p. 13

hammerhead rybozyme ⊗ 🧪 see RYBOZYME

handbag /ˈhan(d)baɡ/ *noun* Also written **hand-bag** 🧪 POP

A form of commercial, catchy, dance music.

From the notion that a follower of this music might be expected to place her *handbag* on the floor and dance around it.

References to *handbag* have been recorded in the UK since the early nineties. The music, sometimes described as *girlie* music, is frequently regarded as shallow and populist, and identified with the stereotypical owner of the dance-floor handbag. The noun *handbag* is often used attributively in phrases such as **handbag music** and **handbag DJ**. A related term is *hardbag*, recorded since the mid nineties, which denotes a popular electronic dance music derived from TECHNO and incorporating elements of HARDCORE and *handbag*.

> Off to an utterly superb 90 minute mix of what he terms 'deep, dubby garage.' You wouldn't exactly call him handbag.　　　　　　　—*Mixmag* May 1995, p. 60

> Despite being clinical, their productions are effective and the way they insert scraps of vocal means their work goes down well with certain handbag DJs.　　　　—*Muzik* July 1995, p. 63

> Maggie and Alan have been storming it for two years now, with an uplifting mix which stretches from handbag to hardbag and trance. Upstairs, Christine spins the camp disco. Cool, safe clubbing.
>
> —*The Face* Sept. 1995, p. 167

handism ⦃ see -ISM

happening /ˈhap(ə)nɪŋ/ *adjective* ❄

In slang: trendy, up-to-the-minute, 'hip', that is 'where the action is'.

Formed by shortening the phrase *what's happening* or *where it's (all) happening* and treating *happening* as an adjective. During the teenage revolution of the sixties, the noun *happening* was widely used to mean any fashionable event, especially a pop gathering; the phrase *what's happening?* is a popular street greeting among US teenagers, perhaps originating in the language of jazz.

Happening as an adjective first appeared in California in the late seventies; in her pastiche of Californian life *The Serial* (1977), American writer Cyra McFadden makes one of her characters say:

> Who could live anywhere else? Marin's this whole high-energy trip with all these happening

people…Can you imagine spending your life out there in the wasteland someplace?

The word then became enshrined in teenage 'valspeak' slang, and eventually emerged in the pop and rock music world in the mid eighties. In the UK it is still used mainly in writing for young people, but has also started to crop up in fashionable magazines and newspaper colour supplements.

> Despite general gloom in the entertainment world, nightclubs for the young and seriously trendy are the happening scene (as they say in the business). —*Economist* 5 Oct. 1991, p. 38

> So why the big rush to get on-line? It's all down to status politics; to look happening you have to be hooked up. —*Observer* 20 Nov. 1994, Magazine section, p.100

happy-clappy /ˈhapɪklapi/ *noun* and *adjective* Also written **happyclappy**

noun: An informal and mildly disparaging name for a member of a Christian group whose worship is marked by enthusiasm and spontaneity.

adjective: Belonging to or characteristic of such a group.

The term, associated with the evangelical movement which has come to prominence over the past twenty years, dramatizes a division which exists among churchgoers between a traditional and formulaic style of worship and one which is more spontaneous and informal. Clapping and waving to hymn music with a strong beat, and a marked display of fellowship, are features of this approach to worship, of which the TORONTO BLESSING is an extreme manifestation. Both the noun and the adjective have been used since the early nineties.

> Holy Trinity, Brompton, one of the largest happy-clappy (and one of the poshest) churches in London. —*Independent* 21 July 1992, p. 17

> I can't believe after all I've been through that I actually go to church regularly. I know there's a lot of teasing about happy-clappy, but this music really gets me going.
> —*Independent* 26 Feb. 1993, p. 13

harassment /ˈharəsm(ə)nt/ *noun*

The subjection of a person to aggressive pressure or intimidation through unwanted sexual advances.

Sexual harassment as the term for unwanted sexual advances which are offensive, persistent, or used (illegally) as a means of intimidation, has been current since the mid seventies. Over the last two decades, perceptions of what may constitute *sexual harassment* have become keener, and now include a number of behaviour patterns which might formerly have been classed as 'pranks' or 'jokes'.

This process has been accompanied by a further semantic development, so that the simple noun *harassment* is likely to be used to denote this form of aggressive sexual pressure, especially when employed in the workplace. While the general perception is still that *harassment* is most likely to occur in a man's treatment of a woman, the usage may also be extended to cover a woman's treatment of a man, especially of a (junior) male colleague.

> During my cow year the harassment had graduated from the mischievous sexual expressions and playful jokes of yearling year to vicious and harmful acts.
> —Donna Peterson *Dress Gray* (1990), p. 237

> The increasing emphasis on woman's essential weakness and man's essential bestiality that underlies many of the current debates about rape, harassment and pornography.
> —*New York Times Book Review* 19 Sept. 1993, p. 41

hard-ass /ˈhɑːdas, ˈhɑːdɑːs/ *adjective* and *noun* Also written **hardass**

In slang, mainly in the US:

adjective: Difficult; also tough, uncompromising.

noun: A tough and combative person, especially one seasoned by life and experience.

The adjective *hard* with the noun *ass*, the North American variant of the British *arse*, meaning 'buttocks'. The adjective *hard-arsed* was reported in 1961 as a slang expression meaning 'niggardly'.

The adjective, in occasional use as long ago as the sixties in the work of American writers such as Jack Kerouac and Norman Mailer, appeared intermittently through the seventies and the first recorded use of the noun was at the end of that decade. By the mid eighties both parts of speech had been taken up in popular slang usage and they continue to gain currency on both sides of the Atlantic. The adjective also appears as **hard-assed** and **hardassed**.

Canadian customs are notoriously hard-assed about drugs.
—C. S. Murray *Crosstown Traffic* (1989), p. 52

I felt it my duty to aggravate Sparrow. I was painfully aware that he'd saved my life...I hid my gratitude and played the hard-ass. —Brent A. Staples *Parallel Time* (1994), p. 186

We seem to have a propensity towards easy, popish melodies and angry, hard-ass riffs.
—*RIP* June 1994, p. 36

hardbag POP see HANDBAG

hardcore /'hɑ:(d)kɔ:/ *adjective* and *noun* Also written **hard-core** or **hard core** POP

Originally in the US:

adjective: (Of various types of popular music, especially techno) fast, harsh, or with an extreme form of expression.

noun: A type of fast, harsh music, especially techno.

The use of the adjective in application to music represents a specialization of context. The major general senses—'forming a nucleus or centre' and 'blatant, uncompromising'—are suggested simultaneously.

In the early eighties **hardcore** denoted a fusion of heavy metal sound with punk velocity; it was an extreme and minimalist genre. From the late eighties the term **hardcore techno** began to make its way into the music journals, and it is this musical style and its characteristics—a fast beat, a loud, insistent, harsh synthesized sound—with which the adjective and noun *hardcore* are now most commonly associated. At around the same time **hardcore rap** was first reported, an extreme form of rap which pushes the genre to new stylistic limits.

This has not gone down too well with those labels promoting 'jungle techno' as the new frontier of hardcore. —*i-D* July 1992, p. 13

Since starting out as a hardcore punk band that set land-speed records in 1981, the Pups have picked up quite a few unlikely musical hitchhikers. —*Rolling Stone* 2 June 1994, p. 69

A veritable codex of appropriated signs and signifiers: guns from hardcore rap; fire and bat-winged angels from heavy metal; the anarchy symbols from punk. —*Village Voice* 13 June 1995, p. 68

HCFC see CFC

HDM see COLD DARK MATTER

headcase /'hɛd keɪs/ *noun* Also written **head case**, **head-case** POP

In British slang, someone whose behaviour is violent and unpredictable, or someone who is regarded as being rash or impetuous. Also in jocular or derogatory use: a person who behaves rashly or impetuously on a particular occasion.

Formed by compounding: a *case*, in its sense 'medical condition', of someone who is 'not right in the *head*'; influenced by *nutcase*, which has the same meaning.

First appearing, as **head case**, in a song written in 1966 by the rock singer Pete Townshend, the word did not pass into the general language until the late seventies, although it was reported as British prison slang in 1971. It has increased in currency, on both sides of the Atlantic, during the eighties and nineties.

> One rear echelon corporal who talked about getting stuck into the Iraqis with a bayonet was derided by most of his comrades as a headcase.
> —*The Times* 23 Mar. 1991, Saturday Review, p. 12

> Many of the synths came via a contact in America, who cruised the country armed with the knowledge that there was an English headcase willing to pay top dollar for items which were rare enough and in good enough nick. —*Muzik* July 1995, p. 96

headend /'hɛdɛnd/ *noun*

A control centre in a cable television system, at which the various signals are brought together and monitored before being introduced into the cable network.

A compound of *head* in its senses of 'the front or forward part (of something)' and 'a position of leadership or command', with *end*, so named because the centre is regarded as being at one end of the cable network with its subscribers at the other.

The term first began to appear in general sources in Britain only in the early nineties when the new generation of cable companies began to wire towns and cities. The *headend* contains the equipment to receive terrestrial and satellite television programmes, and to originate material provided (for example) on videotape. The various sources are monitored and controlled in the centre and then injected into the cable network. As many cable companies now provide telephone services, the *headend* usually also contains the exchange switching equipment.

> Carrier signals are sent to a central point known as the *headend*, from which they are retransmitted to all points on the network. —Stan Schatt *Understanding Local Area Networks* (1992), p. 36

> The headend for the Avon system is situated in the northern part of the franchise area at Aztec West and will be the only source of CATV signals.
> —*Cable Television Engineering* Autumn 1993, p. 47

health maintenance organization /hɛlθ ˌmeɪnt(ə)nəns ɔːgənʌɪˈzeɪʃ(ə)n/ *noun phrase* ⊗

Chiefly in the US, an organization providing comprehensive health care in return for a fixed fee.

Health maintenance organizations, commonly referred to by the abbreviation **HMOs**, have, since the mid eighties and increasingly in the nineties, played a significant part in American health care. The term is said to have been coined by President Richard Nixon in 1971. The new concept offered families and individuals the opportunity to take part in MANAGED CARE: almost all their medical needs would be met in return for the payment of a single fixed fee, offering at least a partial solution to the problem of soaring health care costs. It was also felt that this ongoing maintenance would to a considerable extent reduce the individual's need for more expensive treatment at a later stage. The cost-effectiveness of such schemes has been increasingly recognized by large employers, who now offer membership of a *health maintenance organization* as an employment benefit in place of, or as an alternative to, conventional health insurance.

> One example of a best-of-both-worlds technique is the Health Maintenance Organization. At an HMO you pay one annual fee, and the group supplies all your health-care needs.
> —*Time* 3 June 1991, p. 72

> More than 50% of Rochester-area residents are enrolled in health maintenance organizations that employ the 'gatekeeper' concept of managed care. —*Business Week* 18 Nov. 1991, p. 10

> Companies are steering employees away from fee-for-service medicine (with each doctor visit

billed) and into managed care, particularly health maintenance organizations (doctor groups charging an annual fee per patient). This lowers insurance payments.

—American Spectator Feb. 1994, p. 37

health tourism ⬚ see TOURISM

hearing-abled ⦃ see ABLED

hearing dog /ˈhɪərɪŋ dɒg/ *noun* ⬚ ⦃

A dog trained to guide and help the deaf.

The use of guide dogs by the blind is a well-established practice, but more recently it has become apparent that a trained dog could provide assistance to one whose hearing is impaired. *Hearing dogs* are trained to listen for sounds and lead the deaf person to the source of the sound, which may be anything from a doorbell to a smoke alarm; the comfort and security of such a person living alone is thus substantially enhanced.

> To qualify, potential owners of a hearing dog must be severely or profoundly deaf and either living alone or spending much of the day alone. *—Independent* 16 Dec. 1991, p. 13

> An impressive part of Bel's hearing dog repertoire is her ability to differentiate between cars driven by Emma's family members from those driven by others. *—Dog World* Oct. 1993, p. 85

hearing-impaired ⦃ see IMPAIRED

heli-skiing /ˈhɛlɪskiːɪŋ/ *noun* ⬚ ⊕

A form of skiing in which transport up the mountain is by helicopter.

In recent years, the world of winter sports has seen an increasing interest in more adventurous forms of OFF-PISTE skiing. In the nineties, *heli-skiing* has become one of the more popular varieties, with growing numbers of **heli-skiers** being transported by helicopter to the top of a remote and otherwise inaccessible ski-run, to **heli-ski** on untracked and powdery snow. The use of previously empty alpine ranges for this sport has caused some concern among conservationists, but at present **heli-ski** remains a popular and fashionable pursuit.

> Heli-ski daydreams can have an unpleasant edge to them. It is as easy to imagine getting caught in an avalanche or crashing in a helicopter as it is to envision skiing untracked slopes of powder.
> *—Sports Illustrated* 14 Jan. 1991, p. 86

> Wanaka…is also the centre for a big heli-skiing operation, which claims 200 named runs spread among 100 peaks. *—Daily Mail Holiday Action* Summer 1995, p. 30

> Heliskiing is just one of the options for the adventurous skier with a big budget.
> *—Independent* 27 Jan. 1996 (Supplement), p. 15

See also EXTREME

hell, from ⦃ see FROM HELL

helpdesk /ˈhɛlpdɛsk/ *noun* Also written **help desk** or **help-desk** ⌨ 〰

A section of a business or organization, staffed by specialists able to assist customers or users who have problems, principally those relating to computer equipment or software.

The term *helpdesk* is a product of the eighties, when computing moved from being a centralized resource to one distributed throughout organizations. The increasing complexity of personal computers and of the equipment and software associated with them led manufacturers and software companies to set up systems of support and guidance, initially by telephone and fax, but more recently using e-mail.

> And with X terminals, there's the ability to ensure that everyone in a far-flung organization is using the same version of a particular program, solving what could be a nightmare for system administrators and help desk personnel. *—UNIX World* May 1993, p. 48

Helpdesks all over the country are looking at ways of improving their response times and cutting down on the number of calls coming in on their phone lines.   —*Computing* 24 Mar. 1994, p. 22

heptathlon /hɛpˈtaθlɒn/ *noun* ✹

An athletic contest (usually for women) consisting of seven different events.

A modification of *pentathlon*, in which the Greek prefix *hepta*, 'seven', is substituted for the Greek prefix *pente*, 'five'; *athlon* is the Greek for 'contest'.

The *heptathlon* was introduced as an officially recognized multi-event athletics contest for women at the start of the 1981 athletics season, replacing the five-event pentathlon, although *heptathlon* events had been reported outside official athletics in the late seventies. Both the *heptathlon* and the modern *pentathlon* are based on the ancient *pentathlon*, a contest consisting of five exercises which was a feature of the Olympic Games in ancient Greece. The *heptathlon*, which is held over two days, consists of the 100-metre hurdles, high jump, shot put, 200-metre run, long jump, javelin throw, and 800-metre run. The derivative *heptathlete* refers to the athlete who habitually takes part in this event.

Jodi Anderson, our heptathlete, could easily pole vault 13, 14, probably 15 feet.
—*Runner's World* Jan. 1983, p. 54

As the heptathlon and long-jump champion of the 1988 Games, she became the greatest...woman athlete in the world.   —*Time* 27 July 1992, p. 63

heritage tourism ▨ see TOURISM

HFC ♀ ▲ see CFC

high-five /hʌɪˈfʌɪv/ *noun* and *verb* ᴾᴼᴾ

In slang, originally in the US:

noun: A celebratory gesture in which two people slap their right hands together high over their heads; often in the phrase **to slap high-fives**. Hence also figuratively: celebration, jubilation.

transitive or *intransitive verb*: To slap high-fives (with someone) in celebration of something or as a greeting; to celebrate.

A *five* (that is, a hand-slap; compare British slang *bunch of fives* for a hand or fist) that is performed *high* over the head.

The *high-five* was originally a gesture developed for use in basketball, where it first appeared among the University of Louisville team in the 1979–80 season; Louisville player Derek Smith claims to have coined the name. By 1980 it was also being used widely in baseball, especially to welcome a player to the plate after a home run (and in this respect is similar to the hugs and other celebratory gestures used by British football players). Television exposure soon made it a fashionable gesture among young people generally. By the early nineties, the phrase *slap high-fives* had frequently become shortened to **slap five** or **slap fives**. An action noun **high-fiving** exists, which is also used as an adjective.

A month has passed since the election and still Republicans and Democrats are high-fiving.
—*Maclean's* 2 Apr. 1990, p. 11

And I suppose, in our case, John and I should exchange high-fives in squalid thanks to this human talent for forgetting.   —Martin Amis *Time's Arrow* (1991), p. 89

I highfived every Wisconsin starter.   —*Sports Illustrated* 9 Dec. 1991, p. 40

The pool players slapped five and forgave those who had trespassed against them.
—Darryl Pinckney *High Cotton* (1992), p. 185

There is none of that yelling and high-fiving which made trading in futures resemble a contact sport.   —*New Yorker* 20 Sept. 1993, p. 80

High Sierra /hʌɪ sɪˈɛrə, hʌɪ sɪˈɛːrə/ *noun* 🖳

A specification for the file structure of CD-ROMs.

The name is derived from that of an ad hoc group of CD-ROM researchers and developers, which named itself the *High Sierra Group* following a meeting at the *High Sierra Hotel* at Lake Tahoe, California.

Early CD-ROMs (see CD) could only be manufactured to work on one kind of computer, because no universal standard existed for a file structure or higher-level data organization. In response to this problem, the *High Sierra Group* defined a CD-ROM file-format structure in the mid eighties which was immediately accepted as a *de facto* standard. It allows the same CD-ROM to be read and interpreted on Mac, MS-DOS, Unix, VAX/VMS, and many other computer platforms. A modified version of the **High Sierra format** was accepted by the International Standards Organization as the international standard ISO 9660 in 1988.

> The DOS software writes ISO 9660 or High Sierra formats, and the Unix software writes ISO 9660 and native UFS (Unix File System) formats. —*Byte* Mar. 1994, p. 145

> Standards supported…High Sierra and ISO 9660, AppleMac HFS, CD-DA, CD-I, Video CD, CD-Rom XA, MPC-2, Photo CD, Portfolio CD. —*Computer Weekly* 25 May 1995, p. 38

high-top /ˈhaɪtɒp/ *noun* and *adjective* Also written **hightop** or **high top** 🏈

Chiefly in the US:

noun: A soft-soled sports shoe with a laced upper which extends above the height of the ankle; worn for sports such as baseball and basketball and also as a fashion item.

adjective: (Of a sports shoe) of this style.

A back-formation from the adjective *high-topped*; made with a *high* upper part, or *top*.

Before the mid eighties a **high-topped** or *high-top* shoe or boot was likely simply to be a leather one with a high-cut upper. From the late eighties the term *high-top* was used specifically to refer to a type of high-cut sports shoe, worn by basketball and baseball players, which was believed by some to lend greater support to the ankle. Made usually of canvas or a lightweight synthetic material, and also known as a **high-top sneaker**, the shoe was adopted, primarily by young people, as a fashion item, perhaps as a consequence of the widespread enthusiasm in the US for basketball and baseball — the baseball cap was adopted in a similar way. Off the court or field, the *high-top* is frequently worn partially or completely unlaced. Both the style of shoe and the way of wearing it have been adopted in the UK, although the term *high-top* does not yet seem to have crossed the Atlantic; such shoes are perceived in the UK as a particular type of *trainer*, and are usually referred to by their brand name.

> They wore full gangbang gear: designer jogging suits, unlaced Reebok hightops, baseball caps fixed askew over clear plastic shower caps, and sunglasses blacker than their skin.
> —Seth Morgan *Homeboy* (1990), p. 17

> These days, 98 percent of the recruits get off the bus wearing high-tops…Some of them have never owned a pair of leather shoes. —*Esquire* Jan. 1991, p. 44

> A study of 622 basketball players at the University of California at Davis has found that wearers of high-top basketball shoes, including those with inflatable chambers, suffer sprained ankles as frequently as players wearing low-top basketball shoes. —*New Scientist* 28 Aug. 1993, p. 11

highway 🖳 see SUPERHIGHWAY

himbo /ˈhɪmbəʊ/ *noun* Also written **Himbo** 🏈

In slang, a man whose main asset is good looks.

Punningly formed on BIMBO, by replacing the first syllable with the rhyming syllable *him*.

The word *himbo* was a journalistic creation of the late eighties. Applied at that time to young, good-looking men who appeared to lack intelligence and experience, the use of the word was motivated by the need for a masculine equivalent to the *bimbo*. The term survived into the nineties, its durability perhaps a consequence of a generalization of sense. The *himbo* tends now to be, simply, a good-looking man, the term having lost its earlier implications of lack of brainpower. Interestingly, this generalization of sense has not happened to *bimbo*, which has retained its strong connotations of empty-headedness. The *bimboy*, who has made only a faltering appearance so far, may yet become the *bimbo's* real equivalent.

> For that matter so does Eastwood, who, like the other himbos, camped far from hoi polloi at the secluded Hotel du Cap near Antibes. —*Washington Post* 14 May 1990, section B, p. 1

> His Achilles heel has clearly not been vanity, but a willingness to be manipulated by women who, initially captivated by the finely-chiselled profile of this political Himbo, then seek to take control of his life. —*Evening Standard* 28 Oct. 1992, p. 45

hip-hop /hɪpˈhɒp/ *noun, adjective*, and *verb* Often written **hip hop** 🎤 ᴘᴏᴘ

noun: A street subculture (originally among urban teenagers in the US) which combines rap music, graffiti art, and break-dancing with distinctive codes of dress and speech; more specifically, the dance music of this subculture, which features rap (frequently on political themes) delivered above spare electronic backing, and harsh rhythm tracks.

adjective: Belonging to hip-hop culture or its music.

intransitive verb: To dance to hip-hop music.

Formed by combining the adjective *hip* in its slang sense 'cool' with the noun *hop*, which also had a well-established slang sense 'dance'; *hip-hop* had existed as an adverb meaning 'with hopping movements' since the seventeenth century, but *hip-hop* as a noun was a quite separate development. Its adoption as the name of the subculture and its music may have been influenced by the catch-phrase *hip hop, be bop*, chanted by the disc jockey and rapper Lovebug Starsky in the form 'to the hip hop, hip hop, don't stop that body rock'.

Hip-hop originated among young blacks and Hispanics in New York in the late seventies but it—and the term—were first widely publicized in the early eighties. In the US the name was used to refer to the assertive and showy culture as a whole, with its visible and flamboyant street manifestations, and its related dress and hair styles. *Break-dancing*, and *crews* of graffiti artists leaving their ᴛᴀɢ signatures, are typical parts of the *hip-hop* scene. The word was first imported to Britain to refer specifically to the music, when it became popular in clubs in the mid eighties, though the dress and general culture have also since taken root among British urban blacks. Its popularity as a dance music has led to the development of the verb *hip-hop* and the action noun **hip-hopping**; someone who listens or dances to the music or follows the **hip-hop culture** in general is a **hip-hopper**; adherents may consider themselves, or be described as, part of the **hip-hop community** or **hip-hop nation**.

> The look is squeaky clean. In its simplest form, the hip-hopper's kit consists of a hooded baggy top, tracksuit pants and training shoes. —*Observer* 24 Sept. 1989, p. 37

> The patchwork music, anti-melodic vocals and aggressive posturing of hip-hop have transformed rock, creating as complete a musical revolution as rock-and-roll did in the 1950's. —*New York Times* 19 Jan. 1992, section 2, p. 29

> Yo! Do you remember the movie *Wild Style*? It sparked the 1982 explosion of mainstream hip hop culture. —*VIBE* Nov. 1994, p. 114

HIV /eɪtʃʌɪˈviː/ *abbreviation* ⊗

Short for **human immunodeficiency virus**, a name for either one of two retroviruses (properly called **HIV-1** and **HIV-2**) which cause a breakdown of the body's immune system, leading in some cases to the development of ᴀɪᴅs.

The initial letters of *Human Immunodeficiency Virus*.

HIV became the official name for the Aids retroviruses in 1986, after an international committee had looked into the proliferation of names resulting from research in different parts of the world. Colloquially, *HIV* is sometimes called the **HIV virus**, effectively repeating the word *virus*. As people began to appreciate that the virus often lay dormant and symptomless for many years, the term **HIV-positive** began to be used to help distinguish between those with *HIV* and those with Aids; alternatively, someone who has contracted the virus is said to be **HIV-infected** or to have **HIV disease**; collectively, those infected are **people with HIV**. An uninfected person is **HIV-negative**. **HIVIP** (a blend of *HIV* and *VIP*) describes a famous person who has contracted the disease. For the terms **HIV asymptomaticity**, **HIV antibody seronegativity**, and **HIV antibody seropositivity** see the entry for AIDS.

'Treatments'…encompasses spending on better information services for people with HIV about existing and newly-arriving treatment and prophylaxis options.　　*—Outrage* Feb. 1991, p. 22

Although HIV-2 destroys the body's immune system in the same way as HIV-1, it has a very different structure and consequently most of the drugs and vaccines developed or under development are ineffective against it.　　*—Toronto Globe & Mail* 16 Dec. 1991, section A, p. 9

She has become a member of the latest celebrity category: H.I.V.I.P.'s, those who, because of their magical media-friendliness, make this most tragic of diseases somehow hip.
　　—Vanity Fair Mar. 1992, p. 136

So-called 'discordant' couples, where one partner is sick, HIV-positive, or has died of AIDS, while the other is HIV-negative and healthy, are common in the West and also in Africa.
　　—Spin Apr. 1993, p. 77

ho /həʊ/ *noun* Also written **'ho** or **hoe** 📖 🎵

In US derogatory slang (especially among blacks): a wife or woman.

A representation of the pronunciation in black English of *whore* 'prostitute'.

Occasional usage of the word in its original sense 'prostitute' has been recorded since the mid sixties, when it appeared as **whoe**, a form which corresponded more closely to the standard form *whore*. Bob Dylan used the phrase **hot-lipped hoe** in his song 'Tiny Montgomery', written in 1967. It appeared intermittently during the seventies, but it was in the late eighties, when it was taken up in the vocabulary of rap and GANGSTA music, that it gained a real foothold in the language, especially that of black Americans. Since that time it has gained its general application as a derogatory term for a wife or woman, and is frequently found in the phrase **bitches and ho's**.

She considers herself one of the most decent girls in the neighborhood, not a hoe or a junkie.
　　—Vibe Fall 1992, p. 86

A lot of rappers are so busy explaining how good we are at selling drugs and carrying guns, smacking up bitches and ho's that we forget people are listening to us.
　　—The Voice 18 Oct. 1994, p. 6

In the next verse or the one after, there was a lot of stuff about beating the shit out of your 'ho if she hasn't got a meal waiting for you when you get home.　　*—The Wire* Jan. 1995, p. 24

hole-in-the-wall /'həʊlɪnðə,wɔːl/ *noun* Also written **hole in the wall** 〰️ 🔲

In informal British use: a machine, usually installed in an outside wall of a bank, which dispenses cash and gives information about a person's bank account.

The compound has been in use as a fixed phrase in various senses since the early nineteenth century, when it denoted any small, obscure place. In the US it acquired the transferred sense 'a place where alcoholic drinks are sold illegally', which was extended to refer to a small, often shabby restaurant. This usage represents a new specialization of sense.

The term first appeared in the UK in the mid eighties, when use of the machines became available to the mass of the British public. Used alongside the less picturesque terms *cash dispenser*, *cash machine*, and *cashpoint*, it seems to be directly attributable to the literal notion of a space inside a wall, where cash and electronic information are stored. The phrase is not used in this sense in the US, where a *hole-in-the-wall* is likely to be a small restaurant, and where such a machine is known as an *automated teller machine* or *ATM*. The term *hole-in-the-wall* is frequently used attributively in phrases such as **hole-in-the-wall machine** and **hole-in-the-wall cash machine**.

> They believe the men may be responsible for several early-morning 'hole-in-the-wall' raids in London and Kent. — *The Times* 23 Apr. 1992, p. 2

> Multimedia kiosks are already commonplace in the US, and are making headway in Britain. They look like hole-in-the-wall bank machines, but have touch-screen control, a document scanner, a telephone and a video camera. — *Independent* 24 Apr. 1995, p. 23

hollow-fibre bioreactor see BIOREACTOR

home alone /həʊm əˈləʊn/ *adjectival phrase*

(Of a child) left at home unsupervised while the parents are out or away.

Until 1990 this phrase might simply have described anyone who was at home, unaccompanied by others. 1990 saw the release of a Hollywood film entitled *Home Alone*, starring the child actor Macaulay Culkin. It told the story of a little boy, accidentally left behind when his parents went on holiday, who was left alone at home to fend for himself against all the odds. The film was an enormous box office success, its young hero and the poignancy of his situation appealing widely to children and adults (it was followed by a sequel, *Home Alone 2*). The film's title was rapidly taken up and popularized as a label for the hitherto only partially recognized phenomenon of the child left at home, maybe with siblings but without adult supervision, while the parents are away. Several such cases were reported in the media in the early nineties, and such behaviour on the part of parents came to be regarded as serious if not criminal maltreatment of the child or children concerned. The phrase *home alone*, or the hyphenated form **home-alone**, is frequently used attributively, designating such situations or the people involved in them.

> 'Home alone' couple face abuse charges. — *Coloradoan* (Fort Collins) 10 Feb. 1993, section A, p. 1

> Dozens of school children, as young as 12 or 13, are home alone in Vancouver and suburban Richmond while their immigrant parents have returned to jobs and businesses in their home countries. — *Globe & Mail* (Toronto) 21 July 1993, section A, p. 3

home cinema /həʊm ˈsɪnɪmə/ *noun*

A system for showing films in the home which is designed to simulate as closely as possible the viewing conditions in a cinema.

The term is the UK equivalent of the US *home theater*, reflecting the difference in usage between the British *cinema* and the US *(movie) theater*.

A *home cinema* is broadly an enhancement of the television set and video recorder. Now that high-quality reproduction systems are becoming available, large-screen televisions or projection television systems can be combined with surround-sound digital audio to provide a much better approximation to the conditions in which the film was designed to be shown. The move towards *home cinema* has come about largely as a result of the popularity of television, but it is also linked to the lack of local cinemas in many places and to the availability of feature films on video.

> Comet starts a £10 million promotional campaign this week for home cinema and interactive multimedia systems. — *Daily Telegraph* 20 Sept. 1994, p. 14

> Mercifully free of techno-babble, VTV lifts the lid on the latest amazing video, home cinema and TV systems. — advertisement in *Four Four Two* Oct. 1995, p. 61

home page /ˈhəʊm peɪdʒ/ *noun* Also written **homepage**

The file on a WORLD WIDE WEB site which is the one intended for users to access first, whose network location is published for that purpose, and which commonly provides an introduction and index to other elements of the site; more loosely, the personal details of an individual made available on such a system.

Since a principal feature of the World Wide Web is its ability to provide cross-references (links) to an indefinite number of other pages and sites, it is common to arrange information as a hierarchy and to publicize a first point of contact—a *home page*—from which the user can branch out to investigate the material available in more detail. A *home page* is often linked to computer software for searching data held on the system being accessed, the results of such searches being presented in the form of other Web pages. Many individuals now have personal pages in which details of their experience and interests are made available; these are also known as *home pages*.

Most 'home pages' include links both to locally stored information and to other sites.
—American Scientist Oct. 1994, p. 416

A World Wide Web 'homepage' can comprise literally dozens of small graphic files and separate bits of text, access to each of which can count as a hit. *—Economist* 22 Jul. 1995, p. 75

If you want to add images it is best to dump them in that folder too, where they are easily and quickly accessible by your homepage.
—Independent 2 Oct. 1995, Supplement, p. 18

home shopping /həʊm ˈʃɒpɪŋ/ *verbal noun* Also written **home-shopping** ⚒

The purchase of goods from home, especially goods offered on cable television.

The practice of *home shopping*, which is rooted in the mail-order catalogue, was transformed in the US in the early nineties by the opportunities presented by cable television. The cable networks began to feature a new kind of television show, which hovered on the borders between entertainment, information exchange, and advertising. In such a broadcast, frequently referred to as an *infomercial*, consumer goods were promoted, and members of the audience invited to place orders by telephone (payment being made by credit card). The concept and the term were given impetus in the early nineties by a successful cable television company called the **Home Shopping Network** or **HMS**. *Home shopping*, which combined two existing technologies, television and the telephone, became one of several MULTIMEDIA applications collectively known as *interactive services*.

There was at this time a marked lack of interest in this new way of shopping in the UK, where the term *home shopping*, an alternative for the established term *mail order*, still referred in the main to the ordering of goods from printed catalogues. However, this may change with the advent of the INTERNET; **electronic shopping**, the display and ordering of goods over computer networks, looks set to broaden the scope of the *home shopping* of the future.

People respond to junk phone calls, as they use the Home Shopping Network and order from the catalogues that find their way into mailboxes.
—Coloradoan (Fort Collins) 14 Mar. 1993, section F, p. 1

Three of America's largest regional telephone companies—Nynex, Bell Atlantic and Pacific Telesis—have just unveiled plans to form a 'media company' to provide movies-on-demand, interactive entertainment and education, home shopping and other services on high-quality telephone lines. *—Independent on Sunday* 6 Nov. 1994, p. 2

homesitter /ˈhəʊmsɪtə/ *noun* Also written **home-sitter** ⚒

Chiefly in the UK: a person who lives in or takes care of a home by agreement with the usual occupants while they are away, especially as a commercial service.

Formed on the model of *babysitter*.

The concept of **homesitting** was introduced to the UK in the early eighties, having first developed in the early seventies in the US, where it is known as **house-sitting**. It may be a response to a perceived increase in the risk of burglary, which has made people feel anxious about leaving their homes unoccupied while they are away; and it may also be a consequence of the difficulty many experience in taking time off work to attend to various domestic services, particularly at a time when more women work outside the home. Specialized agencies known as **homesitter** or **homesitting agencies** or **services** have grown up in response to this new market.

> She pointed to the growth of 'homesitter' services which, for an hourly charge, will wait for your gasman. —*The Times* 10 August 1990, p. 15

> The best alternative is a homesitter. All our 440 employees are mature and honest, and carefully selected to stay in your home; they look after your animals and possessions…We take the worry out of going away. —*Dogs Today* Dec. 1992, p. 53

home theater ✂ 🜩 see HOME CINEMA

homocore {{ see QUEERCORE

homophobia /həʊmə(ʊ)ˈfəʊbɪə, ˌhɒmə(ʊ)ˈfəʊbɪə/ *noun* {{

Fear or dislike of homosexuals and homosexuality.

Formed by adding the Greek suffix *-phobia* (meaning 'fear' or 'dislike') to the first part of *homosexual*. The formation is objected to by some people on the grounds that *homo-* as a combining form would normally mean 'the same' (as it does in *homosexual*) or that the word was already in use in the sense 'fear of men' (see below).

Homophobia was originally coined in 1920 in the sense 'fear or dislike of men', but as a hybrid formation mixing Latin and Greek elements (Latin *homo* 'man' and Greek *-phobia*) it did not really catch on. The impetus for a completely new word based on *homosexual* rather than Latin *homo* and meaning 'fear or dislike of homosexuals' came from the gay liberation movement in the US in the late sixties, when consciousness of gay issues among the general public was being raised. The term was first used in print in 1969, and then popularized by American writer George Weinberg in articles published throughout the seventies, but did not reach a wide audience until the advent of AIDS turned the phenomenon it described into a growing reality. A person who fears or dislikes homosexuals is called a **homophobe**; the adjective **homophobic** was derived from *homophobia* in 1971.

> Some [homosexuals] even alleged darkly that a supposedly homophobic Reagan administration was deliberately withholding money so that the 'gay plague' would wipe them out. —*The Times* 12 Oct. 1985, p. 8

> The hatred and homophobia in the Oregon Citizens Alliance's attempt to have homosexuality constitutionally declared 'abnormal, wrong, unnatural and perverse'…should be a warning call to all Americans. —*New York Times* 14 Sept. 1992, p. 18

> At some level, the panic also stems not from fear of the other but from fear of the self. It's widely accepted that the most virulent homophobes are often those troubled by their own sexuality; that gay-bashers can frequently turn out to be gay themselves. —*New Republic* 15 Feb. 1993, p. 8

horlicks /ˈhɔːlɪks/ *noun* Also written **Horlicks** POP

In slang, a muddle, a hash, a 'balls-up'. Often in the phrase **make a horlicks of —**, to make a mess or muddle of —.

It is likely that *Horlicks*, the proprietary name for a malted milk-powder and the drink made from it, is used here as a euphemistic substitute for the similar-sounding *bollocks*.

The phrase *make a horlicks of —* first appeared in the early eighties, when it was regarded as one of the characteristic idioms of a group of young affluent Londoners known jocularly as *Sloane Rangers*. During the decade it spread beyond this restricted group to the rest of the UK and to North America. Since the late eighties an intransitive verb to **horlick**, 'to bungle, to create a muddle', has developed.

To start horlicking around with a phenomenon like this is to court confusion.
—*Daily Telegraph* 20 Jan. 1987, p. 12

He thought privately that they would make a fearful horlicks of running the choir.
—Joanna Trollope *The Choir* (1988), p. 122

The divisional commander will be watching closely, and rival regiments with a strong streak of *schadenfreude* wait for him 'to make a major Horlicks'.
—Anthony Beevor *Inside the British Army* (1990), p. 151

hormone abuse ⁅ see ABUSE

horse abuse ⊕ see ABUSE

horsiculture /ˈhɔːsɪkʌltʃə/ *noun* Also written **horseculture** or **horsey-culture** ♣

In contemptuous use in the UK: the commercial development of farmland or open countryside such as wildflower meadows for the pasturing or exercising of horses.

Formed by substituting *horse* for the first element of *horticulture*, by analogy with *agriculture*: a form of 'agriculture' based on the keeping of horses. There is also a deliberate punning reference to a 'horse culture'.

The trend towards reallocating land to the pasturing of horses rather than cattle or arable agriculture was first noticed in the British press and named *horsiculture* in the late seventies. During the eighties and early nineties there was increasing concern about the environmental impact of this development, especially as wildflower meadows were seen to decline rapidly and the number of wildflower species to be seen in the countryside was drastically reduced, while at the same time farmers were forced by the provisions of SET-ASIDE to leave a proportion of their cultivable land fallow.

Local councils and conservation bodies are becoming increasingly worried about the growth of 'horseculture'—a new fashion whereby farmers divide up land and sell small plots for people to graze their horses. —*Daily Telegraph* 20 August 1984, p. 13

The latest threat [to wildflower meadows] is 'horsey-culture'. A father on the outskirts of Birmingham buys a pony for his daughter…Two or more horses…crop the grasses close and turn a meadow into a pasture…The result is grass short as a billiard table tufted with docks.
—*Reader's Digest* June 1994, p. 53

Protectors of the countryside have identified an 'intimidating and unpleasant' new threat to rural Britain: 'horsiculture'. —*Independent on Sunday* 3 July 1994, p. 8

hospital trust /ˌhɒspɪt(ə)l ˈtrʌst/ *noun* ⊗ ⁅

In the UK: a self-governing administrative body within the National Health Service, comprising a hospital, or a group of neighbouring hospitals, which has withdrawn from local health authority control. Also known as an *NHS trust*.

As part of its programme of reform of the National Health Service, the British Conservative government introduced in the late eighties the mechanism by which hospitals could opt out (see OPT OUT²) of health authority control, becoming independent trusts within the health service, with direct funding from central government and with control over their own budgets. Hospitals choosing not to become trusts were categorized as *directly managed units* or *DMUs*. Under the terms of the 1990 National Health Service and Community Care Act a system based on the purchase and provision of medical care was established, according to the principles of the marketplace. Under this system the new *hospital trusts*, as providers, were to compete in the provision of care to the purchasing bodies—area health authorities and FUNDHOLDER general practitioners. Hospitals compete with others in the same district or from another area. The reforms have proved to be highly controversial, anxieties being felt within and outside the medical professions that these new financial imperatives might influence the prioritization of patient care.

A hospital which is managed by a *hospital trust* is sometimes referred to as a **trust hospital**.

Mr Waldegrave…implicitly admitted at a press conference that hospital trusts and GP fund-holders would create a two-tier NHS service. -—*Pulse* 6 Apr. 1991, p. 1

This latest development in the commercialisation of the NHS comes as opted-out hospital trusts begin to report financial difficulties, with one hospital talking of 'holding down patient activity, with all that implies'. —*Observer* 22 Sept. 1991, p. 7

There will be far more pick-and-mix between the sectors. NHS trust hospitals will supplement their incomes with pay beds. GP budget holders will send their patients to private hospitals if they can get the right treatment at a good price. —*Economist* 6 June 1992, p. 30

See also MANAGED CARE

hot button /hɒt ˈbʌt(ə)n/ *noun* ✖ 🏠

A central issue, concern, or characteristic that motivates people to make a particular choice (for example, among consumer goods, political candidates, or social structures).

The image is that of a particular spot or *button* that must be found and pressed to trigger off the desired responses in the people one wants to influence (an image that had existed before in the figurative sense of *panic button*, used in the phrase *hit the panic button*); *hot* here is used in the combined senses of 'current or fashionable', as in *hot news* and *hot fashions*, and 'tricky', as in *hot potato*.

The expression *hot button* originated in salesmanship in the US in the early seventies, referring to the principal desire or motivation of the potential client which the salesman needed to 'hit' to close the sale. By the late seventies it had begun to be used in political contexts, but it was not widely applied to issues of current concern (what the British might have called political *hot potatoes*) until the US presidential campaign of 1984. Since then *hot button* has become a common political term in the US, developing an attributive use as well (in **hot-button issue**, **hot-button word** etc.) in which it means 'central, influential, crucial'. The phrase is occasionally used in Britain, mainly to describe events in the US.

Of the few hot-button issues that truly roil the nation, abortion is certain to get a full workout sooner or later. —*Time* 27 July 1992, p. 31

Crime and immigration, issues they call 'hot buttons'—emotive, thought-free, encouraging blind reaction—have been his political fare. —*Guardian* 21 Oct. 1994, section 1, p. 15

hot dark matter 🧪 see COLD DARK MATTER

hot-desking /hɒtˈdɛskɪŋ/ *noun* 〰️ POP

The practice of sharing desks and workstations between workers, rather than allocating individual private desks.

Hot-desking as a working practice is recorded from the early nineties as a means of saving on-site space and resources; the approach is complementary to the principle of off-site *teleworking* (see TELE-). A person working in this system is said to **hot-desk**; there is also a noun **hot desk** for the office space shared by two or more **hot-deskers**.

As businesses move towards teleworking and hot-desking, such portability could become crucial. —*Independent* 6 Feb. 1995, p. 21

Contractors, temps and hot-deskers who have to fight for available seats can also crowd you out. —*Daily Mail* 19 Oct. 1995, p. 65

Birmingham council…aims to save £50 million on office space by moving 7,000 of its 39,000 staff to working from home or 'hot-desking', where workers who are often out of the office share desk spaces. —*Daily Telegraph* 22 Oct. 1996, p. 12

hotting /'hɒtɪŋ/ *noun*

In British slang: driving recklessly or in a spectacular manner in a stolen car, usually as a form of display.

A noun formed from the adjective *hot*, probably expressing simultaneously the senses 'stolen' (of property generally) and 'fast and powerful' (of cars). There already existed a compound formed on *hot* which is related in meaning: *hot-rodding*, 'driving a car which is modified to give high power and speed', entered the language in the late forties. It seems likely that the development of the noun *hotting* has been further reinforced by the verb *hot-wire* 'to start the engine of (a car) by bypassing the ignition system'.

The word *hotting* was first used in the early nineties to denote a new development in joyriding. The established term *joyriding*, which entered the language in the early years of the twentieth century, began during the eighties to be associated less with the harmless pleasure trip in a borrowed vehicle and more with the improvised urban sport of driving stolen vehicles at high speed. This was taken a stage further in the early nineties in the UK when the stolen cars, often high-performance models, were used for *hotting*, the display of driving stunts such as hand-brake turns performed at great speed on improvised circuits. For a time these activities were associated particularly with an area in the city of Oxford, where residential estates were used on a regular basis for displays of this kind. The media attention focused on these activities helped to popularize the terms *hotting* and **hotter**, used for the driver in such a display. Since the early nineties the term *joyriding* has developed an extended use synonymous with *hotting*. The same period has seen the introduction of the terms TWOC, RAM-RAIDING, and CARJACKING, all of which denote crimes involving stolen vehicles.

> Police moved into the estate...to crack down on 'hotters', the youngsters who steal high performance cars and speed in front of crowds of more than 100.   —*Guardian* 4 Sept. 1991, p. 2

> What started as a campaign against 'hotting'—displays of high-speed handbrake turns in stolen cars—has turned into a dispute over territory.   —*Observer* 8 Sept. 1991, p. 9

house /haʊs/ *noun* Also written **House**

A style of popular music typically featuring the use of drum machines, sequencers, sampled sound effects, and prominent synthesized bass lines, in combination with sparse, repetitive vocals and a fast beat; called more fully **house music**.

An abbreviated form of *Warehouse*, the name of a nightclub in Chicago where music of this kind was first played.

House music was the creation of disc jockeys at the Warehouse in Chicago in 1985 (the term was first used in print the following year, on a record sleeve). It is designed for dancing, and so does away with meaningful lyrics in favour of complicated mixtures of synthesized sounds and a repetitive beat. In 1986, an important offshoot was created, again in Chicago. This music had similar characteristics, but with a distinctive gurgling beat; to start with it was called 'washing machine', which aptly described the sound, and by the end of the eighties it was known as **acid house**. (Despite suspicions to the contrary, *acid house* was not linked with LSD, but more probably took its name from the record Acid Trax, by Phuture—in Chicago slang, *acid burning* is a term for stealing and the style relies heavily on *sampling*, or stealing from other tracks.)

House and *acid house* proved very popular with club-goers and at warehouse parties when introduced in the UK in the late eighties. The craze for **acid house parties**, at venues kept secret until the very last moment, exercised police forces throughout the south of England.

House has spawned a bewildering range of sub-genres, mixing the features of *house music* with other sounds; following on from *acid house*, there was **deep house** (*house* with more emphasis on lyrics and showing the influence of soul music), **hip house** (mixing HIP-HOP with *house*), **ska house** (*house* with Jamaican influences), **techno-house** (*house* blended with TECHNO), **ragga-house** (combining *house* and RAGGA), **ambient house** (mixing *house* with AMBIENT¹ music), and even **Dutch house** and **Italia** (or **Italian**) **house**. As a result, the term *house* has come to be used to refer generically to a whole range of sounds which share its basic characteristics.

> In the aftermath of the first waves of Acid and Balearic, clubbers have been offered, in no chronological order, dance music under the names of...Acid jazz, ska House and hip House ...There's been the Garage and Techno sounds of New York and Detroit respectively, Belgian New Beat,...and, most recently, Dutch and Italian House. It's enough to confuse even the most dedicated clubber. —*Melody Maker* 14 Oct. 1989, p. 48

> Acid House, whose emblem is a vapid, anonymous smile, is the simplest and gentlest of the Eighties' youth manifestations. Its dance music is rhythmic but non-aggressive (except in terms of decibels). —*Independent* 3 Mar. 1990, p. 12

> With the explosion of the rave scene, house music patiently took the back seat to techno but has been on the rise again, incorporating the hypnotic qualities of techno into deep house or trance. —*Urb* 7 July 1993, p. 34

house-sitting ⬚ see HOMESITTER

HTML /ˈeɪtʃtiːɛmɛl/ *abbreviation* ▣

A specification for generating WORLD WIDE WEB pages which enables the viewing software to display text, images, and other resources and to execute links to other such pages; it also allows the user to create and print out documents.

The initial letters of *Hypertext Markup Language* with the first *t* of *hypertext* interpolated. *Markup* (also written *mark-up*) is used here in a related sense to the one in publishing, 'annotations made to text during editing as instructions to the typesetter' (in this case instructions to the computer software displaying the material), and *language* in the computing sense of 'a codified set of symbols and rules'. See HYPER- for an explanation of *hypertext*.

HTML is an implementation of the standard publishing specification SGML and was created in the early nineties as the coding system for the World Wide Web. Codes (commonly called *tags*) embedded in Web pages instruct the user's Web browser (see BROWSE) where to find the necessary resources and how to process and display them. In particular, *HTML* tags called *anchors* allow the browser to display and execute links to other Web pages so that the user can navigate from page to page. A strength of the *HTML* specification is that it is capable of being extended to include support for new types of media and display techniques—such as animated graphics or broadcast audio—as they become available.

> HTML has 'tags' to tell your browser how to lay out the text it is receiving—'text' that can include images, sounds and even live, digital video. —*Computer Weekly* 30 June 1994, p. 26

> Netscape has used the enormous success of Navigator to push its own extensions to the HTML standard. —*MacWorld* Oct. 1995, p. 114

human resources /hjuːmən rɪˈzɔːsɪz/ *plural noun* 〽

The department in an organization which deals with the administration, management, and training of employees; also the area of work dealt with by such a department.

The staff and employees of a business or an organization, *human* in contrast to *material* resources, considered as a significant asset.

The term *human resources* in its earlier sense was readily adopted as a non-sexist alternative to the established *manpower*. It was also welcomed as conveying a notion of value with regard to the people employed. By the early nineties both the plural noun and the singular form *human resource* had gained in currency, especially in attributive use. Formulations such as **human resource management** and **human resource function** developed to denote the office and function which is approximately equivalent to that of *personnel* or the *personnel department*.

In the nineties the term, while becoming increasingly established within the business world, has come to be associated by some with a trend towards euphemistic circumlocution in references to the workforce, perceived also in the development of terms such as *downsize* and *rightsize* (see -SIZE).

> We are seeking a committed personnel professional who will be able to establish and manage the human resources function at the plant.
> —advertisement in *The Times* 8 Mar. 1990, Appointments section, p. 3

> A...study...demonstrates the difficulty women have jumping from 'staff' positions in areas like human resources to 'line'—read 'fast track'—positions in say, finance.
> —*New York Times* 23 Feb. 1992, section 3, p. 23

> We are, of course, living in the age of the human resources manager, a period in which much of the effort has been spent on finding harmless-sounding sobriquets such as downsizing and right-sizing for an ugly phenomenon—mass redundancy.   —*Guardian* 6 Aug. 1994, p. 36

> You will need to be an excellent manager and have skills in human resources and professional development as well as a keen interest in the built environment.
> —advertisement in *Independent* 16 Feb. 1995, p. 31

hump see SPEED BUMP

hydrochlorofluorocarbon see CFC

hydrofluorocarbon see CFC

hydrospeeding /ˈhʌɪdrəˌspiːdɪŋ/ *noun*

A sport in which participants, wearing helmet, flippers, and padded clothing, launch themselves down rapids holding on to a float.

Formed with the combining form *hydro-* 'having to do with water'.

The precursor of *hydrospeeding*, whitewater rafting, has been popular since the early seventies. In the eighties and nineties, however, the taste for increasingly demanding leisure activities exemplified in CANYONING and HELI-SKIING resulted in a modification of the original sport. Those taking part in **hydrospeed**, abandoning the shelter offered by a raft, entrust their safety to protective clothing and a float as they are carried through rapids to calmer water.

> Canyoning and hydrospeed could be said to be more down to earth, but only just. The former involves wearing protective jackets and careering down mountain streams, the latter is even more violent. You cling onto a float and hope that the padding, helmet and luck will bring you safely through some quite vicious water to the other side.   —*City Limits* 2 July 1992, p. 92

> Hydrospeeding is a big hit—where you throw yourself down the rapids with a float, flippers, helmet and lifejacket and get carried along in the torrent.
> —*Daily Mail Holiday Action* Summer 1995, Mountains & Lakes supplement, p. 15

hyper- /ˈhʌɪpə/ *combining form*

In computing: involving the non-linear organization of text or other machine-readable media.

From the Greek prefix *huper-* 'above, beyond'; these approaches to machine-readable media go *beyond* the simple linear structures of conventional material to present the user with a structured and interconnected resource.

The two key terms in this field, **hypermedia** and **hypertext**, were both introduced in the mid sixties. *Hypermedia* is a method of structuring information in a mixture of media (text, video, graphics, sound) in such a way that related items of information are connected together by links or threads called **hyperlinks**; *hypertext* is machine-readable text that forms an interconnected structure in a similar way. These ideas gained little popular currency until the late eighties. By then, growth in the power of personal computers—and the rise of media such as CD-ROM which could contain large amounts of material in multiple formats—

meant that some such organization of the information was not only desirable, but increasingly necessary as an indexing aid to the user. An adjective **hypertextual** and an adverb **hypertextually** were first used in the late eighties; *hyperlink* is also used as a verb and has an adjectival form **hyperlinked**. The term *hypermedia* is frequently treated as a synonym for the related term MULTIMEDIA; however, *multimedia* presentations can be linear and non-interactive, whereas *hypermedia* ones necessitate decisions by the user to select one route through the presentation over another. The advent of the WORLD WIDE WEB in 1991 brought *hypertext* to greater notice, as Web pages are *hyperlinked*; the formatting of Web pages is organized through the **Hypertext Mark-up Language** (see HTML) and the format of the links is controlled by the **Hypertext Transport Protocol** (**HTTP**). In the late eighties, authors began to experiment with non-linear writing in *hypertext* format called **hyperfiction** (with adjective **hyperfictional**), which is sometimes produced collaboratively and may be published online in **hyperzines**.

Hyperfiction is a new narrative art form, readable only on the computer, and made possible by the developing technology of hypertext and hypermedia.
—*New York Times Book Review* 22 Aug. 1993, p. 8

Without the centering hold of a narrative, everything in a hypertext network seems to have equal weight and appears to be the same wherever you go, as if the space were a suburban sprawl.
—Kevin Kelly *Out of Control: the New Biology of Machines* (1994), p. 463

HTML has 'tags' to tell your browser how to lay out the text it is receiving—'text' that can include images, sounds and even live, digital video. —*Computer Weekly* 30 June 1994, p. 26

A new CDROM of his plays and poetry hyperlinks every word that Shakespeare wrote to every other occurrence of those words. —*Information World Review* Dec. 1994, p. 25

That is one reason so many people are excited about the World Wide Web, a so-called multimedia, hyperlinked system for displaying and organizing information on the Internet.
—*New York Times* 24 Jan. 1995, section C, p. 8

Enterzone is a hyperzine of writing, art, and new media. —24 Mar. 1995, online posting

hyperactivity ⊗ ⁅ see ATTENTION DEFICIT DISORDER

hyperkinetic syndrome ⊗ ⁅ see ATTENTION DEFICIT DISORDER

• •

Iceman /ˈʌɪsmən/ *noun* POP

The body of a man from the prehistoric period, found preserved in ice in the mountains of the Tyrol on the Italo-Austrian border.

Archaeology of the prehistoric periods has derived much information from the accidental preservation of bodies. The richest sources for such finds have been peat-bogs, from Tollund in Denmark, which gave its name to the Iron Age *Tollund Man*, to Lindow in Cheshire, where *Lindow Man* was discovered in the early nineties.

The preservative qualities of ice are more commonly associated with the finding of carcasses of animals from early prehistory, but in 1991 the deep-frozen body of a man was discovered by a climber in the mountains of the Tyrol. The first newspaper reports suggested that it was the body of a medieval man; initial archaeological views selected the Bronze Age. However, carbon dating, and the analysis of skin and bone samples, soon made it clear that *Iceman* came from a much earlier period: the view at present is that he can be dated at around 3300 BC. Detailed investigation continues, but meanwhile there is some evidence that linguistically *Iceman* is already recognized as the type of an early survival.

Yet for all the drama attendant on the discovery of the Iceman, he is but a single pixel in a slowly forming picture made of thousands. —*Scientific American* May 1992, p. 115

At the foot of the cliff…remnants of some fallen trees have survived for 3,400 years with surprisingly little decomposition. 'This is the botanical version of the iceman story,' says Larson.
—*Equinox* (Camden East, Ontario) June 1993, p. 94

If the Alps could have its Iceman, as the find is popularly called, then the Andes now has its Icewoman. —*Post* (Denver) 25 Oct. 1995, section A, p. 2

icon /ˈaɪkɒn/ *noun* POP

An object of particular admiration, especially one seen as a representative symbol of something.

A transferred use of *icon* 'a painting or carving, usually on wood, of Christ or another holy figure, which is used (especially in the Eastern Church) as an object of religious devotion'.

This transferred use of *icon* to designate a person or thing viewed both as an object of devotion in a specified area, and a typical example of it, is recorded from the late eighties. The term has become increasingly popular in the nineties, both in retrospective contexts, as when describing someone as an *icon* of a given period, and in usages indicating that a set of ideals and aspirations can be summed up by the identification of their representative *icon*. Together with this development, the simpler transferred use has been maintained: an *icon* as the image of something exemplary.

Chapman's Lake is the icon of Wood Duck lakes. The mist lingers there longer than on any other lake. —*Birder's World* Oct. 1991, p. 37

A latter-day icon of pre-Sixties America, when the richest man ran the town and all was well for those who resided in his kingdom. —*Esquire* July 1992, p. 85

People come to his shows these days not so much to hear him but to be able to see an r & b icon in the flesh. —*Boston Herald* 1 Aug. 1992, p. 26

Everybody has a soft spot for that all-American icon, the ride-'em cowboy.
—*Vanity Fair* Nov. 1993, p. 124

Ifor /ˈaɪfɔː/ *acronym* Also written **IFOR**

A multinational peacekeeping force, administered by NATO, which superseded UNPROFOR in the former Yugoslavia at the end of 1995.

Formed from the first letter of *Implementation* and the first three letters of *Force*.

The DAYTON *accord* of November 1995 opened another chapter in the troubled history of Bosnia, Serbia, and their Balkan neighbours. It was agreed that direct UN responsibility would end on 18 December, when UNPROFOR handed over to a peace *implementation force* (*Ifor*), under the aegis of NATO, with troops wearing their national uniforms rather than the blue UN helmet of UNPROFOR. The task of *Ifor* is to integrate with local organizations as part of the process of handing back control of the regions to civilian governments: by December 1996 it must either withdraw or reconfigure. It is too soon to see whether *Ifor*'s achievement will be more substantial or long-lasting than that of UNPROFOR, but the process is clearly fraught with difficulty.

The issue remains a highly sensitive one for the 20,000 US troops that make up the largest component of the Nato-led Peace Implementation Force (Ifor).
—*Daily Telegraph* 10 June 1996, p. 10

See also BOSNIAN

impaired /ɪmˈpɛːd/ *adjective*

As the second element of a compound: having a reduced capacity in a specified area.

The sense of *impaired* as 'having a reduced mental or physical capacity' is an established one, but in the eighties it began increasingly to appear as the second element of compounds relating to those who were differently ABLED, or CHALLENGED, in a specified area. (**Hearing-impaired** is the most frequently encountered formulation.) Compound adjectives formed in this way have developed an absolute use, as in '*the* class of people affected in this way', and corresponding development of the noun **impairment** has also been recorded.

The increasing familiarity of the form is shown, in the world of computing, by the appearance of *impaired* in compounds indicating the inability of a user to master a particular brand of software.

> An integral part of the school supporting the needs and integration of some fifty plus physically handicapped, delicate and hearing impaired students.
> —*Times Educational Supplement* 11 Jan. 1991, p. 90

> Fully driven menu for the UNIX impaired. —advertisement in *UNIX Review* Mar. 1992, p. 15

> Computerized newsrooms make it possible to 'close caption' newscasts for the hearing imp-aired. —*Rochestarian* Dec. 1993, p. 58

import /ɪmˈpɔːt/ *transitive verb* 🖳

To transfer (data) into a computer from a distant one, or to introduce (data) into one computer application from another.

A specialist or jargon use of the word *import*, 'bringing something into a place'. The implication is always that the data is being brought to the user's computer or application from somewhere else.

This word came into use in the mid eighties. Like EXPORT, it usually now implies the movement of data into an application, most frequently data which is in another format and which has to be translated by the receiving application. So a user may add new records to a database by importing them from a source file which may be text or may be in the format of another database; a desktop-publishing system may *import* text and graphic files in a variety of formats and convert them to its internal representation.

> Most clip art is saved in medium resolution brush format, and includes a single image ready to import directly into your DTP package. —*CU Amiga* May 1992, p. 184

> Neither program can directly import word processing documents—text is either typed in or imported through the clipboard. —*New Media* Aug. 1994, p. 80

impro /ˈɪmprəʊ/ *noun* Also written **improv** 🄿ᴼᴾ

A form of live entertainment based on improvisation and interaction with the audience.

Impro has been a colloquial abbreviation of *improvisation* among actors for some time, but it was only after the publication in 1979 of Keith Johnstone's book *Impro: Improvisation and the Theatre* that *impro* as a basis for live entertainment was developed into a theatrical genre in its own right. In the late eighties it became a popular form of fringe entertainment, allowing the audience to dictate the course of events by suggesting themes and developments, and this idea was even incorporated into television shows, most notably *Whose Line Is It Anyway?* which showcased several rising stars of the genre. The variant *improv* originated in the US in the late seventies.

> For Ron, nothing is rehearsed. Ron just happens. He comes from the Second City Improv Club in Chicago where even the bar bills are made up on the spot. —*The Times* 30 Aug. 1989, p. 14

> Comedy as a form of sport—it's billed as 'raw and gladiatorial' as teams of impro celebrities and new players challenge each other to perform fast, furious and frivolous improvised games on audience suggestions. —*Time Out* 31 Mar. 1993, p. 51

incestuous abuse ⁅ see ABUSE

inclusivism /ɪnˈkluːsɪvɪz(ə)m/ *noun* 〖

The principle or practice of being inclusive, especially of seeking to incorporate disparate or unreconciled elements in a single system or theory.

Formed by the addition of the suffix *-ism*, to denote a principle, system, or ideological movement, to the root form of the adjective *inclusive*.

Inclusivism as a newly defined philosophy or methodology is potentially very broad in its application. However, during the eighties the term was adopted particularly within two distinct fields: in architecture and theology. The term has been applied to some examples of post-modernist architecture to denote a broadness of reference and style, which may be contrasted with the purist approach of earlier modernist schools. In theology it represents the view that the underlying truth which may be seen as common to all religious experience should be expressed through a single faith; at the same time *inclusivism* has been used to refer to a movement towards inter-denominational unity and an attempt to open church doors to wider membership. There are indications that the term is now being taken up in general usage. In the same period **inclusivist** has developed as a noun, denoting an exponent of *inclusivism*, and as an adjective.

> There is not an '80s' style of housing as such unless it is called 'inclusivist'. Housing designs should be drawn from a much wider scope, as opposed to exclusivist schools of thinking like Bauhause, who draws from a narrow field of design.
> —*Financial Times* 16 Apr. 1988, Weekend supplement, p. 12

> Inclusivism has been propounded by some theologians. This is the view that people can be saved in many traditions…but one tradition contains the normative way of salvation.
> —K. Ward *Vision to Pursue* (1991), p. 172

> The picture that I received is of a university that has lost its way on the search for truth, dabbling in this and that, uncritically accepting anything in the name of a new goddess called 'inclusivism' and teaching men and women so.
> —*Drew Magazine* Winter 1992, p. 3

inconvenienced 〖 see ABLED

info- /ˈɪnfəʊ/ *combining form* ▣

Used as the first element in words relating to information.

Info has been a popular colloquial abbreviation of *information* for most of this century, but it was only with the increasing influence of information technology and the vogue for snappy combining forms that compounds began to appear. **Infosphere**, the whole area of information management and supply (now rarely used except as a US trade mark with an initial capital) was recorded in 1971. Further coinages followed at the beginning of the eighties. **Infotainment** is the presentation of information as entertainment on television and through MULTIMEDIA; the word is sometimes applied pejoratively to news bulletins which overemphasize entertainment at the expense of information. An **infomercial** is a television or video commercial presented in the form of a documentary (see HOME SHOPPING). **Infotech**, an abbreviation for information technology, was coined in the UK. If a mass of indigestible information is presented to a person all at once, the perpetrator is said to be guilty of an **infodump** (a *dump* is an old-fashioned computer term for a mass of detailed data about a system), and the recipient may suffer from an **infoglut**. In Canada, **infocentres** provide accommodation and other tourist information.

In the nineties, the rapid expansion of interest in the INTERNET and online communications spawned several terms: **infobahn** (formed on the German word *autobahn*) is a colloquial—and usefully short—descriptor for the *information* SUPERHIGHWAY; an information network on the *infobahn* may be called an **infonet; infosystem** describes any computer-based information system; someone who rides the *superhighway* in search of information or entertainment is an **infonaut** (formed on words like *astronaut*).

A large number of organizations have used *info-* as the first element of their names, and many such terms are trade marks.

John Mayo's essay on infotech trends and the physical limits that constrain them, and Anne Branscomb's on property rights in information, are two of the best overviews available.

—Whole Earth Review Summer 1991, p. 13

We've got tabloid television (news as infotainment), we've got trash television (talk shows as confessional), and now we've got reality TV, cop and crime shows.

—Independent 6 Jan. 1992, p. 12

The Saturday morning schedule became clogged with half-hour infomercials in which bouncy spielers and venal stars appeared on fake talk-show sets for in-depth discussions of hair products, vegetable juicers and fat-burning systems.   *—New York Times* 27 Dec. 1992, section 9, p. 3

An important cyberpunk forebear was the film 'Blade Runner', whose near-future milieu…is, in the intensity of its visual infodumps, like a template for a cyberpunk scenario.

—John Clute & Peter Nicholls *The Encyclopedia of Science Fiction* (1993), p. 288

It was the phrase 'road kill on the information superhighway' that got me paying particular attention to the number and variety of highway metaphors that have appeared in print and conversation lately, inspired by the term 'information highway.' Although I guess now we're supposed to say 'infobahn.' It seems there's a new infobahn cliché everyday.

— Dr. Dobb's Journal June 1994, p. 160

information cruncher 🖥 see CRUNCHER

information highway 🖥 see SUPERHIGHWAY

information superhighway 🖥 see SUPERHIGHWAY

in-line skates 🎿 see ROLLERBLADE

inner child /ˈɪnə tʃʌɪld/ *noun* ⊗ 🍴

A person's supposed original or 'true' self, especially when regarded as damaged or suppressed by negative childhood experiences.

The essential person regarded as a *child* existing *within* the shell of an adult.

The notion of the *inner child* developed in the United States, where it is still chiefly used. Although the term is recorded from the sixties, its current popularity is associated with psychological jargon of the eighties, and particularly with theories of CODEPENDENCE. In this context, 'getting in touch with' one's *inner child* is seen as a healing process whereby damage done in the past can be assuaged, as well as a key step in achieving true well-being.

At Bridgewater [Addiction Center], I never spent much time 'getting in touch with my inner child' or exploring my 'codependency' or my 'adult child' status. It must have been the milieu that prevented us from using that kind of language. When you're in a place with bars on the windows and concertina wire capping the wall, buzzwords and pop psychology can seem mightily irrelevant.

—Newsweek 20 Jan. 1992, p. 8

The cult of the abused Inner Child has a very important use in modern America.

—Robert Hughes *Culture of Complaint* (1993), p. 8

Spend an Holistic, Healing, Restorative weekend at our inaugural residential workshop including learning the Sacral Breath of our joyful Inner Child.

—advertisement in *Kindred Spirit* Autumn 1994, p. 61

Instants 🎵POP see SCRATCH CARD

intelligent agent 🖥 see AGENT

interactive /ɪntərˈaktɪv/ *noun* 🖥 🎿

A jargon term in the museum exhibition field for a (frequently computer-based) exhibit which encourages a user to respond in some way in order to demonstrate a principle or communicate information.

A back-formation from the adjective, as an elliptical contraction of phrases such as *interactive exhibit* or *interactive multimedia*.

The adjectival form began to be employed in the late sixties to describe computer systems which accepted user input and responded to it immediately, so that the user could enter into a dialogue with the system to direct its operation rather than have it simply carry out some predetermined task. By the early eighties, computer-controlled video systems permitted the viewer to make selections or respond to questions and varied the programme accordingly. Such systems have been used extensively in computer-based training and to a lesser extent in museum exhibits. The adjective *interactive* became something of a buzzword, frequently employed in phrases like *interactive video*, *interactive technology*, or *interactive exhibit*. By the early nineties, the noun had begun to be used in the museum field, frequently to refer to MULTIMEDIA exhibits with which visitors could interact. It is often applied to any display technique—not necessarily computer-based—that requires or encourages a response from a visitor, such as role-playing or dressing in costume, experiments in science centres, or even a simple lift-up flap on a display panel that reveals the answer to a question.

> He was still doing the kind of thing you had to start out with, cheap simulations and interactives, where you never got to make your own dramatic *statement*.
> —Frederik Pohl, *Outnumbering the Dead* (1990), p. 44

> The message from interactives can sometimes be confused and people may take away erroneous ideas from an exhibit. —*Museums Journal* Feb. 1993, p. 30

> Computer interactives have been described as the museum equivalent of sound-bite politics, part of the 'let's have a plasma-ball and call it a science centre' syndrome.
> —*Interpretation* Aug. 1996, p. 3

interactive services ▨ ▲ see HOME SHOPPING

interface agent ▣ see AGENT

interleukin /ɪntəˈluːkɪn/ *noun* ▲ ⊗

A general name for a class of proteins which are secreted by the white blood cells ('leukocytes') in the body to act as chemical messengers between them, particularly at places where the immune system is attacking disease.

The name *interleukin* was proposed in 1979 in order to tidy up the naming of various substances known to act as chemical messengers in the complicated immune system of higher animals, including humans. About a dozen types are known at present, which are given suffix numbers and frequently abbreviated. For example, **interleukin-2 (IL-2)** acts to stimulate the growth of certain T cells, specialized types of white blood cell, which themselves control the B cells that produce the antibodies that attack specific disease toxins. Various drugs derived from *interleukins* are being investigated as treatments for cancers (especially those affecting HIV-infected individuals), to reduce the inflammation in rheumatoid arthritis and the common cold, and to treat sepsis ('blood poisoning'). During the eighties, their possible anti-cancer effect produced much excitement among researchers, but side-effects discovered during clinical trials in the late eighties meant the first such products were only put on the market in 1992; the failure of trials in 1994 of an antisepsis drug has further put back their acceptance.

> Still in the laboratory are a number of other growth factors, including a passel of interleukins, which stimulate early-stage white blood cells.
> —*Scientific American* Feb. 1991, Vol. 264, No. 2, p. 110

> Melatonin was combined with the immune-boosting drug Interleukin-2 to treat advanced cancers of the digestive tract. —*Life Extension Update* Sept. 1993, p. 1

Laboratory tests with a recently discovered immune system messenger called interleukin 12 (IL12) indicate that this one molecule may effectively combat AIDS, cancer, and many parasitic infections. —*Science News* 20 Aug. 1994, p. 120

Internet /ˈɪntənɛt/ *noun*

An international computer network, consisting of a large number of individual computers and computer systems connected by telecommunications circuits.

A shortened form of *internetwork*, itself a compound of *inter-* and *network*, meaning 'a set of networks linked together', reflecting the fact that most of the computer systems linked to the *Internet* are themselves networks of computers. The shortened form is now likely to be understood as reflecting the development of NET.

The abbreviated term *internet*, uncapitalized, began to be used in the early seventies; it was a shorthand term for the communications circuits and their controlling software which linked together the separate computer networks comprising the US military ARPANET system. By the early eighties, the number of linkages had grown greatly to include many universities and other research bodies; by then the word had gained an initial capital letter, referring to the set of computer systems connected in this way as a single unique entity. From the early nineties onwards, the *Internet* grew extremely rapidly to connect many millions of users worldwide, fuelled by the rapid increase in the ability of individuals, commercial companies, and government agencies to connect to the system, and in particular by the explosive growth of the WORLD WIDE WEB carried on it. The word is often abbreviated to *Net*.

The network of networks—the Net, also known as the Internet—links several million personal computers around the world. No one knows exactly how many millions are connected, or even how many intermediate nodes there are. —Kevin Kelly *Out of Control* (1994), p. 464

The latest survey of North American public libraries shows twenty one percent of them offering some form of Internet access to users, with thirteen percent actually providing direct customer access. —*Library Manager* Jan. 1995, p. 5

The Internet lay in the shadows until the arrival of software that could give it wings, from Web browsers to Internet telephones, payment schemes and search services. —*Economist* 25 May 1996, Software Industry Survey supplement, p. 4

intertext /ˈɪntətɛkst/ *noun*

Language or text which is 'intermediate', in sharing the features of two different language forms, or 'intermediary', in its relation to the reader and the text, as a commentary or exegesis.

The concept of a text or language which exists both between and beyond existing texts or existing language forms was first introduced in the late sixties in the post-structuralist notion of **intertextuality** 'the relationship between especially literary texts'. The concept rested on the view that every piece of writing exists within a web of existing allusions and stylistic references. It was further developed during the seventies and eighties in the philosophy of deconstruction, which held that the significance of a text lay in its relationship with other texts, rather than in its interpretation of the concrete world. The notion of the *intertext* had by the mid eighties been carried over into the field of linguistics, where it was used to denote a text or a form of language which is transitional between two or more existing forms. For example, it may denote a text produced by a non-native language-learner as part of his or her *interlanguage*, a linguistic system which contains elements of both the native language and the target language. The term *intertext* is also used to denote a commentary or exegesis, offered as a comment on or interpretation of a text.

And intertextuality...proves that all texts are related to all other texts. Indeed not only does it demonstrate the universality of the pattern of allusion, quotation, cross-reference, parody and parallelism which has always kept us scholars in business and in research grants; it also shows philosophically that authors do not write writing at all, but that writing writes authors. —Malcolm Bradbury *Unsent Letters: Irreverent Notes from a Literary Life* (1988), p. 218

A small detail—as provided by the presence of an Homeric intertext—can totally transform the final view we take of the whole poem. —*Greece and Rome* 1991, Vol. 38, No. 1, p. 90

This notion of the intertext provides a powerful way of understanding both archaeological texts and the non-verbal text of the archaeological record that the archaeologist reads to construct his or her text. —Christopher Tilley *Interpretative Archaeology* (1993), p. 12

See also POST-STRUCTURALISM

intifada /ˌɪntɪˈfɑːdə, ˌɪntəˈfɑːdə/ *noun* Also written **intifadah** 🄰

An Arab uprising; specifically, the Palestinian uprising and unrest in the Israeli-occupied area of the West Bank and Gaza Strip, beginning in late 1987.

A direct borrowing from Arabic *intifāḍa*, which literally means 'a jumping up', itself derived from *intafaḍa*, meaning 'be shaken' or 'shake oneself': the metaphor is that of shaking off the yoke of an oppressor, a concept with a long tradition in Islam.

The word *intifada* first appeared in English-language reports about events in the Lebanon in 1985. Following the Palestinian uprising of December 1987, it was commonly applied to that conflict, and quickly came to be used in press reports without its meaning being explained. When the *intifada* died down in the mid nineties, the term was sometimes applied to other conflicts.

The *intifada* in Gaza and the West Bank is in its third year. Now that we have started, we can go on for three years as well if we have to. —*The Times* 22 May 1990, p. 9

Palestinians in the Occupied Territories are deeply concerned about 'the intifada generation'—the boys, now men, who came of age throwing stones at Israeli soldiers.
—*Vanity Fair* May 1994, p. 183

intranet /ˈɪntrənɛt/ *noun* 🄻

A communications network, private to an organization, which employs the same technology as the INTERNET.

Formed from the prefix *intra-*, 'on the inside, within', and *net*, short for *network* (see NET).

It became evident to many organizations in the mid nineties that the same technology which makes the WORLD WIDE WEB so easy to use could equally well be applied to their internal information networks. Such networks quickly became common. The value of *intranets* for companies lies in their comparative simplicity, replacing proprietary systems with a limited number of widely used and supported techniques, such as Web *browsers* (see BROWSE), and their ability to create a comprehensive communications system for comparatively little effort. Some definitions imply that an *intranet* can also be connected to the Internet, or make use of Internet circuits, while others stress its total separation: the word is new enough that its meaning has not yet quite settled down. A sign of its acceptance is the creation of compounds, such as **intranetworking**.

Intranets may be used entirely in isolation from the outside world...or, as is more likely given the benefits of doing so, they may be hooked up to the global Internet.
—*Computer Weekly* 15 Feb. 1996, p. 41

The Web is cool, snazzy, sexy, and that puts business off; but in Intranet form, companies can exchange information without employees surfing Star Trek sites and without nasty loopholes in their network security that can be exploited by corporate rivals.
—*Information World Review* Apr. 1996, p. 36

That division will provide both home telecommuting and business Internet-access services, as well as intranetworking connections for business-to-business communications.
—*Edupage* 14 July 1996, online newsletter

intrapreneur /ˌɪntrəprəˈnəː/ *noun* 🅆

An employee given the freedom to work independently within a company with the aim of introducing innovation to revitalize and diversify its business.

Punningly formed on *entrepreneur* by substituting the Latin prefix *intra-* in the sense 'within, on the inside' for its first element *entre-* (or by clipping out the middle part of *intra-corporate entrepreneurship*: see below). The result is a hybrid word made up of Latin and French elements.

The concept came from the US management consultant Gifford Pinchot in the late seventies; at first he named it *intra-corporate entrepreneurship*, but then proposed *intrapreneur*, which gained wide acceptance in the mid eighties, largely as a result of his book *Intrapreneuring: why you don't have to leave the corporation to become an entrepreneur* (1985). This introduced the verbal noun **intrapreneuring** to join his **intrapreneurship**. The corresponding adjective is **intrapreneurial**; the view that employees of large corporations should be encouraged to use their skills in this way has been called **intrapreneurialism**; the alternative noun **intrapreneurism** is also found. With changes in management approaches in the nineties, the term seems to have been largely superseded by others, such as EMPOWER and its derivatives.

A one day briefing on intrapreneurship: developing entrepreneurs inside Australian organisations.   —*Courier-Mail* (Brisbane) 21 May 1988, p. 27

Empowerment…means increased participation by employees in their workplaces, with a view to encouraging initiative and a spirit of internal entrepreneurialism, or 'intrapreneurism', among workers.   —*Independent on Sunday* 4 Apr. 1993, Business supplement, p. 15

in your face /ɪn jɔː 'feɪs/ *interjection* and *adjective* Also written **in-your-face** POP

In slang use:

interjection: An exclamation of scorn or derision.

adjective: Bold or aggressive; blatant, provocative.

Perhaps influenced by phrases formed on the word *face* which convey a notion of directness, confrontation, or rejection, such as *in the face* (as in 'she looked me in the face'), *to (a person's) face* ('she said it to my face'), and *to throw (something) in (a person's) face* ('his lies were thrown in his face'); there may also be a sense of the aggressive crossing of the normal personal space boundaries by another person so that he or she is literally 'in your face'.

The exclamation *in your face* was first used in the US in the mid seventies. Adjectival use quickly followed, especially in sports journalism to describe bold, confrontational moves in games such as American football or basketball. By the mid eighties the adjective had been adopted in general slang use, and it has continued to grow in currency throughout the nineties. It is used both attributively, when it is usually hyphenated, and predicatively (as in 'her behaviour was really *in your face*').

The voters are saying, 'In your face, Bush!' They are saying, 'In your face, Clinton!' That's because the voters are stressed out.   —*New York Times* 6 June 1992, p. 23

In L.A., the cars become sort of weapons. They express anger with their horns, by cutting people off, by not letting people in. It's in your face.   —*New York Times* 9 June 1992, section C, p. 11

An aggressively political storyline, so in-your-face it'll bloody your nose, that tests the very limits of acceptability.   —*Interzone* Mar. 1995, p. 33

A broad canvas of British artists, the provocative, in-your-face double act Gilbert and George and Turner Prize winner Damien Hirst infamous amongst them.
                                                —*Independent* 21 March 1996, section 2, p. 2

Irish box /ʌɪrɪʃ 'bɒks/ *noun*

An EU-designated fishing ground located largely in Irish territorial waters.

This area of Irish territorial water gained a high profile in the mid nineties when, under the directives of the EUROPEAN UNION's common fisheries policy, it was opened to Spanish and Portuguese fishing vessels.

The village—one of those worst hit by the European Union decision to let Spanish trawlers into the 92,000 sq mile 'Irish box' from next year—is at the centre of a campaign to make the Government quit the EU's common fisheries policy.   *—Independent on Sunday* 15 Jan. 1995, p. 17

Officials emphasised that the admission of the Spanish fleet to the Irish box did not mean their quotas had been increased.   *—Guardian* 29 Dec. 1995, p. 2

Iron John POP 【 see MYTHOPOETIC

Islamic Jihad /ɪzˌlamɪk dʒɪˈhad/ *noun*

A group of Muslim extremist organizations in the Middle East influenced by the teachings of the Iranian Imam Khomeini.

The word *jihad*, a direct borrowing from the Arabic in which the literal meaning is '(a) struggle', has been used in English since the middle of the nineteenth century to mean 'a holy war or warfare, especially for the defence or propagation of Islam'. A *jihad* may be undertaken to defend Islam against external threats or to spread the religion among non-believers. It may also refer to an individual Muslim's private struggle against resistance to the rule of divine law.

Islamic Jihad is an arm of Hezbollah, an extremist Shiite Muslim group which was created after the Iranian revolution of 1979, led by Ayatollah Khomeini (1900–89). Both *Islamic Jihad* and Hezbollah, which still has close links with Iran, are based in Lebanon. The activities of *Islamic Jihad* were drawn to the attention of the West during the eighties when, as part of its campaign for the liberation of Palestine, the group held a number of European and American hostages in captivity for several years. The hostages were finally released as part of an apparent intention on the part of the group to disconnect Western countries from its campaign against Israel. This opposition to Israel and a high-profile role in the Israeli–Arab conflict came to characterize the activities of the group in the nineties. A Palestinian branch of *Islamic Jihad*, known as **Palestinian Islamic Jihad** or **PIJ**, is associated with the Gaza-based Palestinian organization HAMAS, both groups rejecting the Israel–PLO peace accord of 1993.

They realise it doesn't pay, said Thomas Sutherland, a Scots-American academic released from his Lebanese captivity along with Terry Waite on November 18th. The men were held by Islamic Jihad, a faction of the Iranian-backed Shia group, Hezbollah.   *—Economist* 23 Nov. 1991, p. 90

The rejectionist stand embodied by Hamas and Islamic Jihad…is anathema not just to Israel but to moderate Palestinian leaders.   *—Coloradoan* (Fort Collins) 14 Feb. 1993, section A, p. 11

Islington person /ˈɪzlɪŋt(ə)n ˌpəːs(ə)n/ *noun* POP

A derogatory term for a middle-class, socially aware person of left-wing views, a resident of North London and in particular the borough of Islington.

Islington person (sometimes also **Islington man**), harking back to the *parlour pink* of a previous generation, is represented as typifying a supporter of NEW LABOUR who, while rejecting the brash self-interest of ESSEX MAN, is nevertheless similarly insulated by material wealth from the harshest pressures of modern society.

Just as Essex Man, the distinctive lager-swilling Tory entrepreneur, represented the 1980s, Islington Man—more properly Islington Person—may turn out to be the most potent composite of the late 1990s.   *—Independent on Sunday* 17 July 1994, p. 15

Islington N1, butt of the rightwing press for many years, has a new caricature—Islington Person, symbolised by Tony Blair and the chattering classes surrounding him.   *—Guardian* 19 July 1994, section 2, p. 2

At the time of his election the Labour leader was portrayed as the ultimate Islington man.   *—Independent* 9 Nov. 1995, p. 3

-ism /ˈɪz(ə)m/ *suffix* 【

A specific use of an existing suffix.

In the eighties and nineties, the suffixes *-ism* and -IST became particularly productive in the field of POLITICAL CORRECTNESS. The noun ABLEISM, recorded in print from 1981, is one of many serious and not-so-serious formations; other examples include **bodyism**, **faceism**, and **sizeism**, which are concerned with an inappropriate concentration on the physical appearance, **beardism**, the prejudice that may be shown by the clean-shaven, and **handism**, or discrimination based on whether a person is left- or right-handed. **Alphabetism** reflects discrimination based on the alphabetical position of a name within a given list.

Some of the terms coined reflect further a refinement of thinking. **Womanism** has been suggested by some who feel that the current connotations of **feminism** are not limited to a particular group, and over-concentration by society on the rights and interests of the young has been described as **youthism**.

The existence of less than serious coinages should not obscure the serious intent behind this use of -*ism*, but in the later eighties and nineties there is a view that the productivity of the suffix has been taken to extremes.

Studies on the so-called face-ism index...found that pictures of men tend to emphasize the head, while those of women tend to emphasize the entire body.
—*International Journal of Public Opinion Research* 1991, Vol. 3, p. 367

Yes, there is a cure for 'youthism', Germaine Greer's word for a culture hooked on kids.
—*Vanity Fair* Jan. 1992, p. 78

Perhaps the Left might consider a new crime of decade-ism, prejudice against poor, dead decades that cannot answer back. —*Guardian* 8 Oct. 1993, section 2, p. 2

I have the right to challenge sizeism and bodyism alongside racism, sexism and ageism.
—*Guardian* 23 Mar. 1994, section 2, p. 2

Nick Cohen's article on shaving...is the most appalling example of beardism.
—*Independent on Sunday* 31 July 1994, p. 16

PROFESSOR, LEFTIST...but tired of cliches, sloppy thinking, and PC holier-than-thou-ism.
—advertisement in *New York Review of Books* 23 Mar. 1995, p. 71

-ist /ɪst/ *suffix* 〔〕

Forming personal nouns (and in some senses related adjectives) denoting a person who subscribes to a principle or practice regarded in the light of POLITICAL CORRECTNESS.

Since the eighties, the suffix -*ist*, like the related -ISM, has been particularly productive of nouns and adjectives held to reflect a degree of political incorrectness, such as **ableist** (see ABLEISM) and **sizeist**. The suffix is also used, as with **people-ist**, to form adjectives and nouns denoting what is seen as a more appropriate focus of attention.

As with -ISM, the politically correct productivity of -*ist* is sometimes regarded less than seriously.

Why must we look like what society dictates is fetching? Because we live in a looks-ist world.
—*Out* Summer 1992, p. 55

And I guess you asked whether I am a feminist—I'm a people-ist.
—*The World & I* Mar. 1993, p. 309

item /ˈʌɪtəm/ *noun* POP

A couple in a romantic or sexual relationship.

An extension of *item* meaning 'an individual unit', also coloured by the sense 'a piece of news'.

Use of *item* to mean 'a couple' in this sense can be traced back to the beginning of the seventies, but it is in the eighties and nineties that the term has become an established one for a couple whose relationship is now publicly recognized.

I regard our relationship—our special relationship—as over, Xavier. We've stagnated as an 'item' in both gossip-column and personal-growth terms.
—M. Bishop *Count Geiger's Blues* (1992), p. 279

I know this sounds a bit Mills & Boon…but Penny and I are an item.
—*Guardian* 9 Nov. 1994, section 2, p. 9

We used to hang out together but I think people wanted us to be more of an item than we wanted to be. —*New Musical Express* 28 Oct. 1995, p. 69

• •

J

jaggies 🖳 see ANTIALIASING

JANET 🖳 see NET

Japanimation /dʒəpanɪˈmeɪʃ(ə)n/ *noun* 🐾 POP
Animated cartoons produced in Japan.

Cinematic animation has been associated primarily with the Disney Studios and their cartoon characters and feature films such as Mickey Mouse, Donald Duck, *Snow White and the Seven Dwarfs*, and *Bambi*.

In the seventies and eighties, animation moved away from the child-centred Disney tradition to a mingling with naturalistic adult film (*Who Killed Roger Rabbit?* was an example of this). Meanwhile other traditions of animation were becoming commercially available: *Japanimation*, noted for its high-tech productions and sexually explicit story-lines, was one example of these; another is *anime* (the term used in Japanese), an animated film or television series, chiefly science fiction, frequently characterized by violence, eroticism, or anarchy.

Central Park Media is rolling out its 'Japanimation' collection—sexy high-tech cartoons…best known for tough and often nude female characters. —*Playboy* Dec. 1992, p. 24

Randeep Ramesh and Robi Dutta look behind the sex, lies and videotape of Japanimation.
—*Guardian* 6 Aug. 1993, section 2, p. 15

An annotated list, with capsule reviews and addresses to obtain…gray market Japanimation videos. —*Alternative Press* May 1995, p. 93

Java /ˈdʒɑːvə/ *noun* 🖳

A proprietary name for a programming language, used to create networking applications, especially interactive elements within WORLD WIDE WEB pages.

Named in allusion to *Java* coffee, a favourite drink of many US computer programmers, and intended to reflect the richness and strength of the language.

The *Java* language was first developed in 1990 by software engineers at Sun Microsystems as a control language for consumer electronics products. Though unsuccessful in that context, in 1995 its ability to run on many types of computers made it a good choice for extending the capabilities of those who wished to BROWSE the World Wide Web; users could download small programs (APPLETS) that would run on their own systems to carry out functions such as graphics animation, secure communications, or manipulation of data. Sun wrote a Web browser called **HotJava** entirely in *Java*. Though designed to be secure, some users and industry experts have expressed concern that such applets might allow VIRUSES or other malicious programs into users' systems.

The latest workstations build on Sun's market momentum, thanks to its new Java software which promises to turbocharge the Web through its 'applet' technology.
—*Edupage* 7 Nov. 1995, online newsletter

These tools…include an HTML Web page editor with drag-and-drop page editing that can be used to create Web pages incorporating Java applets.
—*Data Communications International* Jan. 1996, p. 118

Whereas Web pages are static documents, Java applets are real programs that you can control like any other software. —*Economist* 25 May 1996, Software Industry Survey supplement, p. 9

jelly shoes /'dʒɛli ʃuːz/ *plural noun* 🔀

Brightly coloured sandals made of moulded plastic.

A *shoe* made of clear brightly coloured moulded plastic which looks like *jelly*.

Jelly shoes were promoted initially for children. *Jellies* (or **jelly sandals**) then became an adult fashion item which conveniently combined a smart appearance with durability as beachwear: they were not spoiled by salt or sand, and could be kept on in the water.

Shown below are fluorescent hot-water bottles…and children's jelly shoes.
—*Woman's Journal* Mar. 1990, p. 145

Jelly shoes. This summer's best sandals…stand up to sand and stay on in the water.
—*Details* June 1991, p. 27

jet-skiing /'dʒɛtskiːɪŋ/ *noun* ⚽

A sport in which a jet-propelled vehicle like a motorbike is ridden across water.

Jet-skiing, like HELI-SKIING, reflects the increased taste of the late eighties and nineties for EXTREME *sports* which combine speed and excitement with the use of developed technology. The **jet-skis** used by **jet-skiers** are one example of the kind of THRILLCRAFT typical of fashionable leisure activities.

He had bought a thirty-acre estate overlooking the Hudson River and filled it with every toy he could think of: a motorcycle and an all-terrain vehicle, guns and boats, electric guitars and motorized Jet Skis. —*Vanity Fair* July 1991, p. 64

Please can she have more pocket money to go jet-skiing again?
—*Guardian* 7 Sept. 1993, section 2, p. 12

A jet-skier was critically injured when he was hit by a powerboat during a water-skiing competition. —*Independent* 22 May 1995, p. 2

Concessions on both sides of the island rent a variety of vehicles that allow you to take part in more-adventurous activities, including jet-skiing. —*Texas Monthly* June 1995, p. 101

JIT 〰 see JUST-IN-TIME

Joe Sixpack /dʒəʊ 'sɪkspak/ *noun* Also written **Joe Six-pack** 📈

In the US: a mildly derogatory term for the type of an average blue-collar man.

Current in the US since the early eighties, *Joe Sixpack* is a name which supposedly evokes the average blue-collar man, whose favourite drink comes in a six-pack of beer, and whose interest in intellectual, artistic, and social matters is limited.

Beery Joe Sixpack, who used to watch the games on TV in his undershirt, went out and bought a multiband radio to listen to commentary about his team's multiflex defense, replaced his old cable system with a multidirectional antenna, snacks on multigrain cereals and has changed his name to Joseph Multipack. —*New York Times Magazine* 23 Feb. 1992, p. 20

They are Chablis drinkers who have somehow persuaded themselves that they are Joe Sixpack and publicly come on that way, denouncers of privilege who, if their life depended upon it, couldn't tell you who paid for the last 10 crabcake canapés they just dipped in that delectable mustard-mayonnaise. —*Newsweek* 27 Apr. 1992, p. 74

This is food any Joe Six-Pack can purchase. —*USA Weekend* 17 Oct. 1993, p. 16

Sirius and others on the magazine decided to put together *A User's Guide To The New Edge*, a primer intended to help Joe Sixpack get virtual. —*Observer* 22 May 1994, Life section, p. 64

juice box /'dʒuːs bɒks/ *noun* 🔀

A small carton with attached plastic straw containing a single portion of fruit juice.

From the early nineties *juice boxes* have become an increasingly popular item for packed lunches and picnic meals. The small square sealed box can be packed and carried without danger of spillage, and insertion of the plastic straw allows the contents of the box to be drunk without difficulty; the box can afterwards be thrown away. *Juice boxes* of this kind have been marketed as providing a healthy drink, but their disposable packaging has been criticized as damaging to the environment.

> Environmentally unfriendly juice boxes have been snubbed in favor of old-fashioned whole milk in a reusable thermos. —*New Age Journal* Apr. 1991, p. 60

> It was my usual light lunch: five sandwiches, two fruits, two juice boxes, some cookies, and celery sticks with peanut butter.
> —Eric Lidros and Randy Starkman *Fire on Ice* (1992, revised edition), p. 27

jungle /ˈdʒʌŋg(ə)l/ *noun* 🎵 POP

In full **jungle music**: a type of popular dance music which is characterized by fast, prominent, rhythmic drumming and chanting and by the emphatically urban concerns of its lyrics.

The music is thought to be named for its characteristic drumming and chanting, supposedly redolent of the *jungle*. Additionally, the urban concerns of the lyrics are associated with the concept of the *urban* or *concrete jungle*.

Jungle developed as a new musical style in the UK in the early nineties. It represents a fusion of TECHNO, which contributes a synthesized, electronic sound, RAGGA, with its chanting reggae vocals, and the urban rap element of HIP-HOP. In *jungle* these elements are fused to form a vibrant hybrid, an energetic street sound which nods towards the eclecticism of *world music*. The derivatives **junglism** and **junglist** have developed in the same period, *junglism* denoting the culture associated with *jungle*, and *junglist*, which has developed both as a noun and an adjective, denoting a performer or supporter of *jungle* and describing something as being of or related to *jungle*. In the mid nineties references have been made to **intelligent jungle**, a development of *jungle* in which the ragga vocals are dropped in favour of a layer of harmony superimposed over the drums and bass.

> If I say what jungle music's like, it makes it so banal. It's an attitude, very happy and organic, while hard-core techno is banging your head against a wall. —*Rolling Stone* 2 June 1994, p. 20

> Jungle, an exclusively homegrown, London-based hybrid, incorporating elements of soul, hip-hop and especially ragga, whose overloading bass-lines and rumbling vocal style are ever more prominent. —*Independent on Sunday* 17 July 1994, Review section. p. 20

> The junglists are in for a treat, too, with three firing drum 'n' bass versions of this track.
> —*Echoes* 30 Sept. 1994, p. 6

> Ditching the ragga elements and mixing ear-friendly melody and harmony over rattling rhythms lubricated by severe dub bass, intelligent jungle is high on the tip sheet for '95.
> —*Select* Mar. 1995, p. 26

> It's this intelligent strain of drum 'n' bass which appeals to the techno-reared ears and feet of the mostly-white ravers here, whereas ragga-jungle's ghetto-centric menace is more attractive to the black and hispanic youth of the hip hop and dancehall scene. —*Muzik* July 1995, p. 41

jungle fever /dʒʌŋg(ə)l ˈfiːvə/ *noun* POP

A jocular or derogatory term for a burning desire to engage in an interracial sexual relationship.

A transferred sense of *jungle fever*, 'a severe form of malaria', in which the *fever* is caused not by mosquitoes but by the heat, likened perhaps to the tropical heat of the *jungle*, of sexual passion.

This transferred sense of *jungle fever* represents a jocular and somewhat politically incorrect usage which has entered the language since the release in 1991 of the film *Jungle Fever*, in which a black man has a relationship with a white woman.

Jungle fever is the code term, taken from the Spike Lee film of the same name, for a black man's desire to sleep with a white woman. —*New York Times Magazine* 17 Nov. 1991, p. 95

The week after we returned from Catalina was spent convincing him that I'd slept with him out of affection and respect, not out of Jungle Fever.
—Armistead Maupin *Maybe the Moon* (1992), p. 184

'Latinos are fast becoming a hot, must-have accessory for powerful non-latinas,' the headline says. The accompanying copy block asks the question: Jungle fever (fiebre de la jungla) or real love? —*Boston Globe* 12 June 1996, p. 71

just-in-time /dʒʌstɪnˈtʌɪm/ *adjective* and *noun* Also written **just in time**

adjective: Relating to a manufacturing system in which components are delivered at the time required for assembly, in order to minimize storage costs.

noun: The just-in-time system.

The adjective represents an attributive use and a specialization in sense of the adverbial phrase *just in time*, in its sense 'at the last possible moment'. The noun has developed elliptically from this use of the adjective.

This new industrial system was introduced to Europe and the US in the late seventies from Japan, where it had developed within the motor manufacturing industry. The components required for a particular stage in the manufacturing process are supplied along with a card bearing specifications, a KANBAN, which assists the worker in the identification and use of the component and triggers a fresh supply. This results in the delivery of components and production of parts in appropriate quantities at the appropriate time, with a consequent reduction in the costs of storage and the creation of surplus. The system is frequently applied as part of the KAIZEN philosophy of continuous improvement. Advantages to the manufacturer may, however, be counterbalanced by disadvantages to the supplier, who has to ensure that materials are supplied to the correct specification, in the correct sequence, and at the precise time, with no room for error. The abbreviation **JIT** has been in use since the mid eighties. In the nineties some non-manufacturing applications of the term have been recorded, such as **just-in-time printing** and **just-in-time retailing**.

The essence of just-in-time is that the manufacturer does not keep much inventory on hand—he relies on suppliers to furnish parts just in time for them to be assembled.
—*Fortune* 2 Apr. 1984, p. 13

The drive chain works something like this: just-in-time stock control (to free up cash to repay debt) improves manufacturing quality (because defects show up, and must be fixed, more quickly).
—*Economist* 14 Sept. 1991, p. 97

K

kaizen /ˈkʌɪzɛn/ *noun*

A Japanese business philosophy of continuous improvement in working practices and personal efficiency; hence, an improvement in performance or productivity.

A direct borrowing from the Japanese, in which *kaizen* means 'a change for the better; an improvement', from *kai* 'revision; change' and *zen* '(the) good'.

Use of the term in English has been recorded since the mid eighties, when the philosophy was brought to the West by the expanding Japanese motor manufacturing industry. The methodology involves ongoing assessment of working practice, often through QUALITY CIRCLES and continuous restructuring of jobs, resulting in increased efficiency and productivity, and reduced boredom and greater influence over the manufacturing process for employees. The emphasis of the approach, which is frequently practised alongside JUST-IN-TIME and the KANBAN system, is on continuing improvement. By 1990 recognition of the philosophy and use of the term had spread beyond motor manufacturing into the general business vocabulary of North America and the UK.

In many ways, Xerox's emphasis on technology that evolves echoes the Japanese principle of *kaizen*, or gradual, unending improvement. —*Scientific American* June 1992, p. 80

Having absorbed the renowned Toyota Production System—just-in-time manufacturing, *kaizen* continuous on-the-job improvements, the *kanban* system of instruction cards carrying information between each process and from the factory floor to suppliers and—he was ready to start making cars. —*Independent* 28 Dec. 1992, p. 8

kanban /ˈkanban/ *noun* 〽

In industry: a card or sheet displaying a set of manufacturing specifications and requirements which is circulated to suppliers and sent along a production line to regulate the supply of components. Hence also: a coordinated manufacturing system employing such a card.

A direct borrowing from the Japanese, in which *kanban* or *kamban* means 'a sign, a poster'.

The **kanban system**, which was brought to the West in the late seventies by Japanese motor manufacturers, ensures that components arrive from suppliers at the time they are required for assembly, thus minimizing factory storage and surplus. The *kanban* card is an integral part of JUST-IN-TIME manufacturing. The two terms are closely associated; indeed *kanban*, when used attributively in *kanban system* or elliptically to denote the system itself, is almost synonymous with JUST-IN-TIME. By the early nineties the word *kanban* was used in the jargon of business and manufacturing with no need for an accompanying gloss.

Material passed through many different processes in its transition from a blank board to a finished printed circuit assembly...including three kanbans.
—*Professional Engineering* July 1991, p. 34

Like most other Japanese businesses, Asahi operates on the Kanban—or just-in-time—principle of stock control, which reduces stockholding to the absolute minimum.
—*New Scientist* 2 Oct. 1993, p. 35

karaoke /karəˈəʊki, karɪˈəʊki/ *noun* 🎤 ᴾᴼᴾ

A sound system with a pre-recorded soundtrack of popular music without the vocal part which allows an individual to sing along with it, often recording his or her performance on tape or video. Also, the pastime of singing to this kind of system.

A Japanese compound word which literally means 'empty orchestra'.

Karaoke was invented in Japan and is extremely popular with Japanese business people visiting bars and clubs on the way home from work. The word is recorded in English from the late seventies and the concept was successfully introduced in the US and UK during the early eighties, although not taken up with such popular enthusiasm as in Japan; its peak of fashion in the West has now passed. The word is often used attributively, especially in **karaoke bar** or **karaoke club** (where *karaoke* is the main form of entertainment) and in **karaoke machine**, the jukebox on which the accompaniments are recorded. Many pubs and clubs have **karaoke nights** in which *karaoke* is the principal entertainment. Use of the term has more recently been extended to recordings of plays, in which one actor's part is left for the user to provide.

The idea of the karaoke bar is very simple. You get roaring drunk, chat up the bar girls and sing maudlin popular songs, dreadfully out of tune. —*Daily Telegraph* 19 May 1989, p. 15

Sunday nights tone down a notch, with an older, more yuppified clientele showing up for the karaoke night. —*Transpacific* Jan. 1992, p. 117

We now get 'Karaoke Macbeth' on CD-ROM. Just decide the part you want to play, as well as the act and the scene, and the programme will automatically cue you into the computer-animated production.   —*Computer Weekly* 19 Aug. 1993, p. 52

The grand prize is an impressive $5,000 plus a Pioneer home-laser karaoke machine—presumably so the winner can prepare to defend their title.   —*Toronto Life* June 1994, p. 12

karoshi /ka'rəʊʃi/ *noun* 〰️ ⊗

In Japan: death caused by overwork or job-related exhaustion.

A Japanese word, formed from the elements *ka* 'excess', *rō* 'labour', and *shi* 'death'.

Since the late seventies, a number of words (such as KAIZEN) relating to efficient business practices entered the Western business vocabulary from the thriving and expanding world of Japanese markets. More recently, however, Japanese society has looked more critically at its work-oriented culture, and *karoshi* has been identified and discussed since the late eighties. A sharper focus may well be given to this by growing pressures on the Japanese economy: the idea of a 'job for life' is now less of a certainty, and the phenomenon of redundancy is becoming known. Awareness of the dangers of *karoshi* is now paradoxically likely to be accompanied by new anxieties about job security: it is not clear what the long-term effects will be.

Daunted by the prospect of toiling for years to buy a tiny house only to end up victims of *karoshi* (death from overwork), young Japanese are spending more and more of their time—and money— jumping into fads and subcultures.   —*Economist* 28 Mar. 1992, p. 134

Actually, in the first half of 1990 the families of *karoshi* victims reported more than 1,200 cases to an independent *karoshi* hotline.   —*New Republic* 11 May 1992, p. 5

Execs might note the recent news that in Japan karoshi—death from over-work—is now the second leading cause of death after cancer.   —*The Face* Oct. 1994, p. 35

keyhole surgery /kiːhəʊl 'səːdʒ(ə)ri/ *noun* ⊗ 🔺

Surgery carried out through a very small incision, using fibre-optic devices to observe the effect of laser scalpels or tiny instruments.

Formed by compounding: *surgery* done through a hole which is so small that it is likened to a *keyhole*.

The colloquial phrase *keyhole surgery* was first used in print in the late eighties, shortly after the surgical technique itself, more formally known as *minimally invasive surgery*, had come into use. This followed pioneering research over the previous decade, itself based on the advances in fibre optics that made it possible. The technique is now in wide use for what would otherwise be major operations, reducing trauma and decreasing the time patients spend in hospital.

The first operation in Britain to remove a kidney…by minimal invasive surgery, or 'keyhole' surgery in popular jargon, was carried out in Portsmouth.   —*The Times* 17 May 1990, p. 20

Keyhole surgery is used extensively in knee operations, with minimal scarring and faster recovery, and is being tried in hernia repair, although this is still controversial.
    —*Guardian* 23 June 1994, section 2, p. 2

kicking /'kɪkɪŋ/ *adjective* 🅿️POP

In slang: exciting, lively; great, excellent.

Perhaps influenced by the phrase *alive and kicking* 'very active; lively'.

Use of the adjective has developed from a specialized sense of the verb applied since the late eighties to a fast, lively, musical beat, which may be said to **kick**. Some generalization of sense has followed; there is evidence of the adjective being applied to people, places, and even clothing, in either sense or both simultaneously. The word's development may be compared with that of the earlier *jumping*, which has been used in a similar sense since the late thirties.

The joint was kicking.   —*Sun* 13 June 1991, p. 23

The essential monitor of house music, its beats per minute, has increased over the last few years, and some tracks now 'kick' at to up to 138bpm. Raymond Clarke, 20, the fastest dancer at the agency, said: 'The music doesn't work if it's slow. You need a loud bass, a kicking track; you get such a rush you want to explode'.   —*Independent* 6 Mar. 1992, p. 6

The tone is set with fantastic, serious scorcher of kicking syncopated supernova from ORQUESTA REVE called 'Mi Salasa Tiene Sandunga'.   —*Straight No Chaser* Summer 1995, Issue 32, p. 38

kick-start /'kɪkstɑːt/ *noun* and *verb* 〰 POP

noun: An impetus given to get a process or thing started or restarted.

transitive verb: To give a kick-start to (a process or thing).

A figurative use of *kick-start* in the sense 'an act of starting an engine by the downward thrust of a pedal, as in older motorcycles'.

In recent years (particularly following the slump at the end of the eighties) the notion of giving a *kick-start* to something which is seen to be flagging has frequently been given expression. The term has been particularly associated with the financial and political world of the recession, with particular economic theories being presented as ways in which to *kick-start* the economy, but the image of giving impetus to a process which appears to have stalled is now applied to a variety of situations.

The argument that a Tory victory would so underpin sterling that the government could quickly kick-start the economy by cutting rates is doubly flawed.   —*Financial Times* 11 Apr. 1992, p. 32

Now I need to go back to the beginning—of October, that is—because that month was Stamp Month in Canada, and it was given the fashionable 'kick-start' on the first day with the issue of two stamps to delight the followers of the Space theme.   —*Gibbons Stamp Monthly* Jan. 1993, p. 65

With lots of new ideas this high profile branch is an excellent place to kick-start your career.   —advertisement in *The Grocer* 23 Mar. 1996, p. 72

killer application /ˌkɪlə aplɪˈkeɪʃ(ə)n/ *noun* ▣

In marketing jargon, a product of technology which is so good, or which contains features so advanced or innovatory, that it is irresistible to potential purchasers.

The word *killer* is used here in its figurative sense of something which is 'impressive, formidable, or excellent'.

The term *killer application* appeared at the beginning of the nineties to refer to a piece of software which so attracts potential users that they feel they cannot do without it and which in some cases causes them not only to buy the application, but also the equipment to run it on. The best known example of this is perhaps *VisiCalc*, the first spreadsheet for personal computers, which was not only highly successful in itself but persuaded many people to buy Apple computers just to run it. The term quickly became applied to any kind of innovative technological product, employing *application* in the more general sense of 'the use to which something can be put'. In computing, the phrase is often abbreviated to **killer app**.

Most pundits point out that every technology needs a killer app to kickstart its acceptance.   —*Personal Computer World* May 1993, p. 518

After years of evangelizing ISDN, U.S. phone companies may finally have the 'killer application' that will stimulate demand for digital telephony.   —*Byte* June 1994, p. 25

Having initially been transformed by microelectronics, the consumer-electronics industry must now struggle to dream up new 'killer applications' as lucrative as personal stereos and video recorders.   —*Economist* 23 Mar. 1996, p. 15

killer bimbo ▨ see BIMBO

killing field /'kılıŋ fiːld/ *noun* 📷

A place of mass slaughter.

In the wake of the Vietnam War, the Communist guerrilla organization the Khmer Rouge took power in Cambodia in 1975, and in the next four years, under their leader Pol Pot, undertook a forced reconstruction of Cambodian society. This involved mass deportations from the towns to the countryside, and the executions of many thousands of Cambodians as 'bourgeois elements' in what became known as the *killing fields*.

Events in Cambodia, and in particular the scale of killing, were reported by a number of Western journalists, but it was with the release in 1984 of the film *The Killing Fields* that the phrase passed into the language. From the early nineties, the term has been used not just in reference to Cambodia, but to denote any site of large-scale killing; in the transferred use the genocidal connotation is now dominant, while the original sense of the second element of *killing field* as indicating a rural rather than an urban area has lost its distinctive force.

As many as 50,000 Armenians were murdered in this little killing field.
—Independent 4 Apr. 1992, Magazine section, p. 23

2,000 men and women…traveled from all over the country to stage a massive protest at the killing fields and end these pigeon shoots once and for all. *—Animals* Nov. 1992, p. 22

The tens of thousands of ritualised revenge-killings that have in recent times transformed Haiti into a killing field. *—Focus* Aug. 1995, p. 40

kinesiology /kɪˌniːsɪˈɒlədʒi, kʌɪˌniːsɪˈɒlədʒi/ *noun* ⊗

A therapeutic technique in which physical conditions are diagnosed using tests which identify imbalances in muscle strength, and treated using touch as a means of correcting imbalances in the body's energy system.

The term *kinesiology* to mean 'the study of the mechanics of body movements' was coined in 1894, but its use in this specialized sense is of much more recent origin. **Applied kinesiology**, as it is also called, has been used from the late eighties as one of a range of alternative health care techniques: the process involves testing muscle strength to locate weaknesses in internal organs, especially as a result of allergic reaction.

The term *kinesiology* is also used for processes intended to remedy the effects of DYSPRAXIA in relation to learning difficulties: the theory here is that the difficulties perceived result from inadequate stimulation of one side of the brain, and that this can be remedied by appropriate exercise.

The growing interest in natural remedies and health care has ensured that both forms of *kinesiology* have been promoted by **kinesiologists** and other advocates, but their efficacy is still a matter of debate among practitioners of traditional medicine.

Testing is done by means of applied kinesiology, which uses the body to indicate the product it will accept or reject. *—Here's Health* Dec. 1990, p. 53

A variety of massage therapists, applied kinesiologists, and physical therapists around the country do excellent work and can really help many back problems. *—Dressage & CT* Apr. 1993, p. 19

Kinesiology is said to be the fastest growing natural care system in the world, using muscle testing to 'read' the body and bring about balance by enhancing the body's natural healing abilities.
—Kindred Spirit Sept. 1995, p. 84

knowbot 💻 see –BOT

K/S 🐾 📷 see SLASH

L

Ladette POP ⦃ see NEW LAD

lambada /lam'bɑːdə/ *noun* ▨

A fast and erotic dance of Brazilian origin, in which couples dance with their stomachs touching; also, the rhythmic music to which it is danced.

A Brazilian Portuguese word which literally means 'a beating, a lashing'.

The *lambada* has been danced in Brazil for many years, but its existence was first acknowledged by the English-speaking world in 1988, when the dance re-emerged in São Paulo, perhaps in response to the craze for 'dirty dancing' (after the film of the same title, 1987). A French disc called 'Lambada' was a hit throughout Europe in 1989, and North and Central America soon responded to the tide of interest. A verb **lambada** also exists. So popular did the dance become that the word has entered the language in a metaphorical sense: if your nerves or feelings are **doing the lambada** it means that you are very agitated.

> A spokesperson for CBS's Epic records described the lambada as 'an alternative to sex in the age of AIDS'. —*Esquire* Jan. 1991, p. 84

> I'm trying to act and sound calm...but my nerves are doing the lambada as I frantically work to come up with some kind of an answer. —*Coloradoan* (Fort Collins) 28 Mar. 1993, p. 1

> Monica nipped off to a trendy Latin-American club and lambada-ed out the door with a sexy Italian called Giorgio. —*Guardian* 3 May 1993 section 2, p. 10

Lamivudine Ⓧ see AZT

lamping /'lampɪŋ/ *noun* ▨

A form of hunting, practised at night, which makes use of a bright light to illuminate or dazzle the hunted animal.

The verb *to lamp* was used in the 19th century in the sense 'to light as with a lamp'. In the new hunting sense *lamping*, a noun formed from the present participle of the verb, represents a specialization of context. *Pit-lamping* and *pit-lighting* developed in the same hunting sense in Canadian English in the early years of the century, formed on *pit-lamp*, a Canadian miner's lamp.

The term *lamping* was first recorded in this sense in the mid eighties, and refers to a form of poaching in which the prey is illuminated by the beam of a bright light. This also dazzles and confuses the animal, which is then brought down by a hunting dog or by a weapon, usually a gun. There is evidence of the manufacture of specialist **lamping equipment**, which includes guns fitted with spotlights. This suggests a growing commercialization of this stealthy nocturnal activity. Those who engage in *lamping* are known as **lampers**.

> The lampers had split up, though still within contact distance (working two men and a dog to a beam). —*BBC Wildlife* July 1985, p. 326

> A warning to other farmers not to approach poachers was made this week after he was shot in the back with a shotgun without warning...'We have had problems in the past with lamping, but it is just something that happens when you live on the urban fringe'. —*Farmers Guardian* 7 Aug. 1992, p. 8

> We are led into the nocturnal world of Ashcroft and Ninepenny Wood, Kent, and come face to snout with the badgers and the foxes, as well as the lampers and the diggers. —*New Scientist* 22 Aug. 1992, p. 39

LAN /lan/ *acronym* 🖳

Short for **local area network,** a system of linking together computers, usually in the same office or building, so that they can communicate and share resources.

The initial letters of *Local Area Network*.

The first *local area networks* were developed in the seventies; by the early eighties, the acronym *LAN* was being used as a pronounceable word in its own right. With the irresistible move away from mainframes to stand-alone personal computers and workstations during the eighties and nineties, the *LAN* soon became an essential component of the corporate computing environment. *LANs* are now being used extensively to link users to large corporate databases using client-server technologies, to tie them together in workgroups, and to connect them to the world outside the office by electronic mail, fax, voice mail, videoconferencing, and other techniques. To permit portable computing and avoid the need to cable buildings, **wireless LANs** are sometimes installed, which transmit data over radio or infra-red links. Some smaller networks avoid the need for a dedicated central *server* by making all the computers connected to the network equal partners; each user on such a **peer-to-peer LAN** (see PEER) can determine which of their resources are to be made communally available. In the nineties there has been a significant tendency for the term *LAN* to be replaced in compounds and everyday speech by the more general terms *network* and *networking*; *LAN* seems destined to return to being a specialist term.

> We've installed and continue to support a number of varied network environments—from LANS to WANS. —*New York Times* 17 Oct. 1989, section C, p. 13

> On the peer-to-peer LAN, each workstation can become a server for the printer connected to it. —*Computer Buyer's Guide* Mar. 1992, p. 20

> The fact is that the low throughput and high prices of today's wireless LANs are keeping a tight lid on user enthusiasm. —*Data Communications International* 21 Mar. 1995, p. 146

landfill /'lan(d)fɪl/ *transitive* or *intransitive verb* 🌳

To dispose of (refuse) by burial at a landfill site; to fill (something) with landfill.

A verb formed from the noun *landfill* in its senses 'a site where refuse is disposed of by burial under layers of earth', 'the action of disposing of refuse by burial at such a site', and 'material disposed of at such a site or material used to level an excavated site'.

The noun was first used in American English in the early years of the century, but it was not until the late eighties that a first use of the verb was recorded. The verb is frequently used within the context of waste management, and it is also used as a euphemism for the verb *dump*. As part of the heightened awareness of environmental issues in the eighties and nineties, concerns have been expressed about pollution, especially from the seepage of toxic substances through the earth and into the water supply. The noun **landfilling,** formed on the present participle of the verb, is used in the same senses as the noun *landfill*.

> The true foe of degradability is landfilling. —*New York Times* 28 Nov. 1989, section A, p. 24

> By late 1986 LAWPCA had landfilled 10.6 acres with sludge. —*Public Works* Oct. 1991, p. 67

> Sewage sludge heavily contaminated with toxic metals is unsuitable for use as a fertilizer. Instead, it has to be landfilled, creating a pollution threat to water, or incinerated, risking the release of toxins into the air and concentrated in the ash which itself has to be dumped. —*Earth Matters* Autumn 1992, p. 10

> We're talking about millions and millions of pounds' worth of equipment being landfilled every year without any real thought as to how that equipment could be recycled. —*Independent* 13 Nov. 1995, section 2, p. 14

latte /'lɑːteɪ/ *noun* ▓

A drink of steamed milk with a shot of strong coffee.

From the second element of the Italian *caffè latte* 'coffee with milk'.

Since the early eighties, first in America and more recently in Britain, coffee as a drink has become increasingly fashionable, with varying forms now readily available. In the last decade, numerous speciality coffee bars have appeared, as have espresso stands at the roadside and in stations and airports. The earlier form **cafe latte** has now largely given way to the more familiar *latte* as the order given by a customer, and **Latteland** has even been coined as a jocular name for Seattle, in reference to the popularity of *latte* there.

> Newcomers are easily hooked on lattes (espresso mixed with a generous portion of steamed milk). —*New York Times* 19 Jan. 1992, section V, p. 10

> Beverages like espresso macchiato, cafe latte, and granitas are becoming the drinks of choice. —*Hispanic* Mar. 1994, p. 38

> I would love to take Dalí out for a cup of latte. —*Spy* Sept. 1994, p. 50

laxative abuse ⟨⟩ see ABUSE

league table /'liːg teɪb(ə)l/ *noun* ⟨⟩

In the UK, a listing of schools, hospitals, or similar institutions, showing their rankings according to defined measures of performance.

A *table* of those seen as competitors within a *league* in the sense of 'a group of contestants of comparable ability'.

The term *league table*, associated first and perhaps primarily with the sporting world, has in Britain in the nineties increasingly been used in the fields of health and education. The publishing of *league tables* to allow the public to assess given standards of performance is closely linked to the introduction of CHARTERS for specified areas and has formed part of the same debate. Particular concern has been expressed that the comparisons drawn inevitably focus on particular aspects of performance, and may not make sufficient allowance for the role of an individual institution within its own community.

> Whether it is Citizen's Charter or Passenger's Charter, school examination league tables or health service waiting lists, the result is the same. Service delivery is to be monitored as never before, as information is seen as the key to developing motivation and customer satisfaction. —*Independent* 16 Apr. 1992, p. 18

> School welfare officers fear the new truancy league tables may risk stigmatising some schools and pupils as criminals and dens of crime. —*Times Educational Supplement* 5 Mar. 1993, p. 3

lean /liːn/ *adjective* ⌁

Of a business or a sector of the economy: 'slimmed down' or rendered more efficient or competitive through the reduction of unnecessary costs or expenditure.

The use of *lean* in application to business or to the economy was first recorded in Britain in the early eighties, as part of the vocabulary of the free market and popular capitalism promoted by the Conservative government under Margaret Thatcher. Reduction of costs was sought in a number of ways, including greater manufacturing efficiency explored in such systems as JUST-IN-TIME. A *lean* business was also seen to be one which had shed excess expenditure, including that on staff, and the term, which survived the recession of the early nineties, came to be associated particularly with downsizing (see -SIZE). A number of formulations based on *lean* were engendered, with associations sometimes of aggression (**leaner and meaner**) but usually of health and fitness, as in the most common, **leaner and fitter**.

> Industry was now leaner and fitter and in a much better position to compete. —*Observer* 6 Feb. 1983, p. 20

> Lean production enables volume carmakers to go into exotic markets and win niches there. —*Economist* 22 Sept. 1990, p. 19

> In a similar vein, leaner-and-meaner companies tell us they are avidly cutting costs. —*New York Review of Books* 7 Mar. 1991, p. 46

Such observations as: 'We've slimmed down to the tune of 150 people' and 'Er, we think you'll find us a much leaner and fitter organisation,' are popular. —*Independent* 30 Mar. 1993, p. 25

legacy /'lɛgəsi/ *noun* 🖳

Used attributively to describe computer software that has been in service for many years and which has become expensive and difficult to maintain but on which the business using it still depends.

A figurative sense of the word, with the implication of an unsatisfactory *legacy* from past generations of programmers.

The large numbers of mainframe computer systems installed in the last two decades or so have left many large companies with substantial amounts of old software which was written within their own organizations to meet their special needs. The cost of replacing it is often prohibitive, so it has to be kept running. However, the cost of maintaining it is also very great, since it is often written in outdated computer languages, in many cases the people who wrote it have long since moved on or retired, and sometimes it is no longer obvious how it works. The problem is made worse because much of such software coded the year as two digits instead of four (to save space and because nobody expected it still to be in service so many years later) and so will go seriously wrong on 1 January 2000 (see MILLENNIUM BUG). Such software is variously called a **legacy application**, **legacy code**, **legacy software**, or a **legacy system**.

Furthermore, users are only redeveloping legacy software when it provides down-to-earth cost benefits. At the moment, when users re-engineer, it is by using limited serviceable tools to retain some of the legacy applications investment. —*Computing* 3 June 1993, p. 27

Many offices have hardware and software that was once state-of-the-art but would now not look out of place in an IT antiques roadshow. Euphemisms range from legacy systems to heritage computing, and the items are not confined to midrange systems or mainframes.
—*Computer Weekly* 15 Sept. 1994, p. 32

As the twenty-first century approaches, more than half of all US programming and software engineering jobs involve some kind of maintenance of legacy systems.
—*Computer* Apr. 1995, p. 70

lesbian chic 🔛 📖 see LIPSTICK LESBIAN

le Shuttle /lə 'ʃʌt(ə)l/ *noun* Also written **Le Shuttle** 🎲

The shuttle service providing for the transport of motor vehicles on trains through the Channel Tunnel. Also, a train used for this service.

Le, the definite article in French, and *shuttle* 'a train, bus, or other form of transport going to and fro over a short route continuously'.

Construction of the Channel Tunnel, a railway tunnel under the English Channel, linking the coasts of England and France, was begun in 1987; the tunnel was opened in 1994. Terminals near Folkestone in England and Calais in France enable motor vehicles to be loaded on to *le Shuttle* for the journey through the 49-km (31-mile) tunnel.

Franglais won the day. Hoping to appeal to both French and British passengers, Eurotunnel is to call its car-train service Le Shuttle. —*Economist* 11 July 1992, p. 71

The chateau is just 30 minutes drive from Calais, and only a short journey from Folkestone, via Le Shuttle. —*She* Apr. 1996, p. 140

See also EUROSTAR

level playing field /lɛv(ə)l 'pleɪɪŋ fiːld/ *noun phrase* 〰️ 📷

A sphere of activity which offers no advantage to any particular side (a playing field which is not level may offer unfair advantages to the home side, who will be familiar with it).

Since the eighties, the image of a *level playing field* as providing a situation in which a number of contestants could compete without any of them being unfairly advantaged has become increasingly popular in the worlds of business and politics. The term is now regarded as something of a cliché, and a number of instances suggest scepticism that the implied equality of opportunity is to be readily achieved.

> That is not a level playing field. It is not even just a home-field advantage. It is like asking their competitors to play ball in a swamp. —*Washington Journalism Review* May 1990, p. 24

> A perfect example of the flawed thinking emanating from some quarters in Washington, replete with clichés about level playing fields and competitiveness.
> —*International Affairs* 1991, Vol. 67, p. 334

> They are still not providing a level playing field in terms of opportunities for women.
> —*Accountancy* Nov. 1995, p. 22

life, get a 🔲 see GET A LIFE

lifestyle /ˈlʌɪfstʌɪl/ *noun* and *adjective* Also written life-style ⚡ 🔲

In marketing jargon:

noun: The sum total of the likes and dislikes of particular customers or a section of the market, as expressed in the products that they would buy to fit their self-image and way of life; a marketing strategy based on the idea of appealing to this sense of self-image and way of life.

adjective: Using or belonging to this strategy of marketing; (of a product) fitting into or conceived as part of such a strategy, appealing to a customer's sense of lifestyle.

A specialized use of the compound noun *lifestyle* in the sense 'way of life', itself a concept of the sixties.

The concept of *lifestyle* merchandising goes back to the mid seventies, but was particularly in evidence in the second half of the eighties, as advertisers attempted to cash in on and shape the demand for fashion goods, interior decorations, foods, and sports equipment that expressed the new awareness of *lifestyle*. At the same time a movement in the very opposite direction, away from conspicuous consumption and consumerism, was also under way; this movement urged a simpler and greener *lifestyle* on Western societies. Both the consumers of yuppie *lifestyle* products and the followers of this movement towards simplicity have been called **lifestylers**.

> Creative talents in marketing have grasped the concept of lifestyle so insistently that it is changing the face of the high street, the commercials break, even the media.
> —*Creative Review* Jan. 1988, p. 14

> Swissair has gone life-style with its series of 'customer portraits' (would you buy a second-hand seat from this man?). —*International Management* Mar. 1990, p. 60

> The centre is built on a hilltop amid a broadleaf wood and is home to a community of proselytising alternative lifestylers. —*Holiday Which?* Mar. 1991, p. 97

> The latest lifestyle choice for the vibrant elderly is the 'retirement village', an American invention pitched somewhere between Club Med and Brookside, destined to become the apple of every estate agent's eye. —*Independent* 16 Jan. 1995, p. 19

Liffe /lʌɪf/ *acronym* Also written LIFFE ⚡

Short for **London International Financial Futures Exchange**, a financial institution which deals specifically in *futures*, 'stocks, or contracts for stocks, sold for future delivery'. Also, the index published by the Exchange.

The inital letters of *London International Financial Futures Exchange*.

The *London International Financial Futures Exchange*, much more commonly known by the abbreviation *Liffe*, was established in London in 1982. Its growth as the decade advanced and into the nineties is attributable to an increasing interest in the buying of futures as a form of investment with risk attached but with high returns.

> Last year almost 30m contracts were traded on LIFFE, the London International Financial Futures Exchange.   *—Economist* 29 June 1991, p. 96

> Why does Liffe, which is, after all, Europe's biggest futures market with turnover topping £100 billion on a busy day, still rely on face-to-face dealing?   *—Guardian* 13 Aug. 1994, p. 32

> On Liffe the March 10-year bund future reached 100.15 but slipped in the afternoon.
>   *—Financial Times* 11 Jan. 1996, p. 32

lipstick lesbian /lɪpstɪk ˈlɛzbɪən/ *noun* POP

A lesbian of glamorous or manifestly feminine appearance.

This phrase, which is recorded from the mid eighties, contains within it an element of conscious contradiction. The implication is that the prototypical lesbian eschews such enhancements as lipstick, and thus one who uses it is of a distinct type, either one who maintains a feminine role or one who opts for glamour; associated phrases are *glamour dyke* and *designer dyke*.

In recent years, **lipstick lesbianism** has been associated with the choice of many politically active women to look and to dress in a style representing a conscious breaking away from a conventional stereotype.

The *lipstick lesbian* may also be regarded as a proponent of *lesbian chic*, an overtly feminine and glamorous style adopted by lesbians in the nineties.

> All these gorgeous women are getting into it, from the elegant lipstick lesbians to the post-punk baby dykes.   *—This Mag.* Nov. 1994, p. 12

> Ever since pretty young Beth Jordache first kissed her lady tutor on *Brookside*, gay girls have become rather fashionable…and the opportunity to write about 'lipstick lesbianism' and 'designer dykes' has not gone unseized.   *—Daily Telegraph* 16 May 1995, p. 19

> Much as lesbian activists disdain the press's tendency to classify them as either 'diesel dykes' or 'lipstick lesbians', gay women delight in the nuances of their image.
>   *—Independent on Sunday* 2 July 1995, p. 23

> The advent of lesbian chic blew the old stereotype of crop-haired dykes in army fatigues and workboots out of the window and finally brought the heterosexual population in on the secret every gay woman has always known: lesbians are just as likely to wear Nicole Fahri as Milletts and to be found sporting waist-length tresses as a number one crop.
>   *—Independent* 29 Dec. 1995, Supplement, p. 7

LISTSERV /ˈlɪstsəːv/ *noun* Also written **listserv**

The trade mark of a computer application which supervises electronic mailing lists; more generally, any such application, or, loosely, the mailing list itself.

A compound of *list*, short for *mailing list*, with an abbreviated form of *server*; the name was truncated to fit the eight-character limit on the mainframe system on which it was first created.

Electronic mailing lists have proved an excellent tool for distributing messages, newsletters, and other topical material by e-mail to subscribers over computer networks, particularly the INTERNET. The *LISTSERV* program, which carries a trade mark in the US, automates housekeeping for the list administrator, managing subscription lists, despatching documents to subscribers, optimizing deliveries to minimize network usage, maintaining archives and responding automatically to e-mailed requests for information. As well as sending messages from the administrator, it can also be set up to permit a subscriber to e-mail a message to it which it then forwards to all other subscribers, a system conceptually very similar to that of

Usenet NEWSGROUPS. The program was originally developed in the mid eighties as free software for the BITNET system, but from 1993 onwards has been commercially marketed. The term *listserv* is also used as a generic term for any mailing list management system; an alternative term is **list server**.

Sending an e-mail message to a colleague or posting a message on a listserv is today's equivalent of running down the hall to a colleague's office or phoning an expert to pick his or her brain.
—*Information World Review* Dec. 1994, p. 46

So many people wrote in to talk about their problems that *Soundprint* created a LISTSERV—an on-line discussion group for listeners nationwide—which was still going on months after the broadcast. —*Minnesota Monthly* Jan. 1995, p. 152

You can freely subscribe to a mailing list (also called listservs) if you want to stay informed via e-mail on a particular genre of music or a band. —*Alternative Press* May 1995, p. 22

living will /ˈlɪvɪŋ wɪl/ *noun*

A document written by a person while still legally fit to do so, requesting that he or she should be allowed to die rather than be kept alive by artificial means if subsequently severely disabled or suffering from a terminal illness.

The concept of the *living will* was first discussed in legal circles in the US in the late sixties. The documents themselves acquired legal status in several states during the seventies, and by the end of the eighties most states in the US recognized them. The *Patient Self-Determination Act*, which came into force in December 1991, required state governments to clarify their laws on patients' rights to accept or refuse treatment. The term *advance directive* is now often used in the US and the UK as a synonym for *living will*, but more properly is a prior statement of refusal to permit certain specific types of medical treatment. Interest in the idea only began to grow in the UK in the late eighties and no specific legislation has been put in place. However, by the mid nineties it had become accepted, as a result of a number of court cases reaffirming common law, that the wishes of patients could be binding on doctors; following a request from the House of Lords Select Committee on Medical Ethics, the British Medical Association issued new guidelines to this effect in April 1995.

Most of the presentations at the Hemlock conference had been about passive euthanasia, or letting people die: hospices, living wills, plug-pulling. —*Harper's Magazine* Apr. 1994, p. 75

New guidelines concerning advance directives, sometimes known as 'living wills', stress that doctors who force unwanted treatment on patients face legal action for assault.
—*Guardian* 6 Apr. 1995, section 1, p. 8

LMS see OPT OUT²

local management of schools see OPT OUT²

London International Financial Futures Exchange see LIFFE

love dove see ECSTASY, LOVED-UP

loved-up /ˈlʌvdʌp/ *adjective*

Intoxicated by the drug ECSTASY.

From the popular idea that Ecstasy is an aphrodisiac (one of the colloquial names for an Ecstasy tablet is *love dove*).

A term recorded from the early nineties, particularly in descriptions of participants of RAVES. The term implies both the condition of extreme intoxication which might earlier have been described as *stoned*, and the sense of euphoria and well-being associated with Ecstasy.

Yet the first people I met in it were British: fine, upstanding members of Her Majesty's Army, all set

for a night's raving and loved-up to the eyeballs with something you can't get from the NAAFI.
—*The Face* Feb. 1992, p. 72

Although the majority of 'loved-up' ravers will pass through a night happy and unscathed, there will always be a number who run into trouble either health-wise, because they don't heed the warning signs, or because they have been unlucky to get busted. —*DJ* 6 July 1995, p. 41

loyalty card /ˈlɔɪəlti kɑːd/ *noun* 📈

An identity card issued by a retailer to its customers so that each individual transaction can be recorded in order to amass credits for future discounts or other benefits.

Loyalty cards made their appearance in the nineties, as part of a consumer incentive policy whereby particular stores sought to ensure that customers would naturally return to the same source for future purchases; the retailer is also provided with statistical information about the customer. While in the eighties the marketing of *affinity cards* by banks and building societies appealed to the social conscience by stressing the benefit to the charity receiving a proportion of the money spent while using the credit card, in the nineties the appeal of the *loyalty card* is directly to the pocket, and by implication to the good sense and thrift of the customer.

In Ontario…, Ultra Mart and Miracle Mart…are providing shoppers with 'affinity' or 'loyalty' cards, which, when scanned through computerized checkouts deduct savings on advertised specials.
—*Canadian Living* (Toronto) Sept. 1993, p. 23

All the big supermarket groups have experimented with loyalty cards giving rebates or discounts tied to spending levels. —*Independent on Sunday* 23 Jan. 1994, p. 3

All the other major supermarket chains are developing loyalty cards.
—*Daily Telegraph* 15 May 1995, p. 14

luvvy /ˈlʌvi/ *noun* Also written **luvvie**

In jocular and mildly derogatory use: an actor or actress.

A respelling of the affectionate term of address *lovey*. The development of *luvvy* as a noun reflects the stereotype of an actor or actress as a demonstrative person given to using endearments as a form of address.

When the term first entered the language in this sense, at the start of the nineties, it was used especially of actors or actresses considered to be particularly effusive or affected. It was also, in its earlier usage, associated with the actor or actress who, in his or her need to find work, has to accept parts within second-rate productions. The term thus represented a kind of dramatic 'froth'. However, it is now used increasingly broadly of members of the acting profession in general; and as the use has broadened it has become less derogatory, although still not entirely neutral. This extension of use may have been accelerated by the use of **luvvies** as a title for a column on theatrical gossip in the British satirical magazine *Private Eye*. The derivatives **luvviedom** and **luvviness** have developed to represent the world of the *luvvy* and the state or quality of being one. The adjective **luvvyish** has also been recorded.

Actors are always saying that the stage is the loneliest place in the world and I'd always thought it was hyperbolic luvvy talk. —*Daily Telegraph* 24 Mar. 1992, p. 16

Margaret Courtenay and Peter Baylis as the outdated old luvvies and Oliver Cotton as the radical young Robertson figure, seem to have worked out what the play is about.
—*Spectator* 19 Dec. 1992, p. 91

The neurosis doesn't appear to be a straight case of inverted luvviedom—the 'I'm-so-nervous-tell-me-I-was-fab' school of drama queens.
—*Independent on Sunday* 26 June 1994, Review section, p. 26

Lymeswold /ˈlaɪmzwəʊld/ *noun* 🟧

The trade mark of a type of English blue cheese, soft in texture and mild-tasting.

An invented name, intended to evoke associations of the English countryside, with the final syllable echoing *wold*, 'a piece of high uncultivated land'. Ultimately, it may represent an alteration of *Wymeswold*, the name of a town in Leicestershire.

One of a number of new cheeses produced in the early eighties, *Lymeswold* (unlike the German CAMBOZOLA) failed to establish itself in an expanding market, and in 1992 was withdrawn from sale.

> The first new English cheese for 200 years was launched yesterday…Lymeswold is the first soft blue cheese to be produced commercially in Britain.   *—Daily Telegraph* 28 Sept. 1982, p. 6
>
> The man is as mild as Lymeswold.   *—Guardian Weekly* 4 Sept. 1988, p. 24
>
> On April 27th Lymeswold was ignominiously withdrawn from the market. The French must be cackling over their Camembert.   *—Economist* 2 May 1992, p. 103

lymphadenopathy syndrome Ⓧ see AIDS

• •

Maastricht /ˈmɑːstrɪxt/ *noun* 〰️ ⌂

An agreement reached between the heads of government of the twelve member states of the European Community at a summit meeting held in Maastricht, an industrial city in the Netherlands, near the borders with Belgium and Germany, in December 1991. The **Maastricht Treaty** was designed to pave the way towards economic, monetary, and political union within the European Community; it also contained a protocol regarding social and employment policy in member states.

Initial steps towards European economic and political integration were first envisaged in 1957 in the Treaty of Rome, and the European Community was established ten years later. The *Maastricht Treaty* represented the next major development in plans for European unity. Following the agreement reached in December 1991, progress towards ratification of the treaty was impeded by a number of factors. Principal among these were disagreements over steps towards a SINGLE CURRENCY, and the disinclination on the part of some member countries, notably Britain, to accept certain directives set out in the SOCIAL CHAPTER. *Maastricht*, which was seen by some as representing a threat to national sovereignty, was widely discussed in British newspapers in the early nineties, especially the *opt-out clause* (see OPT-OUT¹) and the principle of SUBSIDIARITY asserted by Britain as conditions of ratification. The treaty was eventually ratified in October 1993 and came into effect on 1 November that year; nevertheless *Maastricht* did not win total acceptance within the newly defined EUROPEAN UNION, and it was subjected to further scrutiny in the spring of 1996 at the EU's inter-governmental review conference, known informally as **Maastricht 2**.

The term *Maastricht* came to be adopted by both pro-Europeans and EUROSCEPTICS as a code word for the political philosophy of each camp. Formulations such as **Maastricht-friendly**, **Maastricht-weary**, and **anti-Maastrichtian** appeared, along with suggestions for **Maastricht-minus**, a less ambitious version of the treaty. Even in the US the word *Maastricht* has been used to convey the notion of endangered national sovereignty.

> Sadly, Britain has been on the wrong foot over Europe from the beginning. It will never really influence things until it gets on to the right foot. Maastricht, for all its shortcomings, is the place to start. Mr Major should sign on for EMU, and lead the campaign for a central bank with complete independence to pursue price stability.   *—Economist* 23 Nov. 1991, p. 16
>
> In the European Community, resistance to closer integration through the Maastricht treaty also reflects suspicion at the pace of change, and worry about losing even more control over local

community life. 'Euro-this' and 'Euro-that' seem to mean even more adaptation to new rules, new competitors and new values: time for time-out.

—*Globe & Mail* (Canada) 7 Nov. 1992, section D, p. 6

Those green articles of NAFTA, the pack snarls, represent the most fundamental threat to sovereignty ever faced by this nation—an 'economic Maastricht', no less.

—*Insight on the News* (Washington) 11 Oct. 1993, p. 29

If Britain adopted such a strategy, it could wreck next month's summit of EU leaders in Florence and delay the 'Maastricht 2' talks on Europe's future which began in March.

—*The Times* 12 May 1996 (electronic edition)

MacBride principles /məkbrʌɪd 'prɪnsɪp(ə)lz/ *noun* Also written MacBride Principles 📖

A code of conduct which recommends that firms located in Northern Ireland should pursue a conscious policy of ensuring that their recruitment achieves a balanced representation of the local community. The code was initially formulated for and suggested to companies from the US.

Named after Seán *MacBride* (1904–88), Irish statesman and promoter of human rights, who first advocated the code of conduct. The son of John MacBride, who was executed for his part in the Easter Rising of 1916, and the actress Maud Gonne, he was chief of staff of the IRA at the age of 24, going on to become, in 1950, president of the Council of Foreign Ministers of the Council of Europe, and in 1977 president of the International Commission for the Study of Communication Problems, set up by UNESCO.

The *MacBride principles* were created in 1976 as part of an attempt to secure jobs for the Catholic minority in Northern Ireland. Discrimination against Catholics in local government, employment, and housing had led to violent conflict and, from 1969, the presence of British army units in an attempt to maintain civil order. Sectarian violence led to the imposition of direct rule from London in 1972. Against this unsettled background it was recognized that US companies, as major employers in Northern Ireland, might have a role to play in promoting civil rights and thus reducing one of the major obstacles to peace in the province. Against the background, in the nineties, of the DOWNING STREET DECLARATION, the application of the *MacBride principles* is still being actively pursued.

America's Irish lobby has campaigned hard for the MacBride principles, and several states have made them mandatory on local companies. —*Economist* 8 April 1989 (BNC)

If any further evidence is needed to underline the growing possibility of a US-British rift over Northern Ireland, Clinton emphasises his support for the 'MacBride Principles', which would require American firms based in Northern Ireland to abandon their operations there unless they complied with strict anti-discrimination criteria. —*Today* Dec. 1992 (BNC)

The New York Comptroller, Mr Alan Hevesi, has urged the British government and unionist politicians to accept and apply the MacBride Principles on fair employment.

—*Irish Times* 9 July 1994

See also MITCHELL PRINCIPLES

MACHO /'matʃəʊ/ *noun* Also written macho 🔬

A compact object of a kind which it is thought may constitute part of the dark matter in galactic haloes.

An acronym formed as a pun on WIMP. Various expansions of it are given in the literature, including *massive astrophysical compact halo object*.

It is suggested that haloes of matter must exist around spiral galaxies, like our Milky Way, in order to explain why they rotate. In order to explain why these haloes had not been observed directly, it was suggested in the late eighties that they might contain matter in the form of massive, dense objects. Such *MACHOs* could include *black holes* (objects so massive that their gravitational pull stops light escaping) or *brown dwarfs* (dim stars with the mass of a large planet). Hence their full name: they are thought to be small but massive astronomical objects in the haloes around galaxies. Recently, groups of astronomers claim to have detected them because they are massive enough to bend the light from distant objects. This matter is believed to form only a small part of the *dark matter* (see COLD DARK MATTER) which astronomers are sure must exist in the universe.

> MACHOs could be either dim stars (brown dwarfs) each with about the same mass as Jupiter, or black holes each with a mass up to a million times that of our Sun
> —*New Scientist* 19 Mar. 1994, Inside Science, p. 4

> The light curves of the lensed stars show a slight discrepancy from the shape predicted for MACHO lenses but closely fit the predictions for LMC-star lenses.   —*Sky & Telescope* Dec. 1994, p. 13

mad /mad/ *adjective* POP

In slang: remarkable, unusual, or exciting.

A use of the established adjective in the sense of 'wildly light-hearted, exuberant'; the usage may also be comparable with the development in the eighties of *wicked* as a term of approbation.

A term of approbation used particularly among participants in the dance-music and RAVE culture of the nineties.

> The superlative of the hour was not 'awesome' or even 'cool' but 'mad' as in 'mad house party'.
> —G. Donaldson *Ville* (1993), p. 14

> There was a mad B-Boyin' jam with the French Crew Actual Force representing with mad flavas.
> —*Represent* Apr. 1995, p. 26

mad cow disease ⊗ 【 see BSE

magainin /mə'gʌɪnɪn/ *noun* ⊗ 🔋

Any of a group of peptides with antimicrobial properties.

A compound of the Hebrew word *māgēn*, meaning 'shield', with the chemical suffix *-in*.

Because disease organisms quickly become immune to antibiotics, intensive research is being directed not only towards finding new ones, but also towards discovering new classes of antibiotics which act in different ways to the older ones. In the mid eighties, a substance was found on the skin of the African clawed frog which helped it fight infection; this substance was named *magainin* by its discoverer. More recently, a related compound *squalamine*, which seems to have a similar effect, has been found in the immune defence system of a shark. The way these compounds work suggests that they may also be helpful in fighting diseases of the immune system, such as HIV and AIDS.

> Michael Zasloff...shot to fame in the late 1980s when he publicised his discovery that African clawed frogs (*Xenopus laevis*) contained a chemical in their skin that helped them fight infection. He called this chemical 'magainin', the Hebrew word for shield.
> —*New Scientist* 30 Apr. 1994, p. 27

> Substances from the dogfish shark and the African clawed frog may be used to fight sexually transmitted diseases, including AIDS, scientists said Sunday. Dr. Leonard Jacob of Magainin Pharmaceuticals of Plymouth Meeting, Pa., said the compounds, called magainins or squalamines, have already passed preliminary testing and are being tested, or soon will be tested in humans.
> —*Washington Times* 12 Feb. 1996, section A, p. 7

Magic Eye ▢ ▨ see AUTOSTEREOGRAM

magic realism /madʒɪk 'riːəlɪz(ə)m/ *noun* 🦔 【

A literary style in which realistic techniques such as naturalistic detail and narrative are combined with surreal or dreamlike elements.

A translation of the German *magischer Realismus*, a term coined in 1924 by Franz Roh and used in 1925 in the subtitle of his book *Nach-Expressionismus*. The German form was used from the twenties to describe the work of members of the *Neue Sachlichkeit* group of German painters, which tended to depict fantastic or bizarre images in a precise representationalist manner. The English term *magic realism* was first recorded in the 1930s, and was used largely to refer to a style of painting which combined elements of realism and fantasy.

By the early eighties use of the term had been carried over into literature and this transferred sense became dominant in the eighties and nineties. It was applied to a literary genre deriving from the work of the Argentinian writer Jorge Luis Borges in the sixties and seventies, and associated strongly with the work of other Latin American writers such as Gabriel García Márquez, and with European writers including Italo Calvino, Angela Carter, and Salman Rushdie. By the nineties, use of the term had broadened to include any writing which contained elements of both realism and fantasy but which would not originally have been seen to belong to the genre of *magic realism*. The term **magic realist** is used both as an adjective, and as a noun denoting a practitioner of *magic realism*.

> The magic realist mode frees him from any obligation to make the incidents he devises probable or in any way convincing. —*Sunday Telegraph* 18 Feb. 1990, p. 50

> He searches for a suitable way in which to decorate a 'trade' paperback of yet another Latin American 'magic realist'.
> —*Highways & Transportation* (Appointments & Events Supplement) Aug. 1991, p. 110

> Where the folk tale meets the 20th century we get a form of storytelling often known as magic realism, an expression that should be a contradiction in terms. The task of the author is to convince us that the world of wolves and forests and strange transformations can take on the world of tanks and guns and reinforced concrete without surrendering its elemental vitality, and hence its validity. —*New York Times Book Review* 21 Nov. 1993, p. 9

magnetic resonance imaging ⊗ 🔬 see MRI

maiasaur /'mʌɪəsɔː/ *noun* 🔬

A large duck-billed dinosaur.

Formed from the modern Latin genus name *Maiasaura*, from the Greek elements *maia* 'good mother' and *saura* 'lizard'.

The twentieth century has seen an explosion of interest in dinosaurs (see DINO-), in terms both of popular culture and of scientific discovery. *Maiasaurs* are among many new species to be recorded, but are notable for the interpretation placed on the circumstances of the find after which they have been named.

The original find was of a presumed nest containing numerous young. This accorded well with the theory that dinosaurs provided parental care after their young hatched, much as modern birds do today, and the dinosaur was named *good mother lizard* in recognition of its qualities (and in implied contrast to the 'tyrant lizard' or tyrannosaur).

The maternal *maiasaur* features (alongside the predatory RAPTORS) in *Jurassic Park*, but more recently some doubt has been thrown on the interpretation of the find, with the suggestion being made that the development of the young would have allowed them to forage for themselves. In April 1996, an article questioning the case for extended parental care in dinosaurs was entitled 'Bad Mother Lizard'.

> You and I are obviously aware that dinosaurs, wildly popular as a motif in toys, games, books, clothing, interior design, and foodstuffs, are often inaccurately represented. We sense somehow that despite the maiasaurs' reputation for attentive parenting, the 'good mother lizards' didn't iron their kids' clothes like Mrs Sinclair of TV's *Dinosaurs*. —*Discover* May 1992, p. 82

> Although embryos have been discovered in the nests of maiasaura, the so-called 'good-mother lizard,' it would be the first such find among the big herbivores. —*Guardian* 23 Dec. 1993, p. 3

> That is…the outstanding issue concerning Horner's good mother lizard. Maiasaurs may have, like oviraptors, protected or incubated their eggs. But did they tend their helpless hatchlings?
> —*Earth* Apr. 1996, p. 23

MailMerge /ˈmeɪlməːdʒ/ *noun* and *verb* Also written **mail-merge**, **mail merge**, and **mailmerge** ▣

noun: A proprietary name for a program that draws on a data file (containing names, addresses, and possibly other information) and a text file to produce multiple copies of a letter, each addressed to a different recipient; the facility for doing this.

transitive verb: to carry out such a process on (data).

Referring to the technique of *merging* the data and text documents together to produce the letters.

It was recognized very early in the development of word processors that a valuable function would be to automate the process of dispatching circulars or advertising material to a large number of recipients. It was also quickly realized that by embedding commands within the text it would be possible not only to address each letter personally, but also to change the text itself to suit the circumstances of each recipient. It is now common to link *mailmerge* systems to databases of information, say about customers, in order to produce sophisticated mailings based on the information held; this now forms the basis of a substantial industry. The noun *mailmerge* was first used in the early eighties, initially (as a proprietary term) in capitalized form. It is now widely employed as a generic term, and is frequently used attributively. The verb appeared later in the decade, together with the adjective **mailmerged** and the verbal noun **mailmerging**. Occasionally, an action noun **mailmerger** appears.

> To send a letter to lots of people, you can 'mailmerge' it.   *—Which?* June 1991, p. 352

> Despite the bad smell that Reader's Digest mailshots have given it, mailmerge is one of the main things that makes word processors useful.   *—Personal Computer World* Jan. 1992, p. 410

> Michael Hewitt finds that low-cost Symantec Q&A is a star mailmerger.
>   *—Personal Computer World* Feb. 1994, p. 504

Majorism /ˈmeɪdʒərɪz(ə)m/ *noun* ▣

The political and economic policies of the British Conservative politician John Major (b. 1943, Prime Minister 1990–7).

Use of the suffix *-ism* to denote a policy identifiable with a particular politician is long-standing—*Gaullism* is a notable example—but gained in currency in the eighties when the terms *Reaganism* and *Thatcherism* were very widely used. *Majorism*, which was first used of John Major's economic policies during his period as Chief Secretary to the Treasury under Margaret Thatcher, came, after he succeeded as Prime Minister, to imply a difference between his policies and those of his predecessor, particularly when contrasted with the zeal of Thatcherism. As time went on *Majorism* came to denote a more moderate form of the promotion of a free market economy which characterized the Thatcher years. It also came to represent a moderate or centrist position, the Conservatism of BACK TO BASICS and the *Citizen's* CHARTER, separated by CLEAR BLUE WATER from the Conservative Right. For many, however, the term *Majorism*, which is used fairly freely by journalists as a code word for a range of characteristics, has remained unsatisfactorily vague.

The derivative **Majorite**, though much less common than *Thatcherite*, is used both as a noun, denoting a supporter of John Major's policies, and as an adjective.

> Empowerment will be the theme for the 1990s, giving Majorism a distinct difference from Thatcherism by addressing the problems of public service provision.
>   *—Parliamentary Affairs* 1991, XLIV, p. 573

> Portillo has made a judgement about the ground upon which the Tory Right—of which he is now self-consciously the leader—must fight back against eclectic Majorism.
>   *—Guardian* 12 Feb. 1994, p. 25

> He is now a fully fledged Majorite.   *—Economist* 18 Feb. 1995, p. 30

managed care /'manɪdʒd kɛː/ *noun* Ⓧ

A system of health care designed for the efficient management of resources.

Since the mid eighties, concerns about the rising costs of health care have focused on the management of available resources. Originating in the US, the concept of *managed care* involves an essentially proactive approach to preventive medicine, together with the development of systems such as HEALTH MAINTENANCE ORGANIZATIONS, intended to ensure that medical needs are paid for through a regular fixed charge rather than by the payment of a fee for specific services rendered.

In developed countries, which in the nineties have recognized the dual problems of soaring health costs and an ageing population, *managed care* represents an attempt to maximize the resources available by the application of concepts of business efficiency. The approach has caused some debate on the principles involved, and whether the result will be to provide what are regarded as the essentials of health care at an affordable cost for 'consumers' and taxpayers.

Managed care plans such as HMOs...put a case manager on the side of the patient.

—advertisement in *New Republic* 18 May 1992, p. 2

Bottom line: Managed care buys us little in the way of savings but may cost us much in terms of quality of care. —*Money* Apr. 1993, p. 117

Companies are steering employees away from fee-for-service medicine (with each doctor visit billed) and into managed care, particularly health maintenance organizations (doctor groups charging an annual fee per patient). This lowers insurance payments.

—*American Spectator* Feb. 1994, p. 37

Mandelbrot set /'mand(ə)lbrɒt sɛt/ *noun* ▣

A particular set of complex numbers which has a highly convoluted fractal boundary when plotted.

A compound of the name of Benoit B. *Mandelbrot*, a Polish-born American mathematician, who investigated the concept as part of his wider research into fractals in the seventies, and *set*, in its usual mathematical sense of 'a collection of entities all having some property in common'.

The *Mandelbrot set* is a mathematical construct that could not have been drawn before the age of high-speed computers with graphical abilities, since the number of calculations necessary to produce even a crude representation of it is very large. Of all the fractals, this one has caught the imagination more than any other, perhaps because of its particularly intricate shape and because it is surprising that something so remarkably complex should be produced by so simple and easily-understood a process. At one point in the late eighties it became something of a craze among computer users; it was reproduced on posters and in magazines, and many computer programs were written to display it. Much time was spent exploring it—as with all fractals, it can be enlarged indefinitely to reveal progressively finer detail. Its attractiveness was greatly increased by representing areas around the set by various colours to indicate the degree of divergence of each point from the set; it is not obvious from looking at such a coloured image that the *Mandelbrot set* itself is actually represented by the black core of the picture.

Monster curves, strange attractors, Mandelbrot and Julia sets—these are just some of the exotic fractals you'll generate on your PC. —*Science News* 1 Feb. 1992, p. 80

If you zoom in on the edges of the Mandelbrot set you find little copies of the butt, warts, disk, and stinger, some of the copies wound around into gnarly spirals, all swathed in diaphanous veils and gauzes of the loveliest imaginable colors.

—Rudolf Rucker, R. U. Sirius, & Queen Mu *Mondo 2000* (1993), p. 10

The fascinating thing about the Mandelbrot set, and fractals in general, is that the smaller the set of values you examine, and the greater number of iterations you use, the more complex the results. —*Guardian* 12 Aug. 1993, section 2, p. 17

marketeer /mɑːkɪ'tɪə/ *noun* ⋀ 【

A specialist in marketing; a person who is involved in the action or business of promoting and selling products, including market research and advertising.

From the verbal noun *marketing*; this represents a new formation and a new sense. (The existing noun *marketeer*, formed on the noun *market*, was used in the nineteenth century to mean 'one who sells in a market; a market-dealer'; later uses include those denoting a supporter of Britain's entry into the *Common Market* and a supporter of the FREE MARKET.)

Businesses have always used marketing of various kinds to promote their products, but the eighties and nineties have seen the establishment and growth of marketing departments within a much broader range of organizations. No longer associated only with the selling of consumer goods, marketing departments, frequently known formerly as *publicity departments*, now aim to promote *concepts*; and these are directed towards people newly regarded as *customers*. At a time of reduced government spending, cultural organizations have had to learn how to promote their activities to potential funders; HOSPITAL TRUSTS must now promote themselves within the new health service; and charities need to sell themselves to potential donors. It is into this increasingly market-led world that the *marketeer*, a *marketer* with specialist skills, has been born.

> Analysis of the over-55s—a group of consumers currently much observed by marketeers—shows that they can be segmented into four distinct sub-groups.
> —*Financial Times* 22 Sept. 1988, p. 28

> A year after Desert Storm, the celebration continues—especially on Madison Avenue. If you're feeling nostalgic on the Gulf War's first birthday, the marketeers are ready to touch that feeling.
> —*Mother Jones* Jan. 1992, p. 16

See also MISSION STATEMENT

market makers ⋀ see SEAQ

marzipan layer /'mɑːzɪpan ˌleɪə/ *noun* ⋀ 📰 【

In the jargon of the British Stock Market: the stockbroking executives ranking immediately below the partners in a firm. Also, by extension, those people deemed to rank just below the highest echelon of a community.

A figurative use of *marzipan layer*, the layer of almond paste which lies beneath the sugar icing on a rich cake. Although it is not the top layer, it is nevertheless rich and somewhat luxurious.

Figurative use of the noun *marzipan* to denote a range of coverings or embellishments is well established. Specific use of the compound *marzipan layer* within the world of the Stock Market was first observed in the early eighties. Use of the term, and the alternative **marzipan set**, has now spread beyond the City to other contexts characterized by a hierarchy of influence or expertise. It is used of those who have not yet reached the top but are likely to do so, unlike those whose careers have been blocked by a GLASS CEILING. More generally, the term is now applied to young professional people who already have some of the attributes of wealth and power to which they aspire.

> Graduate scientists take (often non-scientific) jobs in industry and commerce. Many of the best and brightest go into the City and join the Marzipan Set (above the cake but below the icing).
> —*Observer* 26 Apr. 1987, p. 8

> Britain's 'Marzipan layer' already spend far more of their disposable income on housing and education than their German and French peers.   —*Sunday Telegraph* 29 Mar. 1992, p. 40

> The spill-over effect of resurgent prosperity in many Hong Kong economic sectors has not yet percolated down, from the top level of collectors, to the 'marzipan layer' which has produced so many new middle-range collectors.   —*Christie's International Magazine* June 1992, p. 14

massively parallel /'masɪvli ˌparəlɛl/ *adjective* 🖳

Of or relating to a computer which consists of many individual processing units, and which is thus able to carry out simultaneous calculations on a substantial scale.

The first computers operated serially: instructions were carried out one by one by a very small number of processors (commonly just one) operating on data within a single shared area of working memory. This approach, with modifications, worked well for thirty years, but the ever-increasing demands for processing power, changes in the nature of the problems that needed to be solved, and greater knowledge of the way the human brain processes tasks, led to a new method being invented. A **massively parallel computer** consists of a large number of individual processors, often thousands or even millions of them; each processor is given one small part of the problem to execute and the results are then combined. The processors are often simple, with a small amount of memory built in to each one; the complexity of the machine arises from the very large number of interconnections which can exist between the processing elements, which is similar to the way neurons are linked together in the brain (an early such computer with about 64,000 processors was called the *Connection Machine* for this reason). Such computers are particularly suited for running NEURAL nets and for processing visual information, where the system can act simultaneously on a large number of elements within the image. The technique is often called **massively parallel processing** (**MPP**).

> Cray Research, the world leader in supercomputing, has been under threat from firms selling massively parallel processing (MPP) machines built out of microprocessors.
> —*Guardian* 5 Oct. 1993, p. 23

> Rutgers University has acquired one of the largest 'massively parallel' computers on any college campus in the world, allowing the university to take its place at the forefront of research in such futuristic areas as 'voice identification' systems and high-performance computing.
> —*Star-Ledger* (Newark, New Jersey) 10 May 1994, p. 19

math(s) abuse 🅰 see ABUSE

max /maks/ *noun* and *verb* 🅿🅾🅿

noun: In the US slang phrase **to the max**: totally, completely, to the highest degree.

transitive or *intransitive verb*: In US slang, to do (something) to the limit; to excel, to perform to maximum ability or capacity, to peak. (Often as a phrasal verb **max out**.)

Max has been an abbreviated colloquial form of *maximum* since the middle of the nineteenth century, and it seems occasionally to have been used as a verb at that time. Both the phrasal uses result from the tendency for 'in' expressions to become fixed phrases among a particular group of people and then be picked up as phrases by outsiders. *Out* can be added to almost any verb in US slang.

The phrase *to the max* may have originated in US prep school slang in the late seventies (it is first recorded in print in the *Official Preppy Handbook* in 1980), but was at first particularly associated with the speech of young Californians. In the late eighties it appeared on occasion in British sources, but as a conscious Americanism. The verb *max out* has its roots in US prison slang, where it has been used in the sense 'to complete a maximum prison sentence' since at least the mid seventies. In the eighties and nineties, it has been used in a wide variety of different contexts, including the financial (giving or spending to the limit of one's resources), the physical (for example, exercising to the limit of one's endurance), and cases in which it simply means 'to peak'. The phrasal verb is the foundation for an adjective **maxed out**, at the limit of one's abilities or endurance.

> Compared to other areas, our patients have a multitude of problems…If we had three more centers like this we could fill them up easily. We're maxed out.
> —*New York Times* 5 Nov. 1991, Section B, p. 2

187

Like athletes who push their bodies to the max, dancers are no strangers to physical break-
downs.   —*Diabetes Forecast* May 1994, p. 19

Mb ▣ see MEG

Mbyte ▣ see MEG

medicide ⊗ ⦃ see DOCTOR-ASSISTED SUICIDE

meg /mɛg/ *noun* ▣

One megabyte (1,048,576 bytes) of computer memory or storage.

This term came into use in the early eighties, when personal computers began to appear with
fixed disks and with large enough amounts of memory for the memory size to have to
be expressed in megabytes rather than kilobytes. The usage remains informal, being much
more common in speech and in writing addressed to computer specialists than in formal
language, where the term is either spelled out in full or the abbreviations *Mb* or *Mbyte* are
used.

> This computer fever has been running through segments of our society for years now. It's a strange
> kind of lust: K hunger, meg hunger; spirals into the deepest and most deviant recesses of software
> releases and expensive peripherals...The mark of the hacker beast.
>   —B. Sterling *Hacker Crackdown* (1992), p. 182

> Akai S1000 8 meg, latest software, version 4.4.   —*Melody Maker* 25 Mar. 1995, p. 58

mega /'mɛgə/ *adjective* POP

In colloquial use: very large or important; on a grand scale; great.

From the Greek *megas* 'great'. The adjective was probably formed because the highly
productive combining form MEGA- was sometimes written as a free-standing element
(as in *mega star*) and the first element later came to be interpreted as a word in its own
right.

Mega has been in colloquial use, especially in the entertainment industry, since the early
eighties. At first it was used mainly in variations on *megastar* and *megastore*, describing a
person as a *mega* bore or a development as a *mega* project. By the mid eighties, it had also
started to be used predicatively (as in 'that's mega'). At the end of the decade, *mega* was
taken up as a favourite term of approval among young people, with a weakening of sense to
'very good' (a similar story to that of *great* two decades previously).

> I got the gabardine there. I must say that I think that it's absolutely mega. I got it in Auntie Hilda's
> shop—for a quid.   —*Guardian* 3 Aug. 1989, p. 34

> If you shoot colour negative film though, you shouldn't push it because you'll have mega problems
> finding a lab who'll process it and you may also get colour shifts.
>   —*Photo Answers* June 1991, p. 23

mega- /'mɛgə/ *prefix* ▣ ⚡ ⚗

The first element of a wide variety of compounds and blends, with the general
meaning 'very large' or 'very great' (but see below for specific meanings in different
subject fields).

From the Greek *megas*, 'great', and used either with that meaning or in the sense in which it
is used in scientific units of measurement, 'a million times'. Because of the binary nature of
computing, in that field *mega-* always refers to a multiple of 1,048,576 (as in *megabit* and
megabyte).

The prefix *mega-*, used in the sense 'great' since at least the seventeenth century, became
a common prefix in units of measurement in the late nineteenth century. In the past
twenty years, as a result of the relentless quest for superlatives in popular writing and

entertainment, a very large number of terms using it have been derived, many of them trade marks or otherwise proprietary; a substantial proportion are used once and never seen again.

Recent technical uses include **megapixel** (multiples of a 'computer million' of *pixels*, or picture elements, as a measure of the ability of a computer screen to display detail), and **megabase** (one million pairs of DNA bases, used in investigations of genes and especially in the Human Genome Project). Large functional circuit blocks within a semiconductor chip, such as a microprocessor, are called **megacells**. Concerns among conservationists over the rapid rate of extinction of species in the wild led to the concept of the world as a single huge preservation area or **megazoo**.

In a large number of recent formulations the element *mega-* is used to indicate a superlative. A substantial proportion of these terms are associated with the arts and show business. A **megabook** is a book expected to be a **megahit**, perhaps making somebody **megarich**; to achieve this may require **megahype**—extensive promotion which is unlikely to be too scrupulous about facts. A film may be a **megasmash**, catapulting its leading actors to **megastardom**; it may have needed a **megabudget** to achieve the effects on which its success depends. A large sporting event or spectacle is sometimes a **megaevent**. A glitzy fashion show may depend on **megamodels** to give it the requisite glamour.

In commerce, a **megafirm** is a large business, especially one formed by amalgamation of other firms, possibly through a **megamerger** (a term particularly applied to corporate takeovers in the mid eighties); only such large organizations or governments are able to execute **megaprojects**, characterized by great size, cost, or complexity; an international market for goods or services may be called a **megamarket**; a very large airline is sometimes called a **megacarrier**; organizations or individuals may be fundamentally affected by **megatrends** (substantial changes in circumstances of many kinds); a **megastore** is a very large retail store, often on the outskirts of a town or city, with its own parking facilities; several such, together with entertainment and other facilities, may constitute a **megamall**; the concept has spilled over into religion in the US, where worshippers may attend a **megachurch**, a large multi-purpose centre with social and educational facilities as well as religious ones.

The term **megastate** is either applied specifically to California, the most populous of the United States, or to concentrations of supernational power, such as the European Union; a **megaplex** is a huge city conurbation or industrial area. The rubbish from such a **megacity** may end up in a **megadump**.

In the eighties and nineties, some people began to take **megadoses** of vitamins and mineral supplements in expectation of health benefits (the word is linked to the term *megavitamin therapy*, first used by Linus Pauling in 1970). The word has also come to be used more loosely for a large amount of anything.

With an estimated 40 percent of American adults downing $3 billion worth of vitamins…physicians and nutritionists are becoming concerned about megadoses.
—*Coloradoan* (Fort Collins) 21 Feb. 1993, Section E, p. 4

At either end of the waterfront, ore-bearing ships, enormous in their own right, lie dwarfed by the industrial megaplex they have travelled here to serve.
—*Canadian Geographic* July/Aug. 1993, p. 44

Perhaps more important, the preparation for, and actual hosting of this mega-event provided a unique opportunity for community development, both in economic and social terms.
—*Tourism Management* Oct. 1993, p. 382

I got talking to a Creative Affairs executive from RKO pictures about how influential American movies were abroad, but the megasmashes tended to be trash.
—Peter Theroux *Translating LA* (1994), p. 103

Britain's biggest building societies yesterday disclosed that they are trying to put together a mega-merger that would create a force to rival the Halifax-Leeds and Abbey National.
—*Guardian* 8 Mar. 1995, Section 1, p. 17

Megan's Law /'miːg(ə)nz lɔː/ *noun* ⟨⟨

A law requiring that communities be notified if convicted sex offenders become resident in the area.

Seven-year-old Megan Kanka was raped and murdered in New Jersey in 1994; the man charged with her murder was a convicted paedophile who had moved into the street in which she lived. In the wake of the killing, a public campaign was launched to make it statutory for the authorities to notify communities when convicted sex offenders become resident in an area.

The law, known as *Megan's Law*, was first passed as a New Jersey statute which permitted state authorities to notify communities when convicted sex offenders move in, but did not require it. In May 1996 President Clinton signed a tougher form of the legislation, which made notification mandatory. In the following year, the possibility of *community notification* of this kind was being actively considered in Britain.

Megan's Law is seen by its supporters to offer proper protection to families and their children. Others however have argued that the process infringes civil rights and risks making former offenders the target for vigilantes. There is also a view that the effect will be to drive former offenders underground, and thus increase rather than reduce potential dangers.

Kanka family…attend Clinton signing of tougher Megan's Law.
—heading in *The Detroit News* 18 May 1996 (electronic edition)

'Megan's Law', operating in New Jersey, means that the police inform the entire community when a known paedophile moves into the area. —*Daily Express* 19 Feb. 1997, p. 10

Old offences, some of them no longer criminal, are being resurrected as dozens of states enact their own versions of California's recently passed Megan's Law.
—*Daily Telegraph* 6 Mar. 1997 (electronic edition)

The Home Office had been considering the idea of 'community notification', now widespread in America since the introduction of the so-called Megan's Law in many states.
—*Daily Telegraph* 1 Apr. 1997 (electronic edition)

men's movement /'mɛnz muːvm(ə)nt/ *noun* POP ⟨⟨

A movement aimed at freeing men from traditional views of the male character and role in society.

The earliest uses of *men's movement* (and the more colloquial *men's lib*) occur in the early seventies, in conscious contradistinction to the *women's movement* of the period. In the eighties and nineties, however, the term has found fresh currency, in particular through MYTHOPOETIC attempts to redefine the male role.

Vision quest—A notion borrowed from the initiation rites of American Indians, mainly by the nascent men's movement. Through solitude, fasting or the intense physical experience of the sweat lodge, individuals seek understanding of their unrecognized selves.
—*New York Times* 4 Jan. 1990, p. 26

Maybe if she hadn't made fun of those ridiculous calico vests her ex-husband wore, a whole generation of drum-beating groundpawers could have been saved the embarrassment of the men's movement. —*Minnesota Monthly* Feb. 1994, p. 13

Shelley had long been interested in the 'dream work' that the men's movement likes to explore, and had encouraged Richard to be receptive to 'alternative' ideas.
—*Independent on Sunday* 28 May 1995, Review section, p. 14

mentally challenged ⟨⟨ see CHALLENGED

menu /'mɛnjuː/ *noun* 🖵

A list of options within a computer program, either permanently displayed on the screen or which can be called up by the user, showing the commands or facilities available.

A specialized sense of the word, implying that the user is choosing commands as one might select from a restaurant *menu*.

An important part of the system of visually-oriented computer displays which became available in the early eighties is the ability to call up lists of commands by a click of the mouse or a press of a key, so that users can identify the action they want by browsing among the menus without having to learn a complex language of commands. Most such applications now have a row of main menu headings (the **top-level menu** or **main menu**) permanently displayed at the top of the screen in an area called the **menu bar**. Selecting one heading causes a more detailed list of options to appear, a **submenu**; because this appears to drop down or be pulled down from the heading, it is often called a **drop-down menu** or a PULL-DOWN *menu*. In a variant of the system, a list called a **pop-up menu** appears at the cursor when a mouse button is clicked. Applications operated by means of menus are said to be **menu-driven**.

> It also includes three programs which are applications in their own right, complete with full-screen displays, mouse support and drop-down menus.
> —*What Personal Computer* Issue 29, Dec. 1991, p. 118

> Help is on the menu bar of almost every Windows application.　　　—*Compute* Oct. 1993, p. 51

> You can access any work instantly from the main menu and designate up to 99 bookmarks.
> —*CD-ROM World* Apr. 1994, p. 30

> Drag-and-drop and pop-up menus are now considered a more integral part of the interface.
> —*Microsoft Developer Network News* May 1994, p. 16

Mercosur /'mɜːk(ə)sjʊə/ *noun* 〰️

A common market agreement permitting the movement of goods and services between Argentina, Brazil, Paraguay, and Uruguay.

Formed from a contraction of Spanish *Mercado del Sur* 'Market of the South'.

Since the early sixties, a number of Caribbean and South and Central American states have attempted to set up common market organizations which would bring both political cooperation and mutual economic and financial benefit. The Latin American Integration Association, an economic grouping of South American countries having as its ultimate aim the creation of a common market, was instituted in 1981, and a decade later the *Mercosur* agreement was signed between Argentina, Brazil, Paraguay, and Uruguay. The agreement was fully implemented in 1995.

In the second half of the twentieth century the formerly strong Latin American economies have all suffered from severe problems. It remains to be seen whether the free movement of goods and services permitted by *Mercosur* between its signatories will make a substantial difference to the prevailing economic and financial conditions.

> Argentina, Uruguay, Paraguay and Brazil aspire to unify their economies in the group they call Mercosur.　　　—*Economist* 24 Aug. 1991, p. 45

> The four members of the Mercosur group, whose economies account for nearly half Latin America's gross domestic product.　　　—*Guardian* 2 Jan. 1992, p. 9

> The big success...is Mercosur: Brazil, Argentina, Paraguay and Uruguay. In theory, from next January it will be a full customs union, with a common external tariff wall and free trade inside it.　　　—*Economist* 26 Nov. 1994, p. 74

mercury abuse 🌱 see ABUSE

metal dectorist ✴️ see DETECTORIST

Metroblade ✴️ see ROLLERBLADE

Michelangelo /ˌmʌɪk(ə)lˈandʒələʊ/ *noun* 🖫

One of the best-known computer VIRUSES, *Michelangelo*, which affects IBM-com-patible computers by destroying any data on the hard disk, is programmed to activate every year on 6 March, the birthday of Michelangelo (1475–1564).

A few months ago, PC owners were alerted to the imminent arrival of the Michelangelo virus, which threatened to trash electronic files. —*MacUser* Nov. 1992, p. 268

Michelangelo, which first appeared in 1991, is programmed to lurk inside only IBM-compatible computers. —*Post* (Denver) 5 Mar. 1995, p. 6

microbrewery ✖ see BREWPUB

Middle England /mɪd(ə)l ˈɪŋglənd/ *noun* 🏠

The middle classes in England outside London, especially as representative of conservative political views.

Middle America as a term for the middle class in the US, especially as a conservative political force, was originally coined in the late sixties in reference to what was seen as Richard Nixon's natural political constituency, and has since become an established term. *Middle Britain* (from the late seventies) and *Middle England* (from the early eighties) are terms evoking a comparable world of stable, middle-of-the-road conservatism and decency; a typical **Middle Englander**, while likely to be contrasted with the urban radicalism of ISLINGTON *person*, is seen as less brash than ESSEX MAN in asserting essentially right-wing beliefs.

Travel away from the double-glazed cul-de-sacs of middle England and it is not hard to find the bottom tenth. They mostly live on the brutalistic council estates beloved of town-planners in the 1960s. —*Economist* 12 Sept. 1992, p. 29

A battle is on…between Middle England—the sensible heart of the British middle classes—and Islington Person, the politically correct voice of the chattering classes. —*Daily Mail* 18 July 1994

Those deeply engrimed faces smeared with mud and woad, those matted dreadlocks, itchy just to look at, do not endear the eco-campaigners to middle England. Yet this new protest movement, The Land is Ours, believes it will draw in ordinary people as never before. —*Independent* 26 Apr. 1995, p. 19

MIDI /ˈmɪdi/ *acronym* Also written **Midi** or **midi** 🐾 🖫

noun: An interface which allows electronic musical instruments, sequencers, and synthesizers to be interconnected and controlled by a computer.

adjective: Making use of this kind of interface.

An acronym, formed on the initial letters of its official name, *Musical Instrument Digital Interface*.

The **MIDI interface** was invented in the US in 1983 at a time when increasing use was being made of electronic instruments in both classical and popular music. The interface allows descriptions of sounds created by **MIDI instruments** (including **MIDI keyboards**; more generally **MIDI devices**) to be input into a computer, stored (as **MIDI files**), manipulated, combined with other sounds, and replayed through a synthesizer (under the control of a **MIDI sequencer**); many **MIDI channels** can be controlled simultaneously. Such **MIDI systems** have made possible some of the most characteristic musical genres of the eighties and nineties; the interface is also now used extensively in computer-based multimedia. Despite this, *MIDI* remains largely the province of specialists.

The latest studio at the BBC Radiophonic Workshop contains many different synthesisers, samplers and sound sources, all connected together and linked to a full-size keyboard and a powerful computer by MIDI. —*New Scientist* 21 Dec. 1991, p. 39

The 16 bit Cyber Audio Card redefines the sound card standard for stereo CD quality sound with 32 simultaneous voices, 16 MIDI channels and IMB sound ROM containing 128 sampled instruments.   —advertisement in *Wired* Dec. 1993, p. 17

One of the differences is that the MIDI output device 'knows' how to process its sounds when it receives commands from the MIDI file/player, for example how fast to decay a piano waveform. This information is not stored in the MIDI file itself.   —20 Feb. 1995, online posting

mifepristone /mɪfɪ'prɪstəʊn/ *noun* ⊗

The generic name of a drug which can be given in the early stages of pregnancy to induce abortion.

An invented word based on elements of its full chemical name: *mife* is a re-ordered abbreviation of *aminophenol*; *pr* is taken from *propyne*; and *it* represents *oestradiol*. The last element is the chemical suffix *-one*, indicating a derivative compound.

Mifepristone was put on the market in France by the French pharmaceutical firm Roussel Uclaf in September 1988 as an oral drug to induce abortion in early pregnancy, initially under the name **RU–486** (formed from the initials of the firm and a numerical code). Following considerable controversy involving anti-abortion groups in the US, France, and West Germany, the firm suspended sales the following month, but was then ordered to start again by the French government on health grounds. The drug was later licensed in Britain and Sweden but put on the list of banned imports by the Bush administration. Perception of the negative connotations of the drug as an ABORTION PILL has affected the use of the name *RU–486*, and the drug is now largely referred to by its generic name. In 1992 the debate over its use was complicated when it was shown that *mifepristone* could also act as an emergency *morning-after* contraceptive. In 1994 American patent rights were donated to a planned-parenthood research organization in New York; clinical trials began in the US against considerable opposition by anti-abortion groups.

The French drug RU 486 (mifepristone) is one of the most controversial compounds in the world. It is prescribed in France to terminate pregnancy, and is under study in many other countries.
                    —*Sarasota Herald-Tribune* (Florida) 15 May 1991, p. E3

The French-made drug, mifepristone...can be used for women who are up to nine weeks pregnant.   —*Daily Telegraph* 18 Jan. 1993, p. 4

Nationwide clinical trials for the controversial French abortion pill RU486 (also known as mifepristone) are coming to a close this month.   —*Atlantic* Aug. 1995, p. 14

Mighty Morphin Power Ranger POP see POWER RANGER

millennium bug /mɪ'lɛnɪəm bʌg/ *noun* ▣ ⋰✲

In informal usage, the coding of dates in software using only two digits for the year, which will cause errors to occur when the century changes.

A *bug* in the common computing sense of 'a mistake, an error' which will take effect at the *millennium*.

Over the past 25 years or so, it has been common for computer programmers creating applications to store only the last two digits of the year in records, as '81' for '1981'. It was not expected that the software would still be in use in the year 2000, and in any case severe limitations on computer memory and storage space were a more urgent consideration. However, when the year changes to 2000, all such software will turn the date back to 1900, with catastrophic implications for any function which calculates time-dependent information, such as pensions entitlements, investment income, or liability for debt. In the mid nineties the issues raised, and the extremely large cost of correcting the problem, have come to receive wide attention and to be appreciated by government and the business community. Various names have been given, such as **millennium virus**, the *Year 2000 problem*, and **millennium bomb**, but *millennium bug* is currently the most common.

The cost of fixing the millennium bug will be so high that many companies facing failure will try to dump businesses with dud systems on rivals, leading auditor Coopers & Lybrand warned last week. —*Computer Weekly* 18 July 1996, p. 15

Last year, companies got a hint of what it might cost to put this right when the Gartner Group, a Connecticut-based computer consultancy, calculated that removing 'millennium bugs' from the world's computers and software would cost anything up to $600 billion over the next four years, more than $10m per average medium-sized firm. —*Economist* 3 Aug. 1996, p. 59

MiniDisc /'mɪnɪdɪsk/ *noun* Also spelled **minidisc** 🖳

A recordable small CD.

The European spelling of *disc* is usual, even in the US, because it is based on the spelling of *compact disc*, itself a trade mark. In its capitalized form, the name is a trade mark.

The *MiniDisc* was invented by Sony, partly to form the basis of a high-quality portable disc format and partly to be a contender in the market for digital recorders against Philips's DCC format. It uses a two-inch diameter disc and is capable of recording and of playing back pre-recorded material for up to an hour at a time.

Sony yesterday made a bid to win the 'Nintendo generation' back to music with the launch of the MiniDisc—a miniature compact disc for portable players. —*Independent* 18 Nov. 1992, p. 2

The minidisc wants to do to the cassette tape what the CD did to the LP: kill it dead. The MD itself is about half the size of a CD and permanently housed in its own cunning plastic case. —*Esquire* Mar. 1994, p. 35

minimally invasive surgery ⊗ ⚕ see KEYHOLE SURGERY

misper /'mɪspə, 'mɪspə:/ *noun* 🎙 🎖

In police slang: a missing person.

The compound *missing person* 'a person whose whereabouts are unknown (and who is being sought)' is recorded from the nineteenth century, and it seems likely that the contraction to *misper* by those officially involved in trying to trace such people is of some duration. The term came to wider public notice in Britain in 1994, when horrified attention was given to the discovery of the bodies of twelve young women in Gloucestershire, killed and buried over a period of years.

Considerable publicity attended the arrest of a Gloucester builder, Frederick West (who committed suicide in prison), and the subsequent trial and conviction of his wife Rosemary on a number of charges. In discussions of the case, one of the main focuses of alarm was the realization of how many of the young women had become *mispers* without their disappearance being registered by those who knew them as a cause for concern.

He…leaves the sister of a 'misper' in peace rather than ask 'And how did you feel?' —*Guardian* 29 Sept. 1995, section 2, p. 7

mission statement /'mɪʃ(ə)n steɪtm(ə)nt/ *noun* 〰

A declaration made by a company of its general objectives and principles of operation.

A *statement* made by a company of its *mission* to the public.

The *mission statement* has won an important place in the business jargon of the last decade, although opinions are still divided as to the real value of such expressions of aspiration. On the positive side, *mission statements* are regarded as combining responsibility to the public and motivation for employees in their explicit statement of a company's aims and aspirations. However, many *mission statements*, while perceived by the issuing company as a valuable publicity tool, are arguably not detailed enough to amount to more than a vague expression of intent.

A mission statement was introduced to give the business more focus, in line with its real strength: 'Protecting life and property from fire'. —*RTZ Review* June 1992, p. 19

Ask yourself if you really want to own shares in a company with a New Age 'mission statement,' or a board of directors that reads like an A-list cocktail party rather than a corporate board.
—Maclean's 17 Apr. 1995, p. 46

Those who are tempted to laugh at corporate visions, and the fluffy mission statements that invariably accompany them, are reminded that such world-beating companies as British Airways and Coca-Cola take them deadly seriously. *—Economist* 6 May 1995, p. 91

Mitchell principles /ˌmɪtʃ(ə)l ˈprɪnsɪp(ə)lz/ *noun* 📷

Six recommendations urging all sides involved in the conflict in Northern Ireland to renounce violence and to agree to a process of disarmament before entering into all-party negotiations.

The US lawyer and senator George J. *Mitchell* from 1995–6 chaired a group investigating procedures by which disarmament in Northern Ireland could be achieved.

The group formulating the *Mitchell principles* was set up as part of the PEACE PROCESS, in the wake of the DOWNING STREET DECLARATION.

A decision…would place enormous pressure on Sinn Fein to affirm its commitment to the six Mitchell principles so that the party could rightfully claim a place at the table.
—Irish Times 25 Jan. 1996, p. 12

Mr Adams, the Sinn Fein president, sought to gain the initiative before an Anglo-Irish summit in London tomorrow. He said…'I'll sign up to the Mitchell principles provided everybody is doing it and provided they are within the context of proper all-party talks.'
—Daily Telegraph 21 May 1996 (electronic edition)

See also MACBRIDE PRINCIPLES

mixed dark matter 📷 see COLD DARK MATTER

mobile /ˈməʊbʌɪl/ *noun* 🎲 POP 📷

A mobile phone.

With the development of cellular phones at the end of the seventies, mobile phones were increasingly used. The *mobile* in fact became a symbol of success in the eighties, being particularly associated with the 'yuppie' culture: possession (and frequent public use) of a *mobile* was taken as indicating status.

The coming of the recession, and increasing criticism of the disturbance factor involved in calls being made and received in public places, meant that the *mobile* was looked at more critically. But the practical value of the device has made its mark; while no longer a status symbol as such, possession of a *mobile* is now likely to be seen as a sensible precaution contributing to efficient communications and personal security.

Not only does the system take messages if a cellphone is switched off, but it will also automatically replay them as soon as the mobile phone becomes available. If you have not yet invested in a mobile, then you are missing out on one of the best things that has happened to personal communications in a long time. *—InterCity Magazine* Feb. 1992, p. 9

Rather than phone from the airport, Lewis had hired a mobile along with the car but then when they'd tried to use it, it hadn't worked. *—Iain Banks Crow Road* (1992)

Phone rechipping and reprogramming has enabled thieves to establish a growing black market and some insurance companies are now refusing to cover mobiles left in cars unless locked away. *—BBC Top Gear Magazine* Aug. 1994, p. 199

Mockney /ˈmɒkni/ *noun* POP ⓵

A humorous or derogatory term for: a form of speech perceived as an inauthentic and affected imitation of Cockney in accent and vocabulary. Also, a person adopting this form of speech.

Formed from a blend of *mock*, 'false', and *Cockney*.

Mockney is recorded from the end of the eighties as a form of pseudo-Cockney often deliberately adopted to conceal a speaker's privileged background, in a manner reminiscent of the adoption by CRUSTIES of a form of dress which suggests a more unconventional lifestyle than is in fact the case. *Mockney* is often used attributively (as in **Mockney accent** or **Mockney speech**), and it seems likely that if the phenomenon survives, a full adjectival use will develop.

In interview, Mick Jagger may be the world's most famous Mockney (compare his current roadie's slur to the polite vicar's son enunciating in blurred sixties' clips).

—*Guardian* 7 Oct. 1994, section 2, p. 11

Then they let Mr C out of his cage to waggle his fingers in an entertainingly daft fashion and they became The Present, taking mockney accents and tabloid-baiting E anthems to the top of the charts while Blur and Pulp were still in short trousers.

—*New Musical Express* 28 Oct. 1995, p. 54

Twentieth-century boy: Damon Albarn strikes a chord for mockney everywhere.

—caption in *Independent* 1 Dec. 1995, supplement, p. 13

Moldovan /mɒlˈdəʊvən, ˈmɒldɒvən/ *noun* and *adjective*

noun: A native or inhabitant of independent Moldova. Also, the official language of Moldova.

adjective: Of or relating to Moldova or its people.

Moldova is the Romanian form of *Moldavia*, the official name of the former Soviet Republic.

Following the collapse of Communism in Eastern Europe in 1989 and the subsequent break-up of the Soviet Union, the majority of the former Soviet Republics gained independence and enjoyed a renewed sense of national identity (but see CHECHEN). Moldova, a small country lying between Romania and Ukraine, became independent as a member of the Commonwealth of Independent States in 1991. Along with a number of other countries such as Belarus (formerly Belorussia), it marked its independence by a change in the official form of its name from *Moldavia* to *Moldova*. It had been a part of Romania until it was ceded to the Soviet Union in 1940, and its language is Romanian. As a Soviet Republic it officially adopted the Cyrillic script for its written language (Romanian uses the Latin script), but on its independence Moldova restored the use of the Latin script and adopted the name *Moldovan* for its official language.

Both Moldovans and Russians say that the matter will not lead to war between Russia and Romania. —*Economist* 6 June 1992, p. 46

Moldovan was made the official language (written in Latin script) in 1989 but the use of Russian and Ukrainian in official business is permitted. —*Whitaker's Almanack 1995*, p. 959

monty /ˈmɒnti/ *noun*

In British slang: **the full monty**, everything which is necessary or appropriate, 'the works'.

He [Ben Elton] invented Monty, which meant nothing at all. 'I gave it the full Monty', for example.

—*Sunday Telegraph* 27 May 1990, p. 19

When conducting a funeral he wears the full monty; frock coat, top hat and a Victorian cane with metal tip. —*Guardian* 13 Jan. 1995, p. 24

morning-after pill ⊗ 🔬 see ABORTION PILL

morphing /ˈmɔːfɪŋ/ *noun*

A computing technique used to produce the special effect of smoothly transforming one film image into another by encoding both images into digital form and by gradually manipulating parts of the first image to correspond with comparable parts of the second.

Formed from *morphē*, a combining form based on Greek *morphē*, 'form, shape', as in *metamorphosis*.

References to *morphing* have been recorded since the start of the nineties, since when this new computing technique has created something of a revolution within the world of film. It has been adopted by makers of feature films, advertising films, and pop videos; in each case the transformation from one image to another appears to the viewer to be entirely smooth and flawless, a factor which encourages, in fantasy feature films, the suspension of disbelief, and which enhances the product and message in promotional videos. The technique, used in its early days to notable effect in the popular 1991 film *Terminator 2*, was crucial to the success of the POWER RANGERS. It was also used in a 1991 video promoting Michael Jackson's song *Black and White*, which featured the *morphing* of the faces of men, women, and children of differing racial groups.

The process and action of *morphing* are sometimes referred to by the noun **morph**, which also denotes the image or character created by *morphing*. The verb **morph** has also developed, as a back-formation from *morphing*. It is used transitively in the sense 'to alter or animate (a computerized film image) by transforming a digital representation', and is also used intransitively of a person or thing transformed by the process.

Both noun and verb are also used figuratively, to suggest a process of transformation or metamorphosis from one state to another as if by *morphing*.

The 'morphs' have a photo-realistic appearance, because the computer transforms shadows and reflections. It also ensures that there are no visual breaks as the image changes.
—*Daily Telegraph* 16 Mar. 1992, p. 30

ILM had employed computer generated imagery and advanced morphing techniques to transform actor Robert Patrick into a variety of wholly digital and puppet creations in his role as the shape-shifting liquid metal terminator in James Cameron's blockbuster film.
—Don Shay and Duncan Jody *The Making of Jurassic Park* (1993), p. 48

Other TV ads for Republicans across the country are using special effects to morph their Democratic opponents' faces into the visage of President Clinton.   —*Time* 10 Oct. 1994, p. 28

She proved quite capable of morphing from sixties rock icon to seasoned song stylist.
—*New York* 10 Apr. 1995, p. 91

mosh /mɒʃ/ *intransitive verb*

To dance in a violent and reckless manner at a rock concert, often jumping up and down and colliding with other dancers and crashing into the walls or to the floor.

The word may be a development of *mash*, in its sense 'crush, pound, or grind to a pulp'.

Moshing is a phenomenon of the rock scene—especially heavy metal and HARDCORE, and louder indie bands—of the eighties and nineties, in which concert audiences express their involvement with and appreciation of the music through energetic physical activity in the **mosh pit**, the area in front of the stage. Further forms of such activity are STAGE-DIVING and SLAM DANCING. Though these activities carry the risk of physical injury, they are an exuberant expression of enthusiasm rather than aggression. Concern has however been expressed about the vulnerability of those attending these concerts, and there has even been a reference to **post-moshing syndrome** or **PMS**, which is associated with injuries, ranging from bruises and pulled hair to broken bones, sustained by **moshers**.

A recent gig...erupted into a near riot when overeager moshers careened out of the slam pit, felling bystanders.   —*Rolling Stone* 22 Mar. 1990, p. 26

A reputation for mayhem quickly grew up around their live shows...A young, crazed Asian girl with a pierced tongue, bellybutton and god knows what else joyfully got her front tooth knocked out in the mosh-pit melee.   —*Alternative Press* Jan. 1992, p. 51

By 1991, alternative *was* the mainstream. Moshing, long relegated to hardcore haunts, was suddenly *de rigueur* at rock venues.   —*Rolling Stone* 10 Dec. 1992, p. 43

The younger rock audience breaks through video-era impersonality with moshing, one of the most tactile participatory rituals in music history.   —*New York Times* 7 Aug. 1994, p. 24

mouse /maʊs/ *verb* 🖳

transitive verb: To carry out (an operation) by using a mouse.

intransitive verb: To move around a computer screen or carry out an operation by means of a mouse.

A verb sense which has developed directly from the noun *mouse*, a term for the standard pointing device employed in graphical applications and operating systems, first applied in the mid sixties.

This usage, applied to a number of different aspects of the action of using a mouse, began to appear in technical contexts in the late eighties. It occurs most commonly in phrasal constructions such as **mouse across**, **mouse one's way**, and **mouse over**.

A setting is retained…and does not need to be keyed (or moused) in for each session.   —*Computer Buyer's Guide* 1989, p. 85

Mouse your way over to the window, click on it, and you're looking out.   —E. Kraft *Reservations Recommended* (1990), p. 258

Moving the mouse over it makes the taskbar appear; mousing away makes it vanish—no clicks necessary.   —*Microsoft Systems Journal* Aug. 1994, p. 5

mouse potato /maʊs pəˈteɪtəʊ/ *noun* 🖳 ᴘᴏᴘ

A slang term for a person who spends an excessive amount of time in front of a computer, especially one who uses it online.

An alteration of the older slang phrase *couch potato* (a person presumed to have the physical shape of a potato caused by too much slouching on a couch in front of a television set), using *mouse* in the computer sense of 'a pointing device'.

This is one of a cluster of terms which have developed in reference to an all-absorbing interest in computing—others include PROPELLER-HEAD and OTAKU. Though this phrase has a certain euphony, it is as yet uncertain whether it will have the staying power of *couch potato*.

Freddie is a mouse potato, an Internet addict.   —*Guardian* 3 Sept. 1994, Weekend, p. 67

Hollywood producers, media moguls and bankers have come together to create interactive entertainment for the mouse potato masses of the future.   —*The Face* Jan. 1995, p. 96

Confirmed mouse potato Raphael Needleman can't wait for the convergence of TV and the Net.   —*Digital Dispatch* 20 June 1996, online newsletter

move the goalposts /muːv ðə ˈgəʊlpəʊsts/ *verbal phrase* ᴘᴏᴘ

To alter the basis or scope of a procedure during its course, especially so as to fit adverse circumstances encountered.

A figurative usage in which the *goalposts* stand for conditions already set which are *moved* or amended; the notion is one in which an agreed target is changed after the action has begun.

Move the goalposts (less frequently, *shift the goalposts*) has been current since the late eighties, and provides a useful image for the idea of making an important (and usually unheralded) alteration to terms and conditions previously agreed. In contextual usage, there is often an implication that the process is undertaken with the deliberate intention of disadvantaging a particular person or group.

Many companies have, in recent years, moved the corporate goalposts so that those who used to qualify no longer do so.   —*Dimensions* Spring 1989, p. 34

Only Lilley and Redwood, like naughty schoolboys, try to move the Euro-goalposts still further.
—*Guardian* 15 Oct. 1993, p. 20

The goalposts have been shifted enough already. In the first match at Lake Nona in 1990, the total number of points at stake was 16. At Dalmahoy in 1992 it was increased to 18 and at The Greenbrier two years ago to 20. This year, it is up to 28.
—*Daily Telegraph* 15 March 1996 (electronic edition)

MPP 💻 see MASSIVELY PARALLEL

MRI /ɛmɑːˈrʌɪ/ *acronym* ⊗ 🔩

Short for **magnetic resonance imaging**, a technique which provides sectional images of the internal structure of the patient's body by plotting the nuclear magnetic resonance of its atoms and converting the results into graphic form by computer.

The *image* is based on the varying *magnetic resonance* of the atoms making up the body.

MRI was developed in the mid seventies as a diagnostic technique which would do away with the need for exploratory surgery. At first it was known as the **nuclear magnetic resonance** (**NMR**) technique or *zeugmatography*, but *magnetic resonance imaging* (a phrase first used in 1977) and the abbreviation *MRI* (first used in 1983) are now the established terms. The technique works by passing a small amount of high-frequency radiation (radio waves) through the soft tissues of the body in the presence of a strong magnetic field. The nuclei of the hydrogen atoms in the body—protons—will absorb radiation by vibrating in tune with it (the *resonance* of the name). By scanning these temporary absorptions of energy a picture of the body can be built up; the machinery required to do this is an **MR scanner**. *MRI* produces a clear image of soft tissue even if it is obscured by bone, and without exposing the patient to harmful radiation; it has become one of the foremost diagnostic techniques of the late eighties and nineties and is probably the biggest breakthrough in diagnostic medicine since the discovery of X-rays. The main limitation on its use is that the scanning equipment and the computing power needed to present the results are very expensive.

MRIs are like CAT scan machines, but they create images by placing a patient in a strong magnetic field.
—*Baltimore Sun* 7 Mar. 1990, section C, p. 10

To plan an approach, the surgeon examines the latest magnetic resonance imaging (MRI) scans taken of the patient's head. Each image represents a 'slice' of the head, 3 to 5 millimetres thick, cut as if the patient's head were a loaf of bread.
—*New Scientist* 30 Mar. 1991, p. 37

mule /mjuːl/ *noun* 🍾

A person acting as a courier for illegal drugs.

A transferred sense of a *mule* as 'a beast of burden'; there is also likely to be a notion of the secondary meaning, 'a stupid person'.

The use by drug traffickers of people whose role is to transport illegal drugs is of course of long standing, but in the eighties and nineties a number of high-profile cases have brought to public attention a particular category of such couriers.

The *mules* (or more fully **drug mules**) are usually young, female, and in need of money, and the typical account given involves recruitment (for what appeared to be a generous sum) of young women who are not experienced travellers on the selected route. The *mules*, travelling individually or in pairs, are expected to carry packages of drugs through airports and other customs points: such packages are sometimes concealed internally by *mules* acting as STUFFERS or *swallowers*.

Routes taken by the *mules* inevitably run through countries, such as Singapore and Thailand, where penalties for drug-trafficking are particularly severe, and in extreme cases may include life imprisonment or death. *Mules* caught carrying drugs in these circumstances are themselves subject to such penalties, but are unlikely to have any information about the organization which might be of help to them: they are evidently regarded as expendable by those who recruit them.

Customs officials explain that arresting these 'mules' does little to stem the flow of drugs, and the women tell heart-breaking stories about the circumstances that pushed them into becoming drug-runners. —*Daily Mirror TV Weekly* 3 Oct. 1992, p. 18

Police also think the couple may have been lured 'unwittingly' into a classic drug mule scenario. It often starts with a recruiter in Toronto approaching prospective couriers, usually younger people short on money…The mules are normally kept on a short rein and their movements restricted. —*Toronto Star* 26 June 1994 (Weekend Supplement), p. 2

The trial has highlighted the use of 'white mules' to smuggle drugs out of Thailand. —*Daily Telegraph* 29 Feb. 1996, p. 9

multiculti /mʌltiˈkʌlti/ *adjective* and *noun* Also written **multi-culti** POP {{

adjective: Multicultural; of or relating to multiculturalism or multiculturalists.

noun: Multiculturalism; a multiculturalist.

An abbreviation and alteration of *multicultural*.

This colloquial usage has been recorded in the US since the early nineties. Use of the term creates an informal tone, which converts multiculturalism from a serious political issue to something more familiar and accessible.

Dug Jessica Hagedorn's novella…about a Filipino American woman coming of age to black music and California kitsch. Discovered the multiculti in me and loved her fiercely. —*Village Voice* 3 Dec. 1991, p. 51

Up come the conservatives, wringing their hands in the manner of the late Allan Bloom over rap, rock-'n'-roll, and the unearned Dionysiac ecstasies of mass multi-culti. —Robert Hughes *Culture of Complaint* (1993), p. 79

Jane Smiley's satire of a Midwestern university is like a big college party to which everybody's invited. They're all here—the whole multi-culti, crazy-quilt gang that makes up modern academic life in America. —*Entertainment Weekly* 19 May 1995, p. 56

multi-gym /ˈmʌltɪdʒɪm/ *noun* Also written **multi gym, multigym** ⊗ ⊠ ⊛

A piece of exercise equipment which is designed for use in several ways exercising all or most of the muscles in the body. Also, a room containing several pieces of exercise equipment.

The need to bring weight-training and gymnastics equipment outside the confines of the professional gymnasium, and the demand for increasingly sophisticated equipment, were features of the fitness-conscious eighties. They led to the development of the *multi-gym*, a facility for the exercise of a number of different muscle groups.

Designed for use at home or in a gym, the piece of equipment known as a *multi-gym* is a sophisticated development of single-purpose machines such as the exercise bicycle or rowing machine, offering the opportunity to work, simultaneously or sequentially, on a number of different muscle groups.

The term *multi-gym* also denotes the exercise room offered by fitness clubs and increasing numbers of hotels, which is equipped with a selection of weights and exercise machines each designed with particular muscle groups and fitness needs in mind.

He showed me his presents. He had: a multi gym, Adidas football boots. —Sue Townsend *The Growing Pains of Adrian Mole* (1984), p. 134

Sports facilities including indoor swimming pool, tennis court, multi-gym, sauna and sunbeds. —advertisement in *Country Life* 24 May 1990, p. 45

multimedia /ˈmʌltɪmiːdɪə/ *noun* Also written **multi-media** ⊑

The concept of a (computer) system that combines text with audio, video, and still images to create an interactive application; frequently used attributively to describe such a system, for example **multimedia computer** or **multimedia PC**. It is also employed more loosely to refer to any communications technique that involves more than one medium of expression.

The advent of the CD-ROM (see CD) and faster personal computers have permitted the presentation of information on computers to progress beyond text. Using the HTML system of tagging and with suitable audio playback equipment in the computer, applications can be developed so that users see and hear a range of types of material relevant to the subject, most commonly in a way that is under the control of the user. Such systems are now in widespread use in encyclopedias and educational products (the term is now often used in the publishing industry to denote involvement in ELECTRONIC publishing), for promotional material and demonstrations, and in games. The term has been extended in scope to cover other types of computer-mediated communication, such as videoconferencing and the WORLD WIDE WEB, in a development sometimes called **hypermedia** (a blend of *hypertext* and *multimedia*).

> For consumers, the effects of the new chips are most evident in software for presenting movie-style video and combinations of video, sound and text, known as multimedia programs.
> —*New York Times* 4 Mar. 1994, section D, p. 4

> With the new Electronic News Gathering (ENG) systems, each journalist will have a multimedia PC and will call up the video footage from the server to his or her desktop.
> —*Independent* 9 Oct. 1995, section 2, p. 14

See also INTERACTIVE

multi-speed /ˈmʌltɪspiːd/ *adjective* 📇

Progressing at various speeds towards a common goal.

Multi-speed (particularly in the phrase **multi-speed Europe**) is a term that in the nineties has been used in discussions of an ultimate economic and monetary union of Europe, and in particular in association with the prospect of a SINGLE CURRENCY and Britain's *opt-out clause* (see OPT-OUT¹). The essential concept is of individual nations proceeding at varying speeds towards a common goal, although it is still a matter of debate among supporters and opponents of the key MAASTRICHT *Treaty*, as to whether such an approach is in fact tenable.

> The Maastricht treaty already implies a multi-speed Europe in its progress towards a single currency. —*Independent* 29 Oct. 1992, p. 26

muon-catalysed fusion 🧪 see COLD FUSION

mythopoetic /ˌmɪθəʊpəʊˈɛtɪk/ *adjective* 📇 {{

In the US: designating an approach to self-understanding by men which employs activities such as storytelling, poetry reading, and enactments of ritual. Frequently in the phrase **mythopoetic men's movement**, and also designating the approach, followers, and practices of this movement.

This usage represents a new development of sense of the established adjectives *mythopoetic* and *mythopoeic*, 'myth-making'.

In the eighties, perhaps in part as a consequence of the changes in society brought about by feminism and varying employment patterns, the traditional male role was re-examined. In his book *Iron John*, Robert Bly devised the prototype of a contemporary male: a man able to acknowledge within himself both the caring and emotionally expressive NEW MAN and the primitive hunter-gatherer. Bly is also acknowledged as the founder of the *mythopoetic men's movement*, which from the mid eighties has attempted to rediscover and redefine the male role through the exploration of art, mythology, and poetry, a quest conducted through conferences and workshops held for the purpose. This may be seen as part of the broader movement generally referred to as the MEN'S MOVEMENT.

> Shopping for...tea bags satisfies the mythopoetic masculine soul, which houses a repressed hunter-gatherer. —*Boston Globe Magazine* 22 Sept. 1991, p. 10

> He takes pains to distinguish his approach from that of the 'mythopoetic men's movement' led by

Robert Bly. He condemns Bly's 'essentialism', which assumes that 'manhood begins with a timeless, unchanging core of qualities that all men ultimately possess'.

—*New Republic* 19 Apr. 1993, p. 31

The 'mythopoetic' work that attracted Richard to the men's movement—working with myths and poems as metaphors—has a good deal of similarity to theatre work, and sometimes the two cross over. —*Independent on Sunday* 28 May 1995, Review section, p. 14

●●

N

NAFTA /'naftə/ *noun* Also written Nafta 〰

Acronym for **North American Free Trade Agreement**, an agreement to remove trading barriers between the US, Canada, and Mexico over a ten-year period.

The eighties and nineties have seen the establishment of a number of international agreements to expedite trading conditions between various countries. The early nineties saw the introduction of the MERCOSUR agreement between Argentina, Brazil, Paraguay, and Uruguay, and in 1995 the *World Trade Organization*, or *WTO*, replaced *GATT* (the *General Agreement on Tariffs and Trade*). Free-trade agreements, as MAASTRICHT has shown, are by their nature likely to arouse anxieties over sovereignty, and *NAFTA* met with considerable political opposition especially in the US, before finally coming into effect in January 1994.

NAFTA promises...the elimination of all tariffs and other barriers to trade among its three members. —*Economist* 24 Aug. 1991, p. 45

Those green articles of NAFTA, the pack snarls, represent the most fundamental threat to sovereignty ever faced by this nation—an 'economic Maastricht', no less.

—*Insight* 11 Oct. 1993, p. 29

The debate is as much about what kind of nation we want to be as it is about the virtues of free trade. A surprising number of arguments against Nafta rely on hoary stereotypes.

—*New York Times* 2 Nov. 1993, section A, p. 23

NAFTA helped to fuel a surge in Hispanic pride in areas far afield from the straight-laced world of big business. —*Hispanic* Dec. 1995, p. 26

nagware 🖳 see -WARE

nanny state /nani 'steɪt/ *noun* 🗄 ❪❪

A derogatory nickname, according to which government institutions are seen as authoritarian and paternalistic, interfering in and controlling people's lives in the same way as a nanny might try to control those of her charges.

The nickname *nanny state* is first recorded in an article by the Conservative politician Iain Macleod in *Spectator* in 1965. The implication is that a welfare state is ready to limit an individual's freedoms if this can be argued to be for the individual's own good. Under the Conservative government of Margaret Thatcher in the eighties the term acquired a new emphasis as the ethos of individualism and enterprise was presented as a better alternative to spoon-feeding from the *nanny state*. The term survived the Thatcher administration and continues to be used in this wider, but always disparaging, sense.

A measure of privatisation of adoption is called for, with a diminution in the powers of...ideological apartheiders of the nanny State. —*The Times* 28 Sept. 1989, p. 17

Despite Patten's disclaimer in his article, the Conservatives seemed to be demanding a monopoly over the idea on the grounds of its consonance with traditional Conservative doctrine. In a negative sense, they argued that active citizenship was a healthy return to old values which had been submerged by passive reliance on the 'nanny state'.   —*Parliamentary Affairs* Apr. 1991 (BNC)

Those who are likely to object more are those who complain about the 'nanny state' and its propensity to take responsibility out of the hands of individuals.

—*Independent* 23 July 1996, section 2, p. 3

nano- /ˈnanəʊ/ *combining form*

Used as the first element in a variety of compounds relating to the building of devices or substances on a molecular scale.

From the Greek *nanos*, 'dwarf', which is used in English as a combining form in terms of measurement meaning 'reduced by a factor of one thousand million', as in *nanometre* or *nanosecond*. Because one nanometre is approaching atomic dimensions, the combining form has acquired the looser sense of 'relating to molecular proportions'.

Research began in the seventies into the creation of molecules and machines which are built up from their atomic components. This field was first called **nanotechnology** in the mid seventies, but interest in the possibilities of actually implementing such ideas did not become widespread until the mid eighties, from when it grew rapidly. **Nanotechnologists** are working on creating **nanomachines** built to atomic dimensions. This proposed **nanomachinery** includes tiny manipulators, worked by on-board computer logic, that can manufacture materials by pushing atoms about (**nanofabrication**, resulting in **nanostructures**) or which can enter the human body to undertake repair from within. A major area of **nano-technological** research is the controlled creation of complex molecules, such as drugs, analogous to the processes of protein fabrication within the human cell, and of perfect materials with immense strength (this area is often called **molecular nanotechnology** or *molecular manufacturing*). Another area of work is the creation of **nanocomputers**: extremely tiny mechanical computing devices. The techniques may in short be referred to as **nanotech**. Though such concepts were taken up eagerly in the science-fiction community (which has been responsible for coining some of its more esoteric vocabulary), the indications are that the techniques could be practical, though as yet scarcely beginning to be implemented.

More generally in physical chemistry, a **nanocrystal** is a very small perfect crystal, conventionally less than 100 nanometres across; a **nanotube** is a tiny tube formed from a hollow cylinder of atoms (a variant on a *buckyball*, see BUCKMINSTERFULLERENE); interactions between atoms and molecules happen on a **nanoscale**; materials of varying composition formed from particles of *nanocrystal* size may form a **nanophase** or a **nanocomposite**.

The performance of nanoscale registers and logic units...suggests that nanomechanical RISC machines can achieve clock speeds of up to 1GHz and execute instructions at around 1000mips.

—*Personal Computer World* May 1993, p. 484

Drexler's ultimate model for a nanocomputer wouldn't use electricity at all. Instead, it would contain 'rod logic'—a crisscross pattern of sliding rods, one molecule thick, each fitted with stops that interact with the others.   —*Wired* Dec. 1993, p. 87

Tristan and Suze, lovers who have linked themselves by semi-sentient nanotech hair so that they need never be more than six feet apart, are an especially fine touch.

—*Interzone* Apr. 1994, p. 61

Fullerenes can be formed in hydrocarbon flames. We have now found that carbon nanotubes and nanoparticles, along with soot particles containing fullerene-like shells, can also be formed in this way.   —*Nature* 25 Aug. 1994, p. 603

'Nanotechnologists' talk of molecular assembly lines, by which devices are constructed piece by piece using hi-tech tools to position atoms and molecular fragments and then 'weld' them in place with lasers or beams of electrons.   —*Guardian* 17 Nov. 1994, OnLine section, p. 11

narcoterrorism /ˌnɑːkəʊˈtɛrərɪz(ə)m/ *noun* Also written **narco-terrorism**

Violent crime and acts of terrorism carried out as a by-product of the illicit manufacture, trafficking, or sale of drugs, especially against any individual or institution attempting to enforce anti-drugs laws.

The word *narcoterrorism* came into the news in the mid eighties. Large quantities of highly profitable drugs such as cocaine and heroin were being produced illegally in some Central and South American countries, principally Peru and Colombia. It had become clear that the influential producers, or 'drug barons', were in alliance with guerrilla and terrorist organizations to defeat any attempts to enforce anti-drugs laws. Alleging government collusion with *narcoterrorism*, some US authorities favoured intervention in the affairs of foreign countries to stop the flow of drugs into their own country; in view of the serious and rapidly growing problems of drug abuse and drug-related crime within the US in the second half of the eighties, some argued that to manufacture drugs at all was itself a **narcoterrorist** act. In the late eighties and nineties reports centred on the Medellín, and later the Cali, areas of Colombia, where a government determined to stop the drug traffic was the target of repeated attacks. Though the most notorious of the **narcoterrorists**, Pablo Escobar, was shot dead in December 1993 the problems continue.

> The United States wants to crack down on Peruvian 'narco-terrorists', but...the Peruvian government sees these coca-growing peasants as a critical source of income.
>
> —*Utne Reader* Mar. 1992, p. 19

> 'It was important to get Escobar because he was the most defiant of the narcoterrorists, but this hardly means the end to violence or narcoterrorism in Colombia', explains Terry McCoy.
>
> —*Hispanic* Apr. 1994, p. 12

National Lottery /naʃ(ə)n(ə)l ˈlɒt(ə)ri/ *noun* Also written **national lottery** 〰
POP
〰

A state-controlled lottery established in the UK in November 1994.

The British *National Lottery* was established under the watchful eye of Oflot (see OF-) in November 1994, administered by the business consortium Camelot. It has proved to be extremely successful, with the high numbers of tickets and SCRATCH CARDS sold creating very substantial weekly jackpots; these are on occasion, if there are no winners, carried over in a ROLLOVER jackpot to the following week.

Some concern has been expressed that the *National Lottery* is diverting money away from the charities; it is felt that the amount forwarded to charities through lottery proceeds is substantially less than the direct donation it has significantly replaced. The betting industry has also reported losses. Additionally some people have expressed concern at the size of the lottery wins, feeling that excessive wealth acquired so suddenly can create pressures and problems for the recipients.

Others, however, feel that the sums involved encourage participation which in turn creates, besides the prize money, substantial proceeds for distribution to deserving institutions, including charities. These proceeds are allocated to successful applicants through five distributing bodies: the National Lottery Charities Board, the Sports and Arts Councils, the National Heritage Memorial Fund, and the Millennium Commission.

> A cancer charity has been forced by the 'ferocious' success of the National Lottery to scrap its scratch cards. —*Daily Telegraph* 30 Mar. 1995, p. 3

> The Millennium Commission is being asked to provide £50 million from national lottery funds to revitalise Britain's coastline. —*Daily Telegraph* 12 February 1996 (electronic edition)

> Welfare claimants are estimated to be spending £140m of their state benefits on national lottery tickets every year. The disclosure has prompted demands that winners on benefit should pay back part of their prizes to the state. —*Sunday Times* 28 July 1996 (electronic edition)

Native /'neɪtɪv/ *adjective* 🏠 ⁅

Forming compound nouns, and their related adjectives: (of or denoting) a specified indigenous people in contrast to a more recent immigrant and/or colonizing population (typically of European origin).

The use of *Native* in this context represents a conscious attempt to recognize the original status of the indigenous peoples of countries which were later colonized. (In Canada, the term *First Nations* for these peoples is used with similar intent, and the term **non-native Canadians** for immigrant peoples has also been recorded.)

The best-known formulation of this kind is **Native American,** which since the seventies has been regarded as the appropriate designation of those less acceptably called *American Indians.* In turn, **Native American** itself has been seen by some as too all-embracing: members of such peoples from that part of the North American continent comprising Canada have increasingly chosen to specify themselves as **Native Canadians.** This refinement has been accompanied by the proliferation of further forms, such as **Native Australian** and **Native Hawaiian;** it is too soon to say how many of these will acquire preferred term status.

> The site's only remaining Native American tribe, the Osage, will continue to control the land's mineral rights. —*Nature Conservancy* May 1991, p. 28

> The native Hawaiians attributed volcanism to the actions of the goddess Pele.
> —*Scientific American* Aug. 1992, p. 19

> Native Canadians needed a good deal of help to shift from a nomadic hunting/gathering existence to a settled agricultural one, and they did not consistently receive it. Government aid was sporadic, cheese-paring, and patronizing. —J. M. Bumstead *Peoples of Canada* (1992), p. 139

> Aotearoan Maoris, Australian Aborigines, and Torres Strait islanders joined native Hawaiians and the First Nation Peoples of Canada and the United States to discuss the preservation and nurture of indigenous cultures. —*Church Times* 13 Oct. 1995, p. 2

nature tourism ✕ POP see TOURISM

near-abroad /nɪərə'brɔːd/ *noun* Also written **Near Abroad** 🏠

A collective term for the independent republics which were part of the former Soviet Union.

A translation of the Russian phrase *blizhnee zarubezh'e;* the notion is of an area which is both close at hand and distant, and which is seen as coming within Russia's sphere of influence.

A term coined in 1992 in the Russian periodical *Izvestia,* and used particularly in Russia to designate former fellow republics of the Soviet Union.

> Since the giddy days of 1991, when the republics scattered like schoolchildren at recess, independent life in what Russians call the 'near abroad' has proved tougher than anticipated. Euphoria has slowly been replaced by disgust at the hardships of post-Soviet life.
> —*Time* 25 July 1994, p. 40

> Of course, countries in Russia's so-called Near Abroad which do perhaps face a threat are not even considered. —*Guardian* 8 Mar. 1995, section 2, p. 4

> Presumably, Russian diplomacy toward the 'near abroad' would therefore be motivated to turn from the relatively benign present attitude to one of trying at a minimum to embrace Ukraine and Belarus within a tighter alliance than the loose Commonwealth of Independent States (CIS) structure of today. —*New York Review of Books* 21 Sept. 1995, p. 74

See also CHECHEN

near-video-on-demand 🖵 🔬 see ON-DEMAND

necrotizing fasciitis /'nɛkrətʌızıŋ fası͵ʌıtıs/ *noun*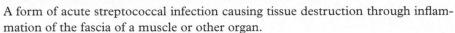

A form of acute streptococcal infection causing tissue destruction through inflammation of the fascia of a muscle or other organ.

Fasciitis, or inflammation of the sheath of fibrous tissue enclosing a muscle or other organ, which *necrotizes,* or causes the death of tissue.

The term *necrotizing fasciitis* came to public attention in Britain in 1994, when an outbreak of the disease, and the death of almost twenty people, was widely reported in the media; the term *flesh-eating disease* was used in reports of its alarming and destructive effects.

'Necrotizing fasciitis', an illness that can eat away fat and muscle at the astounding rate of up to one inch an hour. —*Time* 20 June 1994, p. 54

A 10-year-old boy has died and a 71-year-old woman is seriously ill in hospital after contracting the flesh-eating disease necrotising fasciitis. —*Independent* 13 Jan. 1995, p. 9

nega- /'nɛgə/ *combining form*

Used in words indicating a reduction or absence of the thing identified by the second element of the compound.

Formed from the first element of *negative,* probably with conscious allusion to the contrasting force of MEGA-.

In the early nineties, environmental concerns about excessive (or *mega*) demands on natural resources and the infrastructure began to be expressed in terms delimiting a conscious reduction in such demands. The concept of equating a *megawatt* of electricity saved to a *megawatt* generated was expressed in the designation **negawatt**, and the consequent reduced demand on resources was termed a **negademand**. In ecological terms, *nega-* is now a productive combining form, with discussions of how to reduce traffic congestion including suggestions that drivers should make **negatrips** of **negamiles**.

The concept of 'negawatts'—equating a megawatt of electricity saved to a megawatt of electricity generated—is raised. —*Issues in Science and Technology* Summer 1991, p. 8

Wouldn't this make traffic congestion worse? Not if the public and private sectors work together to develop 'negamile' markets to help to keep cars off the road.
—*New Scientist* 11 Feb. 1995, p. 35

Central to the post-consumerist economy will be the concept of 'negademand'. By saving electricity, or cutting down on driving and shopping trips, for example, consumers will generate negawatts, negamiles and negatrips. —*Independent* 20 May 1995, p. 6

negative equity /nɛgətıv 'ɛkwıti/ *noun*

The indebtedness that occurs when the market value of a property falls below the outstanding amount of a mortgage secured on it, representing a reversal of the favourable situation in which a property is a valuable asset.

The term *negative equity* has been in use in US financial jargon since the fifties, in application to assets generally. In the UK in the nineties it has acquired an extended sense applied specifically to property: an *equity,* the 'net value of a mortgaged property after the deduction of charges', which has acquired a *negative* value.

In the eighties a healthy housing market encouraged widespread investment in property. Many people took on the burden of a large mortgage in order to buy into or increase their investment in this apparently secure market. But with the nineties came the recession, which led to redundancy, a general drop in disposable income, a collapse of the hitherto buoyant housing market, and a sudden marked drop in house prices. People were trapped by *negative equity,* a situation in which they were committed to high mortgage repayments on a house which as a capital asset had dropped in value and which they could not sell. Along with job insecurity, *negative equity* is perceived as damaging to morale and as a significant FEEL-BAD factor. In addition, it has caused a general reassessment of the reliability of property as a source of investment.

For many, the pain was made doubly worse by a phenomenon unimaginable five years before: 'negative equity'. Generations of Britons had been taught to put their money in bricks and mortar.
—*Economist* 24 Oct. 1992, supplement, p. 6

The proportion of house owners with negative equity rose by a fifth over the past year as prices in some regions continued to fall. —*Guardian* 6 Dec. 1993, section 1, p. 7

negative pindown ¶ see PINDOWN

net /nɛt/ *noun* ▣

Used alone, or as one element in a compound, to refer to aspects of computer networking.

The syllable *net* has been used as a stand-alone noun in computing since the early seventies, but only with the huge rise in popularity of networked computer access in the early to mid nineties did it and its compounds become known to a wider audience. **The Net** is increasingly used to mean the INTERNET (see also below).

As the final element of a compound, *net* is commonly employed to form the names of various computer networks, local or global, many of them proprietary terms; the first was **ARPANET**, created in 1969 by the US Department of Defense's Advanced Research Projects Agency; in the early eighties this evolved into the INTERNET; the name **Usenet** appeared in 1980 to refer to a system of online discussion groups or NEWSGROUPS. In the mid eighties **Fidonet** was created to link bulletin board systems (see BBS); **JANET** (the 'Joint Academic Network') links academic institutions in the UK; **BITNET** ('Because It's Time Network') links more than two thousand academic and research organisations world-wide, mainly through electronic mailing lists; **PeaceNet** is a linkage of anti-nuclear activists, and **EcoNet** and **GreenNet** of environmental campaigners. **Cybernet** (see CYBER-), **infonet** (see INFO-), and similar formations are frequently used as generic terms for global information networks, mostly in science-fiction contexts. **Sneakernet** is a facetious term for the process of taking data physically from one computer to another (employing *sneaker* in the US sense of informal footwear). The term **hypernet** has been coined to refer to a computer network which may be used to access *hypermedia* documents (see HYPER-).

The word *net* (often with an initial capital letter, and used attributively) usually relates either to *Usenet* or, more generally, to the Internet as a whole (*Usenet* is a service mainly carried on the Internet but separate from it); sometimes its meaning is broadened to include commercial network services and bulletin-board systems, by no means all of which have Internet access. A **netter** or **nettie** is a regular user of *Usenet* (the latter term in particular is often pejorative in sense). In accessing network systems, people are said to **surf the net** (see also SURF).

Net is now very productive in forming compounds. Another name for an Internet user is **netsurfer** (see SURF); a **nethead** is someone deeply involved with the *net*, possibly to excess; **netiquette** (a compound of *net* and *etiquette*) is the informal canon of good behaviour which all *Usenet* users should adhere to; **netnews** is the content of *Usenet*—the messages, or 'articles', posted electronically by users to newsgroups.

A number of compounds starting in *net* which are used as jargon online are formed with their elements linked by a full stop. This construction, unique to computer networking, is an extension of the use of the stop as a delimiter in computer programming, e-mail addresses, and the names of *Usenet* newsgroups. The most common such formations are: **net.legend** or **net.god** (a person admired for having long experience and great knowledge of computer networks); **net.citizen** (a person belonging to the community of **net.users**, sometimes called a **net.denizen**, or NETIZEN); **net.abuse** (a breach of *netiquette*, such as SPAM; use of the terms **net.cops** and **net.police** suggests an attempt to impose order on what is actually a functioning anarchy).

Beneath their well-publicized surface lies a vast universe of grass-roots on-line bulletin boards, many of them linked into FidoNet, a 10,000-plus worldwide network, as well as smaller networks like PeaceNet and EcoNet. —*Utne Reader* Jan. 1993, p. 120

But sneakernet is still an appropriate option, especially when dealing with service bureaus, clients, or remote offices that may not be connected to your network. —*MacWorld* Dec. 1993, p. 193

All that 'Information Superhighway' hype is beginning to take its toll on increasingly weary net-.denizens. —*Everybody's Internet Update* Apr. 1994, online newsletter

Informal rules of 'netiquette' frown on posting any message as broadly and indiscriminately as the law firm did, and tempers flared when the lawyers insisted they had the right to do so again. —*New Scientist* 9 July 1994, p. 19

Netnews is meant to be read by anyone with access to it. —*Data Communications International* Aug. 1994, p. 8

The importance of BITNET is its reach throughout the world's research establishments. —Howard Rheingold *The Virtual Community* (1994), p. 264

The temptations of surfing are irresistible to new netties but reality takes over. —*Daily Telegraph* 29 Dec. 1994, p. 15

The setup was bugging one particular net.god and that was future UNET founder Rick Adams. —Lee S. Bumgarner *The Great Renaming FAQ v0.90b* 13 Mar. 1995

netizen /ˈnɛtɪz(ə)n/ *noun* Also written **Netizen** 🖳

A person belonging to the community of network users, particularly those connected to the INTERNET.

A blend of NET in its computer networking sense with *citizen*, perhaps indicating someone who spends a good deal of time on the network. There may also be an echo in this formation of the noun *denizen* 'an inhabitant or occupant'.

The word began to appear online in the early nineties, and is still more common there than in print. Though it is often used trivially to mean no more than 'a network user' (and sometimes even dismissively or pejoratively), its adoption also reflects a growing sense that members of the online community have common responsibilities and interests. The attempt by the US government through the 1996 *Computer Decency Act* to impose controls on what could be transmitted over the Internet gave many *netizens* a sense that they indeed belonged to a community, but one that was under threat.

You are a Netizen (Net Citizen), and you exist as a citizen of the world thanks to the global connectivity that the Net gives you. —10 June 1993, online posting

Those who advocate the Internet as a great leap forward in human communication and democracy—the 'netizens'—are keen on participation. —*Guardian* 14 July 1994, OnLine section, p. 4

Several Web sites have set up Valentine's Day pages to put love-lorn netizens in touch. —*Daily Telegraph* 13 Feb. 1996, p. 20

Netscape /ˈnɛtskeɪp/ *noun* 🖳

A proprietary name for a browser (see BROWSE) used to access and display documents on the WORLD WIDE WEB.

Formed from the final syllable of INTERNET and the second syllable of *landscape*; it is employed here figuratively to refer to the 'electronic landscape' of the World Wide Web.

Netscape (in full *Netscape Navigator*) is a trademark of the US company *Netscape Communications Corporation* which was formed in 1994. Within six months, the new application had captured nearly 70 per cent of the browser market. The company has pioneered many techniques that enable the Web to handle moving images, audio, and other techniques; it has incorporated encryption and the programming language JAVA into its browser and through continual innovation has forcefully moved the HTML standard forward. Its supremacy was challenged in 1996 by the decision of Microsoft Corporation to develop a rival series of

Internet-based applications. The term *Netscape* is used interchangeably both for the company and its principal product, and is often used attributively in formations such as **Netscape extensions** (proprietary extensions to the HTML standard) and **Netscape-enhanced** (Web pages designed to exploit these extensions).

> Netscape Network Navigator's core security mechanism is based on RSA encryption and user authentication. —*Data Communications International* Jan. 1995, p. 113

> Netscape has used the enormous success of Navigator to push its own extensions to the HTML standard. Enthusiastic Web-page authors now call their creations 'Netscape-enhanced' as they build nonstandard HTML documents with animations, backgrounds, and the blinking characters that Netscape is known for. —*MacWorld* Oct. 1995, p. 114

> Even the most short-sighted industry watcher knows that the future of the Internet must lie in full multimedia capability, and NetScape seems to be establishing itself as the standard. —*Personal Computer World* Feb. 1996, p. 322

network computer /ˈnɛtwəːk kəmˌpjuːtə/ *noun* 💻

A low-cost personal computer without local disk storage designed to be connected to the INTERNET, a *local area network* (see LAN), or a similar network, from which it would access applications and data.

The *network computer* was conceived and promoted by the US computer company Oracle Corporation. The first machine demonstrated in February 1996 could use either a colour television or a computer monitor as a display device, but had no disk storage, so that it had to DOWNLOAD applications and data from a network, either the Internet or a company INTRANET working on similar principles. The intention was to reduce the cost of the PC, which was seen as an unnecessarily complex device for most purposes, and particularly to break users' dependence on expensive personal copies of applications software. The proposal gained support from some manufacturers and large companies, but some users expressed concern about using remote network connections for their personal computing. The name is frequently abbreviated to **NC**.

> Sometime next year, predict both Mr Ellison and Sun's chief executive, Scott McNealy, companies will release machines (dubbed 'Internet appliances' or 'network computers') that will do nothing more than run Internet software and perhaps a simple word processor. —*Economist* 14 Oct. 1995, p. 106

> The network computer, or NC, will download both a small operating system and applications programs over a network used to access remote 'server' systems holding data and programs. —*Edupage* (online newsletter) 16 Apr. 1996

> But the NC is one of those initially appealing concepts whose glitter fades under the glare of scrutiny. —*Computer Weekly* 11 July 1996, p. 34

neural /ˈnjʊər(ə)l/ *adjective* 💻

Modelled on the arrangement of neurons in the brain and nervous system; used especially in **neural network** (or **neural net**), a computer system which is designed to emulate the brain in its ability to 'learn' to assess large amounts of imprecise data.

The development of computer *neural networks* was founded on the work of mathematicians studying neurophysiology as a model for the construction of automata from the late forties onwards; the term *neural net* as a hypothetical possibility was first noted in 1950 and *neural network* the year after. The various compound terms based on *neural* became much more widely known in the eighties, when advances in semiconductor technology meant that researchers could actually construct such a machine; by the nineties, such systems were being widely used in real-world applications. A *neural network* contains layers of nodes, analogous to neurons in the brain; a large number of connections between the nodes simulate the synapses. Each node accepts several inputs, sums or weights them according to predefined rules and outputs a signal if the inputs exceed a certain value. The nodes may be simple dedicated electronic circuits, or they may be simulations in software within a conventional computer. The strength of *neural nets* is their ability to assess imprecise data and work out whether it matches some pattern or not; they can also be 'trained' to reach correct solutions. The complete device may be called a **neural computer** and the concept **neural computing**; alternatively, using the combining form *neuro-* instead of *neural*, the terms **neurocomputer** and **neurocomputing** have been derived.

A number of special neural networks will be designed and interlinked to create a neural computer...Research into neural computing is now a multi-million pound scientific endeavour.
—*The Times* 25 Mar. 1989, p. 5

Neural nets are in the news again. For starters, Bellcore has announced that it's developing a neural-net computer that processes 100,000 signals per second...Ricoh, the Japanese firm known for printers and photocopiers, has announced a high-speed, hardware-only neural-net computer that will be used as an embedded controller for copiers. —*Dr. Dobb's Journal* Aug. 1992, p. 6

Neural networks can be used for a wide variety of purposes, such as imaging, where applications can be as diverse as using one to interpret the data on customer order forms...or to analyse cloud formations, which a satellite company is doing. —*Computer Weekly* 1 July 1993, p. 14

New Age /nju: 'eɪdʒ/ *noun* and *adjective* Also written **new age** and **new-age** ✦ ⊗ ✖

noun: An umbrella term for a cultural movement (known more fully as the **New Age Movement**), covering a broad range of beliefs and activities and characterized by a rejection of (modern) Western-style values and culture and the promotion of a more integrated or 'holistic' approach in areas such as religion, medicine, philosophy, astrology, and the environment.

adjective: Belonging to, characteristic of, or influenced by the beliefs and activities of this movement.

The term may be used to describe any new era or beginning, but, from the publication of a magazine entitled *Aquarian New Age* in 1908, it also became an alternative name in astrology for the *Age of Aquarius*, that part of the zodiacal cycle which the world is due to enter in the late twentieth or early twenty-first century, and which is believed to signal an era of new spiritual awareness and collective consciousness.

Although *New Age* originated in and remained strongly associated with California and the West Coast of the US, its influence spread throughout the US and northern Europe. Many of the various components that make up the *New Age Movement*—including the wide range of alternative and complementary therapies, the practice of Eastern religions, and the fascination with the occult and parapsychology—are of course not 'new'; and moreover, at first sight, they seem to follow directly from aspects of the hippy movement of the sixties. What made *New Age* different (and in this sense 'new') was that, whereas the hippy movement involved mainly young people and tended to operate in opposition to contemporary Western society, *New Age* was by the early eighties attracting not only an older age group but also middle-class people who had both money and status within society. Such people—some of whom were in fact the hippies of the sixties now grown older—not only gave the movement a reputation for being a kind of 'religion for yuppies', they also, by the late eighties, ensured its rapid growth and extraordinary success in commercial terms, whether it was in publishing *New Age* books on organic gardening or astrological charts, or in promoting crystal healing or water-divining. Members of a more anarchic and youth-oriented group of **New Agers** in the UK were given the label of **New Age travellers** in 1986. They espouse *New Age* ideals by abandoning urban life to lead a nomadic existence.

The general theme within the *New Age Movement* was that in the harsh post-industrial world of the late twentieth century, people had somehow become out of balance both with their own spiritual selves and with nature and the environment as a whole; this theme was strongly featured in **New Age music**. From its first use in 1985, this term was loosely applied to a particular brand of music that tended to be characterized by light melodic harmonies and improvisation, by the lack of a strong beat or prominent vocals, and by the use of such instruments as the piano, harp, and synthesizer. The idea was to create a relaxing or dream-like atmosphere; sometimes sounds were reproduced from the natural world such as 'planetary' sounds and the calls of dolphins and whales. Referring either to the music or the general philosophy, the adjective **New Agey** is often used in a disparaging way.

> The 'New Age'…is, of course, the 'Old Age' and for me, the only hope that we will have any planet left to live on at all. —R. Barr *Roseanne* (1990), p. 182

> Oddly beautiful and intelligently constructed, this is how ambient and New Age musics might be if they were not so bogged down in bloodless nicety. —*Wire* Feb. 1993, p. 51

> A feel-good New Agey spiel tailored to make yuppies feel better about themselves, a designer theology for the millennium, God lite for the free-floating middle class. —*Utne Reader* Mar. 1993, p. 90

> The Harmonic Convergence—a global event in which New Agers gathered at 'power points' to combine their spiritual energy in an effort to save the planet. —*Albuquerque Journal* (New Mexico) 11 May 1993, section B, p. 1

> The collision with the rag-tag army of fossilized hippies, white dreads and old punks who were bobbing along on the free festival circuit created a mutant subculture—labelled New Age Travellers by the Tory press—whose lineage can plausibly be traced back to the Levellers, Diggers and other antinomian religious cults of the 1640s. —*Arena* Sept./Oct. 1994, p. 86

new jack swing /nju: dʒak 'swɪŋ/ *noun phrase* 🐝

A form of dance music combining elements from rhythm and blues, soul, hip-hop, and rap music; a variety of SWINGBEAT.

A *new* form of *swing* music named for the US popular singer Michael *Jack*son, whose producer, Teddy Riley, developed the style.

New jack swing came to popularity in the US at the end of the eighties, and quickly gained ground; the elliptical term **new jack** to designate the music, clothes, and culture associated with the phenomenon developed from it. **New jill swing** is a term for music of this kind for a female performer.

> New jack performers Jodeci and Mary J. Blige, rappers Heavy D and Das EFX, and the Fly Girl dancers of 'In Living Color' have turned hip-hop away from its fixation on high-tech athletic shoes by sporting rugged black military and hiking boots. —*Star Tribune* 26 May 1993, section E, p. 3

> On 'Fountain of Youth' the boxy drum supports a hype New Jack Swing female vocal. —*Rolling Stone* 30 June 1994, p. 72

> The same bubbly swingbeat (or 'new jill swing') rhythms and plush vocal harmonies prevail everywhere. —*Guardian* 26 May 1995, Review section, p. 13

> It still sounds like an Al Green record, not a gussied-up new jack swing record with Al Green's voice on top. —*Newsweek* 13 Nov. 1995, p. 82

New Labour /nju: 'leɪbə/ *noun* and *adjective* 🏛

noun: That section of a Labour Party regarded as combining traditional socialist values with an awareness of people's current aspirations.

adjective: Of or belonging to New Labour.

Labour as a political party which represents the interests of ordinary working people in accordance with socialist traditions, while remaining responsive to *new* ideals and aspirations.

The use of *New* to indicate a fresh political start in a specified area is of course well-established, one of the best-known examples being Franklin Roosevelt's economic *New Deal* of 1932. This use of *New* in the title of a political party is similarly familiar; what became the

British Union of Fascists was originally founded in 1930 by Oswald Mosley as the *New Party*. In America in the sixties, the protest movement evoked by opposition to the Vietnam War gave birth to the *New Left*, a political grouping whose stated aim was to succeed (where traditional liberalism had failed) in winning for ordinary people power over decisions affecting their own lives.

The term *New Labour* came to prominence in New Zealand in 1989, when the left wing of the ruling Labour Party, alarmed by the application of *Rogernomics* (see -NOMICS), separated from the main party to form *New Labour*.

More recently, in the field of British politics, *New Labour* has become the accepted term for that section of the party which accepts with enthusiasm the modernizing approach of the current Leader, Tony Blair (see also BLAIRISM). The seeds of *New Labour* are seen by some as having been sown by the former Leader John Smith, particularly in regard to his OMOV campaign and (perhaps less seriously) the PRAWN COCKTAIL OFFENSIVE. The conflict between the forces of modernization and those (sometimes referred to as *Old Labour*) who felt that essential principles were being jettisoned was demonstrated most clearly in the battle over CLAUSE FOUR.

How strange to find the origins of 'new Labour' in the dying embers of a clapped-out Tory administration. —*New Statesman & Society* 24 Nov. 1995, p. 25

In the end the twenty-first century that Blair fantasises about with new sub-cyber moistness may well be too new, too truly far out, for any old New Labour to cope with. —*ikon* Jan. 1996, p. 58

New Lad /nju: 'lad/ *noun* Also written **new lad** POP

A (young) man who embraces sexist attitudes and the traditional male role as a reaction against the perceived effeminacy or POLITICAL CORRECTNESS of the NEW MAN.

This use of *lad* carries connotations of the British colloquial phrases *a bit of a lad* and *one of the lads*.

The concept of the *New Lad* was first formulated at the start of the nineties, when some, usually young, men were regarded as expressing in their attitudes and lifestyle a revolt against POLITICAL CORRECTNESS, especially in their disregard for the principles of feminism and defiance towards the aims of the MEN'S MOVEMENT of the eighties, as typified in the NEW MAN and the MYTHOPOETIC movement. The *New Lad* is sometimes regarded as expressing a POST-FEMINIST sexism, one that acknowledges new roles for women but simultaneously embraces a male bravado which may be seen as predatory and immature. In the UK in the mid nineties the term has occasionally been used in association with young rock bands and BRITPOP. The adjective **New Laddish** and the nouns **New Laddishness** and **New Laddism** developed in the same period. Most recently the terms **Ladette** and **New Ladette** have been coined for the *New Lad*'s female equivalent, representing the militant feminism also typified by a RIOT GIRL.

I was quite mystified by the New Lad, or rather his motives for trying to be anything more than the neanderthal he always will be. —*Arena* Summer 1991, p. 17

Dave Baddiel, for one, is convinced his New Laddishness appeals to women. 'I've got lots of women friends. They find my honesty refreshing,' he insists.
—*Independent* (Nexis) 14 Apr. 1994, p. 19

If you had to chastise the NME, it would be over their relentlessly trivial insider celebration of the whole Primal Scream/Oasis/Blur drinks and drugs and flattened vowels new laddism, at the expense of any genuine critical or journalistic insights.
—*Guardian* 5 May 1995, Friday supplement, p. 11

And all that new lad rock stuff; they like it, but really it just reminds them of their age.
—*The Face* Sept. 1995, p. 171

New Man /nju: 'man/ *noun* Also written **new man** POP

A man who rejects sexist attitudes, and aims to be caring, sensitive, and non-aggressive and to take a substantial role in his household's domestic routine.

The concept of the *New Man* was first identified in the early eighties. A man thus described was one who demonstrated that men as well as women may be overtly caring and sensitive. He would have espoused the feminist ideals of the seventies and in his own life tried to abandon the traditional male role and the male monopoly of power. He would have been prepared to share in the care of his children and in housework, and he may even have been prepared to give up his job and work as a house-husband. For all these qualities the notional *New Man*, though usage of the term was usually jocular, was broadly welcomed, and men who identified with these aspirations were generally acknowledged as enlightened and progressive individuals.

However, as the decade progressed use of the term began to acquire a derogatory tone. The aspirations of the *New Man* came to be regarded with a POST-FEMINIST ambivalence. His aims were regarded as a form of POLITICAL CORRECTNESS which itself was now increasingly derided. Gradually the *New Man* came to be perceived as lacking the characteristics which make men attractive both to women and to other men. In response to this men sought to recover an acceptable form of masculinity through such endeavours as the MYTHOPOETIC *men's movement*, though by the nineties this too was sometimes mocked, especially by the NEW LADS. By the mid nineties the *New Man* was generally seen as no longer representing a valid role model and scepticism that such a man had ever existed was commonly expressed.

Does the New Woman Really Want the New Man?…The answer, as you might guess, is a frustrated no. —*Chicago Tribune* (Nexis) 3 May 1985, section C, p. 27

The 'new man', that caring, sharing male who is happy to stay at home and look after the children, is still a rare species. —*Independent* 21 Nov. 1991, p. 11

Eight out of 10 women say they prepare every meal in their household, according to a government survey yesterday that casts doubt on the reality of 'new man' culture.
—*Guardian* 25 Jan. 1995, section 1, p. 8

Liam is not what you'd call conventionally good-looking, yet there is something in that bone-structure (= none of your New Man nanciness). —*Select* Mar. 1995, p. 61

New Romantic /njuː rə(ʊ)'mantɪk/ *noun* and *adjective* Also written **new romantic** 🎵 POP

noun: A follower of a British youth cult and fashion of the early eighties which combined elements of punk and glam-rock to form a style in which both sexes dressed in flamboyant clothes and often wore make-up.

adjective: Belonging to or associated with New Romantics.

A *new* type of *romantic*, the term *romantic* making oblique reference to *romanticism*, a movement in the arts originating in the late eighteenth century, which rejected classicism and rationalism and favoured inspiration, subjectivity, and the primacy of the individual.

The cult of the *New Romantic* developed in Britain in the early eighties. Rooted in the music industry, and associated with groups such as Duran Duran and Depeche Mode, its manifestation was most apparent in its code of dress. Romanticism has long been associated with a flamboyant visual aesthetic, and the *New Romantics* created a late twentieth-century style characterized by richly textured and frilly clothing. To this they added some elements from punk such as spiky hair and BODY-PIERCING, and the sexual ambiguity of glam-rock.

In the mid nineties there are indications that **New Romanticism** may be revived in ROMO music and its associated culture.

Any similarity between Brum's Duran Duran and London's so-called New Romantic movement is merely…sartorial. —*Melody Maker* 14 Mar. 1981, p. 30

Brandishing an impudent manifesto which sought to fuse the sexual ambiguity and thunderflashes of glam rock with the surly belligerence of punk, Duran Duran exploded upon a stagnant pop scene on the bespoke shirt tails of the New Romantics. —*Q* Dec. 1989, p. 161

The Pirates Collection of 1980…captured the essence of the New Romantics…Romantic, wayward and defiant it was a best-seller at home and abroad. —*TV Times* 14 Oct. 1990, p. 15

There were three kinds of committed trends at school: the rude boys, casuals into Hawaiian shirts and New Romantics. —Jayne Miller *voXpop: The New Generation X Speaks* (1995), p. 195

newsgroup /ˈnjuːzgruːp/ *noun* Also written **news group** 🖳

One of a number of online discussion forums which together make up *Usenet* (see NET), an informal communications system now mainly carried on the INTERNET but separate from it.

A combination of *news* (the originators of the Usenet system expected it to be used primarily to communicate information of current interest, as an electronic analogue of a notice board or bulletin board) with *group*.

Newsgroups are based around topics. Users can post messages or *articles* to any of the groups and can respond to other people's articles to generate discussion. The distribution system is decentralized, with computers worldwide receiving messages, distributing them to local users and sending them on to other computer systems together with messages originated locally. Some *newsgroups* are moderated, with postings vetted by the moderator, but most depend on the good sense of their participants to maintain order, supplemented by the persuasion and ridicule of other users (see FLAME). The system started in 1980 in the US as an informal network formed from existing UNIX-based systems, connected by public telephone links, initially quite separate from the US Department of Defense network which evolved into today's Internet. By 1996, there were more than 17,000 *newsgroups*, covering a vast range of possible interests, such as computing, health, social issues, local cultures, languages, the arts, recreation, sport, films, and education.

And it is no surprise that young males, with their cultural bent—indeed mission—to master new technology, are today's computer hackers and so populate the on-line communities and newsgroups. —Michael Benedikt *Cyberspace: First Steps* (1991), p. 6

Check the line in the header that says which newsgroups the message has been posted to. If there are a number of them, think to 10 again—do you really want to start a cross-newsgroup flamefest where all the groups get taken over by 'get this crap out of this newsgroup' messages? —*Everybody's Internet Update* Mar. 1995, online newsletter

'Newsgroups'—some 14,000 channels of open discussion, ranging from computer arcana to radical politics (with a lot of sex thrown in for good measure)—look more like a broadcast medium. —*Economist* 8 Apr. 1995, p. 17

news-on-demand 🖳 📷 see ON-DEMAND

new world order /njuː wəːld ˈɔːdə/ *noun phrase* Also written **New World Order** 📷

A vision of the world in which a new political order brings greater peace and stability than that which currently exists.

The notion of a political *new world order*, especially with regard to the maintenance of peace, has been around since the twenties. It was revived in 1991 in the words of the then US President, George Bush, who said, of the prospect of the end of the cold war brought about by the demise of the Soviet Union:

And now, we can see a new world coming into view. A world in which there is the very real prospect of a new world order.

The notion was greeted with some caution by a country which had, for so long, been locked in bitter conflict with its Communist enemy, Ronald Reagan's 'Evil Empire', and commentators in the US and elsewhere went on ironically to test Bush's foreign policy against the assumptions of his *new world order*, the PEACE DIVIDEND, and the VISION THING.

We seek, said George Bush, 'new ways of working with other nations to deter aggression, and to achieve stability, prosperity and, above all, peace.' He was talking of the New World Order—an epic made possible by Mikhail Gorbachev, realised by Saddam Hussein, starring the United States and shortly to be showing in a conflict near you. *—Economist* 22 June 1991, p. 13

This is a crucial period for Africa, when its marginalization in geopolitics and economic affairs has reached a new high. When President George Bush expressed his vision of the 'new world order', Africa was hardly mentioned. *—World Press Review* Aug. 1991, p. 11

Compared to their tech-crazed...cyber-colonels, majors, and captains who are now actually running the digitized New World Order military—the Cold War guys looked like a line of stuffed ducks. *—Wired* (Premiere issue) 1993, p. 96

NHS trust ⓧ 🏥 see HOSPITAL TRUST

NICAM /'naɪkam/ *noun* Also written **Nicam** 🔬

A digital system used in television transmissions, principally in Britain, to provide high-quality stereophonic sound with the video signals.

An acronym formed from the initial letters of *near instantaneously companded audio multiplex*: *near instantaneously* because there is in practice a tiny time lag of about a millisecond before the system can operate; *companded* because the audio range of the signal is compressed on transmission and expanded again on reception using a *compander* (a blend of 'compressor' and 'expander'); *audio*, 'sound'; and *multiplex*, meaning 'the simultaneous transmission of several messages along a single channel of communication' (the system is not limited to audio, but can also carry other types of data).

The *NICAM* system was invented by the BBC in the early eighties, and was first used in 1986, but only became widely available in Britain in the mid nineties. It is also becoming available in many European countries. Using sets equipped with the appropriate decoders, viewers can have stereo sound to accompany television programmes which have been appropriately recorded. Because the sound is transmitted digitally, the quality on both stereo and mono is only slightly less good than that from CDs. The system can also be used to transmit two simultaneous mono sound channels which could be used, for example, to provide a soundtrack in two languages. The word is frequently used attributively, especially in the expression **NICAM stereo**.

Having NICAM Digital Stereo equipped TVs and video recorders (VCRs) provides substantial extra benefits over and above normal monaural TVs and VCRs. *—CD Review* Oct. 1991, p. 86

The most recent evolutionary change in some European countries has been the introduction of NICAM stereo sound to the television broadcast signal.
—EBU Technical Review Autumn 1992, p. 21

Sporting Nicam digital sound, the VHS deck also has NTSC playback, dual Scart connectors and push-jog remotes. *—Camcorder User* Apr. 1995, p. 7

niche /niːʃ, nɪtʃ/ *noun* 〰

In business, a position from which an entrepreneur is able to exploit a gap in the market; a profitable section of the market.

A specialized figurative sense of *niche* (literally 'a recess'), similar to *corner* in its business sense, first used by Frederik Barth in his book *The Role of the Entrepreneur in Social Change in Northern Norway* (1963).

Since the emergence of **niche market** (a relatively small and specialist, but profitable, field in which to sell a product or service) at the end of the seventies, *niche* has been increasingly used in a variety of compounds. The nouns **niche marketing**, **niche marketer**, and **niche marketeer**, and the use of **niche market** as a verb, all appeared in the eighties. **Niche player** (a firm which exploits a *niche*) dates from the mid eighties and **niche product** (a product which one sells in a *niche market*) appeared in the early nineties.

But if you had a real niche fund, say a French authorised second section oil fund for instance, then you could raise interest from foreign investors who wanted into that niche.

—European Investor May 1990, p. 10

Mr Kitayama believes that Japan's banks will fall into two groups: those 'offering the full range of financial services to the entire market' and 'niche players'.

—Economist 2 May 1992 (Survey of World Banking Supplement) p. 49

Niche marketing and strategic alliances can give you greater clout in the markets of the Middle East and Pan Pacific. —advertisement in *Esprit de Corps* (Ottawa, Ontario) Aug. 1994, p. 38

The company now specialises in one of the UK's most substantial niche markets, dealing primarily with individual clients and landed estates. *—Guardian* 26 Apr. 1995, section 1, p. 15

nicotine patch Ⓧ see PATCH

nigga /'nɪgə/ *noun* ᴾᴼᴾ ◖◗

A black man.

A representation of American Black English pronunciation of the word *nigger*.

This and other forms of *nigger* have long been in use within the AFRICAN-AMERICAN community and have been recorded in print since the twenties. However, recent usage of *nigga*, and its plural form **niggaz**, represents a conscious, politically motivated reclamation by blacks of the term *nigger*. This term, which had been regarded as typifying offensive and derogatory attitudes within the white community, was adopted by the black community as a form of self-assertion, with the aim of reducing the term's derogation. (A similar development may be seen in the adoption of the word *queer* by the gay community; see QUEER NATION.) The recent uptake of the term *nigga* has been given impetus by its use in rap lyrics and within the HIP-HOP culture, and by its adoption as a name by some black groups, notably the Los Angeles trio **Niggaz with Attitude** (or *N.W.A.*). Its use is largely restricted to the black community, and both *nigga* and *nigger* remain offensive when used by white people.

Further use of this vernacular respelling of the *-er* element may be seen in terms such as GANGSTA, in the name of the group *Gravediggaz*, and in the formulation *brotha*. Further respellings, such as *dat* for *that* and *tha* for *the*, are similarly used in affirmation of contemporary black culture.

After South Central Los Angeles was plastered with posters promoting N.W.A.'s new '100 Miles and Runnin'' album with the tag line 'Tha Niggaz R Back', some of the most immediate response came not from fans but from alleged white supremacists who were unable to define the posters' origins. *—Los Angeles Times* 15 Oct. 1990, section D, p. 2

These guys were in shock—they had no idea that black people sometimes call each other nigga as a term of endearment. They saw the brothers at the party shouting 'What's up nigga?' to one another and one of my white friends got so excited he started yellin'. 'Hey! How you niggas doing?' The music stopped and everyone looked at them. *—The Face* Sept. 1993, p. 69

Niggas would come to school with them in their back pockets, and I would read 'em and think, 'Oh my God, it's the phattest shit in the world', because it's exactly what hardcore rap is: it's the lingo, it's life, it's the whole life we live. —Brian Cross *It's Not About a Salary* (1993), p. 182

We went through a regular struggle, a lot of niggaz got chopped off in the process, and seein' that, we was able to make us stronger. *—Represent* Apr. 1995, p. 31

no-fly /nəʊ 'flaɪ/ *adjective* ▨

Designating an area in which military, and occasionally civil, aircraft are forbidden to fly; especially in the phrase **no-fly zone**. Also, designating the order to enforce, or the enforcement of, such an area.

The determiner *no* is used elliptically with the verb *fly* to form an adjective, following the model of *no-go*.

Use of this formulation has been recorded since the late eighties. The term *no-fly zone* has been made familiar to the general public through its frequent use in reports of recent conflicts, particularly those of the Gulf War and in the former Yugoslavia. *No-fly* orders are generally imposed by international committees such as the United Nations and are maintained by the interested parties. Such maintenance is sometimes required for some time after the end of active combat; the maintenance of the *no-fly zone* in southern Iraq has involved the US in continuing deployment of resources in Iraq some years after the end of the Gulf War.

> The White House said Saturday that Iraq has moved its missiles out of threatening positions in the 'no-fly zone' of southern Iraq, ending the prospect of imminent U.S. military action.
> —*Coloradoan* (Fort Collins) 10 Jan. 1993, section A, p. 1

> The remaining options appear to be those already agreed and implemented: economic sanctions against Serbia and enforcement of the Bosnia no-fly zone.
> —*Independent on Sunday* 25 July 1993, p. 8

> The incident was part of what has become a long-running cat and mouse game between the US and allied air patrols and the Iraqi military, who keep testing and probing the allied will and capacity to maintain the no-fly zone. —*Guardian* 20 Aug. 1993, section 1, p. 10

> His F16 fighter was destroyed by a Bosnian Serb missile about 90 miles north of Sarajevo as he enforced the United Nations no-fly zone. —*The Times* 9 June 1995, p. 1

-nomics /'nɒmɪks/ *combining form* 〰️ 🗒️

Used as the second element of words denoting 'the economic policies and principles of' (the person indicated by the first part of the compound).

The occasional compounding of the name of a politician with the second element of *economics* is not of course new; the term *Nixonomics* was applied in 1969 to the economic policies of Richard Nixon, and in the early eighties **Reaganomics** was coined to describe the combination of promotion of the free market and reduction of taxation characteristic of the policies of Ronald Reagan.

Since that period, the combining form has become freely productive, with both **Thatchernomics** and **Clintonomics** being coined. While the formation is usually on the surname of the politician concerned, it may be noted that the economic policies of Roger Douglas, New Zealand Minister of Finance from 1984–8, have been designated **Rogernomics**. The individual formations tend not to outlast the political lifetime of the individual politician, but the frequency of the formation (although affected by whether the name will combine euphoniously with *-nomics*) appears to be gaining ground.

> The irony is that it is the failure of Thatchernomics that has forced Britain to hand over one of the major levers of sovereign economic management to the German central bank.
> —*World Press Review* Dec. 1990, p. 25

> A critic of Clintonomics, easy money and high taxes, Mr. Kudlow gave no indication that he would retire from behind the political scenes. —*New York Times* 4 Mar. 1994, section D, p. 1

> 'Rogernomics' so disillusioned the Labour left that in 1989 it split to form New Labour, the electorate revolted, and in 1990 the conservative National Party was returned to power in a landslide.
> —*New Statesman & Society* 24 Nov. 1995, p. 24

Northern blot 🧪 see BLOT

not /nɒt/ *interjection* Also written **not!** 🗯️POP

Used humorously following a statement to indicate that it should not be taken seriously, with the implication that the idea expressed is untrue or the thing postulated unlikely; the equivalent of the older phrase *I don't think*.

Perhaps deriving from usage with an inverted construction in which emphasis is given to the negative by delay, as in the traditional rhyme 'he loves me, he loves me not'.

A number of occurrences of this ironical construction are recorded from the first half of this century, but it seemed to fall into obscurity after 1950. However it has been repopularized in the nineties, largely through the linguistically influential 'Wayne's World' sketches in 1989 on the NBC television programme *Saturday Night Live* (see also BABE), and has become a popular way of expressing an emphatic or ironical negative.

> Including the fabulous *Head Over Heels*, described as 'a seven-part series about a rebellious rock and roller at a girls' finishing school in the Fifties'. That sounds like copper-bottomed quality entertainment—*not.*   —*Observer* 7 June 1992, p. 34

> It's good to know that Apple hasn't lost its knack for making equipment with limited backward compatibility. This is good marketing. It forces you to update everything and keep the economy going. *Not!*   —*MacUser* Feb. 1993, p. 362

not-for-profit /nɒtfə'prɒfɪt/ *adjective*

Not intended to make a profit; non-profit-making.

Increasing use in the eighties and nineties of the mid-fifties compound FOR-PROFIT to describe profit-making organizations has been matched by *not-for-profit*, designating institutions operating in the same areas, but with a different philosophy expressed by their opposite financial aims. The development of both terms may be seen as part of an ongoing debate over the place of privatization in what has been seen as the traditional area of public services.

> I found myself involved with a very complex not-for-profit organization that operates differently from any business I've worked in.
>   —Eva Innes and Leslie Southwick-Trask *Financial Post Turning It Around* (1989), p. 140

> The goal of our not-for-profit corporation is to put a fishing rod into the hands of every young Canadian and plant them squarely on the side of conservation.
>   —*Outdoor Canada* Summer 1994, p. 8

> An incubator is a not-for-profit organization that helps just-hatched companies get off the ground by providing a professional environment.   —*Post* (Denver) 23 Apr. 1995, section G, p. 1

nutraceutical /njuːtrə'sjuːtɪk(ə)l/ *noun and adjective* ⊗ ✕

noun: A food containing health-promoting additives, a functional food.

adjective: Of, relating to, or designating nutraceuticals.

From a blend of *nutrition* and *pharmaceutical*.

The growing commercial interest in FUNCTIONAL FOODS throughout the nineties has been accompanied by the coinage and increasing use of **nutraceutical** as a term which expresses the dual nourishing and health-promoting role of such food. (The alternative term *pharmafood* has also recently been recorded.)

> The notion of food as elixir, hand-me-down from antiquity, has reemerged bearing a new set of names; among them are nutraceuticals, designer foods and functional foods.
>   —*Scientific American* Sept. 1994, p. 86

> Functional foods—also called nutraceuticals and pharmafoods—are medicines to tickle the taste buds.   —*The European* 30 May 1996, Magazine supplement, p. 20

> Japan and other Asian countries, of course, are leading the pack with many nutraceutical products on the supermarket shelves.   —*Food Engineering* July 1996, p. 11

O

October surprise /ɒkˌtəʊbə sə'praɪz/ *noun* 🏛

In the US: an unexpected but popular political act made just prior to a November election in an attempt to win votes.

The term *October Surprise* was originally used during the American presidential campaign of

1980, with reference to the possibility that the embattled Democratic administration of President Carter might succeed in mounting a last-minute popularity coup by achieving the release of the American servicemen held hostage in Teheran.

The release of the hostages was not in fact agreed until the Republican Ronald Reagan had taken office; and in the early nineties the term was applied to an alleged conspiracy whereby it was said that members of the 1980 Republican campaign worked to delay the release of the hostages to benefit their own party. The allegations were not substantiated, and it may well be that with hindsight the **October Surprise conspiracy**, like the **October Surprise theory**, will be seen primarily as exemplifications of conspiracy theory.

Nor would 'an October surprise be sufficient to meet Carter's basic problem—the economy'.
—Christian Science Monitor 5 Sept. 1980, p. 3

Two congressional investigations—one into the goings-on at BCCI and one into the 'October surprise' (the allegations that the 1980 Reagan campaign team conspired to delay the release of American hostages in Iran)—will fuel the public impression that Congress is all talk and inaction. *—Economist* 14 Sept. 1991, p. 45

The October Surprise theory, which holds that the 1980 Reagan-Bush campaign cut a secret deal with Iran to delay the release of the hostages and ensure a Republican victory, has been a mother lode for conspiracy junkies for the past decade. *—Newsweek* 11 Nov. 1991, p. 3

He proved himself wanton and reckless in trying to persuade the country of the October Surprise, by certifying the evidence of so many sicko fabricators that he must himself now be counted in their ranks. *—New Republic* 2 Aug. 1993, p. 47

Of- /ɔf/ *combining form* ⚈

Forming the titles of regulatory bodies for the operations of specified industries.

The first syllable of *Office*.

The development of this productive combining form took place in Britain in the eighties, when the privatization of such former service industries as electricity, gas, rail, and water resulted in the formation of regulatory bodies, or *Offices*, to supervise each industry.

The first of these, **Oftel**, was set up in 1983 as the *Office of Telecommunications* to supervise the operation of the British telecommunications industry after privatization, and others followed, with **Ofgas** (for *Gas Supply*) and **Ofwat** (for the *Water Services*) being established in 1986, and **Offer** (for *Electricity Regulation*) in 1989. The *Office of the Railway Regulator*, which came into existence in 1993, is predictably known as **Ofrail**, and the official regulator for the NATIONAL LOTTERY is **Oflot**. This kind of organization for monitoring standards is not necessarily limited to the world of industry: the full title of **Ofsted** is the *Office for Standards in Education*.

In the nineties, there is increasing evidence of the view that the appropriate name for an official 'watchdog' body should be formed with *Of-*, with more and less serious suggestions including titles for regulatory bodies for banking (**Ofbank**) and the dairy industry (**Ofmilk**).

British Gas wants Ofgas to let the company raise its price for the carriage of its own and its competitors' gas through the national gas grid. *—Economist* 8 Aug. 1992, p. 24

An 'Ofmilk' was essential...Other monopolies such as the gas and telephone utilities had watch-dogs, and so should milk. *—Independent* 19 Nov. 1992, p. 29

Oflot, the lottery watchdog, is being urged to launch an investigation into the running of the game. *—Independent* 13 Nov. 1995, p. 1

offender profiling ⁅ ▲ see PROFILING

Offer ⚈ see OF-

Ofgas ⚈ see OF-

Oflot ⚈ see OF-

Ofrail ⟋ see OF-

Ofsted ⟋ see OF-

Oftel ⟋ see OF-

Ofwat ⟋ see OF-

old age abuse ❨❨ see ABUSE

Olestra /ɒˈlɛstrə/ *noun* Also written **olestra** ⊗ ✖

The trade mark of a synthetic sucrose polyester used as a calorie-free substitute for fat in various foods.

An invented name, probably from *olestr-* derived from a modification of *polyester* or *cholesterol*.

Public anxiety about the harmful effects to health of too much fat and cholesterol in the diet has made the search for substitutes which do not require an effective change of diet one of considerable commercial importance. *Olestra* represents one of the more recent attempts to solve the problem; unfortunately, reports of its ability to pass through the body without being absorbed have been offset by indications that this may have such unpleasant side effects as *gastric leakage*.

> A new fat substitute made with soybean oil is being developed by Proctor and Gamble. The product, called olestra, contains no calories because it can not be absorbed by the body.
> —*Farm Journal* Oct. 1989, p. 26

> In food engineering terms, Olestra is a genuine break-through.
> —*Independent* 22 Jan. 1996, Supplement, p. 4

> Olestra…was approved by the US Food and Drug Administration for use only in crisps, crackers, tortilla chips and other savoury snacks—provided they carry a warning: 'Olestra may cause abdominal cramping and loose stools. Olestra inhibits the absorption of some vitamins and other nutrients.'
> —*Daily Telegraph* 26 Jan. 1996 (electronic edition)

See also TRANS-FATTY ACID

OMOV /əʊˈmɒv/ *acronym* Also written **Omov** ▣

'One member, one vote' as a principle of democratic election within an organization.

Formed from the initial letters of *One Member, One Vote*.

The slogan *one man, one vote* as advocating the principle of universal suffrage is recorded from the mid nineteenth century, but in modern times the understanding of 'man' to mean 'person' is less acceptable. The modification *one member, one vote* (in its avoidance of apparent gender specificity more in tune with the requirements of POLITICAL CORRECTNESS) developed in the nineteen eighties.

The development is associated with a particular situation: the traditional wielding of *block votes* on behalf of their membership by Trade Union representatives within the Labour Party. *OMOV* as a slogan and principle has been a particular focus of interest for NEW LABOUR; the acceptance by the Labour Party and the Trade Unions of the *OMOV* principle has been seen as a central plank of the position of the modernizing forces now represented by BLAIRISM.

> It [the Labour Party] must accept the guiding principle of one-member-one-vote and it must modernise…They don't like Smith's OMOV plans, but they don't like Brown's economic agenda any better.
> —*Guardian* 10 July 1993, p. 29

> With the man preferred by the local party activists safely out of the way, the outcome of the first Omov poll is anybody's guess.
> —*Independent on Sunday* 27 Feb. 1994, p. 4

> It states that without the dreaded OMOV, one member one vote, Labour will simply be written off

as incapable of addressing the massive discontents in the political system.
—*Guardian* 13 July 1994, p. 18

-on-demand /ɒndɪˈmɑːnd/ *combining form* ▱ ▨

Used to form a variety of compounds concerning telecommunications services which are made available when the recipient requests them.

The root term has been used in an adjectival sense since the sixties in phrases such as 'on-demand delivery', but began to be more widely employed in the early nineties as the basis for compounds at the time when telecommunications and cable television companies were seeking to extend the range of their services. The earliest and most common of these terms is **video-on-demand** (sometimes written **video on demand** and often abbreviated to **VOD**), referring to a service in which cable subscribers can ask at any time for video programmes (such as films) to be transmitted from a network centre to be viewed in the home, and which they can freeze, spool forward, or rewind as if they were being replayed from their own video recorders. Such services require a return link from the subscriber to the network centre or HEADEND; as this does not yet exist on most systems, cable operators have devised a variant called **near-video-on-demand**, in which programmes are repeatedly transmitted on a number of channels within a short time of each other, so subscribers can be sure of finding one channel on which the required programme is about to start (the fully interactive system is sometimes called **full-video-on-demand** to distinguish it). Because most demand is for films, the system is sometimes called **film-on-demand** (also called **films-on-demand**) instead. **Fax-on-demand** is a system by which callers can dial a communications system and request it, by means of telephone TONE-DIALLING signals, to transmit informational faxes to their own fax machine; **news-on-demand** is a proposed interactive system for sending news items to cable subscribers for viewing on their television sets. The term also appears occasionally in compounds such as **advertising-on-demand**, **audio-on-demand, shopping-on-demand**, and **games-on-demand**.

> Clever and savvy use of telecommunications, such as toll-free 800 numbers and fax-on-demand, can give your company a cutting-edge image. —*CompuServe Magazine* Jan. 1995, p. 36

> Today a handful of cable TV and telephone companies are conducting interactive television trials, giving a few thousand homes a limited taste of video-on-demand, games, home shopping, advertising, education and information. —*Economist* 1 Jul. 1995, Internet Survey supplement, p. 5

> The report anticipates charges of about $10 a month in addition to current TV-related charges for services such as electronic program guides, near-video-on-demand, video games, cable modem access and home shopping. —*Edupage* 16 Jul. 1995, online newsletter

One Nation /wʌn ˈneɪʃ(ə)n/ *noun* Also (in attributive form) written **One-Nation** ▱

A nation which is not divided by social inequalities.

The concept of *One Nation* in British Conservative thought is seen as originating in the paternalistic form of Toryism advocated by Disraeli, and specifically in its expression in Disraeli's 1845 novel, *Sybil, or the Two Nations*. In the text of the novel, Disraeli described the ultimate result of a divided country:

> 'Two nations; between whom there is no intercourse and no sympathy; who are as ignorant of each other's habits, thoughts, and feelings, as if they were dwellers in different zones, or inhabitants of different planets...' 'You speak of—' said Egremont, hesitatingly, 'THE RICH AND THE POOR.'

In 1950 a group of Conservative MPs, then in opposition, published under the title *One Nation* a pamphlet asserting their view of the necessity of greater commitment by their party to the social services; when the Conservatives were returned to power in the following year, the views expressed had a strong influence on the social policies of the new government.

In the nineties, *One Nation* has returned to prominence in the debate between the left and right wings of the Conservative Party; a debate which has gained force in consideration of the Thatcherite policies of the eighties, which have been held by some to be particularly productive of social division. In such discussions the term is often found attributively, as in **One Nation Conservatism**.

He subscribes to the one nation theory of Toryism, which in the Thatcher years became decidedly unfashionable. —*Country Homes* Oct. 1990, p. 114

Hunt says he has always believed in the social market, which he defines as 'one-nation Conservatism with teeth'. —*Daily Telegraph* 24 July 1992, p. 17

The One-Nation tendency 'seems to be largely dormant' in the present Conservative Party. —*Independent* 11 May 1995, p. 1

open system /'əʊp(ə)n sɪstəm/ *noun* 🖵

A system allowing computer software and hardware from different manufacturers to be used together.

In the past, a computer system has usually been provided by one manufacturer, using proprietary equipment, connections, and software; having once purchased such a system, customers could only get access to innovations introduced by other manufacturers by scrapping their systems and starting again. From the seventies, pressure grew to create standards that would permit equipment and software from any manufacturer to work with that from any other, so that users could pick and choose to get the best value. The first system, **Open Systems Interconnection** or **OSI**, was published in 1977, but the term only began to be widely known in the industry from the mid eighties onward. Latterly it has become something of a buzzword, though progress towards the objective has been slow, with many failures. The critics of the *open system* idea say that there have been so many attempts at standards by various groups that they have become counter-productive. The term is frequently used in the plural, as **open systems**, and in both forms it is employed attributively.

After long efforts, the most notable success of the various 'open' consortia is Motif—a good GUI but not much to show for all the avowed commitment to open systems by so many parties for so many years. —*UNIX Review* Mar. 1992, p. 5

OSI (Open Systems Interconnect), the cumbersome, complex, government and ISO...approved networking protocol is among the corpses. —*Computer Contractor* 22 July 1994, p. 81

Opraf /'ɒpraf/ *noun* Also written **OPRAF** 〰

The regulatory body created in 1993 to supervise the the awarding of franchises to companies wishing to run parts of the former British Rail network after privatization.

An acronym, formed on the initial letters of *Office of Passenger Rail Franchising*.

With the privatization of British Rail in 1993, it became necessary to set up supervisory bodies to oversee the breaking up of the national network. While responsibility for the general infrastructure was lodged (under the supervision of *Ofrail*) with RAILTRACK, *Opraf*'s area of responsibility has been passenger services.

OPRAF's task is to let the new Passenger Rail Franchises which will run Britain's railways in the future. —advertisement in *Guardian* 10 Nov. 1994, section 2, p. 19

The premature departure of a regulator charged with franchising train services (Opraf, or the Office of Passenger Rail Franchising for the frequent traveller) could not have been more badly timed if it had been handled by BR timetable planners. —*Daily Telegraph* 11 Apr. 1996, p. 27

opto /'ɒptəʊ/ *adjective* 🔬

Of or relating to optoelectronics, the branch of technology concerned with the combined use of electronics and light.

The full term *optoelectronic* has been used since the fifties in relation to devices which convert electrical signals into ones carried by light and back again. However, it was not until the beginning of the eighties that the term was abbreviated to *opto*. The word is now used almost exclusively in the phrase **opto isolator** (with **opto isolation** for the technique), a device used to isolate electrical circuits from one another by transferring signals into optical form and back again.

Count inputs protected using a bi-directional opto isolator (voltage polarity insensitive).
—*RS Components: Electronic & Electrical Products* 1992, p. 306

opt-out[1] /'ɒpt aʊt/ *noun* 🖾

An opportunity to opt out of something; an act of choosing to do this.

In the UK in the late eighties, the established term *opt-out* began to be used specifically for the withdrawal of a school or hospital from local authority control (see OPT OUT[2]); references to such institutions as **opt-out schools** and **opt-out hospitals** are frequently found.

A further specialized use developed in the early nineties, following the signing of MAAS-TRICHT in 1991. Disagreement over a number of issues, especially the directives of the SOCIAL CHAPTER, led to the British Prime Minister John Major's insistence on an **opt-out clause**, by which Britain could opt out of support for some parts of the treaty while proceeding with other member nations towards ratification. This was applauded by some as a necessary safeguard of national sovereignty, while seen by others as a failure to embrace the true spirit of the EUROPEAN UNION. Denmark followed Britain in seeking similar *opt-outs*.

Mrs Thatcher, in contrast, saw monetary union as the sharpest constitutional question of all. She went on to argue that the famous opt-out clause, allowing Parliament a further vote before Britain decided whether to join the new Euro-currency, was useless (or worse; a 'trap', she called it at one point). —*Economist* 23 Nov. 1991, p. 36

There might be more opt-outs along the lines Britain demanded at Maastricht. 'Subsidiarity'— code for limiting interference from Brussels—could be more strictly defined.
—*Economist* 22 Aug. 1992, p. 19

The Danish prime minister is to suggest to the summit today that Denmark might have opt-outs from the treaty on the single currency, defence and law enforcement.
—*The Times* 16 Oct. 1992, p. 1

opt out[2] /ɒpt'aʊt/ *intransitive verb* 🖾

In the UK, of a school or hospital: withdraw from local authority control.

A specialized development of the general sense of the phrasal verb *opt out*, 'to choose not to participate'.

The Conservative government, in the late eighties, introduced reforms within the education and health services which encouraged schools and hospitals to *opt out* of local authority control by applying for direct funding from central government and acquiring self-governing autonomy, with control over their own budgets. In the case of schools, a large proportion of the financial and administrative management was to become the responsibility of the governors and head teacher, a system referred to as *local management of schools* or *LMS*; schools that had *opted out* became known as *grant-maintained schools*. Hospitals were encouraged to become self-governing HOSPITAL TRUSTS. The reforms were promoted by the government as a means of reducing the inefficiency and expense of these parts of the NANNY STATE, but were seen by some to create the undesirable prospect of a two-tier system, in which successful institutions are awarded greater funding and thus become stronger at the expense of weaker ones.

The principle of opting out encourages a selfish élitism and it calls in question the relationship between one school and others in its neighbourhood.
—*Times Educational Supplement* 11 Jan. 1991, p. 8

Mr Major personally accused Neil Kinnock of repeating the 'central lie' that hospital trusts were opting out of the NHS. —*Independent on Sunday* 19 May 1991, section A, p. 1

Piqued that an avalanche of grant-maintained schools has not yet occurred, the Government is using fiscal measures to tip the balance and drive more schools to opt out.
—*Times Educational Supplement* 5 Mar. 1993 p. 23

order-driven ∿ see SEAQ

Orimulsion /ɒrɪˈmʌlʃ(ə)n/ *noun* ⚘ 🗛

The proprietary name for an emulsion of bitumen in water, which is used as a fuel.

A blend of the first syllable of *Orinoco* (the bitumen was originally extracted from the Orinoco oil belt in Venezuela), with *emulsion*.

The word *Orimulsion* was trademarked in 1987. Proposals in late 1991 by the British generating companies PowerGen and National Power to use it in several of their power stations were condemned by environmentalists and health workers. Its attraction is that it is comparatively cheap, but compared with other fuels it contains high levels of sulphur as well as some nickel, vanadium, and arsenic. Fears were expressed that plants and animals downwind of the sites would be harmed, even after emission controls were installed, and that the number of cases of respiratory diseases such as asthma would increase. Despite the protests, the government pollution inspectorate licensed two power stations—at Richborough in Kent and Ince in Cheshire—to burn *Orimulsion* in August 1993. Attempts continued into the mid nineties to force a public enquiry into the proposal to convert the Pembroke Dock power station in west Wales to burn the fuel; National Power asserts that emissions from the converted plant would not rise substantially, even with increased output.

National Power is proposing to burn Orimulsion—reputedly the world's filthiest fuel—at two of its oil-fired power stations. —*Earth Matters* Spring 1992, p. 2

The prospectus for the sell-off of the Government's 40 per cent stake in PowerGen says Orimulsion gives the company extra flexibility in oil purchasing. But 'a long-term commitment is likely to require significant investment in plant to reduce emissions.' —*Guardian* 4 Mar. 1995, p. 4

orphan embryo ⊗ 🗛 see FROZEN EMBRYO

orzo /ˈɔːtsəʊ/ *noun* ▨

Pasta consisting of small pieces shaped like grains of barley or rice.

From the Italian *orzo* ' barley', in allusion to the shape.

Orzo (recorded in English from the fifties) is one of a number of forms of pasta which since the seventies have become commercially available, first through speciality shops, and then through general supermarkets. This is a trend which is likely to continue, as pasta is increasingly viewed as a foodstuff which is both quick to prepare and a natural constituent of a healthy diet.

Rice-sized orzo pasta made a novel and pleasant accompaniment.
—*Star-Ledger* (Newark) 25 Dec. 1992, p. 62

This morning in my supermarket I counted 53 different pasta shapes. Six were the tiny variety used in soups and side dishes: stelline, acini di pepe, farfalline, tubettini, orzo and ditalini.
—*Modern Maturity* July 1994, p. 59

More in keeping with the season are grilled shrimp over *orzo* tossed in a very agreeable sort of hellenized pesto. —*Gourmet* Aug. 1995, p. 40

Ossi /ˈɒsi/ *noun* 🏠

A colloquial and sometimes depreciative term used in Germany, especially since reunification, and adopted in English, to denote a citizen of the former German Democratic Republic; an East German.

The German word *Ossi* is an abbreviation of *Ostdeutsche* 'East German', from *ost* 'east'.

On the reunification of Germany in October 1990 the terms 'West German' and 'East German', which denoted the separate national identities of the post-war Federal Republic of Germany and the German Democratic Republic, were, at least in theory, consigned to history; now, once again, there were simply Germans. However, there remained an unofficial recognition of the cultural differences which stemmed from forty-five years of differing political and economic systems. The colloquial terms *Ossi* and WESSI, already in use within Germany, were recognized and adopted worldwide as indicators of this divided heritage, perceived by many to be ingrained. A particular concern, expressed by some in the west, is that economic measures taken to reduce the legacy of unemployment in the east might be at the west's expense.

The *Ossis* want out. The Wall is down.   —*Marxism Today* Mar 1990, p. 7

She rightly lists the many elements of Germany's post-unity despond—including *Ossi-Wessi* friction, soaring unemployment, record state deficits, an upsurge of violence against foreigners and a rush of asylum-seekers.   —*Economist* 10 July 1993, p. 112

In the months after the Wall came down, tales of the Ossi as yahoos were the stuff of countless West Berlin dinner-table conversations. Less affluent West Germans might see their Eastern cousins as a threat to their pay envelopes, or as grifting rubes who expected the state to provide for them.   —*Harper's Magazine* May 1994

otaku /əʊˈtɑːkuː/ *plural noun* 🟦 🔲

In Japan: a derogatory term for socially inadequate young people who are particularly interested in and knowledgeable about computer technology; especially, such people who are obsessed with the trivia of a particular hobby.

A Japanese word meaning (in formal speech) 'your house' or 'your home' (from the honorific prefix *o-* and *taku* 'house, home'), implying poor social skills as shown by excessive or inappropriate formality, and a reluctance to leave the house.

Otaku, recorded from the early nineties, adds a Japanese word to the growing list of vocabulary items for those who would in the eighties have been characterized as 'nerds': in Western culture, ANORAKS, PROPELLER-HEADS, TECHIES, and TRAINSPOTTERS are all seen to share the characteristics of Japanese *otaku* in combining a fanatical interest in technology and the minutiae of a chosen hobby with an inability to socialize.

The otaku are socially inept, information-crazed, often brilliant, technological shut-ins...They relax with sexy manga or violent computer games. They shun society's complex web of social obligations and loyalties. The result: a burgeoning young generation of 100,000 hard-core otaku who are too uptight to talk to a telephone operator but who can kick ass on the keyboard of a PC.
                          —*The Face* Oct. 1992, p. 60

There is also the special type of fan we call otaku—trivia freaks who pride themselves on knowing everything about their favorite subject.   —*Asiaweek* 21 Dec. 1994, p. 38

Now a growing, obsessive market in the West means that 10 to 15 new anime videos are being released in Britain every month, avidly snapped up by fans, or *otaku*—to use the term that's not as offensive here as it apparently is in Japan.   —*Guardian* 4 May 1995, section 2, p. 15

OTE /əʊtiːˈiː/ *abbreviation* 〰️

Short for **on-target** (or **on-track**) **earnings**, a level of pay at which a person is earning to full potential by receiving a basic salary and commission representing best performance.

The initial letters of the phrase.

OTE began to appear as an abbreviation in job advertisements in the early eighties; it is a shorter and euphemistic way of saying 'earning potential with commission'. It differs from *profit-related pay* (PRP) in that the latter depends on the company's trading performance rather than the individual's. Both differ from *performance-related pay* (also abbreviated PRP), often used in non-trading organizations such as the public service, in which salary is partly determined by a general assessment of the individual's achievements. It is not easy to find a rigorous or objective way to do this; various proposals to apply PRP have caused controversy, for example, with British teachers in the mid nineties.

Computers. £30,000 Basic. £60,000 OTE.　　　—*Sunday Telegraph* 1 July 1990, section A, p. 16

Experienced sales person Display advertising £25,000 OTE.

—*Guardian* 24 Apr. 1995, section 2, p. 24

otherly abled {{ see ABLED

out /aʊt/ *transitive verb* {{

To reveal the homosexuality of (a prominent or famous person).

From the notion of causing such a person to *come out (of the closet)* by making a public acknowledgement of homosexuality.

The practice of **outing** first came to public attention in the US in early 1990, when public allegations about the sexual orientation of some famous people were used as a political tactic by gay rights activists; they were concerned mainly about lack of support for the victims of Aids, and about what they saw as the hypocrisy of secret gays legislating against other gays. The word *out* and its derivatives very quickly acquired a currency among gay groups in the UK as well. *Outing* causes considerable controversy because of its implications for personal privacy and the effects on partners and relatives. The controversy was reawakened in the UK in the mid nineties through the activities of the group *OutRage*. In the US, a person who *outs* someone is occasionally called an **outer** or an **outist**.

[Aids] is the new factor that gives outing both its awful appeal and its power and, most precisely, exposes the motives of the outers as terrorism.　　　—*Sunday Times* 6 May 1990, section C, p. 6

A Mr Signorile was our chief 'outist'. He wrote a book called Queer In America in which he defines the limits and explains the purpose of outing.

—Quentin Crisp in *Guardian* 7 Apr. 1995, Friday supplement, p. 3

'I consider outing a supreme act of moral cowardice,' he said. 'In no case I am aware of have the outers offered counselling or support to the person they are outing.'

—*Maclean's* 24 Apr. 1995, p. 32

It's typical of Garber's style that *Vice Versa* is packed with juicy anecdotes about the sex lives of celebrities. She 'outs' dozens as bi—instead of exclusively straight or gay.

—*The Face* Apr. 1996, p. 146

outplacement /ˈaʊtpleɪsm(ə)nt/ *noun* ⚡

The action or process of finding new employment for workers, especially executives, who have been dismissed or made redundant.

From the notion of finding a *placement* for somebody that is *outside* his or her present place of work.

References to *outplacement* can be found from the beginning of the seventies as one of a number of more or less euphemistic usages with which to describe the unpleasant reality of *dehiring*, or dismissal of employees. The term really came to public prominence, however, at the end of the eighties, when a number of businesses reduced their middle management capacity. This in turn gave rise to what has been described as the **outplacement industry**, which involves a more consciously professional approach to the processes of dismissal and redundancy, and active assistance in seeking a new position. Employees whose time with a company is being brought to an end are often offered **outplacement counselling**, and **outplacement executives** provide active help in jobseeking.

But in the world of outplacement, the corporate casualty ward for executives and middle managers who have lost their jobs, the merchandise is not moving the way it once did.

—*New York Times* 24 Nov. 1990, p. 23

Some members from very big companies have left with statutory redundancy pay and no out-placement counselling. *—Independent on Sunday* 10 Oct. 1993, p. 14

He had six months' notice of the move in which to visit outplacement consultants and apply for various positions. *—Accountancy* Sept. 1994, p. 53

outsource /aʊtˈsɔːs/ *transitive* or *intransitive verb* ᴧᴧ

In business jargon: to obtain (goods, especially component parts, or specialist services) by contract from a source outside an organization or area; to contract (work) out.

Outsourcing played a significant role in the drive towards greater cost effectiveness in the manufacturing world of the eighties. Increasing numbers of businesses chose to concentrate their resources on their primary activities, shutting down those secondary and support operations which could be acquired from outside sources. The phenomenon brought with it the need to refine the ordering and supply of components, and the subsequent influence of the Japanese system known as JUST-IN-TIME. As the decade advanced *outsourcing* became a common concomitant of DOWNSIZING, and some concern about its effect on job security was voiced by manufacturing unions.

During the nineties application of the term has spread beyond the supply of components to the purchase of specialist services, especially those requiring high levels of technological or computing expertise. This is perceived as allowing firms to take advantage of the very latest developments and expertise, offered at competitive rates.

It is now fashionable to outsource everything that is not of strategic consequence to the organisation. *—The Times* 9 Jan. 1986, p. 29

BAe's decision to outsource follows a 10-month study of its IT needs, in which an in-house team also vied for the work. *—Computer Weekly* 18 Nov. 1993, p. 1

Another major success for BT has been the winning of a five-year contract with the Woolwich Building Society to connect 600 sites to a new national communications network. The Woolwich decided to outsource the project because, with technology changing so quickly, it was sensible to deal with the real experts. *—BT Review* Feb. 1995, p. 9

oxygenated /ˌɒksɪdʒəˈneɪtɪd, ɒkˈsɪdʒəneɪtɪd/ *adjective* 🌳 ⚗

Of fuel: containining oxygenate additives, compounds such as ethanol, methanol, or one of their derivatives, which reduce harmful emissions such as carbon dioxide.

Discussions of the use of *oxygenated* fuels to reduce the level of harmful emissions appear in the literature from the late seventies. While such ALTERNATIVE FUELS do not attempt the complete reduction of pollutants to which ZERO-EMISSION VEHICLES aspire, they may be ranked with BIO-DIESEL and SUPERUNLEADED fuel in their attempt to address green issues through the medium of modern technology.

Cars and trucks running on fuels containing ethanol or ethers can reduce carbon monoxide pollution by up to 20 per cent. The finding comes from data collected from six US cities which, during last winter, sold only these so-called 'oxygenated' fuels.
—New Scientist 28 Sept. 1991, p. 27

A number of motorists complained last year that they suffered headaches, nausea and dizziness when oxygenated gasoline containing MTBE first arrived at service stations.
—Guardian 18 Nov. 1994, p. 10

ozone depleter 🌳 ⚗ see CFC

. . . .

P

PACE /peɪs/ *acronym*

In the UK: the Police and Criminal Evidence Act, passed in 1984.

The **Police and Criminal Evidence Act** made a number of provisions in relation to the powers and duties of the police and to the treatment of people in police detention. It did this chiefly by standardizing the existing codes of practice regarding the length of time for which the police may detain a subject without charge, which was generally limited in consequence, and by providing the detainee with various rights, including the right to have someone informed of his or her arrest and the right to legal advice. Use of the acronym *PACE* has been recorded since the late eighties.

His observational sample of prisoner interviews, although small, had found the PACE codes of practice were followed to the letter and he argued this showed that it required the sanction of the law to effect changes in interview and interrogation techniques.
—M. Young *Inside Job* (1991), p. 21 (BNC)

The Police and Criminal Evidence Act 1984 (PACE) introduced new procedures to place limits on the length of detention before charge and safeguard the rights of suspects while in custody; these were intended to counterbalance increased police powers.
—*The British Journal of Criminology* Autumn 1991, p. 347

One more stroke like this, Ms Brannigan, and you're going to be in a cell. And if you remember your law, under PACE I can keep you there for thirty-six hours before I have to get round to charging you with obstructing my investigation. —V. McDermid *Dead Beat* (1992), p. 133 (BNC)

paleo-conservative /ˌpalɪəʊkənˈsəːvətɪv, ˌpeɪlɪəʊkənˈsəːvətɪv/ *noun* Also written **palaeo-conservative**

In the US: a person advocating old or traditional forms of conservatism, an extreme right-wing conservative.

Formed from the combining form *paleo-* 'of ancient, especially prehistoric, times' (ultimately from Greek *palaios* 'ancient') and the noun *conservative*.

In the America of the sixties, the term *neo-conservative* (later, and less formally, *neo-con*) was coined to designate Democrats whose approach to a number of traditionally liberal issues was regarded as harder than that of the right-wing Republicans.

In the nineties, the resurgence of the extreme right-wing as an important political force has resulted in a further coinage: the *paleo-conservatives*, or **paleo-cons**, are seen as those marked out even among the right wing as politicians whose attitude to liberal issues is regarded as entrenched, and whose **paleo-conservatism** is characterized by support for traditional moral values and hostility to state intervention.

Instead of common ground, we got demagogues urging that there is only one path to virtuous American-ness: palaeo-conservatives like Jesse Helms and Pat Robertson who think this country has one single ethic. —Robert Hughes *Culture of Complaint* (1993), p. 14

Even the doughty champion of palaeo-conservatism, Pat Buchanan, has fallen victim to the big-government malady. —*American Spectator* Sept. 1994, p. 67

Robertson...unlike Kirk and many 'paleocons', has consistently supported the Israeli right wing over the years. —*New York Review of Books* 20 Apr. 1995, p. 67

Palestinian Islamic Jihad see ISLAMIC JIHAD

Palookaville /pə'luːkəvɪl/ noun POP

An imaginary town characterized by stupidity, mediocrity, and ineptitude.

Formed from the noun *palooka* 'a boxer of only average ability; a stupid or mediocre person' and the combining form *-ville* 'forming the names of fictitious places with reference to a particular quality'.

While *palooka* can be traced back to the mid twenties, *Palookaville* is not recorded until the nineties, in a comment on the end of the former heavyweight champion Charles 'Sonny' Liston's boxing career. Further usages have widened the context: *Palookaville* is now taken as the natural home or destination of the mediocre and incompetent.

The Liston-Wepner saga was Sonny's last stop on his sad, one-way ticket back to Palookaville.
—Boxing Illustrated Oct. 1990, p. 72

Critical buzz, MTV airplay and an endorsement from none other than late night monarch David Letterman combined to shoot this intriguing West Coast band from Palookaville to Platinumland.
—Rolling Stone 30 June 1994, p. 44

This whimsical morass is a genuine trip to Palookaville. *—Time Out* 17 Jan. 1996, p. 172

PALplus /pal'plʌs/ noun

An enhanced version of the existing PAL television system, compatible with it, which is capable of transmitting pictures in the 16:9 wide-screen format now commonly used for films.

Formed from *PAL*, the standard abbreviation for the type of colour television system broadcast in Europe (in full, *Phase Alternate Line*, so called because the colour information in alternate lines is inverted in phase), with *plus*, indicating that the system *adds* features to PAL.

The limitations of the standard 625-line PAL television system have led broadcasters to search for an enhanced system, with better resolution and colour and—in particular—the ability to show wide-screen films made for the cinema. Though the Japanese and European digital high-definition television (HDTV) projects would meet these requirements, many broadcasting companies were loath to suggest such a radical step, which would require studio equipment and existing television sets to be replaced. A strategy group was formed in 1989 to develop a system which was compatible with PAL, so that people with existing sets could continue to receive a conventionally shaped picture. Transmissions started in Germany and the UK in 1995, with other European countries set to follow.

As it was their idea in the first place, the Germans have been most enthusiastic about PALplus and there are plans to start PALplus transmissions there as soon as 1995.
—Personal Computer World Nov. 1992, p. 419

UK broadcasters appear divided over how to implement widescreen transmissions into their schedules, following the announcements by Channel 4 and Granada to begin PALplus services by the end of 1994 and the backing away from the standard by the BBC.
—Television Oct. 1994, p. 19

Pamyat /'pamjat/ noun

A right-wing political movement in Russia.

From the Russian word *pámyat* 'memory'.

The modern state of Russia (for which the official name is the *Russian Federation*) represents the former Russian Soviet Republic; on the break-up of the Soviet Union and the collapse of Communist control in 1991, Russia emerged as an independent state and a founder member of the COMMONWEALTH OF INDEPENDENT STATES or CIS. A new federal treaty establishing the Russian Federation was signed in 1992 by the majority of the Russian republics and other territories.

One of the features of the dissolution of the Soviet Union has been the resurgence of nationalism in a number of the former republics. This is particularly the case in Russia, where the *Pamyat* movement emerged in the late eighties: notably, its assertion of traditional Russian values is characterized by a blend of extreme nationalism and anti-Semitism.

> The most dangerous group is Pamyat, black-shirted extremists whose threats of violence have earned them the name 'monarcho-Nazis'. —*Manhattan, inc.* June 1990, p. 71

> His new investigations detail the terrifying rise of Soviet anti-semitism and, in particular, the sinister Pamyat organisation. —*Sunday Times* 8 Sept. 1991, p. 2

> These hatreds are harnessed by a variety of movements, many of them grouped under an umbrella organization called Pamyat, which preaches a sacred nationalism. —*Time* 13 Jan. 1992, p. 24

Parent's Charter 🄐 ⁉ see CHARTER

park-skating ✖ see ROLLERBLADE

parlour pink 🄐 POP see ISLINGTON PERSON

patch /patʃ/ *noun* ⊗

An adhesive piece of drug-impregnated material which is worn on the skin, enabling the drug to be absorbed gradually over a period of time.

A number of drugs have for some years been administered *transdermally*, 'through or across the skin', by means of the impregnated adhesive *patch* known more fully as a *transdermal patch*. This allows the slow release of the drug over a period of time and avoids the reduction of effectiveness of some orally-administered drugs caused by certain enzymes in the stomach. Use of the *patch* became familiar to the general public with the introduction during the eighties of the **nicotine patch**, which allows the passage of nicotine through the skin into the bloodstream as an aid to those wishing to give up smoking. A number of drugs, which must be soluble in water and oil and non-irritant to the skin, are now administered in this way and the term *patch* is frequently qualified by the name of the drug being administered or the disease being treated, in terms such as **angina patch**.

> Transdermal hyoscine was applied as a patch to glabrous skin behind the ear. —*British Medical Journal* 6 May 1989, p. 1220

> One transdermal patch should be applied twice weekly on a continuous basis. —*Pulse* 6 Apr. 1991, p. 42

> Once the angina patch is removed…the drug concerned, glyceryl trinitrate, clears from the body tissue after 20 minutes. —*Independent* 12 May 1992, p. 15

> Nicoderm is a small, thin 24-hour patch that goes on your upper body and delivers a continuous flow of nicotine through your skin. —advertisement in *US News & World Report* 28 Dec. 1992, p. 5

pathfinder prospectus /ˌpɑːθfʌɪndə prəˈspɛktəs/ *noun* 〰

A prospectus which contains information relating to the proposed flotation of a company but does not state the expected price of shares, and which is issued prior to the official prospectus.

The *pathfinder prospectus*, which is intended to be at once exploratory and trailblazing, provides publicity and advance information about the flotation of a company, and at the same time tests the potential market. The advent of the *pathfinder prospectus* in the early eighties may in part be linked to the privatization of nationalized industries which characterized those years. Publication of such prospectuses is now a standard feature of the business world.

> The pathfinder prospectus for the Government's £5bn sale of shares in BT—due to release its interim results today—is unlikely to make predictions regarding the future regulatory regime and the effect it could have on the telephone company's performance. —*Independent* 1 Nov. 1991, p. 23

The driving school company, BSM Group, steered closer to the stock market yesterday with the publication of the pathfinder prospectus for its flotation. —*Guardian* 1 Oct. 1993, section 1, p. 16

Patient's Charter ⌂ ⁅⁅ see CHARTER

pay spine ⌁ see SPINE

PC ⁅⁅ see POLITICAL CORRECTNESS

PDA ⊐ see PERSONAL DIGITAL ASSISTANT

peace dividend /'piːs dɪvɪdɛnd/ *noun* ⌂

A benefit, especially a financial one, gained from a reduction in spending on defence; a sum of public money which may become available for other purposes in these circumstances.

The term—which was first recorded in the US in the late sixties, at a time when the potential benefits of withdrawal from the war in Vietnam were increasingly acknowledged— gained high profile in the early nineties following the break up of the Soviet Union. The Cold War had resulted over many years in massive defence spending, and it was widely anticipated that the perceived NEW WORLD ORDER would bring with it the benefits of the *peace dividend*, made tangible, and politically advantageous, through tax cuts and increased domestic spending. However the Gulf War, involving massive use of US weaponry, followed hot on the heels of the Cold War, and as the nineties advanced, the war in the former Yugoslavia and continuing conflict in the Middle East reminded the world of the fragility of peace. Though defence budgets in Europe and America have indeed been cut, the *peace dividend* remains elusive.

A further use of the term developed in the UK in the mid nineties, when it was applied to the prospect of peace in Northern Ireland. The PEACE PROCESS had been enhanced by the DOWNING STREET DECLARATION of 1993 and the ceasefire declared by the IRA in the summer of the following year. But here, too, the anticipated peace proved illusory on the resumption of arms by the IRA in the spring of 1996.

Despite talk of a potential 'peace dividend' arising from cuts in the defense budget, 'the cold-war narrative has an astonishingly resilient capability to frame almost any development in the world as indicating a new need for weapons'.

—*Chronicle of Higher Education* 19 Dec. 1990, section A, p. 6

The MoD is a classic case of a landowner which is deserting sites in Hampshire and is expected to desert a lot more as the peace dividend spreads. —*Daily Telegraph* 5 Jan. 1991, p. 4

The 'peace dividend' lies buried in the desert. —*Harper's Magazine* May 1991, p. 63

The 'peace dividend' has already led to the ending of armed road blocks and redeployment of officers from central London. —*Guardian* 8 Mar. 1995, section 1, p. 8

peace process /'piːs prəʊsɛs/ *noun* ⌂

Negotiations towards the peaceful settlement of an established conflict.

Peace process as a term for a sequence of diplomatic negotiations intended to resolve a long-standing conflict is likely to date back to Kissinger's 'shuttle diplomacy' of the seventies; in the eighties and early nineties it was frequently used of negotiations in the Middle East, and was also employed by extension in the area of industrial relations. Most recently, however, the term has become particularly identified with attempts to resolve the situation in Northern Ireland, with the DOWNING STREET DECLARATION seen by many as an important stage in the *peace process* there. The concept involves a view of progression (whether or not this is seen by particular interests as desirable); contextual references often focus on whether or at what rate the *peace process* is moving forward.

We just needed something to kick-start the peace process. —*Newsweek* 13 Sept. 1993, p. 27

The longer the peace process drags on, the more radicalized everyone becomes.
—*American Spectator* Apr. 1994, p. 54

The failure of the timetable for the twin-track peace process, announced before President Clinton's visit, has caused acute disappointment to constitutional nationalists, who genuinely thought a securable, negotiable peace was at hand. —*Sunday Telegraph* 4 Feb. 1996, p. 31

peer-to-peer /ˈpɪətəpɪə/ *adjective* 💻

Denoting a system of computer networking by which two or more computers are connected as equal partners, each sharing processing and control, and each able (given permission) to access the files and peripheral equipment of all the others.

Based on *peer* in its sense of 'equal', as in the phrase *peer group*.

A local area network, or LAN, built on the *peer-to-peer* principle does not need a separate computer to provide network facilities and control communications. For this reason, it is attractive to small groups who need to share resources but who wish to avoid the extra expense of the server.

Whether you use a file server, peer-to-peer connections, or E-mail, networks are the conduit of choice because of their availability and ease of use. —*MacWorld* Dec. 1993, p. 193

Many computer activists preach a new era in the network economy, an era built around computer peer-to-peer networks, a time when rigid patriarchal networks will wither away.
—Kevin Kelly *Out of Control: New Biology of Machines* (1994), p. 45

As attractive as peer-to-peer networking is from the end-user perspective, it can give network managers the jitters because of potential security problems.
—*Data Communications International* Oct. 1995, p. 52

pen /pɛn/ *noun* 💻

A hand-held device used as a writing tool to input commands and data into a computer, via a screen. Chiefly used attributively and in compounds.

After the model of the existing term *light pen*.

In seeking to make computers more portable, manufacturers were hampered by the need to include a keyboard, which could not be radically reduced in size. In the early nineties, it became possible to implement the concept of the *Dynabook*, a visionary seventies design, which envisaged a flat pad acting both as a screen and an input area. The user could write on this with a special stylus, as if with a pen, relying on the computer to translate its movements into commands or electronic text. The first such systems were disappointing, as their ability to recognize handwritten or hand-printed text was regarded as inadequate and the concept struggled to gain acceptance. Such **pen computers** are said to be **pen-based** (or sometimes **pencentric**), with the concept being known as **pen computing**; such machines were briefly called **penputers** (a compound of *pen* and *computer*), though this term seems to have been superseded by PERSONAL DIGITAL ASSISTANT and its abbreviation PDA; the special software needed to interpret the user's input and display the result is called the **pen interface**.

Behind every computer lies an operating system (OS) and penputers are no exception.
—*Sky Magazine* Dec. 1991, p. 79

In turn, this will demand new technologies from the software developers, of which *pencentric* systems...will be the first.
—Edward Yourdon *Decline and Fall of the American Programmer* (1992), p. 273

I am tempted to announce that pen-based computing is dead, but am not sure it was ever alive.
—*Computing* 11 Aug. 1994, p. 20

peopleware 💻 see -WARE

people with HIV and Aids ⊗ see AIDS and HIV

perforin /'pɜːfərɪn/ noun ⊗ 🔋

A protein, released by killer cells of the immune system, which destroys targeted cells by creating pore-like lesions in their cell walls.

As part of the research work on the human immune system, scientists are investigating a number of compounds which are produced by killer cells (T cells) in the blood to destroy cells which are infected with viruses. One such substance is a protein called *perforin*, which—as its name suggests—bores holes in the cell wall and so destroys it. A fuller understanding of the way this protein works may help with the creation of drug treatments against viral infections.

If calcium ions are added to perforin before it makes contact with cells, the protein's killing activity is abolished. —*Scientific American* Jan. 1988, p. 31

The basal level of perforin present even in non-stimulated cells may vary.
—*EMBO Journal* 1990, Vol. 9, p. 381

performance poetry /pə'fɔːm(ə)ns ˌpəʊɪtri/ noun 🦃

Poetry viewed primarily as a medium for public rather than private consumption.

The idea of a poet reciting or declaiming his or her own poetry is of course a very ancient one. Recordings of Tennyson reading his own work exist, and today 'Spoken Word' cassettes and records of poetry are commercially available. *Performance poetry*, however, is a term which implies more than simply the reading by a poet of his or her own poetry. It is seen as a branch of *performance art*, a medium for public rather than private consumption, in which the performance of the poet is an integral part of the process.

Performance poetry is particularly associated with one group of **performance poets**, the 'Liverpool Poets', Adrian Henri, Roger McGough, and Brian Patten, who came together in the sixties in the period of Liverpool euphoria generated by the Beatles, and who since then have published and performed together.

In the seventies other kinds of *performance poetry* proliferated, particularly in association with the burgeoning fashion for rap music; the popularization of West Indian culture in this period brought particular styles of black (and especially West Indian) *performance poetry* to a wider audience. *Dub poetry* is performed extempore, and accompanied by a remixed version of a piece of recorded music, often with the melody line removed and including various special effects; a *toast* is a kind of long narrative poem recited extempore.

In the eighties and nineties a growing perception of the place of poetry in popular culture, and the spread of poetry festivals and similar events, has resulted in a growing interest in the work of *performance poets*.

Cummings's typography, Herbert's pillars and wings, surrealist fal-de-lals, concrete poetry, sound poetry, language poetry, performance poetry are bad Mephistolean bargains.
—*Poetry Review* Spring 1990, p. 68

Not satisfied with being a mere performance poet, Torres wants to blend all sorts of artistry into his work. —*Village Voice* (New York) 9 June 1992, p. 75

Flourishing in the glow of today's poetry revival is the rebirth of 'spoken word'—loosely defined as performance poetry. —*Coloradoan* (Fort Collins) 4 Dec. 1994, p. 18

Peritel 🔋 see SCART

Persian war syndrome ⊗ see GULF WAR SYNDROME

person /'pɜːs(ə)n/ noun 🎗

As the second element of a compound: a man or woman having a specified profession, occupation, or office.

A specific use of *person* 'an individual human being'.

The use of *person* instead of *man* or *woman* as the second element of a compound to avoid sexual distinction is not of course new: **chairperson** is recorded from 1971. However, consciousness of POLITICAL CORRECTNESS in the eighties and nineties has encouraged the development of such forms, and tended to result in a less self-conscious use of many of the resulting compounds. A visitor to a restaurant may expect to be served by a **waitperson** (and may even refer to the activity as **waitpersoning**); watching a local news report, he or she might see an **alderperson** or a **clergyperson** being questioned by a **pressperson**.

This extension has been accompanied by some more jocular usages, notably the suggestion that the opposite of the typical ESSEX *man* might be ISLINGTON *person*. There is also some evidence for **our person** in the sense 'our representative'. On the whole it seems likely that the pattern of increased productivity of such forms will continue, with each formulation in turn passing from striking single-instance occurrence to unremarkable familiarity.

Connie Marshner…served as the point person for the New Right's 'pro-family' agenda.
—*Tucson Weekly* 29 Jan. 1992, p. 2

Unisex waitpersons, all in black and ponytails, move swiftly among the post-modern chairs.
—*Independent* 11 Jan. 1993, p. 16

Walk over to the neighbourhood church or religious institution of your choice and wake up the clergyperson in charge. —*Canadian Yachting* Summer 1994, p. 46

Just as Essex Man, the distinctive lager-swilling Tory entrepreneur, represented the 1980s, Islington Man—more properly Islington Person—may turn out to be the most potent composite of the late 1990s. —*Independent on Sunday* 17 July 1994, p. 15

personal digital assistant /ˈpəːs(ə)n(ə)l dɪdʒɪt(ə)l əˌsɪst(ə)nt/ *noun phrase* 🖳

A small personal computer employing PEN technology.

The word *digital* is used here as a synonym for 'computer'.

The term *personal digital assistant* was used by Apple Computers in 1993 as a descriptive term for their new PEN-*based* computing system: the company wished to avoid the word *computer*, which they saw as inappropriate and off-putting. Though the fortunes of the system have been mixed, perhaps having suffered from an excess of expectations, the term *personal digital assistant* has gained wide acceptance as a generic term for small portable computers, often with pen-based input systems. This is perhaps surprising for a name so anodyne and unwieldy, though it is commonly abbreviated to **PDA**.

This is a PDA, a Personal Digital Assistant or lightweight portable computer which includes, among its many other functions, handwriting and voice recognition. —*CAM* Easter Term 1994, p. 16

The bandwagon that he started shuddered to a halt last year, and although Apple still develops the Newton, which under the Sharp badge does well in Japan, the market for anything called PDA is now close to zero. —*Computer Weekly* 30 Mar. 1995, p. 38

person with Aids ⊗ see AIDS

PGP /piːdʒiːˈpiː/ *abbreviation* 🖳

A computer program which encrypts and decrypts messages for secure transmission over digital circuits.

Formed from the initial letters of the full name of the application, *Pretty Good Privacy*.

The application was developed in the US by Philip Zimmermann in the early nineties, to provide a secure method of transmitting messages and data over the INTERNET, a notoriously insecure medium. It employs a cryptographic technique called PUBLIC-KEY ENCRYPTION and is thought to be almost totally secure against attacks. The US government regards such secure encryption programs as munitions and prohibited its export; however, copies did become available and it is frequently used outside the US. Mr Zimmermann was charged with its illegal export, but the charge was dropped in January 1996. The issues raised by *PGP* are part of a wider controversy in the US about privacy and the right of the government to intercept communications (see CLIPPER CHIP).

It's perfectly possible, in theory, to thwart the government-approved Clipper scheme by using a noncommercial encryption application, such as PGP, to pre-encrypt your messages before sending them through Clipper-equipped devices. —*Internet World* July 1994, p. 93

In certain parts of the Net it is quite common to see messages encrypted with PGP, with a note that the sender's public-key is 'available upon request'.

—Kevin Kelly *Out of Control* (1994), p. 210

If you want real e-mail privacy, use PGP. —*Internet World* Aug. 1995, p. 77

pharm /fɑ:m/ *noun* POP

A place where genetically modified plants or animals are grown or reared in order to produce pharmaceutical products.

Formed from the first syllable of *pharmaceutical*, with a punning play on *farm*.

References to *pharms* as sites for experiments in GENETIC ENGINEERING are found from the early nineties. **Pharming** is now an established activity for the pharmaceutical industry, although the processes involved (in particular the development of genetically modified **pharm animals**) raise ethical and moral questions.

Down on the Pharm. —heading in *Scientific American* Aug. 1990, p. 1990

Others foresee the marriage of cloning with genetic engineering, yielding herds of 'pharm' animals. —*Longevity* Jan. 1991, p. 25

British scientists recently developed Tracey, a sheep capable of producing a human protein used to treat emphysema, while in America scientists genetically altered pigs so they make an anti-clotting drug. There are many other examples of 'pharming' under development in farm animals.

—*Daily Telegraph* 22 Dec. 1993, p. 4

Take the banana. As a pharming product, this tropical fruit is being transformed.

—*Sacramento Bee* 10 July 1996, section B, p. 7

pharmafood ⚡ 🧪 see NUTRACEUTICAL

phat /fat/ *adjective* POP

In slang: excellent, great, 'hot'.

A recent extension of an earlier sense, used of a woman, 'sexy, attractive'. The origin of the word is obscure; it has been suggested that it is formed on the initial letters of *pussy, hips, arse* or *ass*, and *tits*, or on those of *pretty hole at all times*, but these theories have not been confirmed.

The adjective *phat* has featured within the lyrics of rap since the seventies, when it was used to mean 'sexy'. Since then it has been taken up in the vocabulary of HIP-HOP and RAGGA, and in the nineties the extended sense 'excellent' has developed, broadly equivalent to the terms *def*, which also entered the language through the culture of hip-hop, and *hot*. Use of *phat* in this newer sense has in the mid nineties extended beyond the restricted slang of hip-hop and ragga; though still largely restricted to the contemporary music scene, there are indications of an extension of usage to a broader contextual range.

They're just really distinctive—a London crew with a really phat funk sound.

—*The Face* Dec. 1992, p. 68

The Criminal Justice Act put the rave under House arrest. But it's out and it's phat in Oxfordshire.

—*Guardian* 8 May 1995, p. 8

Here he turns in a rough-arsed stomping groove with off-beat disco bass and a phat kick that provide the base for clonky piano, stabby organ and sparse vocal drops.

—*Echoes* 30 Sept. 1995, p. 13

Phoneday /'fəʊndeɪ/ *noun* Also written **PhONE day** 〰️ 🧪

The day, 16 April 1995, which introduced an extensive renumbering of the British telephone system.

Phoneday was the culmination of a long-planned and substantially advertised campaign by British Telecom to adjust the telephone numbering system to the level of demands made on it. As a result of the process, five cities were given completely new telephone numbering schemes, and all other telephone numbers acquired an extra digit. It already seems that the new numbers thus made available will not be adequate to the growing demand for telecommunications services.

On 'Phoneday' next spring…London's 071 becomes 0171, and so on.
— *New Scientist* 17 Sept. 1994, p. 84

Each misdialling caller will be played a recorded message from tomorrow, or Phoneday.
— *Independent* 15 Apr. 1995, p. 1

PhONEday was nothing more than a stop-gap. With more foresight, these second changes…could have been avoided. — *Daily Telegraph* 22 Jan. 1997 (electronic edition)

Photo CD 🖳 see CD

physically challenged ⁅⁆ see CHALLENGED

physician-assisted suicide ⊗ ⁅⁆ see DOCTOR-ASSISTED SUICIDE

PIJ 🖂 see ISLAMIC JIHAD

pindown /ˈpɪndaʊn/ noun ⁅⁆

A system operated in a number of British children's homes in the eighties, whereby children considered difficult to deal with were kept in solitary confinement, usually wearing only nightclothes or underwear.

Formed from the verbal phrase to *pin down*: apparently the staff at one of the homes had repeatedly spoken of the need to *pin down the problem*, and the children themselves subsequently started to refer to the regime as *being in pindown*.

The practice of *pindown* as a way of punishing children in care (especially in Staffordshire) came to light in October 1989, when a High Court injunction was issued forbidding its use by local authorities. It was much written about in British newspapers over a period of about two years from 1990 and became the subject of an independent inquiry led by Allan Levy QC; the official report of the inquiry's findings, co-authored by Barbara Kahan and entitled *The Pindown Experience and the Protection of Children*, was published in 1991. The first recorded use of the word *pindown* was in a log-book entry dated 20 January 1984, quoted in this report; apparently the word was often qualified by an adjective in such terms as **basic pindown**, **full pindown**, **negative pindown**, and **sympathetic pindown**. In the newspapers it was often used attributively (as though itself qualifying a noun), especially in **pindown room**, the barely furnished room containing only a bed, desk, and chair in which children were held in *pindown*.

Grandad died while I was in pin down. My dad came to tell me and he asked the staff if I could go back home for the night to be with my family. They wouldn't let me. They wouldn't even let me talk to my dad. — *Independent* 28 May 1991, p. 4

An 18-year old victim of sexual abuse has broken a three-year silence to tell her ordeal under the infamous pindown regime that operated in Staffordshire children's homes in the Eighties.
— *Observer* 21 Feb. 1993, p. 11

pink pound /ˈpɪŋk paʊnd/ noun ∿ 🖭 ⁅⁆

The perceived buying power of homosexuals as a group.

The *pound* as a symbol of the buying power of homosexuals as a group, symbolized by the colour *pink* (probably because of the colour's long-standing feminine associations, as opposed to 'masculine' blue).

The gay liberation movement of the late sixties and seventies had raised the general public consciousness of gay issues. This was followed in the eighties by a recognition of the gay community as a consumer group, with its own economic strength symbolized by the *pink pound* (occasionally, the **pink dollar**). In the nineties, the **pink economy** is recognized as a substantial element of today's business world.

> The pink pound has never been more fiercely chased. The spending power and brand loyalty of gay consumers are not to be ignored lightly.   —*Independent on Sunday* 6 Feb. 1994, p. 6

> The much heralded boom in the pink economy has increased the number of gay places that lesbians and gays can spend their pink pounds, but with the opening of these offices some of them will be able to earn those pink pounds in a gay environment as well.   —*Guardian* 14 Oct. 1994, p. 4

> *Sensual Classics Too*, out next week, pitches explicitly for the pink pound with a selection of classical favourites suitable for gay men.   —*Daily Telegraph* 13 Mar. 1995, p. 19

pixel ⌨ see RASTERIZE

plastic /ˈplastɪk/ *noun* 〰

Colloquially, credit cards, debit cards, and other plastic cards which can be used in place of money to pay for goods and services.

So named because this form of credit is obtained using a piece of *plastic* which serves as an identity card. Probably abbreviated to *plastic* from the longer *plastic money*.

The explosion of credit facilities and the consequent proliferation of credit cards which people carried in the seventies led to the development of the term **plastic money** in the US in about 1974; by 1980 this was being abbreviated to *plastic* alone, and used colloquially as a collective term for all forms of credit. Thus 'Do you take plastic?' became a common way of asking to pay by credit card.

> 'The acceptance of plastic has reached an all-time high,' John Bennett, senior vice-president of Visa, said. 'Plastic has become a way of life.'
>   —*Globe & Mail* (Toronto) 10 Oct. 1985, section B, p. 13

> When bills can be settled by instant electronic transfer and every shop takes plastic, who needs a pocketful of money?   —*Highlife* (British Airways) May 1991, p. 26

plug-and-play /ˈplʌgən(d)pleɪ/ *adjective* and *noun* Also written **plug and play** ⌨

adjective: Denoting a technique by which additional pieces of equipment or circuit cards added to a computer system are automatically detected and configured without need for skilled intervention from the user.

noun: The concept of this.

A compound of the verb *plug* in its electrical and electronics sense of 'connecting one piece of apparatus to another' (as in *plug in* or *plug together*) and *play*, partly in a figurative sense of 'to operate' (based on the concept of a disc or tape *playing* and so producing output) and partly with the implication that it makes installation child's play.

The name refers to a specification drawn up by a group of manufacturers. The intention was to provide a standard system for PCs by which the often complicated process of installing new equipment (frequently too difficult for many computer users) could be greatly simplified through automatic processes contained in software. The scheme slowly began to be implemented during the nineties, gaining considerable impetus from the launch of Microsoft's *Windows 95* in 1995. The term has become accepted to the point at which a figurative sense of 'simple, easy, uncomplicated' is beginning to appear.

> Although plug-and-play will become fully operational only once a PC has a plug-and-play BIOS, a

new operating system and the add-on hardware, PC users can make themselves 'future-proof' today by buying a PC with a plug-and-play BIOS.   *—New Scientist* 19 Nov. 1994, p. 23

Though products conforming to the new 'Plug and Play' standards were much in evidence, there is little reason to expect that computers will soon be significantly easier to use or understand.
   —New York Times 22 Nov. 1994, section C, p. 8

The [Electronic Business] Co-op…offers a service that allows secure purchases over the Internet without buyers having to set up special electronic accounts in advance. 'It's a plug and play concept for merchants,' says a Dataquest analyst.   *—Edupage* 9 Apr. 1995

PMS 🐡 POP see MOSH

Pogs /pɒgz/ *plural noun* ▓

The name of various children's games played with a set of cardboard or plastic discs, especially a game in which the player strikes a pile of discs with an implement, winning any that flip over. Also in singular form, a trade mark name for a disc used in the games, usually printed with a design or picture and collected and swapped by children.

Formed as an acronym from the initial letters of *passion fruit, orange, guava*, the flavour of a soft drink popular in Hawaii in the 1950s, where the game was played with cardboard bottle tops.

Pogs as the name for a game of this kind played by children, and the trade mark name **Pog** for one of the discs used, are recorded from the mid nineties, although it is clear from the origins of the word that it is a case of the accepted name postdating the game itself, perhaps to a considerable degree.

A group of fourth-grade boys play Pogs during recess.
   —caption in Coloradoan (Fort Collins) 27 Nov. 1994, section C, p. 1

For stuffing Christmas stockings, there are…Pog game pieces, tiny flower presses, and favorite card games such as Authors and Old Bachelor.   *—Minnesota Monthly* Nov. 1994, p. 75

Pogs, a sort of tiddly-winks on steroids, has been named Toy of the Year, just 12 months after its arrival in the UK.   *—Independent* 31 Jan. 1996, p. 3

Police and Criminal Evidence Act ▌ see PACE

policy wonk /'pɒlɪsi wɒŋk/ *noun* POP

In slang: a policy expert, especially one who takes an obsessive interest in minor details of policy.

Wonk as an early term for a nerd or ANORAK has been in use since the early seventies, but *policy wonk* is not recorded until the mid eighties, in terms of the American political scene. A *policy wonk* is one whose expertise in matters of policy may well be genuine, but whose sense of proportion over minor aspects is ill-judged: the interest taken in the chosen field (**policy wonkdom** or **policy wonkery**) has an obsessive quality, and there is often an indication that the high level of theoretical knowledge involved has unfitted the *policy wonk* for dealing with practical realities.

You have to make candidates seem like policy wonks.   *—Reason* Aug. 1991, p. 8

The other path was a slow slog of earnest policy wonkery, of speech after speech on serious issue after issue.   *—New Republic* 27 July 1992, p. 10

She has the lawyerly, analytical mind; he likes to wander off into the thickets of policy wonkdom.
   — Newsweek 28 Dec. 1992, p. 24

The president's furrow-browed band of policy wonks.   *—Washingtonian* June 1993, p. 30

The business world's consummate equivalent of that most unflattering of Washington life-forms, the policy wonk.   *—Economist* 23 Sept. 1995, p. 57

political correctness /pəˌlɪtɪk(ə)l kəˈrɛk(t)nɪs/ *noun* POP

Conformity to a body of liberal or radical opinion on social matters, characterized by the advocacy of approved views and the rejection of language and behaviour considered discriminatory or offensive.

From the adjectival phrase *politically correct* 'appropriate to the prevailing political or social circumstances', which is recorded since the late eighteenth century, but which did not become a fixed phrase until the early seventies.

Use of the phrases *politically correct* and *politically incorrect* (the second a logical development from the first), was given a dramatic impetus in the feminist literature of the early seventies and its campaign against a perceived gender bias. Soon afterwards these phrases were used in relation to a broad range of issues that were held to be sensitive, such as racism, disability, and homosexuality. The eighties brought an increasing consciousness of the rights of members of minority groups and an awareness that language should be used with care to avoid the perpetuation of notions of inequality. This awareness and the *political correctness* it engendered were widely welcomed, and given further impetus in the examination of attitudes prompted by the AIDS epidemic. Insensitivity to these issues was condemned as **political incorrectness**.

However, by the late eighties *political correctness* had come to be seen by many as at best nit-picking and over-sensitive and at worst puritanical and repressive, and as a potential enemy of freedom of thought and expression. Its proponents were held to be the perpetrators of a new kind of bigotry, which might become as pernicious as the prejudices they sought to overturn. At the same time circumlocutions used in an attempt to avoid *politically incorrect* language—ANIMAL COMPANION and *vertically* CHALLENGED are examples—were widely ridiculed. By the early nineties use of the term *political correctness* was almost always pejorative, while the labels *politically incorrect* and *political incorrectness* frequently suggested the notion that the idea or statement was bravely expressed.

The abbreviation **PC** for both *politically correct* and *political correctness* has been widely used in the nineties, almost always ironically or pejoratively, and its derivatives **PC-ery** (modelled on such depreciatory nouns as *quackery* and *popery*) and **PC-ness** have been recorded. To be **non-PC** is frequently considered a positive attribute.

The key to this was found not in her message songs—like many of her ilk, she tends toward smug political correctness. —*Los Angeles Times* 8 Aug. 1986, section 6, p. 22

The bewildering feature of political correctness is the mandated replacement of formerly unexceptionable terms by new ones: 'Negro' by 'black' by 'African-American'; 'Spanish-American' by 'Hispanic' by 'Latino'; 'slum' by 'ghetto' by 'inner city' by, according to The Los Angeles Times, 'slum' again. —*New York Times* 5 Apr. 1994, section A, p. 21

Satirical, hilarious, non-PC, way too smart a la Paglia/O'Rourke...seeks tall...brilliant, handsome aloof arrogant, man's man. —advertisement in *New York Review of Books* 22 June 1995, p. 67

Casting a white actor as Othello is virtually unthinkable these days. But...South Africa's foremost dramatist, Athol Fugard, pointedly braves the charge of political incorrectness in such matters. —*Independent* 10 Jan. 1996, section 2, p. 8

pop-up menu ▣ see MENU

posse /ˈpɒsi/ *noun* POP

A gang of black (especially Jamaican) youths involved in organized or violent (often drug-related) crime in the US. Now more widely, usually in youth slang, one's gang or crowd; a group of friends.

A specialized sense of the existing word, representing a substantial shift of meaning: a *posse* was originally a group of people whose purpose was the enforcement of the law (and in this sense will be familiar to all lovers of Westerns). From here it developed to mean any strong band or company, was taken up in black street slang (see below), and then came to be used specifically by police and journalists for a forceful band operating on the *wrong* side of the law.

The first reports of the criminal kind of *posse* appeared in the mid eighties in reports about the spread of the cocaine derivative CRACK in the US, and the associated rise of drug-related crime there. Originating in black street slang, where it means no more than 'a gang or crowd', the word figured in rap lyrics and in the names of rap groups, and by the end of the decade it had become a fashionable way to refer to a group of one's friends. It may also simply refer to a group of people brought together for a particular purpose.

> May I suggest that the Transport Secretary, together with a posse of ministers, visits Heathrow and Gatwick—not the VIP lounges they are used to, but the terminals millions of ordinary voters clog up hour after hour, day after day. —*Flight International* 25 July 1990, p. 45

> If the streets are home, the gangs are family. Between 30 and 40 drug posses have carved up the city and easily outgun the police with their arsenals. —*Time* 20 Jan. 1992, p. 22

> Expect…to see Manchester's club posses living it up as they lig from party to party.
> —*i-D* 22 Aug. 1994, p. 109

POSSLQ /ˈpɒs(ə)lkjuː/ *noun* Also written **posslq**

A person of the opposite sex sharing living quarters, especially a live-in partner or flatmate.

An acronym, formed on the initials of *Partner* (or *Person*) *of Opposite Sex Sharing Living Quarters*.

The acronym was apparently coined in 1978 by a member of the US Census Bureau, but the term was never officially adopted, and most references to it are ironic. It seems likely that *POSSLQ* will prove ephemeral, or that references will increasingly reflect a historical perspective.

> The Feds, as usual, screwed it up by creating POSSLQ, or Persons of Opposite Sex Sharing Living Quarters, which could refer to married couples as well as unmarried or newborn twins, or just about anybody. —*National Review* (US) 25 May 1979, p. 658

> It's not *terrifically* poetic, as in 'Come Live with me and be my POSSLQ'.
> —*Independent on Sunday* 10 Oct. 1993, p. 25

> At one time numerous words competed: live-in lover, mate, and for heterosexuals, posslq, an acronym for 'persons of opposite sex sharing living quarters'.
> —*Independent* 27 Feb. 1996, section 2, p. 5

post-Aids see AIDS

postcardware see -WARE

post-feminist /pəʊs(t)ˈfɛmɪnɪst/ *adjective* and *noun* Also written **postfeminist**

adjective: Of or relating to the principles and attitudes regarded as formed in the wake of the feminist ideas of the sixties and subsequent decades.

noun: A person regarded as espousing post-feminist principles and attitudes.

The term *feminism*, broadly defined as 'the advocacy of women's rights on the ground of the equality of the sexes', has embraced at different periods a range of different emphases. In the feminist movement of the sixties and seventies in Europe and the US feminists worked for the removal of generally perceived and accepted limitations on women's rights. A central tenet was the idea of unity between women and the advancement of women through sisterhood; this was considered to be more important than issues such as ethnicity and class, which could divide them.

However, during the seventies and eighties the movement became more fragmented. A division arose between mainstream feminists, interested in working to improve the position of women in society as it is, and radical feminists, who felt that any interaction with men tended to result in exploitation. Centred in France, an intellectual feminism associated with psychoanalysis and deconstruction came to prominence. The label *feminism* could no longer embrace these discrete elements and the movement as a cohesive force appeared to have dissolved.

It was, logically, succeeded by a new *post-feminist* age. The era of **post-feminism** has been perceived by many as a time of uncertainty, defined by its lack of identity. The existence of the term does not imply a unified movement, and it may be regarded as significant that instances of the noun *post-feminist* are rare. Any of various surviving elements of the feminist movement may be described as *post-feminist*. Some see the era of *post-feminism* as one in which women enjoy the fruits of their elder sisters' struggles but ignore or reject the ideals from which they sprang. Others regard the period as a time of progress, freed from the shackles of doctrine; they perceive a reformed consciousness of women's rights on the part of men as well as women, and the development of feminism into a tough maturity. Meanwhile the MEN'S MOVEMENT and *New Laddism* (see NEW LAD), both of which have emerged during this period, may be seen to be jostling with the assumptions of feminism.

> It's the fantasy of the post-feminist woman whose 'principles' reward her with material riches but do not involve one moment of sacrifice, regret or self-examination. Another recent version was 'Working Girl'. —*New York Times Magazine* 5 Aug. 1990, p. 12

> Feminism is 'so '70s', the pop culture's ironists say, stifling a yawn. We're 'postfeminist' now, they assert, meaning not that women have arrived at equal justice and moved beyond it, but simply that they themselves are beyond even pretending to care.
> —Susan Faludi *Backlash: The Undeclared War against American Women* (1991), p. 72

> Cold-eyed, clear-headed and glorying in what they do, the difference between these killerettes and, say, the Bond Girls is that they are supposed to represent what is widely viewed as the tough post-feminist persona. —*Guardian* 8 May 1995, section 2, p. 4

> It would be too simplistic to blame work…and I really believe in what *She* is about—a post-feminist magazine for grown-up women. —*Daily Telegraph* 1 Dec. 1995, p. 25

See also RIOT GIRL

post-moshing syndrome 🎵 ᴾᴼᴾ see MOSH

post-structuralism /pəʊs(t)'strʌktʃ(ə)r(ə)lɪz(ə)m/ *noun* Also written **post-structuralism** ⚔ 🔰

An extension and critique of structuralism, which rejects structuralism's claims to objectivity and emphasizes the plurality of meaning.

Formed by the addition of the prefix *post-*, 'after in time', to the noun *structuralism*.

The doctrine of *structuralism* is based on the tenet that structure rather than function is important, and that a concept may be analysed in terms of the contrasting relationships within its conceptual sets. It has been central to thinking in a range of fields, including linguistics, anthropology, literature, the visual arts, and psychology, since the early decades of the twentieth century. *Post-structuralism*, which emerged as a school of thought in French intellectual life in the sixties, initially as a development of structuralism, began to challenge structuralist claims to objectivity and comprehensiveness and increasingly emphasized instead the plurality and deferral of meaning. Associated initially with the philosophers Jacques Derrida and Roland Barthes, and writers such as Michel Foucault, *post-structuralism* had by the late seventies and eighties become very influential in Britain and the US. *Post-structuralism* frequently uses the techniques of deconstruction to reveal unquestioned assumptions and inconsistencies in literary and philosophical language. In the field of critical textual analysis it embraces the deconstructionist emphasis on the instability of meaning and the limitlessness of interpretation. In particular it has, as a development of its own earlier recognition of the relationship between texts known as *intertextuality*, come to reject the concept of authorial authority and adopt in its place the notion of an autonomous INTERTEXT.

The adjectives **post-structural** and **post-structuralist** preceded the formation of the noun *post-structuralism*, initially meaning simply 'pertaining to or designating an analytical approach which emerged after structuralism', but coming to refer specifically to the later theories of *post-structuralism*. The noun **post-structuralist** denotes a practitioner or adherent of *post-structuralism*.

It should…be pointed out that the structuralist and post-structuralist emphasis on the internal structuring of language was self-imposed (rather than the result of blindness to the properties of language as a social phenomenon). —*Archivum Linguisticum* 1976, Vol. 7, p. 152

Itself an echo to Hegel's *Aufhebung* or 'sublation', Derrida's famous neologism, *la différance*, is crucial to the deconstructionist and post-structuralist counter-theology of absence.
—George Steiner *Real Presences* (1989), p. 122

Most post-structuralism may appear to say that the text is autonomous and that literary criticism has no ethical dimension. —*English* 1992, Vol. 41, p. 176

In providing a nonlinear, non-hierarchical, and nonpatriarchal reading experience hypertext is inherently deconstructive and delivers almost all of the desiderata of poststructuralist literary theory. —*Science-Fiction Studies* Nov. 1993, p. 450

post-traumatic stress disorder /pəʊs(t)trɔːˌmatɪk ˈstrɛs dɪsɔːdə/ *noun phrase* ⊗

A condition which develops following exposure to a stressful situation or series of events outside the normal range of human experience. Symptoms include recurrent dreams or memories of the traumatic event, withdrawal, difficulties in concentration, and sleep disturbance.

The adjective *traumatic*, first used to mean 'of, pertaining to, or caused by a wound' (from the Greek word *trauma* 'wound') has been applied to certain types of psychological and emotional disturbance since the end of the nineteenth century.

Post-traumatic stress disorder was identified as a specific syndrome by the psychiatric profession in the early seventies; the term entered the general language in the eighties, especially in relation to veterans of the Vietnam War, who typically suffered stress-related illnesses deriving from repression of the memory of events.

The term *post-traumatic stress disorder*, and the abbreviation *PTSD*, have been used increasingly in the late eighties and nineties. Symptoms of the disorder are now associated particularly with the long-term effects on the victims of accidents and disasters such as the sinking of the passenger ferry *The Herald of Free Enterprise* at Zeebrugge, the terrorist bombing in Oklahoma City, and the massacre of schoolchildren at Dunblane in Scotland. Police, ambulance staff, fire officers, and others attending such disasters may be similarly traumatized. Awareness of *post-traumatic stress disorder* has led to a range of therapies and forms of psychiatric assistance including counselling being made available in the aftermath of such events, in an attempt to prevent the repression by those involved of an appropriate emotional and psychological response.

An examination of symptoms presented by 17 adult women who experienced childhood incest suggests that the long-term effects of incest may be a post-traumatic stress disorder (PTSD).
—*Child Abuse & Neglect* 1985, Vol. 9, No. 3, p. 329

A handful of workers, however, remain physically unable to work. And for at least 10, the explosion lives inside them. They remain in intensive therapy, suffering from incessant post-traumatic stress disorder. —*New York Times* 20 Feb. 1994, section 1, p. 1

power bimbo ▓ see BIMBO

power breakfast ⩗ 📅 see POWER LUNCH

power dressing /'paʊə drɛsɪŋ/ *noun* Also written **power-dressing** ❌

A style of dressing for work and business intended to convey an impression of efficiency and confidence.

The concept of *power dressing* is strongly associated with the business ethic of the eighties, which was broadly perceived as ambitious, tough, and ruthless. The term has been applied to the wearing by men of smart, well-cut suits, but it refers predominantly to a style of dress worn by women as an apparently assertive response to a competitive business environment. In particular the wearing by women of formal, structured suits, which came to be known as *power suits*, was interpreted as an expression of a set of attitudes and attributes including ambition and determination, an assumption of equality with men, and perhaps a desire to break through the GLASS CEILING. The padded shoulder line—a fashion feature linked by many with the apparently glamorous television soap operas *Dallas* and *Dynasty*—was seen as a characteristic feature of *power dressing*.

Indeed, from the perspective of the nineties the large shoulder pad has become a humorous symbol of the ambitious business ethic of the eighties. Disparaging references to the fashions of preceding years are common at any time. In the nineties the workplace provides a less secure, more uncertain environment, and the fashions formerly associated with *power dressing* may be seen to have been replaced by a less assertive code of dress more in keeping with the economic constraints of this decade. The term is still used in the mid nineties, but it has embraced a small shift in meaning; it tends to imply an affluent smartness in styles of dress worn to work, in place of thrusting self-assertion, in keeping both with the modifications of today's fashions and the changed spirit of the times. A further relaxation of the dress code may be seen in the concept of DRESS-DOWN FRIDAY.

The agent noun **power dresser** has developed concurrently as a back-formation of the noun *power dressing*. Use of the intransitive verb **power dress** and the participial adjective **power dressed** dates from the late eighties. There is some evidence in the nineties of a metaphorical use of the noun *power dressing*, applied to cars and their interiors.

> Power dressing for executive women is dead. No-one wants a square-cut, double-breasted jacket with aggressive shoulders now.   *—Dimensions* Spring 1989, p. 26

> She's rolled back the sleeves on her softly-tailored jacket to soften its 'power dressing' overtones.   *—Take a Break* 8 Sept. 1990, p. 23

> Big hair. Big junk bond portfolios. In the 80's, fashion, like finance, went to extremes. At one end were the platoons marching forth to the workplace in those ghastly women's power suits worn with faux bow ties and commuter Reeboks.   *—New York Times Magazine* 24 Oct. 1993, p. 144

> Haughty, power-dressed and still running on adrenalin after a 12-hour day in the office, young professionals in modish suits stalk the aisles of late-opening supermarkets looking for comfort food.   *—Independent* 19 Oct. 1995, Supplement, p. 2

power lunch /'paʊə lʌn(t)ʃ/ *noun* 〰️ 🏛️

A working lunch at which high-level political or business discussions can be held.

Power lunches (and **power breakfasts**) as recognized occasions at which busy and influential people can hold high-level discussions outside the course of the normal working day originated in America at the beginning of the eighties, and soon crossed the Atlantic. To be a **power luncher** in the eighties was a symbol of political and commercial success; it indicated a familiarity with the inner circles of power. In the nineties, the terms may be used with a more ironic inflection, indicating the view that **power lunching** is more concerned with the public demonstration of individual status than with any real achievement through discussion.

> It's the power breakfast, political not literary...The literary types wander into their offices after 10.   *—New York Times* 12 Nov. 1980, section C, p. 1

> The pre-dawn frost was still thick around the early birds of St James's Park when Mrs Thatcher, two members of her Cabinet and two junior Ministers hurried across Parliament Square for

Whitehall's first 'power breakfast'.   *—Daily Telegraph* 30 Jan. 1987, p. 4

Implicit was the notion that most top execs today are mere number crunchers and power lunchers, who have lost touch with the hands-on reality of what their companies produce.
                    —New Yorker 5 Sept. 1994, p. 109

Power lunching at La Trattoria…is enormously popular with lawyers, accountants, bankers and executives whose offices line Front and Reid streets in the capital of Hamilton.
                    —Financial Post 13 Jan. 1996, p. 22

power nap /'paʊə nap/ *noun* and *verb* ▨

noun: A nap, especially one taken in the daytime, intended to refresh a person involved in high-level and important work.

intransitive verb: To take a nap of this kind.

In the mid eighties *power naps* joined POWER LUNCHES and POWER DRESSING as part of the lifestyle of the busy and successful executive in a high-level job; once more, the implication is that as little time as possible is spent on physical refreshment. *Power naps*, however, may be seen less cynically as representing a source of natural refreshment preferable to taking stimulants in order to keep going. In current usage, they are regarded as a sensible way to achieve some relaxation, rather than as merely a demonstration of the pressures of one's successful and busy lifestyle.

From California, the latest way to revitalise yourself is 'power napping'. This is the pinstripe way to keep body and mind together when the pressure is on…A principled power nap every working day is gaining ground as fashionable, even responsible, behaviour. Power nap accessories such as mind-soothing goggles…together with a spate of small, dark rest rooms currently opening in London gyms, have combined to persuade the trend-conscious that this need to nap is a Nineties phenomenon.   *—Daily Telegraph* 16 Aug. 1994 (electronic edition)

Relax, meditate, 'power nap', fall asleep, refresh tired eyes.
            —advertisement in Natural Health Nov. 1994, p. 133

The researchers also would like them to forget about grabbing a cup of coffee to stay alert. How about a power nap instead?   *—New York Times* 27 Dec. 1995, section A, p. 1

Power Ranger /'paʊə reɪn(d)ʒə/ *noun* ▨ ᴾᴼᴾ

A trade mark name for a plastic toy figure resembling any of a group of fantasy characters from the children's television series *Mighty Morphin Power Rangers*. These American teenagers are regularly summoned to change into masked kung-fu heroes to do battle with the evil *Space Aliens* and other villains.

A *ranger*, in the American sense of 'a member of a body of shock troops', conceived as having special *powers*.

The *Power Rangers* followed the *Teenage Mutant Turtles* as an object of enthusiasm among the young. Like the *Turtles*, they appeared in a television series, in which they were regularly summoned by the genie Zordon to change, metamorphose, or *morph* (see MORPHING) into crime-fighting heroes, and the popularity of their adventures was supported and extended by the marketing of a range of toys and other licensed products.

The **Mighty Morphin Power Rangers**, of differing ethnic origins, were evidently intended to conform to standards of POLITICAL CORRECTNESS, but as models for the young the implicit level of violence in their kung-fu practices became the cause of some concern.

The key to the toys' success is television. The characters are all tied in to a series about a group of teenagers able to 'morph' into crime-fighting Power Rangers.   *—Guardian* 31 Aug. 1994, p. 1

They change into super heroes with the cry 'Go! Go! Power Rangers'.
          —Guardian 8 Nov. 1994, Education section, p. 12

Snap up one of these fab Power Ranger key-rings.   *—Sugar* Apr. 1995, p. 4

power user /ˈpaʊə juːzə/ noun 💻

A person, not a computer specialist, who shows considerable skill and ability in using a computer system or software.

A computer *user* who demonstrates a sense of *power* over the computer, in the sense of 'authority, strength, ability'.

The term arose in the eighties to describe those computer users who habitually seek out as much knowledge as possible about a computer system or a piece of applications software, sometimes inducing it to perform feats beyond its apparent capabilities, and who frequently aim at obtaining and using the most recent or highly-specified systems. Such persons appear on occasion to be obsessed by this quest for mastery and so the term is sometimes used pejoratively.

> The home market is being led by the power users, the readers of IT magazines, the people who understand both the technology and the benefits to be gained from using it.
> —*Computing* 19 Aug. 1993, p. 8

> They aim their pitch at 'power users', people compelled by their nature to own the fastest machines and most 'fearful' software. —*Esquire* June 1994, p. 117

prawn cocktail offensive /prɔːn kɒkteɪl əˈfɛnsɪv/ noun phrase 〰️ 📷

A humorous term for the campaign of action instituted by the Shadow Chancellor, John Smith, in the run-up to the British General Election of 1992, to reassure the City as to the budgetary intentions of an incoming Labour government.

An *offensive*, as in a military campaign, in which the *prawn cocktail* symbolized the methodology of using buffet lunches as forums for discussions of financial and economic issues.

With the approach of the General Election of 1992, the Shadow Chancellor John Smith made a conscious effort to establish good terms with City figures who might be thought to view the prospect of Labour's success with some apprehension. His use of lunches in this CHARM OFFENSIVE was noted by the Conservative Michael Heseltine in the House of Commons in February of that year, in a speech which touched particularly on the number of shellfish which had been sacrificed to this end ('Never have so many crustaceans died in vain'), and which had as its culmination the clarion cry, 'Save the prawns!'

> In the mid-1990s there was a paranoia about being left wing, but the prawn cocktail offensive did a lot to demonstrate that the Labour Party didn't have horns. —*Guardian* 30 July 1994, p. 38

pre-Aids ⊗ see AIDS

precompetitive /priːkəmˈpɛtɪtɪv/ adjective 〰️

Relating to or designating an early stage in the development of a commercial idea or product, during which competing companies collaborate.

The notion of a *precompetitive* stage, allowing companies who are natural competitors to combine for the generic stages of research, developed in the early eighties. The practice has to some extent become an established one, whereby large companies may form a consortium to undertake generic research from which they may individually benefit, and which allows investment from official sources.

> There is ample scope for a greater European investment in research at the 'pre-competitive' stage—that is before the competing national industries take up the ideas thus spawned and run with them. —*Financial Times* 16 July 1982, p. 17

> Esprit organises joint research between companies and academic institutions which is

intended to be 'precompetitive', not geared towards specific products.

—*New Scientist* 24 Nov. 1990, p. 16

Initially, the ATP favored the formation of consortia that would conduct 'generic, precompetitive' research, which the member companies could later apply to the development of competing products. —*Scientific American* Sept. 1994, p. 61

pre-embryo /priːˈɛmbrɪəʊ/ *noun* Also written **preembryo** Ⓧ ❙❙

A cell or group of cells which can develop into an embryo. Also, specifically, a fertilized human egg up to fourteen days after fertilization.

In the late seventies references were made in scientific literature to the *pre-embryo*, denoting a cell or group of cells, from non-human mammals, having the potential to develop into an embryo. By the early eighties the term had been applied to the fertilized human egg. Recognition of the human *pre-embryo* as an entity distinct from the *embryo* influenced the legal and ethical debate about the use of the human embryo in genetic and medical research. A legal distinction was made between the *pre-embryo* and the embryo and it was suggested that acknowledgement of the *pre-embryo*, rather than having a scientific base, was made to this end. In the nineties references to the *pre-embryo* are made predominantly within genetic research.

The adjective **pre-embryonic** is used particularly in the phrases **pre-embryonic period** and **pre-embryonic phase** to denote the two-week period during which the *pre-embryo* is considered to exist, before implantation in the womb.

One can distinguish several intergrading phases of human development: the cellular or pre-embryonic phase, the embryonic phase, the fetal phase and finally the phase of vital autonomy.

—*Scientific American* June 1979, p. 42

Such genetic testing could take place in the 'pre-embryonic' period, which spans the first two weeks after the human egg is fertilised. —*New Scientist* 10 Dec. 1987, p. 43

Pre-embryo selection for genetic disorders, genetic susceptibilities, and sex will be available to young couples within a decade or two. Some young couples will use it, particularly if pre-embryo diagnosis...circumvents the emotionally charged issue of abortion.

—Jerry Bishop and Michael Waldholz *Genome* (1990), p. 310

See also FROZEN EMBRYO

pre-loaded /priːˈləʊdɪd/ *adjective* ▣

Relating to software which is already installed on a personal computer at the time of purchase so that it can be used immediately.

As computer operating systems and applications continued to grow in size, the effort of installing them began to be time-consuming and irksome, frequently requiring knowledge or skills the average computer user did not possess. Manufacturers and retailers began to install operating systems and applications on personal computers and to sell them as complete systems, ready to run; this is now commonplace. This approach also has considerable advantages for the software manufacturer, who has the security of bulk sales and generally does not have to provide printed manuals or master disks.

Amstrad forgot only one thing when making this kit utterly devoid of technofear potential—if the software had been pre-loaded, this pack could be marketed as 'no more complicated than setting up your average kitchen appliance.' —*What Personal Computer* Dec. 1991, Issue 29, p. 42

Other developments such as pre-loaded software have also helped to reduce learning curves.

—*Computing* 29 July 1993, p. 8

Software is pre-loaded with on-line documentation.

—advertisement in *Personal Computer World* May 1996, p. 464

prenup /priːˈnʌp/ *noun* 🆙 ❙❙

In informal US English: a prenuptial agreement, signed by both parties before a marriage takes place, establishing the legal claims of one on the estate of the other should the marriage break down.

The development of the term *prenup*, recorded from the beginning of the nineties, reflects the increasingly high profile of *prenuptial agreements* in the eighties. There had been a number of extremely costly divorce settlements, and attention had been focused on claims to a partner's estate by a number of *palimony* suits. (In such suits, a former partner, or 'pal', claimed 'alimony' support.) Originally used only by the very wealthy, it is now increasingly likely that when assets are involved to any degree a *prenup* will be signed.

The De Loreans ($2000-a-month child support in spite of the prenup).
—caption in *Mirabella* Sept. 1990, p. 170

The couple's prenup linked alimony payments to whether the parties remained clean and sober.
—*New York Times* 7 Nov. 1991, p. 10

presence /ˈprɛz(ə)ns/ *noun* ⚡

The position or activity of a business in a particular market.

Formed from a transferred use of the noun in the sense 'maintenance by one country of political interests and influence in another country'.

The use of the noun *presence* to convey the notion of the activity and influence of a business in a particular market dates from the economic expansion of the eighties. The term often appears as the second element of a compound, the area of interest being indicated by the first word.

Saatchi & Saatchi is stepping up its design presence in Britain.
—*Creative Review* Jan. 1988, p. 8

CNN established a brand awareness and market presence that was very difficult for the followers-on to knock out. —*Wired* Jan. 1995, p. 86

In Asia-Pacific...—an area of increasingly dynamic growth—BT is expanding its business presence. —*BT Review* Feb. 1995, p. 6

presenteeism /prɛz(ə)nˈtiːɪz(ə)m/ *noun* ⚡

The practice of being present at one's place of work, especially for more hours than required by one's terms of employment.

Presenteeism is recorded intermittently from the thirties, but in its current use is associated with the FEEL-BAD anxieties of the late eighties and nineties, when increasing job insecurity and concerns about DOWNSIZING have appeared to result in some employees working for much longer hours than required by their contractual obligations. The phenomenon of *presenteeism*, in its more extreme forms, is regarded by many as counter-productive, with belief in the need to be observably present at work for as many hours as possible resulting in an overtired and overstrained workforce, but not necessarily in a significant increase in what is achieved.

'Presenteeism'...is the opposite of absenteeism and consists in people coming early to work and staying late, to demonstrate their commitment.
—*Independent on Sunday* 29 Jan. 1995, Review section, p. 66

The old problem of absenteeism had been replaced by 'presenteeism', with staff continuing to arrive at the office each morning even when sick, because they feared their jobs would disappear while they were gone. —*Daily Telegraph* 24 Nov. 1995, p. 8

prion /ˈpriːɒn/ *noun* ⊗ ⚗

An infectious particle consisting only of protein, which is thought to be the cause of some diseases.

From the descriptive name *proteinaceous infectious particle* by taking the first three letters of *proteinaceous*, 'of or relating to proteins', and the first two of *infectious* and rearranging them.

The cause of a number of apparently similar diseases, of which the best known ones are scrapie and BSE in farm animals and CREUTZFELDT–JAKOB DISEASE in humans, has long been a mystery. All involve degeneration of the nervous system, leading to loss of coordination, dementia, and death. Because they often take years to affect their hosts, the agents have sometimes been called *slow viruses*, though no virus has been found. In 1982 Professor Stanley Prusiner proposed that the infective agent was some unknown protein. The scientific community was sceptical because all other disease organisms use either DNA or RNA to reproduce themselves and it was far from obvious how a protein could do so; it was also unclear how a protein could actually cause disease. More recent research suggests that the disease-causing *prion* protein is a modified form of one which normally exists in the body and which is capable of forcing other molecules of the protein to change form. The word *prion* is frequently used attributively; an adjective **prionic** is occasionally seen.

> Physicians have traced about 40 cases of a prion disease in adults to injections of infected growth hormone administered during childhood. —*Science News* 24 Sept. 1994, p. 202

> Mice inoculated with brain extracts from scrapie-infected animals and from humans infected with Creutzfeldt–Jakob disease have long provided a model for the infectious forms of prion disorders. —*Scientific American* Jan. 1995, p. 37

> There has thus been no sign, in mice producing human proteins, of prionic influence on them. —*Economist* 23 Dec. 1995, p. 126

private key 🖳 see PUBLIC-KEY ENCRYPTION

Producer Choice /prədˌjuːsə ˈtʃɔɪs/ *noun* 🐾 ⚡

A policy which gives programme-makers control over their budget, allowing them to purchase services from other departments or from outside the organization.

The policy known as *Producer Choice* was introduced within the BBC in 1993, under the director-generalship of John Birt. It initiated a system, based on the principles of the marketplace, in which BBC departments compete with each other and with external agencies to provide services to programme-makers. The producer is thus empowered to choose the most competitive tender, whether it be from within the BBC or from the independent sector. The policy has been controversial, many feeling that budgetary constraints have had an adverse effect on innovation and creativity. Associated with a review of BBC over-capacity carried out by John Birt, before he became Director-General, in the early nineties, the policy has also been linked with significant job losses. Along with *bi-medialism* (see BI-MEDIA), *Producer Choice* is regarded as a further manifestation of BIRTISM.

> Like all other areas of the BBC, television drama will not escape the controversial Producer Choice scheme which will force in-house resource departments to compete with external suppliers for business from programme-makers. —*Stage* 17 Dec. 1992, p. 24

> The BBC fought a long and painful battle to prove their mettle. Producer choice and several thousand job casualties later they are a leaner, fitter operation. —*Independent* 20 Feb. 1995, p. 14

> The introduction of the Producer Choice internal market system in April 1993, in which programme departments trade with each other and make charges for services provided. —*Guardian* 22 Apr. 1995, p. 2

profiling /ˈprəʊfʌɪlɪŋ/ *verbal noun* 🎙 ⚖

The process of constructing an outline or 'profile' of a person's individual characteristics.

In the eighties and nineties, the process of *profiling* has become a staple of forensic investigation. The technique of **DNA profiling**, or GENETIC FINGERPRINTING, is now frequently employed to establish the unique physical characteristics of an offender.

More controversially, **psychological profiling** or **offender profiling** may be used to build up a **psychological profile** or outline of a suspected person. (In America, the FBI have set up a unit for *profiling* SERIAL KILLERS.) *Psychological profiling* was initially welcomed with great public enthusiasm (and the technique formed a key theme in the hit nineties television series *Cracker*), but criticism in the course of at least one highly publicized murder trial has led to the process being viewed more cautiously.

> He seems particularly amused by the awe the media have accorded the Bureau's Behavioral Science Unit (B.S.U.) and its vaunted 'profiling' technique, which is supposed to help investigators zero in on the 'type' of person who becomes a serial killer.   *—Vanity Fair* Apr. 1993, p. 126

> The police are building up a new comprehensive system of 'offender profiling' to assist in the hunt for murderers and rapists. The aim is to prioritize suspects for investigation by use of a computerised database of people whose behaviour puts them in the frame for such a crime. Offender profiling was pioneered by the FBI in the United States.   *—Guardian* 10 July 1993, p. 7

> The Lord Chief Justice, Lord Taylor, last night attacked the use of psychological profiling to produce prosecution evidence in criminal trials.   *—Guardian* 2 Nov. 1994, p. 2

propeller-head /prə'pɛləhɛd/ *noun* Also written **propellor-head** POP

A mildly derogatory slang term for a person who pursues an obsessive interest in computers or technology; a boring or studious person.

Perhaps with reference to a beanie hat with a *propeller* on top, as popularized by science fiction enthusiasts.

Propeller-head is recorded from the late eighties as another mildly derogatory term for a person who might otherwise be called an ANORAK, a TRAINSPOTTER, or (in Japan) one of the OTAKU. An adjective **propeller-headed** is also found.

> Then we invited 40 users—novices, propeller-heads, people who swear by Fastback...to visit our office and work with us personally.   *—advertisement in Byte* Dec. 1993, p. 222

> Contrary to my memories of sixth-form breaktime, bridge is apparently *not* a hopelessly anal card game played by propeller-headed losers.   *—Independent* Feb. 1995, Magazine section, p. 56

> It was...an attempt to bring '90210'...to the realm of twentysomething nerds and propeller-heads.   *—Coloradoan* (Fort Collins) 2 July 1995, section C, p. 5

protection factor ⚔ see SUN PROTECTION FACTOR

Prozac /'prəʊzak/ *noun* ⊗

A proprietary name for the antidepressant drug *fluoxetine hydrochloride*; also a dose, in the form of a capsule, of the drug.

An invented name.

References were made in the late seventies to the analgesic effects of fluoxetine hydrochloride, but it was not until the mid eighties that the drug *Prozac* was patented as an antidepressant. Fluoxetine, the effective component of the drug, inhibits the re-uptake in the brain of serotonin, a blood compound which acts as a neurotransmitter and is an important factor in clinical depression. *Prozac* was heralded in the late eighties as an effective new treatment for depression and was increasingly prescribed in the early nineties. Used also to treat some forms of behavioural disorder such as compulsive shoplifting, *Prozac* came to be regarded by many as a wonder drug. However, as the nineties progressed concern was expressed about its perceived effects on a patient's mood and personality, especially as manifested in assertiveness and aggression. Additionally, some patients commented that the drug created a perceived barrier to awareness of their real feelings. Although in the mid nineties it is widely used, it cannot, for these reasons, be universally administered.

> Eli Lilly is battling several lawsuits that claim, on the basis of scant evidence, that the antidepressant Prozac can cause extreme agitation, suicidal tendencies and even an impulse to murder.   *—Time* 10 Feb. 1992, p. 43

> Prozac can make a hormone-addled young adult less sensitive, more confident, less homesick, and able to have a good time at parties.   *—Spy* Oct. 1993, p. 38

> While trying to get myself into some kind of presentable state for the occasion, I swallowed a couple of the Prozacs that a friend gave me a few weeks ago.
> —*Independent on Sunday* 21 Aug. 1994 Review section, p. 34

> Prozac…provides motivation but seems to create a wall in your mind against your feelings so you can't draw on them. I end up feeling narky and frustrated. —*DJ* 6 July 1995, p. 37

psychological abuse ⁣ see ABUSE

psychological profiling ⁣ see PROFILING

PTSD ⊗ see POST-TRAUMATIC STRESS DISORDER

public interest immunity certificate /pʌblɪk ɪnt(ə)rɪst ɪˌmjuːnɪti sə'tɪfɪkət/ *noun phrase*

A formal notice which forbids a witness to give specified information, the disclosure of which is regarded as not being in the public interest.

A *certificate* which guarantees *immunity* for a witness withholding information on grounds of *public interest*.

The principle that the Crown may claim that a witness has a right when testifying to refuse to disclose certain types of information, and in particular to refuse to produce certain types of document, on the grounds that there would be a breach of the confidentiality essential to the functioning of the public service, is an established one in British law. It was not however until the Matrix-Churchill affair of 1992, when the outcome of a trial turned particularly on documents originally withheld through *public interest immunity certificates*, that the term achieved its present high profile.

The circumstances in which the *public interest immunity certificates* (less formally referred to as GAGGING ORDERS) had been signed became a matter of considerable debate and subsequent unease, not fully assuaged by the report in 1996 of Lord Justice Scott's judicial inquiry into the affair. At present it seems safe to say that the question of when a *public interest immunity certificate* should be issued, and on what grounds, is still one likely to cause considerable concern.

> Kenneth Clarke, then the home secretary, signed a 'public interest immunity certificate' (gagging order) refusing Henderson the necessary documents. —*Private Eye* 27 Jan. 1995, p. 26

> So determined is it to keep this paperwork secret that it has threatened to seek a public interest immunity certificate if the court finds against it. —*Independent* 23 Feb. 1995, p. 25

public-key encryption /ˌpʌblɪkiː ɛn'krɪpʃ(ə)n/ *noun phrase*

A method of converting text or other data into a form which cannot be read by unauthorized persons, using a numerical sequence made publicly available for the purpose by the intended recipient.

A system of *encryption*, 'the conversion of data into a code', which employs a *key*, 'instructions for encoding and decoding (data)', which is deliberately made *public* so anyone can use it.

Public-key encryption (also called *public-key cryptography*) makes use of a property of some mathematical functions that it is relatively easy to compute results using them but extremely difficult to work backwards from the result to discover the original numbers; they are called *trap-door functions* because, like a trapdoor, they only work one way. A person or organization wishing to communicate uses such a function to calculate two numbers, one of which is published (the *public key*) whilst the other is kept secret (the *private key*). Anyone wishing to send a secure message uses the *public key* to encrypt it using the same function. Only the person with the corresponding private key can decode the message. The system of *public-key encryption* was developed in the mid seventies. Though in theory such encrypted messages can be broken, in practice they can employ such large numbers in the keys that it is believed there is insufficient computational power in the world's computers to crack them in any reasonable time. The US government has prohibited the export of systems which employ long, safe keys (classing them as munitions of war) but has come under great pressure to relax its embargo so that an international system of secure electronic transfer of financial information can be put in place (the pressure grew in 1995 when permissible systems using short keys were reported to have been cracked by at least two separate groups).

Periodically (say monthly) this usage information is uploaded to an administrative organization for billing, using public-key encryption technology to discourage tampering and to protect the secrecy of this information. —*Dr Dobb's Journal* Oct. 1992, p. 48

The program works through a process called public key encryption, which bypasses the problem of having to somehow tell the recipient of your message what the key is.
—*.net* Feb. 1995, p. 47

Arcane techniques like public key encryption which were until recently the province of obscure mathematicians and hobbyists are becoming essential to the security of big money and international trade on computer networks.
—*Independent on Sunday* 30 Apr. 1995, Review section, p. 14

See also CLIPPER CHIP, PGP

pull-down /'pʊl ˌdaʊn/ *adjective* Also pulldown 🖳

Relating to a list of options in a computer application which appears below a heading when it is selected, and which stays in place only so long as the user wishes.

This term appeared in the early eighties, as a result of the first computer operating systems that used a graphical interface being put on the market. These systems employed a pointer (a mouse), rectangular areas on the screen devoted to individual operations (windows), graphical images to represent activities (icons), and lists of possible actions or tasks (menus). By selecting a menu heading, the user accesses a list of related actions. As the act of selection is like pulling the list down, the menu is known as a **pull-down menu** (in computing, the word is now mainly used in this phrase).

The editors we review here were born to be graphical, replete with well-integrated mouse support, pulldown menus, and dialog boxes. —*UNIX World* May 1993, p. 105

WinGopher provides you with a graphical interface that uses pull-down menus and point-and-click functionality for easy Internet navigation. —*Internet World* July 1994, p. 5

pulse dialling /'pʌls ˌdaɪəlɪŋ/ *noun* 🧪

A system of telephone dialling, in which each digit is transmitted as an equivalent number of electrical pulses.

Dialling which is executed by means of electrical *pulses*, momentary changes in voltage on the line.

This system of transmitting telephone numbers to the exchange equipment is as old as the first automatic exchanges of the late nineteenth century, but the name *pulse dialling* only came to be applied to it in the early eighties in order to differentiate it from the newer electronic method of TONE DIALLING. Even when, as in the UK, a system is wholly electronic, telephone exchanges must continue to accept this method of dialling because many older telephones remain in use.

They work only on the newer digital (tone dialling) phone systems, and not on pulse dialling systems, which a large number of phones still use. —*Which?* Sept. 1991, p. 303

push the envelope /pʊʃ ði 'ɛnvələʊp/ *verbal phrase* 🗯️POP

To go beyond established limits; to do something new, to pioneer.

A phrase which probably derives from the aeronautical and aerospace industries, in which the *envelope* is the boundary line on a graph representing an aircraft's capabilities.

Push the envelope has been used since the late seventies as a mode of expression that covers both the extension of scientific and technical knowledge, and the breaching of accepted limits of toleration. A person who *pushes the envelope*, deliberately or inadvertently, is one who is going beyond the known limits, with the risk that this entails.

She had read that people could lose a great deal of blood and keep on functioning, but when they started to tip over, everything went at once. And she had to be pushing the envelope.

—Stephen King *Gerald's Game* (1993), p. 343

In Canada, if we had let over-zealous censors run amok, we might never have had the pleasure of Kids In The Hall…For an in-depth look at how the Kids continue to push the envelope of conventional comedy, check on Andy Ryan's profile on page 17. —*Campus Canada* Mar. 1994, p. 6

People who push the envelope in the area of reproductive medicine and gender identity can find themselves vilified one year and lionized the next.

—*New York Times Magazine* 27 Nov. 1994, p. 55

I mean, why not be a little risqué?…Push the envelope. —*Sports Illustrated* 29 May 1995, p. 22

PWA Ⓧ see Aids

Q

quad bike /'kwɒd bʌɪk/ *noun* 🃏 ⚽ ⊗

An off-road four-wheeled motorcycle used for sport and recreation.

Quad as an abbreviation of *quadruple*.

Quad bikes (or **quads**) were introduced in the nineties, and have proved popular. **Quad biking** is now a recognized addition to available forms of off-road racing for sport and recreation, although some reservations as to the safety of the vehicles have been expressed.

Farmers looking for new enterprises on their land can provide temporary sites for a range of sports, including traditional ones such as shooting and riding and new activities such as quad bike and motocross tracks, mountain bike courses and angling pools.

—*Countryside Recreation Network News* Oct. 1993, p. 9

Quads were designed as leisure vehicles in response to the many law suits from Americans injured on three-wheeled trikes, the theory being that four wheels would be more stable than three. Unfortunately, because quad bikes have such a high centre of gravity, increased further by the need to stand up out of the saddle at speed, that isn't necessarily so.

—*Daily Telegraph* 5 Nov. 1995 (electronic edition)

Fancy mounting a seriously chunky four wheel-drive motorbike, easing your arse into a juicy seat and zooming along at high speed? Then quad biking is for you.

—*Venue* (Bristol and Bath) 5 July 1996, p. 15

quality circle /'kwɒlɪti sə:k(ə)l/ *noun* 🌾

A group of employees which meets regularly to consider ways of resolving problems and improving production in an organization.

The *quality circle*, which has its roots in Japanese industry, is based on the belief that it is workers rather than senior managers who are the most familiar with the details of a company's working practice and therefore the best qualified to suggest improvements. *Quality circles*, frequently referred to by the abbreviation *QCs*, have become a feature of Western industrial practice since the early eighties, introduced by the Japanese firms which established companies at that time in North America and the UK. The emphasis is on participation and cooperation in problem-solving, this forming part of a continuous quest for improvement based on the Japanese business philosophy known as KAIZEN.

Few of the numberless improvements made in the flow of work in office or factory, by 'quality circles' for example, can be patented. —*Policy Options* (Halifax, Nova Scotia) Jan. 1990, p. 27

Despite these apparent non-fits, we hypothesized that, with some modifications, the participative problem-solving approach of QCs can be most advantageous in construction, too.
—*International Journal of Project Management* Feb. 1991, p. 21

This first volume in a series of four shopfloor manuals aims to provide details of the basic improvement tools used by quality circles in Japan in the Kaizen, continuous improvement, activities.
—advertisement in *Metalworking Production* Sept. 1991, p. 2

The quality of life movement of the 1970s and the emulation of Japanese management of the 1980s have made quality circles a popular and often incorrectly applied management tool.
—*IEEE Annals of the History of Computing* Winter 1994, p. 91

quality time /ˈkwɒlɪti tʌɪm/ *noun* 🧪

Time spent productively or profitably, especially with reference to time spent by working parents with their children.

In the late seventies the sociological concept of *quality time* developed a specific application: the term is now used to describe the necessarily limited time that a working parent can spend with his or her child. The view is a positive one: although the time itself is limited, it is regarded as productive and profitable to the relationship; the implication is that a limited amount of time which is planned and structured, and during which the child has the parent's total and focused attention, is just as valuable as notionally unlimited time.

This concept of *quality time*, pioneered in the US, found many supporters when it crossed the Atlantic. More recently, however, there has been some evidence of scepticism: it is claimed by some that the term, which has become a cliché, is little more than a euphemism for a child's having limited time with a parent who is anyway, at the end of a working day, too tired to provide the productive and creative attention envisaged by proponents of *quality time*.

Without the weekend...families would continue to spin in divergent directions with no time together, much less the often-discussed 'quality time'. —*Atlantic* Nov. 1991, p. 10

With both parents...holding down jobs, home life had been reduced to a mad scramble at the end of the day to cram in shopping, laundry, cooking, mending—and, oh, yes, communication. Quality time had become a bitter cliché: a concentrated forced effort to make up for irretrievable moments. —*Time* 6 Jan. 1992, p. 41

On the album cover, Penner lists ten things that are important to him. The list includes quality time with his family, healthy children, friendship. —*Today's Parent Toronto!* Oct. 1994, p. 22

quantum chaos 🧪 see CHAOS

queercore /ˈkwɪəkɔː/ *noun* 🧪

A cultural movement amongst young homosexuals which deliberately rebels against and dissociates itself from the established gay scene, having as its primary form of expression an aggressive type of punk-style music (see -CORE). The term is frequently used attributively, and the alternative form *homocore* is also found.

Like QUEER NATION, *queercore* represents the gay militancy of the nineties.

Fueled by the snotty, rebellious spirit of punk, queercore youth have punctured the stilted air of the 'gay establishment' by exposing the clichés and stereotypes present within the gay and lesbian community. —*Spin* Apr. 1993, p. 48

This east London gay/lesbian foursome are noisy advocates of queercore, the movement of aggressively out young gay people. —*Guardian* 25 Feb. 1994, section 2, p. 11

Loud and distorted queercore indie and thrash night with seriously wicked live bands.
—*i-D* Oct. 1994, p. 107

He might rave over a record by...the queercore group The Frogs. —*Wire* Jan. 1995, p. 19

Queer Nation /'kwɪə neɪʃ(ə)n/ *noun* ⚑

The name of a campaigning lesbian and gay rights organization founded in the US in 1990.

The contemptuous slang use of *queer* to mean 'homosexual' has long been regarded as offensive, and earlier supporters of gay and lesbian rights have objected to its use. By the nineties, however, a more militant form of activism reclaimed the word, transmuting what was originally regarded as pejorative into a force for asserting the rights of the group concerned. *Queer Nation* has since developed its own derivatives, with **Queer National** noun and adjective being recorded.

> Queer Nation is in the process of organizing 'Pink Panther' (cf. Black Panther) vigilante groups that could respond physically and immediately to gay- and lesbian-bashing.
> —Lillian Faderman *Odd Girls & Twilight Lovers* (1991), p. 301

> Gay riots exploded in Los Angeles and San Francisco after California governor Pete Wilson vetoed AB 101, a bill that would have outlawed job discrimination on the basis of sexual orientation. After his veto, Queer Nationals and other gay activists hurled police barricades through windows.
> —*Mother Jones* May 1992, p. 63

> Elena used to call herself bisexual, but when she got more involved with lesbian and gay politics, in particular with the in-your-face Queer Nation radicalism of the late eighties, she started using queer.
> —*This Mag.* Nov. 1994, p. 14

See also QUEERCORE

quote-driven 〰 see SEAQ

quote unquote 〰 see AIR QUOTES

•   •

R

racket abuse ⚽ see ABUSE

rad /rad/ *adjective* 〰

In slang (especially in the US): really good or exciting; 'cool', 'hip', AWESOME.

Formed by abbreviating *radical*, itself a favourite term of approval among American youngsters in the eighties and originally a word used in Californian surfers' slang. Such slang terms of approval often get abbreviated to a snappy monosyllable—in the UK *brilliant* became *brill* by the same process.

The longer form **radical** was used from 1968 by surfers to describe a turn or other manoeuvre that was at the limits of control and safety, presumably by extending the political sense of the adjective 'representing the extreme section of a party'; this specific surfers' use was interpreted as the equivalent of *far out* and, like *far out* itself some time earlier, was soon weakened to express no more than approval and admiration for something. In the early eighties, as Californian surfers' slang became diluted and spread to a generation of young Americans through films and other sports such as skateboarding and BMX biking, *radical* and the abbreviated form *rad* began to crop up frequently as the currently fashionable accolade.

> Both magazines are so bent on promoting the 'rad bad dude' image, that aside from the great photos, they have no substance. —*Skiing* Mar. 1991, p. 12

> We met this old dude who was like the president of Maclean Hunter for all of Canada. We hung in his office for a bit and he told us about golf and the importance of advertising and stuff. He was a pretty rad guy (minus the loafers). —*This Mag.* (Toronto) Sept. 1994, p. 40

rage /reɪdʒ/ *noun* POP

Intense anger expressed in an uncontrolled outburst, especially involving unprovoked violence and aggression towards another (frequently as the second element of a compound).

In the late eighties and nineties growing attention has been paid to instances of violence attributed to a build-up of frustration in a particular environment. The term *rage*, as the second word of a compound delineating the specific area of the problem, is frequently used, with the best-known compound ROAD RAGE now being joined by ROID RAGE, and a number of others of a more or less serious kind. Cyclists may drive each other to **cycle rage**. Fights over queues in supermarkets have been described as instances of **trolley rage**, while frustrations on a golf course may result in **golf rage**. The growing list of such formulations reflects a heightened public perception of this kind of random violence as a worrying symptom of life in the nineties.

Dogs such as Dempsey on death row frequently suffer 'kennel rage' from being deprived of their owners for long periods, and become frustrated, aggressive and anti-social.
—*Guardian* 10 Mar. 1994 p. 10

Courts should be given power to order 'rage counselling' for aggressive motorists.
—*Independent* 20 Apr. 1995 p. 9

What is this thing called rage? Random violence committed by 'ordinary' people is a growing phenomenon. —*Guardian* 6 Jan. 1996, Outlook section, p. 24

An outbreak of supermarket 'trolley rage' ended with a customer sprawled and bleeding over the Mr Kipling cakes. —*Daily Telegraph* 18 September 1996, p. 3

ragga /ˈragə/ *noun* POP

In full **ragamuffin** or **raggamuffin**: a style of popular music derived from reggae and incorporating elements from faster, electronically-based styles, such as HIP-HOP and TECHNO. The full form *ragamuffin* also denotes both the culture associated with this music, and the exponent or follower of the music.

An abbreviated form of *ragamuffin*. The development of the name is probably influenced by the Jamaican *raga raga*, or *ragga ragga*, 'old ragged clothes'.

Ragga, a musical style which has emerged from a fusion of reggae's Jamaican roots with urban hip-hop, is associated particularly with the culture of young Jamaican and English blacks. Its characteristic sound incorporates a gruff, rasping vocal with a strong bass beat. It is related to JUNGLE music, but differs from the latter in its use of a slower drum. Both *ragga* and *ragamuffin* are used attributively.

It has given an identity to second- and third-generation black Britons who feel no desire to assimilate into the mainstream: raggamuffins pepper their talk with thick Jamaican slang, even if their parents were born in Bi.mingham. —*Independent* 11 June 1993, p. 24

The hip hop pioneer goes gruffly raggamuffin to chant this 'ragga sound' euro galloper in its obviously exciting Van Halen 'Jump' chords driven 140bpm Fargetta Remix.
—*DJ* 6 July 1995, p. 56

Conscious Ragga still has that thumping, fractious sound of the rudie but offers lyrics serious enough for dub fans to appreciate. —*Q* Jan. 1996, p. 139

RAID /reɪd/ *acronym* Also written **Raid**

A technique for reducing the risk of failure of disk storage in computer systems by one of a number of related methods involving writing data to a group of disks.

The initial letters of the phrase *Redundant Arrays of Inexpensive Disks*; *redundant* is used here in its engineering and computing sense of 'the duplication of components in an effort to increase reliability'.

The fixed disks used in computers can occasionally fail unexpectedly through a variety of causes; the risks involved are unacceptably high in situations where the data being stored cannot easily be replaced. In 1988 the term *RAID* was coined for a system which replaces a single large-capacity disk drive with a number of smaller (and hence comparatively inexpensive) ones, using a variety of hardware and software methods (designated by appended numbers from **RAID 0** up to **RAID 5**) to ensure that the data can be retrieved intact even if one or more of the disks fail.

> Raid 5 products use inexpensive disks as their storage medium, arranged in drawers of four. Each block of data written to the Raid 5 device is spread across three of the disks, with the fourth being used to record how it was split up. —*Computing* 23 June 1994, p. 4

> Whether you…back up via disk mirroring, RAID, optical jukeboxes, or tape libraries, the ultimate goal of storage management is to ensure that data is there when it's required.
> —*Byte* June 1994, p. 160

Railtrack /'reɪltrak/ *noun* ✍

An authority set up in 1994 to take responsibility for the infrastructure of British railways.

The privatization of British Rail divided the formerly nationalized company (under the supervision of OFRAIL) into a number of regional businesses for passenger and freight transport. It was however seen as necessary to maintain some central authority for the general infrastructure, and *Railtrack* was established, with responsibility for track maintenance and signalling, and for publication of a national timetable.

> A Railtrack spokesman said: 'We will be rebranding the large independent stations, with new Railtrack signs and uniforms, all with the Railtrack logo'. —*Guardian* 31 Mar. 1994, p. 11

> The seasonal excuse of 'leaves on the line' is causing trouble for Railtrack once again.
> —*Independent* 12 Oct. 1995, p. 10

ram-raid /'ramreɪd/ *verb* and *noun* Also written **ramraid**, **ram raid** {{

transitive verb: To break into premises, especially for the purpose of robbery, by ramming a vehicle through a window or wall.

noun: A break-in of this type.

The term *ram-raid* entered the language in the late eighties and soon became a familiar name in the UK for this motorized form of smash-and-grab. In such a crime the vehicle, usually a heavy van, doubles as a battering ram and as a conveyance for the loot, which is then driven away at great speed by the **ram-raiders**. The force and violence of the demolition lend a particularly aggressive note to **ram-raiding**, which, though normally carried out on commercial premises, may also target private homes. *Ram-raiding* has sometimes been carried out not for the purpose of theft but as an act of aggression against establishments, such as nightclubs, from which the perpetrators have been debarred. There is evidence too of the term being extended to include transferred and figurative uses, denoting the acquisition of an object or an idea with the implication of a lack of finesse.

> The night Sly & Lovechild are due to PA at Manchester's Most Excellent, the club doors are ram-raided and trashed by three reprobates in a stolen car, pissed off at being refused entry. —*New Musical Express* 4 Apr. 1992, p. 18

> A cash-dispensing machine was recovered and five men arrested shortly after a ram raid on a branch of the Abbey National Building Society in Herne Bay, Kent.
> —*Independent* 17 Sept. 1992, p. 8

> Private homes are being targeted by ram raiders in the latest crimewave to hit parts of Northavon and Bristol. —*Bristol Journal* 7 Jan. 1994, p. 1

> 'Prophlex' ramraids Killing Joke's 'Change' for its mutant bounding beats.
> —*The Wire* Jan. 1995, p. 54

Ram-raid your best mates' wardrobes and confiscate anything that would look great on you!
—*Sugar* Apr. 1995, p. 5

rape methyl ester 🌱 🔬 see BIO-DIESEL

raptor /'raptə/ *noun* 🔬

A fierce and predatory dinosaur.

A shortening of *velociraptor* 'a small carnivorous dinosaur of the Cretaceous period', a modern Latin word formed from a compound of Latin *velox, velocis* 'swift' and *raptor* (in English 'a bird of prey'), ultimately from Latin *rapere, rapt-* 'to seize'.

The word *raptor* in the sense 'bird of prey' is recorded in English from the nineteenth century, but more recently a second zoological sense has begun to develop. The swift and ferocious *velociraptors*, or *raptors*, are among the most notable of the dinosaurs depicted in Michael Crichton's thriller *Jurassic Park* and the Spielberg film based on it: it was especially from this film that the *dinomania* (see DINO-) of the early nineties developed.

Although *raptors* are still associated particularly with Crichton's book and its sequel, the term has begun to appear in other works of science fiction with a similar setting, and in popular studies of dinosaurs in general.

> Eventually, the baby raptor part of the scene was cut, and Steven decided to change the triceratops hatchling to a raptor hatchling.
> —Don Shay and Jody Duncan *The Making of Jurassic Park* (1993), p. 101

> One of the most sophisticated hunting machines the world has ever known, the dromaesaur—or 'raptor'—was a terrifying dinosaur.
> —D. Carey and J. I. Kirkland *Star Trek: First Frontier* (1995), foreword, p. x

rasterize /'rast(ə)rʌɪz/ *transitive verb* Also written **rasterise** 🖥

To convert an image into a set of points arranged on a grid.

Formed from *raster*, 'a rectangular pattern of parallel scanning lines', itself derived in the thirties from the German *Raster*, 'screen, frame', and used to describe the pattern of lines in a television picture.

Certain kinds of computer systems, particularly some printers and applications, require images to be presented to them in the form of an array of numerical values, each value representing the intensity and colour of one point on a grid. An image in this form is often called a **bit map** (a 'map' of computer 'bits') and an individual point is a *pixel* (a blend of 'picture' and 'element'). Though such images are often digitized from physical images using a scanner, the term *rasterize* is usually restricted to the action of a computer program which translates another kind of internal representation of the image into raster format. Such a program is called a **rasterizer**, and the process is called **rasterization**; the adjective is **rasterized**.

> When you type a character, *Windows 3.1* finds the appropriate TrueType typeface file and calls up the rasterizer, which then scales the font outline. —*PC World* Apr. 1992, p. 125

> PostScript uses a rasterization process to convert whole pages, including fonts and graphics, into one large bit-mapped image. —*Byte* Dec. 1992, p. 134

> The graphics generator essentially takes a series of 2-D pictures of the 3-D scene and rasterizes them individually to display them sequentially, providing the semblance of motion.
> —*NewMedia* Aug. 1994, p. 44

rave /reɪv/ *noun* 🎵 POP

A large gathering with dancing to fast electronic popular music.

A specialized use of the noun *rave* in the sense 'a lively party; a rowdy gathering'.

The typical features of a late eighties or early nineties *rave* were broadly considered to be threefold: the fast, repetitive beat of the music; the very large numbers of people attending;

and the use by many of the **ravers** of RECREATIONAL DRUGS, especially ECSTASY. To accommodate the large numbers these *raves*, which were usually unlicensed, were commonly held in rural locations such as fields and large barns. Owing to the prevalent use of drugs and in an attempt to avoid police raids, organizers would keep the venue secret until the very last moment, *ravers* acquiring the information through an underground network.

In the mid nineties the **rave scene** is still associated with the use of drugs. But as the decade has advanced *raves* have changed in nature, becoming smaller in size and more mainstream. Many are now licensed gatherings and are recognized as venues for known groups and bands.

> When you're at a rave there's 10,000 ravers going mental—you can't beat the energy.
> —*New Musical Express* 31 Aug. 1991, p. 18

> Now, the music is in the charts, there are licensed raves all over the place, and the punters know they can go and dance the night away in a place which is not a fire hazard.
> —*Daily Telegraph* 4 Nov. 1991, p. 19

> For many youngsters, fun doesn't come any better than the raves and nightclubs where Ecstasy, amphetamines and other drugs complement the hypnotic music and incandescent lights.
> —*Guardian* 28 Feb. 1995, section 2, p. 15

RDU ⊗ ✖ see RECREATIONAL DRUG

Reaganomics 🏛 see -NOMICS

realo 🌳 🏛 see FUNDIE

reboot /riː'buːt/ *verb* and *noun* 🖥

transitive verb: To restart (a computer) by reloading its operating system into working memory; to cause (the system or a program) to be reloaded in this way.

intransitive verb: (Of a computer) to be restarted by reloading its operating system.

noun: An act or instance of restarting a computer in this way.

A compound of *re-*, 'again', with an abbreviated form of *bootstrap* 'to initiate a fixed sequence of instructions which initiates the loading of further instructions and, ultimately, of the whole system'; this in turn is named after the process of *pulling oneself up by one's bootstraps*, a phrase which is widely supposed to be based on one of the eighteenth-century *Adventures of Baron Munchausen*.

Bootstrap processes have been used in computing since the fifties, but it was not until personal computers became widespread from the early eighties that the noun *bootstrap* and the corresponding verb were commonly abbreviated to *boot* and the form *reboot* appeared. The difference in sense between *boot* and *reboot* is that the latter usually implies restarting after a power failure or fault, or following some change in the hardware or software configuration of the system. There is early evidence of the figurative use of *reboot*.

> According to technical support, if you have the DOS screen-saving option loaded, the only way to safely run Windows is to reboot. —*Computer Shopper* July 1993, p. 335

> Rebooting my system without SHARE.EXE got Setup Wizard to work correctly.
> —*Byte* Oct. 1993, p. 144

> The new dongle must then be inserted, with the Atari rebooted so that the alternate program can be loaded from the relevant floppy! —*Keyboard Player* Sept. 1994, p. 18

recovered memory /rɪ'kʌvəd mɛm(ə)ri/ *noun* ⊗ ⚕

Repressed memory, especially of childhood sexual abuse, recovered (or apparently recovered) during psychoanalysis.

In the nineties, the view that suppressed memories of trauma can be retrieved or 'recovered' by therapy in later life has been particularly associated with treatment of those believed to have suffered from childhood sexual abuse. The results of such therapy have often been bitterly controversial, and **recovered memory syndrome** is often taken as synonymous with FALSE MEMORY SYNDROME.

'Recovered memory syndrome', in which children and adults 'discover' under therapy that they were abused as children, is one of the most painful issues dividing American families.
—*Sunday Times* 14 Nov. 1993, p. 22

Proponents of recovered memory believe that the mind has remarkable powers of repression: that it can bury all memory of traumatic abuse, even abuse sustained over many years.
—*Independent on Sunday* 9 Oct. 1994, p. 22

recovery movement ⊗ ❙❙ see CODEPENDENCY

recreational drug /rɛkrɪ'eɪʃ(ə)n(ə)l drʌg/ *noun* ⊗ ✖

A drug regarded as a source of pleasure and enjoyment for one's leisured moments.

A *drug* taken for *recreational* rather than medicinal purposes.

Recreational drugs encompass a wide range of narcotic and hallucinogenic drugs, from a traditional 'hard' drug such as cocaine, through LSD, ECSTASY, and magic mushrooms, to marijuana. The term was originally employed in its literal meaning to distinguish the form of use from that of medical necessity, but in the eighties it came increasingly to reflect the view that it was possible to have intermittent and pleasurable recourse to stimulants of this kind without the user becoming addicted, or being seen as part of the 'drug scene'; **recreational drug users,** or **RDUs,** are not those who followed the sixties injunction to 'tune in, turn on, and drop out', but those who regard the preferred drug as something which can enhance without damaging the chosen lifestyle.

Amazing how many different supposedly intelligent species chose a downright poison, ethanol, as their recreational drug of choice. —Vonda N. McIntyre *The Entropy Effect* (1981), p. 95

The biggest wave of recreational drug use since the hyped-up psychedelia of the late sixties.
—*Guardian* 7 Sept. 1993, section 2, p. 2

A brisk trade in coke, the recreational yuppie drug-of-choice.
—Margaret Atwood *Robber Bride* (1993), p. 436

Unlike drug takers in past decades, RDUs don't identify with one particular sub-culture:...in the Seventies punks took speed—they wouldn't touch dope because that was for hippies; in the Eighties cocaine was cool until it was eclipsed by Ecstasy...Now the boundaries have disintegrated. —*Independent on Sunday* 28 Jan. 1996, p. 3

red ribbon ⊗ see AIDS

red route /'rɛd ruːt/ *noun* ♞

A traffic management scheme (marked by red lines along the edge of the road) designed to ease congestion on main roads in London.

A pilot *red route* scheme took place between Highgate and Limehouse in 1991; despite local objections, especially from shopkeepers who felt the restrictions damaged their trade, it was thought successful and the concept was incorporated into the Road Traffic Act 1991. The traffic management scheme of a network of *red routes* throughout the capital aims to relieve congestion and to improve conditions for people living and working alongside the roads concerned, particularly through TRAFFIC CALMING and by increasing on-street parking. The first new *red route* opened on a stretch of the South Circular Road in south-west London in March 1995 and the network is expected to be complete by the year 2000.

The pilot scheme for the 'red route' plan to improve London's traffic flow on key routes has drastically cut journey times and improved the reliability of bus services, Derek Turner, the Traffic Director for London, said yesterday. —*Independent* 20 Oct. 1992, p. 6

Despite calls from environmentalists for a more radical approach to traffic control through the active discouragement of car use and the development of public transport, the Government is pressing on with the kerbside management of 315 miles of Red Route.

—*Evening Standard* 22 Mar. 1995

re-engineering 🖵 〰 see BUSINESS PROCESS RE-ENGINEERING

repetitive strain injury /rə‚pɛtɪtɪv 'streɪn ɪndʒəri/ *noun phrase* ⊗

Injury to muscles or tendons arising from continuous repeated use of particular muscles, especially during keyboarding. Commonly abbreviated to **RSI**.

A rapid increase in the number of keyboard users generated by the advent of computers brought the phenomenon of *repetitive strain injury* to public attention in the early eighties. The most common component of the condition is an inflammation of the tendons in the wrist and hands, causing pain and sometimes loss of function, known by the medical terms *tendinitis* and *tenosynovitis*. Although the term *repetitive strain injury* has been applied to a number of sports-related activities, it was in its application to tasks in the workplace and especially to keyboarding that the condition received considerable media interest in the eighties and early nineties. This was largely as a result of the legal controversy surrounding citation of the condition as grounds for industrial compensation and health insurance claims. Though fully recognizing the components of the condition, the medical profession was divided on the question of whether the undeniable symptoms were evidence of permanent physical injury. As a consequence the use of the umbrella term *repetitive strain injury* and its abbreviation *RSI* was considered by some members of the legal profession to be invalid in compensation and insurance claims. Most employers now acknowledge the condition as an occupational health problem, and attempt to safeguard their workers from it. Alternative terms are *work-related upper limb disorder* and (in the US and Canada) *cumulative trauma disorder*.

There've been lots of scary accounts of VDU hazards, ranging from repetitive strain injury (RSI) to eyesight damage, and even long-term risks from radiation emissions.

—*What Personal Computer* Dec. 1991, p. 106

RSI is a serious occupational hazard for the dippers and spongers of the Staffordshire pottery industry. —*Independent* 6 Jan. 1992, p. 13

A judge's ruling that repetitive strain injury (RSI) was a 'meaningless concept' has been slammed by medical experts and union leaders. —*Computer Weekly* 4 Nov. 1993, p. 12

The Health and Safety Executive now lists work-related upper-limb disorders (another name for RSI) as the main health problem associated with working with VDUs.

—*Independent* 5 Mar. 1996, section 2, p. 10

reskill /riːˈskɪl/ *transitive verb* Also written **re-skill** 【|

To retrain (workers) in the skills required by a modern business.

The verb *reskill* and the verbal noun **reskilling** entered the language in the early eighties as synonyms for *retrain* and *retraining*, but ones used in the particular context of the business and industrial worlds of the late twentieth century. Those in work may be *reskilled* in new procedures, for example in technology, in management, or on the shop floor, while the unemployed may be offered *reskilling* in preparation for a return to work. *Reskilling* may also be offered as part of a redundancy package.

Earlier this year, it ran a 10-week reskilling course for its developers that concentrated on object-orientation. —*Computing* 18 Nov. 1993, p. 16

The Left…believes that the Government should play a greater role in providing child care, care for the elderly, crime prevention and training and reskilling the unemployed.

—*Daily Telegraph* 3 Nov. 1994, p. 7

retro /ˈrɛtrəʊ/ *noun* and *adjective* ▓

noun: A style or fashion that harks back to the past, a throw-back; a movement to revive past styles; a style of popular music which consciously avoids technical innovations.

adjective: Reviving or harking back to the past; nostalgically retrospective.

Although the combining form *retro-* has a long history in English, forming words with the meaning 'backwards-' on Latin roots (such as *retrograde*), it was actually through the French word *rétrograde* that this word reached English. The French began to abbreviate *rétrograde* to *rétro* specifically in relation to fashion in the first half of the seventies, when the styles of the thirties were revived by Paris designers. The abbreviation stuck in French, and it was only the abbreviated form that was borrowed into English.

The earliest uses in English closely follow the developments in France, and use the word both as a noun and as an adjective, as was already the case in French. As nostalgia in a number of cultural areas, especially music, became increasingly fashionable in the eighties and nineties, both the adjective and the noun were used to form compounds such as **retro-chic, retro-culture**, and **retro-rock**.

> Claire is dressed today in bubble gum capri pants, sleeveless blouse, scarf, and sunglasses: starlet manqué. She likes retro looks, and she also once told us that if she has kids, 'I'm going to give them utterly retro names like Madge or Verna or Ralph'.　　—D. Coupland *Generation X* (1991), p. 15

> Clothing popular in the late '60s and early '70s is now retro-chic; and 'Hair' is in the midst of a national tour.　　—*Boston Globe* 29 May 1994, p. 1

> I am so f?!kin' bored with the music coming out recently and the whole trend towards retro, whether that be 'What does grunge really mean other than 70s rock bands.'
> 　　—*RIP* June 1994, p. 92

reverse-engineer /rɪˌvəːsɛndʒɪˈnɪə/ *transitive verb* 🖳

To examine (a product) in order to ascertain details of construction and operation, especially with a view to manufacturing a similar product; to make (something) by this method.

From the notion of *reversing* the normal sequence of design and manufacture so as to derive the design from the completed product.

The usual process of creating a piece of computer software is to write it in a highly stylized form of text (called *source code*) and then to turn it into numerical instructions which the computer can understand (the *executable code*) by passing it through another computer program called a compiler. It is possible, with difficulty, to work backwards: to take an existing piece of software and determine what the original instructions were. The reasons for doing this may be legitimate: old software may no longer have its source code available, so **reverse-engineering** is the only way to recreate it so it can be amended; or it may be vital to find out how a program operates so another program can be made to work with it. On the other hand, the reasons may be unethical or even illegal: a firm may *reverse-engineer* competitors' products to find out how they work and steal their ideas. The latter practice gave rise to controversy and law suits during the eighties and nineties; the European Union published its European Software directive in 1993 outlawing all *reverse-engineering* except in certain well-defined circumstances. These terms are beginning to be used in other areas beside computing, and also figuratively, in a sense of 'determining how something operates'. The adjective is **reverse-engineered**.

> The flourishing international trade in pirated and reverse-engineered software threatens the health of U.S. software producers.　　—*Scientific American* Nov. 1990, Vol. 263, No. 5, p. 100

> Things churn so fast that innovative substitutions…reverse engineering, clones, third party add-ons that make a weak product boom…all conspire to bypass the usual routes to dominance.
> 　　—Kevin Kelly *Out of Control* (1994), p. 193

> Today, marketers reverse-engineer a consumer's choice to infer why a decision was made.
> 　　—*Wired* Mar. 1995, p. 172

revisit /riːˈvɪzɪt/ *verb and noun*

transitive verb: To reconsider or re-experience (something).

noun: An act of reconsidering or re-experiencing something; a second visit.

The earliest and literal sense of *revisit* in the sense 'to visit again' has been current from the late fifteenth century; since the early seventies, a number of figurative instances in the past participle (particularly in the area of language studies) have been recorded. A secondary sense, 'to reinspect, to re-examine', was current between the early sixteenth and early eighteenth centuries.

One of the most familiar contextual uses of *revisit* as a verb concerns the notion of a departed spirit coming back to his or her former world, as in Hamlet's question to the ghost of his father,

> Revisit'st thus the glimpses of the moon…?

The association of nostalgia for formerly loved and known surroundings has been emphasized by such uses as the title of Evelyn Waugh's 1945 novel *Bridehead Revisited*, which was brought to renewed public attention by a successful televisation in the eighties.

Since the mid eighties, in the field of literary and theatrical criticism, the verb and its associated noun have been used to describe the way in which selected events in a person's past life may be reconsidered and re-evaluated; this process of **revisitation** may cover not simply events in one's personal past, but subjects on which a view has been formed, which it may now be appropriate to submit to further consideration.

> As Victor Navasky points out in this excellent revisit, there never was such an ineffectual creature as a Hollywood communist. —W. Sheed *Essays in Disguise* (1990), p. 161

> A superb tragicomedy in which Neil Simon unflinchingly revisits the time in his childhood when he and his brother had to live as humbled supplicants among richer relatives.
> —*Time* 6 Jan. 1992, p. 78

> Those days are revisited in a six-hour frolic made for British TV and airing on PBS this week.
> —*Post* (Denver) 10 Jan. 1994, section E, p. 1

> The lingering and still pervasive grip of this phenomenon, seen in feminism as well as the 'curial' style of dissenting prelates, justifies a revisitation. —*LayWitness* Sept. 1994, p. 11

ribozyme /ˈrʌɪbəzʌɪm/ *noun*

A type of RNA (ribonucleic acid) which is capable of acting as an enzyme.

A blend of the first part of *ribonucleic* with the second part of *enzyme*.

It was discovered in the early eighties that in some circumstances RNA could act as an enzyme, catalysing reactions within the body without itself being changed. Such *ribozymes* are being intensively researched in the hope that they may form the basis for novel drugs that could deactivate unwanted genetic material, such as the retroviruses which cause HIV infection and AIDS, or the mutant genes which give rise to genetic disorders. *Ribozymes* are found in two varieties, named for the shapes of their molecules as **hairpin ribozymes** and **hammerhead ribozymes**; it is the latter which are currently being investigated. The area of research is sometimes known as **ribozymology**.

> If CSIRO and its commercial partners…can find a way of delivering specific ribozymes into misfunctioning cells, they will have found a way of curing many of the world's ills.
> —*Nature* 7 Dec. 1989, p. 612

> The enzyme-like agent is *only* a modified nucleoside—not a 'proper ribozyme', or folded chain of RNA nucleosides that binds a substance to foster a specific biochemical reaction.
> —*Science News* 22 Dec. 1990, p. 390

rightsize see -SIZE

ring-fence /'rɪŋfɛns/ *transitive verb* 〰️

To protect or guarantee the safety of (funds).

A transferred use of the verb meaning 'guard securely, (as if) by enclosing with a ring-fence'.

Since the late eighties, considerable attention has been paid to the degree to which funds can be protected, particularly in cases where the liability of the parent company may be involved: in the UK, events such as the collapse of Mirror Group Newspapers and major losses by Lloyds increased the degree of public interest and concern. The term is also frequently used in the context of money allocated for a particular purpose: a grant made for one specific end is often said to be **ring-fenced** from the main budget of which it forms a part, and cannot subsequently have money taken from or added to it.

> The European Fighter Aircraft, to cost £22 billion over a number of years, has been 'ring-fenced' from the current spending battles. —*Daily Telegraph* 24 July 1992, p. 20

> Their liability will be limited; and previous Lloyd's losses will be 'ring-fenced'.
> —*New Yorker* 20 Sept. 1993, p. 92

> The retail group ring-fenced Athena last week and placed it into administrative receivership, leaving creditors of the subsidiary nursing heavy losses.
> —*Independent on Sunday* 1 Jan. 1995, p. 22

ring of steel /rɪŋ əv 'stiːl/ *noun phrase* 🛡️

A form of civil protection which provides for the effective sealing off of city centres through closed-circuit television, control zones, and restricted access.

A protective *ring* conceived as having the strength of *steel*.

The system of installing a *ring of steel* of this nature, to provide for increased security at periods of risk, was developed in the mid seventies by security forces in Northern Ireland in Belfast and other towns and cities. The question of a *ring of steel* in a town or city is often a controversial one; subjectively, it may be regarded as an image of protection or of repression, and the increased security it brings may also be offset by a concomitant reduction in trade. In mainland Britain, the possibility was raised of establishing a *ring of steel* around the City of London after the IRA's bombing of the Baltic Exchange in 1992.

> The forts are a ring of steel designed to hem in, survey, control, and intimidate the nationalist population. —*Harper's Magazine* May 1993, p. 8

> What can the law do to help the protection of the City of London and those who work there? The Government and senior police officers have so far resisted calls for a 'ring of steel', Belfast-style protection, with closed circuit television, control zones, and very restricted access.
> —*CA* June 1993

riot girl /'rʌɪət ɡəːl/ *noun* Also written **riot grrl** 🧷 🎸

A young militant feminist. Frequently in attributive use.

A *girl* as a young woman who expresses her feminism through rebellious behaviour characteristic of a *riot* against accepted public order.

The *riot girl* movement began in America in the early nineties. Members typically focus on sexual harassment and the exploitation of women, and express their resistance especially through the medium of aggressive punk-style rock music.

> The main way riot girls express themselves is through dozens of girl fanzines. The small, Xeroxed-and-folded booklets are filled with grrl talk, art and articles.
> —*Gazette* (Montreal) 28 Sept. 1992, section C, p. 3

> When the Riot Grrl movement began in America in 1991, its intention was to redress the balance of power via the punk rock underground using slogans (words like 'rape' and 'slut' written in black marker pens on exposed stomachs or bare arms), fanzines, meetings and women-only shows.
> —*Guardian* 15 Apr. 1995, Weekend section, p. 37

rip /rɪp/ *transitive verb* 🔀 ⁅⁆

In colloquial use, especially in North America: to attack verbally; to criticize severely.

Probably a shortened form of the colloquial phrasal verb *rip into*, first recorded in Australian English in the forties, which has the same sense.

This punchy and expressive verb has been recorded since the early eighties.

> Quisenberry might have been inclined to complain about his teammates' goofs, but he said: 'I won't rip my teammates.' —*Globe & Mail* (Toronto) 10 Oct. 1985, section C, p. 2

> Tenants rip sentences in 'reign of terror'…as a Manhattan judge imposed light jail terms on two landlords. —*Daily News* (New York) 23 May 1986, p. 7

ritual abuse ⁅⁆ see ABUSE

river abuse ⚘ see ABUSE

RME ⚘ 🜊 see BIO-DIESEL

road hump ⚘ see SPEED BUMP

road-kill /ˈrəʊdkɪl/ *noun* Also written **road kill, roadkill** 🔀 ⁅⁆

In colloquial use in North America: the killing of an animal by a vehicle on a road; an animal killed in this way. Also, a person or thing resembling such an animal; a helpless victim.

The term *road-kill* was first recorded in the late seventies. The majority of references to *road-kill* in its primary sense make implicit acknowledgement of its value to the driver of the vehicle involved. It is perceived by many as a sport or even a form of hunting, according to the type of animal killed. The adjective **road-killed** is used to describe animals killed in this way.

By the early nineties transferred and figurative usages had been recorded. A tatty hairstyle or clothing may be referred to as *road-kill*, as may someone or something perceived as being a helpless victim, effaced or about to be effaced by some powerful force, such as a sports team destined for defeat or a person with outdated computing equipment.

> His kitchen-knife physique, sour face and a hairdo resembling a road-kill toupée.
> —*Time* 15 June 1992, p. 71

> Tom Squier is out there on the highway every day, staring through the windshield of his Dodge Dakota pickup, looking for road kills. Perhaps a nice snake or frog. Or, if he's lucky, maybe a possum, squirrel or bird. —*Virginian Pilot & Ledger Star* (Norfolk, Virginia) 6 July 1993, section D, p. 1

> To avoid becoming roadkill on the digital highway, get a faster modem.
> —*Denver Post* 2 Jan. 1994, section H, p. 5

road rage /ˈrəʊd reɪdʒ/ *noun* ⁅⁆

A driver's uncontrolled aggressive behaviour, apparently caused by the stresses of modern driving.

Road rage is probably the best-known of the forms of RAGE which in the eighties and nineties have become a feature of modern urban life. Instances of *road rage* have included not merely the feeling of intense anger and aggression towards another driver, but the physical expression of these: beatings-up and actual killings have been attributed to the phenomenon. Advice on how to avoid violence in this situation has included the recommendation to adopt a non-aggressive stance in response, and to avoid eye contact. More recently the growing familiarity of the term has occasioned some anxiety, in case the attribution of violent behaviour to *road rage* should seem to lessen the responsibility of the aggressor.

> Bad-tempered drivers are now suffering from Road Rage, and the next time someone beans a BMW driver with a tyre lever he'll be able to plead diminished responsibility and get off with a caution. —*Computing* 13 July 1995, p. 14

There's nothing new about road rage—people have been going berserk on the highway for generations. What is new is the expression itself, and it's an apt diagnosis. *Rage* is an old corruption of the Latin *rabidus*, which meant mad, applied to both dogs and humans; and road rage sufferers have lost their reason as well as their tempers.   —*Independent on Sunday* 13 Aug. 1995, p. 21

A driver was jailed for 18 months yesterday for a 'road rage' attack after which a pensioner died.   —*Guardian* 8 Dec. 1995, p. 4

Advice on how to deal with road rage is to be included in the new edition of the Highway Code in July. The increasing number of cars on the road and the growing evidence of stress lies behind the decision.   —*Daily Telegraph* 27 May 1996 (electronic edition)

rock /rɒk/ *noun* POP

In the slang of drug users, a crystallized form of cocaine which is smoked for its stimulating effects; an earlier name (especially on the west coast of the US) for CRACK. Also, a piece of crack in its prepared form, ready for smoking.

Named after its *rock*-like appearance and consistency.

The first recorded uses of *rock* date from the early seventies, but the word did not begin to appear in the newspapers or become known to the general public until the middle of the eighties. Then a number of west-coast newspapers reported raids on **rock houses** (the same as *crack houses*: see CRACK). By the mid eighties, *crack* had become established as the name for the drug itself, and *rock* seemed to be dying out in this sense, but it remained current as the name for a piece of the drug ready for smoking.

It's amazing now. You walk around Notting Hill or Stonebridge and you can hardly score ganja any more. All you see is rock and smack…There are certain geezers who go up to someone who's never touched it, give him a rock, and build him up 'til he gets a habit.
                                                       —*Sunday Correspondent* 8 Apr. 1990, p. 4

Rock houses—single-residence structures, stark and choked with filth, where rock cocaine, also known as crack, is sold and smoked—were springing up like weeds on otherwise nice neighborhood streets.   —Daryl F. Gates *Chief: My Life in the LAPD* (1992), p. 266

When he was arrested in March last year police recovered 54 'rocks' of crack.
                                                       —*Daily Telegraph* 30 Jan. 1995, p. 5

Rogernomics 〰️ 🗄 see -NOMICS

roid rage /'rɔɪd reɪdʒ/ *noun* ⊗

Heightened aggression towards others as a side-effect of taking anabolic steroids; an outburst of intense anger resulting from this.

Perhaps a conscious alteration of ROAD RAGE.

Instances of *roid rage* have been reported since the early nineties as one of the side effects of *steroid* ABUSE by athletes, especially bodybuilders: it appears that as well as increasing muscle size, **roids** (anabolic steroids) result in an excess of aggression.

'Roid rage', the heightened state of violent aggression induced by excess testosterone, is everywhere.   —Camille Paglia *Sex, Art, and American Culture* (1992), p. 81

Leigh documents the 'roid rages' of a man who, she says, is basically a bully.
                                                       —*Guardian* 17 July 1993, Weekend section, p. 9

Rollerblade /'rəʊləbleɪd/ *noun* Also written **Roller-blade**, **Roller blade**, and with a lower-case initial 🔀 ⊕

The trade mark for a type of roller-skate with wheels set in one straight line beneath the boot, giving an appearance and action similar to that of an ice-skate. The noun has given rise to the verb **rollerblade**: to roller-skate using skates of this type.

Formed after *roller-skate*, with the notion that the wheels form a *blade*.

Rollerblades, first sold commercially in the early eighties in the US and patented in January 1985, were devised as a means of training for ice hockey on dry land. However it was as an activity in its own right that **rollerblading** became popular in the late eighties. By the early nineties its popularity had soared and the manufacturers had begun to enjoy considerable commercial success. The majority of **rollerbladers** skate for fun, but they also *rollerblade* for exercise and as a means of transport. *Rollerblades* allow skating at great speed, and a *rollerblader* weaving between the cars is a not uncommon sight in the city streets of the nineties.

Although skates of this type are now produced by other manufacturers, the brand name *Rollerblade* has become a generic term. The shortened form *blades* for the skates and the verb *blading* and agent noun *blader* have been in widespread use since the early nineties. *Rollerblades* are also called *in-line skates* and the activity *in-line skating* or *street-skating*. In Britain, where London's Hyde Park is a popular venue for the sport, it is sometimes called *park-skating*. The manufacturers of *Rollerblades* have also developed an adaptable skate called the *Metroblade*, which incorporates a detachable *blade* section.

As the nineties have progressed increasing anxiety has been expressed about the dangers attached to *rollerblading*, both for the *bladers* themselves and for those whom they pass at great speed on pavements, in streets, or in parks.

> A college kid was skating across the four lanes of Mass. Ave. on Day-Glo-blue Rollerblades, wearing electric-camouflage harem pants. *—Atlantic* Sept. 1992, p. 70

> Late autumn might seem a strange time to go blading across the country.
> *—Gazette* (Montreal) 6 Nov. 1994, section A, p. 4

> I'm a community-health nurse, and I can't help thinking about the public-health implications of the in-line skating craze. Emergency rooms are now keeping track of injuries sustained by Rollerbladers, and the number is soaring. What about injuries to nonskaters caused by careless bladers? *—Newsweek* 31 July 1995, p. 16

> The rollerblade craze has taken a new turn in Brighton where people have been hanging on to cars to be towed along the seafront. Police have warned that the stunt—known as rollersurfing—is dangerous and illegal. *—Daily Telegraph* 25 Aug. 1995, p. 9

rolling news /'rəʊlɪŋ njuːz/ *noun* 🎛

A twenty-four-hour radio news service.

While the term is recorded since the early eighties, proposals in the UK for a *rolling news* service came to the fore after the Gulf War of 1991, during which almost continuous news broadcasts and assessments had been given. The idea has been particularly associated with the streamlined approach to news broadcasting associated with BIRTISM and the development of BIMEDIA: it has proved controversial, with doubts being expressed as to whether outside times of crisis enough 'hard' news would be available for the service to be worthwhile, and anxieties about resulting pressure on frequencies for other programmes surfacing. To date, *rolling news* has still to make its appearance in the UK.

> The strenuous debate over the BBC's plans for a rolling news radio service appears to have had a happy outcome or at least happier than might have been feared.
> *—Guardian* 15 Oct. 1993, section 2, p. 7

rollover /'rəʊləʊvə/ *noun* Also written **roll-over** 〰 📷 POP

The process whereby a jackpot which has not been won in the weekly draw of the National Lottery is carried over to the following week.

A specific use of an existing noun in the sense 'the extension or transfer of a debt or other financial relationship'.

The establishment of the British NATIONAL LOTTERY in November 1994 set up a number of conditions of practice. One of the more controversial of these has been the *rollover*, whereby, if there is no winner for a particular week, the prize money is added to the jackpot for the following week. The amount of money involved in the **rollover jackpot** thus created has been a particular factor in increasing existing anxieties about the size of lottery wins.

If there is no winner after a total of four roll-overs, then the accumulated jackpot will be shared among the next tier of winners—those who have matched five numbers plus the bonus number.

—*Daily Telegraph* 5 Dec. 1994, p. 1

The lottery is proving a serious affair—£5bn has been spent on tickets, since its launch in November 1994, and next week's rollover jackpot will be an estimated £20m.

—*Independent* 29 Dec. 1995, p. 1

Romo /'rəʊməʊ/ *noun*

A 1990s revival of the NEW ROMANTIC movement in pop music. Also, a follower of this.

Formed from a blend of the first syllables of *Romantic* and *Modernist*.

Romo is a development of the mid-nineties, and is characterized by music, especially of the electronic kind, inspired by that of the early 1980s. *Romos* who follow such music have adopted a flamboyant style of dress and make-up in keeping with the trend.

There is something uncannily similar in the way New Romantic was a reaction to the scruffiness of punk and the way Romos dismiss the Britpop bands as 'looking like a bus queue'.

—*Observer* 7 Jan. 1996, Review section, p. 9

Romo is a resuscitation of the New Romantic 'movement'—that golden age of tartan and peroxide before pop got a conscience.

—*The Times* 29 Jan. 1996, p. 15

rotating wall bioreactor ⚠ see BIOREACTOR

rotisserie /rə(ʊ)'tɪs(ə)ri/ *noun*

In the US: a game, originally using baseball statistics but now extended to other sports, in which participants create imaginary teams by 'buying' actual players and scoring points according to their real performances. Frequently used attributively in **rotisserie league**. (*Rotisserie Baseball League* and *Rotisserie Basketball League* are trade marks in the US.)

Apparently from the name *La Rotisserie*, a restaurant in Manhattan, New York City, where the league was devised.

Since the beginning of the eighties, *rotisserie* has gained in popularity in the US.

You may wonder just what this rotisserie craze is that has swept baseball fandom nationwide.

—*Fort Collins* (Colorado) *Triangle Review* 29 Apr. 1993, p. 23

The Fabulous Sports Babe knows everything about sports. This includes the ones she thinks are phony (fantasy football, rotisserie leagues).

—*San Francisco Chronicle* (Nexis) 21 Nov. 1996, section E, p. 7

See also FANTASY FOOTBALL

Route One /ruːt 'wʌn/ *noun* Also written **route one**

In British football, the use of a long high kick upfield as an attacking tactic.

Route One as an expression for 'the most direct route'; perhaps also with allusion to a BBC quiz show of the sixties, *Quizball*, where teams of footballers and other sports players could score a 'goal' by answering one hard question (*Route One*) or up to four correspondingly easier questions (*Routes Two* to *Four*).

Since the late eighties, *Route One* has been used attributively, and somewhat derogatorily, to denote a style of football which relies primarily on a long high kick upfield as an attacking tactic, rather than on silky and skilful interpassing.

My biggest disappointment is that we ended up playing 'route one' football in the last 20 minutes.

—*Today* Dec. 1992

router /'ruːtə; in the US 'raʊtə/ *noun*

An electronic device used to connect local area networks, or LANS, ensuring that messages are delivered to their intended destination by the most appropriate circuit.

Routers are sophisticated, and expensive, devices which actively manage the connections between local area networks. They direct network traffic by the most appropriate route (and can change the route if, for example, a circuit fails), can translate the format of messages to suit the needs of the networks on either side and can filter out unwanted messages according to pre-determined rules. The technique is called **routing**; messages which cannot be processed by a *router* are said to be **unroutable**.

> Cisco has launched a remote access router which is said to extend the enterprise internetwork to remote sites where true routing was previously too costly and too difficult to manage.
> —*Computer Weekly* 1 July 1993, p. 15

> There are access routers in branch offices and backbone routers in regional offices and central sites. —*Computer Weekly* 24 Feb. 1994, p. 32

RSI Ⓧ see REPETITIVE STRAIN INJURY

rubisco /rʊˈbɪskəʊ/ *noun* Also **Rubisco** or **RUBISCO** 🧪

A plant enzyme, ribulose 1,5-bisphosphate carboxylase, which catalyses the fixing of atmospheric carbon dioxide in photosynthesis, and also the oxygenation of the resulting compound in photorespiration.

A partial acronym, formed from the *r* and *u* of *ribulose*, the first three letters of *bisphosphate*, and the *c* and *o* from *carboxylase*.

If there is one substance which is vital to life on Earth, it is *rubisco*, because nearly all plants rely on photosynthesis to convert water, carbon dioxide, and sunlight into the chemicals of life. Oddly, it can also catalyse the opposite reaction that undoes photosynthesis; even though in higher plants the carbon fixing process is the more important, this makes photosynthesis inefficient. Since its identification in the early eighties, *rubisco* has been the subject of research to see if its efficiency could be improved or whether the reverse process might be suppressed. This could lead, by GENETIC ENGINEERING, to plants that were more productive.

> The Earth's most abundant enzyme, ribulose bisphosphate carboxylase, better known as rubisco, 'fixes' carbon dioxide by converting it to the reactive chemical 3-phosphoglycerate.
> —*New Scientist* 22 Dec. 1990, p. 12

> Ellis and his colleagues soon realised that the genes encoding rubisco were similar to the genes for a doughnut-shaped protein called GroEL, which is produced by many bacteria.
> —*New Scientist* 10 Dec. 1994, p. 27

RU-486 Ⓧ see ABORTION PILL, MIFEPRISTONE

• •

S

s- /s/ *prefix* 🧪

Identifying any one of a number of (so far not experimentally identified) sub-atomic particles which the theory of supersymmetry suggests are the boson equivalents of known fermion particles.

The first letter of *supersymmetry*.

Physicists from Einstein onwards have been attempting to link the four fundamental forces of nature—electromagnetism, the strong and weak nuclear forces, and gravity—as part of their attempt to create a comprehensive theory of the way the universe works (which physicists only slightly jokingly call a *Theory of Everything*). Cosmologists are also extremely interested in such a theory, as it could have profound implications for our understanding of the first few instants of time and space at the Big Bang, when the universe was created.

All sub-atomic particles have been divided into two types called bosons and fermions on the basis of their properties. In 1974, Julian Wess and Bruno Zumino proposed the supersymmetry theory, in which every one of these fundamental particles would have a counterpart of the other type.

In the early eighties, physicists had to find names for all these new particles; they adopted the convention that the boson equivalents of fermions had an initial *s*- added: the **selectron** is the boson analogue of the electron, the **squark** of the quark, the **slepton** of the lepton, and the **sneutrino** of the neutrino. More generally, such supersymmetric particles are called **sparticles**.

In supersymmetric theories, the spin-1/2 electron has a partner called the selectron.
—Richard Morris *The Edges of Science: Crossing the Boundary from Physics to Metaphysics*
(1990), p. 89

Calculations show that the presence of squarks and qluinos and all the other new particles required by supersymmetry would change the way that interaction strengths change with energy just enough to bring theory and experiment back into agreement.
—Steven Weinberg *Dreams of a Final Theory* (1993), p. 243

Supersymmetry predicted that every bosonic particle should have a supersymmetric twin: a sparticle.
—Stephen Baxter *Ring* (1994), p. 94

SAD Ⓧ see SEASONAL AFFECTIVE DISORDER

saddo /ˈsadəʊ/ *noun* POP

A person regarded as socially inadequate, unfashionable, or otherwise contemptible; a nerd.

Formed from *sad* in the slang sense 'socially inadequate, pathetic' and the suffix -*o* (used to form slang or colloquial variants or derivatives, perhaps originally representing a jocular use of the interjection *oh*).

Saddo made its appearance in the first half of the nineties as a derogatory term for someone regarded as socially inadequate or unfashionable. A *saddo* shares some of the nerdish characteristics of an ANORAK or a TRAINSPOTTER, but does not necessarily have the interest in or knowledge of technology which distinguishes the TECHIE.

It is now widely acknowledged (except by saddoes) that *Dr Who* stopped being good after Jon Pertwee in 1974.
—*New Musical Express* 9 May 1992, p. 60

Take to faxing your boyfriend instead of phoning him. Only saddos use phones.
—*Sugar* Nov. 1994, p. 36

He actually met his wife through CompuServe, but is not a saddo in spite of this.
—*.net* Dec. 1994, p. 68

What kind of finicky, diet-obsessed saddo would heed the frequent warnings printed in bold: 'The Chef may blaze cooked vegetables with butter. When ordering your vegetables please ensure you ask for NO added butter.'?
—*Independent on Sunday* 27 Aug. 1995, Reai Life section, p. 6

safe haven /seɪf ˈheɪv(ə)n/ *noun*

A protected zone in a country designated for members of a religious or ethnic minority.

The term *safe haven* in this specific sense came to public attention in the aftermath of the Gulf War of 1991, when (following further persecution) *safe havens* were established in northern Iraq for the Kurds, many of whom fled to Turkey and Iran after coming under attack by Saddam Hussein's troops. More recently, events in former Yugoslavia, and in particular the implementation of ETHNIC CLEANSING, caused *safe havens* to be proposed and set up by the United Nations for minority groups in particular areas; subsequent events demonstrated the practical difficulties of providing real protection for those seeking shelter in the designated **safe zones** or **safe areas.**

An abortive post-war uprising, and the terrified exodus that followed, persuaded the American-led alliance to set up a 'safe haven' for the Kurds in northern Iraq. —*Economist* 31 Oct. 1992, p. 17

Deployed nearly a month ago as a 'humanitarian mission', 2,500 French legionnaires and marines succeeded in establishing a safe zone in Rwanda's southwest. —*Time* 25 July 1994, p. 36

NATO warplanes yesterday buzzed Bihac, and only darkness and failure to find their targets prevented air strikes intended to silence Serb shelling of the 'safe haven'.
—*Star-Ledger* (Newark) 26 Nov. 1994, p.1

safe sex /seɪf 'sɛks/ *noun* Ⓧ ᴘᴏᴘ

Sexual activity in which precautions are taken to ensure that the risk of spreading sexually transmitted diseases (especially AIDS) is minimized.

The term *safe sex* (or **safer sex**, as some preferred to call it) arose in the early eighties, as first American society, and later other societies as well, started to face up to the threat of Aids and think of ways in which it might be controlled. Awareness was commonest at first in the gay community, but by the second half of the decade the message was being communicated to all sections of society through health advertising and the term had become common. The main elements of *safe sex* as highlighted in government advertising campaigns were avoidance of promiscuity (by having a single partner) and the use of a condom as a barrier to the exchange of 'body fluids' during intercourse.

Part-parody, part safe-sex education, her presentation uses a combination of home movies, slides, vignettes. —*Mediamatic* Summer 1990 (Edge 90: Special Issue), p. 230

John Bowis, the impressively girthed health minister, was in a Soho café for the launch of 'Cruise Cards', promoting 'safer sex'. —*Daily Telegraph* 20 Feb. 1995, p. 23

See also DENTAL DAM

safety abuse ⦃ see ABUSE

sampling /'sɑːmplɪŋ/ *noun* 🎝 📷

In electronic music, the technique or process of taking a piece of digitally encoded sound and re-using it, often in a modified form, as part of a composition or recording.

A specialized use of *sampling*, which would normally be used in the context of quality control or the taking of statistical samples.

Sampling became an important technique in musical composition (especially popular music) in the mid eighties, as a direct result of the advances in electronics and musical technology which followed from the development of the synthesizer. The music which developed from these techniques (including HOUSE and TECHNO) has a patchwork quality, since it is formed from many different sequences of modified sound. Since the end of the eighties, when the legal question of who owns the copyright for **sampled** music first hit the headlines, it has been a controversial issue for the music industry. Associated terms include **sample** (a noun and verb), the adjective *sampled* (used of a sound or a whole sequence of music), and the noun **sampler** (the electronic instrument—actually a musical computer—which is used to sample sounds).

Advanced Midi Amiga Sampler, High Quality Sound Sampler & Midi interface including all neces-sary Software…The sound is stunning, too. All effects are sampled, and very atmospheric.
—*CU Amiga* Apr. 1990, p. 43

Anyone can play instruments into the computer, recording each part one at a time, and seamlessly mix in digital samples from other people's recordings. Such 'sampling' is sometimes called creative recycling. —*Economist* 21 Dec. 1991, p. 16

Welcome to the brave new world of the Sample Police, an amorphous, ever-growing music patrol, most of whose members work for music publishers, record companies, or independent sample-clearance firms. —*Vibe* Fall 1992, Preview issue, p. 38

S & F 🐑 ᴘᴏᴘ see SEX AND SHOPPING

satanic abuse ⟨⟨ see ABUSE

SBS ⓧ see SICK BUILDING SYNDROME

scally /ˈskali/ *noun* ᴘᴏᴘ

A chancer, a rogue.

Formed as an abbreviation of *scallywag* in the same sense.

Scally as a term for a rogue or rascal originated in northern dialect, but is now moving into a more general slang use (although still particularly associated with the Lancaster and Liverpool areas).

A scally is one of the lads, a sexist, lazy, good-for-nothing. —*The Face* Feb. 1991, p. 38

With his Liverpudlian accent and exaggerated male swagger, Charles seemed to live up to his scally from the alley persona. —*Guardian* 4 Mar. 1995, p. 2

Maybe even *now* some rat-faced scally is flogging bits of what could have been *Brookside*'s storyline from a fly-by-night market stall. —*ikon* Jan. 1996, p. 45

SCART /skɑːt/ *acronym* Also written **Scart** or **scart** ⚗

A 21-pin connector used to send and receive video and audio signals between parts of a video system.

An acronym formed from the initial letters of *Syndicat des Constructeurs des Appareils Radiorécepteurs et Téléviseurs*, the European manufacturers' group which designed the connector.

With the growth in the seventies and early eighties in video equipment such as cassette recorders and cameras, the need was recognized for a connector which provided a comprehensive series of links between such components. The *SCART* connector format was agreed in the early eighties and is now standard on most television sets, video recorders, laser disc players, and satellite receiver decoders. It allows various formats of video and its associated stereo audio to be transmitted down one cable, together with control signals. The Pye and Philips companies called the connector the **Euroconnector** and this name is often used in Europe. Another name for it in Europe is the **Peritel** connector (French *Péritel*, from *péritélévision*), a word coined in the early eighties but now rarely used, which describes a piece of electronic equipment linked to a television set.

To play the sound through a stereo TV, you will need a SCART lead. —*Which?* Nov. 1991, p. 653

Those widescreen sets now in use can be either retro fitted with decoders or have a box plugged into their Scart sockets (a feature which should also ensure they'll be usable with any future digital transmission format). —*Television* June 1994, p. 20

Schengen /ˈʃɛŋ(ə)n/ *noun* 〰 📷

An agreement on border controls signed in Schengen, Luxembourg, in June 1985 by France, (West) Germany, Belgium, the Netherlands, and Luxembourg, and later by a number of other countries.

Relaxation of border controls among member countries is a key strategy of the EUROPEAN UNION, and was brought into effect by the **Schengen agreement** in 1985. Since then, *Schengen* has formed a number of compounds.

Signatories to the agreement, or **Schengen countries**, have developed the **Schengen Information System**, a computer network for criminal intelligence. The land area occupied by signatories to the **Schengen Treaty** may be regarded as a single **Schengenite** unit, or **Schengenland**, inhabited by **Schengenites**.

One reason why Italy is being gently debarred from the Schengen club is that its immigration laws are lax. —*Economist* 16 Sept. 1989, p. 56

A Schengen official said yesterday that the corollary of abolishing internal borders was the need to strengthen Schengenland's frontier with the rest of the world. —*Guardian* 8 Mar. 1995, p. 7

While the Schengen agreement is dismantling borders in Western Europe, they are avidly being restored all over the Baltics and CIS. —*Independent* 6 May 1995, p. 36

scratch card /'skratʃ kɑːd/ *noun* POP

A card with a section or sections coated in an opaque waxy substance which may be scratched away to reveal a symbol indicating whether a prize has been won in a competition.

Scratch cards were introduced in America in the early eighties, and have since become familiar both when sold as a gambling device (in Britain, particularly as linked to the NATIONAL LOTTERY, in the *Instants* game), and as a consumer incentive, when issued free.

He is proposing a form of telebingo involving scratch cards with winning numbers shown on screen during selected ad breaks. —*Independent* 12 May 1993, p. 17

screen saver /'skriːn seɪvə/ *noun* Also written **screen-saver**

A program which, after a set time, replaces an unchanging screen display with a moving image to prevent damage to the phosphor. Also, a graphics image displayed by such a program. The term is recorded from the beginning of the nineties.

Screen-saver programs protect your monitor's display by blanking the screen. —*Compute* Sept. 1993, p. 126

Enter the screen saver. It doesn't matter what it displays, as long as it's a moving image, so it doesn't damage that precious phosphor. —*Computing* 18 Nov. 1993, p. 11

The screen-savers include Hopping Elephants, Man With Baby Carriage and Queen Victoria. —*Guardian* 22 Sept. 1994, OnLine section, p. 7

scrollable /'skrəʊləb(ə)l/ *adjective*

Relating to text or images on a computer screen which can be moved to bring other parts of them into view.

The concept was originally that of a scroll of paper viewed as though through the screen, which could be progressively unrolled to bring other parts of it into view.

The root term *scroll* came into use in the early seventies, and was originally applied to text; early displays added new text at the bottom of the screen, moving up the text already there to make room. It was a considerable advance when systems were devised that permitted the user to reverse the process to see material which had vanished off the top of the screen. With the rise in the early eighties of displays that used graphical concepts to aid interaction with the computer, it was possible to permit scrolling from side to side as well as up and down; control of such *scrollable* material is usually by means of **scroll bars**: narrow bars located at the side of the display containing the image of a cursor or *thumb* which can be moved to control which part of the image or document is displayed.

The opening screen is taken up mostly by a blank page, edged by rulers and scroll bars. —*Personal Computer World* June 1992, p. 268

With a click on the remote control, viewers will be able to summon a pop-up vertical menu along the left side of the screen offering scrollable choices of interactive services. —*Wired* Dec. 1993, p. 132

SCSI /'skʌzi/ *acronym* Also written **scuzzy**

A standard method for connecting external or ancillary devices (disk drives, scanners, printers) to a computer system.

Formed from the initials of *Small Computer System Interface*: *small computer system* because it was originally designed to be used in personal computers, and *interface* in the standard computing sense of 'an electrical device that permits pieces of equipment to be connected together'.

The specification for *SCSI* was worked out during the early eighties and published as a US standard in 1986. Its original purpose was to provide a fast connection between computers and peripheral equipment (particularly disk drives) that would be independent of the type of computer system. Soon afterwards, additional features were added that permitted up to seven such devices to be connected in sequence to the one interface (a process called *daisy-chaining*), each separately accessible. The interface has become extremely popular in the nineties and, despite its name, is now commonly used in large systems with considerable amounts of storage. The various generations of the standard, which continues to evolve, are known by numerical suffixes: **SCSI-1**, **SCSI-2**, and **SCSI-3**. As is common with abbreviations, it has become a word in its own right with its original components forgotten, so that the phrase **SCSI interface** is now sometimes seen.

> SCSI is indeed a capable way of daisy-chaining up to seven intelligent peripherals to a computer, ranging from huge hard disk drives to DAT tape drives to printers to scanners.
> —*Computer Shopper* July 1993, p. 66

> Four SCSI devices, four separate SCSI cards, four slots, four IRQs, four DMA channels, four sets of ports, four levels of frustration. —*Computer Shopper* July 1993, p. 74

> You will have to get a SCSI-2 controller card. —*Electronic Musician* Oct. 1994, p. 71

SEAQ /'si:ak/ *acronym* Also written **Seaq** 〰

Short for *Stock Exchange Automated Quotation* system, a computer system for the display of share prices and transactions on the London Stock Exchange.

SEAQ was introduced by the Stock Exchange as part of the revolution in trading methods in 1986 usually called the *Big Bang*, in which trading moved away from the Stock Exchange floor to computer terminals in brokers' offices. Access to SEAQ is limited to firms called *market makers*, who must quote prices at which they will both buy and sell shares. Because dealings are prompted by responses to quoted prices, the *SEAQ* system is said to be *quote-driven*, as opposed to the *order-driven* system on some other stock exchanges. The trading system of *SEAQ* (and its counterpart, **SEAQ International**, which deals with foreign stocks) is said to have contributed greatly to that market's rapid growth, though a recent report has argued that the rules of access restrict competition.

> The Eurobond business ran off to London long ago. Since SEAQ International, the London Stock Exchange's automated quotation system for foreign shares, began 18 months ago to take more interest in Swiss equities, trading in Swiss shares has been leaving home too.
> —*Economist* 5 Oct. 1991, p. 114

> Less liquid companies which have only one market maker...do not qualify for a continuous quotation on SEAQ. —*Accountancy* Oct. 1993, p. 99

seasonal affective disorder /si:z(ə)n(ə)l əˌfɛktɪv dɪsˈɔːdə/ *noun phrase* Ⓧ

A depressive state associated with late autumn and winter and thought to be caused by a lack of light.

Seasonal affective disorder (abbreviation **SAD**) was identified in the early eighties. It comprises a form of depression which tends to occur during the same season (usually late autumn and winter) every year, and is characterized by loss of motivation, a tendency to sleep for abnormally long periods, and often a craving for foods rich in carbohydrates.

> Two-thirds of people who have a recently recognized syndrome, seasonal affective disorder (SAD), crave carbohydrates and gain weight when they are depressed.
> —*Scientific American* Aug. 1986, p. 57

> In the fall and winter Robert receives...two hours of light therapy daily to treat the seasonal

affective disorder.   —*Atlantic* Sept. 1992, p. 66

A real euphoria accompanies tanning beds. They're warm, comforting and produce the same effects as light therapy in seasonal affective disorder.

—*Independent* 22 Nov. 1995, section 2, p. 6

selectron 🜹 see s-

semi-skimmed /sɛmɪˈskɪmd/ *adjective* and *noun* ⊗ 🔀

adjective: Of milk: from which some but not all of the cream has been skimmed.

noun: Semi-skimmed milk.

In the early eighties, concerns about the ill effects of fat and cholesterol led to the commercial marketing of milk in which fat levels had been reduced. *Semi-skimmed* milk was developed as a product which is seen as healthier than *full cream* or *whole milk*, but which (unlike *skimmed milk*) has not reduced its fat content to the absolute minimum.

Semi-Skimmed has less than half the fat of whole milk.

—advertisement in *Reader's Digest* June 1990, p. 143

Semi-skimmed and skimmed milk contain just as much calcium as silver top (whole) milk, so you won't be losing out there either.   —*Slimmer* Dec. 1992, p. 93

Gold-top milk was once thought a luxury, but in 1993 sales were overtaken by skimmed and semi-skimmed.   —*Independent* 24 Nov. 1995, section 2, p. 8

serial killer /sɪərɪəl ˈkɪlə/ *noun* 🍴

A person who commits a series of similar murders with no apparent motive.

The notion of a murderer who commits a series of killings for no apparent motive other than his own satisfaction is well-established: the *Whitechapel murders* committed by *Jack the Ripper* in the late nineteenth century constitute an early and notorious example of **serial killings**.

The term *serial killer*, initially a technical term used in America by the Federal Bureau of Investigation, came to prominence in the eighties in the wake of a number of notorious cases, notably the crimes eventually traced to Theodore Bundy and John Wayne Gacy.

It is characteristic of the *serial killer* that he (rarely she) will carry out for his own gratification and over a period of time a number of killings using a similar method; typically, the victim will not come from the killer's personal circle, but will have been a stranger before being selected as a target. In the eighties the FBI set up an institution for PROFILING *serial killers*; this organization was brought famously to public attention by the fictional account given by the book (later an Oscar-winning film) *The Silence of the Lambs* by Thomas Harris.

Part of the calculated dementedness of the antisitcom *Married with Children* is the star family's surname, the same as that of notorious serial killer Ted Bundy.   —*ArtForum* Apr. 1990, p. 176

His homicidal heroes…technically straddle the boundary between what the FBI labels 'spree killers' and 'serial killers.'   —*Post* (Denver) 4 Sept. 1994, section F, p. 8

I re-visited the road at the time to co-write a book about the serial killer Charles Sobhtraj, who preyed on pot-trail stragglers, siphoning their passports and travellers cheques, while posing as their friend and drugging their chai.   —*Guardian* 20 May 1995, Weekend section, p. 55

Mass killings like Dunblane, he said had been split in recent years into three broad groups: mass murders, spree killings, and serial killings.   —*Independent* 14 Mar. 1996, p. 3

See also MISPER, SPREE KILLER

serial monogamy /sɪərɪəl məˈnɒɡəmi/ *noun* 🍴

A mode of life characterized by a sequence of monogamous affairs with different partners.

With a conscious allusion in the coinage to *serial killing*.

Serial monogamy, recorded from the beginning of the seventies, has been increasingly used in the eighties as the appropriate term to describe a lifestyle which provides for commitment to one sexual relationship at a time, but implies a regular change of sexual partner. A **serial monogamist**, while sleeping with a number of people, conducts each affair on the basis of some personal knowledge of the partner, and remains faithful to that partner during the lifetime of the relationship.

The public, of course, ate up this serial monogamy, though not uncritically.

—Premiere Mar. 1992, p. 104

But her problems really began when she embarked on a period of serial monogamy.

—Guardian 22 Jan. 1994, Weekend section, p. 9

While having a monogamous relationship is safer, the speakers warned students against 'serial monogamy' as a form of Russian roulette.　　*—Virginia Gazette* 21 Dec. 1994, section A, p. 3

server 🖳 see CLIENT-SERVER

set-aside /'sɛtəsʌɪd/ *noun* 🌱 〰

Land that has been taken out of agricultural production to reduce crop surpluses. Also, the policy that provides for this.

Set-aside as the term for a portion of land or produce reserved by government order for a special purpose has been current in the United States since the early forties. In the United Kingdom, however, the specific use of the term came to public notice in the eighties, in the context of attempts by the European Community to reduce such produce surpluses as the 'beef' and 'butter mountains' and the 'wine lake'. The policy involves the payment of subsidies to farmers for agreeing to take land out of cultivation. The result, while reducing the surplus, has been to generate debate: while there has been an agreed environmental benefit in terms of wildlife, some hostility has been shown towards what has been seen as paying for work not to be done; concerns as to non-agricultural uses of *set-aside land* for purposes such as HORSICULTURE have also been expressed.

Set-aside land—those sterile, bare acres that farmers have turned over to grass because Europe simply grows too much food.　　*—Country Living* Aug. 1990, p. 54

Local conservationists back the scheme, because at present the area is flat, college-owned land once intensively farmed but now put into set-aside.　　*—Independent* 2 Jan. 1992, p. 5

In preparation for tomorrow's European election, politicians of all parties have been wrestling with the intractable agricultural problem of 'set-aside'.　　*—Guardian* 8 June 1994, section 2, p. 7

[A farmer] has outraged his village neighbours with plans for a commercial 'green' cemetery offering environment-friendly burial in set-aside farmland.　　*—Independent* 5 May 1995, p. 4

set-top box /'sɛttɒp bɒks/ *noun* 〉〈 ⛏

A digital decoding device used to connect a domestic television set to a source of signals, such as a cable network or communications satellite.

A compound of the common phrase *set-top*, as in 'set-top aerial', with *box*, a general and often slightly dismissive term for any mysterious electronic device, as in *black box*. The partial rhyme and brevity of the phrase almost certainly contributed greatly to its acceptance, even though the unit is commonly placed under, and not on, the television.

This phrase, recorded from the early eighties, became increasingly common in the nineties, when cable operators and broadcasters had developed systems for transmitting digital television signals that needed to be decoded before they could be viewed on a conventional set. The boxes also frequently handled the decryption of pay channels. Other such devices, more formally known as *home communications terminals*, have been proposed to handle interactive viewing, such as HOME SHOPPING or *video*-ON-DEMAND, in which signals from the viewer must be passed back to the originators of the programmes.

Cable operators will install set-top boxes to convert compressed digital video to the analogue NTSC signals needed by existing TVs.　　*—New Scientist* 12 Mar. 1994, p. 18

These home communications terminals will soon feature robust graphics and full user interactivity as well as MPEG-based video, all controlled and managed by an open-architecture operating system running on a set-top box such as the one being developed by Power TV.

—Computer May 1995, p. 20

Will BSkyB build a proprietary system into the set-top box its viewers will buy, forcing them to acquire a second box if they want to receive the BBC's digital channels.

—Economist 11 May 1996, p. 33

sex and shopping /sɛks ənd ˈʃɒpɪŋ/ *adjectival phrase* Also written sex-and-shopping 🐿 ᴘᴏᴘ

A genre of popular fiction in which the characters enjoy a lifestyle characterized by glitzy commercial success and possession of the latest consumer goods, together with frequent and explicit sexual encounters.

Sex and shopping relies on blending the elements of commercial success and high fashion with scenes of explicit sexuality. *Sex and shopping* novels (often CELEBRITY NOVELS, and within the critical literary world more crudely described as **S & F**, for 'shopping and fucking') had their main success in the expansionist eighties; with the coming of the recession, much of their unquestioned bestseller status was relinquished to the more domestic world of the AGA SAGA.

She's [Julie Burchill] been contracted by Chatto's sister company, Bodley Head, for two S&F books. *—Blitz* Jan. 1989, p. 38

A Parliamentary Affair…reads like the dream diary of a provincial teenager who's overdosed on 'bonkbusters' and 'sex and shopping' novels. *—Guardian* 19 Jan. 1994, p. 18

Sex-and-shopping row: sequel looms. *—heading in Independent on Sunday* 7 Aug. 1994, p. 4

I'm not talking about people who write sex and shopping. *—Daily Telegraph* 20 Mar. 1995, p. 6

See also BONKBUSTER

sex-positive /sɛksˈpɒzɪtɪv/ *adjective* 🔀

Characterized by a positive attitude towards sexual instincts and desires.

Since the mid eighties, the term *sex-positive*, as indicating a positive attitude to sexual instincts and desires, has been increasingly used in the context of female sexuality; the extended compound **sex-positive feminist** has been recorded. The opposite of *sex-positive* is *sex-negative*.

The terms that [health care] people use these days about AIDS education…are *sex-negative* and *sex-positive*. We are very concerned about whether education encourages or accepts sexuality as a positive thing or whether it says DON'T DO THAT. *—Spin* Oct. 1989, p. 91

According to the artist, these are 'sex-positive' paintings about female desire. *—New Yorker* 11 May 1992, p. 14

A one-time anti-pornography activist…[she] eventually migrated to the 'sex-positive feminist' camp. Rather than damn pornography, she set out to improve it. *—Rolling Stone* 19 May 1994, p. 72

sexual abuse ⁅ see ABUSE

SGML /ˈɛsdʒiːɛmɛl/ *acronym* 🖵

A specification for tagging text stored on a computer in a generic format which separates the structure of the material from its intended appearance and identifies its elements in a way which can be analysed by computer.

An abbreviation of the initial letters of *Standard Generalized Markup Language*, with *markup* (also written *mark-up*) in the sense in which it is normally used in publishing, 'annotations made to text during editing as instructions to the typesetter', and *language* in the computing sense of 'a codified set of symbols and rules'.

SGML grew out of an American initiative in the late seventies which became an international standard in 1986. It is now used extensively in publishing to specify the nature of the various parts of the electronic text of a manuscript, and so indirectly to indicate how they should be printed. It is also employed widely in specialist applications such as databases, reference works, and product documentation, where the ability to code and so process elements of textual material in great detail is invaluable. An implementation of *SGML* forms the basis of the tagging of WORLD WIDE WEB documents through a scheme called HTML.

> The study predicts that the steady growth for SGML-based software is due in part to the shift toward electronic delivery of massive amounts of documentation required in manufacturing, military, telecommunications, and service fields. —*Byte* Mar. 1993, p. 32

> SGML tags and defines the content of information, transforming single, sprawling files into a series of manageable 'data objects.' —*Globe & Mail* (Canada) 28 Dec. 1993, section B, p. 10

> The book is coded in the Hypertext Mark-up Language, HTML, an extended multimedia version of the industry-standard SGML (Standard Generalised Mark-up Language). —*Guardian* 24 Mar. 1994, section 2, p. 19

shelfware 🖳 see -WARE

shift the goalposts 📰 see MOVE THE GOALPOSTS

shock jock /'ʃɒk dʒɒk/ *noun* 🐸 📰

A radio disc-jockey who is deliberately offensive or provocative.

A *jock* or *disc-jockey* who makes deliberate use of a *shock* effect.

The phenomenon of the *shock jock* developed in America in the second half of the eighties. *Shock jocks*, who quickly attained considerable notoriety, characteristically employ deliberate offence or provocation when dealing with controversial issues; being abusive to callers is also a feature of their programmes. *Shock jock* radio crossed the Atlantic in the nineties, but although it attained a high profile, the indications at present are that **shock-jockery** may be less to the British than the American taste.

> The airwaves bristle with the sexual dis of shock-jocks, stand-up sociopaths, metal marauders, and rough rappers. —*Village Voice* (New York) 16 Oct. 1990, p. 38

> Caesar is enjoying a burgeoning reputation as the British version of the American 'shockjocks', who have established themselves on naked confrontation and outrageous opinions, but he's at pains to point out that he isn't really like that at all. —*Guardian* 23 Jan. 1995, section 2, p. 12

> Shock-jockery was formally interred three months later with the September sacking of Terry Christian and Caesar the Geezer. Both had 'transgressed the standards of taste and decency expected by the public'. —*Independent* 12 Feb. 1996, section 2, p. 2

short sharp shock /ʃɔːt ʃɑːp 'ʃɒk/ *noun phrase* 🗝 🍴

A regime intended to deter by the immediate impact of its severity.

The term is recorded from the end of the fifties, but in the UK attained a high profile in the early eighties. A recommendation of a regime that would present a *short sharp shock* to young offenders, with consequent deterrent effect, was put to the Conservative Party Conference by the then Home Secretary, William Whitelaw, in October 1979. The *short sharp shock* regime, which typically features a tough military-style discipline, soon became a staple of the law and order debate, but there has been increasing scepticism as to its ability to reduce the likelihood that those subjected to it would reoffend.

Use of the term has now broadened somewhat to include any punitive measure intended to make an immediate impact on the person to whom it is administered.

New Hall and Send detention centres, formerly the homes of the notorious short, sharp shock experiments have become respectively a women's prison and a training prison for men.

—Vivien Stern *Bricks of Shame* (1987), p.27

The detention centre is meant to be a short sharp shock.   —*Independent* 26 Feb. 1993, p. 13

short-termism /ʃɔːt'tɜːmɪʒ(ə)m/ *noun* ⟋

Concentration on short-term projects for immediate profit at the expense of long-term security.

Short-termism is recorded from the mid eighties as a largely critical term for economic and managerial practices which are seen to provide immediate but ephemeral benefits at the expense of long-term security. **Short-termists** are seen by their critics as those who deliberately pursue short-term rewards through **short-termist** policies which cannot provide the necessary basis for long-term economic recovery.

The growing friction between industry and the City over the alleged 'short termism' of financial institutions' investment attitudes.   —*Independent* 12 Nov. 1986, p. 18

There has been talk of BTR floating off its US interests…This appears short-termist and fraught with tax and US legislative hurdles.   —*Observer* 25 Nov. 1990, p. 26

Shuttle, le ✖ see LE SHUTTLE

sibling abuse ⦃⦄ see ABUSE

sick building syndrome /sɪk 'bɪldɪŋ ˌsɪndrəʊm/ *noun phrase* ⊗

The set of adverse environmental conditions found in a building in which the environment is a health risk to its occupants, especially because of inadequate ventilation or air conditioning; also, the set of symptoms (such as headaches and dizziness) experienced by the people who live or work there.

There is both a figurative and an elliptical quality to the use of *sick* here: architects and designers try to treat the symptoms caused by poor design, although it is not the *building* that is *sick*, but the people who use it.

Architects first wrote about large, centrally ventilated buildings as *sick buildings* in the early eighties and the set of vague symptoms suffered by people who used such buildings had become known as *sick building syndrome* by 1983. Commonly reported symptoms included headaches, dizziness, nausea, chest problems, and general fatigue; most could be attributed to poor air quality or actual air pollution within the building. By the nineties, architects were beginning to design low-rise, naturally ventilated offices that avoided the problem. The term is sometimes abbreviated to **SBS**.

Airtight and chemical-laden, office environments may cause 'sick building syndrome', a condition characterized by fatigue, nausea, and respiratory illness.   —*Garbage* Nov. 1990, p. 43

The Inland Revenue plans to move 2,000 workers out of the block in Bootle, Merseyside, which is allegedly suffering from sick building syndrome.   —*Guardian* 1 Apr. 1995, p. 2

sig /sɪg/ *noun* ▣

Text at the end of an e-mail message or similar online communication identifying or giving information about the writer, often in an individualistic way.

The first three letters of *signature*.

Since the early days of online communications, users have been ornamenting their electronic signatures—normally appended automatically to the end of messages by their mailing software—with quotations, personal information, or pictures painstakingly drawn using standard text characters. Because the file containing a person's *sig* message on Unix systems is called **.sig** (said as 'dot sig') this form of the term is often used; as it is appended as a *block* of text, the term **sig block** is also common. Opinions are mixed about these expressions of the writer's personality, some considering they enliven NET culture, others feeling they are unnecessary and a nuisance, particularly if they are large.

> The composition of one's sig can be quite an art form, including an ASCII logo or one's choice of pithy sayings; but many consider large sigs to be a waste of bandwidth, and it has been suggested that the size of one's sig block is usually inversely proportional to one's longevity and level of prestige on the net. —Eric S. Raymond (ed.) *The New Hacker's Dictionary* 1993, p. 376

> Load up one of the .vew files, type in your .sig in the message area and then save the .vew file to your custom views directory. —15 Mar. 1996, online posting

SIMM /sɪm/ *acronym* Also written **Simm** or **simm** 🖳

A small printed circuit board containing one or more random-access memory chips, designed to be easily installed into a computer.

Formed from the initial letters of *Single In-line Memory Module*: *single* to emphasize that the circuit board is a single unit, regardless of the number of memory chips it actually holds; *in-line* referring to the practice of placing the chips in a row on the circuit board; and *module*, 'a standardized part or independent unit'.

Since the late eighties *SIMMs* have become the standard way of installing the working memory of a computer. The system was designed to make such installation easy for non-specialists: the modules are small and clip into sockets. Unfortunately, it also makes them extremely easy to steal: following a sudden rise in price of memory chips in the mid nineties because of shortages, many large companies were systematically raided to steal the *SIMMs* from their computers.

> Depending on its design, one SIMM can represent 256K, 1MB or 4MB of memory. After installing four 4MB SIMMs, you would have a total of 16MB of working memory or RAM.
> —*New Jersey Computer User* Jan. 1994, p. 7

> One Simm module—the size of your little finger—is worth up to £200, bears no means to identify it, and can be removed or inserted in a matter of seconds. —*Independent* 24 Apr. 1995, p. 15

single currency /ˈsɪŋg(ə)l kʌr(ə)nsi/ *noun* 🗞 📧

A unified currency proposed for the use of all member states after the economic and monetary union of Europe.

The concept of a *single currency*, as replacing the former national currencies of member states, has always been central to plans for a EUROPEAN UNION, and has always been a focus for controversy. More narrowly, this has centred on the choice of names for the future European currency units (EURO being agreed in December 1995 for the note, and CENT in April 1996 for the coin), but increasingly the *single currency* has come to symbolize the whole question of the relationship between national sovereignty and economic and monetary union.

> His downbeat judgment pleased some MPs who share his doubts about the wisdom of a European central bank and single currency by the late 1990s. —*Guardian* 13 May 1991, p. 1

> The Maastricht treaty already implies a multi-speed Europe in its progress towards a single currency. —*Independent* 29 Oct. 1992, p. 26

> Germany has always bought into the idea of the single currency and the almost inconceivable abandonment of the mark mainly as the price for political union.
> —*The Times* 25 Sept. 1995, p. 42

-size /saɪz/ *suffix* 🖳 🗞

Used in a variety of compounds relating variously to a physical change in size (of a product), a change in the number of employees in an organization, or an alteration in the size and nature of computer systems.

The first formation in *-size* was the verb **downsize**, employed from the mid seventies to refer specifically to the process of making cars smaller; it has more recently been used in other literal contexts. From the late eighties onwards it has taken on two other meanings. One is to make an organization leaner and more efficient by reducing the number of its employees (the term quickly became regarded as a euphemism for 'dismissal' or 'redundancy'). The other is in computing, in which it relates to the transfer of computer applications from a larger machine, particularly a mainframe, to a smaller one, such as one of a network of personal computers or workstations. The related action noun is **downsizing** and the adjective is **downsized**. In the late eighties the verb **rightsize** appeared, and quickly took on a euphemistic sense in business similar to that of *downsize*; from the early nineties, it has also been used in computing to refer to the process of choosing the most appropriate computer architecture for the job in hand, rather than just assuming that *downsizing* was the solution. **Upsize**, referring to the movement of applications or databases from a smaller system to a larger one, is occasionally found, almost always in computing contexts.

> As downsized companies seek temporary help to fill in where ousted employees have left gaps, temping and consulting have boomed. —*U.S. News & World Report* Nov. 1991, p. 66

> That the economy is unable to absorb these job-seekers shows an economy struggling to recover from recession, still hamstrung by continuing layoffs, restructurings and downsizings by companies trying to slim down even further. —*Bottom Line Personal* 30 July 1992, p. 5

> The theory of downsizing—transferring processing from expensive centralised processors to cheap desktop machines—seems simple enough. But the practicalities and issues surrounding its implementation are frequently complex. —*Computer Weekly* 19 Nov. 1992, Supplement, p. 7

> The East Dyfed Health Authority has benefited from upsizing its patient administration system to a client-server environment. —*Computing* 9 Sept. 1993, p. 11

> The group expects to save $5 million annually by consolidating operations now spread across 11 buildings in suburban Monrovia into a single Seattle facility and 'rightsizing' the employee count from 525 to 400. —*Christianity Today* 25 Apr. 1994, p. 45

sizeism ⦃ see -ISM

sizeist ⦃ see -IST

skell /skɛl/ *noun* ⦃

In New York, a homeless person or derelict, especially one who sleeps in the subway system.

Perhaps formed as a shortening of *skeleton*.

Skells are one example of what is recognized as a growing trend of the eighties and nineties: an increasing number of homeless people living rough in urban environments.

> Other New Yorkers live there…eating yesterday's bagels and sleeping on benches. The police in New York call such people 'skells'. —*New York Times Magazine* 31 Jan. 1982, p. 21

> The delirious, crazy people whom cops call 'skells', the down-and-outs, the grungy and hopeless, garbage-heads who use any foreign substance known to man to alter reality. —*Newsday* (New York) 22 Feb. 1988, p. 6

skimmed ⊗ ✗ see SEMI-SKIMMED

slacker /'slakə/ *noun* ⦃

A person regarded as being one of a large group of people, especially the current generation of young adults, who are perceived to lack a sense of direction in life.

The word *slacker*, 'a shirker, an indolent person', was used in Richard Linklater's film *Slackers* (1991) to denote a former student who is unable to move beyond the student lifestyle and who has no apparent career aspirations; such a person is likely to have a dead-end job or no job at all. This very quickly became a popular notion and *slacker* in this sense has gained rapidly in currency as the nineties have advanced, applied not only to former students but in general to young people who lead apparently unmotivated lives. *Slackers*, as a phenomenon of the late twentieth century, form a part of GENERATION X. As a generation they are perceived to have been lulled into political and cultural apathy by the products of capitalism and by continuous television entertainment such as that provided by MTV. It might also be acknowledged that they have become young adults at a time of recession and shrinkage of the job market, in contrast to the *drop-outs* of the sixties with whom they might be compared. The *twenty-nothings* and *twentysomethings*, they are felt to have considerably lower expectations than had the two preceding generations, the *thirtysomethings* and the *baby boomers*. The term **slacker beat** has been used in music to denote a dissonant and aimless sound. The culture associated with *slackers* is known as the **slacker culture** or **slackerdom**, and the language **slackerspeak**.

The year began with 'Loser' Beck's slacker anthem of self-loathing.
—*Post* (Denver) 18 Dec. 1994, Magazine, p. 6

The tone is set by graphic artists and wannabe musicians and common-or-garden slackers off to drink great cheap beer on Dad's money. —*Wired* Jan. 1995, p. 104

'It's certainly a reaction to the slacker thing, which was so "anti-style",' says Paul Tunkin, promoter of the London club Blow Up. —*Guardian* 20 Jan. 1995, Friday, p. 7

This is anti-Slacker culture—camcorder and karaoke, mobile phone and electronic organiser—in all its lethargic, tedious detail. —*Empire* May 1995, p. 50

slam dancing /'slam dɑːnsɪŋ/ *noun*

A form of dancing to rock music in which participants deliberately collide violently with one another.

Dancing in which participants *slam* into each other.

Slam dancing (originally associated particularly with punk rock concerts) is, like *moshing* (see MOSH) and STAGE-DIVING, a phenomenon of the eighties and nineties rock scene, in which involvement and appreciation are expressed through violent activity. The essential emotion in those who choose to **slam dance** or **slam** is enthusiasm rather than aggression, but the forcible contact during a **slam dance** with other **slam dancers** or **slammers** carries with it the risk of damage as well as intrusion into another's personal SPACE.

For most girls, it was virtually impossible to see a band at a hardcore show because the front of the stage was dominated, always, by muscular, lean, sweaty boys stage-diving and slamming around. —Donna Gaines *Teenage Wasteland* (1990), p. 200

Now that Nirvana has brought slam-dancing to MTV, the mosh pit is getting a lot of attention.
—*Option* July 1992, p. 31

The clientele...includes a disproportionate number of green-Mohawk-coiffed, body-pierced, leather-clad slam dancers. —*Globe & Mail* (Toronto) 14 June 1994, section A, p. 3

slaphead /'slaphɛd/ *noun*

In slang: a bald or shaven-headed person.

Perhaps with the notion that the *head* can be *slapped* directly without the protection of hair (the term *slap head* as school slang for a fashionable flat-top haircut was noted in the mid eighties).

Slaphead emerged in the nineties as a slang (and chiefly derogatory) term for someone who, either through natural hair-loss or by fashion choice, has very short hair or very little hair. The adjective **slapheaded** and the noun **slapheadedness** have also been recorded.

The current rage in London, Paris, Berlin and New York is the Slaphead look...A Slaphead is someone (and there are no gender-based limitations here) who is bald either by nature or by choice—yes, by choice! —*Gazette* (Montreal) 16 July 1991, section F, p. 2

He carried out the robbery to pay for his £5,000 hair transplant. The judge gave him a lenient one year sentence: no doubt he thought that for such a young man, the stigma of slapheadedness could provoke temporary insanity. —*Independent on Sunday* 18 Sept. 1994, p. 22

You thought technoheads all lived in space podules and fusewire-filled bedrooms. Let the slap-headed vegan bleep merchant prove you wrong. —caption in *Select* Mar. 1995, p. 108

Attention British hair loss sufferers! This amazing new technique developed in North Shields will end your slaphead nightmare forever. —advertisement in *FourFourTwo* Oct. 1995, p. 24

slapper /'slapə/ *noun* POP

In slang: a contemptuous term for a woman regarded as promiscuous, a tart.

Probably formed from the verb *slap* (*slapper* is recorded in dialect use with the sense 'a big, strapping woman'); it has also been suggested that the word may represent an alteration of *schlepper* (of Yiddish origin) 'a worthless person'.

Slapper as a derogatory term for a promiscuous woman, especially one who is no longer young, has been current since the beginning of the nineties.

A real old slapper!...Like a 32-year-old...one of your mum's old mates who always used to come round your house when you were young and you always fancied her and she starts coming on to you later. —*New Musical Express* 10 Oct. 1992 (BNC)

Good looking, affluent male, 30, seeks beautiful, well-educated, old slag/slapper, 21–35. —*Time Out* 31 Mar. 1993, p. 130

She was...wearing a very short skirt. If I'd have done that, everyone would have said, 'Oh, look at that old slapper!' —*Observer* 19 Mar. 1995, p. 34

slash /slaʃ/ *noun* POP

A genre of popular fiction, chiefly published in fanzines, in which male characters who form an established partnership are portrayed as having a homosexual relationship. It is frequently used attributively, as in **slash fiction**.

Formed from *slash* 'an oblique printed stroke, /' used between the adjoining names or initials of the characters concerned, as in 'Kirk/Spock'.

While semi-serious suggestions that a romantic relationship might exist between two bonded male characters are far from new, *slash* as a genre seems to have originated among fans of the sixties science-fiction series *Star Trek*, in stories centring on the relationship between Captain Kirk and Mr Spock (*K/S* is an alternative name for the genre). Discussions of **slash fiction**, and the **slash zines** in which such stories typically appear, occur in accounts of science fiction and fanzines from the early nineties.

Slash fiction is written mostly by women, to the intense disgust of many straight men and to the amusement of the gay community. —R. Rogow *FutureSpeak* (1991), p. 313

She said that 1967 marked the debut of 'slash zines', named for their generic label, 'K/S', which refers to the names of Captain Kirk and Mr Spock, who always have sex in them. —Jane & Michael Stern *Encyclopedia of Popular Culture* (1992), p. 481

Consider the case of so-called slash lit, amateur fan magazines in which fans imagine explicitly romantic and sexual relationships between male characters in the popular media. —Marjorie Garber *Vice Versa* (1995), Introduction, p. 32

slaughter /'slɔːtə/ *transitive verb* POP

To criticize with great severity.

A figurative use of the sense 'to kill in a ruthless manner or on a great scale'; perhaps also coloured by an earlier figurative use, 'to defeat utterly'.

In the nineties this sense of *slaughter* has gained some currency. The notion is one of making a severe and stringent criticism of a person or organization in response to the perceived infraction of some standard or rule; there is often also an implication that the severity of treatment of the offender may include the imposition of penalties. A person who has been

slaughtered is one who has been subjected to so comprehensive a criticism as to be effectively defenceless against it.

ICI was hit here recently by a broker cutting estimates, and in New York Phillip Morris was slaughtered for a minor blip in its 20 per cent growth rate.

—*Investors Chronicle* 23 Oct. 1992, p. 6

Oh no…wait! You can't put that, I'll get slaughtered, I didn't mean it.

—*90 Minutes* 15 Apr. 1995, p. 41

After the first death the coroner slaughtered us. He likened us to a mafia operation and said that we were openly selling drugs.   —*Mixmag* May 1995, p. 86

sleazebag /'sliːzbag/ *noun*

A sordid or despicable person, especially someone considered morally reprehensible.

A number of compounds based on *sleaze* 'squalor, sordidness' were coined in the US during the early eighties. These include the approximately synonymous *sleazebag* and **sleazeball**, and SLEAZE FACTOR.

The most conspicuous sexual harassers…are obviously outrageous sleazeballs.

—*New York Times* 15 Oct. 1991, section C, p. 13

My guess is that the FDA finally caught up with the sleazebag from Oxnard who was fronting the operation and nailed him with a cease and desist.

—Armistead Maupin *Maybe the Moon* (1992), p. 4

sleaze factor /'sliːz faktə/ *noun* 📁 POP

The sleazy or sordid aspect of a situation, especially as involving politics.

Sleaze factor was applied initially, in US politics, to scandals and alleged corruption involving officials of the Reagan administration. The term was coined by American journalist Laurence Barrett, as a chapter heading in his book *Gambling with History*; it remained current throughout the Reagan administration and became a familiar expression which was also used to describe political events outside the US. In the UK in the late eighties and nineties it has been applied to a number of scandals, resignations, and instances of alleged malpractice associated with successive administrations, such as the *cash for questions* affair, in which certain MPs admitted to having accepted money for asking specified questions in the House of Commons.

For a presidency that prides itself on the ethics of its personnel even the appearance of a 'sleaze factor' is awkward.   —*Guardian* 23 Oct. 1994, p. 14

Although Tory disunity and uncertainty about Britain's economic prospects are undoubtedly the main reasons underlying voter discontent with the Government, the 'sleaze factor' is almost certainly making an independent contribution.

—*Daily Telegraph* 9 June 1995 (electronic edition)

sleep mode /'sliːp məʊd/ *noun* 💻

In computer jargon, a state of a computer system in which only those parts of it needed to respond to some external stimulus and return the remainder to full operational status are supplied with electrical power.

Because of the limited energy capacity of their batteries, it has been common since the late eighties for portable computers to contain circuitry that switches them into a standby state if they have not been used for a pre-determined period of time; the only circuit remaining active is one which monitors external activity (such as the user pressing a key) which restores the system to its active state. Fuelled by a mixture of environmental concern and by organizations' worries about the high energy costs of maintaining large numbers of computers in full readiness at all times, manufacturers began in the early nineties to incorporate similar circuits in mains-powered computers, workstations, and monitors.

Another portable [computer] feature that is migrating to the desktop is power management—or 'sleep mode' capability—which produces substantial savings for PCs that are turned on but are not in use. —*New York Times' Review of Computers* 8 Nov. 1992, p. 22

These PCs incorporate a number of the energy-saving features of laptop computers, including a flat-panel display and an automatic sleep mode that powers down to less than 20 watts when the computer isn't in use. —*Compute* Oct. 1993, p. 42

To combat this power drain, the AT&T hardware used in the AT&T, DEC, and Solectek adapters has a 'sleep mode' option that stops power consumption except when sending or receiving data. —*Data Communications International* 21 Mar. 1995, p. 80

slepton 🧪 see s-

slice-and-dice /ˈslʌɪsən(d)dʌɪs/ *noun* 💻 🍴

The process of assembling something by cutting down and reshaping sections of a larger whole. It is often used attributively, as in **slice-and-dice capability**.

A figurative use from the idea of food preparation in which raw ingredients are *sliced* and *diced* into the required shapes and sizes.

This application of *slice-and-dice* has been current since the early nineties, and is now particularly associated with electronic management of data. In this area the term is a favourable one, but the idea of quick preparation of given ingredients may in some contexts carry a more critical implication of the mechanical assembly of processed elements.

The inevitable slice-and-dice cliches continue unabated. —*Syracuse New Times* 11 Nov. 1992, p. 16

Borland and Microsoft offer similar slice-and-dice functionality where any spread sheet enthusiast would really need it. —*Byte* Dec. 1993, p. 144

However, other products also lay claim to some of the slice-and-dice capability in which OLAP products excel. —*Accountancy* Nov. 1995, p. 72

smart /smɑːt/ *adjective* 💻 🧪

Of a machine: able to react to different conditions; computerized, intelligent. Of a drug: capable of increasing intelligence.

A figurative use of *smart* in the sense 'clever'.

The first use of *smart* in this sense was in the term **smart bomb**, dating from the early seventies, referring to the concept of a radio- or laser-guided weapon which could home in accurately on a target; the phrase received considerable exposure during the Gulf War of 1991. Such guided munitions are also known generically as **smart weapons**. As part of the US Strategic Defense Initiative (the 'Star Wars' programme) it was proposed in 1988 that small missiles code-named **smart rocks** could be used to fight off an attack.

From the beginning of the eighties, *smart* became a fashionable marketing word for anything with a hint of intelligent control. The **smart card** is a plastic bank card or similar device with an embedded microprocessor, holding personal data or financial information. A **smart building**, or **smart house**, is one with a central computer providing integrated control of environmental services such as heating. A **smart car** is able to locate itself automatically through guidance signals received from the roadside. **Smart phones** provide computerized facilities for automatic dialling, network connections or identification of incoming calls. A **smart highway** (or **smart road**) is one which monitors traffic flows and provides feedback to motorists.

It has been suggested that certain compounds, named *nootropics* in the seventies, could be used to improve human memory or increase intelligence; much pharmaceutical research has been directed at finding them. Such *cognitive enhancers* are commonly called **smart drugs**. They became very fashionable in the late eighties and nineties; in the form of **smart pills** or **smart drinks**, they were even dispensed at clubs and other functions from a **smart bar**.

A new generation of 'smart phones' with built-in computers, screens, and modems will soon let our fingers do the banking, the bill-paying, and the shopping. —*Discover* Dec. 1991, p. 76

Orotic acid is now included in the lengthy list of 'smart drugs' and 'cognitive enhancers' that are increasingly found on sale in the less scrupulous 'health food' stores, despite the lack of evidence for either their need or their effect. —Steven Rose *The Making of Memory* (1992), p. 192

On the other side of the door is...the Smart Bar, which sells an enigmatic selection of 'nutrient' cocktails and 'cognition-enhancing' pills: Razzo Blast, Tootsie Roll, X-Tra's, Party Pilz and, for a special 'mental and sensory charge', Smart Navel. —*New Scientist* 17 Apr. 1993, p. 20

So far, nobody actually lives in a smart house. —Kevin Kelly *Out of Control* (1994), p. 168

SME /ˈɛsɛmiː/ *acronym* 〰️

A business which is regarded as small or medium-sized by virtue of its turnover or number of employees; the commercial sector consisting of such firms.

The initial letters of *Small (and) Medium-size Enterprise(s)*.

The abbreviation came to public notice in the early nineties at a time when greater recognition was being given to the important role played in commerce by smaller firms. For example, the EUROPEAN UNION has launched a six-year scheme called the **SME initiative** to help firms employing fewer than 250 people, and with an annual turnover of less than £15 million, to take advantage of Europe's single market and to gain international competitiveness.

SME account for 94 per cent of employment in the important wood and cork industries, and in the food, drink and tobacco sector.
—*Geographical Magazine* Feb. 1991, Analysis education supplement, p. 5

Nowhere has the failure to address properly what defines the needs of an SME been so marked as in the question of funding requirements, particularly during the argument about the benefit of short-term versus long-term funding. —*Guardian* 11 July 1994, section 1, p. 12

Micro businesses are usually too small for the SME lobby to worry about, but deserve more attention. —*The Times* 25 Sept. 1995, p. 42

smiley /ˈsmʌɪli/ *noun* 🖳 POP

More fully **smiley face** or **smiley badge**: a round cartoon-style representation of a smiling face (usually black on yellow), used as a symbol of the drug culture, especially in connection with *acid* HOUSE.

In online usage: a representation of a face created out of text characters, used to indicate emotion in e-mail messages.

Formed by abbreviating *smiley face* to its first word and treating this as a noun.

The black-on-yellow *smiley* first appeared as a hippie symbol of peace and happiness in the early seventies and enjoyed a revival in the US (especially in California) later in the decade, but it was really its association with *acid house*, and in particular the suggestion that it was being used as the symbol of drug users, that brought it into the news in the late eighties. The *smiley* symbol has also been used in ways that are unconnected with drugs: for example, it was used for the 'Glasgow's Miles Better' promotion in 1983 and it was the official symbol of the Lord Mayor of London's theme 'Service with a Smile' in 1985–6.

In the early eighties, the name began to be applied in electronic mail and other online communications to a shorthand representation of a smiling face formed from text characters. This and other representations are also known as *emoticons* (from *emotion* combined with *icon*). Dozens of *smileys* have been invented, but representations of frowning, quizzical, and smiling faces are the most common.

Acid house fashion, modeled after punk's once-vogue wardrobe of combat boots and camouflage pants, mixes paisley head scarves, RayBans and torn jeans with the mainstay smiley face.
—*American Speech* Vol. 66, No. 3, 1991, p. 318

But irony, misunderstood, easily bursts into flaming, so a whole subculture of typographical 'emoticons' or 'smileys'…has sprung up to signpost the jokes, followed by a sub-sub-culture which eschews emoticons as a sign of lazy and inadequate use of language.

—*Independent on Sunday* 16 Jan. 1994, p. 22

smoke and mirrors /'sməʊk ən(d) mɪrəz/ *noun phrase* Also written smoke-and-mirrors

An explanation or demonstration which is essentially deceptive; something fraudulent or insubstantial.

Smoke and mirrors as used by a conjuror to create an effect.

Since the beginning of the eighties, *smoke and mirrors* has been used as an image of something not only inherently insubstantial, but also typically involving an intent to deceive through an impressive appearance. The growing use of the phrase may reflect growing public awareness of the techniques of news management.

The lengthy, expensive prosecution was a smoke-and-mirrors job, and Stone appears to know it. —*New Yorker* 13 Jan. 1992, p. 75

In January, 1992, deeply concerned about a flood of stories questioning its condition, O&Y released its own flood of financial information. But the move backfired. It missed out on the details people needed to know. It looked like smoke and mirrors. —*Saturday Night* Feb. 1993, p. 14

The grandstanding of Congress, claiming taxpayer money will no longer fund these types of caucuses, is in fact so much smoke and mirrors. —*New Jersey* Apr. 1995, p. 89

smoker /'sməʊkə/ *noun*

A vent in the ocean floor at great depth from which erupts a plume of superheated seawater, rich in minerals.

The name derives from the nature of the plume, which is opaque and looks like the *smoke* from a factory chimney.

Smokers are formed at ridges deep in the oceans where the plates of the Earth's crust are moving apart, allowing molten rock to escape through cracks to form underwater lava flows and volcanoes. Seawater, under immense pressure at these depths, penetrates the cracks. It is heated in contact with the rock, dissolves minerals from it and is then forced back up into the sea, where the water cools and the dissolved minerals come out of solution, forming a dense cloud. The colour of the *smokers* depends on the type and amount of the dissolved minerals and they are called more specifically **black smokers** or **white smokers**. The *smokers* excited the scientific community in the late eighties when it was discovered that bacteria lived near them, feeding off the minerals and obtaining energy from the hot water. A whole ecosystem of animals was found to live on these bacteria. Such ecosystems are unique because they exist independently of the heat from the sun that sustains all other living things on the planet.

At white smokers little sulphide material is discharged, and the main precipitate is barite.
—Philip Kearey & Frederick Vine *Global Tectonics* (1990), p. 265

He saw colonies of bacteria living off a 'black smoker' and off these live blind shrimps, giant clams, tubeworms; weird creatures that live where there are no riverine nutrients, no daylight, no seasons. —*Guardian* 14 Oct. 1993, p. 12

snack abuse Ⓧ see ABUSE

snail mail /'sneɪlmeɪl/ *noun* Also written snail-mail and snailmail

A mocking or sarcastic slang term for the ordinary postal system, emphasizing its slowness compared to electronic mail; a communication sent by conventional post.

Snail, as the type of something very slow, presumably also chosen for its rhyme with *mail*.

The term *snail mail* has undoubtedly been in use among various online communities for more than a decade, though nobody seems to know who coined it or when. It is now common on the INTERNET and in other electronic forums and has begun to appear in printed sources; it is sometimes employed as a verb in the form **snailmail** and as an adjective **snailmailed**.

> The cost of e-mail is an advantage that increases in importance as the cost of snail-mail and the more expensive delivery services...increase. —*Whole Earth Review* Summer 1991, p. 8

> The editorial/letters page doesn't admit to more than a snail mail address, while I have to read the small print...to find fax (and telex) numbers! —*Guardian* 23 June 1994, OnLine section, p. 4

sneakernet 🖳 see NET

sneutrino 🧪 see S-

snowboarding /'snəʊbɔːdɪŋ/ *noun* ⚽

The practice or sport of sliding downhill on a **snowboard**, a wide ski resembling a wheelless skateboard.

Snowboarding appeared in the mid eighties, and by the early nineties had joined the ranks of fashionable winter sports, with **snowboarders** practising their chosen activity (including **snowboard racing**) in North America and Europe, and an International Federation for the sport having been established. The enthusiasm for *snowboarding* as a recognized sport looks set to continue.

> For those who want to test their skill at the vogue sport (and culture) of snowboarding, the resorts are more than willing to help you become a 'shredder', as the expert boarders call themselves. —*Hispanic* Jan. 1994, p. 96

> The International Ski Federation has sanctioned snowboarding as a World Cup event next season, the first step toward the sport becoming an Olympic event. —*Sun* (Baltimore) 20 Mar. 1994, p. 15

> Once you've chosen your equipment, some key snowboarder words will be thrown at you: 'Are you goofy or regular?' Don't panic: goofy means right foot leading, regular means left foot forward. —*Daily Mail Ski Magazine* Feb. 1995, p. 82

> See also FREERIDE

soccerene 🧪 see BUCKMINSTERFULLERENE

social chapter /səʊʃ(ə)l 'tʃaptə/ *noun* 🏛

That part of MAASTRICHT dealing with social policy, and in particular workers' rights and welfare.

In December 1989, eleven European member states signed the *social charter*, a document dealing with social policy, and in particular workers' rights and welfare, which later became the basis for the *social chapter* of the MAASTRICHT *Treaty*. The *social chapter*, among other points, recommends the adoption of a minimum wage: the British government, which at present exercises an *opt-out* (see OPT-OUT[1]) from this part of the treaty, has argued vigorously as to the adverse effects on employment likely to result.

> The treaty's social chapter is probably the single most difficult area. Because it deals with areas of everyday life that everyone can relate to it is politically high-profile. —*Independent* 5 Dec. 1991, p. 12

> Mr Major...promised that he would protect British industry from excessive labour market regulation with his famous opt-out from the social chapter. —*The Times* 1 June 1993, p. 17

social cleansing 🏛 see CLEANSING

socially responsible investment 📈 see ETHICAL INVESTMENT

software agent ▢ see AGENT

software piracy /sɒf(t)wɛː 'pʌɪrəsi/ *noun* ▢ ⩗

The systematic illegal copying of computer software for financial gain.

With the rise of the personal computer in the eighties, many people sought to obtain software applications cheaply by purchasing versions which had been illegally copied. In some countries where copyright law was non-existent or ineffective a substantial industry grew up producing copies not only of the software itself but also of its packaging and manuals, often to a standard that was difficult to distinguish from the original. Considerable efforts have been made to stamp out *software piracy* by associations of manufacturers, both through law enforcement and by various technical methods to prevent copying; most of the latter have proved counter-productive or ineffective. A distinction is usually made between *software theft*, which refers to organizations or individuals making unauthorized copies of applications for their own use without payment to the copyright owner, and *software piracy*, as an organized and commercial counterfeiting activity.

In China, as in Eastern Europe, the concept of software piracy is not widely understood.
—*Byte* July 1992, p. 6

Most senior executives believe software piracy is a serious threat, but almost half of those polled in [a] recent survey admit that illegal copying still thrives in their firms.
—*Computer Weekly* 28 Oct. 1993, p. 23

Software pirates are now using all the latest technology, such as compact disc burners and high performance PCs, to increase counterfeiting activities.   —*Computer Weekly* 12 Jan. 1995, p. 10

SoHo /'səʊhəʊ/ *acronym* Also written **SOHO** or **Soho** ▢ ⩗

Concerning small businesses, often involving only one person, operating from an office or from home; the commercial sector comprising such businesses.

Formed from the initial letters of *Small Office, Home Office* and usually capitalized in imitation of the area of the same name (which itself is an abbreviation of *South (of) Houston*) on the fringes of Greenwich Village in New York, containing many converted industrial premises used as home offices or studios.

With the advantage of computers and good telecommunications, linked to substantial changes in the organization of businesses which involved shedding many staff, such as DOWNSIZING, it became much more common from the late eighties onward to find individuals running businesses from small offices or a room at home converted into an office. It became part of the marketing strategy of many computer manufacturers to target such small firms with products designed for them. The term itself is recorded from the early nineties and is usually restricted to computer marketing contexts.

Bob Hay, chief executive of Fast, warned the Government that when the Copyright Design and Patents Act was passed in 1988 there was no small office/home office (Soho) marketplace.
—*Computer Weekly* 23 June 1994, p. 16

Thrifty SoHo buyers often think they're getting more for their money by buying a larger box.
—*Computing* 6 Oct. 1994, p. 12

The people I feel sorriest for are the tyro SOHO buyers, who make up an increasing share of PC purchasers.   —*Computing* 12 Jan. 1995, p. 10

solvent abuse ▯ see ABUSE

sorted /'sɔːtɪd/ *adjective* 🔧

In slang: well-organized or controlled; fully prepared or equipped (specifically, supplied with illicit drugs); 'together'.

A figurative use with the notion of the essential elements of a person or situation having been *sorted out* and put into order.

Sorted as a general term of approbation indicating that a person or thing is regarded as fully prepared to deal with any situation encountered is a usage which has become familiar in the first half of the nineties; the even more approving **well sorted** is also found.

A dealer wanders around. He pulls out a plastic bag from his pocket…'Are you sorted? It's good stuff, it'll keep you going all night,' he says. —*Independent* 23 Dec. 1991, p. 5

Late 900s are reliable and well-sorted and most earlier models should have had major modifications carried out. —*Super Bike* Jan. 1993, p. 28

If he's a waster then get yourself out of there and get a life. If he's sorted then take a leaf out of his book and 'chill out'. —*Independent* 9 Mar. 1995, p. 23

Peterlee is sorted, it's mad because you can do what you want. —*Daily Telegraph* 3 Nov. 1995, p. 7

sound bite /'saʊnd baɪt/ *noun* and *verb* Also written **sound-bite** or **soundbite** ✖ ⌂

noun: A short, pithy extract from a recorded interview, speech, or discussion, used for maximum punchiness as part of a news or party political broadcast; also, a one-liner deliberately produced to be used in this way.

transitive verb: To reduce (opinions or debate on an issue) to a series of sound bites.

The use of *bite* here both puts across the idea of a snatch of soundtrack taken from a longer whole and includes undertones of the high-tech approach to units of information (*bytes*).

Use of the technique and the term, first recorded in the early eighties, has increased throughout the eighties and nineties, reflecting pressures on airtime and a view among broadcasters that the public will not follow more than a few seconds of speech from any single interview. The US presidential campaign of 1988 used *sound bites* to great effect on the campaign trail and in televised debates between the protagonists. This was mirrored in the 1992 campaign, which also saw the first use of *sound bite* as a verb. Public misgivings about the *sound bite* have grown during the nineties, and are strongly associated with the view that the technique has an adverse effect on the quality of public debate.

Though Perot made frequent reference to his disdain for 'sound-biting' this issue or that, sound-bite them is precisely what he did. —*Tucson Weekly* 24 June 1992, p. 3

Mr Maples called for 'killer facts'—soundbites to be repeated 'ad nauseam' to prove the success of Government policy in all areas—such as 'one million more patients treated annually since NHS reforms'. —*Daily Telegraph* 22 Nov. 1994, p. 2

Consider this Birtian *aperçu* from last Friday's speech: 'In the era of the soundbite and the tabloid headline, a stray remark, a poorly-judged phrase on a Sunday can build by Tuesday into a cacophony of disputation and political crisis.' —*Guardian* 8 Feb. 1995, section 2, p. 9

Southern blot ⛯ see BLOT

sovereigntist /'sɒvrɪntɪst/ *noun* and *adjective* Also written **sovereignist** ⌂

noun: In Canada, an advocate of the independence of Quebec from Canada.

adjective: Of or belonging to sovereigntists or their views.

Formed from *sovereign* or *sovereignty* with the suffix *-ist*, or from the Canadian French *souverainiste*.

The *sovereigntist* view, which advocates a relationship between Quebec and Canada allowing for political independence while retaining some economic links, was formulated at the beginning of the eighties by René Levesque, the separatist leader of *Parti Québecois*, who was at that time Premier of Quebec. In a referendum held on 20 May 1980, the proposal was rejected, but convinced *sovereigntists* retained the view that separation was desirable. The question remains on the political agenda, and in the nineties the sovereigntists have experienced some political resurgence.

As a sovereigntist, Lalonde says her first duty will be to defend Quebec's interests and explain its position to Canadians. —*Homemaker's Magazine* (Toronto) Nov. 1993, p. 94

The already harsh political debate between federalists and separatists will probably become even more bitter and twisted, as the separatists continue to prod for that still-missing backlash issue to serve their cause and the federalists continue to slam-dunk every little proposal that comes out of the sovereigntist camp. —*Globe & Mail* (Toronto) 23 Mar. 1995, section A, p. 29

It is sovereigntists' turn to issue gloom-and-doom pronouncements about the likelihood of a No referendum vote. —*Maclean's* 24 Apr. 1995, p. 18

space /speɪs/ noun **◖◗**

The freedom to think, act, or be oneself.

A specific use of an existing noun, with a particular notion of the sense of *personal space* 'the area around an individual where encroachment by others causes anxiety or uneasiness'.

The sociological term **personal space** was coined in the thirties, but it is in the eighties and nineties that the concept of having one's own *space* has really developed in the general vocabulary, with particular stress on the degree to which others may try to encroach on this essential freedom. Contextually, the *space* needed by a person or special interest group is often defined in terms of those who might be expected to intrude upon it.

She is—invasive. An expert in intimacy. She reduces my space.
—A. S. Byatt *Possession* (1990), p. 270

He tries, he really tries, not to needle people, to respect their rights, not to intrude on their space.
—Lyn Barber *Mostly Men* (1991), p. 117

I'm the sort of punter who needs my own personal space, y'know?
—Irvine Welsh *Eurotrash* (1994), p. 23

spam /spam/ noun and verb Also written **Spam** 🖳

noun: In online jargon, the undesirable practice of posting the same message repeatedly to a large number of Usenet newsgroups.

intransitive verb: To post a spam.

A figurative use of the trade name of a US brand of tinned meat (see below).

The world-wide Usenet system (see NET) consists of many thousands of subject-based discussion forums called NEWSGROUPS. It is improbable that any widely-disseminated message could be relevant everywhere it appears and the usual reason for **spamming** is to advertise, which is a grave breach of online custom. In the US the word *spam* became associated with the practice through the highly-repetitious *Monty Python* restaurant sketch, in which *Spam* appears to be served with everything:

Don't make a fuss, dear. I'll have your spam. I love it. I'm having spam spam spam spam spam spam spam baked beans spam spam spam and spam!

The term reached a wider public in April 1994: two US lawyers aroused great controversy when they posted a message to thousands of newsgroups to advertise their services in obtaining Green Cards (US immigration permits); other *spams* are the 'Make Money Fast' chain-letter scam and the advertising by a New York legal firm of their credit-renewal services. The person who *spams* is a **spammer**. The offence is strictly so called only if the message is individually posted to each newsgroup instead of being *cross-posted* (cross-referenced so users only have to DOWNLOAD it once); if it is cross-posted, but to excess, the usual term is *velveeta* (named after a US brand of processed cheese).

What the Arizona lawyers did that fateful April day was to 'Spam' the Net, a colorful bit of Internet jargon meant to evoke the effect of dropping a can of Spam into a fan and filling the surrounding space with meat…And all over the world, Internet users responded spontaneously to answering the Spammers with angry electronic mail messages called 'flames'. Within minutes, the flames—

filled with unprintable epithets—began pouring into Canter and Siegel's Internet mailbox.
—*Time* 25 July 1994, p. 51

The alt.current-events.net-abuse Usenet newsgroup is the place to discuss spamming and other obnoxious advertising. —*Everybody's Internet Update* Feb. 1995, online newsletter

sparticle ⚗ see s-

spazz out /'spaz aʊt/ *verbal phrase* 🎵

To lose physical or emotional control, to be overcome. Also, to display symptoms of this.

Probably formed as an alteration of *space out*, influenced by *spaz* as a slang abbreviation for *spastic*, or *spasm*.

Spazz out is recorded from the mid eighties as a term for losing physical or emotional control, especially as the result of an intense emotional experience. To be **spazzed out** is to be overcome.

Rooks the toughie…spazzing out at the sight of New Jersey!
—Paul Theroux *O-Zone* (1986), p. 418

One of the boys broke stride, then stumbled. 'Philo!' barked Edgar. 'Stop spazzing out.'
—Armistead Maupin *Significant Others* (1987), p. 256

He gets all spazzed out when he talks about it at home.
—*Fort Collins Triangle Review* (Colorado) 4 Nov. 1993, p. 14

Special K /'spɛʃ(ə)l keɪ/ *noun* Also written **special k** 🎵

A name for the anaesthetic and pain-killing drug ketamine, when used illicitly as a hallucinogen.

Formed from the adjective *special* and the initial letter of *ketamine*, perhaps with punning allusion to *Special K*, the trade mark name for a breakfast cereal manufactured by Kellogg's.

Special K has been used as an illicit hallucinogen from the mid eighties; it appears to have become increasingly fashionable in the RECREATIONAL DRUG scene of the nineties.

Two substances in vogue at gay clubs: Special K and crystal Methedrine, or methamphetamine.
—*Out* Summer 1992, p. 48

Heroin became really big there, and Special K in the club scene. —*i-D* Aug. 1995, p. 32

They could buy heroin, cocaine, crack cocaine, PCP, ecstasy—a new form of methamphetamines, marijuana, LSD, and Special K—that new drug used by veterinarians as an anesthetic for cats. The agents called the place a candy store for drugs.
—*Star-Ledger* (Newark) 5 Nov. 1995, section 1, p. 6

speed bump /'spiːd bʌmp/ *noun* 🌳

A transverse ridge in the road to control the speed of vehicles.

Speed bumps (in the UK also known as *humps*, *road humps*, or *speed humps*) are among a number of TRAFFIC CALMING measures, introduced in recent years, which are intended to moderate the flow and speed of traffic in towns and residential areas. The overall value of such measures is still a matter of debate, but in the meantime the term *speed bump* appears to be establishing itself in the language as a figure of speech for a temporary impediment which may give pause for thought.

Thousands of pounds are to be spent laying speed bumps across a scenic city centre road—in a bid to deter boy racers in souped-up cars. —*Evening News* (Edinburgh) 20 Apr. 1992, p. 7

A few speed bumps down the timeline of rock past the new wave of new wave and the return of baggy, and it seems the obvious revival has been overlooked. —*MOJO* Feb. 1995, p. 96

speed camera /'spi:d kam(ə)rə/ *noun* 🌳

A roadside camera, triggered by speeding vehicles, which takes either video footage or a photograph of the offending vehicle with a record of its speed.

Speed cameras were introduced in the first half of the nineties, and have proved to be one of the more successful TRAFFIC CALMING measures of the period, although unpopular with many motorists. This is particularly the case where conviction for speeding results in endorsement of the driver's licence and the imposition of penalty points, with automatic suspension of the licence once a given number of points have accrued. Although it is common practice that not all *speed cameras* are loaded with film all the time, the possibility that infringements of the speed limit may be automatically recorded and penalized has had a deterrent effect on speeding motorists.

About 6,000 motorists a week are incurring fines and licence endorsements after being caught speeding on film by 'Gatso' speed cameras.　　　　—*Daily Telegraph* 22 Aug. 1994, p. 2

speed hump 🌳 see SPEED BUMP

spell-check /'spɛltʃɛk/ *verb* and *noun* Also written **spell check** 🖳

transitive verb: To check the spelling of (a word or a document) using a program which compares the words in a text file with a stored list of acceptable spellings.

noun: A check of the spelling of words in a text file carried out automatically; a program or facility for doing this.

Being able to check the spelling of words was one of the most prized facilities in the word processor programs that began to appear for microcomputers at the end of the seventies. They quickly became standard, despite limited vocabularies, an inability to spot correctly-spelled but inappropriate words, and a tendency to suggest unsuitable replacements for unknown ones. At first, they were called **spelling checkers**, but the noun was soon abbreviated to **spell-checker** in the US and this form is now frequently used also in Britain. The verbal noun is **spell-checking**.

I always wondered if he had a special spell check on his word processor for dirty words.
　　　　　　　　　　　　　　　　　　　　　　—*Tucson Weekly* 1 Jan. 1992, p. 2

Those of you who don't own spell checkers, get one.　　　—*New Republic* 19 Apr. 1993, p. 22

When I spell-checked a page in DOS, I simply pressed the Alt and F2 keys and then the number 2.　　　　　　　　　　　　　　　　　　　　—*Daily Telegraph* 19 Dec. 1994, p. 28

A journalist needs a spelling checker and a word counter, but rarely a set of drawing tools.
　　　　　　　　　　　　　　　　　　　—*Personal Computer World* Feb. 1995, p. 456

spin doctor /'spɪn dɒktə/ *noun* 🎬

A senior political spokesperson employed to promote a favourable interpretation of events to journalists.

In US politics, *spin* is interpretation, the bias or slant put on information when it is presented to the public or in a press conference. This in turn is a sporting metaphor, from the *spin* put on the ball, for example by a pitcher in baseball. *Doctor* comes from the various figurative uses of the verb *doctor* (ranging from 'patch up, mend' to 'falsify').

The phrase *spin doctor* was first recorded in political journalism in the mid eighties and had become a buzzword by the end of the decade. It is now a standard part of the political vocabulary of the English-speaking world. The activity of a *spin doctor* is **spin doctoring**; the verb to **spin doctor** is also sometimes found, as is the adjective **spin-doctored**.

In a day when people across the country are sick and tired of packaged, polished spin-doctored candidates, I think she had a lot of appeal.　　　　　—*Chatelaine* June 1992, p. 51

It's no wonder the queen publicly pushed her aside as part of the current effort to repackage and market the man who would be king. But the royals aren't skilled at spin-doctoring.

—*Chicago Tribune* 3 July 1994, section 4, p. 3

The party's spin doctors were alarmed to hear the BBC was covering the speech and delighted to hear that it had not 'made' the news bulletin.　　—*Guardian* 17 Mar. 1995, Friday supplement, p. 3

spine /spʌɪn/ *noun* 〰️

A linear pay scale in which each graded job corresponds to a particular point on the scale, but which allows flexibility for local and specific conditions.

A figurative use of the anatomical term, the image being of a vertical structure which, like the human *spine*, is flexible rather than rigid.

Spine and **pay spine** are recorded from the mid eighties as terms for this form of pay scale; an individual point on such a scale is known as the **spine point**. The context is usually that of a large organization or profession, for which there is an established pay structure within which individual needs can be accommodated.

Each person will be assigned to a point; personnel managers can move groups or individuals up the spine depending on merit or on skill shortages.　　　　—*Economist* 11 Apr. 1987, p. 21

The post carries two responsibility points on the School Teachers' Pay Spine.

—advertisement in *Times Educational Supplement* 10 Feb. 1995, p. 63

Teachers...are also paid a tax free Cost of Living Addition...which ranges currently from just over £3,000 p.a. for single teachers...to around £5,600 p.a. for married, accompanied teachers on Spine Point 9 family accommodation.

—advertisement in *Times Educational Supplement* 10 Feb. 1995, p. 89

splatter /'splatə/ *noun* 🎬

A genre of cinema in which many characters die in a violent or gruesome manner. Frequently used attributively, as in **splatter movie**.

A reference to the violent physical disintegration of bodies which appear to be *splattered* across the screen.

Splatter films as a form of violent cinema have been recognized as a genre since the early eighties; in the nineties, the **splattery** special effects which characterize them may be found in video games. It seems likely that if the V-CHIP is developed as a serious application, **splatter movies** will be among the items blocked.

Laymon is well known in splatter circles as an accomplished schlock writer of pulp nasties.

—*The Times* 22 Nov. 1990, p. 19

The producer of a 'splatter movie' (described as one in which 'blood and body parts are distributed in substantial quantities') set part of the film in a graveyard.

—*Guardian* 16 Nov. 1993, section 2, p. 19

The age-old create-mayhem-on-a-major-scale fantasy is revisited yet again in this splattery shoot-'em-up, which provides the player with about as much noise, breathless action, and people being reduced to bloody pools as it's possible to fit into one computer programme.

—*Empire* May 1995, p. 139

sports bar /'spɔːts bɑː/ *noun* 🎬 ⊕

In the US: a bar where non-stop televised sport is shown.

A *bar* devoted to the broadcasting of *sports*.

Sports bars developed in America in the seventies, and have become increasingly popular with the advent of cable television channels devoted entirely to sport on a twenty-four-hour basis.

More and more, football fans are audible-izing to a growing list of parties thrown by sports bars and hotels.　　　　—*Albuquerque Journal* (New Mexico) 28 Jan. 1993, section D, p. 1

The Grille doesn't even try to look like a north-woods retreat. Its decor is pure sports bar, with televisions everywhere and wait staff in shorts.　　—*Minnesota Monthly* Sept. 1994, p. 30

When cable television companies launched round-the-clock sports channels, sports bars took off in the US in a big way. —*Independent on Sunday* 30 July 1995, p. 20

sports tourism ❌ 🔲 see TOURISM

spousal abuse ❌ see ABUSE

spreadsheeting /'sprɛdʃiːtɪŋ/ *noun* 🔲

The provision or use of a spreadsheet program for the manipulation and flexible retrieval of tabulated data.

The concept of the spreadsheet was invented in the late seventies by analogy with the paper equivalent long used by accountants; the program *VisiCalc* was put on the market in 1979 and was immediately a huge success. However, the generic name **spreadsheet** for this type of application was not coined until the early eighties, when competing products began to appear; it was closely followed by the verbal noun *spreadsheeting*.

Spreadsheeting is not exactly one of the most point-and-click oriented DOS applications.
—*Personal Computer World* Feb. 1991, p. 202

As you go about your business doing non-intensive word processing, databasing, spread-sheeting…the Mac spends more time waiting for you than you spend waiting for the Mac.
—*MacUser* Nov. 1992, p. 32

spree killer /'spriː kɪlə/ *noun* ❌

A person who kills in a sudden, random, and apparently unpremeditated and motiveless manner, especially one who kills a number of people at a single location in such an attack.

Since the early eighties, criminologists have identified two kinds of multiple murderer, the SERIAL KILLER and the *spree killer*. Incidents of **spree killing** have been the subject of wide media coverage and public attention, most recently those at Dunblane, Scotland, in March 1996, and at Port Arthur, Tasmania, in May 1996.

Kohl termed the shooting a 'spree' killing—' walking in, going to one location, killing several people and leaving'. —*Courier-Journal* (Indiana) 19 Oct. 1993, section A, p. 1

His homicidal heroes…technically straddle the boundary between what the FBI labels 'spree killers' and 'serial killers.' —*Post* (Denver) 4 Sept. 1994, section F, p. 8

Mass killings like Dunblane, he said had been split in recent years into three broad groups: mass murders, spree killings, and serial killings. —*Independent* 14 Mar. 1996, p. 3

squalamine ⊗ 🔲 see MAGAININ

Squarial /'skwɛːrɪəl/ *noun* Also written **squarial** ❌ 🔲

A proprietary name for a type of flat diamond-shaped aerial for receiving satellite television broadcasts.

A blend of *square* and *aerial*.

One of the two British companies which sought to develop television broadcasting from satellites, British Satellite Broadcasting, attempted to create an unusual form of receiving aerial which would be smaller and hence less obtrusive than conventional dish aerials. The *Squarial* was a flat diamond shape which was focused on the transmitting satellite by electronic means. Its production was hampered by problems in making it work; when BSB merged with Sky Television in December 1990 to form BSkyB, production of the aerial ceased and it became obsolete when transmissions from the Marco Polo satellite ended shortly afterwards.

BSB announce their small, square satellite dish. Affectionately known as the Squarial, it will be proudly displayed on homes all over Britain from next September.
—*Broadcast* 18 Aug. 1989, p. 4

Often people with more money than sense…end up with Betamax videos, quadraphonic sound, BSB squarials and Delorean sports cars. *—New Scientist* 20 Feb. 1993, p. 51

squark ⚗ see s-

squeegee /'skwi:dʒi:/ *noun* ▨

A person who cleans the windscreen of a car stopped in traffic and solicits payment from the driver. Often used in such fuller forms as **squeegee kid**, **squeegee man**.

An extended use of the noun *squeegee* in the sense 'a rubber-edged implement set on a handle and used for cleaning windows'.

Squeegees have been a feature of urban life since the mid eighties, most frequently among cars stopped at traffic lights. The development of such terms as **squeegee bandit** and **squeegee thug** suggest that the 'service' provided is not always a welcome one, with the unasked-for attention often being regarded as a covertly aggressive act.

The squeegee thugs…have become a scourge of inner-city motorists…The squeegees wait at busy intersections. When cars stop for a red light, the young men carrying long-handled rubber squeegees approach each car in line offering to clean the windshield.
—Crime Beat Jan. 1992, p. 6

Squeegee men hung around a few congested intersections and bridge and tunnel toll plazas, 'offering' to wash windshields for a fee.
—Richmond Times-Dispatch 1 Dec. 1994, section A, p. 21

squeeze /skwi:z/ *noun* ⬚

In North American slang: a girlfriend, boyfriend, or lover.

From the earlier *main squeeze*, originally in the sense of 'a very important person', with a pun on *squeeze* 'a close hug or embrace'.

A term (in use since the early eighties) which focuses on the physical relationship between two people, and is often used in contexts which indicate its temporary or transitory nature.

Renee is in her room now, giggling on the phone with her latest squeeze, a guy named Royal.
—Armistead Maupin Maybe the Moon (1992), p. 13

The star, looking every day of 16 in a blue-and-yellow cheerleader costume, played a bit of guitar…while his new squeeze, the mono-talented Mayte, did some aerobics and donned a pink beret for the appropriate song. *—Guardian* 28 July 1993, section 2, p. 6

She's been cheated on by Tom Cruise in *Cocktail*…and ignored by Michael J. Fox as his virtuous hometown squeeze in *Back To The Future*. *—Premiere* Feb. 1996, p. 32

stage-diving /'steidʒ dʌivɪŋ/ *noun*

The practice, among audience members at a rock concert, of jumping from the stage to be caught and carried aloft by the crowd below.

Stage-diving, like *moshing* (see MOSH) and SLAM DANCING, is a phenomenon of the eighties and nineties rock scene in which great stress is laid on the physical expression of involvement and enthusiasm. **Stage-divers** taking part in a **stage-dive**, like *moshers* and *slam dancers*, may risk at least bruising as a result of their exuberant determination to **stage-dive**.

Onslaught, the Bristol thrash band, are taking steps to prevent their fans injuring themselves by stage diving at their gigs. *—Sounds* 1 Aug. 1987, p. 3

Rock bands playing clubs can count on stage-divers and slam-dancers—now part of virtually any loud and uptempo scene—and arena audiences are eager to stand up, wave and shout.
—New York Times 19 Jan. 1992, section 2, p. 29

The hard-core physical nature of moshing and stage diving brings up the issue of liability.
—Albuquerque Journal Rio 26 Aug. 1993, section F, p. 6

Puffy is flying through the air on a massive stage dive. Landing on a hyper audience he floats on a wave of hands back to the stage. —*Mixmag* May 1995, p. 92

stakeholder economy /ˌsteɪkhəʊldə ɪˈkɒnəmi/ *noun* 〽️ 🖳

An economy in which every member of a society has an interest in its economic progress.

An *economy* characterized by those who are its *stakeholders*, and who have an interest in its success.

The term *stakeholder*, in its original sense of 'an independent party with whom each of those making a wager deposits the sum wagered', has been current since the eighteenth century; the secondary sense of 'a person with an interest or concern in a business or other organization' developed in the mid-twentieth century. The compound *stakeholder economy* was coined in a speech on 8 January 1996 by the Leader of the British Labour Party, Tony Blair, who used the phrase to encapsulate his view of how socialist ideals and economic aspirations might be reconciled in the policies of NEW LABOUR. It has already gained considerable currency among both its proponents and its critics.

Tony Blair will today begin to map out the main themes of Labour's campaign pitch for the next general election. He promises to develop a 'stakeholder economy' in which everyone can participate. —*Daily Telegraph* 8 Jan. 1996, p. 4

A stakeholder economy, according to the prime minister, implies a return to a corporatist state, with government intervention in the running of industry, increased rights for trade unions and a powerful role for special interest groups. —*Financial Times* 11 Jan. 1996, p. 5

stalker /ˈstɔːkə/ *noun* 〖

A person who follows or pesters someone (often a public figure) with whom he or she has become obsessed.

A specific use of the noun *stalker* in the sense 'a person who pursues another', from the verb to *stalk* 'to approach (game, prey, or an enemy) stealthily'.

The phenomenon of the *stalker* who follows or pesters a celebrity has been recognized since the early eighties, and in the nineties has become increasingly high-profile, with a concern that the end of the obsession may well be violence against the victim.

The general perception is that a *stalker* is likely to be male and his target female, and not necessarily distinguished by public celebrity. In the last years there has been a growing debate as to whether **stalking** should be categorized as a criminal offence (as in some American states it already is); this question is frequently discussed in the wider context of 'crimes against women'.

I have been the victim of a stalker since 1988. The man who is stalking me has repeatedly been ordered by the courts to have nothing to do with me.
—*Homemaker's Magazine* Mar. 1993, p. 12

This week the media have been using the word 'stalker' to describe the sort of obsessed fan who follows tennis stars around. —*Independent on Sunday* 13 June 1993, p. 23

The attacks on Kerrigan and Seles, and the stalking of other women, are alarmingly looking more like a trend than isolated incidents. —*Coloradoan* (Fort Collins) 8 Jan. 1994, section A, p. 1

Stalkers thrive on seeing their victims, on knowing they have impinged on their victim's lives. For the quarry of a determined stalker, there is no hiding place. —*Independent* 6 Jan. 1996, p. 17

Watching or following a person could become a criminal offence under proposals being examined by the Home Office, after mounting public concern that Britain's present laws on stalking fail to protect women. —*Sunday Telegraph* 4 Feb. 1996, p. 1

statementing /ˈsteɪtm(ə)ntɪŋ/ *noun* 〖

In the UK, an official assessment of a child as having special educational needs.

The formal process of *statementing* the special educational needs of a child has been current since the early eighties, and forms part of the debate as to whether children recognized as having such needs should be educated separately, or integrated into mainstream education. The term has gained linguistic acceptance; literature on the subject now often refers to **statemented** children, and by back-formation there is a verb to **statement**.

At the heart of the problem is the new system of notifying local authorities and the education department of children with handicaps, known as 'statementing'.
—*The Times* 12 Apr. 1985, p. 2

The aim is to direct a greater proportion of resources towards children without resort to formal assessment and statementing, in anticipation that this will enable support staff to offer direct help to a greater number of children. —*ACE Bulletin* Jan. 1991, p. 11

Pupils with learning difficulties are 'statemented'. —*Guardian* 1 Jan. 1994, p. 20

Expenditure on statemented pupils in mainstream schools has more than doubled in three years.
—*Times Educational Supplement* 10 Feb. 1995, section 2, p. 8

stealth bra 🔋 see CAR BRA

steampunk /'stiːmpʌŋk/ *noun* 🐀 POP

A subgenre of science fiction set in an industrialized, nineteenth-century society.

Formed by replacing the first element of *cyberpunk* (see CYBER-) with *steam* to indicate the period (the *steam age*) during which *steam* was the main source of mechanized power.

Steampunk effectively takes the notion of urban counter-culture and high technology, but transports the timeframe back to the Victorian age, when the introduction of *steam* represented the latest technological development. The *steampunk* subgenre has been developing since the mid eighties; the term is recorded since the beginning of the nineties.

His newest works are taking a turn from cyberpunk to steampunk, following in the footsteps of many other s.f. writers. —*Science Fiction Age* Jan. 1993, p. 74

We wanted our cyberspace to have a 'steampunk' feel and a sense that the whole thing was held together with bailing wire and hot glue. —*Science-Fiction Studies* Nov. 1993, p. 455

[His] steampunk sagas are characterized by a romantic vision of Victorian London as it should have been, a playground for eccentrics, fantastic devices and sinister occult conspiracies.
—*Interzone* Oct. 1995, p. 59

step aerobics /stɛp ɛːˈrəʊbɪks/ *noun* ⊗ ⊕

A type of aerobics involving stepping up on to and down from a portable block.

A form of *aerobics* which employs a *step* for the necessary exercise.

Aerobics, a way of taking vigorous exercise designed to increase the body's oxygen intake, became a widespread fitness craze in the early eighties. *Step aerobics* as a form of this was introduced in America in the late eighties, and similarly achieved considerable popularity, although after the initial enthusiasm some concern has been expressed as to the possible dangers involved in repetitive movement of this kind.

The latest trend in aerobic training—Step Aerobics!
—advertisement in *San Francisco Chronicle* 25 Aug. 1990, section C, p. 1

Step aerobics is a fun way to lose weight and trim your legs—and because it's a low impact exercise, injury risk is low. —*Slimmer* Dec. 1992, p. 93

Helen is off at the health club doing step aerobics. —*Successful Retirement* May 1994, p. 63

stereogram 💻 ❌ see AUTOSTEREOGRAM

steroid abuse 〖 ⊕ see ABUSE

sticky /'stɪki/ *noun* ▨

An informal term for a Post-it Note.

A specific use of the noun meaning 'something that adheres'.

Post-it Notes, small pads of paper of varying size, each sheet of which can be peeled off and stuck to another surface, have been a popular item of stationery since their introduction in the early eighties. The informal *sticky*, deriving from their most recognizable characteristic, is now often used in place of the proprietary term *Post-it Note* to denote the means of leaving an annotation, either in the form of a piece of paper or electronically.

> As you happily plaster recycled stickies on your desk and walls, remember that the glue added to the back renders the paper difficult to recycle again. —*Garbage* Mar. 1991, p. 64

> I mentioned how much I liked Stickies, little Post-It style notes you can paste electronically on the screen for reminders, to-do lists or anything else you might use the actual scraps of paper for. —*New York Times* 21 Feb. 1995, section C, p. 9

stonking /'stɒŋkɪŋ/ *adjective* ᴘᴏᴘ

In slang: considerable, very impressive; exciting.

From the noun *stonk* in the senses 'a marble; a military bombardment', ultimately perhaps of imitative origin, mimicking the sound of impact.

Stonking as a term expressing enthusiastic appreciation is recorded from the early eighties, and there is an adverb **stonkingly**. More recently, something regarded as *stonking* may be described as a **stonker**.

> Last year...the gals...decided to hook up for a special concert...and had such a stonkin' good time they decided to reunite for a tour. —*Rage* 13 Feb. 1991, p. 43

> Stonking value for anyone wanting to take their first steps into home cinema. —*What Hi-Fi?* Oct. 1993, p. 61

> The most outrageous Diablo yet with more power, less weight, a stonking 207mph maximum speed and a production run of only 150 cars. —*BBC Top Gear Magazine* Aug. 1994, p. 4

> There is some real innovation going on in places like 'Rhythm Dog', which makes a heavy-bassed stonker of a techno tune a bit different with tribal sounding piano. —*Mixmag* May 1995, p. 112

stormwatch ᴘᴏᴘ see -WATCH

streamer /'striːmə/ *noun* ▣

A form of tape transport, used mainly to provide backup storage, in which data may be transferred in large quantities without interruption while the tape remains in motion.

From the notion of something which maintains a continuous flow.

The growth in size of stored data on personal computers in the early eighties, particularly the introduction of hard disks, provoked the design of a system which could be left to run continuously while backing up data; this was a more convenient process than having repeatedly to remove and insert a succession of floppy disks, which was then the only alternative. The system was based on a cassette tape, and the system was known variously as a **streamer tape**, a **tape streamer**, or just as a *streamer*. The second of these quickly became established as the formal term for the device, with *streamer* the common abbreviated form. The action noun **streaming** (in full **tape streaming**) is also common.

> However there are some cases in which the sheer bulk of new software, or some other reason, means that it may be preferable to employ an alternative upgrade mechanism, such as a streamer tape. —*ICL Technical Journal* Nov. 1990, Vol. 2, No. 2, p. 428

> TapeXchange is an innovation in the tape streaming marketplace. —advertisement in *Computing* 10 Jan. 1991, p. 13

A tape streamer is a device which will back up the complete contents of your hard disk so that you can store it securely away from the machine. —*Which?* Oct. 1992, p. 53

street-skating ▓ see ROLLERBLADE

street style /'striːt staɪl/ *noun* ▓ ᴾᴼᴾ

A style inspired by contemporary urban culture.

This attributive use of the noun *street* was established in earlier compounds, such as *street credibility* and *streetwise*, and continues to gain in force and colour.

The term *street style*, which has been recorded since the early eighties, originally in the US, conveys a notion of informality and toughness. It has been used with reference to various elements of contemporary culture, but in the eighties it had a notable application in the world of fashion. By the mid eighties the fashion establishment had taken elements seen as characteristic of *street style* and reinvented them for the catwalks, where the term came to denote an offbeat, avant-garde style characterized by audaciousness and assertive informality. The informality of *street style* represented a conscious contrast to the conventions of high fashion, and the style's adoption by the fashion establishment created a conceptual contradiction which was broadly acknowledged. The fashion industry has proved less successful in assimilating elements of GRUNGE, which shares some of the attributes of *street style* but is more perverse and less accessible to the designer's craft.

Use of the term in application to contemporary music developed during the eighties and continues to be current in the nineties. In music it similarly suggests assertiveness and individuality. The term has also been used in relation to contemporary literature which is perceived to be brash and survivalist.

Madonna exploded onto MTV with a brazen, insolent, in-your-face American street style. —Camille Paglia *Sex, Art & American Culture* (1992), p. 6

Wear loud layers of skin-tight clothes for a bold street style. It's time to get funky! —*LOOKS* July 1992, p. 10

It took mainstream designers a mere year to appropriate the subculture street style of teens and 20somethings. —*Chatelaine* Mar. 1993, p. 6

Like primitive art, once of interest only to ethnographers, street style, once the province of sub-culture, is now regarded as fit for study and praise. —*Independent on Sunday* 21 Aug. 1994, Fashion supplement, p. 32

The *New Yorker* could pretend it cares about street style and people under 40, and Jay McInerney scored yet again as an insightful chronicler of youth. —*i-D* Aug. 1995, p. 30

stressed out /'strɛst aʊt/ *adjectival phrase* ▐ ᴾᴼᴾ

In colloquial use, debilitated or exhausted as a result of stress.

The use of *stressed out* since the early eighties, to indicate an extreme degree of debilitation or exhaustion, may be taken as an indicator of the perception of stress as constituting one of the main pressures of modern life.

Half of Britain's personnel managers admit to having to push stressed-out employees into taking holidays. —*Daily Telegraph* 1 May 1990, p. 9

If you're holidaying in Bangkok and are totally stressed out by the traffic and noise, blissful relief is at hand. —*Options* Aug. 1993, p. 85

I really think the parents are stressed out, poor and then they've got this little ankle-biter who constantly wants attention. —*Richmond Times-Dispatch* 10 Oct. 1994, p. 12

All programmers who worked on that project…are so stressed out that the sight of a piece of pink paper will give them a stroke. —*Computer Quarterly* Winter 1994, p. 10

stuffer /'stʌfə/ *noun* ▐

A person who smuggles drugs by concealment in a bodily passage such as the rectum or vagina.

A specific use of the noun for someone who *stuffs* drugs into a bodily passage.

Since the early eighties, customs officials have found drug-smuggling (sometimes by MULES) involving internal bodily concealment of drugs. The counterpart of the *stuffer* is the *swallower*, who swallows the drugs sealed in a bag which can subsequently be excreted and recovered.

> The customs teams delicately refer to such smugglers as 'the swallowers and stuffers'.
>
> —*Listener* 28 July 1983, p. 3

> 'Stuffers', as opposed to 'swallowers', will use any orifice available.
>
> —*Independent* 29 Sept. 1992, p. 13

subsidiarity /səbsɪdɪˈarɪti/ *noun* 🏛

The principle that a central authority should have a subsidiary function, performing only those tasks which cannot be performed effectively at a more immediate or local level.

A specific use of the noun, the general meaning of which is 'the quality of being subsidiary'.

Subsidiarity, which is recorded since the mid thirties, was originally used primarily in discussions of ecclesiastical polity with particular reference to the role of the papacy. Since the early eighties, however, the specific sense has come to prominence in the debate on the EUROPEAN UNION, and the question of how national sovereignties can be reconciled with any proposed federal structure. The principle of *subsidiarity* was asserted by Britain as a condition of her ratification of MAASTRICHT, but it is not yet clear to what degree this view of the role of a central European authority will be implemented. It may be noted that the term occurs less frequently now than in the earlier part of the nineties, perhaps because the debate has polarized, and those of EUROSCEPTIC persuasion are more likely to recommend complete withdrawal from Europe than to seek modification of the planned structure.

> The 'principle of subsidiarity'—a meaningless or even misleading phrase in English—is being discussed in the European Parliament in connection with eventual revision of the Treaty of Rome. It is defined to mean that the European Community's activities should be limited to those which are better performed in common than by member states individually.
>
> —*The Times* 18 Sept. 1982, p. 7

> There might be more opt-outs along the lines Britain demanded at Maastricht. 'Subsidiarity'—code for limiting interference from Brussels—could be more strictly defined.
>
> —*Economist* 22 Aug. 1992, p. 19

> Europeans invented the concept of subsidiarity in order to juggle the competing demands for centralization by Brussels' Eurocrats versus the jealously guarded power of civil servants working for the EC's member countries.
>
> —*Maclean's* 7 Nov. 1994, p. 15

substance abuse ▮▮ see ABUSE

sunberry ▨ see TUMMELBERRY

sun protection factor /ˌsʌn prəˈtɛkʃ(ə)n faktə/ *noun phrase* ▨

The ratio of the time it takes skin to burn when wearing a sunscreen compared with the time it takes to burn without one. Also, a measure of sunscreen effectiveness. Often abbreviated to **SPF**.

In the last years, anxieties have grown about the long-term effects of sunburn, and in particular the development of skin cancer as the result of excessive exposure to ultraviolet light. In the nineties, use of the term *sun protection factor* (sometimes simply *protection factor*) reflects a public desire for specific information as to the levels of effectiveness for **sun protection** of the many *sunscreens* and *sunblocks* commercially available.

> It's nonsense to think that you won't get a tan by using high Sun Protection Factors (SPFs) when first exposing your skin to the sun.
>
> —*She* May 1991, p. 104

Providing you use an adequate level of sun protection there's no reason why you can't enjoy the benefits of the sun and come home sporting a healthy glow.

—Wedding & Home June 1994, p. 73

Wear...a hat with a wide brim and sunscreen with a Sun Protection Factor (SPF) of 15 or higher.

—Golf Digest Aug. 1995, p. 16

superbug /ˈsuːpəbʌg/ *noun* ⊗

A strain of bacteria that has become resistant to antibiotic drugs.

Since the introduction of penicillin during the Second World War, the number of available antibiotics (many of them now prepared synthetically) has increased dramatically, and they are widely prescribed. Since the late seventies, however, it has been noticed that a number of bacterial infections have now adapted to the degree of being resistant to antibiotics. Development of such *superbugs* has been associated with the reported resurgence of diseases such as tuberculosis. Currently the question of how to deal with *superbugs* is a key one in the field of immunology.

Suggestions for coping with the ever increasing number of serious infections from superbugs are better late than never, but we'll never keep up with the bugs. *—Time* 3 Oct. 1994, p. 12

Multiresistance has been with us for a long time in some harmless bacterial strains, but multi-resistance and tuberculosis is a relatively new combination in the microbe world. The most developed and the most deadly variety of multiresistant TB is able to fight even our most sophisticated medication. These superbugs were first noticed in New York, San Francisco, Los Angeles, and other large U.S. cities, and they're moving fast. *—Georgia Straight* 12 Oct. 1995, p. 16

The disease is caused by a type of bacteria that succumbs quickly to penicillin. This time, however, penicillin proves useless against what doctors will call a 'superbug'—a strain of pneumococcus that is resistant to several antibiotics. *—American Health* Oct. 1995, p. 51

superhighway /suːpəˈhʌIweI/ *noun* ▣

One of a number of projected national high-speed, high-capacity telecommunications networks linking homes and offices and permitting the transmission of a variety of electronic media, including video, audio, multimedia, and text.

A figurative use of *superhighway*, which has been employed in the US since 1925 to mean a road designed for large numbers of fast-moving vehicles.

The word *superhighway* took on its figurative sense about the time of US Senate hearings on the idea in 1989, usually in the phrase **information superhighway**. The development of a nationwide high-capacity telecommunications network has become a key policy of the Clinton administration, and proposals to create a national system were published in 1993. The argument in favour is that individuals and businesses increasingly need good communications and easy access to information; such a network would also facilitate a wide range of domestic services not readily available at the moment, such as HOME SHOPPING, -on-demand services (see -ON-DEMAND), and *telebanking* (see TELE-), though surveys have not shown high levels of interest on the part of the public. Similar proposals are at various stages of development within the European Community, Canada, Australia, Britain, Japan, and elsewhere. The proposal has given rise to extensive comment and discussion, as well as huge claims for its significance, so much so that the sarcastic variant **information superhypeway** has been coined. The concept has been given many other names, such as *data superhighway, digital superhighway, electronic superhighway, information highway, info highway*, and *infobahn*, but *information superhighway* is the most common usage. In the US, this term is frequently abbreviated to **I-way**.

Vice-President Al Gore yesterday unveiled the Clinton administration plan for a 'superhighway' that would allow information to flow freely to and from homes, schools, businesses and other institutions at high speeds. *—Star-Ledger* (Newark) 22 Dec. 1993, p. 8

She said she saw blackboards being replaced by computer screens, with pupils at every school in

Britain linked by cable to an information 'superhighway' allowing them access to a world network of knowledge.   —*Daily Mail* 2 Jan. 1995, p. 28

While the computer industry has wittered on about the Internet and pooh-poohed the 'information superhypeway', cable operators have been quietly creating the real superhighway in green plastic pipes outside our front doors.   —*Computing* 6 Apr. 1995, p. 13

superscalar /suːpəˈskeɪlə/ *adjective* 🄳

Of a computer microprocessor, able to execute more than one instruction at one time.

The term is a modification of one common in mathematics, in which a *scalar* quantity is one which represents magnitude only, as opposed to a *vector* quantity, which represents both magnitude and direction. The term *superscalar* is a marketing buzzword generated by prefixing the superlative *super-* to *scalar*.

A *scalar* processor is one which is capable of processing a collection of data (a *scalar*) at one time, as opposed to a conventional microprocessor, which can only handle single items of data at a time, and is called a *vector* processor; a vector computer is one in which data must proceed in a linear direction through the processor, as against a scalar one in which multiple strands of data are processed in parallel. The perpetual quest for greater speed in computing systems led designers in the eighties to create RISC (Reduced Instruction-Set Computer) chips; in the late eighties, this evolved into a system in which two or more such RISC circuits were placed together on one chip and so could execute more than one instruction at a time. Though the practical design of such chips poses substantial problems, particularly when an instruction in one part of the processor has an effect on one in another, such chips began to appear on the market in the late eighties and look set to be the key to fast personal computing in the foreseeable future.

One approach to executing multiple instructions simultaneously is the so-called 'superscalar' route…Superscaling involves building two, three, or more 'pipelines' that fetch instructions and process them, assembly-line style, at the same time.   —*UnixWorld* Aug. 1991, p. 72

Almost everyone has underestimated the difficulty of implementing these superscalar designs.
                                                              —*Byte* Dec. 1992, p. 128

The problem with a traditional superscalar or parallel approach is that the chip has to check for interdependencies, and the more parallel instructions sent to the chip, the more scope there is for 'bubbles' where the chip has to process one tiny bit of the code while the rest waits up.
                                        —*Personal Computer World* Aug. 1994, p. 222

supertwist /ˈsuːpətwɪst/ *adjective* 🄳

Concerning varieties of liquid crystal display (LCD) used in portable computers in which to change state the plane of polarized light passing through the display is rotated by at least 180 degrees.

Formed on the noun *twist*, referring to the rotation, or twisting, of light as it passes through the liquid crystal, with *super*, 'superlative or improved quality' (the system is a development of an older and less effective method).

Liquid crystal displays have been a feature of various battery-powered devices—digital watches, calculators, portable computers—for many years, mainly because their power consumption is low. Each element of the display consists of a layer of a liquid, which has some crystalline properties and is normally transparent, sandwiched between two layers of polarizing material. When a small voltage is applied between the front and back of the sandwich, the crystals in the liquid change orientation, rotating the plane of polarized light and stopping light passing through. Older LCDs put light through a 90-degree twist, which produces a relatively low-contrast display. Newer LCDs rotate the polarized light by 180 degrees (*supertwist*) or by 270 degrees (**triple supertwist**) to improve contrast. An adjectival form **supertwisted** and a noun **supertwisting** are sometimes used.

Once the keyboard has been folded into position, the...supertwist LCD screen is revealed.
—Computer Buyer's Guide & Handbook 1989, VII. vi. p. 63

Backlit triple supertwist LCD, VGA display. *—advertisement in Atlantic* Feb. 1992, p. 109

Supertwisted nematic liquid-crystal display: the best image quality is achieved by displays that include crystals with a 270° twist angle. *—New Scientist* 31 July 1993, p. 36 (caption)

superunleaded /suːpəʌnˈlɛdɪd/ *adjective* and *noun* 🌱 🚗

adjective: Designating petrol with no added lead, but with an octane rating similar to that of leaded petrol and higher than that of ordinary unleaded petrol, achieved by the addition of aromatic hydrocarbons.

noun: Superunleaded petrol.

Unleaded motor fuel, developed in the sixties, has become increasingly popular with the development of widespread concern about the effects of pollution on the atmosphere. Motorists were encouraged to have their vehicles converted to its use. Wider use, however, was accompanied by criticism of performance, and this resulted in the development in the late seventies of a *superunleaded* fuel, with the addition of benzene and similar compounds to enhance performance; these additives have themselves been seen as a cause of pollution, and the value of the enhancement has been questioned.

Michael Stone slid the Mustang up to the superunleaded pump at Buckley's Texaco.
—G. Gordon Liddy Monkey Handlers (1990), p. 298

Super-unleaded petrol contains a far higher 'aromatic content' than premium unleaded, including aromatics such as benzene, which is linked to cancer and leukaemia.
—Guardian 21 Mar. 1995, p. 1

supply-sider /səplʌɪˈsʌɪdə/ *noun* 💹 🏭

A supporter of an economic policy of low taxation and other incentives to produce goods and invest.

A specific use of a noun formed by adding the agent suffix *-er* to the adjectival compound *supply-side* 'pertaining to the supply side of the economy'.

Supply-sider as a term for one who advocates the principles of **supply-side** economics is recorded from the early eighties; the views of *supply-siders* found considerable support in the US and the UK in the Reagan and Thatcher years. The recession at the end of the eighties has raised substantial questions about the durability of the apparent economic success achieved in those years, but more recently the debate about levels of taxation has surfaced again, particularly in the US, in the ongoing discussion as to how best to stimulate the economy.

He thought it would be useful ammunition for twitting the pro-spending liberals, not realizing...that the same argument could be used against the supply-siders' proposed tax cuts.
—New York Times Book Review 17 May 1992, p. 9

Something did go wrong with federal revenues since 1990...There is an *additional* revenue loss of $38 billion that isn't accounted for in CBO's economic model. Aha! say supply-siders. This mysterious 'technical' loss surely proves Kemp's thesis—raise taxes and the rich will find ways to pay less of them. *—New Republic* 15 Mar. 1993, p. 6

No one actually thinks Dole cares about 'values' issues; nor do supply-siders—the GOP's other radioactive cluster—think he really wants to cut taxes. *—Newsweek* 8 May 1995, p. 47

surf /səːf/ *intransitive* or *transitive verb* 💻

Used in a variety of compounds, mainly connected with computing or communications, to indicate 'riding', as though on a surfboard.

In the mid eighties young people began to ride on the outside of trains for excitement. The practice of **surfing** (sometimes known more fully as **train surfing**) seems to have begun among poor youngsters in Rio de Janeiro and by the late eighties had spread to some US cities as well. In the late eighties it also started to become a problem in the UK, with a number of incidents in which young people were killed. There were also reports from the US of children **lift-surfing** (riding on the roofs of apartment-block lifts).

More recently, the term **channel-surfing** has been used to denote the activity of switching between channels on a television set to see what is available (see also GRAZE).

Following the rapid increase of interest in the INTERNET in the early nineties, the term has been extended to cover the area of activity known as *browsing* (see BROWSE) the NET for information or entertainment; a person who *surfs* the Internet is a **netsurfer** and the activity is **netsurfing** (the terms *cybersurfer* and *cybersurfing* (see CYBER-) are also used).

Criminals spy on users of telephones or cash machines by **shoulder-surfing** to obtain their authorization codes, either by peering over their shoulders while they type them in or by watching through binoculars from a distance. Such criminals are called **shoulder-surfers**.

What has become known as 'train surfing' is killing 150 teenagers a year in Rio, and injuring 400 more. —*Chicago Tribune* 5 May 1988, p. 28

'Shoulder surfers' spy on users of telephone credit cards to capture their 14-digit authorization codes, then sell the codes on the street moments later.
—*Philadelphia Inquirer* 11 Oct. 1992, section A, p. 1

The duo channel-surfs all day looking for 'cool' videos. —*USA Weekend* 3 Oct. 1993, p. 10

Customers ranging from terrified beginners to hardened cybernauts can now...sit down to a Cappuccino and Danish before embarking on a guided netsurf of the Internet at one of eight terminals under the user-friendly instruction of a member of staff.
—*Computer Weekly* 8 Sept. 1994, p. 1

sussed /sʌst/ *adjective* POP

In slang: in the know; well-informed; aware.

Formed from the verb *suss* 'work out; grasp, understand', ultimately deriving from an informal abbreviation of *suspect* or *suspicion*.

Sussed is recorded from the first half of the eighties as an expression of approval for someone regarded as thoroughly in the know and aware of the latest fashions and trends. A *sussed* person is one whose up-to-dateness is based on a grasp and understanding of the world around, and who is competent to deal with any situation that may arise.

While Morrissey relished in his melancholy and encouraged withdrawal and introspection, The Farm were sussed, street-wise and perfectly maladjusted. —*The Face* Feb. 1991, p. 34

Cooper is the sussed young teacher you never had but he's by no means a fave with the establishment. —*The Voice* 18 Oct. 1994, 24 Hours supplement, p. 3

The unemployed of the nineties aren't just those who didn't pay attention at school...but highly qualified and sussed young people. —Jayne Miller *voXpop* (1995), Introduction, p. 1

sustainable /sə'steɪnəb(ə)l/ *adjective* 🌳

In the environmental sense: of an activity or the use of a resource able to be sustained over an indefinite period without damage to the environment; of a resource that can be used at a given level without permanent depletion; renewable.

The adjective *sustainable* has been used in relation to conservation since the mid seventies; especially in the phrase **sustainable development**, it became one of the environmental buzzwords of the eighties as the green movement succeeded in focusing public attention on the long-term effects of energy use and industrial processes in Western societies. The corresponding adverb **sustainably** and the noun **sustainability** also became popular in these contexts.

It was host...to an environmental meeting in Bergen at which ministers from ECE's member countries discussed practical steps to promote 'sustainable development'.
—*EuroBusiness* June 1990, p. 64

This country is now pledged to move towards sustainability; that is, to conserve resources, to curb pollution, and to achieve the better balance between demand and supply that will protect the environment not only for us, but for our descendants.

—The Oxfordshire Bulletin (CPRE) Nov. 1992, p. 1

Sustainable tourism sees tourism within destination areas as a triangular relationship between host areas and their habitats and peoples, holidaymakers, and the tourism industry...Sustainable tourism aims to reconcile the tensions between the three partners in the triangle, and keep the equilibrium in the long term. *—Journal of Sustainable Tourism* 1994, Vol. 2, Nos. 1 & 2, p. 102

swagger portrait /'swagə pɔːtrɪt/ *noun*

A commissioned portrait of a prominent or wealthy person intended to represent the sitter's role, power, or status.

A *portrait* of a person who is shown as *swaggering* in an assertion of self-importance; there is probably also a notion of the adjectival use of *swagger* 'smart or fashionable'.

The term *swagger portrait* for this style of picture is found in the vocabulary of the art world from the first half of the eighties, but the application is of course retrospective. As was demonstrated by the exhibition held at the Tate gallery in 1992, examples of the *swagger portrait*'s flamboyant and striking representations of the wealthy and powerful can be traced back to at least the eighteenth century.

It is more instructive to consider the distinctions between Henri and those two American emperors of the swagger portrait. Henri made far fewer concessions to his sitter's taste, borne out by the small number of commissions he received. *—Smithsonian* May 1984, p. 148

The Swagger Portrait belongs as much to the history of style as it does to the history of art.
—Daily Telegraph 28 Oct. 1992, p. 18

swallower see STUFFER

swaption /'swɒpʃ(ə)n/ *noun*

The right to enter into a swap contract at preset rates at an agreed future date.

Formed from a blend of *swap* and *option*.

Swap contracts provide for **interest-rate swaps**, transactions in which two rates of interest on a certain principal are exchanged; the usual form for such agreements is that two parties have agreed to pay each other interest on a purely notional principal amount for a specified period of time, one paying at a fixed rate and the other at a floating rate. *Swap contracts* and *interest-rate swaps*, like *swaptions*, have been part of the jargon of the Stock Exchange since the early eighties, but in the nineties have come to wider public notice as events such as the spectacular failure of Barings have focused attention on financial terms associated with the DERIVATIVES market.

The ideal applicants should have gained...experience in trading/marketing swaps, options and swaptions. *—Financial Times* 20 Mar. 1991, p. 14

The London headquarters of Barings was struggling with the division that championed derivatives—financial instruments that use the public's massive bet on securities to create a parallel universe of side bets, some straightforward (like futures) and the arcane (like swaptions).
—Time 13 Mar. 1995, p. 42

swingbeat /'swɪŋbiːt/ *noun* Also written **swing-beat**

A form of dance music combining elements of rhythm and blues, soul, HIP-HOP, and rap music.

Swing 'jazz or dance music with an easy flowing but vigorous rhythm' and *beat* 'in popular music, a strong rhythm'.

Since the late eighties *swingbeat*, particularly as exemplified by NEW JACK SWING, has found wide popularity in the US; success in the UK has been less immediate.

You could probably count the number of *really* good swingbeat tracks (or New Jack Swing as Americans prefer to call it) on the fingers of one hand...though it seems that British dance music fans have given this new musical cross between hip hop and soul a fairly cool reception.
—*Record Mirror* 3 Feb. 1990, p. 33

The same bubbly swingbeat (or 'new jill swing') rhythms and plush vocal harmonies prevail everywhere. —*Guardian* 26 May 1995, Review section, p. 13

Their catchy alternative to swingbeat—part techno, part punk vocals—has won them support slots with East 17...and with Menswear. —*The Face* Aug. 1995, p. 25

swipe /swʌɪp/ *noun*

An electronic device for reading magnetically encoded information, as on a credit card or an identity card, usually incorporating a slot through which the card is passed.

From the idea of *swiping* a card rapidly through an electronic reader.

Swipe cards, with a magnetic strip holding encoded information, have been in use since the early eighties. They are now a common feature of modern life, both for their role in facilitating electronic banking, and for their capacity to increase the physical security of buildings by providing a mechanism whereby automatic access by *swipe* can be limited to those identified as having permission to enter an area.

An electronic swipe automatically clears the transaction. —*Observer* 22 Apr. 1990, p. 35

The Mechanical Engineering building will only be open to those with the appropriate 'swipe card'. —*Gazette* (Imperial College) June 1992, p. 3

A Blackburn reader was told his credit card would not be validated in a French swipe machine and had to pay in cash. —*Holiday Which?* Mar. 1995, p. 82

switch /swɪtʃ/ *noun*

In the US: a computerized link between financial institutions and points of sale, enabling goods to be paid for by debit card using EFTPOS (Electronic Funds Transfer at Point of Sale); in the UK (as *Switch*), the trade mark for a computerized EFTPOS system set up in 1988.

A *switch* in telecommunications has long meant a routing device (a telephone exchange is commonly called a *switch* within the industry); the choice of the name *switch* was probably also influenced by *packet-switching*, a standard mode of data transmission in which a message is broken down into parts or *packets*, each of which is separately routed or *switched* through the communications network.

The first point-of-sale computer system was set up in the US in the second half of the seventies, when the State of Iowa established a statewide *switch* network. The debit card system known by the trade-marked name *Switch* in the UK was launched by the Midland Bank, NatWest, and the Royal Bank of Scotland in October 1988 and has now extended to more than twenty banks and building societies. Using this system, shoppers need only a plastic debit card called a **Switch card** to pay for goods or buy cash (see CASH-BACK); the appropriate sums are transferred electronically from the purchaser's account to the retailer's. The *switch* was thought of in the early eighties as the herald of a cashless society in which a debit card would be all anyone would need to carry; although the *switch* systems are reasonably successful, this appears increasingly unlikely, and the technology may be overtaken by *electronic cash* systems (see ELECTRONIC).

Though similar systems have been tried on a much smaller scale by Hy Vee and Dahl's, both in Iowa, Publix is the first supermarket company to own not only the in-store terminals but also the crucial switch that channels the messages from varied sites to the appropriate banks.
—*Supermarket News* 2 July 1984, p. 1

Last year there were 169m Switch transactions in the UK and the scheme now has 20 member banks and building societies in place of the original three.

—*Financial Times* 11–12 Apr. 1992, p. 14

sympathetic pindown [see PINDOWN

sysop /'sɪsɒp/ *noun*

An informal name for the **system operator** of a computer *bulletin board* or BBS.

An abbreviation of the full name.

In the computing sense, the term *system operator* probably derived from the aviation industry, where it had been in use since at least the mid seventies for the person who controls or monitors any form of complex electronic equipment. With the rise in BBS systems in the early eighties, the term was rapidly abbreviated and applied to the person who ran such a system. It also describes someone who mediates or chairs discussion forums which form part of larger communications systems.

Unlike most systems operators (sysops), who go online as a hobby and grow into it, Miller knew from the start that he wanted to operate a BBS as a business. —*Wired* Sept. 1993, p. 345

If only a single filesystem is to be backed up while the rest of the machine functions normally, then that filesystem can be unmounted and mounted in an area to which only the system operators have access. —*Computing* 27 Jan. 1994, p. 20

Unlike forums, however, newsgroups contain no message sections or separate file libraries, and many are unmoderated (meaning they're not reviewed or systematized by a sysop). —*CompuServe Magazine* Jan. 1995, p. 23

systems software see APPLET

• •

T

tag /tag/ *noun* and *verb*

In HIP-HOP culture:

noun: A graffito, usually consisting of a decorated nickname, word, or initial, made by a graffiti artist as a personal 'signature'.

transitive verb: To decorate (a place or object) with graffiti; to leave (one's graffiti signature) in a public place.

A figurative use of *tag* in the sense of 'label'.

Graffiti *tags* first started to appear in the streets of New York during the first half of the seventies—and began to be called *tags* in print in 1980—but the practice of **tagging** did not spread far outside large American cities until the mid eighties. Then it was the popularization of hip-hop culture as a whole that involved youngsters in constructing these highly decorated nicknames, often on very visible public buildings. The person who paints a *tag* is known as a **tagger**; graffiti artists sometimes work in teams and a particular *tag* can belong to a **tag team** rather than to an individual **tag artist**.

Vandals have imported graffiti materials from America to ape New York 'tag teams'—gangs who vie to leave their personal trademarks in daring or eye-catching places. —*Daily Telegraph* 3 May 1990, p. 4

Taggers, typically, come up with their own logo, and the more they can get it around town, the higher the status with their friends. —*Post* (Denver) 2 Jan. 1994, Magazine, p. 12

Somebody was tagging the subway walls at the White Hart roundabout, in west London...They subsequently caught a youth in a nearby park, hands and jacket covered in silver paint...and put him in a police cell at Southall police station. They returned to find the cell wall had acquired a beautiful tag, precisely matching the White Hart subway work of art.

—Guardian 22 Feb. 1995, section 1, p. 20

Tamil Tiger /'tamɪl tʌɪgə/ *noun* 📷

A member of a Sri Lankan guerrilla organization seeking the establishment of an independent state in the north-east of the country for the Tamil community.

A guerrilla fighter who shows the strength and ferocity of the *tiger* in attempting to establish a separate state for the *Tamils*, a Dravidian people of Sri Lanka.

The *Liberation Tigers of Tamil Eelam* (*LTTE*) came into being in 1972 as a Sri Lankan guerrilla organization dedicated to the foundation of a Tamil homeland, *Eelam*. Since the late seventies Tamil separatists, known as *Tamil Tigers* or simply **Tigers**, have been fighting a virtual civil war for control of provinces in the north and east of the country, where there is a Tamil majority.

He was a member of the Tamil Tigers, the guerrilla group that wants a separate state in north-eastern Sri Lanka. *—Economist* 24 Aug. 1991, p. 41

A suicide bomber, identified by police as an Indian Tamil, set off a cartload of explosives that killed 22 people in Colombo yesterday in what was widely seen as Tamil Tiger (LTTE) separatists' answer to Sri Lanka's plans for power-sharing. *—Sun* (Baltimore) 8 Aug. 1995, section A, p. 7

Naval gunship escorts fought off the initial attack by the guerrillas' Sea Tigers' wing.

—Daily Telegraph 1 Apr. 1996 (electronic edition)

tape streamer 💾 see STREAMER

taqueria /'tɑːkəriːə, takə'riːə/ *noun* 🔀

A restaurant specializing in Mexican food, particularly tacos.

From the Mexican Spanish word *taqueria*, formed from *taco* and the suffix *-ia* indicating a place set aside for a particular activity.

For an earlier generation, the popularity of the *pizza* as a form of fast food led to the spread of *pizzerias* in Europe and America. As Mexican food became popular in the America of the eighties, a similar pattern followed: *taquerias*, where customers could be sure of getting *tacos* and other Mexican dishes, began to be a familiar sight.

Levine...had said something about going out for lunch to a local taqueria.

—New Yorker 8 May 1989, p. 41

In San Francisco, where I live, patrons in a local taquería championed their own personal favorites. *—Newsweek* 2 Nov. 1992, p. 12

Explore the used-book stores and hip barrooms around Valencia and 16th Streets. You'll find a *taqueria* on every corner. *—Wired* Jan. 1995, p. 152

tariff /'tarɪf/ *noun* 🔣

A sentence determined according to a series of scales suggesting standard (minimum) penalties for certain categories of crime.

Formed as an extension of use for an existing noun in the sense 'a table of fixed charges'.

The use of *tariff* in legal parlance to mean a scale suggesting the standard minimum penalty for a specified category of crime, to be used as an unofficial means of calculating a sentence or damages, is recorded from the late fifties.

In the eighties and nineties, however, the term has undergone further development, and is now used to indicate a sentence determined according to the unofficial scale. Most recently, the term has come to particular public attention in Britain in its use to designate minimum sentences set by the Home Secretary in a number of high-profile cases.

In my judgment natural justice requires that the prisoner be told what the judges have recommended, and anything the trial judge has said about relative culpability, in such time that he can make representations before the Home Secretary fixes the tariff period.

—*The Weekly Law Reports* (BNC) 1992, volume 3

The Home Secretary dismissed a recommendation from the home affairs select committee that his role in setting the tariff of years to be served by murderers be ended.

—*Daily Telegraph* 6 August 1996 (electronic edition)

tayberry ⬛ see TUMMELBERRY

techie /'tɛki/ *noun* 🔲

An expert in or enthusiast for technology, especially computing; a technician.

A diminutive form of *technician*.

The term has evolved several times in different contexts, but a main sense today (first recorded in the US at the beginning of the seventies) denotes an expert in computing, telecommunications, networking, and related areas, or an enthusiast for these subjects. It is often used pejoratively or dismissively in reference to the supposedly narrow technical skills such people possess, to the extent that it is unlikely that they would use the term to describe themselves unless in self-deprecation or defiant humour. The word is frequently used attributively and shows signs of becoming an adjective in phrases such as 'this is too techie for me'.

Over the years, bulletin board systems, or BBSs, have appealed to techies, but not to businesses. —*UnixWorld* Aug. 1991, p. 95

While senior managers have the highest regard for the techie when they fix a problem, the warm glow usually lasts just a couple of days. You won't find boffins in the boardroom.

—*Management Today* Sept. 1991, p. 114

This is a techie book that aims to teach you how to use PGP to encrypt, send and receive e-mail messages. —advertisement in *.net* June 1995, p. 85

techno /'tɛknəʊ/ *adjective* and *noun* 🐸 🔲

adjective: Of popular music, making heavy use of technology such as synthesized and sampled sounds and electronic effects.

noun: A style of popular music with a synthesized, technological sound and a dance beat.

From the first element of such compounds as *techno-pop* and *techno-rock*: see TECHNO-.

Techno, which first appeared in the late eighties (and remained popular well into the nineties) represents a synthesized, electronic, futuristic style which has evolved through links with other musical forms. *Techno* may also appear as the second element of compounds: **ambient techno** is a blend of *techno* with AMBIENT sounds, and **ragga-techno** is a combination with RAGGA that evolved into JUNGLE.

The DJs mix a seamless flow of continental techno tracks whose celestial organ melodies, fragmented disco diva vocals, science-fiction soundtrack samples and relentless tribal percussion hint at the gamut of human behaviour. —*Guardian* 22 Oct. 1993, section 2, p. 8

But today, techno means atmospheric chill-out music designed for home listening as often as it does party music. There are even techno clubs where people sip tea rather than take Ecstacy and loll about on mattresses rather than leaping about on the dance floor.

—*New York Times* 13 Mar. 1994, section 2, p. 32

The album...established the Cornwall, England, native as the pioneer of ambient techno, a musical style that converts the energized electrobeats and keyboard surges of dance-floor techno into slower, more tranquil sound washes. —*Rolling Stone* 30 June 1994, p. 72

techno- /'tɛknəʊ/ *combining form* 🖳 🧪

The first element of many compounds relating to those industrial techniques which use advanced or specialized methods, especially computing.

Though compounds formed using *techno-* have been in use for four hundred years, vigorous use of *techno-* as a combining form in word-building dates from the mid sixties onwards (**technophobe** and **technophile** were both coined in this period). Growth of technological industries and the swelling impact of their products on daily life was increasingly associated with nervousness about the effects of this; a high proportion of these new *techno-* words deal not with aspects of technology itself, but with attitudes to it, as in a group of words from the first half of the eighties. **Technofear** is a dread of the effects of technological developments. **Technobabble**, the incomprehensible and sometimes frightening language of the new technologies, especially computing, was joined by **technospeak**, with a similar but less vehement meaning. **Technostress**, a psychiatric illness arising from stressful work in a technological environment to which one is ill-adapted, was the subject of a book by the US psychologist Craig Bord in 1984. A **technofix** is a technological 'fix' or solution to a problem, possibly decided upon without considering whether there might be a more appropriate low-tech alternative; the word **technoindustrial** describes high-technology industries, particularly those related to computing.

A series of words, more or less pejorative, describing individuals fascinated or obsessed by technology were created in this period, including **technohippy** (a high-tech equivalent of the 1960s hippie), **technojunkie** (one 'hooked' on technology, especially computing), **technonerd**, **technoweenie** (in the sense of the US slang word *weeny*, an objectionable person, but with reduced force), and **technowizard** (someone highly knowledgeable about technical matters, especially in computing; this seems not to have the negative undertones of the others).

Ambivalence towards the fruits of technology is shown in the **technothriller**, a work in which some technological situation plays a pivotal plot role and in which attitudes to technology are polarized to the extremes of threat or fetish; examples are the novels of Michael Crichton and Tom Clancy, and the James Bond films (critics refer to works at the worshipful end of the *technothriller* spectrum as **technoporn**). The use of VIRTUAL *reality* techniques to simulate sexual activity is sometimes called **technosex**.

Since the beginning of the eighties, *techno-* has also been used with the names of styles of popular music, as in **techno-funk**, **techno-pop**, **techno-rock**, and **techno-soul**, to designate variations of these styles characterized by the use of synthesized sounds and an insistent dancebeat (see also TECHNO). More recently the dance scene has developed a spiritual dimension through **technoshamanism**, in which drugs, ecstatic dancing, and music are used to create a trance state among participants; related adjectives are **technoshamanistic** and **technoshamanic**.

Technostress…is harder on older employees than younger generations raised on technology.
—*Village Voice* 18 Sept. 1990, p. 79

Computer people speak a language all their own. So do plumbers, librarians and accountants, but somehow the jargon of their trades doesn't irritate the rest of us…as much as technobabble does. —*New York Times* 8 Oct. 1991, section C, p. 5

All it takes is one technomaniac spouting mystical acronyms and letter/number sequences of various models to send the uninitiated screaming to the door. —*Jazziz* Nov. 1991, p. 100

He dubs this the 'technoburb', describing it as 'a hopeless jumble of housing, industry, commerce, and even agricultural uses', with no boundaries. —*Amicus Journal* Summer 1992, p. 18

Now, while my oldest son Alex is a typical computer techno-weenie, his youngest brother most decidedly is not. —*Byte* June 1992, p. 102

Few women, she says, enter the techno-nerd world of MIDI, and even fewer have spent the last few years crawling around Oakland warehouses to wire their own computers from surplus scraps. —*Mother Jones* Sept. 1992, p. 17

First a gentle opener, then a techno-funk piece, followed by the *de rigueur* slushy vocal number:

that's the standard procedure these days, and the uninspired way these tracks are written and performed does raise questions of integrity. —*Jazz: the magazine* 1992, No. 12, p. 61

But unless there is a move away from dazzling, big science techno-fixes towards a renewed emphasis on healing as an art, patients' well-being will be no better served.
—*Time Out* 31 Mar. 1993, p. 12

Although there was a lot of technofear, the local employees caught on very quickly.
—*Accountancy* Oct. 1993, p. 45

The hot subject for techno heads on the Net right now is encryption. —*i-D* Oct. 1994, p. 20

The DJs consider themselves the technoshamans of the evening. Their object is to bring the participants into a technoshamanic trance, much in the way ancient shamans brought members of their tribes into similar states of consciousness. —Douglas Rushkoff *Cyberia* (1994), p. 123

techno-bhangra  see BHANGRA

technology transfer /tɛk'nɒlədʒi ˌtransfə:/ *noun*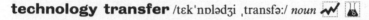

The transfer of new technology from the originator to a secondary user.

The most common usage of this term refers to the process of licensing new techniques or processes which have been developed in universities and research centres to industrial firms for exploitation. Many universities maintain offices whose purpose is to put researchers in touch with organizations which can commercialize their discoveries and which help negotiate licensing agreements; in the US, these are frequently called **technology transfer offices**. It also refers to the process by which industrialized countries provide information on new or appropriate technologies to less-developed countries as part of aid programmes, most commonly through providing people who have the specialized knowledge or experience; in this context, the term sometimes has emotive connotations of exploitation or control. It has also been used by the US government to refer to the conversion of industries from weapons manufacture to other fields.

The vague language relating to 'technology transfer' and equitable sharing appear to be code words for compulsory licensing and other forms of property expropriation.
—*New York Times* 14 June 1992, p. 6

Isaiah's hopeful prophecy that nations would beat their swords into plowshares...was an early expression of what today is called technology transfer.
—*Post* (Denver) 2 Jan. 1994, section A, p. 22

tele- /'tɛli/ *prefix*

Widely used as the first element of compounds relating to telecommunications, particularly in words for concepts which have been transformed by the use of computer-mediated communications and information technology.

One series of new words in *tele-* relating to *computer-mediated communications* began in the mid seventies with **telecomputer** (a computer able to make use of telecommunications), followed later in the decade by **telematics** (the long-distance transmission of computerized information). In the eighties, communicating with businesses by computers and telephone links developed with **teleshopping** (shopping conducted from home using a computer and a telephone) and **telebanking**. Some office workers began to **telecommute** or **telework**: to work from home while communicating with the office and elsewhere via data links; people who do this are **telecommuters** or **teleworkers**. The concept of the **telecottage** came from Scandinavia in the late eighties: a room in a rural area filled with equipment for **teleworking**, available for shared use by local residents; working from one of these is known as **telecottaging**. A purpose-built residential and business area designed for **telecommuting** may be called a **televillage**. Distance-learning using telecommunications is sometimes called **tele-education**; the convergence of the television set and the computer has given rise to the **teleputer**. The concept of **teledemocracy** (citizens linked by computers and communications to elected representatives through an 'electronic town hall') came to public notice as a result of Ross Perot's advocacy for the idea during his candidature for the US Presidency in 1992.

Another series of new words are those with the sense of 'action at a distance', beginning with **teleoperator** in the mid sixties (at first, a machine with which a person could undertake work at a distance, but now the person doing the operating). This idea is closely associated with the concept of **telepresence** (the use of remote control and feedback of sensory information to produce the impression of being in another place) dating from the early eighties, with its adjective **telepresent**. **Telerobotic** (concerning a machine or mechanized system whose operation is controlled remotely through the use of telecommunications) was coined in the early eighties; **telerobot**, **telerobotics**, and **telerobotically** followed later in the decade. In the late eighties, the concept of **telemedicine** developed, in which information on a patient is relayed to a distant location where specialized diagnosis may be made; medicine and robotics began to converge in the nineties with **telesurgery** (carrying out operations using remotely-controlled robotic instruments). Sharing a VIRTUAL *reality* space with others at a distance through telecommunications is known as **televirtuality**; what many would consider the ultimate such experience is the concept of **teledildonics** (the use of virtual reality to mediate sexual interaction between computer users not physically in the same place).

Alongside this new technology, the old ones continued to give rise to *tele-* compounds: **telemarketing**, the marketing of goods or services through unsolicited telephone calls (carried out by **telemarketers**), became an established selling technique (the words date from the early eighties). A site that links satellite and Earth communications is a **teleport** (originally the name of the first such site in New York, a name formed presumably from *port* in the sense of 'a large commercial trans-shipment area', and not related to the common— and much older—science-fiction concept of an instantaneous transportation device). A co-ordinating centre for *telemarketers* is called a **telecentre**. An unsuccessful attempt was made in the UK in the early nineties to create a second-generation short-range digital telephone service that linked users to the public telephone service, generically called **telepoint**.

Many of the tractors were equipped to be teleoperated from indoor stations, their decision algorithms handling the details while the human operators watched screens below.
—Kim Stanley Robinson *Red Mars* (1992), p. 113

A term has already been coined for the hypothetical virtual-reality sex—'teledildonics'—in which two people can meet each other's virtual images, have a sensational experience and then log off from each other without even having to call a taxi.
—*Globe & Mail* (Toronto) 11 Apr. 1992, section C, p. 1

We don't have all the specialized tools for you to use the lab telerobotically, so you'll have to go there in person. —Kevin Anderson & Doug Beason *Assemblers of Infinity* (1993), p. 72

The year was not without victims in the mobile phone arena. Hutchison Telecom closed Rabbit, the only telepoint phone service that stayed the course into full operation.
—*Guardian* 5 Jan. 1994, p. 12

Mayor Richard Riordan announced a grandiose plan to relieve congestion by extensive 'telecommuting'—working from home with computers and faxes. —*Time* 14 Feb. 1994, p. 33

Trials are taking place in eight Welsh surgeries to test 'telemedicine'—a down-the-line, dial-a-diagnosis way for allowing a consultant to see patient and GP in a video conference without moving from his/her hospital chair. —*Guardian* 24 Feb. 1995, Friday supplement, p. 24

telnet 🖳 see NET

temporarily abled 📗 see ABLED

teraflop /ˈtɛrəflɒp/ *noun* 🖳

In computing, a processing speed of a trillion (a million million) floating-point operations per second.

Formed from the combining form *tera-* in its usual sense in units of measurement, 'a trillion times', and a 'singular' form of the acronym *FLOPS*, 'floating-point operations per second' (the *s* being dropped as though it were there to mark the plural form of a regular noun *flop*).

One way to determine the speed of a computing system is to measure how fast it can carry out complicated calculations involving decimal fractions (which are stored in the computer in a special format called *floating-point representation*). It is an indication of the rate at which the field is developing that the computing world of the late seventies spoke of *megaflops* (millions of floating-point operations per second), today measures supercomputers' speeds in terms of *gigaflops*, and is now designing machines that run at *teraflop* speeds.

Cray…has recently launched a crash programme to build a massively parallel 'ultracomputer' that can be scaled up into teraflop territory. —*Economist* 2 May 1992, p. 137

The Concurrent Supercomputing Consortium (CSCC) has recently launched a coordinated attack on the biggest obstacle to effective use of teraFLOPS-scale computer systems by scientists and engineers—getting data into, out of and around such systems fast enough to avoid severe bottlenecks. —3 Feb. 1995, online posting

Thatchernomics 📖 see -NOMICS

there is no alternative 📖 see TINA

third wave /ˈθəːd weɪv/ *noun* Also written **Third Wave** 📖 ❙❙

The current phase of economic, social, and cultural change in which knowledge, especially as stored and disseminated by information technology, is the primary productive force.

A term coined by Alvin Toffler at the beginning of the eighties to designate the *third* such movement in a recognized sequence. The *third wave* thus defined is conceived as following the agrarian *first wave* and the industrial *second wave*. The term is generally used in association with Toffler's analysis, and in contexts which may develop the image of a *wave*.

Third Wave 'postnations' form the newest tier of the global system. Unlike agrarian states, they have no great need for additional territory. Unlike industrial states, they have no need for vast natural resources of their own. —Alvin & Heidi Toffler *War & Anti-War* (1993), p. 248

The Third Wave is crashing over us right now, having started with the birth of a postindustrial, high-technology, information economy in the 1950s. —*New Scientist* 19 Mar. 1994, p. 22

Centre stage were futurists Alvin and Heidi Toffler…whose classic Future Shock warned that society is about to be rocked by a Third Wave. The first created an agricultural society, the second triggered the industrial revolution and the third will centre on knowledge. —*Guardian* 12 Jan. 1995, p. 12

It goes without saying that we are poised on the brink of a postindustrial Third Wave that will sweep through our workplace and home environments, revolutionizing the way we pursue leisure activities, do business, and seek personal growth. —*Interzone* Apr. 1995, p. 4

32-bit /θəːtɪˈtuːbɪt/ *adjective* Also written **thirty-two-bit** 🖥

Concerning a (personal) computer whose central processing unit (microprocessor) is designed to handle instructions and data consisting of 32 binary digits. More generally, relating to any piece of computer equipment which is so designed, or to a software specification based on binary numbers of this size.

A compound of the number *32* with *bit*, in its standard computing sense of 'a binary digit', a number which can take only the values 1 and 0.

Although the concept of a *32-bit* computer processor is far from new, since many mainframe and minicomputer processors have long been able to handle these and greater sizes of binary numbers, it was through personal computers that the term came to more general notice from the mid eighties. Computers with processors which can handle larger binary numbers potentially have advantages of speed and flexibility, since they can work on larger chunks of data at a time and can access greater amounts of system memory. The pressure in the personal computer market since the late eighties has been towards standardizing on systems with such processors, which are better able to cope with the processing and memory demands of visually-based operating systems than earlier 8-bit and 16-bit ones.

> ExpertColor Paint is a simple to use yet powerful color paint program with many extras including 32-bit color, image editing and multiple undo's. —*MacWorld* June 1992, p. 142

> Microsoft says NT will allow users to run their existing DOS-and Windows-based applications under a multitasking, 32-bit system, and will offer a superset of DOS and Windows capabilities.
> —*UnixWorld* Feb. 1993, p. 44

> Your Mac can see only 8 MB of RAM unless 32-bit addressing is turned on, regardless of how much RAM is actually installed. —*MacUser* Aug. 1994, p.133

three-peat /'θriːpiːt/ *verb* and *noun*

transitive or *intransitive verb*: In the US: to win (a particular championship or other event) three times, especially consecutively.

noun: A third success in a particular championship or other event, especially the third of three consecutive wins.

A blend of *three* and *repeat*.

Three-peat derives from American basketball slang, and is first recorded in 1988; since then there is some evidence for the term becoming part of the more general sporting vocabulary. Contextually, and perhaps inevitably, references to *three-peats* are found more often as future hopes than achieved successes.

> If he wins, he will be the first man to three-peat Augusta—and the first in 35 years to three-peat any major—and that means outclassing Nicklaus and Palmer and even Hogan himself.
> —*Sports Illustrated* 8 Apr. 1991, p. 80

> The Bulls couldn't get that last season, but they didn't need it to get their three-peat.
> —*Chicago Tribune* 15 Apr. 1994, section 4, p. 1

> In their quest to three-peat, getting in shape is the name of the game for these World Series champs. —*Healthwatch Mag.* Summer 1994, p. 19

three-strikes /'θriːstrʌɪks/ *adjective* Also written three strikes

In the US, an informal term designating a law whereby a person convicted of three serious felonies is subject to mandatory life imprisonment.

From the terminology of baseball, in which a batter who has had *three strikes*, or has had three fair opportunities of hitting the ball, is out.

In the eighties and early nineties, concerns about law and order resulted in a number of American states passing legislation which introduced *three-strikes* (more fully and explicitly, **three-strikes-you're-out**) legislation. While popular with the conservative right, *three-strikes* legal systems have been criticized on general grounds of the danger to civil liberties, and more specifically in that the definition of what constitutes a serious felony may result in inappropriately draconian punishment for offenders.

> We got a three-strikes law here—three felonies and it's life—so we got guys doing terminal stretches for passing two bad checks and aggravated mopery. —*The Nation* 14 Oct. 1984

> Criminals in California now face life sentences after their third offence under the 'three strikes, you're out' law. —*Independent* 26 Apr. 1995, p. 27

thrillcraft /'θrɪlkrɑːft/ *noun*

Chiefly in the US: any of various types of recreational water vehicles, used in exciting or dangerous water sports, and capable of high speeds.

The use of *thrillcraft* (as in JET-SKIING) reflects the fashion for EXTREME *sports* of the eighties and nineties. As with another such sport, HELI-SKIING, the possible environmental impact remains a matter of concern.

Deborah Glockner-Ferrari…credits the rising popularity of thrill craft—jet skis, parasails and other recreational water vehicles that can annoy cetaceans.   —*National Wildlife* Feb. 1986, p. 10

The commission heard from an industry representative on the subject of jet ski operation, a problem under study along with the impact of other 'thrill craft' on boating safety.
   —*Record* (Bergen County, New Jersey) 25 Sept. 1986, section C, p. 10

Finally in 1991 thrillcraft were banned during the [whale] calving season.
   —*Chicago Tribune* 14 Apr. 1996, Womanews supplement, p. 3

through-ticketing /ˈθruːtɪkɪtɪŋ/ *noun*

A system whereby a traveller passing through several different railway networks can purchase one ticket (a 'through ticket') for the whole journey.

The term *through-ticketing* (recorded from the beginning of the seventies) came to prominence in the UK in the context of the 1993 railway privatization, whereby the formerly nationalized system was divided (under the supervision of *Ofrail*, see OF-) into a number of regional businesses for freight and transport. As full implementation of the new system approached, increasing anxieties were expressed as to the capacity and willingness of the regional businesses to provide for *through-ticketing* from every station, and to date it is still not entirely clear what the long-term picture will be.

Mr Salmon also dispelled fears that commuters would have to buy several different tickets to travel across the network, saying that through-ticketing would continue.   —*Daily Telegraph* 15 Dec. 1994, p. 1

A savage cutback in through-ticketing on trains remained a real threat last night.
   —*Daily Mail* 2 Jan. 1995, p. 33

tiger¹ /ˈtʌɪɡə/ *noun*

A colloquial term, originally a nickname, for any of the more successful smaller economies of East Asia, especially those of Hong Kong, Singapore, Taiwan, and South Korea.

A figurative use of the noun *tiger* to convey the idea of ferocity and energy traditionally associated with the animal.

The development of the East Asian economies, and in particular the **Four Tigers** of Hong Kong, Singapore, Taiwan, and South Korea, has been one of the economic success stories of the last fifteen years. By the late eighties, further **tiger economies**, such as those of Malaysia, Thailand, and the Philippines, had been added to the original four, and in the nineties the *tigers* are seen to have achieved a considerable domination of world markets. The noun **tigerism** has been coined as a term encapsulating the view that the *tiger economies* are likely to prove formidable economic competitors for Britain in the coming years.

It [Hong Kong] is one of the 'Four Tigers'—four nations in East Asia (the others are Singapore, Taiwan, and South Korea) that have experienced massive economic growth in the last two decades.   —*Byte* Jan. 1993, p. 41

The tigers of South-East Asia have built their booms by welcoming foreigners.
   —*Economist* 24 June 1995, p. 16

Suddenly the Conservative Party and Whitehall has been gripped by 'tigerism'—the notion that Britain faces a rough battle for survival in the next millennium against the tiger economies of the Far East, and that only a deregulated, low-tax, free market economy can save it.
   —*Independent on Sunday* 10 Dec. 1995, p. 8

See also DRAGON

Tiger² see TAMIL TIGER

tile /tʌɪl/ *transitive verb* 🖳

To arrange individual application areas in a graphically-based computer display in a rectangular array without overlapping; to cover (part or all) of a computer display with multiple copies of an image arranged in a rectangular grid.

With graphically-based applications which employ multiple windows, it is common to provide a facility to display the windows in a rectangular formation at appropriate sizes so that all can be seen at once. The term can also refer to the process by which a single rectangular image is repeated many times to fill an area of the screen. The technique is referred to as **tiling** and such a display is said to be **tiled**.

> Windows can be stacked, tiled, shadowed, moved, resized.　　*—UNIX Review* Mar. 1992, p. 80

> You can't iconize the windows, but you get tiling, cascading, and other MDI-type activity for free.　　*—Dr. Dobb's Journal* Dec. 1993, p. 82

TINA /'tiːnə/ *interjection* 🏛

An expression of complete unwillingness to consider any other course than that chosen.

From the initial letters of the words *There Is No Alternative*.

TINA, said to be an abbreviation formulated and adopted by the Young Conservatives, is likely to be remembered as an assertion central to the political principles of Margaret Thatcher as Prime Minister. The phrase originally came from a speech of Mrs Thatcher's to the Conservative Women's Conference, 21 May 1980, when she said:

> I believe people accept there is no alternative.

The words **there is no alternative**, and their abbreviation, quickly became catch-phrases, and are permanently associated with the Thatcherite eighties; in the nineties, they have been superseded by later phrases such as BACK TO BASICS. It seems likely that *TINA*, if it survives, will do so as an historical reference to a past period rather than as a current term.

> That was the meaning of TINA, a famous acronym that became a beautiful propaganda weapon. There Is No Alternative grew from a conventional piece of impudent bravado on the part of the monetarists into an assertion that mesmerised the anti-monetarists, terrorising them into spell-bound if curmudgeonly acquiescence. They could think of alternatives, but no Alternative.
> 　　*—Hugo Young* One of Us *(final edition, 1993), p. 205*

tiramisu /tɪrəmɪ'suː/ *noun* Also written **tiramisù** ✖

An Italian dessert consisting of layers of sponge cake soaked in coffee and brandy or liqueur and a filling of mascarpone cheese, topped with cocoa powder.

An Italian word, with the literal sense 'pick me up', from the phrase *tira mi sù*.

The word *tiramisu* entered the English language in the early eighties, when the dessert began to gain status as a gourmet food. The term has now moved from specialized cookery texts to the more general vocabulary; a process no doubt helped by the increasing availability of the dish as a prepared dessert sold in many supermarkets.

> Diners in New York and Los Angeles are getting their first taste of a dessert called Tiramisu.
> 　　*—Nation's Restaurant News* (US) 11 Nov. 1985, p. 4

> The once home-made dessert was light *tiramisù* with fresh mascarpone and barely sweetened coffee.　　*—Decanter* Mar. 1991, p. 107

> Few of the recent Euro-fads have swept Tokyo as thoroughly as tiramisù, which has been trans-formed from a chic dessert to a marketing phenomenon packaged as candy.
> 　　*—New York Times* 13 Mar. 1992, section C, p. 1

> Desserts have foiled the health gestapo, too, with anything made of sexy *mascarpone* an easy

sell. Are they serving *tiramisu* at the drive-in yet? Everybody else is.

—*Minnesota Monthly* May 1994, p. 60

toast see PERFORMANCE POETRY

to die for /tə 'dʌɪ fɔː/ *adjectival phrase* Also written **to-die-for**

An informal expression meaning: extremely good or desirable.

An isolated use is recorded from the late nineteenth century, E. N. Westcott's

Oh! and to 'top off' with, a mince-pie to die for.

However, *to die for* and the alternative **to die** as current expressions date from the beginning of the eighties, as in G. B. Trudeau's

A tad overweight, but violet eyes to die for.

There is increasing evidence of attributive use.

The things he said about Olivier...to die! —M. Riva *Marlene Dietrich* (1992), p. 645

It's impossible not to be seduced by the glorious sound of the Servais—its low register in particular is to die for. —*Globe & Mail* (Toronto) 25 Jan. 1993, section D, p. 2

Excellent Vietnamese fare, including to-die-for softshell crabs.

—*Post* (Denver) 8 Jan. 1995, section D, p. 11

tone dialling /'təʊn dʌɪəlɪŋ/ *noun*

A system of telephone dialling, in which each digit is transmitted as a short burst of a single audio frequency.

With the development of electronic exchanges, a system was adopted by which a telephone handset or other device generated audio tones which were recognized by the computerized equipment at the exchange. This has replaced the older PULSE DIALLING system, though different tone sequences are used in different countries.

They still accept pulse dialling, but they're also geared for tone dialling phones.

—*Which?* Sept. 1989, p. 439

The service is accessible 24 hours a day...using any Group 3 fax machine with tone dialling and loudspeaking capability. —*The BT Small Business Catalogue* Autumn 1995, p. 13

tool- /tuːl/ *combining form*

In computer jargon, used to form compounds relating to software applications or services.

The first word to be formed on *tool-* was **toolkit** in the early eighties, denoting a suite of software applications designed to assist in some task, such as computer-based design or compilation of other programs. An alternative term with the same sense is **toolset**; a person developing such software tools is sometimes called a **toolsmith**. As computer applications became more complicated and visual metaphors became common, the **toolbar** was invented to help users avoid having to traverse the often intricate MENU structures of programs; *toolbars* are sections of a graphically-based computer application containing a number of representations of buttons which call up relevant functions or utilities when clicked with a mouse. A related form, **toolbox**, often refers to a rectangular array of such buttons which can be positioned anywhere on the screen. The term **tooltip** was invented by the Microsoft Corporation to describe a technique for making short messages appear alongside *toolbar* buttons to explain their purpose.

A toolbox on the left edge gives access to the tools for drawing geometrical figures, colouring, text, selecting objects and changing the screen view.

—*Personal Computer World* Mar. 1992, p. 254

So the early toolsmiths writing in C under UNIX began developing idioms at a rapid rate.

—P. J. Plauger *The Standard C Library* (1992), p. 25

Unlike the toolsets of the big four, their products allow developers to send SQL instructions to multiple databases. —*Computing* 19 Nov. 1992, p. 30

Of course, a toolbar is just a dialog with buttons, but SmartPad lets you build 'smart' buttons. Tooltip-like titles you define automatically pop up a few seconds after you position your cursor over a button. —*Byte* May 1995, p. 36

Toronto blessing /tərɒntəʊ 'blɛsɪŋ/ *noun* 🄴

A form of religious ecstasy primarily characterized by mass fainting in association with speaking in tongues, weeping, and laughing.

The *Toronto blessing*, first observed in the Vineyard Church in Toronto, Canada, is taken by those who experience it as evidence of the gifts of the Holy Spirit and a direct expression of divine favour. This expression of religious ecstasy, which soon spread to congregations in Britain, is characterized by the recipient's falling to the ground; weeping, laughing, and speaking in tongues are all associated with it.

Despite being welcomed by many evangelical churches, the extreme emotionalism associated with this manifestation has been regarded with some concern. In December 1995, the Vineyard Church in Toronto, where the *Toronto blessing* first appeared, was refused accreditation by the Anglican hierarchy.

Members of the congregation started falling to the floor, giggling...For the past couple of months, growing numbers of worshippers in growing numbers of churches have experienced this strange form of ecstasy, known as the 'Toronto blessing' after its first appearance in a chapel in Canada. —*Church Times* 12 Aug. 1994, p. 13

Our experience of the so-called Toronto Blessing is that it is the work of the Holy Spirit, bringing many hundreds of people to renewed faith in Jesus Christ, a greater depth of repentance, and a fresh desire to pray and read the Bible. —*Guardian* 30 Jan. 1995, p. 3

What many view as the 'Toronto Blessing' is criticized by others as a dangerous offense. —*Faith Today* (Willowdale, Ontario) Mar. 1995, p. 19

See also HAPPY-CLAPPY

total quality /təʊt(ə)l 'kwɒlɪti/ *noun phrase* 〰

A theory of management based on the principle that every member of staff must be committed to maintaining high standards of work in every aspect of a company's operations.

The concept *total quality* was introduced into the business world in the mid eighties, in the period also characterized by such introductions as JUST-IN-TIME and QUALITY CIRCLES. It is most frequently found in the compound **total quality management** (abbreviation **TQM**), a term for a systematic approach to improving the quality of products and customer service, while reducing costs. In the nineties, *total quality* has been to some extent superseded by BUSINESS PROCESS RE-ENGINEERING as the latest and most fashionable concept, but the principles of *total quality management* are still regarded by many as valuable.

Having opted to make Total Quality a keystone of his company's corporate culture, they began defining quality and relating it to each employee's job content. —*Industrial Waste Management* Oct. 1991, p. 4

The fad of the moment, business process re-engineering...has since upstaged such preceding fads as 'just-in-time' and 'total quality management'. —*Economist* 2 July 1994 (electronic edition)

An empirical study suggests that organizations benefit from Total Quality Management not so much from such touted TQM features as quality training, process improvement, and benchmarking, than from the organizational characteristics that would make a company want to adopt TQM to begin with—open culture, a climate of employee empowerment, and executive commitment to organizational development. —*Infosys* 7 Apr. 1995 (electronic newsletter)

touchy-feely /'tʌtʃɪfiːli/ *adjective* 🔝

Often in derogatory use: given to the tactile expression of one's feelings, motivated by emotion rather than intellect.

Touchy-feely in its literal sense is associated with the development in the sixties and seventies of *encounter groups*, in which members of such groups sought psychological benefit through close contact with one another.

By the early nineties the figurative use of the term was also strongly established, and had extended its range: in a number of instances, *touchy-feely* appears to sum up the attitude implicit in what journalists christened the *caring nineties*, and the values of a NEW AGE society. The noun **touchy-feeliness** has been recorded.

Instead of teaching practical skills, many have offered a rash of new touchy-feely courses designed more to humor students than show them how to manage in the real world.
—advertisement in *New Yorker* 11 May 1992, p. 75

I don't want to sound New Age touchy-feely, but she has almost a sense of responsibility for speaking to its best sentiments, its economic and social potential.
—*Vanity Fair* June 1994, p. 47

We Greens are quite touchy-feely types. But because you go to a Green Party Conference it doesn't mean you want to be hugged all the time.
—*Daily Telegraph* 6 Mar. 1995, p. 1

tough love /tʌf 'lʌv/ *noun* 🔝 🔠

Care and concern expressed by encouraging a person to give up certain behaviours, take responsibility for themselves, and seek self-help.

The concept of *tough love* developed in America in the early eighties as an appropriate way for family members in co-operation with professional carers to deal especially with children and young adults likely to be affected by drug abuse. The climate of the eighties was sympathetic to a view that true concern was best expressed by the setting of standards, rather than by showing indulgence; the aim was to develop a readiness for self-help, and to foster the notion that each person is responsible for his or her own actions.

With growing familiarity, the term developed a transferred use in the political world: *tough love* in this sense would be expressed by restricting state benefits in an effort to combat what has been called the DEPENDENCY CULTURE.

Grappling with teen-age drug abuse...In many cases this means practising 'tough love'...by establishing curfews, enforcing house rules, chaperoning parties and forbidding drugs in the house.
—*Washington Post* 24 Feb. 1981, p. 5

I always told her, 'You let Tracey in your house, everything will be gone'. If they give you hell, you've got to give them tough love.
—*New York Times* 13 Oct. 1991, section 1, p. 42

The governor would also cut off welfare payments to able-bodied mothers after two years, although their children would continue to receive support. Not for nothing is Mr Wilson now being dubbed the 'tough-love' governor.
—*Economist* 14 Jan. 1995, p. 49

Early indications are that 'tough love' reforms now implemented in America are actually working, both in reducing the rolls and in changing the entitlement culture.
—*Daily Telegraph* 12 Oct. 1995, p. 19

tourism /'tʊərɪz(ə)m/ *noun* 🔳 🔝

As the second element of a compound: the organization and operation of holidays with a specified area of interest.

The development of *tourism* as a major industry has from the mid eighties resulted in a number of coinages specifying the particular area of interest catered for in the travel package. Those attracted to the past may indulge in **heritage tourism**. Wildlife and the countryside are the subjects of **nature tourism**; city holidays give the opportunity for **urban tourism**. **Health tourism** provides for those who wish to dedicate their holidays to becoming or remaining fit, while sports enthusiasts can enjoy the opportunities offered by **sports tourism**.

Some more-or-less euphemistic compounds have also developed, all having some implication of an element of exploitation. In Britain, so-called BENEFIT TOURISM has occasioned considerable debate. The term **business tourism** has been coined for the practice of travelling in order to take advantage of the economic deprivation of a chosen area or country. Since the early nineties there have been reports of **sex tourism**, holidays said to be organized to take advantage of the lack of restrictions on sexual activity and prostitution, especially involving the young, imposed by some legal systems.

Those taking advantage of such forms of *tourism* are described in corresponding compounds as **business tourists, health tourists, heritage tourists, nature tourists, sex tourists**, and **urban tourists**.

> Seduced in the giddy late eighties by an apparently meteoric rise in 'health tourism', investors overbuilt the Atlantic and Mediterranean coasts with such a profusion of marine healing centres that supply far outstripped demand. —*Guardian* 20 Nov. 1993, p. 39

> At Yosemite, the wilderness is not the same since heritage tourism leads visitors on horseback into the backcountry bringing radios, football games, and ice for martinis.
> —*Legacy* Jan. 1994, p. 37

> It's a dusty hour's journey by pickup truck, but pasture tourists can also see the original bed for the railroad. —*Post* (Denver) 30 Apr. 1995, section T, p. 4

towelhead /ˈtaʊəlhɛd/ *noun* POP 🔲

A derogatory slang expression for a person who wears a headcloth or turban.

Towelhead is recorded from the mid eighties as a derogatory (and consciously offensive) term for someone who habitually wears a headcloth or turban. It may be compared with an earlier formation *raghead*, of similar meaning, which was recorded in the twenties.

> A film in which an Arab character is addressed as 'towel head' can hardly pretend to have much in the way of spirituality. —*New York Times* 11 Dec. 1985, section C, p. 22

> If you did a brain scan of the British racist mentality, you'd find that, on the whole, we reckon the 'towelheads' have a pretty rough time of it. —*Observer* 3 Feb. 1991, p. 18

toyboy /ˈtɔɪbɔɪ/ *noun* Also written **toy-boy** or **toy boy** 🔲

In British slang: an attractive young man who is 'kept' as a lover by an older person.

Taking advantage of the rhyming syllables: a *boy* who is the plaything or *toy* of an older partner.

The concept of the *toyboy*— the male equivalent of the BIMBO—developed in the early eighties as a regular feature of the language of the tabloids. Normally the *toyboy* is the younger lover of a mature woman, but the word has also been applied to gay relationships, or to any male viewed merely as a sexual plaything; often it is used attributively, with the implication that the person being described is young and attractive. The term has even begun to generate variations: for example, the rock star Madonna was punningly described as the **boy toy** in 1989, because of the motto on her belt-buckle and the overtly sexy image that she cultivated, and this was later applied to other female stars in the same mould. In an interesting reversal of meaning, it is *boy toy* rather than *toyboy* that has caught on in the US to refer to men as well.

> I wonder to myself if now that he is representing Madonna it is okay to think of him as my little CAA agent boy toy. —Julia Phillips *You'll Never Eat Lunch in this Town Again* (1991), p. 540

> An 87-year-old woman ditched her toyboy husband after he threw an ashtray at her in a blazing row. —*Daily Mirror* 8 Sept. 1992, p. 15

> He informs Aunt Elspeth that he has always wanted to be a toy-boy but he was born too early, dammit, unless she is willing to recruit him. —*Guardian* 25 Sept. 1993, p. 68

See also HIMBO

TQM ⟋⟍ see TOTAL QUALITY

traffic calming /'trafɪk kɑːmɪŋ/ *noun* 🌳

The deliberate slowing of traffic, especially along residential streets, by the construction of road humps or other obstacles to progress.

A translation of the German word *Verkehrsberuhigung*.

In the last decades, growing pressure by the increased number of private cars in developed countries has led to pressure on the infrastructure, and various schemes of traffic management for cities (such as the introduction of RED ROUTES) have been considered. *Traffic calming* as a concept was introduced in the late eighties and has quickly become familiar; it is now customary in many residential areas to drive along road surfaces in which SPEED BUMPS have been constructed, and the traffic flow in city streets is often constricted by *chokers*, or periodic street narrowings introduced for this purpose.

Traffic calming, as advocated by **traffic calmers**, is now an accepted part of traffic management policy, but some concerns have been expressed that simply slowing down the flow of traffic leads to an increase of exhaust pollutants in the affected areas; the obstructions themselves in **traffic-calmed** areas may also constitute a hazard to cyclists and a nuisance to bus drivers.

> Surface changes…emphasise to motorists that they are in a traffic-calmed area.
> —*Which* Oct. 1992, p. 33

> Where traffic calming had been introduced, there had been a dramatic decline in accidents.
> —*Cycling Weekly* 16 Jan. 1993, p. 12

> Cyclists in particular are told to take care of 'narrowings and other traffic calming features' but warned that they should ride over the hump rather than avoid it by going along 'a drainage channel at the edge of the road'.　　　　—*Independent* 20 Jan. 1993, p. 5

> Such ambitious goals could not be achieved by cycleways alone: they depend heavily on persuading people out of their cars by a sophisticated system of traffic calming.
> —*Independent on Sunday* 6 Feb. 1994, Review section, p. 67

> The bad news is that 'traffic calming,' the science of slowing down drivers, usually with speed bumps, has hit potholes.　　　　—*High Country News* 27 Nov. 1995, p. 15

trainspotter /'treɪnspɒtə/ *noun* 〰️ 🍺

In British slang: a derogatory term for an obsessive follower of any minority interest or specialized hobby.

An extended usage of *trainspotter* in the sense of 'a person who collects locomotive numbers as a hobby'.

This extension of the established term *trainspotter* is recorded from the late eighties, and like the associated terms ANORAK and GEEK reflects a disparaging view of a person who allows one (especially solitary) interest to dominate his or her lifestyle. The interest and knowledge brought by a *trainspotter* to his or her chosen field are seen as largely negated by the trivial nature of the selected subject area. *Trainspotters* practise **trainspotting** (a term given a high profile by Irvine Welsh's 1993 novel *Trainspotting*, the film of which was released in 1996), and their interests and activities may be characterized as **trainspotterly**; the compound adjective **trainspotter-worthy** has also been recorded.

> For years people have been going around doing the wally voice for anoraks and trainspotters— and when a politician comes along with a similar voice we elect him prime minister.
> —*Guardian* 7 Oct. 1994, p. 10

> With denim trainspotting now a national institution, it's interesting to see the number of vintage jackets being snapped up sporting vintage patches.　　　　—*The Face* Oct. 1994, p. 41

> Trainspotters may jubilate to learn of an upcoming Beatles first: they've released two tracks,

Yesterday and She Loves You, for a non-Beatle compilation. —*Q* June 1995, p. 16

See also OTAKU

trance /trɑːns/ *noun* 🎵

A type of electronic dance music derived from techno, characterized by hypnotic rhythms and sounds.

Music supposedly likely to induce a *trance* by its hypnotic quality.

Trance or **trance music** is a phenomenon of the nineties, deriving from a development of TECHNO, and perhaps particularly associated with attempts to create a state of trance among participants: the music is seen as having a spiritual dimension as well as providing entertainment.

Superb trance house full of spot-on drum drops and trippy noise. —*i-D* July 1992, p. 78

Self-empowerment comes from awareness and tolerance, spirituality and knowledge of self. Much of hip-hop teaches that while other forms of ambient and trance coax it through their restraint. Listen to the music. —*Urb* 7 July 1993, p. 12

One area of growing interest in the current fragmentation of rave culture is tribal elements in trance music. —*Hypno* 1994, Vol. 3, p. 56

transdermal patch ⊗ see PATCH

trans-fatty acid /ˈtranzfati ˌasɪd, ˈtrɑːnz-/ *noun phrase* ⊗ 🔀

A form of unsaturated fat with a changed molecular structure which is now regarded as being potentially harmful.

The fashion established in the eighties for a low-fat diet saw a considerable growth in the development of reduced fat spreads to replace the saturated fats of traditional margarine and butter. A number of such spreads are made with liquid vegetable oils, solidified by the process of hydrogenation, and from the early nineties there has been a growing awareness that this process also results in the production of *trans-fatty acids*, or **trans-fats**, which may in themselves present a risk to health in their effects on levels of cholesterol.

These trans-fatty acids, according to the new study, raised the high-risk LDL cholesterol levels and lowered the protective HDL cholesterol levels of their study subjects. —*Food and Wine* Apr. 1991, p. 110

Our insatiable appetite for foods made with vegetable oil has pushed trans-fat intake to an all-time high. Because trans-fats don't appear on food labels but lurk unnoticed in many foods, stalking this shifty player in the heart-health game takes some know-how. —*Runner's World* Feb. 1994, p. 26

The Co-op will...label margarines which contain trans-fatty acids, which some studies suggest are a worse health risk than butter. —*Independent* 24 Apr. 1995, p. 5

transgenic /tranzˈdʒɛnɪk, trɑːnz-/ *adjective* ⊗ 🔬

Relating to an organism which contains inheritable genetic material which has been artificially introduced from another organism.

To produce a *transgenic* organism, genetic material (DNA) from the donor is injected into embryo cells of the recipient at an early stage in development; the DNA is incorporated into the genetic material of the recipient organism and can be passed to future generations. The process is formally called **transgenesis** but is commonly referred to as GENETIC ENGINEERING, though this term has the wider sense of any change made to the organism's genes, not necessarily ones involving foreign genetic material. *Transgenesis* has aroused immense controversy because of the environmental and health implications of releasing modified organisms into the wild, and the ethical implications of modifying higher animals to turn them into living biological factories, or BIOREACTORS (as has been done with cows, sheep, and goats in order to produce human proteins for therapeutic use). Other procedures involve introducing human DNA into mice so they mimic the human immune response for experimental purposes, modifying the genes of food plants to make them resistant to disease, and changing the DNA of pigs so their organs can be used as human transplants. The field is usually referred to as **transgenics** and the adverb is **transgenically**; a gene which is introduced into another organism in this way is called a **transgene**.

> If the transgene gets into the germ line, researchers say it should be possible to generate transgenic offspring from the chimeric animal.
> —*Genetic Engineering News* 1 Nov. 1994 (electronic edition)

> Indeed, in developing countries, farmers may find the price of transgenics just too high.
> —*New Scientist* 7 Jan. 1995, p. 22

> Transgenesis enabled scientists to add new genes to creatures, but its results could vary even between identical embryos. —*Economist* 8 July 1995, p. 101

trap-door function ⌨ see PUBLIC-KEY ENCRYPTION

trash /traʃ/ *noun* 🎸

Any variety of rock music noted for its throwaway nature.

A use of the noun *trash* in the sense 'rubbish, worthless stuff'.

The term *trash* (more fully **trash rock**) developed in the early eighties, when it was particularly associated with the loud, energetic, and unpolished sound of *garage*. Featuring in the lyrics of David Bowie and Lou Reed, the term is also associated with the kitschiness of glam-rock. In the nineties, many **trash rockers** have moved on to new enthusiasms, but *trash* is still recognized in pop as a term with a broad application.

> The label 'Trash' was coined by the Cannibals' front man, Mike Spenser, who opened the Garage Club as a venue for Trash bands to 'bang their heads against the wall together'.
> —*Harpers & Queen* Aug. 1983, p. 68

> The hideous apparition is…American trash rocker *Dee* from *Twisted Sister.*
> —caption in *Sounds* 29 Dec. 1984, p. 4

> The band's sound is an amalgamation of elements—instrumental, surf, garage, punk and girl group. 'The merging of trash and pop', is how Delran characterizes the result.
> —*Magnet* May 1994, p. 20

trawl /trɔːl/ *intransitive* or *transitive verb* 🎸POP

Make an exhaustive and sometimes indiscriminate search for (a person or thing) within a defined area.

A figurative use of *trawl* in the sense 'fish with a trawl or seine'; a noun *trawl* in the sense of 'an act of searching thoroughly for something' has existed since the early seventies.

This use of *trawl* has been recorded since the early eighties, often with the idea of **trawling** through a number of possible candidates to find a suitable recruit. The later eighties and nineties, however, have seen an extension of contextual use, with an increasing number of references to the need to *trawl* records or files in the hope of finding a relevant piece of information. There has been an inevitable application to the world of computing: electronic searching is well adapted to the process of **trawling** through texts for preselected items, although concerns have been raised as to the threat to privacy incumbent in an individual's facility to make indiscriminate online searches in this way.

> Now scientists are working backwards from the epidemiology, trawling through the genomes of affected families looking for triplet repeats that might be linked with these diseases.
> —*New Scientist* 15 Oct. 1994, Future supplement, p. 9

> V & A researchers trawled annual British music festivals like Glastonbury and Donnington's Monsters of Rock, as well as Manchester raves and North Cornish surfing beaches.
> —*High Life* Nov. 1994, p. 112

> Our Mr Hindle gathered it in a completely non-scientific fashion, trawling around the Net for a

week and seeing what he could find.   —*.net* Feb. 1995, p. 41

Perhaps the biggest threat to privacy comes…from individual technical operators employed by large on-line systems. Often these are shift workers, with little to do in the wee hours but trawl through messages for juicy titbits. The potential for harassment and blackmail is obvious, particularly on users of supposedly private 'adult' services.   —*Focus* Aug. 1995, p. 70

tree house /ˈtriː haʊs/ *noun* 🌳

A structure built among the branches of a tree and occupied by environmental protesters in order to prevent the felling of the tree in which it stands.

In the nineties the *tree house*, for so long the domain of children, has acquired a new function as a strategic defence. A number of environmental campaigns in the nineties have involved attempts to prevent the felling of trees, usually as a means of obstructing redevelopment of urban sites or of impeding the destruction of woodland for the purposes of road-building. A notable example was the campaign to prevent the construction of the Newbury bypass in Hampshire in 1995, during which protesters fought to protect woodland threatened by the building of the road. Many of the protesters conducted their campaign from *tree houses*, also known as TWIGLOOS, built high in the trees and connected by ropes serving as walkways. The vulnerability of these *tree dwellers* was matched by their agility and few met with accidents, even when police and tree fellers moved in to force their eviction.

The felling of oaks in Queen Anne's Ride was halted last month after representations to Buckingham Palace from conservationists and protests from Windsor and Maidenhead council, local residents and activists who camped in tree-houses.   —*Daily Telegraph* 10 Oct. 1995, p. 2

Some protesters are living in tree-houses and others in 'benders' made from branches and canvas.   —*Daily Telegraph* 9 Jan. 1996, p. 5

tree hugger /ˈtriː hʌgə/ *noun* 🌳

A (chiefly derogatory) term for an environmental campaigner.

With the idea of a person who literally *hugs* or embraces a *tree* to prevent its being cut down.

Since the late seventies, one of the main concerns of the green movement has been to prevent tree felling, both in terms of protection for the trees themselves, and with a view to preventing further environmental damage permitted by tree clearing. In countries such as the United States and Canada, where logging is a major industry, anxieties have focused on the destruction of forests; in Britain, the emphasis has been on tree felling to allow road-building, often through what are regarded as sites of environmental and ecological importance. The term *tree hugger*, and the associated noun **tree hugging**, are frequently used to imply sentimentality and emotionalism on the part of those who support such views.

One example of ecofeminism is the tree-hugging movement in India, where women preserve community forests by hugging trees in defiance of approaching bulldozers.   —*Vegetarian Times* Jan. 1991, p. 62

I'm not a tree-hugger, but I believe strongly in preserving environmental resources as a life choice.   —*Canoe* Mar. 1993, p. 59

Perhaps, in time, history will give us a proper title like Enlightenment or Romantics. About all I hear these days is Tree-Hugger and Environmentalist Wacko.   —*Mother Earth News* Dec. 1995, p. 36

trip hop /ˈtrɪp hɒp/ *noun* and *adjective* Also written **trip-hop**

noun: A form of dance music combining elements of HIP-HOP with softer, more ambient sounds, special effects, and allusive lyrics.

adjective: Belonging to trip-hop music.

Formed by substituting *trip* in the sense 'a hallucinatory experience, especially one that is drug-induced' for the first element of *hip-hop*.

Trip hop developed in the nineties as a form of dance music, usually slow in tempo, which brings together elements of a number of genres. HIP-HOP rapping and scratching are combined with softer, more ambient, and psychedelic sounds, special effects (often borrowed from dub reggae), and lyrics which are suggestive and allusive rather than polemical. A person who performs this kind of music is a **trip hopper,** and an adjective **trip hoppy** has been recorded.

All different styles, electro, techno, jazz/funk, dub are being fused/mixed with a solid Hip Hop beat. This hybrid of musical influence has been termed 'Trip Hop' by the media, although anyone involved in the actual music hates this 'nutshell' type of categorization because the spectrum of musical influence is too wide. —*Represent* Apr. 1995, p. 44

Now the whole, jazzy, housey, trip hoppy collection has been put together on one CD.
—*DJ* 6 July 1995, p. 8

Certainly the haunting, heady lyrics of the song (released this month on East West) coupled with Schroeder's lazy delivery add depth and resonance to what could easily be just another (cringe) trip hop tune. —*The Face* Sept. 1995, p. 30

triple supertwist ▣ see SUPERTWIST

triple whammy ▣ ▐ see DOUBLE WHAMMY

troller /ˈtrəʊlə, ˈtrɒlə/ *noun* ▣

A person who posts an inflammatory electronic message.

Probably a transferred use of *troller* in the sense 'a person who fishes by drawing bait along in the water'.

Unlike those who generate the more personally directed *flamage* (see FLAME), *trollers* address their electronic messages, or **trolls,** generally, in the hope that those who read them will 'rise to the bait'. There is a verb to **troll,** and the victim of **trolling** may be described as a **trollee.** *Troller* and its associated terms are still largely unknown outside the electronic community, but with the growth of interest in the INTERNET this is likely to change.

A really simple troll might be to post a message in a Star Trek newsgroup telling participants to get a life, or to post something like '101 Uses for a Dead Cat' in rec.pets.cats. If the troller's lucky, people will rise to his flame bait, sometimes so vehemently that the newsgroup becomes engulfed in a flamewar that completely drowns out all other discussions.
—*Everybody's Internet Update* Mar. 1995, online newsletter

trophy wife /ˈtrəʊfɪ wʌɪf/ *noun* ▉ ᴾᴼᴾ

A derogatory expression for a wife regarded as a status symbol for her husband.

Trophy wife as a dismissive term for the young and attractive wife of an older man is recorded from the late eighties. The *trophy wife* is seen essentially as a BABE or BIMBO who has married a successful older man, often as his second wife; through the marriage she gains access to his wealth, and he gains the status of a man whose power, and by implication sexual prowess, are displayed by his acquisition of a young and attractive woman.

These trophy wives make the fifty- and sixty-year-old CEOs feel they can compete sexually with younger men, the kind of ego boost that doesn't hurt when going up against Young Turks at the office. —*Olivia Goldsmith The First Wives' Club* (1992), p. 126

The use of the term 'trophy wife' in the Melnitzer story is disgusting and medieval. The males (no one else would use such a phrase, and they are certainly not adult enough to be considered men) who were responsible should be horsewhipped.
—*Globe & Mail Report on Business* Mar. 1993, p. 12

It's about three women whose husbands have divorced them and married young 'trophy wives'.
—*Star Ledger* (Newark) 17 Sept. 1995, section 4, p. 2

trust hospital ⊗ ▐ see HOSPITAL TRUST

'tude /tjuːd/ *noun* Also written tude POP

In slang (chiefly North American): attitude, especially involving truculence or arrogance; style, swagger.

Formed as an abbreviation of *attitude* in the same sense.

'Tude is recorded from the end of the seventies, but has come into increased use in the nineties.

> If the 60s gave us a new sexual ethic, the new 'tude gives us a sexual aesthetic.
> —*Village Voice* (New York) 16 Oct. 1990, p. 35

> Bill Hogan drove in from Vegas in a luminescent turquoise custom Studebaker with an evil-looking bullet-nose grille...Forty-three years ago, when it rolled off the assembly line, it was known as a Starlight Coupe. Today, it's a Stude with a 'tude.
> —*New York Times Magazine* 30 May 1993, p. 20

> These two femme contenders from this week's Lollapalooza main stage should have both the tunes and the 'tude to disprove Hynde's gender theories.   —*Toronto Star* 30 July 1994, section G, p. 10

> But even Childress needs something more than a rude 'tude and his own skills.
> —*Sports Illustrated* 27 Mar. 1995, p. 39

See also ATTITUDE

tummelberry /ˈtʌm(ə)lˌbɛri/ *noun* ▓

A dark purple soft fruit produced by crossing the tayberry with another hybrid of raspberry and blackberry. Also, the plant bearing this fruit.

The name of the river *Tummel* in Tayside, Scotland, and the noun *berry*, on the model of the existing *tayberry* (named from the Scottish river *Tay*).

The last twenty years have seen a number of developments in cane fruit. The *tayberry*, a cross between the blackberry and the raspberry, introduced in 1977, was the first of several new hybrid soft fruit to be produced. The *tummelberry*, introduced in Scotland in 1984, represents a further development, being the result of crossing the tayberry with another hybrid of raspberry and blackberry. By 1990 the *sunberry*, another blackberry/raspberry cross, had also made its appearance.

> The Tummelberry, bred by crossing the Tayberry with one of its sister hybrids from the same cross, is an offshoot of the Tayberry, just as the river Tummel is a tributary of the river Tay.
> —*Grower* 7 Aug. 1986, p. 30

> Plenty of soft fruit including sunberries (a long berry that is a blackberry/raspberry cross), tayberries and tummelberries.   —*Guardian* 11 June 1994, Weekend section, p. 42

turf war /ˈtəːf wɔː/ *noun* POP ◖◗

Especially in North America: a dispute over territory between rival groups or departments.

A dispute or *war* over *turf* in the slang sense 'an area regarded as being under the control of a particular person or group, a personal territory' (originally, the streets controlled by a (juvenile) street-gang, or the part of a city in which a particular criminal or detective operates).

The expression *turf war*, which in its literal sense relates particularly to disputes between drug-pushers over the area in which they operate, is recorded in North American speech since the late seventies, and is frequently used figuratively to denote a dispute between two defined groups over a particular sphere of influence.

> In December, turf wars in city hall knocked Los Angeles out of the race for one of the largest urban-renewal prizes to come out of Washington in decades.   —*Economist* 4 Feb. 1995, p. 54

> In New Jersey...a turf war between attorneys and brokers has simmered for more than 20 years.   —*Coloradoan* (Fort Collins) 9 Apr. 1995, section F, p. 17

> Given the number of innocent victims of drive-by shootings typical of turf wars between drug

dealers, it seems to me that serious measures to disarm that trade are worth considering.
—*Mother Jones* Feb. 1996, p. 3

twigloo /'twɪglu:/ *noun* 🌳 📷

A form of temporary shelter made of branches and used especially by environmental protesters.

Probably formed from a blend of *twig* and *igloo*, a coinage which suggests both the material and the shape of the construction.

Twigloos first came to public attention in Britain in 1995, in reports of controversy surrounding the construction of the Newbury bypass in Hampshire. The route of the proposed road, the construction of which involved considerable tree felling, ran through countryside regarded both as beautiful and environmentally important; against these considerations were set the claims of a town overloaded by pressure of traffic. The Newbury scheme became a focus of debate for the whole question of balancing the concerns of the rural and urban communities, and in the course of it numerous protesters established themselves in a number of encampments within the threatened woodland.

The temporary structures which they built to house themselves, and to hinder or prevent tree clearance, included *benders*, or ground-level erections with a superstructure of branches which have been bent over, and a wooden base, and *twigloos*, TREE HOUSES with a similar superstructure, but with a flooring of tarpaulin over netting. A compound form **twigloo house** is also recorded.

She lives in a tree house, known as a 'twigloo', at Slyward Camp.
—*Daily Telegraph* 27 Dec. 1995, p. 4

For the first time, professional climbers are being used…Their task is to climb the trees and use the walkways to grab those in the 'twigloo' houses…They will also cut down the elaborate system of walkways which allows the protesters to move freely between trees.
—*Daily Telegraph* 1 Mar. 1996, p. 4

Twinkie defence /twɪŋki dɪ'fɛns/ *noun* 🍴

An American colloquial term for a legal defence of diminished responsibility in which the defendant's criminal behaviour is attributed to the effects of an unbalanced diet of convenience food.

A legal *defence* based on the assumption that a person's behaviour can be affected by excessive consumption of convenience food, as typified by a *Twinkie*, the trade mark of 'a brand of cupcake with a creamy filling'.

The *Twinkie defence* was first employed in 1979 in a San Francisco Supreme Court murder trial, when it was alleged that the defendant's compulsive consumption of sugar through cupcakes, coca cola, and similarly sweet foods had aggravated a chemical imbalance in his brain. The *Twinkie defence* was disallowed as a legal defence by the US Congress in 1981, and the term is now likely to be used pejoratively, as the type of a defence which seeks to exculpate wrongdoing by the evasion of responsibility.

Blaming the sun for making you kill a man is a lame excuse, on a par with the 'Twinkie' defense.
—*Christian Science Monitor* 18 May 1989, p. 13

The age of the culprit as victim began with the Twinkie defense, which freed the killer of San Francisco Mayor George Moscone and Supervisor Harvey Milk; too much sugar made him do it.
—*Time* 7 Feb. 1994, p. 76

twoc /twɒk/ *noun* and *verb* Also written **TWOC, twock** 📷 🍴

In slang use:

noun: The offence of stealing a car.

transitive verb: To steal (a car).

From the the initial letters of *taking without (the) owner's consent.*

Twoc developed in the early nineties, in police jargon, as part of the vocabulary of car-crime. Media attention paid to such activities as HOTTING and RAM-RAIDING meant that **twoccing** has also had its share of attention. The original implication of the acronym is that the offence centres on the temporary removal of the vehicle from the owner, perhaps for the purpose of joyriding, but it appears that activities of **twoccers** do in fact often result in outright theft.

> Twoc—to rhyme with 'clock'—is police shorthand for the offence of taking and driving away a vehicle without its owner's consent...From the victim's point of view, 'only a twoc' has a very hollow ring to it. —*Oxford Times* 27 July 1990, p. 15

> [He] reckons most joyriders steal cars for fun, not profit, although he recently took a twocked car to a breakers in Manchester which was run by a gang of professional car thieves. —*Guardian* 20 Aug. 1993, section 2, p. 17

> Detectives found the business card in a suspect's wallet...It read 'Smash and grabs, shop windows, drums, TWOC and arson—anything done'. —*Daily Telegraph* 2 Dec. 1994, p. 15

> Nauseating saddoes who'll work double-shifts at £2 per, on the promise that one day they just might get to lob rocket-propelled grenades...at a twoccer on a quiet motorway. —*Interzone* Nov. 1995, p. 52

● ●

U

über- /'uːbə/ *combining form* Also written **uber-**

Forming nouns and adjective with the meaning: the ultimate form of the thing named.

From the German *über* 'over', as in the first element of *Übermensch* 'superman'.

Since the early nineties, *über-* has been recorded as the fashionable first element in a number of forms designating the ultimate or 'super' form of a named phenomenon.

> The new optimism is dangerous because it is building President Clinton up to be someone he cannot be—a mythical savior, the über-boomer, heir to JFK's Camelot legacy. —*Spin* Apr. 1993, p. 66

> Ratings-guzzling *über*-TV show *Cracker* is back to peel away the scabs of post-Hillsborough Britain. —*New Musical Express* 28 Oct. 1995, p. 30

> Add to this a titillating mix of sporty models, (sorry, the trendy word is Über-Babes), and a fetishist's guide to rubber. —*Time Out* 17 Jan. 1996, p. 161

Unabomber /'juːnəbɒmə/ *noun* 📷 POP

The media name given to the perpetrator of a series of mail bomb attacks, carried out in America between 1978 and 1994.

A blend of *university* and *bomber.*

Beginning in 1978, a number of mail bomb attacks, viewed by the Federal Bureau of Investigation as constituting a series carried out by a single person, were made on academic institutions and particularly scientists. The nature of the selected targets gave rise to the name *Unabomber*, and a task force was set up to investigate what were referred to as the **Unabom** attacks.

Over the years of this major investigation, a number of people were killed and injured, but it was not until 1996 that the FBI arrested and charged a suspect. The coming trial is likely to result in exhaustive media coverage of the activities of the alleged *Unabomber* over the last eighteen years.

The stills above are taken from a videotape shown last October at a press conference held by the UNABOM Task Force, a joint operation of the FBI, the U.S. Postal Service, and the Bureau of Alcohol, Tobacco and Firearms that is investigating the 'Unabom' mail bombings, a series of fourteen attacks that have occurred since 1978. Most of the mail bombings have been directed at scientists and professors; last June a geneticist at the University of California at San Francisco and a computer scientist at Yale University were seriously injured in separate mail-bomb incidents.

—caption in *Harper's* Jan. 1993, p. 19

The serial bomber known as Unabomber, whose most recent letter bomb killed a Young & Rubicon advertising executive in December, is still on the loose, and his devices show increased skill.

—*Computer* Apr. 1995, p. 66

The man suspected of being the long-hunted Unabomber was charged yesterday with a single count of possessing the components of a bomb.

—*Daily Telegraph* 5 Apr. 1996 (electronic edition)

Unicode /ˈjuːnɪkəʊd/ *noun* Also written **unicode** 🖳

An internationally-agreed standard for representing symbols in all the world's languages by numerical codes, each consisting of two bytes (sixteen binary digits).

It has been suggested that the element *uni-* stands for 'unique, universal, and uniform character encoding'.

An older system for encoding characters so they can be manipulated by computer, ASCII (*American Standard Code for Information Interchange*) was first agreed in 1963; even its extended international version has no more than 256 possible codes and can only represent the characters in the Roman alphabet. With computer companies selling equipment and software worldwide, this was a severe limitation on their ability to produce international versions. Over a period of six years from 1987, a group of US computer companies (now called the *Unicode Consortium*) produced a new standard which can accommodate more than 65,000 characters, enough to accommodate the symbols used in all the world's languages, including non-alphabetic ones such as Chinese, Japanese, and Korean (the developers even plan to include Egyptian hieroglyphics and Sanskrit in the list of languages). The system is now an international standard and widely accepted.

When multibyte Unicode, which embraces the alphabets, syllabism, and ideographs of all the world's languages, replaces the existing ASCII code, we may well find a wider range of individuals using a much more extensive set of letters and other symbols.   —*Byte* Dec. 1993, p. 302

Although it does not natively support Unicode, Chicago does support multiple code pages and multilingual content for documents.   —*Microsoft Developer Network News* July 1994, p. 5

UNPROFOR /ˈʌnprəfɔː/ *acronym* 🏳

A multinational peacekeeping force administered by the United Nations, instituted in 1992 to mediate in the conflict in former Yugoslavia, and superseded in 1995 by IFOR.

From the initial letters of *United Nations*, the first syllable of *Protection*, and the first three letters of *Force*.

Intensification of the fighting between BOSNIAN *Serbs* and *Muslims* in former Yugoslavia led to the institution, in 1992, of the **United Nations Protection Force**, or *UNPROFOR*.

UNPROFOR, which included contingents from up to 30 countries, was authorized by the Security Council of the United Nations on 21 February 1992. *UNPROFOR* had some success in its peacekeeping mission, but from the first was often unable to prevent what were seen as flagrant violations of apparent agreements, and in particular instances of ETHNIC CLEANSING; at the present time, the United Nations is investigating allegations of war crimes taking place during the period of *UNPROFOR*'s mission. At the end of 1995, with the signing of the

DAYTON *accord*, and the hope of restoration of civilian government, *UNPROFOR* was replaced by IFOR.

> UNPROFOR—the peacekeeping arm of the United Nations—passed out water purification tablets. —*Chicago Tribune* 15 Apr. 1994, section 2, p. 7

> UN officials...are increasingly worried that if no deal is struck by midnight March 31, then the Serbs and Croats separated by UNPROFOR troops in the so-called Zone of Separation in the Krajina will start a struggle to occupy all the strategic points along a one-thousand-kilometer front line. —*New York Review of Books* 23 Mar. 1995, p. 64

> When the war broke out, Bosnia couldn't defend itself and looked to the United Nations for help. But the West activated UNProFor (the U.N. Protection Force) not to silence the Serb artillery surrounding the capital but to deliver bread and medical supplies to the victims. —*Newsweek* 31 July 1995, p. 22

unroutable 🖳 see ROUTABLE

upgradability /ˌʌpgreɪdəˈbɪlɪti/ *noun* 🖳

The degree to which the design of a computer permits improvement of its technical specification by the addition of further components or replacement of those already present with ones of a higher specification.

The ability to upgrade a personal computer became an important issue from the late eighties onwards, as the pace of innovation in microprocessor design outstripped the ability of organizations and individuals to pay the cost of replacing their systems. To meet this need, manufacturers produced systems which were more easily extendible than those of previous generations; in particular, they put the central microprocessor in a special socket so it could be exchanged for one with a higher specification at a later date.

> But with the doubler chip, upgradability has become a vital issue. —*Byte* Dec. 1992, p. 120

> The CompuAdd Express 466/DX2 is the current top-of-the-line model in the company's series of 'scalable' computer systems designed with upgradability in mind. —*Compute* July 1993, p. 17

> Unparalleled upgradability is the current hallmark of Linn's modular approach to system building. —*Q* June 1995, p. 155

upload /ˈʌpləʊd/ *transitive* or *intransitive verb* 🖳

To transfer (the contents of an electronic data file) from a peripheral or subordinate system to a larger or more central one.

The verb **upload** appeared in 1982 to describe the process of sending data to a central storage system from a peripheral device. For example, a user may upload a file to a bulletin board system or to a server on a global network such as the INTERNET. The action is **uploading** or an **upload**. The opposite is DOWNLOAD.

> Some have recently implemented microcomputers in field operations with selected uploading of data to central office mainframes. —*Public Works* Jan. 1992, p. 48

> The story jumped from the crime pages into cyberspace when computer-savvy residents...donated their time to upload information...onto the Internet. —*Coloradoan* (Fort Collins) 17 Oct. 1993, section A, p. 7

upsize 🖳 see -SIZE

urban legend /ˈɜːb(ə)n lɛdʒ(ə)nd/ *noun* 🗯

An unverifiable and usually apocryphal anecdote of some aspect of modern life, widely recounted as if true, which has acquired the status of folklore.

A story with an *urban* setting, as representing modern life, which has come to be regarded as a *legend* 'a traditional story sometimes popularly regarded as historical but unauthenticated'.

Urban legends (or *urban myths*, as they are also called) have been recognized as a form since the early eighties, but there is general agreement that the kind of story indicated by the term is likely to be of very long standing. A typical *urban legend* depicts outlandish or sensational happenings in a plausible contemporary setting; through perpetuation in numerous varying and embellished versions it has acquired the status of folklore.

Urban legends were originally presented as having happened to or been recounted by an acquaintance at several removes: the 'friend of a friend's friend'. More recently, the development of communication via the INTERNET has proved a fertile breeding ground for the dissemination of such stories.

> We all know those horrible and extraordinary things that happened to a friend of a friend's friend; the stories about vanishing hitch-hikers, the ones about poisonous spiders being found in yucca plants...They are called Urban Legends and many of them have been happening to friends of friends' friends for centuries. —*Observer* 15 Feb. 1987, p. 18

> Transposing the action from a Liverpool council estate to a run-down Chicago housing project haunted by a mythical hook-handed killer, Candyman—this intelligently frightening riff on urban myths sets the standard for horror movies of the '90's. —*Time Out* 31 Mar. 1993, p. 57

> These viruses, I was made to understand, are the Net's version of urban myths: no one knows where the rumours start, and the plethora of newcomers...ensure that they spread like wildfire and never go away. —*Guardian* 6 Jan. 1995, Friday supplement, p. 11

> Common urban legends include the belief that collecting the pull tabs off drink cans can earn free dialysis for sick people; that pet alligators flushed down toilets by their owners are alive in sewers...and that the FTC plans to impose a tax on use of telephone lines by computers. —*Internet World* Feb. 1995, p. 87

urban tourism ⁑ see TOURISM

urgicenter /'ə:dʒɪ,sɛntə/ *noun* ⊗

In the US: an EMERGICENTER.

Formed from a blend of *urgent* and *center*, after the earlier *surgicenter, emergicenter*.

A term in the US for an emergency clinic or EMERGICENTER, dating from the early eighties.

> A California group of hospital-affiliated urgicenters. —*Geriatrics* Sept. 1985, p. 96

> Scheduled for completion in September is the medical center's new Urgi-Center, next to the Emergency Department, to serve patients who don't have severe medical problems. —*Mercer Business* May 1993, p. 16

usability /juːzəˈbɪlɪti/ *noun* ▯

The degree to which a software application is easy to use.

In the eighties computing moved rapidly away from being a specialist skill to one employed by a high proportion of workers. Much more than before, commercial software applications needed to be intuitive and easy to understand, particularly so as they continued to grow in complexity. Large software companies began to expend considerable resources researching how new and experienced users reacted to applications. Many established **usability laboratories** in which the reactions of a variety of users attempting to use applications under development were monitored by various survey techniques. This has developed into a subdiscipline within software development called **usability testing** or sometimes **usability engineering**.

> For all the people on the project, usability testing is the most humbling of experiences. You wince as Joe Public makes a total hash of your menu system, deletes a file instead of copying it, or replies N instead of Y to a question. —*.EXE Magazine* Feb. 1989, p. 16

> But, since a squillion-pound system that is unusable is a waste of a squillion pounds, IT managers must ensure that usability is a prime directive in all software development systems. —*Computer Weekly* 22 Apr. 1993, p. 22

Usability engineering is moving up the software development agenda.

—*Computing* 19 Aug. 1993, p. 20

Usenet see NET

· ·

V

vanilla /vəˈnɪlə/ *adjective* 🖥 ✖

Plain, basic, conventional; (of a computer system or software) ordinary, standard, without bells and whistles.

A jargon term derived from the default or standard flavour of ice cream, in particular from the phrase *plain vanilla*, which in its literal sense dates from the fifties.

The figurative use of *vanilla* (originally with reference to sexual activity, as in **vanilla sex**) is recorded from the early seventies. Since the first half of the eighties, however, the term has been applied particularly to computing equipment, denoting a system which is in the form supplied as standard by the manufacturer, without any optional additions or extra equipment, or which is a standard example of its type. It is also applied to software, particularly systems software or complex applications for which enhancements are possible but which are not present.

The specious appropriation of selected fragments of a prestigious literary theory can even make a species of 'vanilla linguistics'...look enticingly 'postmodern'. —*Profession 89* 1989, p. 60

We used vanilla Intel systems, with no unusual hardware or software.
—*UNIX Review* Mar. 1993, p. 59

In its 'vanilla' form, AutoCAD does enable the generation of a limited range of surface entities.
—*CAD User* Apr. 1994, p. 23

Since the late Seventies, the lesbian community has also suffered a painful schism between 'S & M dykes' and 'vanilla' lesbians. —*Guardian* 28 Nov. 1995, Weekend section, p. 7

VAR /vɑː/ *acronym* 🖥 〰

A computer supplier offering additional services (training, customization of equipment or software, pre-sales and after-sales support) in addition to equipment and applications.

An abbreviation of *value-added reseller*, that is, a *reseller* or supplier of computer equipment who *adds value* to the product by providing additional services.

This term grew up in the late eighties to distinguish those suppliers which specialize in providing complete systems and associated services for customers from those which concentrate on selling items of equipment and software at the most competitive prices, frequently by mail order (often referred to disparagingly as *box-shifters*).

High margins are what allow a VAR to put a trained engineer, instead of a glorified sales clerk, on the other end of the support line. —*Sun World* Dec. 1991, p. 16

Relying on another VAR to provide any of these elements raises issues of accountability, reliability and turn-around time. —*UnixWorld* Feb. 1993, p. 22

V-chip /ˈviːtʃɪp/ *noun* ✖ 📺

A computer chip designed to be included in television receivers to prevent children viewing material which is deemed violent or sexually explicit according to rules set by broadcasters and parents.

Originally from the initial letter of *viewer*, but now generally interpreted as standing for *violence*.

As part of the Telecommunications Act, passed into US law in February 1996, manufacturers of television receivers were required to include a *V-chip*, or **violence chip**, in all new sets within one year; broadcasters and cable companies had to implement a classification scheme for programs they transmit, indicating whether they contain material which is considered violent or sexually explicit. The proposal, intended as a way for parents to control their children's viewing, aroused great controversy and was regarded by many as impracticable, not least since it would be at least a decade before all existing sets would be replaced with new ones containing the chip and that a workable classification scheme would be extremely difficult to create; it also raised issues of censorship and First Amendment rights and was opposed by some religious and family groups. Despite these arguments, the scheme has been considered for implementation in other countries, and the European Parliament has passed a directive similar to the US legislation.

> Every programme classified as violent will be 'tagged' with an electronic signal. The V-chip would detect the signal, and if parents choose, block transmission.
>
> —*New Scientist* 14 Aug. 1993, p. 5

> The American and Canadian associations of broadcasters oppose the use of V-chips, arguing largely on constitutional grounds.   —*Edupage* 28 Jan. 1996, online newsletter

> Despite the political enthusiasm, opposition to the technology in Europe is growing, with many in the broadcasting, advertising and electronics industries claiming the V-chip is unnecessary and impractical.   —*New Scientist* 20 Apr. 1996, p. 14

veal crate /'viːl kreɪt/ *noun* 🌳

A partitioned area with restricted light and space in which a calf is reared for slaughter.

The gastronomic view, held strongly in Continental Europe, that meat from calves should be white rather than pink, led to the development of *veal crates*: individual slatted partitions in which young calves are placed to be reared in virtual darkness and with little room for movement. After slaughter, the meat thus produced is very pale.

In the United Kingdom, concern for animal welfare led in 1990 to a total ban on *veal crates*. No ban, however, was placed on the export of live calves to the Continent for **veal crating**, and in recent years there have been an increasing number of violent protests against this practice.

> In 1990, John Gummer, then agriculture minister, ordered a unilateral end to the practice of veal crating—putting week old calves in solitary, darkened crates to produce very pale meat.
>
> —*Guardian* 5 Jan. 1995, p. 8

> William Waldegrave, the Agriculture Minister, has refused to ban shipment of live calves to veal crates unilaterally, saying that it is illegal under EU law.
>
> —*Independent on Sunday* 15 Jan. 1995, p. 3

vedge ▓ see VEG

veejay /viːˈdʒeɪ/ *noun* Also written VJ ▓

A person who presents a programme of videos, especially on television.

Formed from a modification of the existing *deejay* or 'disc jockey', by the substitution of *v* (as the initial letter of *video*) for *d*.

The introduction of **video jockeys**, or *veejays*, dates from the early eighties, and is particularly associated with the field of popular music. *Veejays* present the videos made by groups and individual performers as *disc jockeys* of an earlier era presented records; **VJ-ing** may also include the presentation of advertising videos.

> Not long after its debut, Nirvana's 'Smells Like Teen Spirit' video ran four or five times a day for

weeks. In October 1991, Steve Isaacs, MTV's first grunge veejay, was hired and was put into equally heavy rotation. —*New York Times* 15 Nov. 1992, section 9, p. 9

The latest in talk-show hosts. The online jockey hosts discussions on the Internet. Just like the video jockey (VJ) and the disc jockey (DJ) before. —*Guardian* 30 July 1994, Weekend section, p. 51

When I started I was doing the MTV news which meant I was editing, writing, producing, directing...Now I've moved to just VJ-ing and all the scripts *are* prepared beforehand, but it still isn't easy. —*Select* Mar. 1995, p. 107

veg /vɛdʒ/ *intransitive verb* Also written **vedge**

In slang: to vegetate, to pass the time in vacuous inactivity.

Since the early eighties, the term *veg* has been used to summarize a virtually complete lack of mental and physical activity in what someone is doing: the implication is often that this is less beneficial relaxation than a mindless and negative way of passing the time. **Vegging** or **vegging out** is particularly associated with the kind of television viewing in which the watcher slumps in front of the set and pays little or no attention to the programme being shown. There is an obvious conceptual link here to the development of the term *couch potato* and its associated culture; a person exhibiting this kind of lifestyle may be described as **vegged out**.

When I get home what I really like to do is...veg out. I don't want to interact, I don't want to play games. —S. Brand *The Media Lab* (1987), p. 40

Television viewing is usually done in a very casual manner. We tend to turn on the set, aim the remote, then veg. —*Ottawa Citizen* 14 Dec. 1991, p. 56

So what constitutes leisure time for you? Is it exercising, travel, cultural events, spending time with family, or vegging out in front of the TV? —*Minnesota Monthly* Jan. 1995, p. 86

vegelate /'vɛdʒ(ə)leɪt, 'vɛdʒ(ə)lət/ *noun*

Chocolate which contains a certain proportion of vegetable fat other than cocoa butter.

From the first element of *vegetable* and the final syllable of *chocolate*.

Vegelate was proposed in 1985 as a term to be used within the European Community to designate chocolate containing more than a specified percentage of vegetable fat other than cocoa butter. Since this would particularly have affected the British chocolate industry, considerable opposition was expressed by the UK; the proposal is regarded by EUROSCEPTICS as characteristic of what they see as the bureaucratic dominance of the EUROPEAN UNION. To date *vegelate* remains a suggested term; there is no indication that its use will be accepted or imposed.

In 1985 European Community mandarins criticised the quality of British chocolate and said it should be called 'vegelate'. —*New Scientist* 13 Feb. 1993, p. 52

The European Commission continued to argue over the rules governing chocolate harmonisation— the Germans object to the vegetable fat in British chocolate and want it renamed 'vegelate'. —*Guardian* 17 Mar. 1995, p. 5

vehicle abuse see ABUSE

velociraptor see RAPTOR

velveeta see SPAM

velvet divorce /vɛlvɪt dɪ'vɔːs/ *noun phrase* Also written **Velvet Divorce**

The non-violent separation of formerly united states, especially as applied to the partition of Czechoslovakia in 1993.

Formed on the model of *velvet revolution*: a *divorce* which provides for the peaceful separation of formerly united parties.

Following the VELVET REVOLUTION of 1989, Czechoslovakia subsequently separated into two states, the Czech Republic and Slovakia. This peaceful separation, or *velvet divorce*, which came into effect at the beginning of 1993, has not been marred by any of the violence which has become endemic in the former Yugoslavia (see BOSNIAN).

> Mr Vaclav Klaus, head of the Czech republic...and Mr Vladimir Meciar, the Slovak leader, had agreed in Bratislava, the Slovak capital, to introduce legislation in the federal parliament for what is coming to be known as the Velvet Divorce, after the Velvet Revolution that ended communism in the country. —*Daily Telegraph* 24 July 1992, p. 10

> The Western European public is being sedated with the argument that the use of violence between Czechs and Slovaks is absolutely improbable. Nothing similar to Yugoslavia could possibly occur, it is said—just a 'velvet divorce'. —*Washington Post* 19 Oct. 1992, p. 22

> He now finds himself being invited to Belgium and Quebec, to tell them how you make a velvet divorce. —*New York Review of Books* 23 June 1994, p. 17

velvet revolution /ˌvɛlvɪt rɛvəˈluːʃ(ə)n/ *noun phrase* Also written **Velvet Revolution** 📷

A non-violent political revolution, especially as applied to events in Czechoslovakia at the end of 1989.

A translation of the Czech phrase *sametová revoluce*.

The collapse of Communism in Eastern Europe, symbolized most graphically by the opening of the Berlin Wall in November 1989 and the subsequent reconstitution of a single German state, was also marked by events in what was then Czechoslovakia. A renewed campaign for political change, led by the dramatist and former dissident Václav Havel, resulted in December 1989 in the peaceful overthrow of Communism or *velvet revolution*; the policy of non-violence was successfully maintained in the subsequent VELVET DIVORCE or partition of Czechoslovakia. The term **velvet revolutionary** for a supporter or adherent of a *velvet revolution* has been recorded, but appears rare.

> For 74 years Czechoslovakia achieved a mostly peaceful accommodation between Slovaks and Czechs. As recently as 1989 they were solidly united in the 'velvet revolution' against communist rule. —*Time* 6 July 1992, p. 37

> A playwright who led the 1989 'Velvet Revolution', Havel was Czechoslovakia's first post-Communist president and remains the best-known Czech politician at home and abroad. —*Day* (New London, Connecticut) 27 Jan. 1993

> The thousands who turned up on November 16th in the main square of the capital, Bratislava, to mark the sixth anniversary of the 1989 'velvet revolution' which swept communism aside in what was then Czechoslovakia, were in no doubt. —*Economist* 2 Dec. 1995, p. 42

> 'Velvet Revolution' gathers pace as Serbs rally to oust Milosevic. —heading in *Daily Telegraph* 30 November 1996

Veronica /vərˈɒnɪkə/ *noun* 🖥

A computerized INTERNET tool designed to simplify searches of multiple GOPHER servers.

Acronym for *Very Easy Rodent-Oriented Net-wide Index to Computerized Archives*; perhaps also partly from the name of a character in the US *Archie* comic strip, ARCHIE being another Internet search method (a third system, *Jughead*, was named after yet another character in the same strip).

Though the gopher system for searching out information on the Internet is popular and useful, there are now so many gopher systems that it can be difficult and time-consuming to find the right server and traverse its menu structure. For this reason a search facility called

Veronica has been developed that automatically searches all of gopherspace and returns a list of items matching the search criteria.

> Add Veronica to your gopher bookmarks file as soon as possible.   —*.net* Dec. 1994, p. 44

> Veronica knows all about gopherspace, and updates its contact list every night.
>   —*.net* Dec. 1995, p. 44

vert /vəːt/ *noun* and *adjective* 📝 ⊕

noun: A vertical surface, such as the lift of a ramp or ski-jump. Also, a manoeuvre performed on this.

adjective: Of or belonging to such a surface or such a manoeuvre.

Formed from an abbreviation of *vertical*.

Verts as hazards (or manoeuvres) in skateboarding have been recorded since the late seventies. More recently, the development of such sports as SNOWBOARDING has increased usage of the terms.

> We had skied more than 21,000 feet that day. I know, because one of CMH's traditions is to post the vertical feet—'verts' in heli-ski parlance—skied by each group. The more verts you rack up...the better and harder you skied.   —*Sports Illustrated* 14 Jan. 1991, p. 92

> He did frontside ollie-oops onto the vert wall, frontside airs off of the vert wall to disaster on the seven-foot section.   —*Trans World Skateboarding* Mar. 1992, p. 57

> As you are approaching vert, start turning in a direction parallel to the coping, allowing your momentum to bring your body weight up (almost as if you were about to do a 50–50 stall).
>   —*Inline* July 1995, p. 51

vertically challenged ▌ see CHALLENGED

viatical settlement 〰 ⊗ ▌ see DEATH FUTURES

video jockey ▨ ⚗ see VEEJAY

video-on-demand ▣ see -ON-DEMAND

virtual /ˈvəːtjuːəl/ *adjective* ▣

In computing: not physically existing but made to appear so from the point of view of the user; involving the replication of a physical object by an electronic equivalent.

The word *virtual* has been employed in computing since the late fifties to describe techniques for simulating memory space, disk storage, and operating environments. However, the current usage stems from the development of the phrase **virtual reality** in the early eighties. It refers to a computer-generated visual environment that a person can move about in and interact with, for example by touching or moving 'objects'. Since such **virtual environments** require large amounts of computer power, a realistic simulation is beyond today's capabilities, but at various levels of verisimilitude, such systems are now used in training, medicine, scientific and technical simulations, military exercises, and entertainment. Some employ a DATAGLOVE; others have helmets containing motion sensors and small television screens, which always show what the user is looking at; yet others employ *body suits* which feed back the user's movements to the system producing the displays. Some use all of these, in a *total-immersion* environment. The surroundings generated by such systems are also referred to as **virtual landscapes**, **virtual spaces**, or **virtual worlds**. Some psychiatrists have used *virtual reality* techniques to help individuals overcome phobias, such as fear of snakes or heights, using **virtual therapy**. It is suggested that improved quality of simulation may one day permit **virtual sex** between individuals who are physically separated. Research into **virtual shopping** is taking place in the US; this would permit shoppers to traverse a simulated shopping mall, making purchases as they go, with the goods delivered to their homes later. The associated nouns are **virtuality** and **virtualization**; the verb is **virtualize**. The abbreviation **VR** for *virtual reality* has been recorded since the late eighties.

With the growth in computer-based communications in the eighties and nineties, the word *virtual* also took on a weakened sense referring to the replacement of a physical entity by an electronic equivalent using telecommunications. A **virtual community** is one which 'meets' and interacts through the medium of the NET; in a **virtual classroom** students may be linked to each other and to teachers without being physically present; people may communicate in a **virtual meeting** using videoconferencing or similar techniques; a **virtual office** is one which is simulated by communications links between dispersed employees or freelances; the proposed **virtual corporation** would be a temporary network of independent companies, suppliers, and customers, linked by information technology to share skills, costs, and access to one another's markets; the term **virtual company** has been used in the sense of both *virtual office* and *virtual corporation*.

Variations of virtual-reality technology already have been used to help physicians position beams of radiation…and to aid biochemists seeking to attach drugs to protein molecules.
—*Wilson Quarterly* Summer 1991, p. 125

This spring the Open University is to start a course taught almost entirely on computer networks to explore the possibilities of 'virtual classrooms'. —*Independent* 20 Jan. 1992, p. 15

Television viewers watching BBC news will soon be watching the newsreader sitting in the middle of a virtual newsroom. From 13 April…everything apart from the announcer will have been generated by computer in all news programmes on both BBC channels.
—*New Scientist* 3 Apr. 1993, p. 22

The key to immersive VR is the use of a headset, or 'eyephone', which projects a small image of the virtual world on to each eye. —*Guardian* 14 Jun. 1993, Education supplement, p. 14

Computer networks have created thousands of virtual communities that have been the basis for a participatory democracy, creating fast friendships for millions of people around the world.
—*New York Times* 2 Jan. 1994, section 4, p. 5

The virtual corporation begins to emerge: workers who never go to the office, but who fax, phone, and transmit their work back and forth to one another from remote sites.
—*Minnesota Monthly* Feb. 1994, p. 103

virus /'vʌɪərəs/ *noun* 🖳

A piece of program code that attaches itself to computer applications, executes when they do, attempts to copy itself, and which may cause damage or loss of data.

A figurative use of *virus* based on the ability of the computer *virus* to replicate itself within the computer system.

The concept of computer *viruses* is one of the few cases in which science fiction has genuinely predicted the future. The idea, and the name, were first used in David Gerrold's book *When Harlie was One* in 1972. (The more frequently quoted book *The Shockwave Rider* (1975) by John Brunner actually predicts a *worm* rather than a *virus*—see below.) The first real *virus* was the subject of a computer science experiment in November 1983. Computer *viruses* suddenly became news in 1988, after a series of attacks had led to substantial public anxiety. A large number have since been identified and described by names (see MICHELANGELO), though only a few are seen at all frequently. They are written mainly by malicious pranksters, though the high proportion originating in the eighties in the old Soviet Union satellite countries suggests that some were designed as a form of anti-state sabotage. Many companies have brought out **anti-viral** software of various types; some, called **virus scanners**, *scan* the computer's memory and disk files in search of the digital *signatures* of known *viruses*; others use a variety of techniques for **virus detection**, including monitoring the system for unauthorized activity (these were sometimes called **vaccines** in the late eighties); programs that remove viruses from disks, occasionally called **virus killers**, are said to *disinfect* them. Most personal computers have little security against *viruses*, which are easily transmitted on floppy discs or software downloaded from bulletin boards. Considerable financial loss was suffered as a result of the epidemic, not to mention research time and valuable data.

The problem of combating viruses gave rise almost immediately to a new technical field and an extensive vocabulary to describe types of *virus*: **boot sector viruses** put a copy of themselves on disc so they are run whenever the computer is restarted; **polymorphic viruses** continually mutate to avoid detection; **stealth viruses** hide themselves away by subverting the operating system; **cruise viruses** are designed to attack specific targets, in the way a *cruise missile* does. Commonly, a *virus* is anything that causes unexpected behaviour or leads to damage, but specialists make a careful distinction between *viruses* themselves (which must attach themselves to other programs to operate), *worms* (self-contained programs designed to propagate across networks), *Trojan horses* (programs that appear to be useful but which also do something undesirable), and *logic bombs* (which lie dormant until some action triggers them—they are sometimes used in commercial software to stop it working after a fixed period if a licence fee has not been paid).

Comprehensive virus detection and removal features to protect your software investment. Works with all presently known viruses. —advertisement in *CU Amiga* Apr. 1990, p. 70

Like other anti-virus software, Untouchable is equipped with a TSR monitor for patrolling your system memory. —advertisement in *PC World* Apr. 1992, p. 20

Viruses like the Satan Bug cause concern among computer security experts as they represent a new and rapidly growing class called polymorphic viruses. These change themselves each time they replicate, foiling scanning software which identifies viruses by looking for a characteristic piece of code. —*Computing* 11 Nov. 1993, p. 13

If the scanner doesn't possess identification strings for the virus it will be missed and the scan process will spread the virus. —*VIRUS-L Digest* 5 Jan. 1995, online newsletter

vision thing /ˈvɪʒ(ə)n θɪŋ/ *noun* 📱 ᴘᴏᴘ

A political view encompassing the longer term as distinct from short-term campaign objectives.

Formed by compounding: the *thing* required is *vision* for the future.

In 1987 it was suggested to George Bush, then US Vice-President and setting out on his ultimately successful presidential campaign, that he should turn his attention from short-term political objectives and look to the longer term. Bush's response was

Oh, the vision thing.

The phrase quickly became established, first in connection with Bush himself, and then as applied to other politicians, or in other fields. There is often an implication that a person seeking or claiming a *vision thing* has at best an imprecise grasp of the elements essential to an accurate overview of a given situation.

All the modern technology, tracking polls, highly paid media advisers from Madison Avenue-…cannot invent a message. A rudimentary gesture, in this context, can look like a 'vision thing'. —*Vanity Fair* Sept. 1991, p. 214

He has been genuinely perplexed by the public's desire for him to supply what he calls 'the vision thing'. —George Will *Restoration* (1992), p. 136

John Major followed up his ministerial reshuffle with a sweeping proclamation last night of his government's commitment to ownership, choice and opportunity designed to convince voters that he—not Tony Blair—has the 'vision thing' for the Nineties. —*Guardian* 28 July 1994, p. 1

visually challenged ⁅⁅ see CHALLENGED

VJ 🗙 see VEEJAY

VOD 🖵 📠 see -ON-DEMAND

voice mail /'vɔɪs meɪl/ *noun* Also written **voicemail** 🖳 〰

A system for electronically storing, processing, and reproducing verbal messages left through the conventional telephone network, or transmitted through a digital computer network.

Voice mail systems employ computers that can respond either to the electronic tones transmitted by modern TONE-DIALLING phones or to simple verbal responses. Callers can be directed to a variety of services, hear pre-recorded responses, be connected to specialist staff, or leave messages in someone's **voice mailbox**. Though undeniably useful in reducing the need for telephone receptionists, a factor which has fuelled their widespread introduction since the early nineties, the systems are disliked by many people for their impersonal and sometimes unresponsive nature. The term *voice mail* is also used for recordings of spoken messages sent electronically from one person to another in a similar way to electronic mail; the phrase **voice message** is employed to distinguish any such spoken message from faxes and other data.

> The unit will also read back your electronic mail, synthesised into voicemail by a PC which controls the network for the entire building. —*Guardian* 10 Mar. 1994, section 2, p. 19

> Voice mail, in fact, is a layman's umbrella term used to cover various kinds of telephone messaging. The more annoying sort, where you are greeted with a recording which invites you to start pressing buttons or saying—embarrassingly—'yes' after various beeps, is officially known as 'Automated Attendance'. —*Independent on Sunday* 15 Jan. 1995, p. 25

> This somewhat uneven program provides central control with a unified inbox (actually, 10 inboxes organized as mailboxes) for incoming voice messages and faxes. —*Byte* May 1995, p. 126

voluntary simplicity ✖ see DOWNSHIFTER

voxel /'vɒks(ə)l/ *noun* 🖳

A point in a computer representation of a three-dimensional space containing a numerical value representing some property of that point.

Formed from *volume element* by a blend of the elements *vol* and *el*, after its equivalent in two-dimensions, *pixel*, itself a modified abbreviation of the phrase *picture element*.

A number of technologies require data to be stored about some property of the internal structure of a three-dimensional object. Typical examples are x-ray computerized tomography (CT) machines in medical diagnostics (which build up an image consisting of a series of 'slices' through the body), three-dimensional scanning microscopes, magnetic resonance imaging, seismic imaging systems, and three-dimensional ultrasound scans. All these produce data about sampled points which are arranged on a grid in a three-dimensional space: each of these points is a *voxel*. Through a process called *volume rendering*, or *volume imaging*, this data can be used to produce a two-dimensional image, usually relying heavily on colour, which enables researchers to visualize the data and make inferences from it.

> A voxel's value represents a sample of volume data from real-world scientific or medical instruments. —*Byte* May 1992, p. 178

> Voxel-based imaging is practically a prerequisite for laser scan confocal microscopes, instruments that let biologists peer into living cells in a manner analogous to the way CT lets doctors scan the interior of patients. —*Scientific American* Mar. 1994, p. 83

W

wack /wak/ *adjective* POP

In slang (especially in the US): bad, unhip, harmful.

Possibly derived from *wacky* or *wacko* 'crazy, mad'. The connection with drugs can be seen in *wacky tabacky*, a slang name for the drug of the sixties, marijuana. The implication is both that drugs affect the mind, and that it is *mad* to get involved with them.

Wack seems to have arisen in US street slang, first coming to the media's attention in the mid eighties, especially in connection with the spread of CRACK. It has been used in writing especially in the anti-drug slogan **crack is wack** (or **crack be wack, jack**) notably in a number of mural paintings in New York and other cities.

> Another inscription...warned, 'Crack is wack. You use crack today, tomorrow you be bumming. That's word experience talk.' —*Atlantic* Sept. 1989, p. 75

> 'That was what sparked us to start the band: seeing all these wack people getting paid', explained Gee. 'We knew we could do better.' —*Vibe* Fall 1992, Preview issue, p. 45

waif /weɪf/ *noun* ▨ POP

A fashionable young woman, with clothes and hair suggesting a ragged style, characterized by extreme slenderness and apparent fragility. Also occasionally used of a young man of similar appearance.

Formed from a transferred use of the word in the sense, 'an abandoned child'.

In the nineties, the so-called **waif look** has been made fashionable by such supermodels as Kate Moss. The characteristic elements of extreme youth and slenderness, together with the appearance of vulnerability and fragility, occasioned some concern: with EATING DISORDERS an increasing matter of concern, it was felt that the role model thus offered to the young by the successful **superwaifs** (sometimes contrasted with the more robust *übermodels*) might achieve style at the expense of health. The term is often used attributively of the characteristic appearance or style, and the adjectives **waifish** and **waiflike** are also found.

> She has so many layered waif outfits. —*Premiere* Oct. 1991, p. 107

> The onslaught of ugly models in the women's fashion shows has now been paralleled by an onslaught of unattractive men. Male waifs—underfed, wild-haired, feral types looking enormously uncomfortable...Many seem to be candidates for some form of rehabilitation. —*Esquire* May 1994, p. 119

> One of Stasi's main claims to fame is starting the controversy over the low body weight of superwaif Kate Moss. —*New York* 1 Aug. 1994, p. 28

> There have been many articles...concerning the battle between the asexual waif and the super-sonic supermodel in the fashion world. —*The Face* Sept. 1995, p. 15

waitperson ⁅ see PERSON

waitron /'weɪtrən/ *noun* ⁅

A waiter or waitress.

Formed originally from a blend of *waiter* and the suffix *-tron* (in physics, forming nouns denoting a subatomic particle), with the implication that waiting at table is a mindless, robotic activity; a contrast with the *patron* of a restaurant to whom service is offered may also be intended.

In the early eighties *waitron* may originally have carried derogatory connotations, but by the midpoint of the decade it had joined *waitperson* (see PERSON) as a useful common gender form.

'Waitron!' I made an elaborate semaphore signal across the deck at the girl who'd been serving us. —Armistead Maupin *Maybe the Moon* (1992), p. 160

There's that uneasy silence that settles over almost every boozer-friendly social occasion when the waitron asks if it can bring something from the bar. —*Spy* Feb. 1994, p. 62

We were tiring of the usual haunts that out-of-town writers point to when they're trying to prove that the Twin Cities actually has a 'scene'. Sure, we liked the food, and…even those nasty waitrons who gave us a glimpse of what it means to be cosmopolitan. But amid all the espresso, the pancake makeup, the clove cigarettes, we found there was something missing: bowling. —*Minnesota Monthly* May 1994, p. 15

wakeboarding /ˈweɪkbɔːdɪŋ/ *noun* ⚽

A form of water sport in which participants ride on a short, wide board or **wakeboard**, resembling a surfboad, towed by a motorized craft.

Wakeboarding, also known as *skiboarding*, has become popular in the nineties. Those who **wakeboard** may simply coast over the surface of the water in the wake of the towing boat, or may perform stunts and acrobatic tricks.

Imagine leaping up to 25ft in the air, turning somersaults as if launched from a trampoline and performing contortionist tricks like the *chicken salad grab*—or just drifting from side to side behind a speedboat hopping over its wash. Well that's wakeboarding, the radical alternative to waterskiing. —*Daily Mail Holiday Action* Summer 1995, p. 9

If you've seen *Waterworld* and fancy emulating the water-skiing Smokers, you could try wakeboarding, designed for newcomers to the skiing scene. —*Independent on Sunday* 20 Aug. 1995, Real Life section, p. 7

It's a big move for Innovative Marketing Ventures, which makes and markets skateboards, wakeboards, snowboards and surfboards. —*San Diego Union-Tribune* 4 Sept. 1996, section C, p. 1

See also JET-SKIING, THRILLCRAFT

walker /ˈwɔːkə/ *noun* POP

A male escort paid to accompany a woman in public or at a social engagement.

The concept of a *walker* or male escort employed to accompany a wealthy woman in public, or while attending social engagements, came to notice in the early eighties; it is originally and still chiefly a US practice. A *walker*'s function as escort may sometimes overlap with that of a HIMBO or TOYBOY, but the roles are in fact distinct: the implied relationship of the *walker* to the woman whom he is escorting is non-sexual: his task is to be at her side on public and social occasions.

Alfredo was a well-known 'walker', who spent much of his life escorting wealthy, usually married socialites to society functions and private dinners. —*Los Angeles* May 1990, p. 130

A dependable date for charity events—to which he insists on buying his own tickets, 'going Dutch', as he puts it—Woolley has fallen into the category of 'walker'. He often shows up in paparazzi shots with such ladies-about-town as Eleanor Lambert…Dorothy Hirshon, and Iris Love. —*Vanity Fair* Jan. 1993, p. 133

wannabe /ˈwɒnəbi/ *noun* and *adjective* Also written **wannabee** POP

In slang (originally in the US):

noun: An avid fan or follower who hero-worships and tries to emulate a particular celebrity or type, especially in appearance. Also, more generally, anyone who wants to be someone else.

adjective: Aspiring, would-be; like a wannabe; inspired by envy.

A respelling of *want to be* (as in the sixties song *I Wan'na Be Like You* by Richard M. and Robert B. Sherman), treated as a single word which can operate as a noun (someone whose appearance and manner seem to say 'I wanna be like you') or an adjective.

The noun was first used in the mid eighties to refer to white youths in the US who dressed and behaved like members of black gangs. It was probably most widely popularized, though, by its application to the female fans of the rock star Madonna, many of whom adopted a style of dress and make-up which almost turned them into Madonna look-alikes. There are also the sporting *wannabes*, the people who own all the kit that goes with the sport and manage to look the part, but have not yet the ability to fulfil the role. The adjective *wannabe* developed from 1986 onwards.

> Madonna is the most successful female pop star of her generation—a powerful figure whose mass appeal even triggered the phenomenon of wannabees, girls who not only dressed like her but wanted to be her. —*New Scientist* 15 Feb. 1992, p. 32

> More than any other popular artist, Mr Lee has raised the explosive issue of black-on-black discrimination. In 'School Daze' he parodied resentments between lighter-skinned and darker-skinned black women by having them deride one another as 'wannabes' (as in 'wannabe white') and 'jigaboos'. —*Economist* 26 Dec. 1992, p. 127

> The winning-isn't-everything speeches almost seem like a joke as kids read how a wannabe cheerleader's mother in Texas resorted to murder to make a place for her daughter. —*Star-Ledger* 30 Jan. 1994, p. 6

-ware /wɛː/ *combining form* 🖳

A combining form widely used in computing to construct words describing various kinds of software.

Software itself is recorded from 1960, and in the next two decades various terms identifying a particular type of software were formed on the second element of the word. (An example is *courseware*, software designed for educational use.)

The early eighties saw a rapid increase in the number of terms ending in *-ware*, fuelled by the increasing accessibility of personal computers and the associated rise of electronic bulletin boards (BBSs) for exchanging software and hobbyist information on programming. **Freeware** appeared in 1982 (software which may be freely used and exchanged); the year after came **shareware** (software which may be freely exchanged and used for a trial period but which must be registered and paid for if it continues to be used). Some *shareware* authors include on-screen notices 'nagging' users to register, so their software has come to be called **nagware**; others disable features to create **crippleware**, which requires users to register to obtain the complete working program. Some *freeware* authors request users merely to send them a picture postcard if they like it (such software is called **postcardware**), while others ask for a charitable donation to be made (variously called **donorware**, **charityware**, or **careware**). On occasion, firms distribute free software whose principal purpose is to advertise another, commercial, product; this is called **bannerware**. So many computer magazines in the nineties issued free CD-ROMs each month they had trouble filling them, and some dumped lots of undistinguished software—which became known as **shovelware**—in the space available. (It is difficult to determine when many of these terms were coined as they undoubtedly circulated informally before they ever appeared in print.)

Computer companies' promises of new or updated software so often failed to be met that **vapourware** (**vaporware** in the US) was coined about 1984 to mean products announced but not delivered. Software that is too difficult to use or does not live up to its promised performance is called **shelfware**, because that is where it ends up. The great size of many commercial applications in the nineties caused them to be described pejoratively as **bloatware**; there was a desire among some users to return to small, fast applications, which they dubbed **slimware**. Software which aids or enhances abilities, say for the disabled or in computer simulations, is sometimes called **mindware**.

The growth of client-server computing in the late eighties and nineties, in which individuals' computers are linked to corporate databases through networks, required a new kind of software, **middleware**, to supervise the connections. Changes in business practices in the late eighties and nineties towards workgroups gave rise to **groupware** designed to allow several people to work on the same documents or information at once. The greater emphasis on individual skills and responsibility caused the term **peopleware** to be coined to describe the human resources of the business as opposed to the computing ones (sometimes **liveware** is used with the same meaning).

The key to good design...was to start thinking about 'liveware' (human beings) along with the hardware and software. —*Independent* 1 May 1987, p. 19

Company president David Miller referred to 'dBASE/SQL' as 'the ultimate vapourware, since it's unannounced, undesigned, undeveloped, unknown, has no marketing plan...nor any release date or pricing.' —*Australian Personal Computer* Oct. 1989, p. 26

Government agencies and business organizations must use peopleware along with hardware and software to attack the productivity problem. That means focusing on hiring good people, expanding management skills and encouraging teamwork. —*Governing* Dec. 1991, p. 56

This means more than just buying five copies of brand X CASE tool; there were lots of companies in the late 1980s who did just that, and the five copies ended up as 'shelfware' because nobody could use them.
—Edward Yourdon *Decline and Fall of the American Programmer* (1992), p. 136

For many people, particularly programmers and engineers, the Internet means 'info-booty': shareware and freeware source code, documents, graphics and data sets available by file transfer downloads and from E-mail servers. —*Byte* Feb. 1992, p. 113

Users are only redeveloping legacy software when it provides down-to-earth cost benefits.
—*Computing* 3 June 1993, p. 27

It was the only groupware she'd ever installed—ever *seen*, even—that actually worked, in the sense that it genuinely helped a group manager rather than slowly driving its users bug-house.
—Bruce Sterling *Heavy Weather* (1994), p. 58

If wireless networking is all about freedom, why do net managers feel as if they've been taken prisoner by carriers, middleware vendors, or their own applications?
—*Data Communications International* Jan. 1995, p. 104

warehouse club /ˈwɛːhaʊs klʌb/ *noun* 🔀

A repository offering a wide selection of goods for sale at discounted prices to members of a club. Also, such a club itself.

Warehouse clubs grew up in North America in the early eighties, in response to growing consumer demand for the opportunity to buy economically and in bulk. *Warehouse clubs* are usually sited out of town, and carry a wide range of goods; members of the club pay an annual subscription for the right to shop there.

In the nineties, despite objections from established supermarket chains, *warehouse clubs* spread to the UK. Although well supported, they have not developed the predicted level of popularity, and it remains to be seen whether the phenomenon will be a lasting one.

Warehouse clubs charge a fee to members, but because they have lower operating costs, they are able to sell merchandise at smaller gross margins than supermarkets, department stores and traditional discounters. —*Globe & Mail* 17 June 1993, section A, p. 2

Discount 'warehouse clubs' retailing everything from computers to bulk bags of beef are expected to open throughout Britain following a defeat in the High Court yesterday for the big supermarkets. —*Guardian* 28 Oct. 1993, p. 2

The warehouse club format was supposed to be the future.
—*Independent on Sunday* 26 Mar. 1995, Business section, p. 2

warez /wɛːz/ *plural noun* 🖳

Pirated software or other digital material, usually transmitted via the INTERNET.

A re-spelling of *wares*.

This term is common in some areas online, but only began to appear in printed sources in the mid nineties. Those involved are a subset of HACKERS (sometimes known as **warez doodz**) who obtain early releases of commercial software, break any security codes, and make the material widely available. The motive appears to be largely a pride in achievement, often associated with an anarchistic desire to do down the 'system'; it is rarely undertaken for profit, though this is small consolation to the software houses who see their intellectual property subverted.

> As lame as the warez d00dz are, I find it funny that people...still haven't gotten over the fact that people will always find a way to get the software for free.　　　　—4 July 1995, online posting

> And of course no one ever rats on sites or fellow swappers. No one, that is, except for the Feds or outraged software manufacturers, who are constantly cruising cyberspace for warez sites—and have busted a fair number of the pirates in their travels.　　　　—*Focus* Aug. 1995, p. 13

> The server on which pirated 'warez' are held may be in one country, the server through which they are advertised in another, the seller in a third.　　　　—*Economist* 27 July 1996, p. 71

-watch /wɒtʃ/ *combining form* 🐾POP

Forming nouns (with or without a hyphen, or written as two words) to indicate the act or process of maintaining vigilant observation of the thing indicated by the first element of the word formed.

Formed from the noun *watch* 'a state of alert or constant observation or attention'; originally occurring as the second element of such compounds as *doomwatch*, *skywatch*; perhaps also influenced by such forms as *birdwatching*, *firewatching*.

The use of *watch* in this sense as the second element of a compound is recorded from the fifties, but it is in the eighties that *-watch* has become freely productive as a combining form. The nouns formed (which may be more or less ephemeral) tend to fall into two groups: those relating to studies of the natural world, such as **badger-watch**, **foxwatch**, or **whale-watch**, and those which have connotations of vigilant awareness of the object specified for the purposes of self-defence, such as **hacker watch** or **stormwatch**.

The popularity of *-watch* as a combining form coincided with, and was probably assisted by, its use in the titles of television programmes; a number of the more recent, and jocular, formations make implicit ironic allusion to the notion of applying the standards of observation appropriate to phenomena of the natural world to the object or person specified.

As this use of *-watch* has become established, formations of related verbs (as in to **whale-watch**) have also occurred, and the further combining forms **-watcher** and **-watching** have also developed; these however are likely to have been influenced by such established forms as *birdwatcher* and *birdwatching*.

> The guard would go on 'hacker watch' by making...electronic patrols.
> 　　　　—*The Times* 27 Dec. 1984, p. 3

> Everywhere it seems to be 'Progwatch' time, *Birdwatch* roughly once a fortnight; *Drugwatch* coming up in ten days' time.　　　　—*Listener* 11 July 1985, p. 21

> Badger Watch is a popular TV programme.　　　　—*The Face* 1990 (BNC)

> Knowing how the low-level jet is behaving 'may make the difference between a tornado watch and a thunderstorm watch'.　　　　—*Scientific News* 11 July 1992, p. 29

> Whale-watch advocates point out that the young industry pumps money into seaside communities.　　　　—*National Wildlife* Feb. 1993, p. 10

> Family-sized platters contain an entire chicken or spaghetti for eight...No reservations, so prepare to people-watch while you wait.　　　　—*Minnesota Monthly* May 1994, p. 61

water birth /ˈwɔːtə bəːθ/ *noun* ⊗

A form of childbirth in which the mother is supported in a specially designed pool or tub so that the child is delivered into the water.

Since the late eighties, *water births* have been presented as providing a form of 'natural' childbirth. In the last stages of labour, the mother is supported in a *birthing pool* of warm water, physical circumstances which are held to reduce stress and increase the ease of delivery, and which provide an environment for the baby which corresponds to that of the womb.

Water births, although advocated strongly by some, have been seen by others as a questionable technique from the area of alternative health care. More recently concerns have focused particularly on the alleged possibilities of infection encountered by a newly delivered infant in the water of a *birthing pool*, but it is too soon to say what the long-term view of the pros and cons will be.

> The safety of water births is called into question today by a report of a baby becoming infected by bacteria in the birthing tub. —*Guardian* 19 Aug. 1994, p. 6

> An international conference on water births is to take place in London this weekend, with researchers from 30 countries sharing information. —*Guardian* 31 Mar. 1995, p. 3

watercise ⊗ ⊕ see AQUACISE

way /weɪ/ *adverb* POP

In slang: extremely, very; really.

A use of the existing adverb *way* 'to a considerable extent'.

This slang use of *way* as an intensifier to qualify any adjective, especially to express approval, is recorded from the late eighties.

> When we recorded it originally I doubled up the drums and it sounded way Gary Glitter, way Clash. —*New Musical Express* 21 July 1990, p. 14

> He's way cute. I'd do him. —*Village Voice* 20 Apr. 1993, p. 79

> Savage is way low on her estimate of breeding peregrines North of 60. There are not hundreds of them, as she says, but thousands. —*Up Here: Life in Canada's North* Mar. 1994, p. 44

> See also WELL

wazzock /ˈwazək/ *noun* POP

In slang: a stupid or annoying person.

The origin of this word is unknown, although the final syllable *-ock* may echo the ending of *pillock* in this sense. At the beginning of the eighties, a musical album was issued which was built around the theme of 'Radio *Wassock*': possibly an early variant of the term.

Wazzock as a derogatory expression for a stupid or annoying person is found from the late eighties; the compound **wazzock-like** has also been recorded.

> Kids have gone Yank crazee, overdosing on Trans Atlantic sickness by chewing gum, guzzling popcorn, wearing wazzock-like baseball caps and slurping coke.
> —*New Musical Express* 13 Jan. 1990, p. 35

> She makes the tea and hangs around in the background, on hand lest Winterson get into trouble or find herself shouting at a 'wazzock'. —*Guardian* 18 June 1994, Weekend section, p. 22

Web ⌨ see WORLD WIDE WEB

weight-train /ˈweɪttreɪn/ *intransitive verb* ⊗ ⊕

To exercise using weights.

A verb recorded from the early eighties, in a formation reflecting a growing interest in physical health. Initially those prepared to *weight-train* regularly would have been those professionally involved with sport, but many who now *weight-train* do so on the grounds of health.

I just run and weight-train, that's all there is to it. *—Health & Fitness* Jan. 1991, p. 17

At an age at which many people are preparing for retirement, she feels her productive life has just begun; she weight-trains, plays table tennis. *—Daily Telegraph* 13 Jan. 1995, p. 17

well /wɛl/ *adverb* POP

In slang: extremely, very; really.

A use of the existing adverb *well*, as in such forms as *well able*, *well aware*.

This use of *well* as an intensifier to qualify an adjective, especially in a commendatory sense, is recorded from the mid eighties.

No dress restrictions, music policy is well 'ard with P. Funk, House, Go-Go and Electro cutting it. *—Blues & Soul* 3 Feb. 1987, p. 34

This boy looked in wonder at the polyurethane and leather marvel and offered it the coolest of street compliments. 'Well wicked,' he breathed. *—Daily Telegraph* 9 June 1990, p. 13

They thought our food was well weird. They'd eat burgers and chips, really straight food. We were vegetarians then.
—Richard Low & William Shaw *Travellers: Voices of the New Age Travellers* (1993), p. 20

See also WAY

Wessi /'wɛsi, 'vɛsi/ *noun*

A colloquial and sometimes depreciative term used in Germany, especially since reunification, and adopted in English, to denote a citizen of the former Federal Republic of Germany; a West German.

The German word *Wessi* is formed from *West* 'West'; it is probably an abbreviation of *Westdeutsche* 'West German'.

On the reunification of Germany in October 1990 the terms *West German* and *East German*, which had referred to the separate national identities of the post-war Federal Republic of Germany and the German Democratic Republic, were, at least in theory, consigned to history; now, once again, there were simply Germans. However there remained an unofficial recognition of the cultural differences which stemmed from forty-five years of differing political and economic systems. The colloquial terms Ossi and *Wessi*, already in use within Germany, were recognized and adopted world-wide as indicators of this divided heritage, perceived by many to be ingrained. A particular concern, expressed by some in the west, is that economic measures taken to reduce unemployment in the east might be at their expense.

For the Ossi, the Wessi was an arrogant know-all ruled by an oppressive bureaucracy. *—The Times* 3 Oct. 1991, p. 12

For the Wessi, the Ossi was pot-bellied, lacking in initiative and naive. *—The Times* 3 Oct. 1991, p. 12

In the East, people often speak of arrogant 'Wessis' with fear and loathing; in the West, the idle, scrounging 'Ossis' are mocked. *—Vanity Fair* May 1993, p. 44

Many Germans, both Wessis and Ossis (in local slang), are having difficulty coming to terms with life in the new Germany. *—Guardian* 30 July 1994, Weekend section, p. 20

Wessis befriended through work invite me to their birthday parties or whatever and I'm always the only Ossi. *—Post* (Denver) 8 Oct. 1994, p. 31

Western blot see BLOT

West Lothian question /wɛst ˌləʊðɪən ˈkwɛstʃ(ə)n/ *noun phrase*

The name given to the question encapsulating what is seen as a central flaw in plans for regional devolution: should an area with its own regional assembly also be able to vote in a national parliament on matters concerning other areas of the country.

A *question* originally asked in Parliament by the member for the constituency of *West Lothian*.

In the debates on Scottish devolution in 1977, the Labour MP Tam Dalyell repeatedly posed the question of whether, once a Scottish Assembly had been set up (thus removing from Westminster responsibility for Scottish local government), it would be appropriate for Scottish members of parliament to have a voice in purely English matters.

The same point had been made in 1914 by Arthur Balfour, but Dalyell's persistence in raising the question has in modern times associated the formulation with him, and led to the coinage of *West Lothian question* from the name of his Scottish constituency.

> This minimalist approach may be right for England, but it undermines Mr Robertson's hope that English devolution would solve the 'West Lothian question': after an Edinburgh parliament is established, why should Scottish MPs at Westminster have a voice on issues in England about which English MPs have no say in Scotland? —*Economist* 18 Feb. 1995, p. 29

whale-watch ᴘᴏᴘ see –WATCH

Wheneye /ˈwɛnʌɪ/ *noun* Also written When-eye ᴘᴏᴘ

In slang: a person who exasperates listeners by continually recounting tales of his or her experiences and exploits.

Formed from a respelling of the introductory phrase *When I —*.

A derogatory term, dating from the early eighties, reflecting the exasperation aroused by a speaker's continually recounting experiences or exploits which by implication outshine those of the listener.

> I met my first Wheneye in the corner of a bar overlooking the sea on the north shore of a small island. —*Age* (Melbourne) 8 February 1982, p. 16

> In the Isle of Man...the incomers are known to the locals as the 'Wheneyes' from their habit of harking eternally back to their former lives, saying 'when I was chairman' of this that or the other company. —*Independent* 1 June 1990, p. 19

white-bread /ˈwʌɪtbrɛd/ *adjective* Also written white bread ᴘᴏᴘ

Of, belonging to, or representative of the North American white middle classes; bourgeois; conventional; bland or innocuous.

From *white bread* in its literal sense, with reference to its colour and perceived blandness; perhaps also with a punning allusion to the idea of being *white bred*.

White-bread has been used since the end of the seventies to designate what is seen as characteristic of North American white middle-class society; the term is now likely to be used to indicate what is strait-laced, conventional, and generally lacking in individuality.

> He's our age, and Biff-and-Muffy private schoolish like Claire's brother Allan, and from some eastern white bread ghetto: New Rochelle? Shaker Heights? —Douglas Coupland *Generation X* (1991), p. 79

> In playing Carroll, the working-class Catholic bohemian, DiCaprio never seems like a true street kid. He's too sleek and white-bread and suburban. —*Entertainment Weekly* 21 Apr. 1995, p. 39

> Perhaps too feisty for the currently booming Easy Listening sector, but ultimately too white bread to really grasp the lapels, this Nashville-recorded LP from 1969 is an agreeable thing nonetheless. —*Q* Jan. 1996, p. 148

white information /ˌwʌɪt ɪnfəˈmeɪʃ(ə)n/ *noun* ᴘᴏᴘ

Financial information indicating that a person is creditworthy.

White information is recorded from the late eighties, as a term for information (passed on by a finance house) which provides evidence that a prospective borrower is creditworthy; *black information* would indicate the contrary (and cause the person to be financially *blacklisted*). Both terms are now established, although the contextual use often indicates uneasiness about the ethical aspect of disclosure of what is effectively confidential information, whether or not it is favourable.

People...are likely to be turned down if they refuse to let the card company investigate their borrowings with other lenders...It is part of the preparations to share 'white information' about its borrowers with other lenders. It already shares 'black information' about bad behaviour.

—Independent on Sunday 27 June 1993, Business section, p. 24

Another bone of contention is that finance houses and credit card arms of retail stores register any loan or credit they extend to customers with credit reference agencies. This so-called 'white information' is passed on even when customers have a good repayment history. Banks and building societies have hitherto resisted providing 'white information' to the agencies, restricting themselves to defaults—so-called 'black information'. But some banks have started to pass on 'white information' to their credit card operations. *—Guardian* 19 Mar. 1994, p. 26

white smoker 🦎 see SMOKER

Whitewatergate /'wʌɪtwɔːtəˌɡeɪt/ *noun* 🗂 ᴾᴼᴾ

The name given to circumstances surrounding allegations of financial misconduct in Arkansas in the eighties, involving a commercial land development associated with Bill and Hillary Clinton.

Formed from *Whitewater*, the name of an eighties property development corporation based in Arkansas, in which Governor (later US President) Bill Clinton and his wife Hillary Rodham Clinton were partners; there is also a direct play on the *Watergate* scandal of 1972.

Following President Clinton's first inauguration in January 1993, allegations of financial misconduct during his years in Arkansas began to surface, with particular attention being paid to the **Whitewater** land development involving the law firm with which Hillary Clinton was associated. It seems likely that the coincidence of the name helped with the coinage of *Whitewatergate*, but once coined the term was fixed in the public consciousness by continuing news reports and (on the Republican side) calls for an official inquiry. To date no inquiry has been set up, but *Whitewatergate* remains an unresolved topic of interest for politicians and journalists.

Leach wants a special prosecutor to look into what has come to be known as 'Whitewatergate.'

—Post (Denver) 16 Jan. 1994, section F, p. 1

He could be just the man the Clintons need to put Whitewatergate behind them.

—American Spectator Apr. 1994, p. 8

whoop /huːp/ *noun* 🎲 ⚽

A bump or dip on an off-road racetrack or rally course.

Formed from a shortening of *whoop-de-do* 'a fuss, a commotion', in the motor-cycling sense of 'a very bumpy stretch of road'.

A term recorded from the early eighties, when *off-roading*, or driving on dirt tracks and other unmetalled surfaces, had become established as a popular sport and leisure activity.

The whoops around the back of the track had been made bigger and deeper to almost stadium standards. *—Motocross Rider* June 1987, p. 12

The whoops were very deep and unpredictable and many riders were sorted right out on the first day. *—Courier-Mail* (Brisbane) 15 June 1990, p. 37

In supercross there are no long straights, steep hills and power-robbing sand whoops.

—Motocross April 1993, p. 58

wicked /'wɪkɪd/ *adjective* ᴾᴼᴾ

In slang: excellent, great, wonderful.

A reversal of meaning. There might first have been a catch-phrase or advertising slogan *so good it's wicked* which was later abbreviated to *wicked* alone; however, it is not unusual for an adjective to be used as an 'in' word in the opposite sense to its usual one among a limited group of people, and then pass into more general slang.

In US slang, *wicked* has been used in the sense 'formidable' since the end of the nineteenth century (compare *mean* in British English). A famous example occurs in F. Scott Fitzgerald's *This Side of Paradise* (1920), when Sloane calls for music and announces

Phoebe and I are going to shake a wicked calf.

It was only in the early eighties, though, that *wicked* was taken up by young people (including, and perhaps especially, young children) as a fashionable term of approval, often preceded by WELL. This usage, unlike the earlier slang use, spread outside US English to enjoy a vogue among British and Australian youngsters as well. A children's weekend television programme in the UK took up the theme in its title, *It's Wicked!*

I've been to loads of Acid House parties. We have a wicked time but never, not never, do we take any drugs.   —*Time Out* 18 Oct. 1989, p. 9

We [had] half a dozen old farmers along the other night...They were well wicked, really knocking back the damson and apple wine.   —*Guardian* 27 July 1992, p. 3

wife abuse ⁅⁆ see ABUSE

WIMP /wɪmp/ *acronym* 🔬

Any of several subatomic particles, not yet observed, which are thought to have relatively large mass but to interact only weakly with ordinary matter, and which may be the main constituents of the dark matter of the universe.

Formed from the initial letters of *weakly interacting massive particle*.

It has long been known that there must be much more matter in the universe than we can observe (see COLD DARK MATTER). It has been suggested that types of elementary particle could exist which were massive (perhaps more so than the proton) but which did not interact with ordinary matter except by gravity. These could account for at least some of the missing mass. Though such particles have not yet been observed, theoretical studies suggest they must exist.

They hypothesize that an as yet unobserved class of subatomic particles known as weakly interacting massive particles (WIMP's), created in vast quantities in the early universe, account for the large quantities of invisible mass that seems to exist in large cosmic structures.
                                            —*Scientific American* May 1990, Vol. 262, No. 5, p. 32

Theorists have quite a shopping list of hypothetical WIMPs, bearing outlandish names like gravitinos, Higgsinos, and photinos.   —Paul Davies *Last Three Minutes* (1994), p. 72

wind farm /'wɪnd fɑːm/ *noun* 🌱

A group of energy-producing windmills or wind turbines.

The notion is that the *wind* can be *farmed* to produce energy.

Wind farms were introduced at the beginning of the eighties, and were initially regarded with enthusiasm as a source of power which could be obtained without environmental damage. However, as *wind farms* on a large scale have become more common, concerns have surfaced as to their visual impact and the possible noise pollution resulting from their operation. In the mid nineties, opinions as to their desirability are divided.

Canada's first commercial wind farm...is the latest initiative in the age-old quest to harness the wind as a clean and free source of energy.   —*Equinox* Nov. 1988, p. 38

A facility that will produce clean electricity by burning both domestic and commercial rubbish. We are helping to develop Britain's first commercial wind farm.
                                            —advertisement in *Economist* 9 May 1992, p. 30

One of the biggest countryside groups will throw its weight today behind the growing campaign against wind farms in remote upland areas.   —*Guardian* 26 March 1994, p. 9

Much of the debate about renewable energy in 1994 focused on wind power. There was growing public unease about what wind-farm development actually means for the countryside. The lure of clean, 'green' energy offered by wind-energy developers often skimmed too lightly over the visual impact of wind turbines in wild, remote landscapes.

—*Annual Report 1995* (Council for the Preservation of Rural England) 1995, p. 9

wired¹ /wʌɪəd/ *adjective* 👖

In slang: In a state of nervous excitement; tense, anxious, edgy. Often in the phrase **wired up**.

An extension of an existing adjective, perhaps with the notion of being held as by *wire* in a tense posture; there may also be a reflection of the established phrase *strung up* in the same sense. A rare US slang use of *wired up* in the sense 'annoyed, angry' is recorded from the early part of the twentieth century.

Wired and **wired up** to convey the kind of nervous excitement and anxiety deriving from an inability to relax are recorded from the early eighties. The term may now be used to indicate tension in varying degrees.

He's really wired up. It's fun to see him do the jumping for a change.
—Erin Pizzey *Watershed* 1983, p. 221

If he'd started the week expansive, unsweaty, not noticeably wired, he ended it, several dozen promotional encounters later, travelling at media-speed. —*Independent* 3 May 1990, p. 19

Meditation is an integral part of Buddhism, and days are likely to be structured around this…This appeals to wired Londoners hoping to reduce their stress levels.
—*Time Out* 31 Mar.–7 Apr. 1993, p. 27

He was tense and wired on game days, and he rarely ate a full meal before a game, although before night games he would eat a little bit. —David Halberstam *October 1964* (1994), p. 273

wired² /wʌɪəd/ *adjective* 🖥

Making use of computers and information technology to transfer or receive information, in particular through the Internet.

The term began to be used in the early nineties, when businesses were increasingly taking advantage of advances in computer technology and networking to improve their services or their understanding of their own affairs, and interest in the INTERNET was rapidly rising among both businesses and individuals.

Wired news, including IBM, Microsoft and Apple's new Internet-ready operating systems, plus the truth behind CompuServe and the Net. —*.net* Dec. 1994, p. 6

Whatever happens, librarians need to adjust quickly to these trends—becoming masters not just of commercially published data, but also of all the new, more informal, 'wired' ways that people are sharing information. —*Library Manager* Jan. 1995, p. 4

Build a better Web site, and the wired will beat a path to your door.
—*Data Communications International* 21 Nov. 1995, p. 83

wise use /'wʌɪz juːs/ *noun* 🌱 〰

Especially in the US: environmental policy promoting a controlled use of natural resources.

The philosophy of *wise use* was set out in 1989 in Alan Gottlieb's *The Wise Use Agenda*, which advocated a controlled use of natural resources in preference to attempting to find alternative resources or to preventing such use altogether. This policy has proved a controversial one, with traditional environmentalists viewing supporters of the **wise use movement**, or **wise users**, as effectively representing a threat to the environment, with the term *wise use* seen as a euphemism for commercial exploitation of what should be protected: an approach essentially hostile to proponents of GREEN issues.

For 25 years, environmentalists have driven one ranch after another into non-use classifications such as 'wilderness'. But they've radicalized so many people the Wise Use Movement has arisen to defend commodity production on our federal lands.   —*USA Today* 3 May 1989, section A, p. 10

Now, the exploiters and developers have introduced the euphemism 'wise use' for wilderness destruction.   —*U.S. News & World Report* Nov. 1991, p. 5

The timber industry says plenty of old-growth forest still exists, and that the industry has adopted a 'wise use' policy that will maintain the integrity of the region's forests.
          —*St. Louis Post-Dispatch* 10 May 1992, section A, p. 1

'Wise Use' activists...oppose alleged 'lockups' of federal lands.
          —*Post* (Denver) 15 Jan. 1995, section C, p. 4

wolf-dog /'wulfdɒg/ *noun* ▒ ꜗ

A dog which is a hybrid between a wolf and a dog.

In 1996, reports of the commercial availability of *wolf-dogs* as pets in Britain revived anxieties about DANGEROUS DOGS, not least in that *wolf-dogs*, which are not named in the Act, are therefore not subject to any legal embargo.

The RSPCA has warned the public to steer clear of hybrid 'wolf-dogs' being sold for £400 as Britain's latest family pet and said to be replacing the pit-bull as a favourite with macho dog lovers.   —*Daily Telegraph* 16 Jan. 1996, p. 9

word-crunching ▣ see CRUNCHER

workgroup /'wə:kgru:p/ *noun* ▣

A group of workers engaged in a series of specialized or collaborative tasks who share and process information by means of linked computers.

This term only began to be used to any significant extent in the late eighties. By then it was relatively common for workers in offices to have personal computers linked into local-area networks (see LAN) so they could share resources such as printers. Early usage of *workgroup* often implied little more than a group so linked. However, the sense has shifted somewhat in the nineties as ideas about the role of computers have evolved and as more powerful systems and specially designed software have become available. By the mid nineties it had become a common term describing a group undertaking some collective project—anything from computer-aided design to stock control—whose productivity is dependent upon and enhanced by computer hardware and software that allows them to communicate with each other, schedule tasks, and share information and resources. Such software is now commonly called *groupware* (see -WARE). The term *workgroup* is frequently used attributively, and an action noun **workgrouping** is occasionally encountered, but other compounds are rare.

This means that companies are free to draw the bounds of the workgroup in a much more flexible fashion, so that workgroup colleagues may be in the next room to each other or on opposite sides of the globe.   —*Microsoft Magazine* 1992, p. 21

Workgrouping is the next major growth area and we have put together a platform which allows developers to write workgroup and workgroup-enabled applications easily and effectively.
          —*.EXE Magazine* June 1993, Supplement, p. 1

Only a third of those questioned had some idea of what workgroup computing and groupware mean.   —*Daily Telegraph* 26 June 1995, p. 31

work-related upper limb disorder ⊗ see REPETITIVE STRAIN INJURY

work shadowing /wə:k 'ʃadəʊɪŋ/ *noun* ꜗ

The process of accompanying and observing a person at work, for training or research purposes.

Use of the verb *shadow* in the sense 'to accompany (a person) at work either as training or to obtain insight into a profession' is recorded from the mid seventies.

Work shadowing is recorded from the first half of the eighties, and was initially seen as part a process of work experience in which future employees could familiarize themselves with the workplace. **Work shadow** schemes have grown in popularity, and offer opportunities for research as well as training: a member of a given profession may be **work shadowed** so that the **work shadow** can gain insights into the practices of that profession.

> Llewellyn is an enthusiastic supporter of the workshadow schemes in which undergraduates spend two to five days watching a top executive at work.   —*Daily Telegraph* 6 June 1989, p. 17

> Another, more personal, way to encourage possible recruits: I have been 'work-shadowed' by one of the girls.   —*New Scientist* 5 May 1990, p. 71

> Training courses featured highly...so did more unusual forms of development such as job moves, secondments, project work, task forces, work shadowing.   —*Independent* 23 Mar. 1995, p. 19

World Trade Organization ⚡ see NAFTA

World Wide Web /wəːld wʌɪd wɛb/ *noun phrase* Also written **World-Wide Web**, **Worldwide Web** and with lower-case initials 🖳

A visually-based system for accessing information (text, graphics, sound, and video) by means of the INTERNET, which consists of a large number of 'documents' tagged with cross-referencing links by which the user can move between sources.

The tagged 'documents' within the system form a *web* of links which extends *worldwide*.

The *World Wide Web* concept was originally intended to help particle physicists in various organizations throughout Europe share information; it began to be used for this purpose in 1991. However, it proved so useful a tool that it was taken up much more widely from about 1993 onwards, being responsible by the end of 1996 for almost half of all Internet traffic and with more than twenty million 'documents' available worldwide. Its huge popularity is due in part to its visual appeal, since the ability to mix colour pictures and formatted text permits online electronic publishing of a sort impracticable in print. It is also very much easier to use than the rather forbidding interface presented by older Internet systems. Links, which may be within the same document, the same computer system, or on any other system in the world, are formatted using *hypertext* principles (see HYPER-); accessing the linked material is simply a matter of selecting the link. The term *World Wide Web* is often abbreviated to **Web**, **WWW**, or (less often) **W3**. A single 'document' is usually called a **Web page** (or *page* for short), even if it is longer than can fit on a computer display screen; each page is identified by a unique *Uniform Resource Locator* (URL). A collection of such pages grouped by theme or provider is called a **Web site** (now frequently written **Website**). A user DOWNLOADS and displays pages using software called a **Web browser** (usually abbreviated to *browser*, see BROWSE), frequently finding the pages through one of a number of indexing sites, which employ automated computer software aplications called **Web crawlers** or **Web spiders** to find and catalogue pages. The person who administers a *Web* site is often called a **Webmaster** or **Webmeister** (the gender-specific term **Webmistress** is only rarely used); a document which has been converted to *Web* format is sometimes said to have been **Webized**; the totality of all *Web pages* and the links between them is called **Webspace**.

> This is what is known as a Web spider, crawler, robot or worm. That is, it is an automated technique for discovering and recording URLs in an attempt to map out Webspace.
> —*Computer Weekly* 12 Jan. 1995, p. 47

> Some people believe the Web is the most important advance in publishing since the printing press. Why? Because the World Wide Web makes it possible for anyone to publish electronic books, brochures and other documents with a potentially global audience.
> —*New York Times* 24 Jan. 1995, section C, p. 8

> As a WWW site administrator, or Webmaster, becomes comfortable with the site's basic functionality, more advanced features can be added.   —*Internet World* Feb. 1995, p. 26

> They experience difficulty in separating their website lives from their real lives, and find the freedom of the former infinitely preferable to the limitations of the latter.   —*Interzone* Aug. 1996, p. 60

See also HOME PAGE

WORM 🖳 see WRITE-ONCE

wormhole /'wɔ:mhəʊl/ *noun* 🖾

A concept in cosmology describing a 'tunnel' which might form under certain circumstances to connect two places which are separate either in time or in space.

Some recent theories seeking to reconcile quantum mechanics with gravitation lead to the conclusion that it is possible under certain circumstances (such as during the creation of a black hole) for 'gateways' to open that link different parts of the universe. This is highly speculative, but has been taken up by science-fiction books and films as a way of creating a time machine or a method of faster-than-light travel (the television series *Deep Space Nine* uses this as a core theme). Unfortunately, the indications are that such *wormholes* would shut again before there is time for spacecraft, or even information, to pass through them; many physicists are sceptical because they appear to violate the laws of conservation of energy.

> It turns out that to get through before the wormhole squeezes shut requires the astronaut to travel faster than light. —*Guardian* 12 Aug. 1993, section 2, p. 15

> When viewed very closely space seethes with quantum fluctuations, so much so that 'wormholes' can open up that connect parts of the universe with other parts that are distant in space and time. —Steven Weinberg *Dreams of a Final Theory* (1993), p. 177

> If time travel is possible through a wormhole, the paradox of consistency needs to be addressed. —*Economist* 20 Jan. 1996, p. 96

write-once /'rʌɪtwʌns/ *adjective* Also written **write once** 🖳

Relating to a type of optical storage technology in which data, once it has been written, cannot be erased or modified.

The first recordable optical systems, using a laser to write data to disks and read it back, appeared in the late seventies but did not come into general use until the early nineties, when recordable CDs came on the market. At first, the technology was usually referred to by the rather strained acronym **WORM**, standing for '*write-once*, read-many (times)', but *write-once* is now often used instead. At first, the ability to record large amounts of data on a removable disk outweighed the disadvantage of being able to use disks only once. With the rise of magneto-optical (MO) recording technology, by which disks can be erased and reused, the importance of *write-once* technology has declined somewhat. The lack of standardization between manufacturers' formats has also been a factor in this. Its strength is now seen to lie in archiving, where a record which cannot be erased has particular value; in distributing data in a secure form; and in some commercial situations, where it is important to keep all previous versions of a file as an audit trail. It is now becoming common to have *multifunction* drives which can cope both with *WORM* discs and with rewritable media.

> For the most part, MO has replaced the older WORM (Write Once, Read Many) technology in the market place. —*Computer Shopper* July 1993, p. 272

> A 'write-once' blank disc, or CD-R, is coated with a dye that is altered when struck by a more powerful laser beam. —*New Scientist* 11 Mar. 1995, p. 23

WTO 〰 see NAFTA

WWW 🖳 see WORLD WIDE WEB

• •

X

Xer see GENERATION X

XXXX /ˈfɔːrɛks/ *noun* Also written **Fourex, Four-x** POP

A type of Australian lager (from the trade mark name) manufactured by the Castelmaine firm. Also, in British slang, a humorous euphemism for a four-letter word.

From *Castlemaine XXXX*, the trade mark name of a lager manufactured by the Castelmaine firm.

Castlemaine XXXX was established as a trade mark in 1928, but the simple *XXXX* as a term for the lager is not recorded until the mid eighties. Since then, however, it has become widespread, and a series of advertisements using the catch-phrase **wouldn't give a XXXX for** have given rise to its use as a humorous euphemism for a swear-word (especially 'fuck') in a variety of similar phrases.

> He didn't give a four-X if his water tasted a bit funny, had the odd squiggly bit in it, or was in breach of 'totally unrealistic standards set by bloated Brussocrats'.
> —*Green Magazine* Apr. 1992, p. 11

> Men…have to have eight pints of XXXX and once the barriers are down, they really do enjoy getting together and being teary-eyed. —*Options* Aug. 1993, p. 21

> Most of the world couldn't give a XXXX about it, something that has long rankled with the marketing men who run the game. —*Arena* Dec. 1995, p. 59

Y

Yardie /ˈjɑːdi/ *noun* and *adjective*

In British slang:

noun: A member of any of a number of Jamaican or West Indian gangs (see POSSE) which engage in organized crime throughout the world, especially in connection with illicit drug-trafficking. In the plural, **Yardies**: these gangs as a whole or the criminal subculture that they represent.

adjective: Of or belonging to the Yardies.

The name is derived from the Jamaican English word *yard* (or *yaad*) which originally meant 'a house or home' and came to be used by Jamaicans living outside Jamaica for the home country. The suffix *-ie* is common in nicknames for people from a particular place: compare *Aussie* or *Ozzie* for an Australian.

Although probably active in the UK since the early eighties, the *Yardies* only began to feature in the news in 1986, when they were associated with the spread of drug-related crime in the UK in much the same way as the drug *posses* were in the US.

> The Yardies is a loose association of violent criminals, most of whom originated in Kingston, Jamaica and whose principal interest is the trafficking and sale of cocaine. In Britain they are perceived as a new phenomenon. In America, however, their counterparts, the 'posses', are said to have been responsible for up to 800 drug-related murders since 1984.
> —*Daily Telegraph* 13 Oct. 1988, p. 13

> A less well crafted but much more sussed example of the ghetto novel is Victor Headley's *Yardie* (X Press). —*i-D* July 1992, p. 55

> Those most at risk from Yardie violence were law abiding black communities in inner city areas, he said. —*Guardian* 10 June 1994, section 1, p. 6

year out see GAP YEAR

Year 2000 problem 🖳 ⩘ see MILLENNIUM BUG

yoof /juːf/ *noun* POP

In colloquial speech: youth; young people collectively, especially when viewed by others as a constituency to be catered for in commercial or artistic terms.

Formed from a respelling intended to represent a non-standard pronunciation of *youth*.

Yoof is recorded from the mid eighties as a term for young people collectively, particularly when seen in social and cultural terms. **Yoof culture** (or *culcha*) quickly became a jocular and ironic phrase which for many people summed up a category of the contemporary scene, particularly in the field of broadcasting; the term *yoof* is now likely to be used pejoratively, with an implied scepticism as to the value of attitudes or aspirations to which this label can be applied. The adjectives **yoofy** and **yoofish** have also been recorded.

> The Conservatives made the Criminal Justice Bill into a legal stick with which to beat us and vented their prejudices on yobs, anarchists and yoof culture in general. —*The Face* Jan. 1995, p. 70

> There is more than an element of the trendy vicar scenario at work here, but instead of brightly coloured pamphlets entitled God Is Groovy and Hell's A Bad Vibe, yoofy drug posters cover the wall. —*Guardian* 11 Mar. 1995, Weekend section, p. 75

> Jelly Babies have been redesigned in politically correct 'yoof' guises, wearing baseball caps, trainers and bumbags. It's all a bit much to swallow.
> —heading in *Independent* 26 Apr. 1995, p. 21

> Street-Porter went to the BBC where she created a sheaf of youth programmes…It was there too that the press bestowed its enduring, popular title 'head of yoof', encapsulating a fogyish distaste for television's deference to young people and popular culture. —*Vogue* Dec. 1995, p. 64

youthism ⦃⦄ see -ISM

• •

Z

zaitech /ˈzʌɪtɛk/ *noun* ⩘

Complex financial management, particularly as involving investment in financial markets by a company as a means of supplementing the earnings which it receives from its principal operations.

Formed from Japanese *zaiteku*, a compound of *zai* wealth and *teku* (from English *tech* 'technology').

Zaitech began to appear in Western sources in the mid eighties, as the expanding Japanese economy led to increasing involvement by Japanese businesses in Western money markets. The term occurred widely in the early nineties, but more recently has been less common, a pattern which presumably reflects the concurrent reduction of the economy.

> Big enterprises in banking, transportation, and commerce have maintained extremely labor-intensive services, besides services outstanding in the use of limited numbers of personnel extremely qualified in innovative methods of *Zaitech* as well as of modern electronic communication systems. —M. & H. Schmiegelow *Strategic Pragmatism* (1989), p. 110

> About 70 percent of the $135 billion went for *zaitech*, Japanese slang for financial engineering. —*Playboy* Nov. 1992, p. 166

zalcitabine /zalˈsɪtəbiːn/ noun ⊗

The generic name of the anti-viral drug DDC used in the management of HIV infection.

The ending *-citabine* is apparently a re-wording of the last part of its chemical name, *dideoxycytidine*, with the invented prefix *zal-* added.

The name has been in use since the beginning of the nineties, but the drug is most commonly known as *ddC*, or under its brand name *HIVID*.

> Activists who have fought strenuously for years to ensure that people with HIV gain access to new anti-AIDS drugs quickly last week asked the US government to withdraw approval from one of the drugs—zalcitabine or ddC. —*New Scientist* 2 Oct. 1993, p. 4

> The project compared survival rates between people who were treated with azidothymidine, or AZT, and those treated with AZT plus didanosine or zalcitabine.
> —*Daily Telegraph* 26 Sept. 1995, p. 6

zap /zap/ transitive verb POP

To make more powerful, exciting, or lively; to revitalize; to spice or pep up.

Zap was first used as an onomatopoeic word in comic strips for the sound of a ray gun, bullet, laser, or similar device; as a verb it has meant either 'to kill' or 'to move quickly and vigorously' since the sixties, and more recently it has developed the meaning, 'to use a remote control to move rapidly between television channels'. The current sense is associated with the idea of quick and vigorous movement: the notion is that of making an addition which has an invigorating and revitalizing effect.

This sense of *zap* arose in the late seventies, and became popular in a variety of contexts to indicate that steps had been taken to enhance or enliven the essential effect of a commodity.

> A whole head of garlic is olive-oiled, oven-baked, blobbed with brie, then zapped up with a sprig of fresh thyme on top. —*Western Living* Mar. 1991, p. 81

> Saab brought turbocharging to the mass market long before it became faddish to zap up the performance of shopping buggies by ramming air down their throats.
> —*Independent* 9 Nov. 1991, p. 43

> Large, juicy scallops are sautéed in butter and zapped with garlic.
> —*enRoute* (Toronto) July 1992, p. 72

zero-emission vehicle /zɪərəʊ ɪˈmɪʃ(ə)n ˌviːɪk(ə)l/ noun phrase Also written zero-emissions vehicle ⚘

A motor vehicle which does not emit pollutant gases.

Since the eighties, growing concerns about the effects of pollution on the atmosphere by exhaust emissions have encouraged the development of strategies to reduce or eliminate the perceived damage. The development of BIO-DIESEL, SUPERUNLEADED, and ALTERNATIVE FUEL characterize one area of response to the problem, but a stricter approach suggests that the only acceptable way is to devise a vehicle with *zero emissions*: in effect, one powered by electricity.

By the early nineties, the commercial development of an electric car appeared to be a real possibility, and in 1990 the state of California passed a law stating that by 1998 a minimum number of new vehicles sold in the state must be *zero-emission vehicles*, or *ZEVs*. It remains to be seen whether other states will follow suit, and whether the introduction and development of such **zero-emission cars** will be commercially viable.

> Under present regulations, a Zero Emissions Vehicle (ZEV) is defined…as one producing no tailpipe pollutants, without regard to emissions produced in the manufacture of the vehicle or in generating the electricity to recharge its batteries. —*Popular Science* May 1991, p. 76

> The whisper-quiet, zero emission car has improved the odds that electric vehicles will finally make serious inroads in the US. —*Independent* 6 Jan. 1996, p. 13

Zidovudine Ⓧ see AZT

ZIFT /zıft/ *acronym* Also written **Zift** Ⓧ ⚗

Short for **zygote intra-fallopian transfer**, a technique for helping infertile couples to conceive, in which a zygote (a fertilized egg which has been allowed to begin developing into an embryo) is re-implanted into one of the woman's Fallopian tubes after fertilization with her partner's sperm outside the body.

The technique was first successfully employed in 1986 and the abbreviation appeared two years later. *ZIFT* is a further refinement of GIFT, offering greater certainty of establishing a pregnancy. However, unlike GIFT, it takes fertilization outside the body once again, and is therefore open to the same ethical or religious objections as IVF.

A new variation, zygote intrafallopian transfer (ZIFT), may further improve GIFT's odds. The egg is fertilized in a petri dish, and the embryo is placed in the fallopian tube about 18 hours later. ZIFT has been tried on fewer than 50 couples, so it is too soon to measure its success.

—*US News & World Report* 3 Apr. 1989, p. 75

On this occasion, I was being treated with a variation of Gift, called Zift (Zygote intrafallopian transfer), in which the eggs and sperm are mixed outside the body and then replaced in the tube. —*Independent* 15 Jan. 1991, p. 17

See also GIFT